Rich..An Informal
Guia..y Editor on
Cour..les on tradi-
tional ....gy, Sing Out!, Pickin',
Frets, Mugwi..duced ten albums of tra-
ditional music for Folkways Records, currently part of the Smithsonian/Folkways Archive of
Traditional Music.

THE
BIG BOOK OF
COUNTRY
MUSIC

A BIOGRAPHICAL ENCYCLOPEDIA

RICHARD CARLIN

PENGUIN BOOKS

PENGUIN BOOKS
Published by the Penguin Group
Penguin Books USA Inc., 375 Hudson Street,
New York, New York 10014, U.S.A.
Penguin Books Ltd, 27 Wrights Lane,
London W8 5TZ, England
Penguin Books Australia Ltd, Ringwood,
Victoria, Australia
Penguin Books Canada Ltd, 10 Alcorn Avenue,
Toronto, Ontario, Canada M4V 3B2
Penguin Books (N.Z.) Ltd, 182–190 Wairau Road,
Auckland 10, New Zealand

Penguin Books Ltd, Registered Offices:
Harmondsworth, Middlesex, England

First published in Penguin Books 1995

10 9 8 7 6 5 4 3 2 1

LIBRARY OF CONGRESS CATALOGING IN PUBLICATION DATA
Carlin, Richard.
    The big book of country music: a biographical encyclopedia/
Richard Carlin.
        p.   cm.
    Includes bibliographical references and index.
    ISBN 0 14 02.3509 4
    1. Country music—Bio-bibliography—Dictionaries.   I. Title.
ML102.C7C28   1995
781.642'092'2—dc20
    [B]   94–39275

Printed in the United States of America
Set in Adobe Cheltenham Light
Designed by Ann Gold

To Bob Carlin,
who taught me how to love country music;
and to Richard Kostelanetz,
who taught me how to write dictionaries

ACKNOWLEDGMENTS

Thanks to my agent, John Wright, for advice and operatic interludes; to Jessica Myers Carlin for research assistance and pesto; to all the researchers and scholars who did the leg work that made this book possible; and to my Penguin editors David Stanford and Kris Puopolo for careful line reading.

A Note about the Recommended Recordings

I have made an attempt to list only in-print and currently available recordings; all are available on compact disc unless otherwise noted. All discographies are selective: I have not attempted to list all recordings by every artist—a gigantic task and one that should be undertaken in a separate, "complete" country listing. For some artists it was necessary to list out-of-print items because nothing is currently available. Some of these out-of-print items may be available in used-record stores or libraries, and some may eventually be reissued on CD or cassette. Folkways recordings are technically all still available, although they must be ordered directly from the Smithsonian Institution and can be had only on cassette, with the exception of those listed as "Smithsonian/Folkways," which are available on CD or cassette and are sold commercially through regular stores.

As always, record labels come and go; catalog numbers may change; and what is available today in one format may only be available tomorrow in a different format.

INTRODUCTION:
A SHORT HISTORY OF COUNTRY MUSIC

It is tempting in this time of its greatest popularity to pronounce country music dead and buried. After all, what's the difference between seventies soft-pop-rock and nineties country-corn-kitsch? If GARTH BROOKS outsells Guns 'n' Roses, maybe it's heavy metal that should be called "folk music" and country "mainstream pop." When everybody wants to be a hunk in a hat or a cowgirl in a gingham dress, is it beside the point to look to the roots of one of America's only indigenous musical forms?

Country music is not America's only indigenous music; there are jazz and blues and rock 'n' roll to contend for the crown. But country music has never garnered the critical respect or intellectual prestige of even rock, perhaps because it is so closely associated with its so-called "hillbilly" or "redneck" roots. But, like jazz, country music has a century-old tradition, with myriad styles evolving (and co-existing) over the decades. Like jazz, it is constantly turning back and renewing itself at the source; flirting with mainstream success; crossing over into pop; going into lengthy periods of exile; and ultimately bubbling forth again like an irrepressible voice of the earth.

Like all great American art forms, country music has its roots in commerce; that is to say, it took commercial recording companies and radio stations to nurture the country style. There were settlers both black and white in the Appalachians from time immemorial, and they brought with them two distinct traditions: the European tradition of Anglo-American balladry, story songs, and dance music based on four-square harmonies and fixed forms; and the African-American tradition of blues, work songs, and field hollers, featuring often improvisatory melodies and words accompanied by polyrhythmic, instrumental virtuosity. And like all great American musics, country music is a blending of these black and white elements, with each tradition tapping into the other's root system at enough places that it's impossible to completely disentangle one from the other.

The first commercialization of America's backwoods sounds came in the mid-nineteenth century, thanks to the minstrel and traveling tent shows. Minstrel show music was built around the popularity of a new instrument, the BANJO, whose roots were in Africa. While the banjo was African in its origins, the music played by the minstrels—whether black or white—was an amalgam of traditional English dance tunes and the popular compositions of the day. While originally the minstrel show was created by whites imitating/parodying black manners, and thus could be viewed as an elevation of racism to a mass form of entertainment, the minstrel shows were entertaining, and in a backwards kind of way they proved the value of black culture to a larger audience (just as Pat Boone singing "Tutti Frutti" helped introduce whitebread America in the late fifties to the real thing, Little Richard).

Minstrel shows gave birth to two distinct forms of American entertainment. The larger, more successful troops managed to make a mark in northern cities like Baltimore, Philadelphia, and New York and eventually toured Europe. They began to incorporate other ethnic types found in the nation's large cities—such as stage Irishmen and Germans—eventually maturing into what would be known as vaudeville, with music provided by the composers of Tin Pan Alley. Meanwhile, the backwoods traveling shows continued to tour the South, nurturing hundreds of wannabe banjo and fiddle players, country rube comedians, and assorted semi-professional entertainers.

A second seedbed for country music was—and still is—oddly enough, the rural church. Music was an integral part of church services both black and white, and many churches founded singing schools, to teach the rudiments of harmony through the SHAPE-NOTE SYSTEM (shape-note notation uses different shapes—such as squares, triangles, and so on—to differentiate the scale tones, so that it's not necessary to read music to sing from the hymnal). While the black church evolved an ecstatic, semi-improvisational, and highly emotional take on the tradition of Protestant hymn singing, the white church evolved its own sound, a blend of primitive harmonizing with the nasal twang of backwoods singing. The two traditions would cross-pollinate and fertilize each other, so that eventually a blues-influenced, tightly harmonized music called "blue-grass" would become the ultimate melding of black and white music making.

But it took new technologies and the coming of mass marketing in the twentieth century to really launch country music. In the early days of recording, when heavy and primitive equipment was used to capture sound, almost all sessions were held in the large northern cities and were limited to the sounds and styles familiar to record executives—such as those of light opera, comedic stage vocalists, or watered-down dance bands. Occasionally a fiddle player or vocalist would work his way north—such as the great Texas champion fiddler UNCLE ECK ROBERTSON who made some of the first solo fiddle recordings in 1922—but there was little understanding of or appetite for recording this music.

However, as local dealers began selling phonographs in the South and West, they reported back to the home offices about artists who were popular in their area. One such dealer was the Atlanta-based Polk Brockman, who knew what his customers wanted and had enough clout to be able to suggest that local artists be recorded. One artist that Brockman recommended was a fifty-plus-year-old fiddler and sometime house painter named FIDDLIN' JOHN CARSON; the OKeh label dutifully made a custom record of Carson singing the late-nineteenth-century popular song

"The Little Old Log Cabin in the Lane" for Brockman to sell, but the company didn't even bother to assign a master number or affix a label to the five hundred records that were pressed for him. It was only after the record became a regional hit that the light bulb of commerce went off in the executive's heads, and suddenly they were scouring the countryside for entertainers.

Recording technology was so improved by the late twenties that portable equipment was finally available, and studios could be set up closer to the musicians. In 1927, Victor recording executive RALPH PEER made a now-famous trip to Bristol, Tennessee, near the Virginia border, where he set up a makeshift studio in a local hotel. There he "discovered" two of country's greatest acts: the CARTER FAMILY, a Virginia-based trio that specialized in songs of hearth and home; and JIMMIE RODGERS, a blues-influenced yodeler. Through the Carters came the sound of the white country church, with songs derived from the Anglo-American traditions of balladry; Rodgers was a more progressive voice, a jazz era–influenced vocalist who somehow brought together the lonesome sound of the blues with Swiss YODELING to create something altogether new. Even in imagery the two pioneers represented diametric poles: The Carters were marketed as the ultimate embodiment of the home, while Rodgers was promoted as the "yodeling brakeman," a rambling hellraiser who lived hard and died young.

These two strands—home harmonizers versus bluesy barroom singers—would become the models for much of the country music that followed in the thirties. This was the era of the brother act, beginning with the BLUE SKY BOYS, Earl and Bill Bolick. In their simple harmonizing and sedate instrumental accompaniments, the Boys sounded like they were just sittin' and pickin' on their back porch. Their songs focused on mother, home, and religion; they were the good sons who dutifully plowed the fields and attended church. Meanwhile, Jimmie Rodgers's legacy was also brewing, but on the other side of the tracks. The outlaw railroad man gave birth to hundreds of singing cowboys, from GENE AUTRY through ROY ROGERS and countless others. Although Autry sentimentalized and diluted the power of Rodgers's music and image, his music maintained a vital connection with jazz and blues roots.

Many of the stars of the thirties got their start on the radio, not records. Originally, country music got onto the radio because it was easy for rural programmers to use cheap and accessible local talent. Local announcers could ferret out popular performers and interview them on the air to fill up the dead time between network broadcasts. GEORGE D. HAY, a news reader and radio programmer for station WSM in Nashville in the early twenties, brought a local fiddler named UNCLE JIMMY THOMPSON to the studios to perform on his program; the listener response was so great that Thompson became a regular feature on the weekly show. Hay's program was scheduled immediately following the national NBC broadcast of the Metropolitan Opera out of New York; Hay, taking on the character of a backwoods "solemn old judge," would parody the previous broadcast by extemporizing "You've just heard Grand Opera; get ready for the Grand Ole Opry," and the name stuck.

Soon, a slew of barn-dance programs were operating out of the South and

Midwest. Each program had its own personality, although most were modeled after the traveling tent shows that were still popular in backwoods America. Many country stars began their careers on the radio, where they could establish their unique sound and style, sell songbooks (often by the thousands), and promote personal appearances. Producers like John Lair, who worked for Chicago's *National Barn Dance* and later the *Renfro Valley Barn Dance* out of Kentucky, carefully nurtured the images of his star performers and was thus among the first to sell an image as well as a sound.

One of the most unusual progressive movements of the thirties was a new style brewing in Texas and Oklahoma that would become known as WESTERN SWING. Like all the great country styles, it is an amalgam of different influences, old-style Texas fiddling (always jazz-influenced in its elaborate, syncopated variations) meeting the sound of the big bands. Vocalists like TOMMY DUNCAN sounded like they had their ears glued to Bing Crosby's popular recordings and broadcasts, singing a mixture of blues, pop, and sentimental songs. The Western swing bands were the first country groups to feature drums, barrelhouse piano, and amplified steel guitars. The voice of the jazz age crossed with a country kick crackles forth from the classic recordings of bands like BOB WILLS's Texas Playboys.

Social changes in the thirties also had an impact on the growth and spread of country music. The dust storms in Oklahoma and Texas prompted a mass migration of poor farmers looking for increased job opportunities in Southern California. Meanwhile, black and white southerners in search of better job possibilities were migrating further north, settling in Cincinnati, Cleveland, Detroit, and Chicago, bringing with them their mixture of country and blues music. World War II would increase the forces of displacement; it drew off of family farms thousands of southerners, who, after the war, were deposited back in major ports like New York and San Francisco, many never to return to the rural life.

In the postwar years, country music took two radically different directions. The old string-band tradition was gussied up and energized into something entirely new that would be known as BLUEGRASS, created by fiery mandolinist and high-tenor vocalist BILL MONROE and his classic, late-forties band featuring the revolutionary banjo work of Earl Scruggs, Chubby Wise's swing-influenced fiddling, and guitarist/vocalist Lester Flatt's modern, relaxed style of singing. Although Monroe would record for major labels—first Columbia and then, through the fifties, on Decca (later MCA)—and was a regular on the GRAND OLE OPRY, bluegrass was viewed as, at best, a nostalgic reminder of the old days, and its audience was small, compared to mainstream country.

Meanwhile, a new style was brewing in the small southern and southwestern neighborhood bars known as honky-tonks. These bars were often located on the edge of town and had a somewhat seedy, disreputable atmosphere; they were places where men could go after work to do some serious drinking. To be heard over the considerable racket, musicians began using electrified instruments and performing in small ensembles, featuring GUITAR, bass, and drums, as well as the occasional fiddle and steel guitar. Songs about mother, home, and church were hardly acceptable to an audience drenched in beer and lusting after loose women; a new subject matter needed to be created to suit the new circumstances.

The first great HONKY-TONK star was HANK WILLIAMS, Sr., whose short, troubled life served as both a cautionary tale and model for hundreds of wannabe honky-tonkers. Like Jimmie Rodgers before him, Williams was influenced by black music, learning his first songs in Montgomery, Alabama, from a black street entertainer known as Tee-Tot. His first hit, "Lovesick Blues," was a revival of a jazz-era song, right down to its short yodeling breaks. But Williams would be best remembered for the searing songs he composed, songs that addressed firsthand issues like drinking ("Tear in My Beer," "Honky Tonkin' ") and love gone wrong ("Your Cheatin' Heart"). His songs were sung in the first person and dealt head-on with topics such as adultery and alcoholism, which were previously touched on only peripherally in country music. Williams's songs were cannily marketed by Nashville power broker FRED ROSE and so were among the first to be covered by mainstream pop acts, furthering popularizing country music.

The growth of Nashville as a center of country-music making was intense in the years following World War II. Previously, recording companies had visited the city occasionally for field recording; now major labels established their country-music home bases in the city. The continued influence and success of the *Grand Ole Opry* kept major acts tied to the city, while it also allowed backup musicians to find steady, profitable work there. Recognizing the value of country music, performer ROY ACUFF teamed with veteran music-industry professional Fred Rose to form Acuff-Rose publishers; they were the first to employ professional songwriters to create country songs for the market, and among the first to craft a recognizable country sound, the NASHVILLE SOUND, supervising the production of their artist's recordings and selection of material.

In the mid-fifties, the Nashville Sound grew around two major studios: One was led by OWEN BRADLEY, who worked as a pianist for radio station WSM (the home of the Opry) and became the leading producer for the Decca label; the other was headed by CHET ATKINS, a talented guitarist who worked for RCA. Both men were fans of contemporary jazz and pop and wanted to see country music viewed as the equal of these more socially accepted musics. Both downplayed the presence of traditional instruments such as banjos, fiddles, and even steel guitars for what they viewed as more modern instrumentation, such as tinkling pianos, purling electric guitars, bass, and drums. Atkins used vocal groups like the ANITA KERR Singers or the JORDANAIRES as backups to his country artists, again to give them a slicker, more contemporary sound. Eventually, by the mid-sixties, there was little to distinguish country music from mainstream pop, which was the Nashville Sound's ultimate triumph (or tragedy, depending on your point of view).

The effect of the Nashville Sound is evident in the stories of hundreds of acts and is exemplified in the career of Virginia Hensley, aka PATSY CLINE. Cline began as a pure country vocalist, appearing in cowgirl getup and performing classic honky-tonk hanky strainers like "Walkin' After Midnight." However, after she came under the guiding hand of producer Owen Bradley, she increasingly performed and recorded songs that fit as easily into the mainstream pop repertoire. By the time of her tragic death in an airplane crash, Cline was a full-throated chanteuse, belting out songs that were country in their weepy contents but otherwise were the equivalent of the pop drivel that could be found on the mainstream charts.

Meanwhile, on the edges of the country-music empire, another musical revolution was brewing. Memphis, Tennessee, located miles from Nashville philosophically and musically, was becoming a hotbed for the union of black rhythm and blues and white country. In the early fifties, the city was home to influential disc jockey and later performer Riley B. (B.B.) King, as well as to a number of small labels specializing in the new rhythm and blues sounds. At Sun Records, radio engineer SAM PHILLIPS, who produced many of these black acts, realized that their appeal went beyond the African-American community. If only a white artist could capture the sound, he was certain he'd have a monster act on his hands. That artist materialized in the form of a young teenager who came to his studios to record a custom disc of a sentimental song for his mother. The teenager was ELVIS PRESLEY, and in late 1954 Phillips brought Elvis into the studio to record his first single, which interestingly enough paired a reworked R&B song ("That's All Right") with a reworked bluegrass number ("Blue Moon of Kentucky"), representing in miniature the polarities of a new musical style: ROCKABILLY.

Although Elvis began his career as a country performer, working the circuit of small-time bars, clubs, and fairs as well as appearing on the *Grand Ole Opry* and *Louisiana Hayride* radio programs, just like any other country act, he soon outgrew his country roots to enter the pantheon of mainstream pop. In his wake hundreds of Elvis imitators and admirers sprang up in the South, some recording just a few songs and others (like CARL PERKINS, JERRY LEE LEWIS, and BUDDY HOLLY) refining and expanding on the rockabilly style to create a truly unique music.

The late fifties saw the beginnings of the folk boom on the pop charts, with the Kingston Trio's surprise hit recording of "Tom Dooley." JOHNNY HORTON's recording of "The Battle of New Orleans," set to the old fiddle tune "The Eighth of January," was another surprise hit on both country and pop charts, and a new trend, the saga song, swept country music. These were narrative, pseudo-folksongs (newly composed) celebrating tales of the Civil War or the Old West. They were perfect for the go-go optimism of the turn of the decade, when the Kennedys were recreating an epic Camelot for a nation newly proud and young.

Mainstream Nashville was becoming increasingly conservative politically and as a musical force. With the Nashville Sound fully entrenched, any artist could be transformed from a rough "hillbilly" into a smooth pop crooner. The machinery of Nashville, well-oiled, perfectly in tune with the conservative tastes of the average listener, needed only to be activated to turn country ham into high-quality bologna. The only problem was that the music was soulless; its heart was ripped out to make the music inoffensive—attractive but not alluring.

While mainstream Nashville became increasingly conservative through the sixties, a quiet revolution was brewing along the sidelines. SINGER/SONGWRITER WILLIE NELSON was frustrated and disappointed by his record label, RCA, which tried to mold his music to fit the homogeneous Nashville Sound with little success. Nelson knew that his music could have appeal if he were allowed to perform it on record the way he did in his live shows, but the Nashville power brokers were not convinced that anything that "country" would sell.

At the same time, a new generation of SINGER/SONGWRITER was coming to town, influenced equally by the legacy of Hank Williams and the new music of folk-rockers like BOB DYLAN. Dylan proved that an idiosyncratic, highly personal style of performing could be more successful than a more polished approach. This lesson was not lost on country songwriters like Nelson, WAYLON JENNINGS, and KRIS KRISTOFFERSON, all of whom felt that their individual voices were being stifled by the Nashville establishment.

In the seventies, Nelson and friends would abandon Nashville, many heading to the hinterlands of Texas, there establishing what would become known as OUT-LAW COUNTRY. Meanwhile, the Nashville Sound matured into what has been called COUNTRYPOLITAN music, personified by relatively bland mainstream "pop" acts like BARBARA MANDRELL and KENNY ROGERS. These performers were just as comfortable —if not more so—in a Vegas lounge as they were on the Opry stage, and for many it seemed that country music had lost all contact with its roots.

Meanwhile, way off on the edges of country music, there were some fledgling signs of rebirth developing. One was a revival of interest in bluegrass music, beginning with the urban FOLK REVIVAL in the sixties but then growing deeper in the seventies with the founding of new bands. Young musicians, including RICKY SKAGGS and KEITH WHITLEY, began performing in both traditional and more progressive bands, and their interest in bluegrass blossomed into a wider concern for older country styles. Many of the house musicians of today's Nashville—including dobroist JERRY DOUGLAS and fiddler MARK O'CONNOR—came out of this movement.

In the late sixties, a number of rock bands began flirting with country sounds, forming the short-lived but influential COUNTRY-ROCK movement. The spiritual leader of the movement was GRAM PARSONS, who performed with his own International Submarine Band, then with a revitalized BYRDS, and cofounded the FLYING BURRITO BROTHERS before embarking on a short-lived solo career, cut off by his death due to drugs. The legacy of his music cast a long shadow through the seventies, and his torch was carried by his protégé EMMYLOU HARRIS. Harris began as a LINDA RONSTADT–styled singer whose music turned increasingly country, thanks to the influence of members of her backup band, including ALBERT LEE, RODNEY CROWELL, and Ricky Skaggs.

Skaggs was probably the first bluegrass star to cross over into mainstream country success in the early eighties, paving the way for countless others, including his past partner Keith Whitley as well as VINCE GILL, KATHY MATTEA, and ALISON KRAUSS. But the first true megastar of the NEW-COUNTRY, back-to-roots movement of the eighties was RANDY TRAVIS, who possesses a unique vocal style that hauntingly recalls many of the greatest stars of the fifties. Unlike others who strain to sound country, Travis seems to feel it in his bones (or at least down deep in his vocal cords), so that even on his sappiest recordings he sounds disarmingly authentic.

Travis's success opened the floodgates to the "hunks in hats," hundreds of would-be country crooners who flooded the airwaves with music that blended rockabilly, honky-tonk, and sentimental pop in an increasingly mechanical way.

Still, there were blips of originality among the cowpoke stars, some talented, some simply artfully promoted. Garth Brooks successfully blurred the lines between singer/songwriter, arena rocker, and good ol' boy in his hit recordings and energetic stage shows. While Brooks is talented, there were others whose astonishing lack of talent was nonetheless rewarded with great success, confirming that sometimes, as the saying goes, the proof is in the packaging.

While new country began as a revolt against the homogenized, mainstream country-pop of the seventies and early eighties, it is now in danger of itself becoming a stylistic cliché. The use of similar backing, musicians, songwriters, and producers, in a neat package, has meant that many of today's new acts sound generically like one another. And yet what makes country great is the personality, the undeniable recognizability of its best performers. Performers like TRAVIS TRITT break through by sounding unique, performing material that is different from the pack; but too often, like Tritt, they are sucked into the mainstream, so that their music and presentation begins to take on the sheen of a product rather than a personal message.

But just as the Nashville Sound collapsed under its own weight, so too will this Stepford-wife, new-country music disappear when the next generation discovers that it has become hollow and lifeless. Country music in some guise, under some new form, will survive; and its survival depends on understanding where it's been, why it's been there, and where it's going.

This book attempts to follow that route, celebrating the unique voices and damning those who stood in the way. *The Big Book of Country Music* traces the ups and downs, honoring the innovators as well as the popularizers; both have a place in the history of any musical form. It is an attempt to map out the territory of country music, to take an eclectic, comprehensive look at the great artists, genres, and musical instruments that have shaped the country sound. One of my main goals was to capture the sound—or at least the personality—of the artist in each entry; not just to provide names, dates, and facts but also to talk about styles, influences, and contributions. Like all evaluations, mine allow for a high degree of subjectivity; it should, however, be clear to the canny reader where opinion begins and ends. I hope that a combination of fact and feel, research and impression makes this book a faithful portrait of the many characters who together are country music.

THE BIG BOOK
OF COUNTRY MUSIC

A

◀ ACUFF, ROY

(born 1903, Maynardsville, TN; died 1992)

One of the most important and influential members of the GRAND OLE OPRY, Acuff helped pave the way for the transformation of old-time country music into modern pop-style country. Although he enjoyed brief success as a country singer, Acuff left a lasting mark as a music-business executive.

Born to a middle-class family, the son of a lawyer, Acuff originally hoped to be a professional ballplayer; but a case of severe sunstroke left him bedridden for two years, during which time he took up the fiddle. He formed his first band, the Crazy Tennesseans, in the early thirties, performing on Knoxville radio. They were signed to the budget label American Recording Company (ARC) in 1936, recording their first hit, "The Great Speckled Bird." 1938 brought Acuff's biggest hit, "The Wabash Cannonball," and his first appearance on the *Grand Ole Opry*. At this time, Acuff, at the suggestion of Opry management, changed the name of his backup band to the Smoky Mountain Boys. The band prominently featured the DOBRO, popularizing the instrument in country music. The most famous dobro player associated with Acuff is "Bashful Brother Oswald" (Pete Kirby). Despite the fact that he performed holding a fiddle under his arm, Acuff was primarily a pop crooner, the slight twang in his voice the only hint that he came from country roots. The year 1942 brought his last big hit, the tragic car-crash ballad "Wreck on the Highway." In the same year, recognizing the financial value of country songs, Acuff formed a music-publishing partnership with songwriter FRED ROSE. Acuff-Rose became Nashville's premier song publishers through the fifties and sixties. They also formed the Hickory record label.

In 1962 Acuff was elected to the Country Music Hall of Fame, and in 1974, with the opening of the theme park Opryland USA (providing him with steady work in Nashville), he retired from active touring. Despite increasingly poor health, Acuff continued to perform on occasion at the Opry through the late eighties and early nineties, appearing at a show honoring the career of country comedienne MINNIE PEARL just a month before his death.

Select Discography

Columbia Historic Edition, Columbia 39998. The best overview of Acuff's classic early recordings, including four from his first 1936 session.

Steamboat Whistle Blues, Rounder 23/*Fly Birdie Fly*, Rounder 24. For true Acuff fans, here is a more complete overview of Acuff's classic recordings, including pop ballads and jazzy numbers along with the country standards.

King of Country Music, Bear Family 15652. Acuff's mid-fifties recordings cut for a variety of labels, including gospel numbers and remakes of his earlier hits.

◀ ALABAMA

(c. 1975–ongoing: Randy Yuell Owen [vocals, guitar]; Jeffrey Alan Cook [vocals, guitar]; Teddy Wayne Gentry [vocals, bass]; Jackie Owen [1975–1979: drums]; Mark Joel Herndon [1979–ongoing: drums])

Alabama is a pop-rock-influenced vocal group that was most popular in the early and mid-eighties. They were one of the first vocal bands to introduce a harder, rocking style to country music, while continuing to project a good-time, nostalgic message through their songs.

Originally formed around a quartet of cousins, the group worked as a bar band from the mid-seventies to about 1979, when they recorded their first hit, "I Wanna Come Over," for MDJ Records of Dallas, operated by their then-manager. This was followed by "My Home's in Alabama," cowritten by Randy Owen and Teddy Gentry, which became their first theme song and a top-twenty hit in 1980. That same year they signed with RCA, which released the follow-up, "Tennessee River," and the pop-country "Why Lady Why."

Alabama was notable for its three-person lead (most other country acts focused on a soloist accompanied by an anonymous band); for their long hair (and beards), which would have been unacceptable to country audiences just ten years earlier; and for their prominent use of electric bass and drums, which gave their music a rocking kick that was unlike the middle-of-the-road country of the day. Not surprisingly, their appeal was to a younger audience, although their wholesome good looks and "just country folks" stage presence did help sell them to the more conservative, older country audience.

The group's biggest hit was "Play Me Some Mountain Music," notable for its sunny harmonies and down-home content. Still, this was basically an up-tempo pop song, one that could as easily have been recorded by Three Dog Night.

By the mid-eighties, the group was moving increasingly in a pop-rock direction, going for splashier production with a more heavily amplified sound. By the early nineties, their popularity on the country charts had waned, thanks to the increasing popularity of new country stars. Their sunny harmonies, a vestige of seventies pop, were beginning to sound a bit dated, particularly when compared to the more hard-driving groups and soloists then working in country.

Select Discography

Greatest Hits, RCA Nashville 61040. 1991 collection of their chart-toppers.

Mountain Music, RCA 4229. One of their earlier, less glitzy albums. A good sampling of their sound.

◀ ALGER, PAT

(date and place of birth unknown)

A friend of folksingers Happy and Artie Traum, Alger has become a leading writer of NEW-COUNTRY hits of the eighties and nineties.

Alger first emerged as a guitarist/songwriter/vocalist in several different Traum projects, including the various incarnations of the Woodstock Mountains Revue, a loosely knit group of musicians from the greater Woodstock area including bluegrasser John Herald, the Traums, Maria Muldaur, and others. Alger contributed some of the more country-flavored songs to the group's repertoire, including "Old Time Music" and "Southern Crescent Line." Alger hooked up with folk/country singer NANCI GRIFFITH in the mid-eighties to write songs, and the pair wrote several of her hits, including "Once in a Very Blue Moon" and "Lone Star State of Mind." In 1988 KATHY MATTEA covered "Goin' Gone," a song he had cowritten for Griffith, which launched his career in new Nashville circles. In the early nineties Alger made two solo albums, featuring backup by many big Nashville stars, including Griffith, Mattea, and LYLE LOVETT. In 1994 he signed with Liberty Records and toured with a group of other contemporary country tunesmiths.

Alger's simple guitar style and relaxed vocals all recall his folkie roots. He is the purest link of the folk-Nashville connection that has produced some of the more eccentric of the eighties and nineties new-country stars, including Griffith and Lovett.

Select Discography

True Love and Other Short Stories, Sugar Hill 1029. His "comeback" album from 1991.

◀ ALLEN, DEBORAH

(born Deborah Lynn Thurmond, 1953, Memphis, TN)

Deborah Allen is a SINGER/SONGWRITER who straddles the line between NEW COUNTRY and power pop.

Allen came to Nashville at age seventeen looking for work as a singer; instead, she took a job as a waitress at the local International House of Pancakes. Fate intervened when singer ROY ORBISON stopped in for a short stack; Allen served him and convinced him that she could sing, and he hired her as a backup singer for his next session. She then worked as a singer/dancer at Opryland, where JIM STAFFORD heard her and hired her to be a part of his touring company. She worked with him from 1974 to 1977, during which time she was based in Los Angeles, the home of Stafford's syndicated television program.

On her return to Nashville in 1977, Allen began writing songs, hitting it big with "Don't Worry 'Bout Me," recorded by JANIE FRICKIE in 1980. The song was the first number-one hit for both the composer and the singer. A short time later Allen married songwriter/producer Rafe Van Hoy, and the duo wrote hits for a number of traditional and NEW-COUNTRY stars.

Allen's own recording career got off to a slow start. She made a critically acclaimed LP for Capitol in 1979, combining country, gospel, and folk sounds, but it failed on the charts and her follow-up LP was never released. Four years later, she was signed to RCA, and her husband produced her first album, which yielded the hits "Baby I Lied," "Cheat the Night," "I Hurt for You," and "I've Been Wrong Before."

Guided by her husband, Allen adopted a more commercial approach through the mid- and later eighties. The two began to work as songwriters with a variety of up-and-comers, including a young singer named Kix Brooks, whose debut album Van Hoy produced; and although his debut went nowhere, Brooks later became one-half of the megaduo, BROOKS AND DUNN.

Select Discography

Special Look, MCA 6317. 1989 pop-country recordings.

◀ ALLEN, RED

(born 1930, Kentucky; died 1993)

Red Allen was a BLUEGRASS guitarist/vocalist who was quite influential on the first generation of bluegrass revivalists in the sixties.

Allen first came to prominence as the lead singer and guitarist for the OSBORNE BROTHERS in the mid-fifties. He soon broke away from the band, forming his own band, the Kentuckians. In the early sixties, he recorded and performed with innovative mandolinist Frank Wakefield and also with a new young revival mandolinist, DAVID GRISSMAN. At this time, his band was a little more progressive than traditional outfits although not as far out as some younger players.

In the early seventies, Allen hooked up with progressive banjo player J. D. CROWE to sing lead in the first version of the New South. Allen performed as a band leader through the seventies and eighties and groomed the careers of his three sons, who formed the Allen Brothers band in the mid-seventies. They recorded a couple of albums of more contemporary country and bluegrass compositions in tight three-part harmonies.

Select Discography

In Memory of the Man, Folkways 31073. This out-of-print LP features Red with son Harley and fiddler Curly Seckler on a tribute album to Lester Flatt.

Bluegrass Country, County 704. Early-seventies recordings.

Red Allen with Frank Wakefield. Folkways 2408. Out-of-print early-sixties album that greatly influenced the second-generation bluegrass revivalists. Produced by David Grissman.

◀ ALLEN, REX

(born 1924, Willcox, AZ)

Allen was a cowboy actor and singing star who was most active from the mid-forties through the late sixties. Allen is as well-known for his television appearances and work as a narrator for Disney documentaries as he is for his musical skills.

Born in rural Arizona, Allen was already working the amateur rodeo circuit in his early teens; at the same time, he took up guitar and fiddle playing as a sideline. His smooth, modern singing style won him many fans through radio appearances and at fairs. In his late teens, he traveled west to California on the rodeo circuit. He then crossed the country to take a job as a performer on radio stations in Trenton and Philadelphia, leading to a role on Chicago's popular *National Barn Dance* from 1945 to 1949.

In 1949, he returned to California to host his own radio show and appear in the first of a series of Westerns for the famous C-grade Republic studio. Like GENE AUTRY and ROY ROGERS before him, Allen became a popular star of these horse operas, always accompanied by his horse/sidekick, Koko. He also helped to pioneer the Western genre on television in his *Frontier Doctor* program, broadcast from 1949 to 1950 on CBS TV.

In the early fifties, Allen signed with Decca Records, producing a string of Western hits, including 1953's "Crying in the Chapel." He moved to Mercury in 1961, immediately hitting with the slightly bizarre "Don't Go Near the Indians." He continued to record through the sixties, drawing heavily on cowboy standards like "On Top of Old Smoky" along with his own self-penned Western epics.

He retired from music in the early seventies, just when his son, REX ALLEN, JR., began to achieve some success.

Select Discography
Voice of the West, Bear Family 15284. Nicely produced sessions from the early seventies cut by JACK CLEMENT, including Western standards as well as modern country numbers. No mushy strings or swelling choruses.

◀ ALLEN, REX, JR.

(born 1947, Chicago, IL)
The second Rex Allen was a popular baritone-voiced crooner of the seventies who continued the tradition of cowboy-themed hits that were originally purveyed by his father.

Raised in Southern California, the young singer often traveled with his father on the rodeo/county fair circuit, performing with him from the age of six. After forming amateur bands in high school, and serving time in the military, Allen relocated to Nashville in search of success as a country singer. He had his first break in 1973, when he signed with Warner Brothers. His first hits were in the popular COUNTRYPOLITAN style of the day, including "Goodbye"; a country version of the soft-pop hit "I Can See Clearly Now"; and "Lyin' in My Arms." He recorded an album of Western standards in 1975, many of which were associated with his father, including the hoary old chestnut "Streets of Laredo," BOB WILLS's "San Antonio Rose," and his own composition "I Gotta Remember to Forget You" (an obvious allusion to the old country warhorse "I Forgot to Remember to Forget About You").

1976 brought his first big hit with "Can You Hear Those Pioneers," which he cowrote, firmly in the Western vein. He continued to produce minor hits, alternating Western-flavored numbers with more standard mid-seventies country. His career pretty much faded out during the NEW-COUNTRY movement of the early eighties.

◀ ALLEN, ROSALIE

(born Julie Marlene Bedra, 1924, Old Forge, PA)

Rosalie Allen was one of the most successful cowgirl yodelers of the thirties. She recorded both as a solo act and in partnership with ELTON BRITT from the late thirties through the fifties.

Allen's pedigree is hardly that of a classic Western cowgirl; she was the daughter of a Polish immigrant chiropractor and lived in rural Pennsylvania. But, like many of her compatriots, she was bitten by the cowgirl bug early in her career and was performing on Denver Darling's New York–based pseudo-Western radio show by the time she was in her midteens. Like other cowgirls, the big draw of her act was her spectacular yodeling, featured on her remake of PATSY MONTANA's "I Want to Be a Cowboy's Sweetheart," one of her first hits for Victor. The label paired her with cowpoke Elton Britt, and the two recorded some of the greatest harmony yodeling on disc, including "The Yodel Blues" and "Beyond the Sunset."

In the late fifties Allen tired of touring and took up a job as a disc jockey. In the sixties she opened her own New Jersey–based country record shop. By the eighties she had retired to rural Alabama, her performing days long behind her.

Select Discography

Queen of the Yodelers, Cattle 46. Out-of-print reissue collection of Victor recordings from 1946 to 1951. Includes CHET ATKINS on guitar and Jethro Burns (of HOMER AND JETHRO fame) on mandolin on some cuts.

◀ ALLEN, TERRY

(born 1943, Wichita, KS)

Terry Allen is a contemporary Texas SINGER/SONGWRITER/pianist who gained a cult following in Europe for his offbeat original compositions and gruff vocal style.

Trained as an architect and working occasionally as an art teacher, Allen recorded a number of concept LPs in the seventies and early eighties, collaborated with David Byrne on the soundtrack for his film *True Stories*, and accompanied JOE ELY and Butch Hancock on their recordings. His most interesting LPs are *Juarez*, a 1975 song cycle that relates the story of four Californians who migrate to Mexico in search of a better life, and *Lubbock on Everything*, a double-LP set whose songs are peopled with archetypal Texan misfits and desperados. His best-known songs are "New Delhi Freight Train," covered by Little Feat, and the slightly skewed "Cocktail Desperado," which he performed in Byrne's film. His score for Wolf-Echart's film *Amerasia*, concerning the impact of the United States on Southeast Asia during the Vietnam War, is probably the world's only country-*eastern* record, as it features Allen accompanied by traditional Thai instrumentalists.

◀ ALLEN BROTHERS, THE

(Austin [banjo, lead vocals] and Lee [guitar, kazoo, vocals])

The Allen Brothers were a jazzy duo who specialized in blues and hokum numbers. Their biggest hit was "Salty Dog Blues," with its snappy "hey-hey-hey-hey" chorus.

The Allens were an anomaly in country music; although they were born out in the back country, some fifty miles north of Chattanooga, Tennessee, they were living in the metropolis by their teen years and were well educated (Lee even attended the city's St. Andrews Prep School, which also bred the famous Depression-era writer James Agee). They dressed in natty, double-breasted suits and aspired to be vaudeville stars. Chattanooga had its share of blues-oriented acts whom the Allens undoubtedly heard, including a guitar-playing woman named May Bell, who was a popular performer on the riverboats that cruised up and down the Mississippi, and a group known as the Two Poor Boys, who were familiar street singers and made a few 78s themselves. The brothers were also influenced by jazz-era orchestras and pop crooners, whose jivey vocals were reminiscent of the sis-boom-bah style of college quartets of the era.

They first recorded for Columbia in Chattanooga under the direction of famed producer FRANK WALKER. Their first record, "Salty Dog Blues," sold well, leading to a second session producing another jazz age–influenced number, "Chattanooga Blues," featuring a "wow-wow-wow-wow" chorus echoing their earlier "hey-hey" chant in "Salty Dog," a ragtime-influenced guitar break by brother Lee, and even some strange vocal interjections by brother Austin (who urged his brother to "percolate, mama, percolate," during his guitar solo). Perhaps because it was titled a blues, and perhaps because Walker returned the master to New York along with recordings of black as well as white artists, the company released the record in their race series (reserved for black artists). The brothers were furious and sued. Lee later claimed that their suit was based on their fears that managers would not hire an act to perform in mainstream theaters if they believed its members were black. The unsuccessful suit soured their relationship with the label, and soon after they signed with the rival Victor company.

The Allens recorded prolifically for Victor through the mid-thirties, again focusing on songs that at least had "blues" in the title. These songs were pop-jazz numbers, many with topical themes, including songs that commented on the plight of the farmer ("Price of Cotton Blues") and the rise of mass-market chain stores that were threatening the local mom-and-pop venues ("Chain Store Blues"). They moved into hokum (slightly sexually suggestive) novelty numbers in the second half of their career, including their hit, "(Mama Don't Allow) No Low Down Hanging Around," from 1930, a version of the ever-popular jazz novelty that was widely copied by other country acts. They also re-recorded their first hit, now called "New Salty Dog Blues," which helped keep the song in circulation through the late thirties.

The Depression and the advent of radio conspired to put a bite into the profitability of many recording labels. The Allens, like many other country acts, saw their sales suffer. In the early thirties, they were performing in vaudeville and eventually ended up in New York, where in 1934 they made their last recordings (mostly remakes of their earlier hits) for the smaller, dime-store (budget) label Vocalion-ARC. Older brother Austin remained in the city, but his younger sibling returned to Tennessee, where he eventually became an electrician.

Select Discography

With Banjo and Guitar, Old Timey 115. Copies of this LP reissue of the Allens' early sides may be scarce. Allen Brothers tracks are also available on various anthologies, including the *Roots and Blues* set from Columbia.

◀ AMAZING RHYTHM ACES

(c. 1973–1981: Russell Smith [lead vocals, guitar]; Barry "Byrd" Burton [guitar, dobro]; Billy Earheart III [keyboards]; Jeff Davis [bass]; Butch McDade [drums])

Somewhat ahead of their time, the Amazing Rhythm Aces combined rock, Memphis soul, and country, presaging eighties hybrid bands like SAWYER BROWN.

Formed in the early seventies, the group grew out of the rhythm section of folksinger Jesse Winchester's road band, led by SINGER/SONGWRITER Russell Smith. He supplied their first hit, the up-tempo "Third Rate Romance" in 1975, charting on both pop and country lists. However, they were unable to duplicate this pop success and turned their attention to country with follow-up singles including "Amazing Grace (Used to Be Her Favorite Song)" and "The End Is Not in Sight." Smith left to pursue a solo career in 1981, with little success, and wrote songs in the early eighties for mainstream country stars like CONWAY TWITTY and GEORGE JONES.

Although the group featured some country instrumentation (including Burton's DOBRO), they had a sound similar to mainstream pop acts of the era, including the far more successful EAGLES.

◀ ANDERSON, BILL

(born 1937, Columbia, SC)

Anderson is a songwriter and recording artist whose late-fifties and early-sixties compositions brought a new realism to Nashville songwriting. Known as "Whispering Bill" because of his famous half-recited vocals on his 1963 hit, "Still," as well as the general limitations of his vocal style, Anderson later redirected his career toward being an all-around entertainer, working in television, B movies, and game shows.

Growing up in suburban Atlanta, Anderson was already leading his own country band and writing songs while in high school. With a BA from the University of Georgia and experience as a working journalist, Anderson was hardly just "one of the folks." He pursued a part-time career as a songwriter and performer. His 1958 recording of "City Lights" was heard on local radio by RAY PRICE, who covered it and made it a gold record; Price followed it with another Anderson composition, the typically titled "That's What It's Like to Be Lonesome." Anderson abandoned journalism and began writing for many of the big Nashville recording stars of the day, including JIM REEVES, HANK LOCKLIN, and PORTER WAGONER.

Anderson achieved his greatest success in the early sixties, joining the Opry in 1961. He first topped the country charts with 1962's "Mama Sang a Sad Song" and then crossed over into the lucrative pop market with "Still" in 1963. Other HONKY-TONK classics from this period include "I've Enjoyed as Much of This as I Can Stand," "My Name Is Mud," and "8 × 10." The taste of pop glory encouraged Anderson to seek a wider audience, courting success on TV and in the movies while continuing to record country hits. In the late sixties he recorded some popular duets with JAN HOWARD and, in the early seventies, with Mary Lou Turner, whom he discovered. Mid-seventies hits with Turner included "More Than a Bedroom Thing," "That's What Made Me Love You," and a reworking of the traditional "Where Are You Going, Billy Boy?" In the mid-seventies he made "country-disco" recordings of "I Can't Wait Any Longer" and "Three Times a Lady."

In the early eighties, as his country career waned, Anderson launched two ill-fated gameshows, *Mister and Mrs.* and *Funzapoppin*, while recording for his own Southern Tracks label. He continues to tour, appealing primarily to an older, more conservative audience who remember his bygone hit-making days.

Select Discography
Greatest Hits, MCA 13. Cassette-only reissue of his mid-sixties Decca recordings.

◀ ANDERSON, JOHN

(born 1955, Apopka, FL)

One of the first new traditionalists in country music, Anderson scored some early-eighties hits before lapsing prematurely into pop-country obscurity. He returned with a vengeance with his 1992 megahit, "Seminole Wind."

Anderson performed in a high-school rock band and immediately following graduation moved to Nashville to pursue a music career, performing with his sister Donna. They signed to the tiny Ace of Hearts label, recording a gospel number, "Swoop Down, Sweet Jesus," in 1974. Anderson worked for a couple of years as a songwriter before signing with Warner Brothers in 1977. His recordings in the late seventies featured a hardcore, Texas HONKY-TONK sound. He cowrote a number of traditional rocking country numbers with Lionel Delmore, son of one-half of the famous DELMORE BROTHERS, including the big hit "Swingin'," and covered country favorites like BILLY JOE SHAVER's "I'm Just an Old Hunk of Coal."

Career mismanagement detoured Anderson into a more mainstream pop sound in the mid-eighties, but in 1988 he returned to his roots with the excellent *10* album, emphasizing his original compositions and world-weary vocals set against simple, tasteful traditional accompaniments. Still, Anderson looked like he had been superceded by younger performers like RANDY TRAVIS, until 1992 brought his comeback hit, "Seminole Wind," the kind of Western-myth, cowboy-flavored number that the country charts love.

Although he's had a spotty career, Anderson continues to represent the better side of the new traditionalism, not totally selling out to the arena-rock sound that is luring GARTH BROOKS and ersatz stars like BILLY RAY CYRUS away from their country roots.

Select Discography

Greatest Hits, Warner Bros. 25169. His chart-toppers from the late seventies and early eighties.

10, MCA 42218. Cassette-only reissue of this important 1988 album.

Seminole Wind, BNA 61029. His 1992 "comeback," with his latest big hit.

You Can't Keep a Good Memory Down, MCA 11089. 1994 release.

◀ ANDERSON, LIZ

(born Elizabeth June Haaby, 1930, Rosean, MN)

Anderson is a SINGER/SONGWRITER best-known for hits penned for MERLE HAGGARD, including the bad-guy classics "Lonesome Fugitive" and "My Friends Are Gonna Be Strangers." She also had a brief recording career in the late sixties, during the time of her daughter Lynn's greatest success.

Born in Minnesota near the Canadian border, Elizabeth Haaby took an early interest in music, singing on street corners with her older brother. The family relocated to Grand Forks, North Dakota, in the early forties, where she met her future husband, Casey Anderson. They married in 1946, and their daughter was born a year later. In 1951 the family moved to California in search of better times, and Casey got a job selling cars. Meanwhile, Liz began writing songs, attracting the attention of Casey's co-worker Jack McFadden, who later became BUCK OWENS's manager. McFadden pitched her song "I Watched You Walking" to DEL REEVES, who had some local success with it, but it was 1961's "Be Quiet Mind" that gave Reeves and Anderson their first national hit.

In the mid-sixties, Anderson wrote songs for many California-based country stars. BONNIE OWENS picked up her "Just Between the Two of Us" and recorded it as a duet with Merle Haggard. It was at this time that Haggard heard the song "My Friends Are Gonna Be Strangers," which became a signature tune for him. In 1966 Liz and her husband went to Nashville, where she was signed by CHET ATKINS at RCA Records. Her back-home sound married to her many well-known songs led to a string of moderately successful albums on RCA in the late sixties. After that, the pair settled in Hendersonville, Tennessee, where husband Casey became a song publisher and also cowrote further hits with his wife.

◀ ANDERSON, LYNN

(born 1947, Grand Forks, ND)

Lynn Anderson is a smooth-voiced vocalist whose 1970 hit "(I Never Promised You a) Rose Garden" influenced the nascent COUNTRYPOLITAN movement.

The daughter of HONKY-TONK tunesmith LIZ ANDERSON, Lynn was raised in California and first found success as an equestrian on the local horse-show circuit while working as a singer on *The Lawrence Welk Show*. She signed with tiny Chart Records in 1966, scoring hits with the peppy "Ride Ride Ride" written by her mother. In 1968, she moved to Nashville and, a year later, had a country hit with "That's a No No." She wed producer/songwriter R. Glenn Sutton, who produced her biggest hit in 1970, which hardly sounds like a country song at all. The title song of a successful film, "Rose Garden" brought Anderson widespread exposure to a MOR (middle-of-the-road) audience. A string of pop-country hits followed, although Anderson split from her husband in the mid-seventies. By the early eighties, she had returned to a career as a horsewoman, although she did make an abortive comeback attempt in 1989 with a cover of the Drifters's pop hit "Under the Boardwalk."

Select Discography

Greatest Hits, Columbia 31641. Cassette-only reissue of her early- to mid-seventies goldies.

◀ AREA CODE 615

(c. 1969–1971: Ken Buttrey [drums, vocals]; Wayne Moss [guitar]; David Briggs [keyboards]; Mac Gayden [guitar, French horn]; Charlie McCoy [harmonica]; Weldon Myrick [steel guitar]; Norman Putnam [bass, cello]; Buddy Spicher [fiddle, viola, cello]; Bobby Thompson [banjo, guitar])

Area Code 615 was the first Nashville supergroup made up primarily of younger session players. They were noteworthy for their tasteful instrumental work, which was a far cry from the sanitized strings and reverb-laden choirs heard on much Nashville work of the sixties.

The leader of the group was guitarist Wayne Moss. Like the other players, he had a varied background in country, pop, and rhythm and blues. He worked for many years in BRENDA LEE's backing band before joining the Escorts, led by harmonica player CHARLIE McCOY and also featuring Gayden and Buttrey. Later they became the nucleus of the house band at Nashville's Monument label, taking the name the Music City Five.

Area Code 615, named for the Nashville phone exchange, was formed in 1969 and gained a good deal of attention from the pop press because of their folk-rock style. In the same year, many of these musicians worked on BOB DYLAN's *Nashville Skyline*, one of the first COUNTRY-ROCK albums. The core group was joined by the fine BLUEGRASS fiddler Buddy Spicher and banjoist Bobby Thompson and featured unusual instrumentation including cello, viola, and even the occasional French horn. Area Code 615 recorded two albums, the first all instrumental, the second featuring vocals by Buttrey, before they disbanded. Most have returned to session work, with Spicher also recording an occasional solo album, particularly working with jazz-styled steel guitarist Buddy Emmons.

Moss, along with another Nashville session player, steel guitarist Russ Hicks, formed Barefoot Jerry to continue the progressive country-rock style of Area Code 615. The group also included Jim Colvard (guitar), Warren Hartman (keyboards), Terry Dearmore (bass, vocals), and Si Edwards (drums). They stayed together for about five years, recording for a variety of labels with limited success. Unlike the country-rock groups out of California, this Nashville-based band had a hard time gaining respect either from the conservative country audience or from the mainstream rock press.

◀ ARNOLD, EDDY

(born Richard Evert Arnold, 1918, near Henderson, TN)

Originally a middle-of-the-road HONKY-TONK crooner, Arnold became one of the most successful crossover artists of the sixties, championing the NASHVILLE SOUND on a series of MOR hits.

The son of an old-time fiddler father and guitar-playing mother, Arnold took up the guitar at age ten, abandoning his schooling soon after to help during the Depression years on his family's farm. After performing at local dances, Arnold was hired to perform on local radio, which in turn led to radio jobs in Memphis and St. Louis. A job fronting PEE WEE KING's Golden West Cowboys led to nationwide exposure on the GRAND OLE OPRY. From his early experiences on the farm, Arnold took the nickname "the Tennessee Ploughboy."

In 1944, he signed as a solo act with RCA and had his first string of hits with honky-tonk and cowboy numbers between the late forties and early fifties, including the sentimental "Bouquet of Roses" (1948), the slightly racy "I Wanna Play House with You" (1951), and his Western epic, "Cattle Call" (1955). He wrote or cowrote many of his early hits, including the bathetic "I'm Throwing Rice at the Girl I Love" and "Will Santa Claus Come to Shanty Town?" Much of his early success can be ascribed to his wily manager, Colonel Tom Parker, who later helped another Southern boy make it big (Elvis).

Up to the mid-fifties his accompaniments were fairly spare, featuring the fine steel guitar of Roy Wiggins, who was influenced by Hawaiian artists like Sol Hoopi. However, by the mid-fifties Arnold began to succumb to RCA's house style, molded by producer CHET ATKINS, and his originally plaintive vocal style became increasingly smooth and bland. He also hosted his own syndicated television program and, because of his mainstream good looks and pleasant vocals, was invited to guest on many of the popular fifties variety programs catering to a general audience.

It was in the mid-sixties that Arnold really hit pay dirt with a series of string-smothered recordings tailored for the country charts. With hits like "Make the World Go Away," "Lonely Again," and "Turn the World Around," Arnold successfully wed blue-and-lonesome subject matter with mainstream schmaltz. He proved that a country artist could have broad appeal, encouraging others to take a similar middle-of-the-road approach. His career flagged a little in the early seventies and then picked up steam again in 1976 when he re-signed with RCA.

Although Arnold continued to chart on the country scene into the early eighties, he survived primarily as a nostalgic reminder of mid-sixties pop-country. His legacy was that he proved a country artist could appeal to a mass audience, something that the new Nashville crowd would discover again in the late eighties and early nineties.

Select Discography

Pure Gold, RCA 58398. The sixties and seventies hits, when Arnold's original honky-tonk sound was buried under a ton of strings.

Anytime, Stetson HAT 3086. This out-of-print (but worth-searching-for) album re-issues late-forties and early-fifties recordings, with wonderful steel guitar by Little Roy Wiggins, and Eddy crooning his heart out on his early hits. This LP was orig-inally issued by RCA in 1955.

◀ ARTHUR, CHARLINE

(born Charline Highsmith, 1929, near Paris, TX; died 1987)

Arthur was a pioneering country-boogie and ROCKABILLY singer, full of spunk and sass, who helped break the mold for the next generation of plucky songstresses.

Charline's family was dirt-poor; she was said to be born in a boxcar. Her father rambled around Texas, working as a Pentecostal preacher and performing on the harmonica accompanied by his guitarist/wife. Impressed by the music of ERNEST TUBB, Charline bought a guitar for $4.95 and wrote her first song, "I've Got the Boogie Blues," when she was twelve. (She recorded the song seven years later for Nashville's Bullet Records.) She formed a duo with her sister to perform at community functions and, in 1945, was hired as a performer by a traveling medicine show. Three years later she married bassist Jack Arthur, who performed with the show. He became her manager, taking her to Nashville a year later and booking her into honky-tonks as a sultry diva.

After recording for the small Bullet label, Charline attracted the attention of HANK SNOW's manager, Colonel Tom Parker (who would later take another fireball, ELVIS PRESLEY, and make him famous). Parker got her a contract with RCA, but she was unhappy with their attempt to change her into a demure country chanteuse. Charline refused to wear the standard-issue gingham dress that all country women were meant to don; instead she appeared in pants suits, years before these outfits were considered acceptable, particularly by the conservative country audience. Arthur's stage show featured lots of theatrics, and she loved to shout the bluesy numbers that drove small-town bar audiences wild. Her best RCA recordings were of up-tempo material, including "I'm Having a Party All By Myself," the husband-stealer's warning "Just Look, Don't Touch, He's Mine," and the proto-rockabilly recordings "Honey Bun" and "Burn That Candle."

In the mid-fifties she really raised eyebrows with the then-racy songs "The Good and the Bad" (in which bluesy Charline engages in a dialogue with her sweet-voiced alter ego—with the bad girl winning out) and "Kiss the Baby Goodnight," which could not be performed in its original, unedited version on the GRAND OLE OPRY. In 1957, after continuing battles with her producer CHET ATKINS, Arthur was dropped from RCA and fell into obscurity as a performer, dying penniless and forgotten some thirty years later.

Select Discography
Welcome to the Club, Bear Family 15234. LP reissue of Arthur's mid-fifties RCA recordings, with vintage photographs and complete notes.

◀ ASCH, MOSES

(born 1905, Warsaw, Poland; died 1986)

Moses Asch ran Folkways Records for thirty-nine years, the main (and for many years only) outlet for folk and country music to an urban audience.

The son of noted novelist Sholem Asch, Moses began his career as a sound engineer, working on the sound for Broadway shows like the original *Hellzapoppin'*. His father was friendly with many leading intellectuals of the day, and Asch claimed he took his inspiration to start a record company from Albert Einstein, who suggested that with his background in sound recording Asch could make a valuable contribution to documenting the twentieth century.

Asch first founded the Disc and Asch labels in the late thirties, recording jazz and folk and blues revivalists like PETE SEEGER, WOODY GUTHRIE, and Josh White. During the Second World War, when shellac used in making 78 rpm records was rationed and only established labels could get records pressed, Asch joined forces with the Stinson label for a while. He started Folkways Records in 1947 as a means of documenting all types of music and speech.

From the beginning, Folkways played a central role in the revival of interest in old-time music. In 1952, eccentric filmmaker/record collector Harry Smith approached Asch about issuing a six-record set of recordings from the twenties and thirties that he called *The Anthology of American Folk Music*. Smith had an excellent collection and peerless taste and selected for representation on this set several key country artists, many of whose recordings were long unavailable (or never available in urban areas). These six records were highly prized by the first generation of folk revivalists, who in turn passed along the songs to another generation of performers. Meanwhile, Asch recorded Pete Seeger throughout the fifties when Seeger was blacklisted for his alleged Communist sympathies, and issued albums by traditional artists like BASCOM LAMAR LUNSFORD and Woody Guthrie, to name just two.

In 1959 young folklorist MIKE SEEGER approached Asch about issuing an album he called *Mountain Music Blue Grass Style*; this was the first album of BLUEGRASS music issued for a city audience. Seeger's group, the NEW LOST CITY RAMBLERS, were the first old-time string-band revivalists, and they recorded for Folkways throughout the sixties. Meanwhile, group members Seeger and JOHN COHEN produced albums of traditional country musicians, both rediscovered artists from the twenties and thirties like DOCK BOGGS and newly found masters such as ROSCOE HOLCOMB. Folkways also issued albums by traditional BANJO players WADE WARD and Pete Steele.

In the mid-sixties Asch entered into a distribution agreement with MGM records, which was anxious to cash in on the folk-music craze, and then into a second deal with the educational publisher Scholastic. By 1971, he resurfaced on his own, issuing records on the revived Asch label, and by 1973 he took control of the

Folkways back catalog. He continued to issue records until his death thirteen years later, although by then other labels like Rounder, County, and Arhoolie had become more important in issuing new recordings of folk and country figures.

Because Asch believed that all of his records should remain in print, even if they only sold a few copies each year, all of this material remained available until the time of his death in 1986, influencing many generations of musicians. The Smithsonian Institution, under Ralph Rinzler (late of the GREENBRIAR BOYS), took over the label after his death and has been slowly reissuing the better material on compact disc while keeping everything available through special-order cassettes.

◀ ASHLEY, TOM

(born Clarence Earl McCurry, 1895, Bristol, TN; died 1967)

Ashley was a spirited performer on BANJO and GUITAR and one of the finest of the classic country artists who were rediscovered during the FOLK-REVIVAL years of the sixties.

Born in Bristol, Clarence was raised by his maternal grandfather, Enoch Ashley, in the Mountain City area of northeastern Tennessee (he later legally took his grandfather's surname). He was already performing on banjo and guitar in local medicine shows around 1910 and remained active on the informal tent-show circuit through World War II. He performed on record, usually as guitarist, with a number of bands, including famed old-time trio the Carolina Tar Heels, Byrd Moore and his Hotshots, and the Blue Ridge Mountain Entertainers.

The Tar Heels recorded many sides in the late twenties and early thirties, usually featuring Ashley on guitar and lead vocals, either Gwen or Garley Foster (no relation) on harmonica, guitar, and tenor vocals, and Doc Walsh on banjo and baritone vocal. Ashley claimed to have composed the folk ballad "My Home's Across the Blue Ridge Mountains" for the group, which became popular in the folk-revival repertoire after BASCOM LAMAR LUNSFORD recorded it for the Library of Congress. Ashley also cut solo songs on the banjo, most notably his versions of "The Coo Coo Bird" and "The House Carpenter," that were much-copied during the early days of the folk revival in the fifties and sixties.

Ashley was rediscovered by folklorist Ralph Rinzler at the Galax, Virginia, fiddlers convention in 1960. Rinzler encouraged him to take up banjo playing again, an instrument Ashley had stopped playing in the early forties due to a hand injury. Ashley had himself discovered and tutored a number of younger musicians in northwestern North Carolina, where he had been living, including guitarists Clint Howard and ARTHEL "DOC" WATSON and fiddler Fred Price. Rinzler brought the quartet to New York City during 1961 and 1962 to record a series of influential albums as well as to perform for folk-revival audiences. Watson was such a standout that he was quickly performing as a solo act, recording for the then-major folk label Vanguard Records. Ashley continued to make appearances at folk festivals and in concerts and made one more album before he died in 1967.

Although not as flamboyant a performer as UNCLE DAVE MACON, Ashley had a fine singing voice, a good memory for traditional and sentimental tunes, and a simple but clean playing style on the five-string banjo. His many long years as a performer made him an ideal figure to introduce old-time sounds to a new, younger audience.

Select Discography

Old Time Music at Clarence Ashley's, Smithsonian/Folkways 40029/30. Wonderful early-sixties recordings made by Ralph Rinzler, featuring Doc Watson, Clint Howard, and Fred Price.

◀ ASHWORTH, ERNIE

(born 1928, Huntsville, AL)

Ashworth was a typical mainstream songsmith of the fifties who developed a successful career as a pop-influenced crooner in the early and mid-sixties.

Raised in a midsized Alabama community, Ashworth got his first taste of performing while still in his teens, playing his own material on guitar over local radio. His success prompted him to take a chance on a career as a songwriter, and he moved to Nashville in the mid-fifties, placing songs with stars CARL SMITH and "LITTLE" JIMMY DICKENS, among others, while performing on radio. He signed with powerful song publisher WESLEY ROSE, who got him a contract with MGM, where he recorded under his own name and also under the nom de disc of Billy Worth. These recordings were duds, however, and by 1957 Ashworth had returned discouraged to his Alabama home.

In 1960, Rose lured him back to Nashville with a promise of a contract with Decca Records. Ashworth hit it big with his first release, "Each Moment (Spent with You)," laying the groundwork for the drippy follow-ups "You Can't Pick a Rose in December" and "Forever Gone." In 1962 Ashworth moved to Rose's new record label, Hickory, and the hits kept coming with more hanky-straining WEEPERS, including "Talk Back Trembling Lips" (his one and only number-one hit), "A Week in the Country," "The DJ Cried," and "Sad Face." In 1965, his big break in Hollywood came with an appearance in the forgettable film *The Farmer's Other Daughter*.

By the late sixties Ashworth had fallen off the charts and taken to a life of constant touring on the backstreams of the country circuit and performing on the GRAND OLE OPRY. In the early eighties he performed at DOLLY PARTON's Dollywood theme park in Pigeon Forge, Tennessee.

Select Discography

Greatest Hits, Curb 77483. Reissue of sixties-era recordings.

◀ ASLEEP AT THE WHEEL

(c. 1970–ongoing; original lineup: Ray Benson [guitar, vocals]; Lucky Oceans [steel guitar]; Chris O'Connell [vocals, guitar]; Jim "Floyd Domino" Haber [piano]; LeRoy Preston [drums, vocals])

Asleep at the Wheel is a rocking WESTERN SWING revival band that was most popular in the mid-seventies and is said to have employed over seventy-five musicians in its twenty-plus years of existence. Lead guitarist/vocalist Ray Benson is the motivating force behind this band that will not die, and the only original member left.

Benson's love of Western swing music began when he was a teenager in suburban Philadelphia, playing music with his friend, steel guitarist Reuben Gosfield (aka Lucky Oceans). The duo, along with pianist Danny Levin and drummer/vocalist LeRoy Preston moved to a farm in West Virginia in 1970, forming the nucleus of the original band. Soon they were playing rock and Western swing (but never mixing the styles) at local clubs.

Around 1971, the band began to make waves as an opening act in the Washington, D.C., area. George Frayne (aka Commander Cody) heard them at a local gig and urged them to move to San Francisco later that year. Through 1973 the band was headquartered on the West Coast, continuing to grow in personnel, and finally landed a record contract with United Artists. By this time, Levin was replaced by new pianist Jim Haber, who took the nickname Floyd Domino, in honor of his idols, country tinkler FLOYD CRAMER and R&B stylist Fats Domino.

A tour of Texas in 1974, then a hotbed of progressive country music, led the band to move to Austin and to sign a one-album deal with Epic. In 1975, they finally scored a hit with "The Letter That Johnny Walker Read" on Capitol Records, the label where they scored their greatest success. The band ballooned to eleven members, creating a sound that mixed BOB WILLS's styled Western swing with a little Count Basie and a little Commander Cody. A hard-working touring band, they developed a large following in Europe, while occasionally scoring minor hits. They also had a devoted following on the college circuit, where their nouveau Western style appealed to the latter-day hippie audience.

In the early eighties Benson cut back on the size of the outfit, for financial and artistic reasons. The band had grown so big that it was hard to control and expensive to tour. Through the eighties the band soldiered on, with Benson leading a pack of musicians through Western swing, CAJUN, and country styles. Although no longer the darlings of FM college radio, they found a steady audience on the road, where they had always made their best music. Benson is one of those rare true believers who has been able to keep his band going against the odds and will probably perform with some version of Asleep at the Wheel for many years to come.

Select Discography
Route 66, Liberty 98925. Twenty-year retrospective of their best tracks.
Asleep at the Wheel, Epic 33097. Reissue of their second album from 1974.
The Swinging' Best of, Epic 53049. Early- to mid-eighties recordings.
Live and Kickin', Arista 18698. Late-eighties and early-nineties recordings.

◀ ATCHER, BOB

(born 1914, Robert Owen Atcher, Hardin County, KY)
An early COWBOY actor/performer, Atcher was long associated with Chicago's *National Barn Dance*.

Although he was born in Kentucky, Atcher was raised in North Dakota, the heart of Western song and lore. His father was a champion fiddler, and many other members of the family picked and sang, so he was exposed to both Southern folksongs and songs of the West from an early age. By his late teens, he had moved to Chicago, which at the time had a thriving country-music scene, primarily centered around a number of popular radio shows. Atcher, with his smooth tenor voice and good looks, was a natural for the role of singing cowboy, and he appeared on a number of Chicago-based radio shows from 1931 on, signing with Columbia Records in 1937 (where he remained for twenty-one years).

Atcher's fame grew after he joined the *National Barn Dance* in 1948, where he performed both as a soloist and in duet with a string of partners who all went by the name of Bonnie Blue Eyes. He remained with the Barn Dance (a vital link to the thirties cowboy style that had otherwise disappeared from popular music) for twenty-two years, until it went off the air. Toward the end of his career, Atcher turned his attention to local politics, serving as mayor of Schaumburg, Illinois, (a Chicago suburb) for sixteen years.

◀ ATKINS, CHET

(born Chester Burton Atkins, 1924, Lutrell, TN)

Chet Atkins is one of those maddeningly professional Nashville musicians who, while undoubtedly a great talent on the guitar, has recorded his share of schlock over the years. Plus, as house producer for RCA, he is credited with creating the late-fifties/sixties NASHVILLE SOUND, the mainstream trivialization of country music that drove many traditionalists to despair.

Atkins's guitar style is rooted in the playing of MERLE TRAVIS, the legendary finger-picker who developed a style that combined playing the melody with a flat pick and picking out an accompanying bass line with the thumb. Beginning in the mid-forties, Atkins worked as an accompanist for various country acts (including the CARTER FAMILY and country comedians HOMER AND JETHRO) on radio and the road, and began recording as a soloist in the late forties. His best work was done in this period through the early fifties; his electric-guitar instrumentals set new standards for performance, from 1947's "Canned Heat" to 1949's "Galloping on the Guitar" through his best-known composition, 1953's "Country Gentlemen" (Atkins would help design a guitar for the Gretsch company that was named after this recording).

An appointment as manager of A&R (Artist & Repertoire) at RCA's new Nashville studios in the mid-fifties spelled the end of Atkins's creative career as an instrumentalist. In choosing a house band, he selected pop-oriented players, including the famous pianist FLOYD CRAMER, whose slide-note style epitomized the new mainstream orientation of the Nashville Sound. Atkins also employed vocal groups like the JORDANAIRES and string sections to give his productions a slicker sound. Still, Atkins gave a new professionalism to Nashville's recordings, and he helped mold the careers of ELVIS PRESLEY, the EVERLY BROTHERS, the BROWNS, and SKEETER DAVIS.

Atkins's later recordings are best when he is paired with a musician who inspires him to do his finest work, such as LES PAUL, DOC WATSON, JERRY REED, Merle Travis, or even Scottish rock guitarist Mark Knopfler. He retired from working for RCA as a producer in the late seventies to return to his first love, performing, although his eighties and early-nineties output continued to vary from the sublime to the saccharine.

Select Discography

The RCA Years, RCA 61095. A double-CD set with some gems set among the dross. Hear Chet pick with the Boston Pops under Arthur Fiedler. When you've recovered, there are some decent tracks with Jerry Reed and Merle Travis, along with cuts accompanying DOLLY PARTON.

◀ AUTRY, GENE

(born Orvon Autry, 1907, Tioga Springs, TX)

The first and most famous singing cowboy, Autry transformed the image of the country singer with his introduction of Western garb and mannerisms into his stage persona. In the thirties he was a star of radio, records, and films; from the end of World War II on he was primarily a canny businessman who invested in diverse activities from real estate to baseball to oil. Besides performing many venerable cowboy hits, he wrote or cowrote songs in the sentimental ("That Silver Haired Daddy of Mine"), cowboy ("Tumbling Tumbleweeds," "South of the Border"), and blues ("I Hang My Head and Cry") styles, as well as his famous Christmas/ children's songs ("Frosty the Snowman," "Rudolph the Red-Nosed Reindeer," "Here Comes Santa Claus," and "Peter Cottontail").

Autry began his career as a JIMMIE RODGERS imitator; like so many country performers of the late twenties and early thirties, he was enamored with the Rodgers's sound, which he shamelessly copied. In 1928, supposedly on the advice of famous radio comedian Will Rogers, he traveled to New York in search of radio work. There he was discovered by ART SATHERLY, the early country-music scout who worked for the American Record Company (ARC).

His first hits were with sentimental songs sung in the plaintive style of Rodgers. At the same time, however, Autry began downplaying his rural-farm upbringing while playing up his (nonexistent) roots as a cowboy, perhaps influenced by the increasing popularity of movie cowboys such as Ken Maynard. In 1934 Autry gained his first movie role in support of Maynard in *In Old Santa Fe*. The next year he starred in his first film serial, the unusual *Phantom Empire*, which featured a bizarre mix of science fiction and cowboy antics. He would go on to appear in almost a hundred horse operas, usually accompanied by his favorite horse, Champion. From 1939 to 1956 he starred on radio in Gene Autry's "Melody Ranch," further underscoring his cowboy image.

After serving in the Army Air Corps in World War II, Autry returned to civilian life to find himself supplanted in the public imagination by another civilian-turned-cowpoke, ROY ROGERS, of recent burger-broiling fame. Autry retired from music making in the early fifties to focus on his lucrative business ventures.

Autry's main importance was not his style, which was a typical mix of country mannerisms with the crooning popularized by Bing Crosby; rather, it was his image, with the complete Western garb that helped spread the myth of the cowboy as the last American pioneer. Country stars, who had previously appeared in overalls to emphasize their rural background, suddenly began appearing in cowboy hats and chaps. The romance of the West and the sentimentality of heart-tugging songs made an unbeatable combination. It's no surprise that GARTH BROOKS, country's latest superstar, always appears in a ten-gallon hat.

Select Discography
The Essential, Columbia/Legacy 48957. Fine thirties and forties recordings, featuring swinging Western accompaniments, including previously unissued alternate takes for the collector.

◀ AXTON, HOYT

(born 1932, Comanche, OK)

Axton is a seventies-era SINGER/SONGWRITER who has had more success writing hits for other artists than scoring them on his own. He has worked in a number of styles, from blues to folk-rock to pure country.

Son of noted pop tunesmith Mae Boren Axton (who wrote ELVIS PRESLEY's early hit "Heartbreak Hotel"), Axton was raised in rural Oklahoma and was greatly influenced by the topical music of fellow Oklahoman WOODY GUTHRIE. His first big hit was a reworking of "I Don't Want Your Millions, Mister," a Depression-era song popularized by Guthrie; Axton's version, called "Greenback Dollar," was co-written with Ken Ramsey of the folk revival group the Kingston Trio. Through the sixties Axton wrote countryesque songs for mainstream Nashville acts including FARON YOUNG, JEAN SHEPARD, and HANK SNOW.

Axton's big break into pop music came in 1969 when the rock group Steppenwolf recorded his "The Pusher," which was featured on the soundtrack of every hippie biker's favorite movie, *Easy Rider*. The song did little to endear him to country audiences, however, who failed to realize that the message of the song was that drug dealers are evil. Thanks to this success, he was signed to Columbia in the same year and released an album recorded in a soft-pop, singer/songwriter style.

Axton next penned the ultimate seventies feel-good anthem, "Joy to the World," a megahit for Three Dog Night in 1971. Four years later he followed up with the silly "No No Song" for Ringo Starr, a number-one pop hit. Axton recorded two more folk-country-styled discs in the mid-seventies, scoring minor hits with 1974's "When the Morning Comes" and 1976's "Flash of Fire." A year later, he had moved to a new label, recording another antidrug tune, "Snow Blind Friend," about the evils of cocaine, and producing the hit satire "You're the Hangnail in My Life." Unable to do much on the pop charts, Axton recorded a pure country album in 1979, with minor success on the story songs "Delta and the Dealer" and "Rusty Old Halo"; however, the NEW-COUNTRY movement had not yet been born, and Axton's career stalled out.

In the eighties, Axton worked as a film actor, appearing in a number of Steven Spielberg–produced films, including *Gremlins* and *E.T.*

B.

◀ BAILES BROTHERS

(Homer [fiddle, vocals]; Johnny [guitars, vocals]; Kyle [bass, vocals]; Walter [guitar, vocals])

The Bailes Brothers were a family group centering on Johnny and Walter, whose classic gospel songs (the ever-popular "Dust on the Bible") and sentimental numbers ("Remember Me") have become country standards.

Hailing from a West Virginia farming community, the boys performed together at home and church, where they learned the classic SHAPE-NOTE style of harmony singing that would be echoed in their recordings. Their father was a Baptist preacher, and two of the four sons would eventually follow him into this profession. Johnny was the first successful musician, working with RED SOVINE in 1937 and then hooking up with Skeets and Laverne Williamson (Laverne later gained fame as MOLLY O'DAY) and "LITTLE" JIMMY DICKENS to work out of Beckley, West Virginia, on radio. He also began performing with brother Kyle as a vocal duo; soon after, Walter replaced Kyle, and the Bailes Brothers was born.

In 1942, the two brothers were signed by ROY ACUFF to the GRAND OLE OPRY, where they remained popular performers for six years. They were signed to Columbia, where they recorded many of their classic compositions, including "I Want to Be Loved (But Only By You)," "Oh, So Many Years," and "Give Mother My Crown." All of these recalled the vocal sound and accompaniment of recordings of a decade earlier; in fact, the brothers' vocal style resonated with the age-old mountain ballad singing style, as it was filtered through rural churches.

In 1948, the duo switched to the rival *Louisiana Hayride* program, performing for one more year before the act dissolved. Although Johnny and Walter continued to work sporadically as a gospel duo through the early fifties, Walter curtailed his performing to focus on the ministry. Johnny began managing one of WEBB PIERCE's country radio stations in the late seventies, and Walter, while still a minister, was also performing. He found time to write "Whiskey Is the Devil in Liquid Form," one of those deadly serious gospel numbers that is often satirized by other performers. Homer followed Walter into the ministry, but Kyle went into the air-conditioning business.

Select Discography
Early Radio, Vols. 1–3, Old Homestead 103, 104, 109. Radio broadcasts of the thirties and forties are reissued on this series of out-of-print LPs.

◀ BAILEY, DEFORD

(born 1899, Carthage, TN; died 1982)

One of the most popular performers on the original GRAND OLE OPRY, Bailey is one of those tragic pioneers who never received the recognition that he deserved and spent much of his life in bitter retirement from music making. In his day, he revolutionized harmonica playing, and his 1928 recordings, including the famous "Pan American Blues" with its myriad train sound-effects, influenced generations of musicians. For years, he was the sole black performer on the Opry stage.

Born in rural Tennessee, Bailey's growth was stunted by infantile paralysis, and he suffered from a lifelong affliction of back pain. Bailey was discovered by another early harmonica whiz, DR. HUMPHREY BATE, who had already broadcast over WSM prior to the formal beginnings of the Opry. Bate brought him to the Opry's announcer and motivating force, GEORGE D. HAY, for an audition, and the judge was so impressed that he put Bailey on as the first act on the new Opry program. His talents on the harmonica were awesome, and besides being hired to perform on the Opry, he was among the first artists to be recorded in Nashville, in 1928.

Although Bailey continued to perform on the Opry, the novelty of his few numbers began to wear thin in the thirties, and he was eventually phased off the program by 1941. Bailey blamed racism for the failure of his career; Hay blamed Bailey for his failure to learn new material. Whatever the truth, Bailey spent the final decades of his life an embittered man, turning down offers to appear on Opry anniversary shows, record, or otherwise play. He operated a shoeshine stand in Nashville until his retirement in the seventies.

Select Discography

Harmonica Showcase, Matchbox 218. LP reissue of all eleven of Bailey's original recordings, plus five by D. H. "Bert" Bilbro, a white contemporary of his.

◀ BAILEY, RAZZY

(born Rasie Bailey, 1939, Five Points, AL)

Bailey is a soul-flavored country vocalist whose big hit was "9,999,999 Tears" covered by DICKEY LEE in 1976. Initially a COUNTRYPOLITAN hit maker, Bailey's natural affinity for soul music led him to pursue a career as a blue-eyed soulster.

Bailey was raised in rural Alabama on a farm with no running water or electricity. His father's name was Erastus, nicknamed "Rasie," the name he gave his son. Young Bailey formed his first band in his teenage years, sponsored by the local branch of the Future Farmers of America. He continued to play music part-time as he pursued careers as a truck driver, insurance and furniture salesman, and finally a butcher. He made his first recordings for the tiny Peach label under the producing hand of Joe South in the mid-sixties, followed by two further stabs at recording in the early seventies while continuing to hold his day jobs.

His big break came in 1976 when Dickey Lee covered "9,999,999 Tears"; two years later, he was signed to RCA and had a number of top-twenty hits through the mid-eighties with his original compositions recorded in a pop-country vein, including his first single, "What Time Do You Have to Be Back in Heaven," and 1980's "Loving Up a Storm." In 1981 he had his first number-one country hit, in a rhythm-and-blues vein, with "I Keep Coming Back," followed by the truck-driving anthem "Midnight Hauler." In the mid-eighties he hooked up with soul legend Steve Cropper (of Booker T. and the MGs fame), and the pair cut remakes of Wilson Pickett's "In the Midnight Hour" and Eddie Floyd's "Knock on Wood" along with Bailey's own compositions, all in an R&B style.

◀ BAKERSFIELD SOUND

(c. 1955–1965)

About a hundred miles north of Los Angeles lies the oil-boom town of Bakers-field. In the late forties, many displaced Midwesterners, particularly from Oklahoma, came to the town in search of work. The oil industry provided good jobs that paid well, and soon a local club scene was thriving to cater to the tastes of the displaced Okies. One of the first stars from the area was Okie TOMMY COLLINS, whose band and recordings featured a stripped-down HONKY-TONK sound, thanks to lead guitarist BUCK OWENS, another Okie. Owens was soon a star on his own, leading a hot country combo from the late fifties through the sixties, featuring lead guitar parts and vocal harmonies by Don Rich (who played the newly introduced Fender Telecaster guitar, favored by country rockers like BUDDY HOLLY for its trebley sound) and steel guitarist TOM BRUMLEY. A Bakersfield native named MERLE HAGGARD furthered the roots-oriented style, performing songs about his real-life experiences.

The Bakersfield sound was first captured on record by tiny labels that sprang up in the area but was really given a boost when Los Angeles–based Capitol Records hooked into it. Capitol was a fledgling label in the early fifties that signed Collins and then his protégé Owens and finally Merle Haggard. Half a continent away from Nashville, the Capitol producers pretty much let the Bakersfield groups record without adding the deadening strings and sickly choruses that were a key part of the then-popular NASHVILLE SOUND. The result were some of the finest roots-country recordings of the fifties and sixties.

The Bakersfield sound has recently been revived by NEW-COUNTRY stars like DWIGHT YOAKAM, who have taken the blend of rock, honky-tonk, and traditional country to a new audience.

◀ BANDY, MOE

(born 1944, Meridian, MS)

Hailing from the same town as JIMMIE RODGERS, Bandy was instrumental in launching the mid-seventies revival of HONKY-TONK songs, from his first hit, 1973's "I Just Started Hatin' Cheatin' Songs Today," through 1975's "Hank Williams, You Wrote My Life." At the decade's end, he teamed with JOE STAMPLEY to form the influential country duo Moe and Joe, performing a mix of honky-tonk and hu-morous numbers. They gained some attention in 1984 with their parody of Boy George's stage attire in "Where's the Dress?" complete with a video showing the two performers in MINNIE PEARL–type getups. Bandy's later solo material featured pop-rock flavorings that softened his original honky-tonk edge.

Although Moe was born in Mississippi, his family relocated to San Antonio, Texas, when he was just six years old, and his musical legacy is pure Texas honky-tonk. Both of Bandy's parents were musical, particularly Moe's father, who had his own country band for a while. He encouraged his son to learn fiddle and guitar, but Moe was more interested in pursuing a career as a rodeo rider. After several years of hard knocks and little pay, he abandoned the rodeo life to take up a job as a sheet-metal worker during the day and a honky-tonk singer at night. He formed his first band, Moe and the Mavericks, in 1962 and recorded sporadically for the next decade for many small Texas labels.

In 1972, Moe met record producer Ray Baker, who took an interest in his career. Baker had him record the song "I Just Started Hatin' Cheatin' Songs Today," which was released a year later on GRC Records out of Atlanta. The song shot to number five on the country charts and was followed by similar honky-tonk anthems, including "Honky Tonk Amnesia" and "Don't Anyone Make Love at Home Anymore." In 1975, Bandy cowrote with LEFTY FRIZZELL a song recalling his rodeo days, "Bandy the Rodeo Clown," his last hit for GRC.

In that same year, Bandy signed with Columbia, still under Baker's guiding hand. They continued their string of beer-soaked laments through the early eighties, including "Here I Am Drunk Again," "She Just Loved the Cheatin' Out of Me," "Barstool Mountain," and 1979's duet with JANIE FRICKIE, "It's a Cheatin' Situation." In the same year, Moe made his first recording with Joe Stampley, "Just Good Ol' Boys," the beginning of a string of successful duets with a good-natured, humorous tone, culminating in 1981's top-ten "Hey Joe, Hey Moe."

Although Moe continued to tour (accompanied by his backup band, the Rodeo Clowns) and record through the eighties, he more or less faded from the charts during the onslaught of New Nashville artists.

Select Discography

Greatest Hits, Columbia 38315. Recordings from 1975 to 1981.

Greatest Hits, Curb 77259. Later Bandy output, including remakes of earlier hits.

◀ BANJO (FIVE-STRING)

(c. 1840)

The five-string banjo developed in the mid-nineteenth century, probably derived from earlier African instruments. White minstrel star Joel Sweeney is generally credited with adding the short fifth, or drone, string to the banjo, which previously had been made in four-, six-, eight-, and ten-string models. Early banjos were generally made with wooden bodies and rims, a fretless neck, and a skin head. The original banjo-playing style has been variously called clawhammer, frailing, rapping, or knocking. It involves brushing the back of the hand across the strings while catching the thumb on the fifth string. There are many different varieties of clawhammer styles, from highly melodic to highly percussive.

Around the turn of the century, ragtime players like Fred Van Epps and Vess L.

Ossmann popularized a picked style using three fingers; this style is known as classical or ragtime banjo today. Improved instrument designs helped increase the banjo's popularity. Makers like the Vega company out of Boston introduced new metal tone rings that helped project the instrument's sound, so it could be heard in a band setting. The famous instruments of the teens and twenties, such as Vega's Whyte Laydie and Tubaphone models, were favored by banjoists working both as soloists or in bands.

In the mid-forties, a new style of playing helped transform the banjo from a background (or accompaniment) role to a new prominence as a melody instrument. Two-finger and three-finger picking styles existed among folk banjoists at least from the turn of the century, particularly in North Carolina and the upper South. These evolved into bluegrass-style picking, originally introduced by Earl Scruggs as a member of BILL MONROE's Blue Grass Boys. Here, three fingers are used, with metal picks, to play rapid chord rolls and melody parts. Bluegrass musicians began playing a newly styled banjo marketed by the Gibson company called the Mastertone; it featured further improvements in the design of the tone ring, including a raised head, as well as a full resonator to further increase the instrument's sound.

Although old-time styles continue to be performed today, particularly among urban revivalists, bluegrass-styled banjo dominates commercial Nashville music. The mid-seventies PROGRESSIVE BLUEGRASS movement helped introduce jazz and rock techniques into the banjoist's repertoire; some of the leading practitioners of this latest banjo style include TONY TRISCHKA and BELA FLECK, who leads the jazz-pop band the Flecktones.

◀ BANNON, R. C.

(born Daniel Shipley, 1945, Dallas, TX)

Bannon is a SINGER/SONGWRITER in the COUNTRYPOLITAN style who has been upstaged on the charts by his wife, LOUISE MANDRELL.

Bannon grew up in Texas, where he first sang as a member of his church choir. He moved on to playing rock and roll in local teen groups and then worked the Texas club circuit as a guitarist for a couple of years. He moved to Seattle in the late sixties, taking the name R. C. Bannon after he became a professional deejay in 1968. Five years later, Bannon signed up with MARTY ROBBINS's backup band and eventually worked his way to Nashville. In 1976, he became the deejay at a popular music-city hangout, the Smugglers Inn, where he befriended songwriter Harlan Sanders who recommended him to Warner music as a songwriter.

In 1977, Bannon was signed to Columbia Records, producing only a minor stir on the charts. Two years later, he married Louise Mandrell, and they recorded the hit duet "Reunited," which was written by Bannon with John Bettis, followed a year later by "We Love Each Other." Bannon returned to recording on his own, scoring minor success with 1981's "Where There's Smoke There's Fire" and "Our Wedding Band" a year later. He also supplied more hit songs for wife Louise and cowrote "One of a Kind Pair of Fools" with Louise's sister BARBARA MANDRELL in 1983.

Like the Mandrell sisters, Bannon's work represented the kind of mainstream, glitzy pop-country that was popular in the late seventies and early eighties, but he had less success. Bannon has not been active in the music business since his recording career fizzled in the early eighties.

◀ BARE, BOBBY

(born 1935, Ironton, OH)

A long-time SINGER/SONGWRITER, Bare has passed through many career phases, from country to folk to R&B-styled rock and back to country again. He is best-known for his mid-seventies hit "Detroit City."

Bare was raised in relative poverty on a farm by his father (his mother died when he was just five years old). He began working as a farm laborer when he was fifteen and eventually landed a job in a clothing factory. He played in a local country band, recording his first solo song, "All American Boy," in 1958. The song was a hit when it was released by the Fraternity label a year later under the name Bill Parsons, but Bare did not profit much from it because he had sold his rights to the number for fifty dollars. The record was so successful that Fraternity sent out a stand-in Bill Parsons to lip-sync to Bare's recording on the road.

Soon after, Bare signed with RCA Records, having minor hits with his own "Shame on Me" and "Detroit City" in 1962 and 1963. He recorded an arrangement of the traditional folksong "500 Miles Away from Home," which Bare, folksinger Hedy West, and Charles Williams took credit for as arrangers. He continued to score minor hits on the country and pop charts throughout the sixties. He moved to Mercury in the early seventies but returned to RCA in a more rocking mood in 1972, recording the country hits "Daddy What If" and "Marie Laveau," both penned by Shel Silverstein. Bare was an early fan of then-progressive country song-writers like BILLY JOE SHAVER, KRIS KRISTOFFERSON, and MICKEY NEWBURY. In the late seventies he hooked up with rock promoter Bill Graham, who got him a contract with Columbia Records, which tried to market him as a more mainstream star; however, his pop career fizzled, and he ended up back in country music by the mid-eighties, hosting his own show on the then-fledgling Nashville Network.

Select Discography

Sings Lullabies, Legends and Lies, Bear Family 15683. Reissue of 1973 RCA LP consisting entirely of Shel Silverstein compositions.

Down and Dirty, Columbia 36323. Cassette-only reissue of his later, more pop-oriented recordings.

◀ BATE, DR. HUMPHREY, AND THE POSSUM HUNTERS

(Dr. Humphrey Bate [harmonica], born 1875, Summer County, TN; died 1936; Alcyone Bate [Beasley] [vocals, ukelele, piano]; Buster Bate [guitar, tipple, harmonica, Jew's harp]; Burt Hutcherson [guitar]; Walter Leggett [banjo]; Oscar Stone [fiddle]; Staley Walton [guitar]; Oscar Albright [bass])

The Possum Hunters, led by the harmonica-playing physician Dr. Humphrey Bate, were one of the first old-time string bands featured on the GRAND OLE OPRY.

Bate, a Vanderbilt-educated doctor, led several old-time bands in the Nashville area. He was already performing on Nashville radio in 1924, a year before the *Grand Ole Opry* program began, and he was immediately invited to perform on the Opry as a representative not only of one of Tennessee's finer string bands but also as a respected member of the community. Soon after their Opry debut, the band recorded for Brunswick records. Bate's two children, Alcyone (who began performing with her father when she was thirteen and continued to play with various versions of the band until the early 1960s) and Buster, were prominent members of the group, with other members floating in and out as recording sessions or radio work came their way. After Bate's death, the band continued until the late forties under the lead of fiddler Oscar Stone and then into the early sixties led by Alcyone and guitarist Staley Walton. In the early sixties the band merged with the Crook Brothers, another old-time string band long resident on the Opry.

The sound of the Possum Hunters was fairly typical of middle Tennessee string bands. They were not as wild as the SKILLET LICKERS in their approach to traditional dance tunes, and they favored a repertoire of old-time songs mixed with the sentimental favorites of the day. In a publicity photo taken in the twenties, Dr. Bate is pictured in a rumpled hat and workshirt holding his favorite hunting dog; other band members are dressed in typical "country" getups (banjoist Leggett is wearing a loosely fitted tie, but his shirtsleeves are rolled up and his baggy pants reach only to the knees). Obviously, despite Bates's educated background, the idea was to promote the band as just down-home folks.

Though not the greatest of the classic string bands of the late twenties and early thirties, the Possum Hunters had wide exposure through their residency on the *Grand Ole Opry* and continued to represent an important aspect of country music history for Opry listeners for many decades. Their recordings reveal that Dr. Bate was indeed an able harmonica player, who propulsively played the popular old-time dance tunes of the day.

◀ BEE, MOLLY

(born Molly Beachboard, 1939, Oklahoma City, OK)

A country comedian/singer/actress, Molly Bee has been a popular performer since her preteen years and reached her greatest success in the late fifties and early sixties.

Born in Oklahoma, Bee was raised on a farm in the colorfully named Southern town of Beltbuckle, Tennessee. The family relocated to Tucson, Arizona, when she was ten, and her mother brashly introduced her to singer REX ALLEN, for whom she performed "Lovesick Blues," leading him to recommend her to a local radio station. A year later, the family moved to Southern California, where the young singer/comedian was signed to CLIFFIE STONE's *Hometown Jamboree* radio show and was a regular on it through her teenage years. At the same time, she signed to the California-based Capitol label and began performing on television, working three years with Pinky Lee, followed by two years on TENNESSEE ERNIE FORD's daytime show. She then moved to Ford's more prestigious nighttime program, and also guested on a slew of fifties-era TV variety shows.

In the sixties, Bee took to the glitzy Vegas trail, as did many other contemporary country stars, performing regularly at the area's hot spots. She also toured as a musical-comedy actress and appeared as a solo act at country fairs, rodeos, and clubs. She switched from Capitol to MGM in the sixties, continuing to produce a smattering of hits in country-weeper and light-comedy styles.

After two failed marriages, Bee took time off in the seventies to try to make her union with husband number three work out a little better. But by mid-decade she was recording and performing again, this time for the tiny Granite label, for whom she produced the modest hit "She Kept on Talkin'." After that, however, she disappeared from the charts, although she continued to perform into the eighties.

◀ BELLAMY BROTHERS, THE

(David [keyboards, vocals] born 1945, Derby, FL; Howard [guitar, vocals] born 1941, Derby, FL)

The Bellamy Brothers are sweet-voiced harmonizers whose music is an amalgam of country, rock, and mainstream pop.

Born in rural Florida, their father was a farmer who played DOBRO and fiddle in an amateur BLUEGRASS band. David was the first to make it into the musical bigtime, in the mid-sixties as a member of a rhythm and blues band called the Accidents, backing such far-flung stars as Percy Sledge and Little Anthony and the Imperials. The brothers began performing together in a COUNTRY-ROCK band called Jerico in the late sixties, playing the Southern club circuit until 1971, when they disbanded. The Bellamys then went to work as jingle- and songwriters.

Their big break came in 1975 when JIM STAFFORD scored a hit with David's composition "Spiders and Snakes." They were signed to Warners and had a minor hit with 1975's "Nothin' Heavy." In 1976 they covered the Neil Diamond/Larry Williams' pop anthem "Let Your Love Flow," replete with the Bellamys' sugary harmonies and jangling acoustic guitars. The record was an enormous hit on the country and pop charts. The Bellamys continued to record in this acoustic-rock style through the seventies, scoring minor hits with songs like "If I Said You Had a Beautiful Body Would You Hold It Against Me" from 1979.

In the eighties they turned to more mainstream country sounds, recording a

number of minor hits mostly written by David, including 1982's "Redneck Girl,"
1983's "Dancing Cowboys," and 1986's "Too Much Is Not Enough." In 1987 they
teamed up with the FORESTER SISTERS to record the broadly appealing "Kids of the
Baby Boom," a nostalgic look at growing up in the fifties. The Bellamys continue
to perform into the nineties.

Select Discography

The Best Of, Curb/CEMA 77554. Reissued cuts from the eighties originally on MCA.

◀ BERLINE, BYRON

(born 1948, Caldwell, KS)

Berline is a flashy fiddler credited with introducing Texas or show-style fiddling
into the BLUEGRASS repertoire. He has had a distinguished career in bluegrass, newgrass, and COUNTRY-ROCK.

A country boy with a college education, Berline was the son of an old-time
fiddling father, Luke, and a piano-playing mother. His father was a big fan of Texas
fiddling, and the boy picked up this style when he began to play at age five. He
beat his father in a local contest when he was ten and soon was taking many
regional titles. Meanwhile, an athletic scholarship took him to the University of
Oklahoma, where he began to perform in a college band.

At college, he heard bluegrass music for the first time, when the progressive
band the DILLARDS performed on campus. He met banjo player Doug Dillard after
the concert, and they soon discovered that both of their fathers shared a love of
old-time fiddling. Berline was invited to perform on the Dillards's next album, an
homage to traditional fiddling called *Pickin' and Fiddlin'*. On this album the band
performed many Texas favorites in the ornate competition style that Berline had
picked up playing at countless fiddlers' conventions.

After finishing college in 1967, Berline performed briefly with BILL MONROE before
joining the army. During his stint with Monroe, he recorded "Sally Goodin," originally recorded by UNCLE ECK ROBERTSON in 1922, complete with the many variations
that have made the piece a competition favorite. After he was discharged, Berline
rejoined with Doug Dillard on the West Coast as a member of the country-rock
outfit Dillard and Clark and also sessioned with many bands, including playing
fiddle on the Rolling Stones' "Country Honk," the first version of "Honky Tonk
Woman." He also performed with a reconstituted version of the FLYING BURRITO
BROTHERS in the early seventies, which soon after became the first version of COUN-
TRY GAZETTE.

Thanks to the mid-seventies bluegrass revival, Berline was able to return to
playing acoustic music in a variety of formats. As a bandleader, he recorded bluegrass, PROGRESSIVE BLUEGRASS, and jazz-influenced music; as a member of the trio
Crary, Hickman, and Berline, he recorded in a more straightforward traditional
vein. Berline's jazz-tinged, highly ornamented, and richly improvised fiddle style
influenced an entire generation of fiddlers, particularly those who helped create
the newgrass style, such as Sam Bush.

Select Discography

Dad's Favorites, Rounder 100. Cassette-only recording featuring Berline on a selection of fiddle-contest standards.

Four, Sugar Hill 3773. 1989 recording with Dan Crary and John Hickman; the trio's fourth album (hence the title). Progressive bluegrass meets contemporary country.

◀ BLACK, CLINT

(born 1962, Long Branch, NJ)

One of the superstars of late-eighties country, Black began as an honest-to-God Texas honky-tonker who has gone Hollywood with his marriage to television actress Lisa Hartman.

Born in New Jersey, Black was raised in Houston, Texas, from the age of six months. He played bass as a teenager in his brother's band and began working local clubs soon after. He hooked up with guitarist Hayden Nicholas, who had been working in Los Angeles but returned to Houston in the mid-eighties, and the pair began writing songs together, as well as working at Nicholas's studio to produce a demo tape. The tape landed Black an audition with ZZ Top's manager, Bill Ham, who was able to get him a contract with RCA. Black's first single, "A Better Man," co-written with Nicholas, hit number one, a rare feat for a first recording. It was followed by another chart buster, "Killin' Time."

Black's career has been cleverly managed. He paid homage to old country by recording a COWBOY duet with ROY ROGERS and then followed that with a rowdier-than-thou duo recording with HANK WILLIAMS, JR., on the boozy "Hotel Whiskey." Meanwhile, he kept on racking up the solo hits, including "Put Yourself in My Shoes," an updating of the WESTERN SWING sound in modern cowpoke clothing.

Of late, Black has been more noticeable for his appearances on *Entertainment Tonight*, escorting his glitzy wife, than for his country recordings. Like GARTH BROOKS and other megastars of new country, Black's later recordings show the influence of seventies arena-rock and middle-of-the-road pop, veering away from his HONKY-TONK roots. His 1993 duet recording with Wynonna (Judd) is the kind of sentimental schmaltz that even Barbra Streisand and Neil Diamond would have been embarrassed to record. Still in all, Black's aw-shucks personality and unassuming, straightforward performance style save him from some of the excesses that are creeping into other new country acts.

Select Discography

Killin' Time, RCA 9668. 1989 major-label debut.

Put Yourself in My Shoes, RCA 2372. His best-known recording, glitzier than his debut.

The Hard Way, RCA 66003. Actually, the easy way. Clint stalls out on his third album.

No Time to Kill, RCA 66239. 1993 release.

One Emotion, RCA 66419. More pop-country from the middle of the road.

◀ BLAKE, NORMAN

(born 1938, Chattanooga, TN)

Blake is a pleasant-voiced SINGER/SONGWRITER who was most popular in the mid-seventies for his countryesque songs and superb instrumental skills.

Blake was born in Tennessee but raised in Georgia, and he could already play a number of instruments by his teen years. In the middle to late fifties, Blake played MANDOLIN with a number of BLUEGRASS-flavored bands, including the Lonesome Travelers, who made two albums for RCA. After serving in the Panama Canal in the army, Blake returned to his native Georgia in the mid-sixties to discover that traditional music was on the wane. Determined not to shortchange his talents, he took to teaching GUITAR while playing in a local dance band on the side.

Blake was discovered by June Carter, wife of JOHNNY CASH, who invited him to join her road show in the late sixties. He began performing with both husband and wife, moving to Nashville in the spring of 1969. He was one of the young pickers featured on BOB DYLAN's *Nashville Skyline* album, further enhancing his reputation both as a guitarist and DOBRO player. He toured with KRIS KRISTOFFERSON's band in 1970 and then hooked up with JOHN HARTFORD's seminal country-bluegrass band, which also featured fiddler VASSAR CLEMENTS, dobroist Tut Taylor, and bassist Randy Scruggs. They recorded Hartford's highly influential *Aereo-Plain* album and toured widely. By 1972 the rest of the band had dispersed, but Hartford and Blake continued as a duo, recording *Morning Bugle* together.

Blake's solo career began with a number of low-key albums, featuring both original material and re-creations of traditional bluegrass, country, and old-time songs. His song "Last Train from Poor Valley," featured on his 1974 album *The Fields of November*, was widely covered in bluegrass circles. Blake also showed he was no laggard when it came to hot guitar licks, issuing the all-instrumental *Whiskey before Breakfast* LP in the mid-seventies.

Blake has often performed as a duo with his wife, Nancy, a classically trained cellist. With the addition of bluegrass fiddler James Bryan, who had previously played with BILL MONROE, they formed a trio called The Rising Fawn String Ensemble. Although the name didn't stick, the group continued to perform together informally throughout the eighties. Bryan was the perfect foil for Blake; not a flashy fiddler, but a very talented one, his almost cerebral approach to bluegrass fiddling matched Blake's own increasingly soft-edged approach.

Both Blake and his wife continue to record and tour, although they have never really been able to break out beyond a cult following into mainstream country success.

Select Discography

Back Home in Sulphur Springs, Rounder 0012. Cassette-only reissue of 1972 debut solo album.

Slow Train through Georgia, Rounder 11526. CD compilation drawn from various Rounder releases.

Natasha's Waltz, Rounder 11530. CD compilation taken from various albums cut with wife Nancy and fiddler James Bryan.

Just Gimme Somethin' I'm Used To, Shanachie 6001. 1992 release with wife Nancy. *Blake & Rice*, Rounder 0233/0266. Two albums cut with hot picker Tony Rice, from 1988 and 1990, respectively.

◀ BLANCHARD, JACK, AND MISTY MORGAN

(Blanchard born 1941, Buffalo, NY; Morgan born Mary Morgan, 1945, Buffalo, NY)

One-hit wonders of the seventies, Blanchard and Morgan are best remembered for the novelty song "Tennessee Birdwalk."

Although they were both born in Buffalo, and both were childhood prodigies on the keyboards, Blanchard and Morgan didn't meet until they were working in two clubs located a block apart in Hollywood, Florida. By then Blanchard had become an adept performer on slide guitar, DOBRO, and lap steel, as well as keyboards and synthesizer, while Morgan mostly stuck to the keyboards and vocal work. Blanchard had recorded a couple of country singles on his own, with little success, before meeting and marrying Morgan. The two formed a duo, more or less out of desperation, after Blanchard's band dissolved, hitting it big in 1970 with the screwball "Tennessee Birdwalk." They followed this with the even stranger novelty "Humphrey the Camel" and the more straightforward country "You've Got Your Troubles, I've Got Mine," both in the same year as their original megahit.

Although they continued to place minor hits on the charts until the mid-seventies, they were never able to equal their first fluke successes. Blanchard increasingly turned to writing humorous pieces for newspapers and drew his own comic strip, and the two continued to write songs individually and together, occasionally placing a number with another country artist.

◀ BLUE SKY BOYS, THE

(Bill Bolick born 1917, Hickory, NC; Earl Bolick born 1919, Hickory, NC)

One of the archetypical brother acts of the thirties, the Blue Sky Boys were perhaps the purest vocal-harmony duo ever. Lacking the bluesy style of the ALLEN, CARLISLE, or DELMORE BROTHERS or the raw excitement of the Monroe Brothers, the Blue Sky Boys performed a combination of sentimental and traditional songs in tight harmonies that would have a lasting impact on country music (the LOUVIN BROTHERS and JOHNNY AND JACK) and early rock and roll (the EVERLY BROTHERS).

The boys were raised in the mountainous western section of North Carolina on a small family farm. They learned their repertoire of traditional songs from family members, gospel hymns from the local church and mail-order hymnals, and sentimental songs from the recordings of twenties country artists like KARL AND HARTY, RILEY PUCKETT, and BRADLEY KINCAID.

Their major period of recording and performing was in the late thirties, beginning with a radio slot out of Asheville, North Carolina, in 1935 along with fiddler Homer Sherrill as the Good Coffee Boys (after their sponsor, JFG coffee), followed by a stint in Atlanta as the Blue Ridge Entertainers. It is said that Victor scout Eli Oberstein gave the brothers their new name, the Blue Sky Boys, taking the "blue" from the Blue Ridge Mountains and "sky" from "Land of the Sky," a nickname for the region where the boys were born. The brothers recorded prolifically for Bluebird beginning in 1936, with their close harmonies and slightly nasal voices a trademark of their recordings. Although Bill played mandolin, he was no hot picker, mostly limiting himself to a few fills between verses; Earl's guitar playing was equally sedate.

On their best songs, their carefully worked out harmony arrangements often made for breathtaking effects. On "The Sweetest Gift (a Mother's Smile)" the interplay on the chorus has the two voices echoing each other's part for a truly unique sound; a similar effect can be heard on their popular "Sunny Side of Life."

Although they lacked the overt blues influence of other duos, the Bolicks did have a lonesome, yearning sound that at least implied a blues style. Their classic "Short Life of Trouble" is perhaps the most plaintive recording in the country repertory, and they even managed to imbue such pure country bathos as "The Little Paper Boy" with deep feeling. Even on happy numbers like their radio theme song "Are You from Dixie?" they managed to capture the high, lonesome mountain sound.

The brothers were more or less inactive in the fifties, returning to recording in the early sixties for Starday and then retiring again until the old-time music revival of the mid-seventies brought them back to the studio. Even though Starday added a fuller country band to their accompaniment, the sound and style of the Bolicks's music never really changed. Oddly enough, the closest vocal style to the Bolicks is the Everly Brothers, who both in tone and style sound remarkably like the earlier duo, although their choice of material obviously is far different.

Select Discography

In Concert, 1964, Rounder 11536. Live recording from their first reunion in the early sixties.

Radio Shows, Vols. 1 and 2, Cooper Creek 120/121. Forty songs cut between 1946 and 1947 for radio broadcast, including comic skits and advertisements. A priceless time capsule.

◀ BLUEGRASS MUSIC

(c. 1948–present)

Sometimes called "country music on overdrive," bluegrass music is often caricatured as high-speed, high-pitched, high-energy music. Taking its name from the legendary band led by mandolinist BILL MONROE in the late forties, bluegrass is actually more than just fancy picking and breathless singing. It is a music of great emotional power that borrows from country, gospel, HONKY-TONK, and, more recently, jazz and rock to form a unique musical union.

All bluegrass bands owe a debt to Bill Monroe, who brought together a group of five musicians to form the first classic lineup of his Blue Grass Boys in 1946. These included Lester Flatt and Earl Scruggs on lead GUITAR and BANJO, respectively, fiddler Chubby Wise, Monroe on mandolin and high tenor vocals, and bass player Cedric Rainwater. Scruggs had evolved a unique method of playing the five-string banjo: a three-finger picking style that changed the instrument from primarily an accompaniment to a melodic lead instrument. Flatt developed a new way of playing guitar accompaniments, using bass runs rather than chords as fills to bridge the gaps between chord progressions. Monroe was a fire-breathing mandolin player and Wise a fiddler influenced as much by WESTERN SWING as he was by old-time styles. Vocally the group offered a strong contrast between the relaxed, almost crooning lead vocals of Flatt with the intense, high-pitched harmonies and leads of Monroe. They also recorded as a gospel quartet, dropping the banjo, and were perhaps the first band to borrow from traditional SHAPE-NOTE, backwoods church singing to record gospel in an entirely new way. It is not an exaggeration to say that Monroe's band—vocally and instrumentally—not only invented bluegrass but also became the model that every other band has emulated.

When this band performed on the GRAND OLE OPRY, their effect was immediate and revolutionary. Bands like the STANLEY BROTHERS who had been playing in a more traditional style immediately switched to bluegrass; FLATT AND SCRUGGS left the Monroe fold to form a less mandolin-oriented ensemble. Monroe continued to work through the fifties, composing many classic bluegrass tunes and songs while refining the overall sound.

In 1959 MIKE SEEGER recorded a number of groups for an anthology for Folkways Records called *Mountain Music: Bluegrass Style*. While a few urban players had been aware of bluegrass before this LP was issued, this opened the floodgates, with many groups forming in urban centers, including New York, Boston, Baltimore, Washington, D.C., San Francisco, and Los Angeles. So-called "progressive" bluegrass was born, a wedding of traditional bluegrass instrumentation with a broader palette of material. Banjoist BILL KEITH, who briefly performed with Monroe, introduced "melodic" bluegrass banjo, almost eliminating accompaniment chords from his playing. Bands like Washington, D.C.'s COUNTRY GENTLEMEN, Boston's Charles River Valley Boys (who recorded an LP of Beatles songs redone in bluegrass arrangements), Los Angeles's KENTUCKY COLONELS (with Clarence and Roland White), and New York's GREENBRIAR BOYS all represented a new approach to the bluegrass style.

The older acts, like Monroe, the Stanleys, and Flatt and Scruggs, had eked out a living through the fifties existing somewhere on the edge of country music. The FOLK-MUSIC REVIVAL, along with the growth of PROGRESSIVE BLUEGRASS, helped them gain a larger audience, although they still remained definitely on the fringes of country music. Flatt and Scruggs came the closest to widespread popularity, thanks to their appearance on TV's *Beverly Hillbillies* and the soundtrack to the film *Bonnie and Clyde*. By the end of the decade, Scruggs was pursuing a COUNTRY-ROCK audience performing with his sons, while Flatt formed a more traditional bluegrass band.

The seventies brought a second wave of bluegrass innovators. These bands and solo acts tended to emphasize flashy instrumental work over vocals. COUNTRY COOKING out of Ithaca, New York, featured the twin banjos of TONY TRISCHKA and Pete

Wernick on original bluegrass-flavored instrumentals (the band never recorded vocals). DAVID GRISSMAN, once a mandolinist with RED ALLEN, began recording what he called "dawg" music, a synthesis of swing and bluegrass. NEW GRASS REVIVAL, under the leadership of mandolinist Sam Bush, combined the energy of rock (and the lack of subtlety of heavy metal) with bluegrass instrumentation.

In the eighties, Bill Monroe began to gain the wide acceptance that his stature as the "father of bluegrass music" deserved. Meanwhile, progressive bluegrassers began returning to more traditional material while traditionalists showed the influence of the influx of the progressive crowd. The NEW COUNTRY explosion featured many ex-bluegrassers, most prominently RICKY SKAGGS, KATHY MATTEA, and VINCE GILL. They brought many traditional bluegrass songs and their instrumentation into mainstream country music. Bands like the JOHNSON MOUNTAIN BOYS arose as virtual clones of traditional bluegrass outfits, recreating the look, style, and sound of a generic fifties bluegrass ensemble. Meanwhile, the NASHVILLE BLUEGRASS BAND and others continued to broaden the bluegrass repertory while remaining true to the roots of the music.

◀ BOGGS, DOCK

(born Moran Lee Boggs, 1898, Dooley, VA; died 1971)

Boggs was a blues-influenced banjo player and vocalist who recorded in the twenties and was rediscovered by MIKE SEEGER during the FOLK REVIVAL of the sixties.

Raised in a traditional mountain community, Boggs's entire family was musical, and particularly fond of the BANJO. Boggs began playing the instrument at the age of twelve, the same year he was introduced to coal mining, work he would pursue for the next forty-one years. Originally he played in the traditional "frailing" or "clawhammer" style; however, he was impressed by the bluesy playing of a local black banjoist who picked the strings with two fingers and a thumb. This would become Boggs's mature style, perfectly suited to his repertoire of blues-flavored songs, including his adaptations of traditional songs like "Country Blues" and "Mean Mistreatin' Mama."

After his wedding in 1918, Boggs continued to play the banjo, despite the fact that his religious wife frowned on what she considered to be the "devil's music." His fame spread locally and in 1927 he was approached by a scout from Brunswick Records to make some recordings. He recorded twenty-four songs in 1927 and 1928, but, discouraged by his wife's continued disapproval, he abandoned the instrument soon after, not picking it up again until his retirement from mining in 1954.

In the early sixties, folklorist Seeger came to the mountains looking for some of the older recording artists. By this time Boggs was a legendary figure, thanks to his unusual recordings, which were more blues-oriented than those of most other white pickers. However, no one knew if he was still alive or active until Seeger found him still living in Norton, where he had made his original recordings. A series of albums of music and interviews followed, and Boggs was soon performing at the Newport Folk Festival and on the folk-revival circuit.

Boggs was a unique musician for a number of reasons. His picking style was more modern than many mountain players of his generation, although not as advanced as Earl Scruggs–style or BLUEGRASS picking. The intensity of his singing and his choice of material was unique in that he avoided almost entirely the dance music and upbeat songs usually associated with the banjo, preferring blues numbers that expressed the troubles that he had experienced as a coal miner. Although some younger pickers emulated his style, Boggs's playing and singing was unique, and he made no concessions to build a bigger audience. His music was like that of blues great Skip James, also rediscovered in the sixties: difficult, thorny, and definitely an acquired taste.

◀ BOGGUSS, SUZY

(b. Susan Kay Bogguss, 1956, Aleda, IL)

Bogguss is a perky, well-scrubbed singer who got her big break singing at DOLLY PARTON's Dollywood theme park.

Bogguss seems to have stepped out of a Norman Rockwell America; her father was a machinist and her mother a secretary, and in her teen years she passed through the rituals of scouting, cheerleading, and, yes, she was even homecoming queen in high school. She also took up guitar and singing as a teenager, a hobby she carried with her to Illinois State University, where she studied art. After graduation in 1978, Bogguss hit the road with some friends, performing informally throughout the western states. After an abortive trip to Nashville in 1981, Bogguss returned to try to break into music making in 1984. Two years later, she was the lead attraction at Dollywood, selling a self-made cassette offstage, and attracted the attention of Capitol Records, which signed her in 1987.

Bogguss's first hits were remakes, beginning with her 1987 redo of the pop standard "I Don't Want to Set the World on Fire" followed by a rather tepid reading of PATSY MONTANA's classic "I Want to Be a Cowboy's Sweetheart." Her best-selling effort so far is her 1991 collection *Aces*, featuring the title hit along with covers of "Someday Soon," written by Ian Tyson (of IAN AND SYLVIA fame), and NANCI GRIFFITH's "Outbound Plane." She also released a duet recording with country star LEE GREENWOOD on "Hopelessly Yours," a two-hanky WEEPER. In 1994 she paired with legendary guitarist CHET ATKINS, performing pop-country songs.

Bogguss is one of those eternally upbeat singers whom you can't help but like, despite the fact that she has a little-girl sound that can annoy. Her 1992 rendition of JOHN HIATT's "Drive South" reduces his gritty Southern-roots anthem into cotton candy, a trick, unfortunately, that seems to be her forte as an artist.

Select Discography

Somewhere Between, Liberty 90237. 1989 debut.

Aces, Liberty 95847. Her third, and still best, album.

◀ BOND, JOHNNY

(born Cyrus Whitfield Bond, 1915, Enville, OK; died 1978)

Author of more than five hundred songs, many of them country and cowboy standards, Bond was a sidekick to singing cowboys GENE AUTRY and TEX RITTER in hundreds of horse operas on the big and small screens.

Raised on a number of small Oklahoma farms, Bond can remember listening to his parent's Victrola, and he was particularly fond of "The Prisoner's Song" and "The Death of Floyd Collins," both tremendously popular recordings by urban country crooner VERNON DALHART. Bond was a member of his high-school brass band, learning the rudiments of music and investing ninety-eight cents in a Montgomery-Ward ukulele. He quickly graduated to the guitar and was playing locally during his high-school years.

At age nineteen Bond made his radio debut out of Oklahoma City, and three years later he was hired by JIMMY WAKELY, who led the Western trio called the Bell Boys. In that same year, 1937, Bond made his first solo recordings for Columbia Records, including his classic cowboy ballad "Cimarron" and the country WEEPER "Divorce Me C.O.D." In 1940 Wakeley's group was hired en masse to back popular cowboy star Gene Autry on film and on his popular "Melody Ranch" radio show, a relationship that lasted sixteen years. Meanwhile, in 1943, Bond hooked up with Tex Ritter, with whom he would star in numerous horse epics, tour, and form a music-publishing company, called Vidor Publications.

In 1953, Bond and Ritter were hired to host the syndicated *Town Hall Party* television show, giving them national exposure for the next seven years, while Bond continued to work TV and radio with Autry, SPADE COOLEY, and Wakeley. He also began writing prolifically, adding to his catalog many country classics such as "I Wonder Where You Are Tonight," "Gone and Left Me Blues," and "Tomorrow Never Comes." In 1960 his song "Hot Rod Lincoln" was a major rock-and-roll hit for him on Autry's Republic record label. He had one further hit with 1965's tongue-in-cheek classic "Ten Little Bottles," issued by Starday.

In the 1970s he retired from active performing to focus on music publishing. He also wrote two books, a biography of Ritter and his own memoirs.

Select Discography

That Wild, Wicked but Wonderful West, Starday 147. Reissue of mid-sixties cowpoke songs.

The Best of Country, Richmond 2155. Cassette-only reissue of recordings from I-know-not-where.

◀ BOONE, DEBBIE

(born 1956, Hackensack, NJ)

Sure, go ahead and laugh. But face it, this clean-cut diva was one of the biggest country and pop stars of the late seventies and early eighties, showing once again that, in America, anyone can be famous (even if it is only for fifteen minutes).

The daughter of Pat "Isn't That a Shame" Boone, Debbie comes to her musical "talents" naturally; her grandfather was legendary country showman RED FOLEY, adding to her musical pedigree. Pat ripped off some of the greatest rock songs of the late fifties and sanitized them for white-bread America before becoming a born-again Bible thumper. Young Debbie followed in Dad's footsteps, first shooting up the charts in 1977 with "You Light Up My Life" (which at least isn't as grotesque as KENNY ROGERS's later variation on the theme, "You Decorated My Life"). She had a couple more country hits, including the number-one 1980 ode "Are You on the Road to Lovin' Me Again" (written and produced by the same team that created "You Decorated My Life"), before she found Christ in 1982 and began cutting religious albums for the Word label. Since there is a God, we can thank him (or her) for taking both Debbie and Pat into the fold and pulling them (mercifully) off commercial radio.

Select Discography

The Best of Debbie Boone, Curb/CEMA 77258. All the hits (that you can stand) in one place at a low, low price.

◀ BOWEN, JIMMY

(born c. 1936, Texas)

One-time ROCKABILLY star Bowen has become one of Nashville's most successful producers, molding the careers of REBA McENTIRE and discovering and shaping GARTH BROOKS.

Bowen started out as a musician, working with famed guitarist Buddy Knox in a group known as the Rhythm Orchids, which they formed while still in college in 1955 at West Texas State. They made some recordings for Norman Petty (who also recorded and produced BUDDY HOLLY), which were leased to Roulette in 1957. The pair had a two-sided hit: "Party Doll," credited to Knox, and "I'm Stickin' With You," credited to Bowen. Bass-playing Bowen was only a marginal singer, however, and, after recording one album for Roulette, his career as a performer ended.

By the mid-sixties, Bowen had relocated to Los Angeles, where he became a house producer for Reprise Records, then owned by crooner Frank Sinatra. He produced big hits for the label, including Dean Martin's mellow classic, "Everybody Loves Somebody Sometimes." Following this work, he ended up at MGM in the mid-seventies, but by the time that label fizzled out, he was tiring of the fast-paced Los Angeles lifestyle. He moved to Nashville in 1977 and a year later was running MCA's country division. He moved from there to Elektra, where he shaped the career of EDDIE RABBITT and the resurgence of HANK WILLIAMS, JR.

In 1984, he was hired by music whiz kid Irving Azoff to return to MCA. He played a central role in molding Reba McEntire into the glitzy, and more mainstream, act that she became. In the early nineties, he moved to Capitol Records, which had little if any country roster. He immediately discovered and nurtured Garth Brooks, who he built into a megastar, one who tops both pop and country charts.

Bowen's background in country, rockabilly, mainstream pop, and rock demonstrates the diverse styles that have been brought to bear on today's NEW COUNTRY.

His talent for identifying new stars and for carefully grooming and marketing them shows that country, like pop, is a megadollar business, one that depends as much on shrewd marketing and packaging as it does on musical ability.

◀ BOXCAR WILLIE

(born Lecil Travis Martin, 1931, Sterret, TX)

Boxcar Willie is a pseudo-hobo who is, frankly, not much of a musician. However, he made a reputation, first in England and Europe and then in America, mainly off of his carefully crafted stage character.

Although his father was a railroad worker, Willie never worked on the rails, despite his colorful name. He had a number of professions while pursuing his avocation, a love of music, ranging from deejay to mechanic to flight engineer. In the mid-seventies, he decided to scrap it all for the life of an entertainer, relocating from his native Texas to Nashville and taking on his hobo persona. Scottish agent Drew Taylor caught him performing at a local club and arranged for several English tours, where the locals were wowed by his repertoire of train sound effects. In 1979 he returned triumphantly to the United States, premiering on the GRAND OLE OPRY and receiving a standing ovation for his kitschy act. He had a minor hit in 1980 with his "Train Medley." He followed this with a number of half-sung, half-spoken novelty numbers, including 1982's European hit "Bad News," which also charted on the lower ends of the U.S. country charts.

Willie's act is a combination of hokey renditions of hoary old chestnuts and his "stories" of his life as a "rambling hobo." He always appears in a calculated costume including a floppy hat, ratty overalls, and a smudged face. As such, he represents the ultimate triumph of image over substance, and for those who prefer to enjoy the myth of country life (rather than its reality), Willie certainly fits the bill.

Select Discography

Boxcar Willie, MCA 39052. Ultra-cheap cassette-only issue featuring WILLIE NELSON (believe it or not) on a couple of cuts.

◀ BOYD, BILL

(born William Lemuel Boyd, 1910, near Ladonia, TX)

Boyd was a WESTERN SWING pioneer who led the Cowboy Ramblers along with his brothers. Boyd's music focused on bluesy and novelty numbers, often with a cowboy theme. He later appeared in many Hollywood-produced, B-grade horse operas and ended his career in the sixties as a country deejay.

Boyd was one of thirteen children born to Lemuel and Molly Jared Boyd, both originally of Tennessee. The family migrated to Texas around 1902, settling on a large ranch. There the young Boyds were exposed to hard work and music; both parents were singers and many of the ranch hands played music in the evening. Bill got his first guitar through a mail-order catalog and was soon performing with his younger brother Jim (born 1914). When the Depression hit Texas, the family relocated to Dallas, where Bill began working a series of odd jobs from laborer to salesman while pursuing music on the side. Brother Jim enrolled in the technical high school, where he met Art (born Audrey) Davis, a talented musician who played clarinet, fiddle, and mandolin and would become a key member of the Cowboy Ramblers.

While Jim and Art were getting their act together, Bill got his first radio job as a member of a trio known as the Alexanders Daybreakers, who played for a local early-morning show. By 1932 the Daybreakers had become the Cowboy Ramblers, moved to station WRR, and the brothers were reunited. They were signed to the Victor budget label, Bluebird, in 1934 and would continue to perform together for nearly twenty years.

Through the thirties, the Boyds made classic Western swing recordings for Bluebird, including blues like "Fan It" and "I've Got Those Oklahoma Blues," instrumentals like "Beaumont Rag" and "New Steel Guitar Rag" (picking up on the popularity of BOB WILLS's recording of "Steel Guitar Rag"), and novelties like the silly "Wah Hoo," complete with animal sound effects. They also recorded the obligatory COWBOY SONGS, including "The Strawberry Roan" and "The Windswept Desert." The band was a small, tight unit, focusing on Davis's fine swinging fiddle, with the brothers on guitar and bass, along with piano, banjo, and, on later recordings, accordion and steel guitar. Younger brother John played steel guitar on several of their later recordings and formed his own band, the Southerners, in the late thirties. He continued to perform until his death in 1942.

During the forties, the two brothers relocated to Hollywood, following in the footsteps of other Western swing bands who had found lucrative work in Southern California. They also appeared in a number of the inane, comic-book Westerns that small Hollywood studios produced by the bushel during this period. In the late forties and early fifties, Jim formed his own band, the Men of the West, to cash in on the cowboy craze.

In the fifties, the broadcast of live music on the radio was gradually edged out by records, and the two brothers switched to working as deejays. Bill retired in the early seventies, while his brother Jim was still working part-time as late as 1975.

Select Discography
Bill Boyd and His Cowboy Ramblers, RCA Bluebird 5503. Wonderful, out-of-print two-LP set.

◀ BRADDOCK, BOBBY

(born 1940, Lakeland, FL)

Braddock is a country songwriter most famous for cowriting TAMMY WYNETTE's tearjerking hit "D-I-V-O-R-C-E." He pursued a sporadic solo career as well.

Born in Florida, Braddock began his career as a pianist, working in local bars and clubs before moving to Nashville where he gained work as a studio musician. He began performing in MARTY ROBBINS's backup band in the early sixties, writing "While You're Dancin' " for him, a 1965 hit. He left Robbins soon after, signing up with Tree Publishing run by session musician and music-city mogul Buddy Killen.

Working with various partners, including Sonny Throckmorton and Curly Putnam, he wrote numerous hits, including 1967's "Ruthless," recorded by the STATLER
BROTHERS, Wynette's 1968 hit, "D-I-V-O-R-C-E," the 1976 GEORGE JONES/Tammy Wynette duet, "Golden Ring," and Jones's solo hit, 1980's "He Stopped Loving Her
Today." He also wrote early-eighties hits for T. G. SHEPPARD: "I Feel Like Loving You
Again" (1981) and a duet with KAREN BROOKS on "Faking Love." Most of these
songs were in the classic HONKY-TONK tears-in-my-beer style.

Braddock has had a minor recording career, initially recording for MGM between 1967 and 1969 with hits such as "I Know How to Do It" and "Girls in Country
Music." He returned to wax in 1979 when he signed with Elektra and then moved
briefly in the early eighties to RCA. His style of country heart-draggers fell out of
favor in the NEW-COUNTRY era, and he has since faded from view.

◀ BRADLEY, OWEN

(born 1915, Westmoreland, TN)

Along with CHET ATKINS, Bradley was the man most responsible for the growth
of the NASHVILLE SOUND, moving country away from its roots toward bland, middle-
of-the-road pop. As owner of the famous Bradley's Barn studio and house producer
for Decca in the fifties and sixties, Bradley was responsible for some of country's
biggest hits in this smoother, more commercial style.

Bradley began his career as a piano and guitar player in various pop pickup
bands in and around Nashville. In 1947 he was selected to be the orchestra leader
for radio station WSM, home of the GRAND OLE OPRY. In that same year, he was
approached by Paul Cohen of Decca Records, which wanted to establish a presence in country music. Cohen agreed to guarantee that Bradley could produce
one hundred sessions a year if he would build a studio meeting Decca's specifi-
cations. Bradley built three different studios between 1952 and 1955, the last being
the most famous, a quonset hut that became known as Bradley's Barn. In 1962
Columbia Records purchased the studio when they opened their Nashville recording operation.

Although Bradley recorded everything from BILL MONROE's traditional BLUEGRASS
to ERNEST TUBB's original HONKY-TONK sessions, he is most famous for his late-fifties
and early-sixties recordings of crossover artists like BRENDA LEE and PATSY CLINE.
Traditional instruments like fiddles, guitars, and pedal steel were downplayed—if
they were used at all—on these sessions, replaced by tinkling pianos, soothing
strings, and walls of backup vocals (usually provided by the JORDANAIRES or the
saccharine-sounding ANITA KERR Singers). In 1962 he was promoted to chief staff
producer for MCA (now the parent company of Decca). Through the sixties, he
was country's premiere producer, toning down the rural roots of singers like CON-
WAY TWITTY and LORETTA LYNN and bathing their productions in mainstream-pop
arrangements.

Although best known as a producer, Bradley also had a recording career with
Decca, from 1949 through the fifties. He led an all-instrumental quintet, playing
everything from instrumental versions of country hits to pop schlock. His biggest

hits came with covers of rock numbers, particularly 1958's "Big Guitar"; he even produced two albums of rock covers in the late fifties.

Bradley's younger brother Harold (born 1926, Nashville, Tennessee) worked as a guitarist on many of his brother's sessions, as well as in the WSM house band, before serving as musical director for the JIMMY DEAN television show in the mid-sixties. In the eighties he toured with SLIM WHITMAN, although more recently he has limited himself to working as a music publisher.

◀ BRANSON, MISSOURI

A formerly sleepy town that was best known for its natural springs, Branson has become a center for (mostly older) country and pop performers who have built lavish theaters there to present their music.

The Branson story has been oft-told: how this town of some 3,700 inhabitants, nestled in the foothills of the Ozarks, was first put on the map by Harold Bell Wright in his 1907 best-selling romance, *The Shepherd of the Hills*; and how things heated up a little further when the minor-league theme park, Silver Dollar City, opened in 1960, followed by a couple of music clubs, most notably Presley's Mountain Music Jubilee, said to be the first country-music attraction in town, which opened its doors in 1967.

In the old days, country acts continued to perform for their core audience long after their hits dried up, primarily by hitting the road for a grueling round of one-nighters. Many wished they could stay put in one place and let their core audience come to them. ROY CLARK had often vacationed in the Branson area and figured it would be as good a place as any to open a year-round music theater. He set up shop in 1983 and continues to offer one of the better music shows in the area. Soon Clark brought other older country stars to the area, including MEL TILLIS. Both had long been off the country charts, but they proved to be major draws in Branson. They opened their own palatial theaters, with architecture and floor shows reminiscent of the best (or worst, depending on your taste) Vegas kitsch. A second wave of musical immigrants, such as Andy Williams and Wayne Newton, came from other mainstream musical genres and discovered that Branson was hospitable to their talents as well. The number of theaters multiplied, and the town's main drag became a glittering strip of marquees and neon.

A featured segment on *60 Minutes* hosted by a bemused Morley Safer in 1989 cemented the town's growing reputation as middle America's country entertainment mecca. A highlight of Safer's report was his interview with Japanese violin virtuoso Shoji Tabuchi, who has become one of the town's major attractions. Tabuchi doesn't just play music—from Mozart to Broadway tunes to high-speed BLUE-GRASS standards—he puts on an entire spectacular show, including lasers, smoke bombs, genies emerging from bottles, and magic carpets. Tabuchi's wife serves as the show's genial emcee, and his teenage daughter provides entertainment as a singer and dancer. Tabuchi's show is typical of the redneck/Las Vegas mixture that makes Branson such an enormous success; when WILLIE NELSON opened a theater to simply play music, the result was a total financial failure.

Another Branson standout are the Baldknobbers, a rural hayseed comedy troupe reminiscent of the tradition of "kountry korn komedy" immortalized by TV's HEE HAW. The Baldknobbers had actually been performing in Branson long before the town ascended to its now legendary status. And, of course, their show features leggy chorus girls along with backwoods rubes, to appeal to everyone in the family!

Branson stands apart from such prepackaged amusement attractions as Dollywood (the theme park built by DOLLY PARTON in rural Tennessee) and even Nashville's Opryland USA, in that it was a real town that simply grew like Topsy. As such, it gives strong testimony to the strength of country music's core audience, and it will undoubtedly continue to prosper long after NEW COUNTRY slips off the pop charts. With an estimated five million visitors annually, Branson has become America's second favorite vacation destination off the interstates. Don't be surprised when the GARTH BROOKS pavilion opens there in the year 2015!

◀ BRITT, ELTON

(born James Britt Baker, 1917, Marshall, AK; died 1972)

An amazing yodeler, Britt was a singing cowboy who enjoyed success in B movies, early television, and as a radio and recording star.

Britt was the son of a champion fiddler/small-time farmer and learned to play guitar on a five-dollar Sears-Roebuck model. At age fourteen, he was discovered while playing in a local amateur show and was hired to perform on radio station KMPC, Los Angeles, fronting the pseudo-country band the Beverly Hillbillies under a stage name. He began recording almost immediately with this group and as a soloist, and in 1937 broke with the band to sign a contract with RCA, which would last for more than twenty years.

Britt's best recordings, from the late thirties through the late forties, were primarily made in New York. RCA had yet to establish a studio in Nashville, so it was not unusual for the country star to record in the Northern music capital. Many of his recordings feature some of the city's finest sidemen, including pop/jazz instrumentalists, giving them an unusual quality for country sides of the era.

Britt's 1942 patriotic ballad, "There's a Star Spangled Banner Waving Somewhere," was the first country recording ever to go gold (sell a million copies), although it took two years to achieve this feat. This led to an invitation from President Roosevelt to perform at the White House. Other popular recordings include 1948's "Chime Bells," where Britt yodels up a storm, including a final high falsetto note that is held for a breathtakingly long time. He also recorded many duets with ROSALIE ALLEN, including 1949's "Quicksilver."

Britt's recording career continued through the fifties but was upstaged somewhat by his film and television work. He retired from active performing between 1954 and 1968 but returned to perform occasionally during the last four years of his life.

◀ BROOKS, GARTH

(born 1962, Tulsa, OK)

Brooks's phenomenal success in the early nineties is a combination of genuine talent, shrewd marketing, and being in the right place at the right time (with the right act). His neo-country act draws so much on mid-seventies folk-rock and even arena rock (in its staging) that it's hard to think of him as a pure country artist. The fact that his recent albums have shot to the top of the pop charts, outgunning Michael Jackson, Guns 'n' Roses, and Bruce Springsteen, underscores the fact that Brooks is a pop artist dressed in a cowboy hat. Still, Brooks draws on genuine country traditions, particularly the HONKY-TONK sound of GEORGE JONES, and he has managed to popularize country music without diluting the sound.

Brooks's mother, Coleen, was a small-time country singer who worked sporadically in their native Oklahoma on recordings and radio. Brooks himself grew up interested in sports, playing football, basketball, and track in high school, and entering Oklahoma State on a track-and-field scholarship, with a specialty in javelin throwing. His guitar-playing career began in high school and continued in college, where he worked college-area clubs performing a mix of James Taylor folk-pop and country. He made his first trip to Nashville in 1985, without success, returning home with his college-sweetheart wife, Sandy Mahl. Returning to Nashville in 1987, Brooks attracted the attention of Capitol Records and producer Allen Reynolds.

His first album was successful, but the follow-up, *No Fences*, really began Garth-mania. It sold 700,000 copies in its first ten days of release and stayed on the pop charts for over a year. His third album, *Ropin' the Wind*, entered the pop charts in the number-one position, the first country album ever to do so. Brooks's hit singles from these albums combined country bathos ("If Tomorrow Never Comes," a ten-hanky WEEPER about a husband's recognition of the value of his marriage) with neo–HONKY-TONK ("Friends in Low Places," a cleverly humorous song with its tip-of-the-hat bass vocals recalling George Jones) and even with feminism, as in "The Thunder Rolls," which tells the story of a cheating husband (and a physically abusive one whose depiction in the music video ruffled quite a few conservative Nashville feathers).

Brooks's performing style captured the attention of the major media. Learning a lesson from the arena rock stars of his youth, Brooks built a special set featuring large ramps enclosing the band (enabling him to dramatically charge up and down around his backup musicians) and even installed wires attached to a harness he wears so he could swing out over the audience, in shades of Ozzy Osbourne–like theatrics. With his portable mike neatly hooked to his ten-gallon hat, Brooks is one of the most mobile and energetic of all country performers, although recently he has adopted such schmaltzy tactics as waving and winking at the audience and blowing air kisses at his fans.

Brooks's 1992 album, *The Chase*, reflects a further nudging toward mainstream pop, particularly in the anthemic single, "We Shall Be Free," whose vaguely liberal politics also sent shivers of despair through the conservative Nashville musical community. Less successful than his previous releases (although it still sold several million copies), Brooks followed it with 1993's *In Pieces*, featuring a safer selection of high-energy honky-tonk numbers and even the odd "American Honky-Tonk Bar Association," in which Brooks beats up on welfare recipients, a shameless attempt to cater to country's traditionally conservative audience.

After a much publicized "fling," Brooks has become the model family man, at one point indicating he would give up performing so he could spend more time with his wife and child (but he soon after decided that he would be a better father if he took to the road with wife and child in tow). Brooks's "aw, shucks, ma'am" interview style masks a canny performer who knows exactly the public image he hopes to mold.

Despite these caveats, the music he has made is not half bad, in a pop-rock way. He has taken characteristic country sounds and made them more accessible to a pop audience, undoubtedly opening some ears to more traditional performers.

Select Discography

Garth Brooks, Liberty 90897. Debut LP from 1989.
No Fences, Liberty 93866. The big kahuna that put Garth on the charts.
Ropin' the Wind, Liberty 96330.
The Chase, Liberty 98743. Garth as soulful SINGER/SONGWRITER.
In Pieces, Liberty 80857. Garth's return to form and another megaseller.

◀ BROOKS, KAREN

(born Dallas, 1954, TX)

A talented SINGER/SONGWRITER, Brooks enjoyed minor chart success in the mid-eighties but has never had the following that she deserves.

With a voice midway between EMMYLOU HARRIS and ROSANNE CASH, Brooks has had a strong following among other country performers. Another graduate of the Texas school of country songwriting, Brooks first cut her teeth in the Austin, Texas, country-folk scene that also nurtured JERRY JEFF WALKER, TOWNES VAN ZANDT, and Gary P. Nunn, a producer/performer who was briefly her husband. RODNEY CROWELL heard her performing in Austin and hired her as a backup vocalist for his band in the late seventies.

She left Texas for a farm outside of Nashville in 1981 and was signed to a contract with Warner Brothers a year later. She had a minor hit with "New Way Out," her first single, followed by more solid success with 1983's "If That's What You're Thinking" and "Walk On," and 1984's "Born to Love You" and "Tonight I'm Here with Someone Else." A year later, she cut a duet with JOHNNY CASH on "I Will Dance with You," but after that the hits dried up. Soulmates Harris and Rosanne Cash had hits with her compositions: "Tennessee Rose" and "Couldn't Do Nothing Right," respectively.

Brooks has retired to raise quarter horses and cattle on her Tennessee farm, although she returned to the recording studio to make a duet LP with Randy Sharp in 1992.

Select Discography

That's Another Story, Mercury 512232. 1992 LP with Randy Sharp.

◀ BROOKS AND DUNN

(Brooks [lead guitar, vocals] born Leon Eric "Kix" Brooks, 1955, Shreveport, LA;
Ronnie Dunn [guitar, vocals] born Tulsa, OK, 1953)

Brooks and Dunn have been called country music's answer to Hall and Oates, and indeed there are many similarities between them: Front man Ronnie Dunn is the looker of the two, sings most of the lead vocals, and writes much of their material, while lower profile (and shorter) Kix Brooks romps across the stage in a modified Chuck Berry duckwalk while strumming his Stratocaster. And like Hall and Oates in the mid-seventies through early eighties, these guys are a veritable hit-making machine, churning out country anthems from the get-go.

Both were frustrated performers who were struggling to get their careers on track when a canny Arista Records producer Scott Hendricks brought them together to become a duo. Brooks was a Louisiana-born SINGER/SONGWRITER who had spent some time working in Alaska on the pipeline before settling in Nashville to a successful career as a songmaker. He had written a number of country hits, beginning with JOHN CONLEE's "I'm Only in It For Love" (1983), which he cowrote with the team of Rafe Van Hoy and his singer/songwriter wife, DEBORAH ALLEN. Van Hoy went on to produce Brooks's debut album for Capitol in 1988. The recording did nothing on the charts. Meanwhile, Brooks continued to write with a variety of partners, including Dan Tyler (with whom he wrote "Modern Day Romance," a 1985 hit for the NITTY GRITTY DIRT BAND), while pursuing (unsuccessfully) a solo career.

Dunn came out of Oklahoma, a hotbed for country performers (GARTH BROOKS, REBA McENTIRE, and ALAN JACKSON, to mention a few). Originally pursuing a career as a Baptist minister, he was led astray by the local honky-tonks where he performed on guitar. The lanky Westerner won a Marlboro talent contest in 1988 (he does resemble the Marlboro man); one of the contest's judges was Hendricks, who brought Dunn together with Brooks to write some songs for a solo album. The pair clicked, and they debuted with the mega–dance hit "Boot Scootin' Boogie" in 1990. Since then they have been rarely off the charts, with their nouveau HONKY-TONK anthems like "Brand New Man" and 1992's "Hard Workin' Man."

Select Discography

Brand New Man, Arista 18658. 1991 debut album.
Hard Workin' Man, Arista 18716.
Waitin' on Sundown, Arista 18765. 1994 release.

◀ BROWN, MILTON

(born 1903, Stephenville, TX; died 1936)

One of the fathers of WESTERN SWING, Brown was a vocalist who combined jazz-styled phrasings with the popular manner of a crooner.

Brown began his career as a cohort of BOB WILLS, forming a band in 1931 known originally as the Alladin Laddies, which became the famous Fort Worth (later

LIGHT CRUST) DOUGHBOYS in 1932. Brown soon struck out on his own, as did Wills. From 1934 until his death, he led one of the first and hottest bands in Western swing, the Musical Brownies, who were far more hard-edged than Wills's band at the time. The band featured a swinging fiddler (originally Cecil Brower, who was replaced in 1936 by Cliff Bruner), a jazz-styled pianist, Fred Calhoun, and legendary steel guitarist, Bob Dunn, whose rapid-fire, staccato bursts of sound were unequaled at the time. Dunn is said to have been the first player to use an electric instrument on a country recording, and certainly his unique playing style made the instrument stand out. The group further capitalized on this novelty by doubling the fiddle lead with the steel guitar, an effect that was often imitated on other Western swing and later country recordings. The band's repertoire was heavy on blues, jazz, and pop standards, with the occasional country number thrown in. They avoided ballads, perhaps because they worked primarily as a dance band and probably also because Brown's vocal style, a combination of Cab Calloway–styled jive and Bing Crosby–styled smooch, was ill-suited to slower numbers. When Brown died in a car accident, his brother, guitarist Durwood, managed to keep the band going for a few years, but most of the key members soon defected to other outfits or to lead their own ensembles.

◀ BROWN, T. GRAHAM

(born Anthony G. Brown, 1954, Arabi, GA)

Motown-influenced hit maker of the mid-eighties, Brown brought a younger audience to country in the days before GARTH BROOKS.

Brown formed his group, playfully called Rack of Spam, when he was still a student at the University of Georgia. Originally a soul-flavored R&B outfit, the band was also highly influenced by the soft pop-rock of the EAGLES, spiritual granddaddies of most of today's NEW-COUNTRY artists. Coming to Nashville in 1982, Brown was soon in demand for cutting jingles (when he became a star, he continued to perform the Taco Bell theme in concert) as well as country-flavored demos. He signed to Capitol in 1984, first charting in 1985 with his own "I Tell It Like It Used to Be," which he describes as a cross between GEORGE JONES and Otis Redding. His first number one was "Hell and High Water" from a year later, cowritten with Alex Harvey, a top Nashville tunesmith famous for writing early-seventies COUNTRY-POLITAN hits like "Delta Dawn." Brown followed up with two other number-one songs, "Don't Go to Strangers" and "Darlene," and a remake of Redding's "(Sittin' on the) Dock of the Bay." He also enjoyed a movie career as a character actor in Hollywood.

Brown's career was sidetracked by his increased dependence on alcohol. In the early nineties he attempted a comeback after drying out, but it was a failure.

Select Discography

The Best of T. Graham Brown, Liberty 97520. Recordings from the late eighties and early nineties, not his earlier hits.

◀ BROWNS, THE

(Ella Maxine born 1932, Sampi, LA; Jim Edwards born 1934, Sparkman, AK; Bonnie born 1937, Sparkman, AK)

The Browns were a popular fifties country trio who performed a mix of light country and pop schmaltz (their big hit was an English-language version of Edith Piaf's "Les Trois Cloches") and later jumped on the early-sixties FOLK-REVIVAL bandwagon. Their smooth harmonies and refined good looks made them natural crossover artists in the era of the NASHVILLE SOUND; many of their recordings can hardly be distinguished from mainstream pop of the fifties and sixties.

The Browns were not dirt-poor country folks; their father operated a sawmill, and for a while Jim Ed studied forestry with the idea that he would take over the family business. However, his sister Maxine was ambitious and longed for a career as an entertainer. The two had been singing together since junior high school and began performing together in the early fifties on Little Rock radio station KLRA after winning a talent contest sponsored by the station. They eventually worked their way up to being featured on the larger KWKH's *Hayride*, which also originated out of Little Rock. They made some early recordings for the local Abbott label in 1954 and 1955 that feature some nice country harmony singing, including their own composition, "Looking Back to See," along with lots of country novelty songs. Their backup on these sessions included the guitar of JIM REEVES (who would later encourage RCA to sign the group) and slide-note piano playing of FLOYD CRAMER.

In 1955 younger sister Bonnie joined the act, and the group toured as headliners with the *Ozark Jubilee*. Thanks to Reeves, they got a contract with RCA, and the group had a hit with a cover of the LOUVIN BROTHERS' "I Take a Chance" in 1956. They were inactive on the recording scene for a few years while Jim Ed served in the army (although another sibling, Norma, temporarily joined to help out with touring) but scored a big pop and country hit in 1959 on his return with the saccharine "The Three Bells," a cover of Edith Piaf's "Les Trois Cloches."

Some more pop-country hits followed, as well as covers of traditional folk songs, such as 1961's "Groundhog," performed in the manner of the popular folk-revival groups of the day (such as the Kingston Trio or Peter, Paul, and Mary). In 1963 they were invited to join the GRAND OLE OPRY, but internal disagreements in the group, sparked by the marriages of the two women, led to the group's breakup in 1967. Jim Ed had already recorded successfully as a soloist in 1965 and continued his solo career on RCA through the early eighties, appearing regularly in the late sixties at Lake Tahoe as a lounge singer. He also scored as a partner with HELEN CORNELIUS from 1976 to 1981. His first hit with Cornelius was the slightly racy "I Don't Want to Have to Marry You," followed by other country-pop heartache numbers (even a cover of Neil Diamond's three-hanky WEEPER "You Don't Bring Me Flowers"). Maxine made a successful solo single in 1968 ("Sugar Cane Country" issued by Chart) but soon retired from performing.

Select Discography
Greatest Hits, RCA 55979. Budget-priced compilation of Jim Ed's duet hits with Helen Cornelius.

Rockin' Rollin' Browns, Bear Family 15104. LP reissue of cuts from 1957 through 1964; exactly why they called this collection of mushy pop-folk "Rockin' Rollin' " is a mystery.

◀ BRUCE, ED

(born Keiser, AR, 1939)

A SINGER/SONGWRITER with a long career, Bruce began in the ROCKABILLY-filled fifties recording for Sun Records, became a country songwriter in the sixties and seventies (writing the classic "Mama, Don't Let Your Babies Grow Up to Be Cowboys," a 1978 hit for Waylon and Willie), and then scored his own number-one country hit with "You're the Best Break This Old Heart Ever Had" in 1982.

Arkansas-bred Bruce made his first recordings in the then-popular rockabilly style for Sun Records in the late fifties; he then recorded teen pop for Sceptre in the early sixties. Moving to Nashville, he placed his first country hit with Charlie Louvin, 1965's "See the Big Man Cry." Thanks to his enterprising wife and manager, Bruce picked up a good deal of work doing jingles, his down-home voice gracing ads for everything from burgers to coffee to military service.

By the mid-seventies, Bruce was recording country material for United Artists, including the first version of "Mama." (The song originally warned against young girls marrying guitar players, but Bruce realized that cowboys was even better.) He also penned "The Man That Turned My Mama On" and "Texas (When I Die)," both mid-seventies recordings by TANYA TUCKER. In the early eighties, he signed with MCA, scoring his sole number-one country hit in 1982. At the same time, he enjoyed minor success portraying cowpokes on television, including the short-run return of the classic *Maverick* program.

Oddly enough, in the late eighties the rockabilly revival brought renewed interest to Bruce's first recordings; many of these listeners were unaware of his more mainstream country career.

Select Discography

Greatest Hits, MCA 27139. Budget-priced cassette-only reissue of early-eighties tracks.

◀ BRUMLEY, TOM

(born 1935, Powell, MO)

Brumley is a pedal steel guitarist who helped BUCK OWENS create the famed BAKERSFIELD SOUND in the early sixties and then became one of the pioneers of COUNTRY-ROCK when he helped RICK NELSON form the Stone Canyon Band.

The son of noted songwriter Albert Brumley (who composed "Turn Your Radio On," among other gospel-tinged numbers), Brumley began playing country music from an early age, taking up the steel GUITAR as a youngster after hearing JERRY BYRD, one of the early, legendary players of the instrument. He worked locally with his four brothers in a HONKY-TONK band until he was drafted into the army.

On his return, he settled in California, eventually hooking up with Buck Owens and becoming a full-time member of Buck's backup group, the Buckaroos, in 1963. He remained with Owens during his greatest recording years and developed a style of steel playing that was far from the maudlin, weepy style of mainstream Nashville; instead, his playing had a rocking edge that helped drive the music.

In 1969 he left Owens and with Nelson cofounded the Stone Canyon Band, generally credited with being among the first country-rock outfits. He continued to perform with Nelson for sixteen years, playing in pop-rock, country, and even rockabilly styles. After Nelson's death, Brumley more or less retired to instrument building, although he occasionally continues to do session work.

◀ BRYANT, BOUDLEAUX AND FELICE

(Boudleaux born 1930, Shellman, GA; died 1987; Felice [Scaduto] born 1925, Milwaukee, WI)

The Bryants are the most famous of all country songwriting duos. They penned hundreds of country classics, including the perennial BLUEGRASS favorite "Rocky Top," along with most of the EVERLY BROTHERS' late-fifties hits.

Boudleaux Bryant's first love was classical music; as a classical violinist, he worked for a year with the Atlanta Symphony before turning to jazz, leading a series of small combos. While touring the Midwest, he met and befriended an elevator attendant at Milwaukee's Shrader Hotel; she was Felice Scaduto, and the couple were married soon after World War II. At about the same time, he joined HANK PENNY's band as a country-styled fiddler and began writing country songs with his young wife.

Their first hit was "Country Boy," recorded by LITTLE JIMMY DICKENS in 1949, which led to a contract with FRED ROSE of the powerful Acuff-Rose publishing company. They produced hits for both pop crooners (Tony Bennett's "Have a Good Time") and mainstream country acts (CARL SMITH's "Hey Joe," later covered by Frankie Laine; and a number of hits for EDDY ARNOLD, including "I've Been Thinking" and "The Richest Man," both released in 1955).

In 1957 Fred Rose's son Wesley introduced the Bryants to an up-and-coming country duo called the Everly Brothers, asking them to come up with some teen-styled hits for the pair. They quickly produced "Bye Bye Love," the Everly's first hit, followed by "Wake Up Little Susie" in the same year; "All I Have to Do Is Dream," "Bird Dog," and "Problems" in 1958; and "Take a Message to Mary" and "Poor Jenny" in 1959. Their success with the Everlys led other teen popsters to cover their material, including BUDDY HOLLY ("It's Raining in My Heart") and BOB LUMAN ("Let's Think About Living"). In these songs the Bryants combined classic country sentiments of love gone wrong with teen angst; even the nonhits, like the Everlys' "Love Hurts" (later covered by ROY ORBISON and GRAM PARSONS), have had a long shelf life because of this classic combination.

In the sixties, with the growth in power and influence of the New York–based Brill Building songwriters, the Bryants returned to writing primarily for country performers, penning SONNY JAMES's 1964 hit "Baltimore" and ROY CLARK's 1973 hit "Come Live with Me." In 1979 they made their first recording, the unusually titled

Surfin' on a New Wave, on the tiny DB label. After attempting a few other recordings for small labels, the Bryants realized their true strength was in songwriting, not performing their own material.

◀ BRYANT, JIMMY

(born 1925)

Bryant was one of the hottest country-jazz guitarists of the fifties, often recording with steel guitarist SPEEDY WEST.

Originally a child prodigy fiddler, Bryant took up the GUITAR to amuse himself while recuperating from a wound he received in World War II. He settled in Los Angeles after the war, working in the vibrant local country bar and club scene. Singer TEX WILLIAMS heard him perform and invited him to session on his 1950 recording of "Wild Card." CLIFFIE STONE, who was the host of Los Angeles's influential "Hometown Jamboree" radio program, hired the guitarist soon after to work in the show's backup band. It was there that he met the talented steel guitarist Speedy West, and the two were soon paired on instrumentals, earning the nickname the Flaming Guitars. Bryant and West signed with Capitol and recorded many jazz-influenced instrumentals, including Bryant's original compositions, which had colorful names like "Frettin' Fingers" and "Stratosphere Boogie"; on "Jammin' with Jimmy," through the miracle of overdubbing, Bryant played a duet with himself on swinging fiddle and guitar. Additionally, the two worked on many fifties-era West Coast country recordings for Capitol and other smaller labels.

West left California in the late fifties to work in Oklahoma, but Bryant continued to record as a soloist for the West Coast–based Imperial label. He also produced recordings by other country acts and wrote the country standard "Only Daddy That'll Walk the Line."

◀ BUFFALO GALS, THE

(1974–1979: Susie Monick [banjo]; Carol Siegel [mandolin]; Martha Trachtenberg [guitar, vocals]; Sue Raines [fiddle]; Nancy Josephson [bass])

One of the first all-female, revival BLUEGRASS bands, the Buffalo Gals spotlighted progressive banjoist Susie Monick (born 1952), whose noodling instrumentals recalled the work of her contemporary, TONY TRISCHKA.

The band was formed originally when Monick, guitarist Debby Gabriel, and dulcimer player Carol Siegel were undergraduates together at Syracuse University. Siegel took up MANDOLIN, and they formed an old-time/bluegrass trio. Gabriel decided to pursue a career as a painter and was replaced by vocalist/guitarist Martha Trachtenberg and bassist Nancy Josephson. By 1974 fiddler Sue Raines was on board, and the quintet was playing bluegrass clubs and folk festivals.

The band's notoriety came mostly from their all-female makeup. It was not only unusual for women to play bluegrass but women were rarely even showcased as hot pickers, and these women could certainly hold their own with any of the other PROGRESSIVE BLUEGRASS bands of the day. By 1976 new members Lainie Lyle on mandolin and fiddler Kristin Wilkinson had replaced Raines and Siegel, and the band relocated to Nashville. At about the same time, Monick released a solo BANJO LP, *Melting Pots*, an experimental mix of far-out instrumentals and Celtic-flavored banjo sounds. The band went through more personnel changes before it finally folded in 1979.

Of late Monick has been performing as a mandolin and button accordion player in State of the Heart, a country-folk ensemble led by Nashville songwriter Richard Dobson.

◀ BUMGARNER, SAMANTHA

(born Samantha Biddix, c. 1880, Silva, NC; died 1960)

Bumgarner was an early country banjoist, fiddler, and vocalist who is best known for twelve recordings made in April 1924 with guitarist Eva Davis for OKeh records, among the earliest old-time recordings. She was probably the first banjoist, male or female, to record in this style. In 1928 she appeared at the first Mountain Dance and Folk Festival, which was organized by another legendary banjoist, BAS-COM LAMAR LUNSFORD, in Asheville, North Carolina. She was a favorite at this festival for the next thirty-one years until her death. The daughter of an old-time fiddler, Bumgarner was a talented performer on both BANJO and fiddle and won numerous contests in her day, an unusual feat at the time for a woman. She continued to perform throughout the fifties, gaining regional fame as a performer of traditional banjo tunes and songs.

◀ BURNETT AND RUTHERFORD

(Richard D. Burnett born 1883, Elk Spring Valley, KY; died c. 1989; Leonard Rutherford born c. 1900, Somerset, KY; died 1954)

Burnett and Rutherford were an old-time BANJO and fiddle duo who were prolific and popular recording artists in the middle to late twenties. Their style was somewhat smoother than some of the more backwoods units that recorded at the time, and their repertoire included sentimental and novelty songs along with the older traditional numbers.

Burnett was a talented musician who played the dulcimer, banjo, and fiddle from an early age. Both his father and grandfather were dedicated churchgoers, and Burnett remembers singing hymns from the age of four. He also picked up the traditional songs and tunes of the south-central Kentucky region where he was born. Burnett lost both parents by the time he was twelve, a fact he immortalized in his sentimental ballad "The Orphan Boy," which became one of his most popular numbers.

Burnett began working as an oil-field hand around 1901. Six years later, when returning from work one night, he was robbed and shot in the face; the bullet struck his optic nerve, blinding him. Unable to continue work, he fell back on his musical skills and became a wandering performer. Around 1914 he approached a

local family, the Rutherfords, to ask them if their young son Leonard could serve
as his companion and guide. The fourteen-year-old was already proficient on the
fiddle and would be a valuable addition to the street-corner act. The parents
agreed, and the Burnett and Rutherford duo was born. Burnett takes credit for
teaching Rutherford music and for training him to play note-for-note along with
his banjo. This made their performances much tighter and less chaotic than many
of the other old-time performers of the day.

By the mid-twenties, the duo was in great demand throughout the Kentucky-
Tennessee-Virginia area. In 1926 they were performing in Virginia when a local
store owner heard them perform and recommended them to Columbia Records.
Their first recordings were made soon after under the supervision of legendary
A&R man FRANK WALKER, who oversaw many of Columbia's "hillbilly" records,
including the classic sides made by the SKILLET LICKERS. Burnett's expressive vocals
and Rutherford's smooth fiddling made these records stand out, and the duo recorded many of them again, first for Columbia and later, with the addition of
guitarist Byrd Moore, for Gennett.

Burnett's older style of performing—including a good deal of clowning around
on stage (he even worked up a vocal imitation of the sound of the Jew's harp to
accompany his banjo playing)—irritated the younger, more serious Rutherford. By
the late twenties, they had begun to record with other musicians, although they
continued to perform together sporadically until Rutherford's death. The Depression effectively ended their recording careers, but they were still well-known street
performers into the early fifties. Later Burnett took up chair caning and retired
from music.

Burnett and Rutherford's recordings were quite influential throughout the South.
Rutherford's fiddling featured many blue notes, slides, and complicated syncopation that forecast the BLUEGRASS fiddle style of some twenty years later. Burnett's
energetic banjo playing and singing (and his older-style fiddling, highlighted on
recordings made without Rutherford) make their recordings some of the most
memorable and enjoyable of the old-time style.

Select Discography
Ramblin' Reckless Hobo, Rounder 1004. Cassette-only reissue of their best
recordings.

◀ BURNETTE, DORSEY

(born 1932, Memphis, TN; died 1979)

Along with his famous brother Johnny, Burnette was one of the pioneers of
ROCKABILLY before moving into a more mainstream country career as a songwriter.

The Burnette brothers were raised in a house full of country music, and Dorsey
remembered traveling to Nashville with his dad to hear the GRAND OLE OPRY. Both
brothers took up musical instruments at an early age and were playing in pickup
bands of various types throughout the region by their high-school years. Uncertain
if music could be a career, they both trained as electricians while still pursuing

musical interests; they even traveled to New York in the early fifties to appear on *Ted Mack's Amateur Hour*, taking first-place honors four times.

By 1954 they were working in Memphis at Crown Electric, which had previously employed another local musician, ELVIS PRESLEY; they befriended another Crown employee, guitarist Paul Burlison, and formed the Burnette Trio, playing for local dances and at bars and clubs. After Elvis hit it big, they recorded a couple of jazzed-up country tunes under the new name of the Rock 'n' Roll Trio for Coral Records, including a swinging version of the DELMORE BROTHERS's "Blues Stay Away from Me" and the Trio's most famous recording, "Train Kept a-Rollin'," later covered by the Yardbirds in the 1960s and Aerosmith in the 1970s.

Discouraged by their relative lack of success, the brothers relocated to the West Coast. Here they teamed up with young RICKY NELSON, providing him with a number of hits, including "Waitin' in School" and "It's Late." Meanwhile, they recorded both individually and as a duo. Dorsey had hits with "Hey Little One" and "Tall Oak Tree" in the early sixties, while Johnny had solo hits with the teenybopper numbers "You're Sixteen" and "Dreamin'" before dying in a boating accident in 1964.

Dorsey moved from label to label from the late sixties until his death, while also supplying hit songs for country performers like ROGER MILLER and GLEN CAMP-BELL. He had a couple of minor hits in the country-WEEPER style and penned some gospel standards, the best-known being "The Magnificent Sanctuary Band." His biggest hit was 1975's "Molly I Ain't Getting Any Younger," released by the Melo-dyland division of Motown Records. Shortly after issuing "Here I Go Again" in 1979 on Elektra/Asylum, Dorsey died of a heart attack. His sons Billy and Rocky Burnette have performed as rockabilly revivalists, and Billy briefly served as guitarist for Fleetwood Mac after Lindsey Buckingham jumped ship.

Select Discography

Rock 'n' Roll, Richmond 2134. Cassette-only reissue of his pop-rock recordings.

◀ BURTON, JAMES

(born 1939, Shreveport, LA)

Burton is a highly influential session guitarist who has had a great impact on country, rock, and pop music. His sharp, stacatto picking and bluesy stylings made him one of the most loved and most copied of all guitarists. In his long career he has recorded with hundreds of artists, from RICK NELSON and ELVIS PRESLEY to GRAM PARSONS and EMMYLOU HARRIS.

Although originally strictly a country guitarist, Burton first made his mark in his 1957 duet with Dale Hawkins on "Suzie Q"; he then signed on with BOB LUMAN, who at the time was briefly recording in a teen-star style (he would later go country). Along with bassist James Kirkland, Burton was hired to accompany the young teen star Ricky Nelson and played on most of his late-fifties and early-sixties hits beginning with "Hello, Mary Lou."

In 1964 Burton returned to playing country, accompanying BUCK OWENS and

MERLE HAGGARD on many of their classic Capitol recordings, helping to bring a
ROCKABILLY edge to the nascent BAKERSFIELD SOUND. In 1969 he was signed by Elvis
to be his accompanist, and he remained with the King until his death. Meanwhile,
Burton accompanied Gram Parsons on his two solo albums and helped form
Emmylou Harris's Hot Band upon Parsons's death. Along the way, he made some
solo recordings that reveal that his personal taste runs, unfortunately, to the worst
kind of pop-schlock.

Burton's guitar of choice was the Fender Telecaster, and he helped popularize
this instrument in both rock and country circles. He used the Telecaster's biting
tone to emphasize his own propensity for cleanly played bursts of notes. He was
one of the first electric guitarists to work consistently in country, and through his
association with Parsons he was also one of the shaping voices of COUNTRY-ROCK.

◀ BUSH, JOHNNY

(born 1935, Houston, TX)

A protégé of and sometime accompanist to WILLIE NELSON, Bush had a series of
late-sixties and early-seventies hits, primarily with covers of Nelson's songs.

Born in Houston, Bush relocated to San Antonio when he was twenty-seven
years old and got a job performing at a local HONKY-TONK, originally as a singer/
guitarist. He switched to playing drums soon after, playing informally with Nelson
before linking up with RAY PRICE, with whom he toured as a member of his backup
group, the Cherokee Cowboys, for three years. He returned to working with Nelson
in 1966, leading his backup group, the Record Men, and also signed as a singer
to the local Stop label. He remained with the label for three years, producing hits
with covers of Nelson's "You Ought to Hear Me Cry" and "What a Way to Live"
in 1967, followed by "Undo the Right" and "You Gave Me a Mountain" in 1968
and 1969, respectively. In 1972 he signed to RCA and had his biggest hit, a cover
of Nelson's "Whiskey River."

However, Bush soon fell out of public favor, eventually recording a few more
hits, including his minor 1977 hit "You'll Never Leave Me Completely," for the
smaller Starday/Gusto label, a Nashville-based BLUEGRASS-oriented outfit. By the late
seventies, vocal-cord injuries made it difficult for Bush to speak, and he had to
limit himself to performing for only short periods at a time, effectively ending his
career.

◀ BUTLER, CARL AND PEARL

*(Carl born 1927, Knoxville, TN; Pearl Dee Jones born 1930, Nashville, TN; died
1988)*

The Butlers were a husband-and-wife team who produced a string of hits in the
mid-sixties in classic country-harmony style.

Butler was originally a solo recording artist, first charting in the early sixties with
the HONKY-TONK throwbacks "Honky Tonkitis" (1961) and "Don't Let Me Cross

Over" (1962). The second recording featured an uncredited Pearl on harmony vocals. After the song hit big, the duo followed up with a number of similar-sounding WEEPERS, from 1963's "Loving Arms" to 1969's "I Never Got Over You." Most of their recordings were made in typical mid-sixties Nashville style, i.e., burdened with schlocky strings and mainstream pop accompaniments that did little to enhance their basically down-home performances. In 1967 the duo appeared in the B-grade epic film *Second Fiddle to a Steel Guitar*. In the seventies they retired from performing.

◄ BYRD, JERRY

(born 1920, Lima, OH)

Byrd was a pioneering Hawaiian-flavored steel guitarist who helped make the instrument a central part of country music in the fifties.

As a youngster, Byrd took up the lap steel guitar, influenced greatly by musicians who played in the Hawaiian style, complete with wide tremolo and sweeping glissandi. Although he worked professionally as a painter before enlisting in the army, he also found time to work as a musician on the side, often with the Pleasant Valley Boys. After his discharge from the service at the end of World War II, he joined ERNEST TUBB's Troubadours for two years, then signed as a solo artist in 1949 to Mercury.

Byrd's recordings became famous for their remarkably clean picking and high level of virtuosity, even though his material tended toward the crassly commercial. Whereas many players bubbled and burbled, Byrd managed to produce clean melodic lines, a warm romantic tone, and flawlessly executed phrases even when performing the kind of "shores-of-old-Waikiki" numbers that make grown folks weep. However, as the fifties wore on and the newly introduced PEDAL STEEL GUITAR gained popularity in country music, Byrd refused to give up his simpler style and found it increasingly hard to find work. Eventually he retired to Hawaii, where he worked for a while in the mid-sixties as bandmaster for the Bobby Lord television show. He has become a champion for the traditional Hawaiian style of playing and continues to occasionally record and perform.

◄ BYRDS, THE

(1964–1973; original lineup: Roger [Jim] McGuinn [guitar, twelve-string guitar, vocals]; David Crosby [guitar, vocals]; Gene Clark [guitar, vocals]; Chris Hillman [bass, vocals]; Michael Clarke [drums])

The Byrds were one of the most influential folk-rock groups of the sixties and they later helped popularize COUNTRY-ROCK with their classic album, *Sweetheart of the Rodeo*.

Roger McGuinn was the leader of the group; he had previously been part of the FOLK REVIVAL, working as an accompanist for the Chad Mitchell Trio and the Limelighters before settling in Los Angeles. David Crosby had also been a member of a professional folk band, Les Baxter's Balladeers, while CHRIS HILLMAN's background was in BLUEGRASS, as the leader of the Hillmen, which included the Gosdin brothers. All of the group's members were active in the Los Angeles folk scene, and all were inspired by the Beatles to take up electric instruments. The band was originally called the Beefeaters and then the Jet Set before they finally settled on the Byrds.

From the beginning, the group's repertoire reflected a folk and country orientation. They were among the first to record and popularize BOB DYLAN's songs on the pop charts, beginning with their first hit, 1965's "Mr. Tambourine Man." The same year, they took PETE SEEGER's "Turn Turn Turn," a folkie setting of the book of Ecclesiastes, to number one.

GENE CLARK left the group in 1966 because of his fear of flying; he hooked up with Doug Dillard soon after to form the country-rock outfit Dillard and Clark. The band, now led by McGuinn and Crosby, took a decided psychedelic turn, scoring with the spacey anthem "Eight Miles High" along with the parody of life as a teen idol, "So You Want to Be a Rock and Roll Star." However, Crosby soon left the group to form the pop trio Crosby, Stills, and Nash, leaving the Byrds a three-member group, with McGuinn, Hillman, and Clarke. They recorded their first country-rock tunes for their album *The Notorious Byrd Brothers*, although they were still experimenting with psychedelia.

In 1968 the band's transformation was completed by the addition of guitarist GRAM PARSONS, who had previously performed with the International Submarine Band, an early country-rock group. The new Byrds, with McGuinn, Hillman, Parsons, and drummer Kevin White, along with guests CLARENCE WHITE and JOHN HARTFORD, recorded *Sweetheart of the Rodeo*. The album included remakes of country classics like "(An Empty Bottle, a Broken Heart, and) You're Still on My Mind," as well as Parson's neocountry ballad "Hickory Wind," pointing the band in the direction of a country-rock fusion.

Determined to pursue country-rock music further, Hillman and Parsons left the band and formed the FLYING BURRITO BROTHERS. Session guitarist Clarence White came on board with the remaining Byrds along with bassist John York (later replaced by Skip Battin). This new version of the band continued to record country and folk-rock material, lasting for four years, producing the hits "Ballad of Easy Rider," a folkie-esque tune sung by McGuinn for the soundtrack of the film *Easy Rider*, as well as the minor 1971 hit "Chestnut Mare." In 1975 the original five-man Byrds reunited for an album for Asylum Records, but the old group magic was gone.

In the mid-seventies, McGuinn went solo, recording a couple of poorly received albums, and toured with Bob Dylan's Rolling Thunder Review. In the early eighties, he reunited with Hillman and Gene Clark to form a trio that was plagued by Clark's bouts of depression and continued fear of flying. Later that decade, Hillman formed the DESERT ROSE BAND, Clark went back to a solo career (and eventually committed suicide), and McGuinn continued to perform sporadically as a solo artist; longtime fan Tom Petty produced his solo album in 1992. When Columbia issued a boxed set of the Byrds's classic recordings, McGuinn, Hillman, and Crosby reunited to record a couple of new tracks.

Select Discography

The Byrds, 46773. Four-CD retrospective set.

Twenty Essential Tracks, Columbia 47884. If you can't afford the boxed set, how about buying this single CD and sampling the best of the best.

Sweetheart of the Rodeo, Columbia 9670. Hear the record that started it all.

C.

◀ CACKLE SISTERS, THE

(c. 1935–c. 1950: Mary Jane, Carolyn, Lorraine, and Eva DeZurick)

The DeZurick Sisters were amazing trick yodelers who specialized in all kinds of barnyard and natural sound effects.

Born on a dairy farm in Royalton, Minnesota, to a Dutch farming family of six girls and a boy, the original duo was made up of elder sisters Mary Jane and Carolyn, who undoubtedly honed their skills while working among the various farm animals. Signed on to the *National Barn Dance*, their popularity brought them to the attention of feed manufacturer Ralston-Purina, which hired them in the mid-forties to perform their harmonized chicken-cackling act on the GRAND OLE OPRY. In order to maintain their ties with WLS, the station that broadcast the Barn Dance, they took the name the Cackle Sisters for their Opry appearances. When the older sisters got married, they began using their younger sisters to fill in; Lorraine came to the fore after the Second World War, introducing a new element to their act: rapid-fire, stacatto vocalizing that was called "machine-gun" or "triple-tongue" yodels, giving the act a final burst of popularity in the early fifties.

◀ CAJUN MUSIC

A revival of interest in the traditional music of southern Louisiana in the seventies and eighties led to a rediscovery of Cajun music, the songs and dance tunes performed by the descendants of the original French Acacians who settled the area. Elements of the Cajun style have been introduced into mainstream country music from time to time, and in turn, through the influence of radio and recordings, country music has also reshaped contemporary Cajun sounds.

The Acacians originally hail from the island of Acacia, a French colony off of Canada (now known as Nova Scotia). When the French ceded the island to the British in 1713, the settlers moved south to what was then still French territory in Louisiana. There they came into contact with English, Spanish, and African-American settlers and developed a unique language and a distinct musical style. During the nineteenth century, the musical styles of Europe—waltzes, quadrilles, cotillions, mazurkas—came to the area and entered the musical repertoire. While in the eighteenth century, the fiddle and triangle had been the primary musical instruments, the nineteenth century introduced the accordion and its many relatives and, later in the century, the GUITAR.

Although Cajun music has a distinctive, immediately recognizable sound, it's easier to hear than describe in words. As you might suspect from Cajun music's polylingual and polymusical roots, the result is a musical gumbo that reflects a variety of influences. The fiddle and accordion are the two most prominent instruments, and both are played rhythmically, with a heavy emphasis on the beat, rather than primarily melodically. Songs tend to be made up of lyrical fragments, often sung in Acadian French, usually on the topics of good times (dancing, courtship, food and drink) or bad ones (heartbreak). The dance styles are a mix of popular European dances of the nineteenth century, such as polka, waltz, and quadrille, and the ever-present two-step, known throughout the rural South. Of course, there are many different varieties of Cajun music, and most recent performers have been influenced by country (particularly in their vocal styles) and rock and roll (in instrumentation and a heavy emphasis on the backbeat).

Cajun music was first recorded in the twenties when the record industry was quickly discovering the commercial potential of music directed at specific regional groups. Fiddlers Dennis McGee and Saday Courville made the first, legendary twin-fiddle recordings. In the thirties and forties, WESTERN SWING and pop styles swept the area, and several Cajun musicians—notably fiddler Leo Soileau in the prewar era, who led the first band to feature drums with a jazzy feeling; and fiddler/bandleader Harry Choates after the war, who wrote the big country and Cajun hit "Jole Blon"—modernized Cajun music to reflect these outside influences.

In the post–World War II era, Cajun sounds occasionally crossed over into the country charts. HANK WILLIAMS had a hit with the Cajunesque "Jambalaya," and Rusty and DOUG KERSHAW began recording for both country and Cajun markets. Meanwhile, the FOLK REVIVAL of the late fifties and early sixties led to a renewed interest in more traditional Cajun music. Groups like the NEW LOST CITY RAMBLERS added Cajun music to their act, and traditional family bands like the Balfa Brothers from Mamou, Louisiana, were successful on the festival and folk-revival trail. Accordionist Nathan Abshire, who had originally recorded in the thirties without much success, was rediscovered and became a big attraction on the concert scene.

Cajun music's sister sound, known as Zodico or Zydeco, also gained new popularity in the seventies and eighties. Zydeco is the wedding of African-American blues and jazz styles with Cajun dance and song; its proponents are mostly African-American Creoles. One of the greatest Zydeco musicians was Clifton Chenier, an accordionist who recorded extensively through the sixties and seventies.

Cajun and Zydeco revival bands began springing up in the seventies to cater to a more educated, upscale market. Fiddler Michael Doucet was one of the most active of the younger Cajun musicians; eventually he formed the group Beausoleil, which wed Cajun sounds to folk-rock instrumentation. Their music was celebrated in the lyrics of MARY CHAPIN CARPENTER's first big country hit, "Down at the Twist and Shout" (the band also performed on the track). Other popular Cajun and Zydeco revivalists include Rockin' Dopsie and the Twisters (who appear on Paul Simon's *Graceland* album), Rockin' Sydney (popularizer of the much-recorded "My Toot Toot"), and Jo-el Sonnier.

◀ CALLAHAN BROTHERS, THE

(Walter T. ["Joe"] [guitar, lead vocals] born 1910, Laurel, NC; died 1971; Homer C. ["Bill"] [mandolin, guitar, bass, harmony vocals] born 1912, Laurel, NC)

A popular brother duo of the thirties, the Callahans featured both traditional ballads and sentimental songs and newer blues and jazz-influenced, pop-swing material in their repertoire. Their songbooks and radio broadcasts were quite influential in the South, Midwest, and Southwest through the 1940s.

Born in the mountains of western North Carolina, the brothers absorbed the traditional dance music, balladry, and religious songs that were performed in the region. After performing locally for various functions, they made their professional debut at the 1933 Asheville, North Carolina, folk festival, emulating the yodeling style of JIMMIE RODGERS. They were immediately signed by a Knoxville radio station and a year later made their first recordings for the budget American Record Company (ARC) label. In 1935 they made one of the first recordings of the traditional folk blues tune "The House of the Rising Sun," released under the name "Rounder's Luck." They also published a series of songbooks that they promoted through their radio shows and personal appearances, greatly influencing the repertoire of many other traditional musicians.

The Callahans moved throughout the South and West to work for a variety of different country radio programs, including a stint with RED FOLEY on Cincinnati's WLW and another with the country musical comedy act the WEAVER BROTHERS AND ELVIRY, out of Springfield, Missouri, before finally settling in Texas in the early forties, broadcasting simultaneously out of Dallas and Wichita Falls. After recording a good deal of traditional material in the thirties, they moved toward more blues- and jazz-oriented sounds in the forties, expanding their band (now called the Blue Ridge Mountain Folk) into a cross between the sound and style of old-time bands like the J. E. MAINER outfits and modern WESTERN SWING orchestras. Their recordings included country-blues numbers like "Step It Up and Go" and "Rattlesnakin' Daddy," a cover of a song by Bill Carlisle (of the CARLISLE BROTHERS).

The Callahans are a link between the old-time country style and the subsequent cowboy and Western acts who emphasized bluesier styles. Though they continued to perform until the early sixties (primarily on radio and in personal appearances), their greatest impact was in the thirties and forties when this period of transition was occurring.

◀ CAMPBELL, GLEN

(born 1936, Delight, AK)

A country-pop vocalist and guitarist best known for a string of mid-sixties crossover hits, Campbell has soldiered on in the country market, although with diminishing success.

Campbell was encouraged by other musicians in his family to take up the GUITAR at age four; by his teens, he was touring with his own country band, the Western Wranglers. At age twenty-four, Campbell relocated to Los Angeles, where he quickly found employment as a session guitarist, scoring a minor solo hit in 1961 with "Turn Around Look at Me." Campbell worked comfortably as a session player in pop, country, and rock, even briefly touring as bassist for the Beach Boys after founding member Brian Wilson suffered a nervous breakdown.

In the mid-sixties, Capitol signed Campbell as a solo artist. The company first tried to promote him as an instrumentalist, releasing an LP of twelve-string guitar instrumentals aimed at a general, pop market. However, it was Campbell's clear tenor, with only a hint of a country twang, that would gain him his hits as a pop crooner. The year 1967 brought his first hit, a cover of JOHN HARTFORD's "Gentle on My Mind," followed by a string of Jimmy Webb–penned soft-country hits ("By the Time I Get to Phoenix," "Wichita Lineman," and "Galveston"). These songs all had pop arrangements, replete with string sections and choruses, and had great appeal to a general audience, as well as success on the country charts. Campbell's career was furthered by his exposure as the guest host for a summer replacement program for the popular *Smothers Brothers* television show, followed by his own variety show in 1969, plus film roles, most notably with John Wayne in *True Grit*.

Soon after, the hits stopped. Campbell returned to the charts in the mid-seventies as more of a country-oriented performer with "Rhinestone Cowboy" and "Southern Nights" but then lapsed again into obscurity. Although he continues to perform both as a vocalist and instrumentalist, Campbell has failed to recapture his early success.

Select Discography
Best of the Early Years, Curb 77441. His sixties-era Capitol hits.

◀ CANOVA, JUDY

(born Juliette Canova, 1916, Starke, FL; died 1983)

Canova was a hillbilly comedian who first performed in New York's nightclubs, then on radio, and finally in a series of C-grade Hollywood comedies.

Canova's character of a backwoods, slightly ditsy, but always lovable rube was the prototype for hundreds of country comics who followed. Canova came from a well-to-do Southern family; her mother was a concert singer who managed her performing children's careers. Judy began her career performing with her family at the age of fourteen, traveling in a musical-comedy revue throughout the South. Known as the Georgia Crackers, Judy, sister Anne (Diana), and brother Zeke (Leon) worked up a novelty act, combining verbal and physical comedy with reworkings of country and novelty songs, eventually hitting New York in mid-1930. In 1931 they became the prime attraction at Greenwich Village's Village Barn, a kind of pseudorustic hangout for New York's Bohemia featuring Western-garbed waitresses and a countryesque floor show. From there they moved into vaudeville and radio and appeared on Broadway with Martha Raye in *Calling All Stars* in 1934.

The Canovas made their first recordings in 1931, including hammed-up versions of folk songs like "Frog Went A-Courtin' " performed by the two girls, and "I Wish I Was a Single Girl Again," Judy's first solo recording. The trio also cut cornball harmony numbers like "Snake-Eyed Killing Dude" along with sentimental favorites such as "When the Sun Goes Down Behind the Hill." They began to publish their own songbooks in 1934.

They first went to Hollywood in 1937 to make films for Paramount, with little success. After a tour of England and more radio work, the trio landed back on Broadway in *Yodel Boy*, the show that launched Judy's solo career. In 1940 she returned as a solo act to Hollywood, starring in her first movie, *Scatterbrain*, produced by Republic Pictures, the same C-grade studio that brought the world the Western adventures of GENE AUTRY and ROY ROGERS. Canova's Republic hits were top grossers, and she became the studio's one and only female star. Most of these vehicles were thin on plot, and all featured pseudo-Western numbers for Canova to show off her blend of vocal gymnastics (including YODELING and jazzy inflections), put to the service of broad comedy.

Canova did not make many recordings, focusing instead on live radio performances. She did have one hit in 1947 with her pairing of "No Letter Today" and the bluesy girls-listen-up ballad "Never Trust a Man." By the mid-fifties, with her film career and radio days behind her, she recorded one album, backed by legendary steel guitarist SPEEDY WEST, issued in 1958, which combined well-worn traditional numbers with the hokey composed material she favored in the forties.

Canova tried to break into television in the sixties, with little success; eventually she retired and, in 1983, died of cancer. Daughter Diana Canova became a TV comedian, starring on the series *Soap* as well as *Throb*, a satire of the pop-music business.

◀ CARLIN, BOB

(born 1953, New York, NY)

Carlin is a traditional-styled BANJO player and record producer who has been active in the old-time music revival scene since the mid-seventies.

Carlin originally played bass with New York old-time string band the Delaware Watergap, and both produced and performed on the 1977 *Melodic Clawhammer Banjo* album. Inspired by John Burke, a group of banjoists had begun to play full melody lines while still using the old-time clawhammer style. (Banjoist BILL KEITH had done a similar thing fifteen years earlier in a BLUEGRASS style.) This album was quite popular among young pickers, although Carlin pretty much abandoned the note-for-note style soon after.

In 1980 he released his first solo album, in which he played in a more traditionally oriented style; his second album offered an eclectic mix of old-time banjo numbers, duets with progressive banjoist TONY TRISCHKA, and adaptations of Rolling Stones songs to an old-time style. A third album featured duets with a number of fiddlers, including James Bryant (a relaxed, old-styled bluegrass fiddler who works with NORMAN BLAKE) and Brad Leftwich. Carlin and Bruce Molsky released a cassette of old-time songs and instrumentals soon after.

As a producer, Carlin has released anthologies of old-time banjo picking as well as a tribute album to fiddler TOMMY JARRELL. He also hosted a traditional music radio program out of Philadelphia for over a decade. More recently, he has been working as an artist-in-residence in community colleges in North Carolina and Virginia while continuing to perform and produce recordings. He is currently producing an album of minstrel-era banjo music, as well as an album of fiddle and banjo duets with JOHN HARTFORD.

Select Discography
Fiddle Tunes for Clawhammer Banjo, Rounder 132. His first solo album.
Where Did You Get That Hat? Rounder 172. Includes duets with Tony Trischka.
Bangin' and Sawin', Rounder 197. Banjo and fiddle duets.

◀ CARLISLE BROTHERS, THE

(Cliff [dobro, vocals] born 1904, near Taylorsville, TN; died 1983; Bill [guitar, vocals] born 1908, Briar Ridge, KY)

Yet another one of the popular brother acts of the thirties, the Carlisles were on the more bluesy end of the spectrum, closer in sound to the DELMORE BROTHERS, for example, than the BLUE SKY BOYS. Cliff Carlisle was the more prolific of the pair and one of the first masters of the DOBRO guitar. He recorded prolifically as a soloist, as an accompanist, and in various combinations with other musicians as well as with his brother Bill.

The duo were raised in the hills of Kentucky, although the family originally hailed from Tennessee, where the elder son was born. Their father led singing schools in rural churches, teaching gospel songs in the traditional SHAPE-NOTE style, but his kids were more interested in the sounds coming over the radio from Nashville. Cliff apparently toured the South as a youngster playing on the vaudeville circuit, specializing in railroad songs and Hawaiian numbers. The novelty of playing the GUITAR with a steel bar to perform pseudo-Hawaiian songs made him an instant success. He signed with the Indiana-based Gennett label when he was twenty-six, initially recording with guitarist Wilbur Ball. Inspired by JIMMIE RODGERS, the pair specialized in blues numbers featuring closely harmonized YODELING. In fact, Carlisle sessioned on some of Rodgers's recordings, providing dobro accompaniment for the famous musician.

The brothers formed their duet in 1931, and they performed together on many recordings for various labels, as well as on radio stations out of Lexington, Kentucky, and Charlotte, North Carolina. They specialized in train songs (such as "Pan American Man" and the hobo numbers "Just a Lonely Hobo" and "Ramblin' Jack") and the blue yodeling that Cliff had originally performed with his first partner; both of these styles showed their debt to Jimmie Rodgers. They also performed comic novelty numbers, including risqué, suggestive songs such as "Tom Cat Blues," and Hawaiian instrumentals, both vestiges of Cliff's vaudeville days. (Some of Cliff's solo recordings in a more rowdy style were issued under the nom de disc of Bob Clifford.) As part of the act, Bill sometimes portrayed a barefoot country hayseed character called Hotshot Elmer. Meanwhile, Cliff continued to perform and record with other musicians, including his original partner, Wilbur Ball, as well as Fred Kirby.

Cliff retired in 1947, and Bill formed a new group called the Carlisles with his wife and children. Taking the name Jumpin' Bill Carlisle, the younger musician made his GRAND OLE OPRY debut in 1952, following his hit with the comic novelty number "Too Old to Cut the Mustard," a Bill Carlisle original. He also wrote a follow-up hit, "No Help Wanted," and the further novelties "Is That You, Myrtle?" (cowritten with the LOUVIN BROTHERS) and "Rough Stuff." Bill continued to record through the late sixties, and had one more hit with another country comedy number, "What Kinda Deal Is This," in 1966.

Select Discography
Cliff Carlisle, Vols. 1 and 2, Old Timey 103, 104. Two out-of-print LPs reissuing Cliff's solo recordings and duets with his brother and Wilber Ball.
Busy Body Boogie, Bear Family 15172. Fifties-era band recordings, mostly led by brother Bill.

◀ CARPENTER, MARY CHAPIN

(born 1958, Princeton, NJ)

Well-educated, slightly ironic, a feminist, and politically liberal, Carpenter is the last person one would expect to be successful on the country charts. The fact that she has enjoyed success shows much about how the definition of country is changing.

The daughter of a *Life* magazine executive, Carpenter was raised in suburban Princeton, New Jersey, for most of her childhood, except for two years during which the family relocated to Japan so her father could oversee the publication of the Asian edition of *Life*. Her mother had picked up the GUITAR during the FOLK REVIVAL of the early sixties and gave her instrument to Carpenter when she expressed interest in learning to play. Her family moved to Washington, D.C., in 1974, and Carpenter spent the year following her high-school graduation traveling through Europe before enrolling as an American civilization major at Brown University.

After college, she began performing in the Washington, D.C., area, playing a mix of pop and rock standards and SINGER/SONGWRITER material, as well as her own songs. She hooked up with guitarist John Jennings, and the duo produced a demo tape that they planned to sell as a cassette at their engagements. This demo led her to an audition for Columbia Records, who signed her and released her first LP in 1987.

From 1987 to 1992, Carpenter developed a cult following, although she was difficult to categorize. FM radio, which at one time had been responsive to singer/songwriters, was now oriented either toward hard rock or oldies. Country stations were not too sympathetic to her material, which tended to be soft-acoustic with an emphasis of women's themes. She did score a minor hit with 1989's "How Do," a brassy, flirtation song told from a woman's point of view, followed by "This Shirt," a song that owes as much to Joni Mitchell as it does to LORETTA LYNN.

Carpenter's breakthrough came with the hit 1992 single, "Down at the Twist and Shout," which immortalized a Washington, D.C.–area folk club where the

CAJUN band Beausoleil often performed. Its snappy Cajun rhythm, well-made performance video, and rocking arrangement sent it shooting up the country charts. She quickly followed up with her 1993 releases, "I Feel Lucky," another uptempo, sassy number, and her cover of LUCINDA WILLIAMS's "Passionate Kisses."

Still, Carpenter's albums have as much acoustic folk on them as country, and her songs often subtly skew traditional country themes. "Going Out Tonight" tells of a woman who is going out to a bar "in search of a friend"; this is almost the polar opposite of the traditional country HONKY-TONK ballad, in which the man is looking to hoist a few brews with a "honky-tonk angel." Of course, Carpenter's audience is largely made up of young, well-educated, professional people (like herself), so it is less surprising that her fans are willing to accept songs that would never have passed muster in country circles just a decade ago.

Despite her high-powered hits, Carpenter's best material remains her softer, more acoustic-oriented songs. "Come On Come On," the title track of her 1992 release, is a near-perfect ballad of lost love and longing, while "I Am a Town" is a nostalgic gem that perfectly captures the feeling of summers long ago spent in sleepy backwaters. When all the boot-scootin' dust settles, these songs will be accepted as her strongest legacy.

Select Discography

Shooting Straight in the Dark, Columbia 46077. Her third album, featuring the breakthrough hit "Down at the Twist and Shout."

Come On Come On, Columbia 48881. Fine 1992 album featuring more chartbusters.

Stones in the Road, Columbia 64327. 1994 return to her folkie, singer-songwriter roots. The hyphen is officially dropped from her name!

◀ CARSON, FIDDLIN' JOHN

(born 1868, Fannin County, GA; died 1949)

A prominent Georgia fiddler, vocalist, and minstrel-show performer, Fiddlin' John Carson single-handedly created the country music industry with his 1923 recording of "Little Old Log Cabin in the Lane" backed with "The Old Hen Cackled." This recording is generally acknowledged to be the first country music record successfully marketed to a country audience, convincing big-city recording executives that there was money to be made in recording traditional performers.

Carson was born in 1868 on a farm in Fannin County, Georgia; his first recording appeared in 1923 when he was fifty-five years old, with about forty years of semi-professional fiddling, singing, and entertaining under his belt. He was a professional entertainer, although he held odd jobs as a painter and carpenter and probably also worked as a subsistence farmer. His music was so popular that he was enlisted by several local politicians, eventually working on the campaign trail with Herbert Talmadge, who repaid the performer after his election as Georgia's governor with a job as an elevator operator in the state capital building.

Atlanta-based furniture dealer Polk Brockman is responsible for launching Carson's recording career. As the local dealer for OKeh records, in 1923 he sent a telegram to New York requesting that they record Carson, because he knew his music would sell well in Georgia. Legendary producer RALPH PEER oversaw the first session but felt the music was so bad that he had the records pressed without labels and shipped copies only to Brockman as a favor. When the records quickly sold out, Peer realized his mistake and quickly signed Carson to the label.

For his first two years of recording, Carson primarily worked as a soloist, using traditional tunings and uneven rhythms in his accompaniments to his own rough-hewn vocals. He also performed as a duo along with daughter Rosa Lee Carson (dubbed MOONSHINE KATE by executives at the OKeh label that recorded Carson), a fine singer in a deadpan country style, who also played the BANJO and GUITAR.

Because string bands were becoming increasingly popular in the mid-twenties, Carson formed his own band, the Virginia Reelers, a floating ensemble of musicians who were mostly younger and played in a more modern style than their leader. Chief among the members of this group were fiddlers Earl Johnson and "Bully" Brewer, banjoists Land Norris and Bill White, and guitarists "Peanut" Brown and Rosa Lee Carson. Many of the band's members doubled or even tripled on other instruments (Brewer played fiddle, banjo, and guitar), so that they might take a different part if one or another of the others was absent. On his band recordings, Carson continues to play using the older tunings and his own unique sense of rhythm, while the band often struggles to follow his lead. The result is a sometimes chaotic meeting of two traditions, the older unaccompanied songster matched with a jazzy, driving string-band sound.

Carson's repertoire reached back into the mid-nineteenth century and was an amalgam of traditional dance tunes, ballads and songs, and recently composed sentimental, comic, and vaudeville numbers. He performed traditional dance tunes like "Cotton-Eyed Joe," "Fire in the Mountain," "Sugar in the Gourd," "Arkansas Traveler," and the like; topical and protest songs such as "The Honest Farmer," "There's a Hard Time Coming," "The Death of Floyd Collins," "Taxes on the Farmer Feeds Them All," and "My Ford Sedan"; nineteenth-century sentimental songs and early–twentieth-century popular and novelty items like his first recording, "Little Old Log Cabin in the Lane" (although Carson transforms it into an almost ancient-sounding celebration of life in the backwoods), "The Baggage Coach Ahead," "When You and I Were Young, Maggie," "Bully of the Town," and "I'm Glad My Wife's in Europe"; and traditional songs such as "Bachelor's Hall," "900 Miles Away from Home," "Old Joe Clark," and "Goin' Where the Weather Suits My Clothes" (John's title for "Worried Man Blues").

Carson set the stage for later country stars in many crucial ways. He was a unique personality who transformed the material that he performed into his own unique sound. His sense of rhythm and tonality, influenced by his boyhood in rural Georgia and his years of professional performing in tent shows and fiddlers' contests, gives even the most recently composed of his songs a country sound. Finally, Carson's music is often both topical and humorous, commenting on the everyday experiences of his listeners. As a performer, Carson came from the people and, although he achieved great celebrity, he never took on airs or acted like a star. His popularity encouraged countless others that they, too, could become country performers.

Select Discography

The Old Hen Cackled and the Rooster's Going to Crow, Rounder 1003. Out-of-print LP reissuing Carson's recordings from the twenties and early thirties. Includes solo recordings, duets with daughter Moonshine Kate, and some of his chaotic band tracks. Sound quality is fine for these older 78s. Annotated booklet includes notes on John's life and achievement and lyrics of songs plus thorough discographical information.

◀ CARSON, MARTHA

(born Irene Amburgey, 1921, Neon, KY)

Carson was one of the great fervent gospel singers of the fifties, who also wrote many famous modern religious numbers, most notably "I'm Gonna Walk and Talk with My Lord."

Born in backwoods Kentucky, Carson got her first radio exposure when she was eighteen years old in Bluefield, West Virginia. Her father was an old-time banjoist and her mother played organ; along with their daughters Bertha and Irene, they formed a sacred quartet that sang at religious revival meetings throughout the South. In about 1938, fiddler Bertha and guitarist Irene, along with younger sister Opal, who played BANJO and MANDOLIN, formed the Amburgey Sisters and began performing on Lexington, Kentucky radio. A stint in Bluefield, West Virginia, followed and they finally joined the famous *Renfro Valley Barn Dance*, where they performed with legendary fiddler/banjoist LILLY MAE LEDFORD in a later incarnation of the Coon Creek Girls. In 1940 the Sisters went to Atlanta's WSB where their act was renamed Mattie, Marthie, and Minnie (for Opal, Irene, and Bertha, respectively); they performed such patriotic wartime ditties as "I'll Be Back in a Year, Little Darling."

In the early forties, the trio dissolved as the various sisters married and moved on to other careers. Opal wed Salty Holmes from the PRAIRIE RAMBLERS, and the two became popular on the GRAND OLE OPRY performing as Salty Holmes and Mattie O'Neill. In the fifties, she took the new name of Jean Chapel and recorded for Sun Records as a sultry ROCKABILLY artist. SAM PHILLIPS of Sun sold her contract to RCA, where she was billed "The Female Elvis Presley" and had a minor hit with "Oo-ba-la Baby" in 1956. Bertha married a defense plant worker and more or less retired, although she returned to performing with her sisters in the early fifties.

In the early forties Martha married country songster and mandolin player James Carson (Roberts), the son of old-time fiddler Doc Roberts, one of the finer old-time recording artists of the late twenties. The two became known as the Barn Dance Sweethearts when they signed up with Atlanta's WSB in the mid-forties and had hits with sentimental numbers such as their cover of the BLUE SKY BOYS' "The Sweetest Gift" as well as the gospelesque "Man of Galilee."

The Carsons split in 1951, and Martha briefly reunited with her sisters. She joined the cast of the *Grand Ole Opry* a year later, bringing her tub-thumping gospel style to the stage of Nashville's premiere radio show. Oddly enough, her fervent singing, a wedding of old-time religious sentiment, black gospel and R&B, and country styles, found a home in the rarefied supper clubs of northeastern cities in the mid-fifties, so much so that she became equally in demand for her appearances at toney venues like New York's Waldorf-Astoria. Her solo recordings increasingly took on fifties pop stylings, in which wall-to-wall orchestrations accompanied Martha's big voice. She even took a stab at rock and roll, covering numbers like Otis Blackwell's "Just Whistle and Call" and "Music Drives Me Crazy (Especially Rock 'n' Roll)," although she sounds less comfortable outside of the country milieu. Carson wrote over a hundred songs, all in a religious vein, including "Let's Talk About that Old Time Religion" and "Satisfied."

Although she continued to perform in the sixties, seventies, and even eighties, Carson's most successful days were in the fifties.

◀ CARTER, CARLENE

(born Rebecca Carlene Smith, 1955, Nashville, TN)

Heir to the famous CARTER FAMILY dynasty, the daughter of June Carter and CARL SMITH, Carlene has been somewhat of an iconoclast in country circles, recording in England in the late seventies and early eighties in a punk-country style, creating a music that she says was "too rock for country [radio] and too country for rock." An energetic singer, Carter is most at home with up-tempo material that has a rock edge to it.

Her mother and father split when Carlene was just two, but from an early age she was immersed in music thanks to tours with the entire Carter clan led by her grandmother, Mother Maybelle Carter. When Carlene was twelve, her mother married JOHNNY CASH, and Carlene joined the Cash/Carter road show, working as a backup singer along with her stepsister ROSANNE CASH. Two ill-fated marriages, at ages fifteen and nineteen, produced two children before she returned to the road show. Carlene headed to LA when she was twenty-two, where she landed a recording contract as a rock singer. The resulting self-named debut album was recorded in London with backup by the punk band the Rumour, and her follow-up improbably featured members of the Doobie Brothers. In 1979 she married Nick Lowe, a British punk-country SINGER/SONGWRITER, whose musical eclecticism contributed to her unusual style.

The early eighties brought her innovative LP, *Musical Shapes*, which featured many of her original compositions. The album wed country influences with a hard-rocking sound, anticipating the NEW-COUNTRY boom of the late eighties, but was a commercial failure on both country and pop charts. By the mid-eighties, her career and third marriage were on the skids, and Carlene was increasingly dependent on cocaine and alcohol, addictions she overcame by decade's end. Her mother and aunts came to England at about this time to tour, and Carlene rejoined them to form a quartet, returning to the country-music fold.

Carter returned to Nashville in the late eighties and recorded her comeback LP, *I Fell in Love*, which was released in 1990. The title track was a minor country hit, and the album combined traditional country songs with Carlene's own brand of confessional songs with an ironic twist. Her follow-up, *Little Love Letters*, featured the clever ROCKABILLY-sounding "Every Little Thing," a perfect example of Carter's ability to honor country traditions while also skewing them slightly.

Select Discography
I Fell in Love, Reprise 26139.
Little Love Letters, Giant 24499.

◄ CARTER, WILF

(born 1904, Guysboro, Nova Scotia)

Better known in this country as Montana Slim, Carter was one of the pioneering YODELING cowboys, Canada's answer to the Western craze.

Carter was one of the few cowboy-styled performers who was not directly influenced by JIMMIE RODGERS, although he was certainly aware of Rodgers's incredibly successful recordings. He took up yodeling after hearing a Swiss yodeler who was performing on the Canadian vaudeville circuit. He was a real cowboy, too, actually having worked as a trail rider in the Canadian Rockies and performing at local rodeos.

Carter's big break came on Calgary radio in the mid-thirties, leading to a contract with Canadian RCA. He began performing in New York later in the decade, taking the stage name of Montana Slim. Although he recorded over five hundred numbers for RCA and its budget Camden label, as well as for countless smaller labels, Carter's skills as a performer were about as slim as his stage name. He makes another slim performer, SLIM WHITMAN, sound positively plump! He's best known for his 1949 recording of "There's a Bluebird on Your Windowsill," the kind of cowboy pop that is treasured as a kitsch classic.

Select Discography
Montana Slim, Hollywood 265. Cassette-only reissue of sixties-era Starday recordings.

◄ CARTER FAMILY, THE "ORIGINAL"

(Alvin Pleasant [vocals] born 1891, Maces Spring, VA; died 1960; Sara Dougherty Carter [autoharp, vocals] born 1898, Flat Woods, VA; died 1970; Maybelle Addington Carter [guitar, vocals] born 1909, Nickelsville, VA; died 1978)

The Carter Family were one of the first and most popular country vocal groups. Their unornamented, nasal harmonies, born and bred in rural church music, are probably the closest we can come to a pure, white Appalachian sound. The group coalesced around Alvin Pleasant (known as A.P.) Carter; his wife, Sara; and his sister-in-law Maybelle. Sara usually sang lead and played the autoharp, with Alvin on bass vocals and Maybelle on tenor and GUITAR. A.P. was a master collector of traditional songs and reworked them into pleasant and memorable melodies that became among the first country music hits, including "Keep on the Sunny Side," "The Storms Are on the Ocean," "Wildwood Flower," "Bury Me Beneath the Willow,'' and their best-known song, ''Will the Circle Be Unbroken,'' an adaptation of a SHAPE-NOTE hymn.

Their first and greatest success came recording under the supervision of RALPH PEER for RCA Victor from 1927 to 1933. Exact contemporaries of JIMMIE RODGERS, with whom they made a few comedy sketch records, the Carters were almost straight-laced in their approach to their music. Unlike Rodgers, who showed strong influences of jazz and blues, the Carters sang as if no African-Americans ever lived in the South. For some, this makes their music excruciatingly bland; for others, beauty lies in the simplicity of their four-square harmonies.

The group continued to record through the later thirties and early forties, even though A.P. and Sara's marriage dissolved in 1932. They gained great exposure in the late thirties while working on XERA, the famous ''border'' radio station that, because it broadcast out of Mexico, was unregulated in the United States and thus had a much more powerful and far-reaching signal than U.S. commercial stations. Various Carter daughters were also getting into the act. The last ''original'' Carter Family performance came in 1943.

In the late forties, Maybelle performed with her daughters (Anita, June, and Helen) as the Carter Family; the girls also performed as a more modern-sounding country act, the Carter Sisters. Mother and daughters became members of the GRAND OLE OPRY in 1950. Meanwhile, A.P. recorded in the early fifties with his two children, Janette and Joe. Maybelle was rediscovered during the sixties FOLK RE- VIVAL and became a popular performer on the autoharp, picking melodies on it rather than just strumming chords. She was also prominently featured on the NITTY GRITTY DIRT BAND's homage to country music, *Will the Circle Be Unbroken?*, in 1971. Although she performed with Maybelle at the 1967 Newport Folk Festival, Sara was mostly inactive after A. P.'s death in 1960. Janette Carter continues to run the Carter Family Homestead in Virginia, which includes a museum with memorabilia of the family's music career plus a dance/concert hall that features BLUEGRASS and country acts. She recorded a duet album with her brother Joe in the seventies.

The Carters were influential for introducing a wide number of folk standards into the country repertoire and for popularizing a smooth, tight harmony style. They were not virtuoso musicians or vocalists; indeed, they sounded much like the folks next door, undoubtedly a large part of their appeal. But their down-home harmonies and simple accompaniments made them models for hundreds of other family bands and helped change the shape of country music from a rural enter- tainment to a popular, mainstream one.

Select Discography

Complete Recordings, Rounder 1064–1072. Following their similar series devoted to Jimmie Rodgers, Rounder is reissuing all of the Carter Family's original Victor recordings in chronological order.

On Border Radio, JEMF 101. Later recordings from their days working out of Mexico.

Country Music Hall of Fame, MCA 10088. Decca-label recordings from 1936 and 1937.

Clinch Mountain Treasures, County 112. Early-forties recordings of the original Carters.

◀ CARVER, JOHNNY

(born 1940, Jackson, MS)

Carver was a mid-seventies country star best known for covering ersatz pop hits of the era (such as "Tie a Yellow Ribbon") and making them palatable for country radio.

Born and raised in Jackson, he began performing as a child in his family's gospel group along with his aunts and uncles. His high-school years found him performing in more of a pop mold, and he took up the life of a touring musician after graduation, eventually settling in Milwaukee. In 1965 he left for California, where he became the lead singer for the house band at the Palomino Club, famed country night spot. Talent scouts from the local Imperial label caught his show and signed him up, leading to his first late-sixties hits, "Your Lily White Hands" (1967) and "Hold Me Tight" (1968).

Carver moved to Imperial's parent label, United Artists, and then to Epic, but he could not equal his first success until 1973, when he signed with ABC's Dot division. There, he recorded a series of countrified covers of middle-of-the-road hits; his slight twang made the songs more accessible for country radio, although his arrangements were hardly breakthroughs, following fairly closely their pop models. After a spate of these cloned hits culminating in 1977's "Livin' Next Door to Alice," Carver moved on to smaller labels, without much success, through the early eighties.

◀ CASH, JOHNNY

(born 1932, Kingsland, AK)

Johnny Cash is one of the most distinctive performers in country music. Drawing on his poor, rural background, Cash created a country-folk music in the early sixties that commented on the plight of the working poor. His uniquely deep voice, with its slight flutter and twang, and the sparse backup of the Tennessee Three, with their primal, oom-chiga beat, sets Cash's work apart from all other country performers. Cash at his best had the unique capability of writing songs that, while stark and simple, sound like they've been around for hundreds of years. In his performances, he combined the primal energy of WOODY GUTHRIE with a more menacing undertone.

Cash's family were poor cotton farmers who were wiped out in the Depression and relocated to a federal resettlement colony in rural Tennessee. He joined the air force in the early fifties and took up the GUITAR while stationed in Germany. On his return home, he borrowed two pickers from his older brother's band, the Delta Rhythm Ramblers, to form the original Tennessee Two (Cash played guitar, backed by a second guitarist and bass; later a drummer was added to make the group the Tennessee Three). Signed to SAM PHILLIPS's legendary ROCKABILLY label,

Sun Records, Cash scored with his country classic, "I Walk the Line" (1956), as well as with some forgettable more rock-oriented sides.

Disappointed with Phillips's commercial orientation, Cash signed to Columbia Records in 1959, where he worked with producer Don Law. Law was sympathetic to Cash's folk leanings and remolded the star to appeal to the nascent FOLK REVIVAL. He emphasized Cash's folk background by having him record topical songs about America's working class, American Indians, legendary figures (such as John Henry), and outlaws. He recorded Cash with the simple backup of his own band rather than adding the strings and choruses typically heard on country recordings of that era.

Cash's big break came with his legendary live concert at California's Folsom Prison (held in 1968), in which he played the classic bad-man song "Folsom Prison Blues," the sympathetic but ultimately tragic portrayal of a condemned murderer. In 1969 BOB DYLAN enlisted Cash's aid for his country LP, *Nashville Skyline*, exposing Cash to a younger, rock and folk-pop audience. In the same year, Cash had his first solid hit with the unlikely tune "A Boy Named Sue," a comic song written by Shel Silverstein.

Throughout the seventies, Cash recorded more mainstream pop-country material while also developing an acting career. Following his Folsom Prison performance and his mid-sixties battle with drug addiction, Cash exploited his image as the Man in Black, emphasizing his years of "hard traveling." He often performed with a large revue, including his wife, June Carter Cash, and members of the CARTER FAMILY, as well as old friends like CARL PERKINS.

In the eighties, Cash had a varied career. He recorded a successful series of LPs with country "outlaws" WILLIE NELSON, KRIS KRISTOFFERSON, and WAYLON JENNINGS. His own LPs have continued in a pop-country vein. Cash signed with producer Rick Rubin's Def-America label (better known for promoting rap and progressive rock groups) in 1994, producing an album featuring traditional folk songs performed with his simple guitar accompaniment. While it was a big improvement over his previous, recent recordings in terms of quality, it failed to find an audience among either rock fans or on country radio.

Johnny's younger brother Tommy (born 1940) initially worked as a deejay and then for his brother's music-publishing company before pursuing a solo career in the mid-sixties; he had his greatest success in the late sixties, leading his band, the Tomcats, with whom he scored a couple of hits, including a remake of the traditional country-blues song "Six White Horses" in 1970. He recorded sporadically during the seventies with moderate success.

Daughter ROSANNE CASH has been one of the most innovative and unusual country singer/songwriters of the last decade. Stepdaughter CARLENE CARTER combines rockabilly and seventies rock styles with a country sound.

Select Discography

Columbia Recordings 1958–1986, Columbia 40637. Anthology of Cash's biggest hits recorded during his most popular period as a performer.

Johnny Cash at Folsom Prison and San Quentin, Columbia 33639. Landmark live recordings made in the late sixties that helped give Johnny his tough-guy image.

The Sun Years, Rhino 70950. Reissue of classic fifties Sun sessions; a good introduction to his pre-Columbia sound.

Come Along and Ride This Train, Bear Family 15563. Fans of Johnny's saga songs will love this set of eighty-seven pseudofolk numbers cut between 1960 and 1977.

The Man in Black, 1954–1958, Bear Family 15517. Takes Johnny through all of his Sun label recordings to his first Columbia sessions; four CDs with notes by Colin Escott.

American Recordings, Def-America 45520. Cash performing traditional songs accompanied by his own guitar in his characteristic rough-hewn style.

◀ CASH, ROSANNE

(born 1955, Memphis, TN)

Daughter of JOHNNY CASH, Rosanne is one of modern country's best singer/songwriters, whose sophisticated take on country music has made her a true innovator, although not a chart-busting hit maker.

Rosanne was raised by her mother in Southern California and did not come directly in contact with her father's music until after high-school graduation, when she joined his road show, initially working in the laundry. She says that her dad gave her a list of "100 essential country songs" and advised her, "You have to know them if you want to be my daughter." She was undecided whether music would be her career and spent some time studying acting in Nashville and New York. She also worked as a secretary in CBS's London office in the mid-seventies.

In the late seventies, Cash began performing with Texas SINGER/SONGWRITER/bandleader RODNEY CROWELL, and the two were wed in the early eighties. Crowell served as her producer, recording her debut LP, *Right or Wrong*, with his primal ROCKABILLY band, the Cherry Bombs, as accompanists. This was followed by *Seven Year Ache*, which netted her two number-one country singles and established her as a sophisticated singer/songwriter. Cash has gone on to produce song cycles reflecting her own dialogue with country-music traditions (*King's Record Shop*), and her 1993 album, *The Wheel*, which documents the breakup of her marriage, raises questions about the romantic myths promoted by popular and country music.

Cash is a thoughtful songwriter who approaches country themes from a new perspective. "Most country songs go something like, 'Oh honey you left me and now I'm sad.' but I'm more interested in the hidden agenda, 'Oh honey you left me and why did I want you to do that?' " Cash has tackled difficult issues with songs like "Rosie Strike Back," which encourages women to stand up to abusive spouses.

Like many other NEW-COUNTRY performers, Cash feels free to move between styles, from driving rockabilly and HONKY-TONK to intense ballads. She shares with her father an ability to express deep feelings through her vocals, and also an honesty and directness that gives their work a slightly disturbing edge. Perhaps it is for this reason that mainstream fame eludes her while her work is met with critical acclaim.

Select Discography
Hits 1979–1989, Columbia 45054. All the chart-toppers.
King's Record Shop, Columbia 40777.
Interiors, Columbia 46079. Introspective, singer/songwriter material dominates this collection.
The Wheel, Columbia 52729.

◀ CHARLES, RAY

(born Ray Charles Robinson, 1930, Albany, GA)

Although he's best known to the general listening public as a soul singer, Charles has recorded country music for over a quarter-century, and was one of the first black artists to cross over into the country market. Of course, like many great artists, Charles's music tends to transcend easy categorization, but his deep love for country music shines through all of his best recordings.

It is not surprising that there should be a natural affinity between R&B and C&W artists (besides the fact that both genres are represented by two initials!). In the rural South, black and white musicians have always mixed rather freely, despite segregation, and country music's greatest stars have all been influenced in one way or another by traditional blues, jazz, and R&B. After Charles's trailblazing success in the country arena, many R&B stars of the fifties turned to the country market as a natural extension of their audience in the sixties and seventies. And both R&B and C&W are definitely soulful musical styles, in that both value deeply felt emotions expressed through lyrics that deal with the real-life issues faced by the singer and his or her audience.

Charles has always been an eclectic musician. Beginning in a Nat King Cole–styled trio, performing as R. C. Robinson, he had his first success in the mid-fifties recording what would be called "modern soul" music for Atlantic. In 1959 he scored a minor hit with HANK SNOW's "I'm Movin' On," revealing for the first time his unique take on country sounds. Joining ABC in the same year, Charles took control of his recordings, choosing his own material and arrangements, and issued a series of LPs in pop-soul, jazz, and country styles, beginning in 1963 with the hugely successful *Modern Sounds in Country and Western Music*.

Charles's country hits include "I Can't Stop Lovin' You," a cover of the DON GIBSON classic from the *Modern Sounds* album, "Hit the Road Jack," "Busted," and HANK WILLIAMS's "Your Cheatin' Heart." Charles transformed the pop classic "Georgia on My Mind" into a slow country blues; his performance was so brilliant that he was invited to sing it for the Georgia legislature when it was made the official state song. Through the seventies, Charles recorded in a variety of styles but pretty much settled on country for most of the eighties and early nineties.

If you haven't heard Ray Charles sing, you've probably been locked in a Skinner box for the last forty years; suffice it to say, his blues-inflected, gritty vocals have influenced scores of country singers, both black and white. And although CHARLEY PRIDE is more frequently called the pioneering mainstream black country artist of the sixties, it can be argued that it was Charles who really broke the racial and musical barriers between two of America's greatest musical traditions.

Select Discography

Greatest Country & Western Hits, DCC 040. Ray's great sixties-era recordings for ABC, which launched his country career.

Friendship, Columbia 39415. Duets with country heavy hitters like GEORGE JONES, HANK WILLIAMS, JR., RICKY SKAGGS, MERLE HAGGARD, JOHNNY CASH, and many others. Typical eighties-era sound and production.

◀ CHESNUTT, MARK

(born 1963, Beaumont, TX)

Deep-voiced, broad-chested Chesnutt is another in a long line of hunks of the month who tip their ten-gallon hats toward GEORGE JONES.

Raised in Beaumont, Texas, Chesnutt came from a musical home; his dad had been a local country crooner before giving up his dreams of making it big to open up a used-car lot. At age sixteen, Chesnutt began performing locally, filling in with day jobs as necessary but mostly pursuing a performing career. He worked locally for twelve years, releasing his first single on a small Houston label; the song was "Too Cold at Home," written by country song-slinger Bobby Harden. After his record was released, he managed to get it to GEORGE STRAIT, whose drummer had previously played in Chesnutt's band. Strait passed it along to producer Tony Brown at MCA Records. Brown liked what he heard and signed Chesnutt, re-recording the song and releasing it in summer 1990 as the title song of Chesnutt's debut album. Buoyed by Chesnutt's pleasant voice and he-man looks, the song hit big, and soon Chesnutt was being compared to GARTH BROOKS as the "next big thing."

Actually, his second album was far superior, with Chesnutt revealing more of an individual personality on such Texas-styled, light-hearted numbers as "Bubba Shot the Jukebox" and traditional WEEPERS like "I'll Think of Something." He followed with another collection of honkers and weepers, including the 1993 hit "Almost Goodbye," which literally drips sentimental goo. Chesnutt has become the most prominent of the NEW-COUNTRY performers whose popularity is largely based on their looks rather than the music that they produce.

Select Discography

Too Cold at Home, MCA 10032.

Longnecks & Short Stories, MCA 10530.

◀ CHILDRE, LEW

(born 1901, Opp, AL)

Childre was a popular country comedian and Hawaiian-styled guitarist who performed on the GRAND OLE OPRY for sixteen years.

Originally performing on the backwoods tent-show and vaudeville circuit of the South, Childre developed the rural bumpkin physician character of Doctor Lew, who gave colorful, if slightly outrageous, medical advice to his many "clients." He played GUITAR with a steel bar, emulating the popular Hawaiian styles of the twenties, including in his repertoire such hoary old chestnuts as "I'm Looking Over a Four Leaf Clover," displaying just enough string wizardry to wow his audiences. He joined the Opry in 1945, originally performing with comedian banjoist STRING-BEAN before embarking on a solo career in 1948. He remained with the Opry until 1961. Although a popular stage performer, he rarely recorded.

Select Discography

On the Air, Old Homestead 132. Out-of-print LP reissuing radio transcripts from 1946.

◀ CHUCK WAGON GANG

(1935–ongoing; original members: D.P. ["Dad"], Carrie, Rose, Anna, and Jim Carter)

The Chuck Wagon Gang are one of the most enduring and popular country-gospel harmonizing groups, originally a small-town family group that has blossomed into a big country business.

The Carters were sharecroppers in West Texas and also highly religious; D.P. met his future wife, Carrie, at a singing school sponsored by the local Baptist church. They raised nine children, including two particularly talented daughters, Rose and Anna, who became the center of the family's informal singing group. Along with brother Jim, the group appeared on radio out of Lubbock in 1935 and a year later won the sponsorship of Fort Worth's Bewley Mills, who named the group the Chuck Wagon Gang; at the same time, the group was signed to Columbia.

Although they always featured at least one gospel number in their radio act and in personal appearances, the group started out performing a mix of folk songs, pop, and sentimental numbers, led by the sweet harmonies of the two young daughters. However, listener response was so overwhelmingly strong for their gospel numbers that by 1938 they switched to an all-gospel format. From the traditional backwoods church, they took the call-and-response pattern that was typically used by preacher and chorus; but from pop music they borrowed sweet harmonies and slick instrumentation to achieve a more modern sound. They recorded many gospel standards, including "I'll Fly Away" and "We Are Climbing Jacob's Ladder," and published countless songbooks. A young songster named HANK WILLIAMS borrowed the melody of their 1941 recording of "He Set Me Free" for his own classic gospel song, "I Saw the Light."

In the wake of World War II, country gospel gained new popularity, thanks in part to groups like the Chuck Wagon Gang and in part to a return to traditional values that swept the country. The Gang toured extensively, with some personnel changes over the years. The biggest blow to the group came with the retirement of the two lead singers in swift succession in 1965 and 1967 (Rose retired first, and then Anna wed songster/politician JIMMIE DAVIS, leading to her more-or-less complete withdrawal from the family act). Although family members continue to work in the band to today, it has become more of a business than a family group, with new members brought in to carry forward the Chuck Wagon sound; since 1989, the two lead singers have been professionals recruited specifically to fit the bill.

The Chuck Wagon Gang are an important link connecting the informal past of rural church singing with the modern, glitzy, country-gospel industry. They bridge traditional, unornamented harmony singing with more modern approaches borrowed from pop music in both harmonies and instrumentation. Their many tours, recordings, and publications have kept gospel music alive for a new audience in the postwar world.

Select Discography
Columbia Historic Edition, Columbia 40152. Reissues of their finest recordings from 1936 to 1975.

◀ CLARK, GENE

(born Harold Eugene Clark, 1941, Tipton, MO; died 1991)

Clark was a country-flavored SINGER/SONGWRITER, one of the founding members of the BYRDS, who went on to perform with the Gosdin Brothers, Doug Dillard (in the early COUNTRY-ROCK band Dillard and Clark), and vocalist Carla Olson.

Clark began his career in the Los Angeles–based folk-rock band, the Byrds, contributing some of their better original numbers, including "It Won't Be Wrong," "Set You Free This Time," and "Feel a Whole Lot Better," along with his emotional lead vocals. He quit the band in 1966 due to his fear of flying and recorded an excellent album of original compositions with the traditional-sounding Gosdin Brothers, featuring superguitarists CLARENCE WHITE and GLEN CAMPBELL, arranger/pianist Leon Russell, and the Byrds's rhythm section; however, the album failed on the charts. With Doug Dillard and Bernie Leadon (who would later join the FLYING BURRITO BROTHERS and then the EAGLES), he formed Dillard and Clark, a folk-rock outfit that featured country instrumentation (Dillard's BANJO, BYRON BERLINE's fiddle, plus DOBRO and MANDOLIN) as well as some classic psychedelic sixties touches like electric harpsichord.

In the early seventies, Clark made a number of abortive attempts at solo albums backed by various members of the Byrds, Burrito Brothers, and other West Coast country-rock regulars. He had a genuine knack for the contemporary country song but was recording about a decade too soon to gain much popular success, and most of these recordings went unreleased at the time.

Early in the eighties, Clark rejoined with ex-Byrdsmen Roger McGuinn and Chris Hillman performing as a trio for two critically acclaimed albums, but again his fear of flying limited the success of the trio. In the late eighties, Clark and former Textones vocalist Carla Olson formed an acoustic duo. Always troubled personally and prone to periods of depression, he took his own life in 1991.

Select Discography
Gene Clark with the Gosdin Brothers, Sony Music Special Products 2618. Wonderful 1966 recordings featuring BLUEGRASS backup by the Gosdins, Clarence White, then-

session picker Glen Campbell, and even pianist Leon Russell. This was the first album Clark recorded after leaving the Byrds.

The Fantastic Expedition of Dillard and Clark/Through The Morning, Through the Night, Mobile Fidelity 00791. CD reissuing the two LPs made by Dillard and Clark in the late sixties.

Echoes, Columbia/Legacy 48253. Seventies-era recordings, many unissued at the time.

So Rebellious a Lover, Razor and Tie 1992. Clark's last recordings, made in duet with Carla Olson.

◀ CLARK, GUY

(born 1941, Monihans, TX)

Guy Clark is a Texas SINGER/SONGWRITER who, along with comrades JERRY JEFF WALKER and TOWNES VAN ZANDT, wed HONKY-TONK sounds to contemporary lyrics. His songs have been widely covered by eighties NEW-COUNTRY stars.

Raised by his grandmother (who ran a run-down hotel), Clark learned to play guitar as a youngster, playing primarily Mexican folk songs that he heard in his small Texas hometown. In the sixties he moved to Houston, and he immediately began performing in the vibrant club scene there as well as in Austin and Dallas. Clark moved briefly to Los Angeles in the late sixties (inspiring his song "L.A. Freeway," which later was a hit for Jerry Jeff Walker) and then settled in 1971 in Nashville, where he recorded for RCA in the mid-seventies and Warners later in the decade. His first album, *Old No. 1*, was critically acclaimed, although it did little on the charts. It featured many of his now-classic songs, including "Rita Ballou," "That Old Time Feeling," and "Desperados Waiting for a Train." Clark became a patron saint of the new Nashville crowd, recording with and supplying songs for EMMYLOU HARRIS, RICKY SKAGGS, RODNEY CROWELL, WAYLON JENNINGS, and ROSANNE CASH, among others. In the mid-eighties, he recorded an acoustic-tinged comeback album for the country-BLUEGRASS label, Sugar Hill.

Besides being one of the most prolific and talented of the new Texas songwriters, Clark helped expand the themes of the traditional honky-tonk song beyond boozin', partyin', and cheatin' to more contemporary and literary themes. Many of his songs recount stories from his youth; "Desperados Waiting for a Train" is based on the reminiscences of an elderly oil-well worker who worked at his grandmother's hotel as a handyman. Some are nostalgic, like "Texas-1947" which was a minor hit for JOHNNY CASH in 1975. Many of his songs self-consciously refer to and comment on earlier country roots, as in "The Last Gun Fighter Ballad."

Select Discography

Old No. 1, Sugar Hill 1030. Reissue of Clark's first album from 1975, originally issued by RCA. It features most of his famous songs, including "L.A. Freeway," "Rita Ballou," and "Desperados Waitin' for a Train."

Texas Cooking, Sugar Hill 1031. His second album, originally issued in 1976 by RCA, features many name country stars sitting in, including Emmylou Harris, Rodney Crowell, and Waylon Jennings.

Old Friends, Sugar Hill 1025. 1989 "comeback" album features a star-studded cast, including Rosanne Cash, STEVE WARINER, VINCE GILL, and many of the folks who appeared on *Texas Cooking*.

Boats to Build, Asylum 61442. 1992 major-label recording with lots of new Nashville folks helping out.

◀ CLARK, ROY

(born 1933, Meaherrin, VA)

If ever a musician defined "pickin' and grinnin'," it is the affable Roy Clark, a talented string-bender and star of the oft-maligned country-corn television show HEE HAW. Despite his considerable skills as a guitarist and BANJO player, Clark does not have a definitive style of his own, perhaps because he spent his formative years as a session player.

Clark's father was a rural tobacco farmer who moved his family to urban Washington, D.C., when his son was just eleven. An important center of country-music making, Washington turned out to be the ideal place for the young musician to be raised; he was soon performing locally and won the prestigious Country Music Banjo Championship at age sixteen. Clark spent most of the fifties as a backup musician, first working with JIMMY DEAN and eventually hooking up with singer WANDA JACKSON, for whom he played guitar and wrote arrangements.

Beginning in the late fifties, Clark recorded as a solo artist for a variety of small labels, but success eluded him until he signed to Capitol in 1963. His first hit came the same year with the classic NASHVILLE SOUND instrumental "Tips of My Fingers," featuring the tinkling piano of FLOYD CRAMER, a girly chorus, and acres of strings. Clark was hired to host the short-lived *Swinging Country* TV show, which led to his successful audition for *Hee Haw*. Exposure on this show led to other charting songs, including 1969's schmaltzy "Yesterday When I Was Young" and the clever novelty number "Thank God and Greyhound (You're Gone)." He continued to score hits through the mid-seventies.

A pleasant singer, an affable showman, and a picker who can wow his audiences with his fleet-fingered solos, Clark is a natural for the Las Vegas/dinner club circuit where he has performed for most of the last three decades. He has become a popular attraction in Branson, Missouri, country music's new performance capital, where he has his own theater.

Select Discography

The Best of Roy Clark, Curb 77395. Capitol recordings from the sixties.

◀ CLEMENT, "COWBOY" JACK

(born 1931, Memphis, TN)

Best known for his production work with SAM PHILLIPS at Memphis's legendary Sun Studios, Clement has worked as a country producer, songwriter, and sometime performer.

Clement is a talented musician who can play in a number of styles, from big-band jazz to BLUEGRASS, and who has also had an interest in the more technical aspects of music. He took up music while stationed in Washington, D.C., while in the Marine Corps, performing locally with another country legend in the making, ROY CLARK. He worked briefly in the early fifties with Buzz Busby as a duo called Buzz and Jack, the Bayou Boys, then played Hawaiian-style music in the Washington, D.C., area, and finally returned to Memphis to pursue an English degree at the local university.

Clement hooked up with legendary studio owner Phillips in the late fifties and worked for him as a producer, engineer, and session player until he was fired in 1959. He was Sun's house arranger, working with the other musicians to perfect accompaniments for many classic recordings. He recorded a few singles under his own name, which flopped, and also wrote a couple of hits for Sun artists, including the country WEEPER "Guess Things Happen That Way" and the rocking "Ballad of a Teenage Queen," recorded by JOHNNY CASH. Sun historians Colin Escott and Martin Hawkins call the ballad "arguably the worst song Cash cut at Sun . . . a teen-oriented story song with an ending so sugary it could put a diabetic into a coma."

After leaving Sun, Clement briefly ran his own label, Summer, and then relocated to Nashville, where he was hired as an assistant to CHET ATKINS at RCA. He spent a few years running a studio and label in Beaumont, Texas, before returning in 1965 to Nashville, where he opened a successful music-publishing business and recording studio. He discovered some of the top Nashville stars of the era, including CHARLIE PRIDE and DON WILLIAMS. In the early seventies, he co-owned a record label, JMI, which lasted until about 1974. Later in the decade, he was a successful producer working with country outlaws Johnny Cash and WAYLON JENNINGS and also made a solo album for Elektra records.

◀ CLEMENTS, VASSAR

(born 1928, Kinard, SC)

Clements is a BLUEGRASS fiddler of the fifties and sixties who gained fame as a jazz-influenced soloist in the seventies.

Clements worked through the fifties and sixties with a number of traditional bluegrass bands, including BILL MONROE's and JIM AND JESSE's groups; accompanied country star FARON YOUNG; and also worked for a while in the late sixties with the bluegrass-rock amalgam, the Earl Scruggs Review. His career was given a big boost by BANJO-playing songwriter JOHN HARTFORD, who hired him to tour and record with him in the early seventies; he appeared on Hartford's seminal *Aero-Plain* album. Clements took the jazz and swing elements that were always present in bluegrass fiddling and brought them to the forefront.

In the mid-seventies he made an album (*Hillbilly Jazz*) with steel guitarist Doug Jerrigan and hot-picker David Bromberg for Flying Fish records; this helped revive the WESTERN SWING style while establishing Clements as a solo artist. He made a number of albums through the seventies and eighties in a variety of styles, including bluegrass, jazz, swing, blues, and even COUNTRY-ROCK. He also continued to work as a session musician for a variety of artists.

Clements's fiddling has a slightly nasal sound to it, almost a country twang, reflecting his bluegrass roots. Despite attempts to become the Jean-Luc Ponty of crossover country fiddling, Clements is at his best performing in the traditional bluegrass style.

Select Discography
Hillbilly Jazz, Flying Fish 101.
Grass Roots, Rounder 287. 1991 bluegrass session.

◀ CLEMENTS, ZEKE

(born 1911, near Empire, AL)

Zeke Clements was a cowboy-style star who had a long career, appearing on all three major country-music radio programs. He also supplied the voice for Bashful, the YODELING dwarf, in Disney's *Snow White and the Seven Dwarfs*.

Zeke's career began at age seventeen when he was signed to Chicago's *National Barn Dance*, as a part of Otto Gray's Oklahoma Cowboys touring show. Five years later, he joined the Bronco Busters, the first cowboy-oriented vocal group on WSM's GRAND OLE OPRY program. From about 1933 to 1939, the band was led by the husky-voiced TEXAS RUBY, one of the great yodeling cowgirl singers of the era; she often performed harmony yodeling with Zeke. In the mid-thirties, he made his home on the West Coast, doing radio work, appearing in B-grade Westerns, and recording voiceovers that included his famous role in *Snow White*.

In 1939 Clements rejoined the Opry, becoming a major star in the forties thanks to his wholesome cowboy image and hit songs, including the self-penned "Blue Mexico Skies," "There's Poison in Your Heart," and the all-time country classic, "Smoke on the Water," which he co-wrote and recorded in 1945; it was the number-one country recording of the year and has since become a standard at Western square dances.

In the late forties, Clements moved to the *Louisiana Hayride* radio show for a brief period and then worked a number of smaller Southern radio stations before retiring to focus on his business interests in Nashville at the end of the fifties.

◀ CLIFTON, BILL

(born William Marburg, 1931, Riverdale, MD)

Clifton was one of the first BLUEGRASS revivalists and was instrumental in promoting the music of the CARTER FAMILY and introducing bluegrass styles to urban folk audiences in the United States, Europe, and even Asia.

Clifton's interest in folk music bloomed as a student at the University of Virginia, where he began performing with another folk revivalist, guitarist Paul Clayton. After graduation, the two formed a bluegrass band in 1954, perhaps the first urban group to pick up the bluegrass style. They recorded for Nashville's Starday label and often included songs from the Carter Family repertoire, which Clifton had enjoyed as a youngster; he began playing the autoharp in the style that the Carters made famous, reintroducing this instrument to folk revivalists like MIKE SEEGER, who adopted it himself. He also published a songbook including many gospel and old-time songs that had originally been recorded in the twenties, thirties, and forties, introducing them to a new, musically literate audience.

In 1961 Clifton organized the first bluegrass festival for an urban audience, held outside of Washington, D.C. Two years later, at the height of the FOLK REVIVAL, he left the country to settle in England. Besides performing there and throughout Europe in the then largely unknown bluegrass style, he brought over key U.S. performers, including the NEW LOST CITY RAMBLERS and bluegrass bands led by BILL MONROE and the STANLEY BROTHERS. In 1967 Clifton took his act to the Philippines when he joined the Peace Corps, and performed throughout the Pacific Rim through the mid-seventies, turning up in such far-flung places as New Zealand.

Clifton returned to Britain in the late seventies and toured Europe and the U.S. with bluegrass veterans Red Rector and Don Stover as the First Generation Band in 1978. He continues to record, often in Germany, and to perform, although his style remains frozen in the late-fifties style of the early folk revival.

Select Discography
The Early Years, 1957–58, Rounder 1021. Mercury label recordings with fine backup by Washington, D.C.–area musicians.

◀ CLINE, PATSY

(born Virginia Patterson Hensley, 1932, Winchester, VA; died 1963)
Cline is one of country's best-known vocalists, still celebrated more than thirty years after her death. She was among the first country stars to make the crossover into mainstream pop, and if she had lived she would undoubtedly have become a middle-of-the-road chanteuse. Whether this would have been a step forward or backward for country music depends very much on your attitude toward the increasing commercialization of Nashville's musical product in the sixties.

Growing up in Winchester, Virginia, Cline won an amateur talent contest as a tap dancer at the ripe old age of four; she began singing soon after. Trained on the piano, she performed in the local church choir as well as in school plays. She won an audition with Wally Fowler of the GRAND OLE OPRY when she was sixteen, and so impressed him that he invited her to Nashville; however, she was unable to obtain a recording contract and eventually returned to her hometown. She performed throughout her high-school years, eventually signing with the local Four Star label in 1956. Her fifties recordings were unexceptional, although she did score one hit in 1957 with "Walkin' After Midnight" after performing it on the *Arthur Godfrey Talent Scouts* television program, which led to a contract with Decca Records.

Cline worked with producer OWEN BRADLEY from 1957 to 1960, originally in a fairly standard country mold, gaining moderate success on the country charts. It wasn't until 1961's "Crazy" (written by WILLIE NELSON), followed by "I Fall to Pieces" (cowritten by HARLAN HOWARD and HANK COCHRAN) that her characteristic sad-and-lonesome vocal sound fell into place. A brief two-year hit-making career followed, including "When I Get Through with You," "Leavin' on Your Mind," and the posthumously released "Sweet Dreams."

Cline's death in an airplane accident, along with stars HAWKSHAW HAWKINS and COWBOY COPAS, helped solidify her place in the country music pantheon. She combined a lonesome country vocal sound with fairly smooth, pop-style delivery, thus bridging the gap between HONKY-TONK singer and pop chanteuse. Many country stars cite her as an influence, including LORETTA LYNN, who was befriended by the older performer when she first came to Nashville, and, of course, NEW-COUNTRY star K. D. LANG, who has ventured into the same big-throated pop style that made Cline famous. (Her original backup band, the re-clines, was named in homage to the earlier singer.) *Sweet Dreams*, a Hollywood film based on Cline's life, starring Jessica Lange, was released in 1986.

Select Discography
Her First Recordings, Vols. 1–3, Rhino 70048, 70049, 70050. Her fifties-era recordings for Four Star records, with a ROCKABILLY and country sound.
Greatest Hits, MCA 12. Her essential Decca recordings from the early sixties.
Live, Vol. 2, MCA 42284. Radio transcripts made between 1956 and 1962, including many songs she never cut for Decca.

◀ CLOWER, JERRY

(born 1926, Liberty, MS)

Clower is a country comedian specializing in the kind of rural monologues that have long been staples of tent shows, vaudeville acts, and other backwoods entertainments.

After serving in the army and graduating college with a degree in agriculture, Clower worked for a local chemical company in the sales division. Trying to inspire his coworkers, he developed a series of monologues based on his experiences growing up in the Mississippi woods. Eventually, his friends encouraged him to make his first record, which he released on his own Lemon label, called *Jerry Clower from Yazoo City Talkin'*. It quickly sold eight thousand copies with no national distribution. Clower was signed to MCA in 1971, and his monologues, most notably his "Coon Hunt Story," were immediate sensations on the country charts, earning him a regular spot on the GRAND OLE OPRY. He also earned a spot as cohost of the syndicated *Nashville on the Road* television show.

Besides his humorous monologizing, Clower is an ordained Baptist minister out of Yazoo City, and author of the homily-filled book *Ain't God Good?* He has appeared as an evangelist with Billy Graham and other popular fundamentalist preachers.

◀ COCHRAN, HANK

(born 1935, Isola, MS)

Cochran has played two roles in American music history, first as a country rocker and then as a country songwriter. His performance skills have been overshadowed by his contributions to the repertoires of other hit makers.

Cochran was born in a small town near Greenville, Mississippi, and was educated in New Mexico, where he took a job as an oil-field worker, eventually working his way to California in the early fifties. He continued to work full-time while performing in clubs at night, hooking up with another local singer/guitarist, Eddie Cochran, who had the same last name although he was no relation. The two formed the Cochran Brothers Trio along with songwriter Jerry Capehart, recording in a country style for the tiny Ekko label. Hank's role as backup guitarist was overshadowed by Eddie's famous string bending, so much so that he remains a footnote in the more famous musician's career. The two split when Eddie and Jerry moved to Nashville and switched to a ROCKABILLY style (and fame), while Hank continued to struggle along in the country arena, performing on local shows like the *California Hayride* television program out of Stockton.

In 1960 Hank moved to Nashville to pursue a career as a songwriter and performer. Working with legendary tunesmith HARLAN HOWARD, he wrote Patsy Cline's 1961 megahit, "I Fall to Pieces," and followed it up with "Make the World Go Away," which was successfully waxed by both RAY PRICE and EDDY ARNOLD, who also recorded Cochran's "I Want to Go With You." Thanks to these successes, he was signed as a solo artist to Liberty in 1961, charting a year later with "Sally Was a Good Old Girl" and "I'd Fight the World." He moved to the smaller Gaylord and Monument labels and had a few more hits through the sixties. In the mid-sixties he married country chanteuse JEANNIE SEELEY, producing and writing many of her sultry hits, including her first biggie, "Don't Touch Me" (1966).

In the mid-seventies, WILLIE NELSON recorded Cochran's song "(Angel) Flying Too Close to the Ground," which led to renewed interest in Cochran's career. He recorded a new album for Capitol in 1978 with many of the OUTLAW-COUNTRY musicians in the supporting cast, including Nelson and MERLE HAGGARD, as well as Seely. Two years later, Elektra records released new recordings of his classic sixties country material. Neither album did much to revive Cochran's performance career. In the eighties he returned to the charts as a songwriter, now working with Dean Dillon, penning "Ocean Front Property" and "The Chair" for nouveau country hunk GEORGE STRAIT.

◀ COE, DAVID ALLAN

(born 1936, Akron, OH)

Coe is one of the only seventies-era outlaws who actually has a prison background, but he tries a bit too hard to live up to his image.

Coe spent most of his youth in trouble with the law, ending up in the state penitentiary, where he allegedly killed another prisoner; only the end of the death penalty saved him from the chair. On his release in 1967, he hooked up with legendary country-pop producer SHELBY SINGLETON, who signed him to his SSS label, impressed by the bluesy, soulful original material that Coe had composed while in prison. Coe made two albums that showed a strong soul influence, then switched to a more countrified format, without too much success, before settling into his mature style, which seems to draw from both streams.

In 1974 he was signed to Columbia, where he remained for over a decade. Many of his songs were self-confessional (some might say self-promotional), including the outlaw ballad "Willie, Waylon and Me" about you know who, and 1983's "The Ride," telling of a mystical meeting with the ghost of HANK WILLIAMS. 1984's "Mona Lisa's Lost Her Smile," a typically enigmatic and self-conscious composition, was his biggest "hit." In 1986 he issued an entire album of meditations on the death of his father, even featuring an inner-sleeve photo of his dad decked out in his coffin. In the late eighties, he ran the Willie Nelson and Family general store in Branson, Missouri.

As a songwriter, Coe has placed a number of hits with mainstream country acts, including TANYA TUCKER, who in 1975 recorded "Would You Lay with Me (in a Field of Stone)," which created quite a stir because of its mature theme; and JOHNNY PAYCHECK, who immortalized the 1977 megahit "Take This Job and Shove It."

Select Discography
Biggest Hits, Columbia Legacy 38318. One of many hits collections put out by Columbia featuring mainly his mid-seventies recordings.
The Mysterious Rhinestone Cowboy/Once Upon a Rhyme, Bear Family 15706; *Longhaired Redneck/Rides Again*, Bear Family 15705. Two CDs reissuing four mid-seventies Coe albums.

◀ COHEN, JOHN

(born 1932, New York City)
Cohen is an old-time revivalist, filmmaker, and folklorist who has discovered and recorded many fine traditional musicians.

Born to a well-educated, urban family, Cohen was first introduced to folk music through his older brother Mike, a founding member of the Shantyboys, an early FOLK-REVIVAL band in the late forties. He attended Yale University and then settled into the burgeoning folk music/coffeehouse scene in New York in the mid-fifties. There he met another ex-Yalie, Tom Paley, as well as MIKE SEEGER, and in 1958 the trio became the NEW LOST CITY RAMBLERS, the first and probably most influential of the old-time string-band revivalists.

Cohen performed with the Ramblers through 1972. He also began making field trips to the South. Focusing on the coal-mining communities of Kentucky, he made a film in 1964 called *The High Lonesome Sound*, which introduced master BANJO player ROSCOE HOLCOMB to an urban audience and featured footage of BILL MONROE. He made several other films, including *The End of an Old Song* (1974), featuring ballad singer Dillard Chandler from North Carolina, as well as recording and producing a number of records for Folkways.

In 1972 Cohen formed the Putnam String County Band with fiddler Jay Ungar, guitarist Lynn Hardy (then Ungar's wife), and cellist Abby Newton. The band was one of the more innovative of the old-time revival groups, although it only lasted a year or so. Since that time, Cohen has continued to perform with the Ramblers at their various reunion concerts, while teaching filmmaking at the State University of New York at Purchase. He has also become interested in traditional Peruvian music and has produced a film as well as several recordings of this musical style.

Select Discography

High Atmosphere, Rounder 1028. Fine sixties-era field recordings made by Cohen with wonderful photographs and notes.

◀ COLLIE, MARK

(born 1956, Waynesboro, TN)

Collie is another young SINGER/SONGWRITER who is half-country, half-R&B in his approach. He is a decent original songwriter, although he has yet to make a major dent on the charts.

Born in Waynesboro, a town Collie describes as "halfway between Memphis and Nashville" (musically as well as geographically), Collie originally hoped to join the army but found out that he was ineligible because of his diabetes. He ended up in Memphis, looking for the vibrant music scene that had existed twenty or more years earlier; instead, he ended up bumming around with the few local players he could find. After marrying, his wife encouraged him to move to Nashville in 1986 and try to become a professional performer. Collie landed a bar job at Nashville's Douglas Corner club, playing for a year before he was discovered by MCA producer Tony Brown. Collie's music combines hard-edged fifties HONKY-TONK with a Memphis twist. His first album was particularly strong, featuring the fine lead guitar of legendary string bender JAMES BURTON.

Select Discography

Hardin County Line, MCA 42333. His first album.

Born and Raised in Black & White, MCA 10321. His 1991 follow-up.

Mark Collie, MCA 10658. Third album, released in 1993.

Unleashed, MCA 11055. More mainstream warbling from 1994.

◀ COLLINS, TOMMY

(born Leonard Raymond Sipes, 1930, Bethany, OK)

One of the pioneers of the BAKERSFIELD SOUND, Collins is best remembered for his mid-fifties recordings featuring a young BUCK OWENS on lead GUITAR.

Born and raised in Oklahoma, Collins had his first exposure on local radio before relocating to the Bakersfield, California, area, where many displaced Okies came in search of employment after World War II. He roomed with FERLIN HUSKY and soon became an important member of the local country scene, appearing on the influential *Town Hall Party* radio program, which featured TEX RITTER, Rose and JOE MAPHIS, the COLLINS KIDS (no relation), and many other local country acts. He signed with Los Angeles–based Capitol Records and had his biggest hits in 1954 and 1955 with "You Better Not Do That," "Whatcha Gonna Do Now," "You Gotta Have a License," and "High on a Hilltop," all featuring Buck Owens in the backup band.

Collins's career stumbled after this initial success, although he did manage to return to the charts in the mid-sixties with a couple of singles for Columbia, including "If You Can't Bite, Don't Growl" and "Birmingham" from 1966 and "I Made the Prison Band" from two years later. In the late sixties, he remained popular in Europe, although his U.S. career was pretty much over. Recently, NEW-COUNTRY star GEORGE STRAIT has covered some of his earlier HONKY-TONK numbers, including "If You Ain't Lovin' (You Ain't Livin')."

Select Discography
Leonard, Bear Family 15577. Five-CD set of Capitol, Columbia, and Morgan label recordings, with nicely illustrated booklet.

◀ COLLINS KIDS, THE

(Larry [guitar, vocals] born 1944 near Tulsa, OK; Lorrie [vocals] born 1942 near Tulsa, OK)

Mid-fifties ROCKABILLY stars Larry and Lorrie Collins were prominent in the California country scene. Cutey pie Lorrie was a big-throated belter, while Larry picked a mean GUITAR, and together their wholesome, all-American looks made them the perfect ambassadors of the new rockabilly style to a country audience.

Born and raised in Oklahoma, the Collins family came to California like countless other Okies in search of a better way of life. Larry and Lorrie began performing together as teens, singing in close harmonies while Larry energetically played his custom, double-necked guitar. The two became immediate sensations on the *Town Hall Party* radio program, the most influential country show out of Southern California, where Larry often dueted with country-jazz guitarist JOE MAPHIS.

The Kids were signed to Columbia, where the pair recorded some hot rockers with descriptive titles like "Beetle-Bug-Bop," "Hop, Skip and Jump," "Hoy Hoy," and "Hot Rod"; Columbia also had them commit some teen drivel to wax, including "I Wish" and "Soda Poppin' Around." Lorrie proved she was no shrinking violet on her bluesy covers of standards like "There'll Be Some Changes Made," while Larry showed off his considerable chops on some fine instrumentals. Lorrie even dated RICKY NELSON for a while and went out with Elvis, too!

By the early sixties, the Kids were becoming too old to be cute; Larry's voice changed, making their high-pitched duets a thing of the past. Lorrie recorded some solo country material, showing great potential to be a classy chanteuse, but she retired when she got married. Larry continued working in country behind the scenes, writing a couple of seventies standards (including Tanya Tucker's "Delta Dawn") as well as occasionally acting (he had a cameo in *Every Which Way But Loose*).

Select Discography
Hop, Skip and Jump, Bear Family 15537. Two CDs featuring fifty-nine Columbia
recordings made between 1955 and 1958, as well as some 1961 sessions with Lorrie
belting out four great country numbers, and some solo instrumental sessions by
brother Larry.

◀ COLTER, JESSI

(born Miriam Johnson, 1947, Phoenix, AZ)

The only female SINGER/SONGWRITER associated with the mid-seventies OUTLAW-
COUNTRY movement (thanks to her marriage to primo outlaw WAYLON JENNINGS),
Colter was actually a rather tame mainstream country chanteuse, an outlaw by
association rather than by blood.

Born Miriam Johnson, she was raised in a strict household by her evangelist
mother, who had her playing church piano by the time she reached adolescence.
By her teen years, she was singing professionally; through her sister, who had
married producer/songwriter JACK CLEMENT, she was introduced to twangy guitarist
Duane Eddy, who was looking to record with a vocalist. The two married when
she was just sixteen, and she became part of his road show, performing mostly in
Europe (Eddy's rockin' hits had come a few years earlier in the States, and by the
mid-sixties he was something of a has-been). In 1966 the couple resettled in Los
Angeles, where Miriam Eddy (as she was now known) placed some of her original
songs with DON GIBSON and DOTTIE WEST, before taking the stage name Jessi Colter
(after her great-great-uncle, Jess Colter, a small-time Western outlaw and counter-
feiter). She was signed to LEE HAZELWOOD's Jamie label, but her records failed to
make much of an impression, and she returned to being a housewife briefly before
divorcing Eddy in 1968.

While performing in Phoenix, she met the next man in her life, Waylon
Jennings, and the two were married in 1969. Jennings took her to his label,
RCA, and the two issued a couple of duets, although Colter's solo career was
slow to get started. She moved to Capitol in 1974, and the following year produced
her sole number-one country hit, the treacley "I'm Not Lisa" (*The Billboard Book
of Number One Country Hits* points out that "when put to a slightly different rhythmic pattern, [the first four notes of the song] are the same as the notes in Don
Ho's Hawaiian version of 'Tiny Bubbles' "; that about sums up this number for the
history books!). Despite the fact that this song was an enormous hit, Colter's
album tracks from the time were far superior to it and show her to be an
expressive vocalist not limited to sentimental warbling. She followed this with a
couple of other hits over the next two years, charting on both rock and pop
charts.

In 1976 RCA issued an anthology featuring recordings by Jennings, Colter, WILLIE
NELSON, and Tompall Glaser called *Wanted: The Outlaws*. This clever marketing
ploy gave a name to the seventies artists who refused to participate in the COUN-
TRYPOLITAN sounds of the decade, instead producing a rougher, rowdier, more rock
and roll–oriented sound. The decision to include Colter gave her career a further

jolt, and she spent much of the rest of the seventies touring with her husband and Nelson.

In the late seventies and early eighties, Colter's career slowed down, and she returned to recording primarily for the country charts. Many of her albums of this period had cowboyesque themes. In 1980 she recorded a second album of duets with husband Jennings, called *Leather and Lace*, a rather lackluster affair that was, however, a big seller. She returned to Capitol records in 1982, but her recording career slowed down; in 1985, she issued an all-gospel album under her real name of Miriam Johnson.

◀ COMMANDER CODY
AND HIS LOST PLANET AIRMEN

(c. 1970–1976: George Frayne [aka Commander Cody] [keyboards]; Billy C. Farlow [vocals]; Bill Kirchen [guitar, vocals]; John Tichy [guitar]; Andy Stein [fiddle, tenor saxophone]; Bruce Barlow [bass]; Lance Dickerson [drums])

One of the wackiest of all the bands to come out of the psychedelic era, Commander Cody and His Lost Planet Airmen combined traditional country, WESTERN SWING, R&B, truck-drivin' songs, and a whole lot more into a musical stew that enlivened many college dorms in the seventies. And who can argue with the world's only country band that takes its name from a line by Samuel Taylor Coleridge?

Frayne was an art student at the University of Michigan when he rounded up his first suspects to form the original Lost Planet Airmen. The lineup jelled around 1970, and a year later the band relocated to San Francisco, where they guested on the debut album of another COUNTRY-ROCK outfit, the NEW RIDERS OF THE PURPLE SAGE.

The group was signed to Paramount and released their first and best-known album, *Lost in the Ozone*, which featured their hit remake of Charlie Ryan's "Hot Rod Lincoln." The album consisted of a mix of original material that gently parodied earlier country and swing styles, along with covers of everything from "Twenty Flight Rock" by Eddie Cochran to Ronnie Self's "Home in My Hand." This set the standard for the band's recordings through their Paramount years; their second album featured both odd country-styled numbers like "The Kentucky Hills of Tennessee" and all-out rockers like "Rip It Up."

By the time the band signed to the larger Warner Brothers label in the mid-seventies, they had pretty much played out their hand. The band dissolved after issuing a strong live album based on their 1976 tour of England. Cody went solo and produced a series of rather mediocre recordings before forming a new backup band with ex-Airmen Kirchen and Barlow called the Moonglows around 1980. They had a minor hit with the kitschy "Two Triple Cheese (Side Order Fries)," and the band recorded and toured sporadically throughout the eighties, mostly in England.

Select Discography
Lost in the Ozone, MCA 31185. Their debut LP, featuring many of their best-known numbers, including "Hot Rod Lincoln."
Hot Licks, Cold Steel, and Truckers Favorites, MCA 31186. Affectionate tribute to sixties-era truckers songs.
Too Much Fun: The Best of Commander Cody, MCA 10092. Hits collection.

◀ CONLEE, JOHN

(born 1946, Versailles, KY)

Conlee is a smooth balladeer who was most popular in the late seventies and early eighties for his middle-of-the-road countryesque performances. He also claims to be the only licensed mortician to ever have a number-one country record.

Conlee was born and raised on a farm in Kentucky. He learned to play the GUITAR at age nine, playing rock, pop, and country music for his own enjoyment. After high school, he trained as an undertaker and worked for eight years at the trade (occasionally performing on the guitar at memorial services). In his mid-twenties, he relocated to Nashville, where he was hired by WLAC as a pop-music deejay.

Another deejay at the station got Conlee an audition with ABC/Dot in 1975, and he was signed a year later, recording a couple of singles that had regional success. His big break came in 1978 with his original country WEEPER "Rose Colored Glasses," a story of a deluded, hard-working ol' boy who doesn't realize his girl is cheating on him. This was followed by his first two number-one hits, both in 1979: "Lady Lay Down" and his own composition, "Backside of 30," about a troubled marriage.

Conlee had a few minor hits in the early eighties, culminating with 1983's "Common Man," one of those god-bless-ordinary-folks kind of songs that have immediate appeal to a country audience. He followed it up with some up-tempo hits, unusual for this usually laid-back balladeer, including "I'm Only in It for Love," written by DEBORAH ALLEN, her husband Rafe Van Hoy, and a newcomer named Kix Brooks (later of BROOKS AND DUNN). A year later, Conlee spotted another talented newcomer, Kieran Kane (later of the O'KANES) and recorded his "As Long as I'm Rockin' with You."

Conlee left ABC/MCA records in 1986 after a decade with the label, switching to Columbia although sticking with his producer, Bud Logan. He had a couple more hits in 1988 but soon faded from the scene. His smooth-voiced pop-country was beginning to sound old-fashioned as the NEW-COUNTRY sound took hold. Conlee has a pleasant enough voice and often performs with conviction, but the production values of his recordings vary from okay to downright dreadful, in the forgettable style of late-seventies pop.

Select Discography
Greatest Hits, Vols. 1 and 2, MCA 31229, 31230. His best songs from his first decade of recording.

◀ CONLEY, EARL THOMAS

(born 1941, Portsmouth, OH)

Dubbed "the thinking man's country musician"—probably because his songs tend to have a little more depth than the average pop-country hits and feature more unusual chord progressions (while he himself is a student of art history and Eastern philosophy)—Conley enjoyed a string of hits in the eighties despite his failure to fit into an established country niche.

Born to an impoverished rural Ohio family, Conley originally studied to be an art student and didn't take up songwriting professionally until he was twenty-six. He began commuting back and forth from his native Portsmouth to Nashville, but with little success, and in 1970 relocated to Huntsville, Alabama, where he cut a demo tape with his brother Fred. The two brought it to a local insurance salesman and part-time record producer Nelson Larkin, who signed Conley to his own Prize label; these first recordings were later licensed to GRT. In 1975, after four years of trying, Conley finally dented the country charts with "I Have Loved You Girl (but Not Like This Before)," and continued to graze the lower ends of the charts through the decade's end. In the 1970s, Conley suffered some from the confusion of deejays and fans, who mixed him up with CONWAY TWITTY and JOHN CONLEE, so he went by a variety of names, including the ETC Band as well as just plain Earl Conley (although his family called him Tom) before settling on using his full name.

After a brief stint at Warner Brothers in 1979, Conley signed with Larkin's Sunbird label, recording an album of original songs called *Blue Pearl*; Randy Scruggs, a musician and producer (as well as the son of legendary banjoist Earl Scruggs), worked on the sessions, beginning a long association with Conley. The album yielded a hit with "Fire and Smoke," and Larkin quickly licensed it to RCA. The producer and songwriter moved to the new label together, producing a follow-up hit in 1982 with "Somewhere Between Right and Wrong," a song that featured a rocking beat and horns (although RCA tried to placate country audiences by releasing two versions of the song, one with the horns mixed out). Some country stations refused to play the record because it "promoted" promiscuity.

In 1983 Conley scored a string of hits from his next album, *Don't Make It Easy for Me*, all cowritten with Scruggs. Conley claims that he "programmed himself" through Zen-like meditation to produce radio hits before writing with Scruggs; whatever your feelings about Buddha, the scheme seems to have worked, because the album yielded four number-one country hits for the duo.

Into the mid-eighties, Conley and producer Larkin continued to move his recordings toward a more rock-oriented sound. Always a somewhat sporadic songwriter, Conley increasingly relied on material provided by Nashville's professional hit-making factory. In 1986 RCA convinced him to cut a duet with Anita Pointer, of the R&B group the Pointer Sisters (the Sisters had had a freak country hit eleven years earlier with "Fairytale"); the result was "Too Many Times," which made it to number two.

In 1988 Conley finally broke with producer Larkin, although he didn't go far in selecting a new guiding hand; Randy Scruggs handled the production duties on his next record, along with Nashville pro and session bass player Emory Gordy, Jr. From these sessions came the odd-couple pairing of Conley with sweet-voiced singer EMMYLOU HARRIS on "We Believe in Happy Endings." Conley continued rocking Nashville's boat when for his first 1989 single he chose to release "What'd I Say," a song that featured the phrase "Go to hell" repeated three times. Despite the fact that coproducer Gordy had once edited the word "friggin'" out of a BELLAMY BROTHERS single for fear of invoking the wrath of country deejays, the song was released untouched and went to number one. Conley scored his sixteenth consecutive number one as a solo artist later that year with "Love Out Loud," the last in his long, unbroken string of good luck (matched only by the pop schmoozers ALABAMA).

Gruff-voiced Conley with his oddball songs, minor chords, and love-me-or-leave-me attitude has had less success on the charts of late; but his long reign in the eighties proves that you don't have to perform in a rhinestone-crusted leisure suit to make it in country music. In fact, the audience seems to enjoy the occasional misfit, as long as his rugged individualism doesn't overstep too much the lines of propriety.

Select Discography
Best of Earl Thomas Conley, RCA 6700. Big numbers from his years at RCA.

◀ COOLEY, SPADE

(born Donnell Clyde Cooley, 1910, Pack Saddle Creek, OK; died 1969)

Cooley was a pioneering fiddler/bandleader who led one of the biggest and most popular WESTERN SWING bands.

Cooley was descended from two generations of fiddle players, so it's not surprising that he played for his first dance at the age of eight. His family relocated from Oklahoma to Southern California, where the young Cooley performed with Western-flavored groups, including JIMMY WAKELEY's band. In the mid-thirties, he began picking up movie work in the many C-grade cowpoke epics of the day, working as a stand-in at Republic Pictures for popular cowboy star ROY ROGERS and playing fiddle in a number of films.

In the early forties, Cooley formed his first band, and by the end of World War II they were permanently installed in the Santa Monica Ballroom that Cooley leased as his home base, drawing several thousand cowboy-swing fans a night. Cooley's classic first band featured vocalist TEX WILLIAMS, as well as Joaquin Murphey's hot steel guitar and Johnny Weiss's guitar leads, which were reminiscent of jazz great Charlie Christian. In 1943 they recorded Cooley's composition "Shame, Shame on You," which would be his biggest hit and would become his theme song. The entire band along with singer Williams quit in 1946 to go out on their own as the Western Caravan.

In 1948 Cooley was given his own variety show on a local Los Angeles television station, which introduced country comic HANK PENNY. In the fifties, Cooley's bands grew in size, sometimes numbering over a dozen members, including full string sections, harp, and accordian, and he slowly gravitated toward a more pop-sounding style. Increasing problems with alcohol led to a decline in his popularity later in the decade, and his personal problems came to a head in 1961 when he shot and killed his wife in front of their teenage daughter. Cooley spent the sixties in prison for his crime. He was released to perform at a benefit concert in 1969; following his performance, he died backstage of a heart attack.

Although Cooley's recordings on a whole are more pop-flavored than BOB WILLS's, for a period in the middle to late forties his band defined and helped popularize the Western swing style. True fans of Western swing find his later bands bloated and too far removed from the jazz influences of his youth, but they should not forget that, for a brief period, he was one of the great innovators in this style.

Select Discography

Columbia Historic Edition, Columbia 37467. Great, swinging recordings made just after World War II.

◀ COOLIDGE, RITA

(born 1944, Nashville, TN)

Somewhat of a marginal presence in country, Coolidge is best remembered for her 1970s marriage to KRIS KRISTOFFERSON and the duets they recorded together, and for her MOR hit, 1977's "(Your Love Has Lifted Me) Higher and Higher," a cover of the old pop tune by Jackie Wilson.

Coolidge began performing from early childhood as a member of her father's gospel choir. Her parents also encouraged her to play gospel-styled piano. When she was a teenager, the family relocated to Florida, and after high school she enrolled at Florida State. There she began performing country-rock, blues, and pop with a local band. She moved to Memphis to work for the tiny Pepper record label, which released her first material. She also found work recording jingles.

In Memphis she met the British country rockers Delaney and Bonnie (Bramlett), along with session pianist Leon Russell, with whom she became romantically involved. The quartet moved to Los Angeles, and Coolidge recorded as a backup singer for the Bramletts's first album. Russell got her a job on Joe Cocker's (in)famous "Mad Dogs and Englishmen" tour from 1969 to 1970, which led her to a recording contract with Cocker's label, A&M.

Coolidge's first albums featured a fairly standard mix of pop-rock and countryish material written by the leading singer/songwriters of the day, including NEIL YOUNG, GUY CLARK, VAN MORRISON, and her soon-to-be-husband Kristofferson. The duo met in 1973 and recorded two albums together over the next year, again in a mix of country and light pop styles. Coolidge's career finally took off in 1977 with her cover of "Higher and Higher," in which she transformed Jackie Wilson's exciting sexuality into a cool, almost off-hand tone that made for perfect dentist-office listening.

She recorded another album with Kristofferson in 1979, but their marriage fell apart a year later. Despite a couple of early eighties albums, Coolidge was unable to regain her pop momentum, and her new material had even looser ties to country than her original records. She continues to record and perform sporadically today.

Select Discography
Greatest Hits, A&M 3238. Her big-selling, easy-listening country fluff from the mid-seventies.

◀ COOPER, STONEY AND WILMA LEE

(Stoney born Dale Troy Cooper, 1918, Harmon, WV; died 1977; Wilma Lee born Wilma Leigh Leary, 1921, Valley Head, WV)

The Coopers were a well-known country/BLUEGRASS duo with deep roots in traditional mountain music. The duo enjoyed minor success on the country charts in the fifties and then renewed success on the bluegrass-revival trail two decades later.

Wilma Lee was born into a performing group, the Leary Family, a gospel outfit that was well-known throughout the upper South in the thirties and forties, performing at church-sponsored socials, on radio, and at folk festivals. Her mother was the motivating force behind the group; a talented organist, she arranged the music for her three daughters, with her coal-miner husband singing bass. Beginning at age five, Wilma Lee sang with her family group; by her teens the group had grown beyond the limits of family to incorporate other local singers and musicians, including a young fiddler named Stoney Cooper. The two were wed in the late thirties.

Although they continued to perform gospel with the Leary band, the duo began to perform secular music on their own. They performed in the early forties in the upper South and as far west as Nebraska and had a number of radio jobs on small stations. In 1943 Wilma Lee performed on Chicago radio while husband Stoney worked in a defense plant. Four years later they got their big break when they were hired to join the WWVA *Jamboree* out of Wheeling, West Virginia (WWVA was a powerful station that saturated the upper South and West). They also made their first recordings for Rich-R-Tone Records, a label well-known for its bluegrass recordings, and were signed two years later to the bigger and more powerful Columbia label. They remained in Wheeling for ten years, performing with their band, known as the Clinch Mountain Clan. At this time, they had their greatest country hits with a number of songs either written by Wilma or cowritten by husband and wife, from 1956's "Cheated Too" through 1959's "There's a Big Wheel"; their last country song to hit the charts was a remake of the venerable "Wreck on the Highway" in 1961. They were well-known for sentimental WEEPERS like "Willie Roy, the Crippled Boy" and "I Dreamed about Mom Last Night," and introduced Leadbelly's "Midnight Special" to the country charts. They also continued to record and perform gospel material, giving a hard-driving sound to newly composed hymns like "Walking My Lord Up Calvary Hill." In 1957 they left Wheeling to join the cast of the GRAND OLE OPRY.

The sixties were slower times for the duo as recording artists, although they continued to tour widely. In the early seventies, the renewed interest in traditional mountain music brought their old-style country/bluegrass sound back in vogue, and they remained quite active, although Stoney's health was beginning to deteriorate due to heart problems. After his death in 1977, Wilma Lee kept the band together, continuing to take a more traditional direction and recording for bluegrass revival labels. Daughter Carol Lee also performed with the family band and directed the background singers (known as the Carol Lee Singers) on the *Grand Ole Opry* stage. Although Wilma Lee continued to perform through the eighties, of late she has been less active.

Select Discography

Wilma Lee and Stoney Cooper, Rounder 0066. Bluegrass sessions cut just before Stoney's death.

Classic Early Recordings, County 103. This LP reissues late-forties recordings originally cut for Columbia.

◀ COPAS, COWBOY

(born Lloyd Copas, 1913, Muskogee, OK; died 1963)

One of the great HONKY-TONK singers of the fifties, Copas is best-remembered for singing lead vocal on PEE WEE KING's "Tennessee Waltz," one of the biggest country hits of all times.

Copas grew up on his grandfather's ranch and learned GUITAR and his first songs from his elder relative. By his late teens he was already touring as a musician in a novelty duo with a pureblood Indian named Natchee who played the fiddle. In 1940 the duo broke up when Copas was hired as a single act for the Cincinnati-based radio show, *The Boone Country Jamboree*.

In Cincinnati, Copas hooked up with record producer Syd Nathan, who founded King and related labels in the forties to produce country and R&B acts. Copas recorded a number of hits for King, including "Filipino Baby," "Tragic Romance," "Gone and Left Me Blues," and "Signed, Sealed and Delivered" (not the same as the later R&B hit). These mid-forties hits were early songs in the honky-tonk style that would become increasingly popular after the war. In his performances, Copas wed jazz, blues, and pop influences, making for a hot, high-energy style that anticipated not only honky-tonk but the coming ROCKABILLY craze.

In 1946 Pee Wee King invited Copas to replace the smooth-voiced EDDY ARNOLD in his Golden West Cowboys, getting him his first exposure on the GRAND OLE OPRY. Copas stayed for two years, singing lead on the legendary 1948 recording of "Tennessee Waltz" and securing a place in country history. He then went solo again, with a few more hits, including 1949's "Hangman's Boogie" and 1951's "Strange Little Girl."

Copas's career sagged in the fifties but was revived toward the decade's end when he signed with Starday and returned to his original, stripped-down sound on a number of hits, including the number-one "Alabam'," (1960); "Flat Top" and "Sunny Tennessee" (both from 1961); and his last hit, "Goodbye Kisses" (1963). In that year, Copas had the misfortune to play a benefit concert with HAWKSHAW

HAWKINS and PATSY CLINE. The trio were tragically killed when their chartered plane crashed on the way back to Nashville.

Select Discography
Tragic Tales of Love and Life, King 714. Reissue of a late-fifties album.

◀ CORNELIUS, HELEN

(born 1941, Hannibal, MO)

Cornelius is a mainstream country SINGER/SONGWRITER who is best remembered for a series of duets with Jim Ed Brown released in the late seventies.

Born in Mark Twain's hometown, she was raised in a musical family; her father was a big GRAND OLE OPRY fan, and her brothers were all amateur country musicians. Cornelius began her career as a child performing in a vocal trio with her sisters on the local country-fair circuit. After a number of years working on an amateur level, she got her big break as a soloist appearing on the *Ted Mack Amateur Hour* in the mid-sixties.

However, it took a while for her career to get in gear. After failing to get very far as a solo artist, she took up songwriting, placing minor hits with other female country stars, including LYNN ANDERSON, JEANNIE C. RILEY, and SKEETER DAVIS. She recorded demos for MCA and Columbia and finally was signed in the mid-seventies to RCA, with whom she produced the minor hit "We Still Sing Love Songs in Missouri."

RCA producer Bob Ferguson suggested that the young singer might make a good duet partner for Jim Ed Brown, whose career was in the doldrums at the time. The pair recorded "I Don't Want to Have to Marry You" in 1977 in the sugary COUNTRYPOLITAN style. The song was a number-one hit on the C&W charts. Inspired by this success, they recorded together for the next three years, even doing a country cover of the schlock classic "You Don't Bring Me Flowers," originally cut by Neil Diamond and Barbra Streisand.

In 1980 Cornelius and Brown split to pursue solo careers, without too much success. Cornelius toured the dinner-theater circuit for a while, working with another seventies country artist, Dave Rowland of the DAVE AND SUGAR duo. In 1988 Brown and Cornelius reunited, but by then their style seemed hopelessly outdated, and they fared poorly.

◀ COUNTRY COOKING

(c. 1974–1978: Kenny Kosek [fiddle]; Tony Trischka, Peter Wernick [banjos]; Russ Barenberg [guitar]; John Miller [bass])

Country Cooking, based in Ithaca, New York, was a mid-seventies PROGRESSIVE BLUEGRASS band whose members later spawned many other experimental/newgrass outfits. They were marked by TONY TRISCHKA's and Peter Wernick's dual BANJOS (inspired by the OSBORNE BROTHERS, who used twin banjos on some of their late-fifties and early-sixties recordings), the jazz-influenced fiddle of Kenny Kosek, and Russ Barenberg's progressive GUITAR work. They recorded two influential albums for Rounder in the mid-seventies, and various members performed under different names (including Breakfast Special and the Extended Playboys) and with different lineups throughout the decade.

After the band's demise, Trischka became the most influential of the new, progressive banjoists, recording a series of solo albums that mixed his own somewhat spacey improvised compositions with more traditional numbers. Wernick relocated to the Denver area where he recorded one solo album before forming the influential bluegrass ensemble HOT RIZE. Kosek continued to perform with various bands, as a backing musician, in a duo with Matt Glaser, and as a member of JAY UNGER's band, FIDDLE FEVER. Barenberg went on to become a solo artist, and Miller pursued an interest in blues and jazz guitar on a series of solo albums.

Select Discography

Bluegrass Instrumentals, Rounder 006; *Barrel of Fun*, Rounder 0033. Their two fine albums, now both out of print.

◀ COUNTRY GAZETTE

(c. 1972–ongoing; original lineup: Byron Berline [fiddle]; Kenny Wertz [guitar, vocals]; Herb Pederson [banjo, vocals]; Roger Bush [bass]; late '70s lineup: Alan Munde [banjo]; Roland White [mandolin, vocals]; Joe Carr [guitar, vocals]; Michael Anderson [vocals, bass])

Originally a California-based PROGRESSIVE BLUEGRASS trio, the Gazette became one of the better revival bands of the seventies thanks to the teaming of Roland White (formerly of the KENTUCKY COLONELS) with BANJO whiz Alan Munde.

The group got their first break when they were invited to tour with the last original FLYING BURRITO BROTHERS lineup in 1971 and 1972 as a kind of extension of the band: the original trio of fiddler BYRON BERLINE, guitarist Kenny Wertz, and banjoist Herb Pederson would play a bluegrass set in the middle of the Burrito's act and then join the group for their electric COUNTRY-ROCK numbers.

Mandolinist Roland White came on board in late 1973, after the death of his brother Clarence, with whom he had been playing traditional bluegrass. Munde, who gained fame in the mid-seventies thanks to a solo album titled *Banjo Sandwich*, joined in the same year to replace Pederson, and the two became the nucleus of a new band (at one point, they even recorded as a duo under the band name). The group's greatest lineup was, arguably, its late-seventies roster, with vocalist Michael Anderson and jazz-flavored guitarist Joe Carr joining Munde and White. They recorded two excellent albums, which both contained classic bluegrass numbers along with more recent songs. Anderson was a strong lead singer with a lot of personality whose voice blended perfectly with White's idiosyncratic harmonies, while Munde provided rock-solid banjo playing that was strongly influenced by bluegrass traditions while still incorporating unusual, jazz-influenced chords and runs typical of progressive bluegrass.

This version of the band, like most of its previous lineups, didn't last long, and soon Carr, Bush, and White were recording as a trio, producing a couple of rather lame instrumental albums of standards (marketed as *Festival Favorites* because they were the kind of numbers that are played to death at bluegrass conventions). The band petered out by the late eighties. Munde went back to solo and session work, and White soon after hooked up with the NASHVILLE BLUEGRASS BAND, one of the most distinguished of the new traditional bands of the eighties. In the early nineties, Munde assembled a new Country Gazette lineup without White.

Select Discography
American & Clean, Flying Fish 253. Early-eighties lineup with excellent lead singer Michael Anderson on a selection of mostly newly written songs.
Strictly Instrumental, Flying Fish 446. Later incarnation of the band with Munde and White joined by talented dobroist Gene Wooten along with fiddler Billy Joe Foster.
Keep on Pushing, Flying Fish 70561. Early-nineties band without White.

◀ COUNTRY GENTLEMEN, THE

(1959–1969; original lineup: Charlie Waller [lead vocals, guitar]; John Duffey [tenor vocals, mandolin]; Eddie Adcock [baritone vocals, banjo]; Tom Gray [bass vocals, bass])

The Country Gentlemen were Washington, D.C.'s premiere BLUEGRASS band during the first decade of the FOLK REVIVAL; they were also the best-known of the second-generation, so-called "progressive" bands who helped broaden the bluegrass style by introducing new material to the repertoire and new instrumental techniques.

The original band was formed out of the pieces of another Washington-area group, Buzz Busby's Bayou Boys. When most of the group's members were injured in an automobile accident, banjoist Bill Emerson hired a couple of local players to finish out their gigs, including guitarist Charlie Waller, MANDOLIN player John Duffey, and bassist Larry Lahey. The pairing of Waller and Duffy proved to be an inspired choice; Waller's laconic lead vocals (in the style of country crooner HANK SNOW) were a perfect match for Duffey's high-energy and unusual tenor harmonies, plus both were able players on their instruments. The group changed its name to the Country Gentlemen in 1958 and signed with Starday Records, a Nashville-based label that was dedicated to traditional bluegrass.

Emerson left the band soon after, and, after a brief period during which bluegrass scholar Pete Kuykendall filled his shoes, Eddie Adcock came on board in mid-1959. Adcock had been playing electric guitar in local bars to make a living, but he had previously worked with BILL MONROE and Bill Harrell (one of the first performers to venture beyond the bounds of the traditional bluegrass sound). Adcock was also an excellent baritone vocalist, and the trio of Waller, Duffey, and Adcock became one of the most powerful and distinctive in all of bluegrass.

MIKE SEEGER, another Washington-area denizen who had come under the spell of bluegrass music, introduced the group to Folkways Records, an urban outfit that employed him as a producer and whose sales were mostly concentrated among the fledgling folk revivalists. In 1959 Seeger oversaw their first recording, an album that featured primarily older mountain songs in keeping with the label's folk orientation, although the group also covered LEFTY FRIZZELL's country hit of the same year, "Long Black Veil," a bold move for a bluegrass band (the song has since become a bluegrass and COUNTRY-ROCK standard). They would record three more LPs for the label, becoming the best known of all bluegrass groups among the urban revivalists.

After their first album was released, the band reached its classic lineup with the addition of bassist Tom Gray. Another innovative musician like Adcock, Gray avoided the boom-chick patterns of traditional country styles, instead adapting jazz licks and walking bass lines borrowed from bluegrass guitar. The importance of the bass was further emphasized in the band's recordings, particularly when the harmonies came in full force and the other instruments dropped back.

The band was influential for a number of reasons. Unlike traditional bluegrass bands, they did not feature a fiddle player, which was a conscious decision to give them more of a "chamber-grass" feeling (for this reason, many other urban bluegrass bands also went fiddleless). Waller's solid GUITAR solos were prominently featured, another innovation that would influence future revival bands, such as the KENTUCKY COLONELS with Clarence White. Duffey's mandolin work combined the high energy of Bill Monroe with a more sophisticated, bluesy feeling; he was among the first to emulate Jesse McReynold's (of JIM AND JESSE) style of crosspicking. Adcock's banjo playing went beyond the rolls of Earl Scruggs to include jazzy melodic riffs. Vocally, the band could not be beat; Duffey set the standard for every bluegrass tenor in the revival scene with his highly ornamented harmony and lead vocals. And, in terms of repertoire, the band both expanded the bluegrass realm backward to include folk classics and added to the field with original compositions like "Red Rocking Chair" (cowritten by Duffy and William York).

Gray left the band in 1964, ending their classic era, and although the band continued to be active on the bluegrass circuit, they were less evident on the mainstream folk scene. Duffey retired in 1969 due to an internal management dispute; within a few years, he had rejoined with Gray to form the SELDOM SCENE, the best-loved bluegrass band in Washington, D.C., in the seventies. In 1970 Adcock left to form the II Generation, a progressive bluegrass band that was more instrumentally oriented, leaving only Waller to carry the Country Gentlemen torch. The band signed with another urban folk label, Vanguard, in the early seventies and began a long period of success with many new members passing through, including the return of Bill Emerson, young RICKY SKAGGS, JERRY DOUGLAS, Doyle Lawson (later leader of Doyle Lawson and Quicksilver), and many other budding progressive bluegrass stars. The band continues to record for Rebel Records today under Waller's leadership.

Select Discography

Country Songs, Old and New, Smithsonian Folkways 40004; *Folk Songs and Bluegrass*, Smithsonian Folkways 40022. These two CDs reissue the Gentleman's first two Folkways albums from 1960 and 1961, respectively. This is the so-called "classic" group, and these albums were highly influential on the urban folk/bluegrass revival.

The Country Gentleman Featuring Ricky Skaggs, Vanguard 73123. Reissue of an album originally recorded about 1976. At the time, Skaggs was just a young blue-grass fiddler on the rise.

Twenty-Five Years, Rebel 1102. One of the more recent versions of the band celebrating a key anniversary.

◀ COUNTRYPOLITAN

(c. 1970–1985)

After the pernicious effects of the NASHVILLE SOUND had rendered country music into a bland reflection of middle-of-the-road pop, the seventies drove what seemed to be the final nail into country music's coffin with the development of country-politan, or crossover, country artists. It was obvious that the influence of rock, pop, and even disco could no longer be ignored by the country music establishment, which was more comfortable with Dean Martin–era crooning. Younger artists were pushing for a more contemporary sound. But rather than returning to its pure country roots for inspiration, the professional music establishment turned to pop styles and countrified them.

The movement began with soft-pop singers who tried to move a little more toward a rock sound. LYNN ANDERSON's upbeat "(I Never Promised You a) Rose Garden" is a good example of a pop-ish song that came out of the country charts. The instrumentation was pure pop, and Anderson's little-girl mewing was perfect for the soothing sounds of MOR radio (despite the fact that the song's message was hardly upbeat). The ultimate lounge-style country hit would have to be CRYSTAL GAYLE's "Don't It Make My Brown Eyes Blue," with its tinkling piano and oh-so-pleasant vocals. Even RITA COOLIDGE, wife of outlaw KRIS KRISTOFFERSON, got into the act with her cover of "Higher and Higher," taking a sexy R&B hit and sucking the life out of it so it would be acceptable to middle America.

In the mid-seventies, countrypolitan tried to jump onto the disco-pop band-wagon. DOLLY PARTON made a much noticed attempt to cross over, releasing the perky "Here You Come Again" and posing in leather pants and more "contemporary" clothing. (Remember that in country music image is often part of the message, so that country women were always pictured in gingham dresses until the mid-sixties; Parton's choice of disco clothing to represent her "new" sound was quite controversial in Nashville.) Late-seventies star EDDIE RABBITT represented the perfect blend of pop-rock and country styles, although it's hard to figure out what makes a song like "I Love a Rainy Night" country.

KENNY ROGERS was the ultimate countrypolitan star. Coming from a folk-pop background (he had been lead singer of the sixties group the First Edition), Rogers had a husky voice, sexy good looks, and a knack for choosing soft-pop ballads that gave the female members of his audience the screaming meemies. Again, his dress style indicated a basic change in the country audience; no rhinestone-encrusted Nudie suits or ten gallon hats for this cowboy, but, rather, ready-to-wear disco clothes, complete with unbuttoned shirts, chains, and bell bottoms. Rogers's act found a natural home in places like Vegas, where middle-of-the-road

America (i.e., "country") audiences come to enjoy sanitized entertainment and just a little sin.

While the countrypolitan movement was in full flower, stirrings of revolt could be felt in two areas. The so-called outlaws turned their backs on Nashville, heading to places like Austin, Texas, to create a new music by focusing on older country styles. Meanwhile, the BLUEGRASS revival was sweeping through the folk community, and many of these younger pickers would become the NEW-COUNTRY stars of the eighties and nineties.

◀ COUNTRY-ROCK

(c. 1968)

Country-rock is the granddaddy of today's progressive or NEW COUNTRY. In the sixties, many rock acts were rediscovering the joys of real country music, as opposed to the watered-down pop sounds that were coming from Nashville. Even the Beatles helped point the way, with their recording of BUCK OWENS's hit "Act Naturally" (remember, Liverpool was a seaport town, and country music came across the ocean on many merchant ships, so that HANK WILLIAMS was as big an influence on John Lennon and company as Little Richard).

Probably the first and most important country-rock LP was the BYRDS's 1968 release, *Sweetheart of the Rodeo*. This West Coast group had always included folk and SINGER/SONGWRITER material in their act; many of the original members had performed in FOLK-REVIVAL groups in the early sixties. In 1968 new member GRAM PARSONS brought with him a love of country material, which he had expressed in his previous, short-lived group, the International Submarine Band, another early country-rock outfit. *Sweetheart* featured country standards, along with compositions by BOB DYLAN and Parsons in a country style, performed by the band with some of the better, younger Nashville sessionmen. While this version of the Byrds was short-lived, this album became a model for later country-rock ensembles.

A year later, Bob Dylan gave the movement added legitimacy by releasing his *Nashville Skyline* LP, in which he took on the voice of a mellow-sounding country crooner and dueted with JOHNNY CASH. Young Nashvillians like multi-instrumentalist NORMAN BLAKE and steel guitarist PETE DRAKE were used for these sessions; these musicians knew country roots but were influenced by more progressive sounds. Dylan was universally respected in the rock world, with every twist and turn in his career carefully inspected. Giving his approval to the country-rock movement undoubtedly encouraged others to try out this new style. Another influential LP, oddly enough, was Ringo Starr's *Beaucoups of Blues* recorded in Nashville in 1971; Ringo had sung lead on "Act Naturally" with the Beatles, and somehow his sad-sack vocals perfectly fit mainstream country songs. Steel guitarist Pete Drake approached Starr with the project and produced all of the tracks using Nashville's young talent.

Out of the remnants of the folk-rock group, Buffalo Springfield, emerged the band POCO, featuring Rusty Young on PEDAL STEEL GUITAR, along with Jim Messina, Richie Furay, and Randy Meisner. Their theme song, "Pickin' Up the Pieces," on their first LP, stated their mission quite clearly: to "pick up the pieces" of country tradition and modernize them for a new, young, hipper audience. Meisner would soon leave to help form RICK NELSON's Stone Canyon Band, another pioneering countrified ensemble. (Meisner later formed the EAGLES, who began their recording lives in the country-rock style, although they later veered off into a decidedly pop/rock sound.) The NITTY GRITTY DIRT BAND was another West Coast band that began its life in rock and converted to country-rock in the late sixties. Another short-lived West Coast country-rock outfit was Nashville West, featuring guitarist Clarence White, lead singer Gib Guilbeau, and drummer Gene Parsons. They lasted from about 1967 to 1968, before White and Parsons went to the Byrds. Guilbeau sessioned with country-popster LINDA RONSTADT and was a member of one of the later incarnations of the FLYING BURRITO BROTHERS.

Gram Parsons and Byrds bassman CHRIS HILLMAN formed the most influential West Coast country-rock band, the Flying Burrito Brothers, in the early seventies. Their first two LPs, made while Parsons was still with the group, are considered classics today, combining traditional country subject matter and sounds with a decidedly new outlook. When Parsons left the band, he had a short solo career, before an untimely death; and he helped launch the career of COUNTRY-ROCK vocalist EMMYLOU HARRIS, who would later "cross over" in the mid-eighties to become a pure country act. Chris Hillman later formed the progressive country band, the DESERT ROSE BAND.

Even San Francisco hippie band the Grateful Dead got in on the country-rock act on their early-seventies releases *Workingman's Dead* and *American Beauty*. Both albums feature songs with distinct country flavorings, along with the purest harmonies ever laid down by this usually loud and grungy outfit. Jerry Garcia, who began his career as a bluegrass banjoist and would from time to time return to this format in the seventies and eighties with his informal group, OLD AND IN THE WAY, took up the pedal steel guitar at this time to get that true country sound.

The importance of country-rock cannot be overstated. It not only opened country music to a new audience, the young, highly literate audience of contemporary rock, but it also helped remind country of its roots in WESTERN SWING, HONKY-TONK, and BLUEGRASS, pointing the way to a new musical form based on these roots. While COUNTRYPOLITAN and even seventies crossover country tried to "modernize" country music by employing cushy choruses and sappy strings, the country-rock crowd was showing that the real strength of country music lay in its strong lyrical content and its stripped-down sound. The country-rock revival would lead, in turn, to interest in other types of country music, as evidenced by the revival of ROCKABILLY in the mid- to late seventies.

◀ COUSIN EMMY

(born Cynthia May Carver, 1903, near Lamb, KY; died 1980)

Cousin Emmy was an audacious and often outrageous singer/instrumentalist who was a major star of country radio in the late thirties and early forties. Emmy made a comeback during the FOLK REVIVAL of the sixties, performing for a new, urban audience.

The daughter of a fiddling tobacco farmer, Emmy was a born performer who used her talents to her own advantages: "Mama would leave me in the tobacco patch and tell me to do one row, [and] I'd sing and dance and slap my legs and entertain the seven other kids to git them to do my work for me." Taking up the fiddle at an early age, Emmy won the prestigious National Old-Time Fiddlers Contest in Louisville in 1935, the first woman to take this award. Helped by her performing cousins, the Carver Brothers, Emmy began performing professionally. Her first radio job was with the powerful *Wheeling* (West Virginia) *Jamboree* as a member of Frankie Moore's Log Cabin Boys. In 1937 she formed the first Kin Folks Band (a name she used for many years for her backup group), broadcasting first out of Louisville. By this time, besides playing fiddle and banjo-guitar, Emmy was also playing a slew of popular instruments, and even handsaw and rubber glove (by slowly releasing air out of an inflated glove, she could play "You Are My Sunshine," a trick she continued to use throughout her career).

Emmy was a loud, raucous performer in the tradition of UNCLE DAVE MACON. She was probably the first female country performer to drop the demure, gingham-and-lace image promoted by the male executives of country radio. She dyed her hair platinum blond, wore bright red lipstick, and dressed in an exaggerated country style. She was unafraid to draw attention to herself and thus forecast the visual style of later performers like DOLLY PARTON.

Emmy moved to St. Louis in 1941, where her local radio broadcasts were heard by a university professor who invited her to participate in his lectures on ancient balladry. In 1947 she made her first impact on the urban FOLK REVIVAL through recordings supervised by noted folklorist ALAN LOMAX, introducing several traditional folk songs into the folk-revival repertoire, including "Free Little Bird" and "I Wish I Was a Single Girl Again."

Emmy appeared in a few B-grade cowboy flicks in the late forties and fifties and also performed at Disneyland. Her adaptation of the traditional banjo song, "Reuben/Train 45," which she called "Ruby (Are You Mad at Your Man?)," was the first hit for the OSBORNE BROTHERS in 1956, establishing that act on the country circuit. In the 1960s, Emmy performed on PETE SEEGER's *Rainbow Quest* television program and made her final LP backed by the old-time revival band, the NEW LOST CITY RAMBLERS, in 1967.

Select Discography
Cousin Emmy with the New Lost City Ramblers, Folkways 31021.

◀ COWBOY SONGS

Although Western literature has been popular in America since the days of James Fenimore Cooper and Zane Grey (right up to today with Louis L'Amour), cowboy songs were discovered by urban America with the publication of JOHN A. LOMAX's *Cowboy Ballads* in 1908, followed by several other collections. Lomax introduced such classics as "Home on the Range" and "Git Along, Little Doggies," providing the backbone for cowboy singers' repertoires for decades to come, and also solidifying the image of the cowboy as a lonesome songster.

Although not in the cowboy mold per se, JIMMIE RODGERS was also influential in developing the cowboy repertoire. His combination of a black, blues-influenced repertoire and vocal style with white sentimental songs and simple GUITAR accompaniments was influential on dozens of country performers, including a young GENE AUTRY, the first "cowboy" star. Rodgers's characteristic Swiss yodel also became an integral part of many cowboy acts, although there is little evidence that cowboys came from Switzerland!

The middle to late thirties saw a blossoming of cowboy and cowgirl acts, influenced by successful movie serials starring Autry and other singing cowboys. These "horse operas," so called because they combined hokey music with fanciful plots of the Old West, were hugely popular in rural America, because they reinforced images of a simpler, happier time when good guys wore white and bad guys were always successfully run out of town. Groups like the SONS OF THE PIONEERS and the GIRLS OF THE GOLDEN SOUTHWEST were two of many who exploited the cowboy imagery and repertory. These bands took thirties and forties vocal harmonies and wed them to cowboy themes, giving the odd impression that the Andrews Sisters might have felt at home working at the O.K. Corral. Even the WESTERN SWING bands, who had previously dressed in natty, uptown clothing, began emphasizing their cowboy connections; Western swinger BOB WILLS even starred in a number of C-grade Westerns in the forties.

With cowboys came cowgirls, particularly the popular PATSY MONTANA and ROSE MADDOX. Montana wore a full-fringed outfit while singing the popular "I Want to Be a Cowboy's Sweetheart," appealing to both male and female listeners.

ROY ROGERS and TEX RITTER would continue the image of the singing cowboy for a new generation on television and in films in the fifties and sixties (Rogers's "Happy Trails" was even covered by sixties heavy-metal rockers Quicksilver Messenger Service). The popularity of Walt Disney's *Davey Crockett* would also further the cowboy myth. Country performers began wearing increasingly flamboyant cowboy garb, culminating in the famous Nudie suits of the sixties with their garish rhinestones, embroidery, and exaggerated flared pants.

The good-guy cowboy of the thirties through fifties gave way to the outlaw cowboy of the seventies, most notably in the music of WILLIE NELSON and WAYLON JENNINGS. Nelson even created a musical tale of the Old West, *Red Headed Stranger*, a song cycle that changed the cowboy image to fit the idea that, in fact, the cowboy lived by his own rules, just as Nelson as SINGER/SONGWRITER refused to obey the "rules" of mainstream Nashville. The early seventies also saw COUNTRY-ROCK bands cut in a cowboy mold, such as the NEW RIDERS OF THE PURPLE SAGE, a Grateful Dead spinoff group that got its name from Roy Rogers's second backup group (who in turn borrowed their name from one of Zane Grey's most popular novels).

The singing cowboy continues to be popular in folk and country circles, although he is more likely to be seen behind the wheel of a pickup truck than on horseback. Folklorist Doug Green has revived a forties-style cowboy combo with the retro band RIDERS IN THE SKY, which has become a popular act on the GRAND OLE OPRY stage. Nearly every male country star appears wearing a cowboy hat as at least a nod to the Western heritage.

◀ CRADDOCK, BILLY "CRASH"

(born 1939, Greensboro, NC)

Craddock got his start in the fifties in ROCKABILLY and teen pop before becoming a country artist in the seventies. He was dubbed "Mr. Country Rock" in the seventies not because he played in the style of the FLYING BURRITO BROTHERS but because he remade fifties and early-sixties rock songs in a country style.

Billy was raised on a farm near Greensboro in relative poverty. When he was eleven his older brother began teaching him GUITAR, and Craddock debuted as part of a country duo during his high-school years, playing with another brother, Ronald. Eventually the duo expanded into a foursome called the Four Rebels, who played rockabilly and upbeat country music. Billy also earned his nickname "Crash" in high school, thanks to his enthusiasm for tackling the opposing team's players on the football field.

In 1959 a field scout for Columbia caught the Four Rebels act and signed Billy to the label. Columbia brought him to Nashville, but instead of recording country or even straight rockabilly, they decided to mold him into a teen idol, in the style of crooners like Fabian. The results were far from awe-inspiring, although fans of rockabilly have rediscovered these recordings today. Oddly enough, Billy's greatest success in this phase of his career was in the Australian market, where he was hailed as the new ELVIS PRESLEY.

After his teen-pop career faded, Craddock returned to North Carolina to work in construction. Although he continued to perform locally, he spent most of the sixties in semiretirement, until a local pharmaceutical manufacturer named Dale Morris caught his act in 1969. Morris enlisted record producer Ron Chancey to engineer Craddock's comeback sessions, released on his own Cartwheel label. Billy's first hit was a countrified version of the old rocker "Knock Three Times," released in 1971, followed by remakes of "Ain't Nothin' Shakin' (but the Leaves on the Trees)" and the teeny-pop ode "Dream Lover."

Craddock's early-seventies success interested ABC Records, who bought out his contract and released his first number-one country hit, the cutesy "Rub It In" in 1974. (Some country stations refused to play this ode to suntan oil because they thought the lyrics referred to another kind of rubbin'; a few years later, Craddock made an answer song "You Rubbed It in All Wrong," and then remade his original hit as an ad jingle for the muscle-soothing compound Absorbine Junior in 1986.) Recognizing a good thing, ABC had him record more rock remakes, including his next number-one, a cover of the Leiber/Stoller classic "Ruby, Baby."

By the mid-seventies, the novelty of doing old pop hits in a country style was wearing thin. Craddock began moving into a more mainstream country style, crafting one final hit with the country WEEPER "Broken Down in Tiny Pieces," featuring background vocals by JANIE FRICKIE, who was then working as a session singer. In 1977 he left ABC Records for Capitol and broke off his relationship with longtime producer Chancey. He managed to score a few more late-seventies hits, beginning with 1978's "I Cheated on a Good Woman's Love" and the saccharine "If I Could Write a Song as Beautiful as You" from a year later. In 1980 he returned to his old pattern of recording rock songs with a remake of "Sea Cruise." He left Capitol in 1982 and recorded an album three years later for Dot. Today he continues to record and perform, primarily focusing on the Australian market, where he remains a living legend.

Select Discography

Billy "Crash" Craddock Sings His Greatest Hits, MCA 663. Cassette-only reissue of his ABC recordings from the seventies.

◀ CRAMER, FLOYD

(born 1933, Shreveport, LA)

If one person can be said to be central to the NASHVILLE SOUND, it would have to be pianist Floyd Cramer, whose slip-note style of playing virtually defines the easy-listening/pop hybrid that dominated Nashville from the late fifties through the mid-sixties. Although CHET ATKINS as a producer crafted the sound, Cramer's presence on literally hundreds of sessions, as well as his own solo hits, solidified it.

Cramer was raised in tiny Huttig, Arkansas, learned piano at the age of five, and first played professionally for local dances while still in high school. He joined the *Louisiana Hayride* radio program as a staff accompanist upon his graduation from high school in 1951. He worked briefly for the Abbott label and then teamed up with Chet Atkins as house pianist at RCA, recording behind a young ELVIS PRESLEY, JIM REEVES, and countless others. Influenced by the GUITAR picking of Mother Maybelle Carter and the piano playing of Don Robertson, he developed his characteristic slip-note style of playing, in which he imitates the sliding from note to note that is possible on guitar or fiddle by hitting one note and almost immediately sliding his finger onto the next key. Like Atkins, Cramer was influenced by the light jazz of fifties acts such as Nat King Cole.

Cramer recorded a number of ROCKABILLY/bluesy titles in the late fifties, including his first hit "Flip, Flop and Bop" issued in 1957. He scored his biggest hits in the early sixties, including 1960's "Last Date," "San Antonio Rose" (a cover of the BOB WILLS classic) and "On the Rebound," both in 1961, and finally "Stood Up" from 1967. In the sixties he made countless recordings of everything from pop-schlock tunes like "Smile" and "My Melody of Love" to covers of HANK WILLIAMS favorites like "Lovesick Blues." He reemerged from obscurity in the late seventies on an album featuring him playing eight different keyboards (through the miracle of overtracking), including synthesizer.

But it is as a studio pianist that Cramer will always be famous. The slightly blue sound of his piano work, which is almost immediately recognizable, is a signature on some of Nashville's best (and, lamentably, also much of its worst).

Select Discography
The Best of Floyd Cramer, RCA Nashville 56322. Tinkling tunes to relieve those weary ol' nerves. Pass the martinis, Billy Bob.

◀ CROWE, J. D.

(born 1937, Lexington, KY)
Crowe is a progressive BANJO player who led one of the most influential BLUE-GRASS bands of the seventies.

Crowe began his career as banjoist in JIMMY MARTIN's country-bluegrass backup band, the Sunnysiders. He quickly established himself as one of the more innovative bluegrass banjo players, with an interest in rock and roll and blues as well as straight country. After leaving Martin, he formed his band, the New South, in the early seventies along with brothers Larry and TONY RICE on GUITAR and MAN-DOLIN, respectively. They signed to Starday in 1973, already playing amplified instruments and drawing on contemporary singer/songwriters for material as well as traditional bluegrass numbers, all the marks of PROGRESSIVE BLUEGRASS playing. Crowe's most influential album was his 1975 debut on Rounder Records, when the band featured Tony Rice on guitar, RICKY SKAGGS on mandolin, JERRY DOUGLAS on DOBRO, and Bobby Slone on fiddle. This album did much to boost Rice's, Skagg's, and Douglas's careers among young bluegrassers, while the band's style influenced countless other progressive outfits.

In the late seventies, KEITH WHITLEY, who had previously performed with Skaggs, joined the band as lead vocalist, and the group began to draw more on a HONKY-TONK repertoire based on Whitley's ability to recreate the sounds and styles of LEFTY FRIZZELL and Lester Flatt. Other important alumni of the New South of this era are Sam Bush and Jimmy Gaudreau.

Crowe rejoined with Tony Rice, along with bluegrass "superstars" Doyle Lawson (guitar, vocals), Bobby Hicks (fiddle), and Todd Phillips (bass) to form an unnamed supergroup that recorded two aptly named "Bluegrass Albums" for Rounder in the mid-eighties. These were straightforward, return-to-roots efforts for these artists, all of whom had achieved fame and fortune in a more progressive arena.

Select Discography
J. D. Crowe and the New South, Rounder 0044. This album, featuring Ricky Skaggs and Tony Rice, was an important and influential seventies release for the progressive bluegrass movement.
You Can Share My Blanket, Rounder 0096. Features Keith Whitley.

◀ CROWELL, RODNEY

(born 1950, Houston, TX)
NEW-COUNTRY SINGER/SONGWRITER Rodney Crowell combines rock, R&B, and HONKY-TONK influences. For a while the husband of ROSANNE CASH, Crowell's career has been spotty; he's never quite made it as a performer, although his songs have

been covered by many new and old country artists, and he's produced a variety of acts.

Crowell performed with his father in a local country bar-band when he was growing up. He moved to Nashville in the mid-seventies in search of a recording career and ended up performing as a lounge singer. In 1975 he was hired by EMMYLOU HARRIS to play in her Hot Band, where he worked for two years not only as a musician but as an arranger; Harris also recorded several of his songs, including "Leaving Louisiana in the Broad Daylight" and "Bluebird Wine." His songs began being covered by country and pop acts, including big names like CRYSTAL GAYLE, JOHNNY CASH, and the OAK RIDGE BOYS; and rocker Bob Seger scored a hit with his "Shame on the Moon," which led to Crowell's solo recording contract in 1977. Two years later he wed Rosanne Cash, with whom he recorded several duets (and for whom he produced several albums), until their marriage ended in the early nineties.

Crowell's albums have always been a grab bag of musical influences; he's even worked with Booker T. Jones (of the famous Memphis soul group, Booker T and the MGs). His music has been described as "country shuffle," and his attitude (as singer and songwriter) is just slightly left of center. Crowell's subjects are typical country ones—loving, losing, leaving, cheating—but are told in a modern, frank way (such as on "I Know You're Married," a flirtatious cheating song). Crowell has also inherited the confessional style of many seventies pop singer/songwriters, documenting his stormy relationships in songs like "Till I Gain Control Again" and "Things I Wish I'd Said," a ballad lamenting the loss of his father.

Select Discography

The Rodney Crowell Collection, Warner Bros. 25965. Selected from his first solo recordings.

Diamonds & Dirt, Columbia 44076. Honky-tonk classics performed with a beefed-up rocking sound.

Life Is Messy, Columbia 47985. 1992 album inspired by Crowell's breakup with wife Rosanne Cash.

◀ CURB, MIKE

(born 1944, Savannah, GA)

Curb has been a wunderkind pop producer, then the leader of the ersatz Mike Curb Congregation, a Nixon-era vocal combo that took the Ray Coniff approach of creating inoffensive, listenable music to new heights (or depths, depending on your point of view). He later became a successful producer of pop-country acts.

Curb first burst onto the musical scene in 1964 as the creator of the Honda jingle, "You Meet the Nicest People on a Honda," forming the ersatz pop group the Hondells to market it as a hit song under the name "Little Honda." He became the "voice of his generation," at least to Madison Avenue and Hollywood types, who discovered he was one of the few young musicians who understood the bucks that could be made out of the craze for youthful sounds. He scored a number of (in)famous Hollywood B-grade youth flicks, including *Wild Angels* and *Riot on*

Sunset Strip before taking over the ailing MGM label in 1970, immediately dropping innovative acts like Frank Zappa and the Velvet Underground and replacing them with the far more successful (although musically repugnant) Donny and MARIE OSMOND. He also started his Mike Curb Congregation, becoming one of the few young groups that President Nixon actually could enjoy.

When he left MGM in the mid-seventies, Curb established his own production company, signing a string of the less-offensive, more pop-oriented country acts, including DEBBIE "You Light Up My Life" BOONE, the BELLAMY BROTHERS, and rockin' country acts like SAWYER BROWN. In the eighties, he was involved with the megasuccess of the JUDDS and set up his own Curb label to promote mainstream country acts.

◀ CURLESS, DICK

(born 1932, Fort Fairfield, ME)

Curless is a northeastern country singer who achieved his greatest success in the mid-sixties with his truck-driving ode "A Tombstone Every Mile." His career has been rather erratic, due to continuing health problems.

The backwoods of Maine have long been strong grounds for country music; like many other northeasterners, Curless was bitten by the then-prevalent COWBOY-SONG bug as a youth. His father was a guitarist who taught him his first chords, and he began playing locally when he was a teenager. When the family relocated to Massachusetts, he gained his own radio show as the Tumbleweed Kid when he was just sixteen and used his high-school graduation money to buy a fancy cowboy suit. When he was eighteen, he moved back to Bangor, Maine, and formed a country-and-western group, the Trail Blazers, to play at local bars.

Drafted into the Korean War, Curless entered a new phase of his career performing on Armed Forces radio as the Rice Paddy Ranger, a kind of cowboy-meets-the-Orient character that he created. He even wrote a cowboy ballad called "China Nights" about the tough conditions in Korea. On his discharge in 1954, he returned to Maine and to performing locally; three years later, he got a big break when he performed MERLE TRAVIS's hit "Nine Pound Hammer" on the *Arthur Godfrey Talent Scouts* show, leading to some work in Vegas and Hollywood. However, ongoing heart troubles led him to retire to Maine a year later, where he worked as a logger before he set out once again to conquer the music world on the West Coast.

Curless's Hollywood days in the early sixties were far from successful, and soon he found himself back in Maine playing the local nightclub circuit. Bangor-based radio personality Dan Fulkerson talked him into recording a truck-driving anthem that he had written ("A Tombstone Every Mile"), and the pair issued the song on their own label, Allagash, in 1965. At the time, TRUCK-DRIVING SONGS were all the rage (thanks to the recordings of DAVE DUDLEY), and the tune became a regional hit, leading to a contract with Capitol's Tower subsidiary. Curless and Fulkerson produced a series of hits in a similar hard-life-on-the-road vein, including "Six Times a Day" (1965), "Tater Raisin' Man" (1966), and "Travelin' Man" (1967). Capitol introduced him to country singer BUCK OWENS, and Curless toured as part of Owens's country extravaganza, the All American Show, performing for two years all across the country.

However, in 1968, his bad health caught up with him, and Curless was forced again into retirement for a year. He returned with yet another trucking anthem a year later, "Hard, Hard Travelin' Man," followed in the early seventies by more gear-crunching numbers, including the colorfully titled "Drag 'Em Off the Interstate, Sock It to 'Em J.P. Blues." Although long off the charts, the baritone-voiced, eye patch–wearing singer continues to have appeal on the club circuit, particularly in his native New England.

◀ CURTIS, SONNY

(born 1937, Meadow, TX)

Curtis has been a star in ROCKABILLY and straight country, best known for his stinging lead GUITAR work and the hit rockin'-country anthems that he composed, including "I Fought the Law."

Originally a session musician working in Lubbock, Texas, Curtis worked out of Nashville in the late fifties in SLIM WHITMAN's backup band. He was called back to Texas by old friends Jerry Allison and Joe Mauldin, the former Crickets, who had returned home after breaking up with BUDDY HOLLY. Curtis joined them under the Crickets name, along with guitarist Glen D. Hardin, and they continued to work in a light, pop-rock style. The new Crickets broke up in 1965, and Curtis became a busy session guitarist, working with everyone from WILLIE NELSON to CRYSTAL GAYLE and, in the eighties, RICKY SKAGGS. A re-formed Crickets led by Curtis and featuring countrified British guitarist ALBERT LEE recorded in the early seventies. The band continues to perform today in various incarnations, often with Curtis at its helm.

Television trivia buffs please note: Curtis also had a career writing jingles and TV theme songs, his most famous composition being "Love Is All Around," the theme from the seventies hit comedy *The Mary Tyler Moore Show*.

Select Discography
The Liberty Years, EMI 95845. Reissue featuring mostly Curtis's teen-pop hits recorded with the Crickets between 1961 and 1971.

◀ CYRUS, BILLY RAY

(born 1961, Flatwoods, KY)

Cyrus, the "achy breaky" kid, has inspired much controversy in country circles, thanks to his hunk-of-the-month looks, gyrating hips, and Michael Bolton–esque hairdo. Attacked by fans of NEW COUNTRY as a flash in the pan, Cyrus may indeed be a one-hit wonder. But he has also proven that savvy marketing, combined with a clever choice of material, can lead to megasuccess.

Cyrus is the grandson of a preacher and began singing in his family's gospel group before attending school. An early enthusiasm for sports led to a baseball scholarship at Georgetown College. He says that, at age twenty, he heard an "inner voice" that urged him to take up music; with his brother he formed a band, Sly

Dog, which played locally in the Kentucky/Ohio region in bars and small-time clubs. A fire destroyed their equipment in 1984, and Cyrus relocated to Los Angeles in search of a movie career. Eventually, he abandoned this plan and relocated to Huntington, West Virginia, where he returned to singing in local clubs. He would travel to Nashville in his free time, persistently visiting every agent and publisher who would give him the time of day. He finally hooked up with promoter Jack McFadden, who got him a job opening for REBA McENTIRE, leading to his contract with Mercury Records.

Cyrus's rush up the pop and country charts in 1991 is an example of canny marketing on the part of Mercury's PR department. They decided they would launch his first single, "Achy Breaky Heart," by introducing a new line dance, the Achy Breaky, in country dance clubs. These clubs have become popular in big cities and small towns alike and are a natural place to reach country fans. The dance paved the way for the song, which was also accompanied by an excellent video that showed Cyrus performing in a torn T-shirt while dancers enthusiastically performed the new steps. Thanks to exposure on VH-1 and other mainstream video channels, Cyrus achieved success on the pop charts as well as in country circles.

Cyrus's rather limited voice, and his often schlocky material, made his debut album an easy shot for critics of the new Nashville's tendency to prepackage any good-looking singer into the latest fad. Even other new country stars, like TRAVIS TRITT, attacked Billy Ray's gyrating stage presence (while at the same time Tritt himself took to wearing tight leather pants) on the basis that Billy Ray was not a true country star. His patriotic gut-thumper "Some Gave All," a revisionist look at the Vietnam War, was the album's second, though minor, hit, reminding us that Billy Ray was catering to the more conservative spectrum of the country audience.

The debate over whether Cyrus belongs in the country or pop category reveals how much new country has been influencing the pop charts, and also the strength of country marketing in the more traditional pop and rock markets. Cyrus will probably disappear quickly (his 1993 second album has been less successful than his first outing), due to a lack of real talent to go along with his hunky looks. But as an example of successful marketing, Cyrus will continue to influence the way record companies, radio, and video channels package future country stars.

Select Discography

Some Gave All, Mercury 510635. The album that started the craze.

It Won't Be the Last, Mercury 514758. More muscle-pumping music from the he-man country star.

D.

◀ DAFFAN, TED

(born Theron Eugene Daffan, 1912, Beauregard, LA)

Daffan was an early steel guitarist and HONKY-TONK songsmith who is best remembered for his 1939 hit, "Truck Drivin' Blues," introducing the trucker as a country-music hero.

Born in Louisiana, Daffan was raised in Houston, where from a young age he developed a keen interest in electronics, leading him to open one of the first electric musical-instrument repair shops. The newly introduced electric steel guitar was particularly fascinating to the young musician/engineer; he even formed an amateur Hawaiian-style band called the Blue Islanders to play local gigs so he could practice. WESTERN SWING star MILTON BROWN patronized Daffan's shop and also convinced him to become a full-time musician. Daffan first worked with the Blue Ridge Playboys, led by guitarist FLOYD TILLMAN, in 1934.

Daffan's songwriting career got off to a good start with "Truck Drivin' Blues," a big hit for Western swing bandleader Cliff Bruner, who featured Texas honky-tonk singer MOON MULLICAN as his lead vocalist. This led to a contract with Columbia for Daffan and his band, the Texans, and to their 1940 hit "Worried Mind." This song was followed by similar bluesy numbers, mostly on the themes of lovin', losin', and leavin', classic honky-tonk topics. These include 1943's WEEPER "Born to Lose," the good-ol'-boy-gone-bad song "Headin' Down the Wrong Highway" (1945), and the fine jump number "I've Got Five Dollars and It's Saturday Night" (1950). After World War II, he briefly had a steady job at the Venice Pier Ballroom near Los Angeles, but in 1946 he returned to Houston.

In the fifties, Daffan's career as a performer slowed down, even though he continued to write hits in the beer-soaked style that made him famous. In 1958 he joined forces in Nashville with Canadian HANK SNOW to form a publishing company, and he turned his attention to the business side of songwriting and promotion. He returned to Houston in 1961 to continue working on the business side of the industry. That same year, Joe Barry had a million-selling hit with a remake of Daffan's "I'm A Fool to Care," previously recorded about a decade earlier by LES PAUL and Mary Ford.

◀ DALHART, VERNON

(born Marion Try Slaughter, 1883, Jefferson, TX; died 1948)

Dalhart was one of country's first superstars, cutting over five thousand 78 rpm records, although because of his highly trained voice he is an acquired taste at best for the true fan of country music.

Dalhart was the son of a rancher who worked the rich land of northeastern Texas. Young Slaughter worked as a cowhand in the region, but his true love was for the light classical and operatic music of the day. He entered the Dallas Conservatory of Music and then moved to New York, landing a job with the Century Opera Company in 1913. He took his stage name from the names of two tiny Texas towns, Vernon and Dalhart, where he had worked as a cowpoke.

Dalhart first recorded as a popular tenor, not a country singer, beginning with the Edison label in 1916 and then moving to Victor, using over a hundred pseudonyms. He did everything from comic novelties to "darkie" dialect disks to light classics, without much success. Then, in 1924, he recorded "The Wreck of the Old 97," which he learned from the rough, backwoodsy recording made a year earlier by blind fiddler HENRY WHITTIER. The record would sell over twenty-five million copies over the next two decades, becoming the first big country music hit. It was backed by "The Prisoner's Song," the sentimental number Dalhart would re-record several more times, earning, it is said, over a million dollars in composer's royalties.

Dalhart's heyday was between 1925 and 1931. He worked with several accompanists, beginning with CARSON ROBINSON (who accompanied him on GUITAR and supplied many of his better songs) and fiddler ADELYNE HOOD, and then, when Robinson went out on his own, guitarist FRANK LUTHER. His repertoire was made up of what the record companies termed "old familiar tunes"—that is to say, a smattering of traditional songs along with popular songs of the late nineteenth and early twentieth century, along with topical numbers, such as the ever-popular "Death of Floyd Collins" (written by Robinson). He sang with an exaggerated hillbilly twang, although to modern ears he hardly sounds like a country singer; his mainstream training shines through even when he tries to put on an aw-shucks, backwoodsman's act.

The Depression put a crimp in Dalhart's career, although he continued to record through 1939, when he made his final records for the budget Bluebird label. Meanwhile, his earlier records were reissued on various budget labels, sold both by dime stores and the popular mail-order catalogs that reached thousands of rural Americans. In the forties, Dalhart relocated to Bridgeport, Connecticut, where he eventually became a hotel clerk; he died of a heart attack in 1948.

Select Discography

"The Wreck of the Old 97" and Other Early Country Hits, Old Homestead 167. Out-of-print album reissuing some of Dalhart's best-loved country material, with excellent annotation.

◀ DALTON, LACY J.

(born Jill Byrem, 1948, Bloomsburg, PA)

A former folk-rocker who has had a long and bumpy career, Dalton's music emphasizes her working-class background and the difficulties women face in a man's world.

Dalton comes from a solid working-class background in the midst of rural Pennsylvania. Her father was a sometime mechanic, sometime hunting guide, while her mother worked as both a beautician and waitress. Both were active amateur country musicians, giving their child an early indoctrination in country balladry. Interested in art during her high-school years, Dalton enrolled at Brigham Young University as an art major; she lasted only a year and a half in school and then began performing with a friend in local coffeehouses. She passed through Minnesota, returned home to Pennsylvania, and then headed out to California, where she fronted a folk-rock band called the Office, managed by her future husband, John Croston.

The band never really took off, despite some record label interest, and Dalton's personal life went on the skids when her husband was paralyzed in a freak accident; after a few painful months, he died. Dalton was left pregnant and unemployed in Santa Cruz. Although she continued to play her music, she had to fill in with many menial jobs.

In 1978 Dalton recorded an album in a friend's garage; she was able to sell locally about three thousand copies. A local deejay passed a copy along to Columbia Records, where her songwriting abilities impressed veteran country producer BILLY SHERRILL. Sherrill suggested a name change, and Jill Byrem became Lacy J. (for Jill) Dalton; the last name came from a singer she admired, Karen Dalton. With a husky voice somewhat reminiscent of the bluesy style of rocker Janis Joplin, she did not fit exactly into the country mold; but the country charts were ripe for something new, and her first single, 1978's "Crazy Blue Eyes," which she also cowrote, was moderately successful. Her 1980 remake of the hoary old chestnut "Tennessee Waltz" was a bigger hit.

Through the eighties, Dalton produced a body of work centering on a number of concept albums, often dealing with the difficulty that the rural poor, particularly females, face in making a living. This streak began with 1980's "Hard Times" and included her 1986 album *Highway Diner* with its hit "Working Class Man," and 1989's *Survivor* with the title song, "I'm a Survivor." (Between 1986 and 1989, Dalton struggled to overcome a growing problem with alcoholism.) It's unusual for country songs, particularly those performed by female performers, to be so directly autobiographical and topical; in this way, Dalton considerably broadened the palate of material available to women in country music.

Select Discography

Survivor, Liberty 94059.

Greatest Hits, Columbia 38883. Billy Sherrill–produced hits from the early eighties.

◀ DANIELS, CHARLIE

(born 1943, Wilmington, NC)

Daniels is a flashy fiddler who leads a solid COUNTRY-ROCK band. He is best known for his 1979 country/pop hit, "The Devil Went Down to Georgia."

Raised in rural North Carolina, Daniels played fiddle and GUITAR in a number of amateur country and BLUEGRASS bands before turning professional at age twenty-one. His first group was a rock-and-roll instrumental ensemble called the Jaguars, who recorded in 1959 under the hand of producer Bob Johnston, later a leading country and folk producer for Columbia Records. The group had been together in one form or another for eight years when Johnston urged Daniels to come to Nashville to work as a session musician and songwriter (Daniels had already placed one song, "It Hurts Me," with ELVIS PRESLEY). Daniels sessioned on a number of landmark recordings, including BOB DYLAN's *Nashville Skyline*, and toured with folkie poet Leonard Cohen. He also served as producer for the folk-rock group the Youngblood's *Elephant's Memory* album.

After recording a solo album for Capitol, Daniels formed his Charlie Daniels Band in 1972, inspired by the success of the Allman Brothers. Daniels played lead guitar (and occasional fiddle) along with Don Murray (aping the twin-guitar approach of the Allmans), Joe DiGregorio played keyboards, Charlie Hayward bass, and Don Murray drums (he was replaced six years later by Charlie Marshall). Their first big hit was "Uneasy Rider," a 1973 recording that told of a hippie who accidentally strayed into a back-country bar, with the "rednecks" the butt of the joke. (In 1988 Daniels remade the number for his country audience, now casting the hippie as an honest "good old boy" who wanders into a gay bar.) A year later, they had another hit with the gut-thumping anthem "The South's Gonna Do It."

By the end of the seventies, it was clear that the rock audience was turning away from Southern bands, so Daniels shifted into a more country-oriented direction. His biggest hit in this mold was 1979's "The Devil Went Down to Georgia," full of flashy fiddle effects (not played by Daniels on record), along with the requisite pounding beat and screeching lead guitar to appeal to his core rock audience. The song was an enormous hit and remains the number most closely associated with him today.

Through the eighties, Daniels increasingly aligned himself with the core country audience, although he failed to produce a follow-up to his megahit. By the end of the decade, he was recording anthems advocating lynching as a cure for social ills and calling for the assassination of Gorbachev. Luckily, these numbers received little airplay, even on conservative country radio.

Daniels was recently invited to remake "The Devil" with master fiddler MARK O'CONNOR, featuring TRAVIS TRITT singing the lead role. A miniseries, no doubt, will follow.

Select Discography

A Decade of Hits, Epic 38795. All the songs you remember, and a bunch you don't, too.

◖ DARBY AND TARLETON

(Tom Darby [guitar, vocals]; Johnny James Rimbert "Jimmy" Tarleton [steel guitar, vocals])

Darby and Tarleton were a legendary country duo of the twenties, particularly loved for Jimmy Tarleton's expressive and exquisite steel GUITAR playing, which had great influence on the next generation of pickers.

The duo worked in South Carolina's textile mills. Tarleton was undoubtedly the more talented of the pair; early on, he took up the BANJO but could play many instruments well. A fine singer with a clear voice, he apparently traveled around the country performing, covering lots of ground between South Carolina, New York, and California. He first began playing guitar with a bottleneck slide in the blues style popular in the South, but then he met a Hawaiian guitarist when he was bumming around the West Coast at the time of World War I, and he quickly adopted novelty effects from that musical style.

Exactly when and where Darby and Tarleton met and first performed together is unknown. In April 1927, the duo made their first recordings for Columbia Records in New York, with Darby playing guitar and singing lead vocals and Tarleton on steel guitar and providing tenor harmonies. At their second recording session, also held in 1927, the duo recorded two traditional folk-blues numbers ("Birmingham Jail" and "Columbus Stockade Blues") both arranged by Tarleton, who received a seventy-five-dollar arranger's fee for the two numbers, which have since become folk and country standards.

The duo continued to record together through the early thirties for a variety of labels, until the Depression caused a slump in the country-music industry. Tarleton also recorded without Darby. Their brand of bluesy duets was quite influential on later brother acts, from the ALLEN BROTHERS to the DELMORE BROTHERS.

Select Discography

Sing the Blues, Old Timey 112. Out-of-print album reissuing their twenties and thirties recordings.

◖ DAVE AND SUGAR

(1975–1982)

Dave and Sugar was country music's mid-seventies answer to Tony Orlando and Dawn: a smooth vocal trio singing mainstream pop numbers to a soft-rock accompaniment.

Dave Rowlands was a California-born vocalist who got his first professional work touring with a later version of the vocal quartet the Four Guys. After working as a session vocalist, he was hired as a backup singer to tour with CHARLEY PRIDE, which was his first job working in a country format. Recognizing the popularity of country in the mid-seventies, and admiring the music of other mainstream COUNTRYPOLITAN singers like KENNY ROGERS and BARBARA MANDRELL, he formed his first Dave and Sugar trio with backup singers Vicki Hackman and Jackie Franc (other female session singers would take the role of Sugar over the years). Their second record, 1976's "The Door Is Always Open," was a number-one country hit, and it opened the door to more light-pop offerings, including 1977's "I'm Knee Deep in Loving You" and their final number one, 1979's "Golden Tears" (the kind true country fans shed when they heard this record).

The hits dried up after the trio switched to Elektra Records in 1981 (just as the countrypolitan boom was waning). A few years later, Dave hit the trail as a solo vocalist, touring with other stars of seventies country, including HELEN CORNELIUS. He can still be heard occasionally in supper clubs.

◀ DAVIES, GAIL

(born Patricia Gail Dickerson, 1948, Broken Bow, OK)

Davies is a SINGER/SONGWRITER who had her biggest country hits in the late seventies and early eighties. Somewhat ahead of her time, Davies brought a rootsy California sound and a feminist sensibility to her country music, similar in style to the recordings of LINDA RONSTADT and EMMYLOU HARRIS.

Davies was born the daughter of an amateur country singer/guitarist who performed in the manner of ERNEST TUBB. Her parents split when she was five, due to her father's increasing alcoholism, and her mother took her and her two brothers to Washington State, where she married Darby Allan Davies. Along with her brother Ron (later a successful pop songwriter who wrote "Long Hard Climb" for Helen Reddy and "It Ain't Easy" for Three Dog Night) Gail began performing in a country-rock vein as a teenager. The duo relocated to Los Angeles and recorded an LP that was never released. In L.A., Davies met and married a jazz musician and began singing in that style.

In the mid-seventies, Davies returned to country songwriting and performing. Encouraged by the more progressive country songwriters, such as HOYT AXTON and movie-star-turned-singer Ronnee Blakely, Davies began performing on L.A.'s country circuit. Deemed too traditional for the more progressive L.A. clubs, she went to Nashville in 1975, where her music was rejected as too pop! Finally, though, she was signed to Epic/Lifesong in 1978 and released her first LP, a mixture of original compositions and country classics, a year later.

Davies's songs were unusual because they combined a country sensibility with an ambivalence toward the difficulties of growing up in a country household. "Bucket to the South," her best song from this period, relates her ambivalent feelings toward her father, who was a role model as a guitarist but unreliable as a parent. She also had a hit with her remake of the classic fifties tearjerker, "Poison Love." Further hits followed in the early eighties, including "Blue Heartache," "It's a Lovely, Lovely World," and "Singin' the Blues." Unlike more mainstream country female acts, who were still dressing in gingham and lace, Davies projected a more relaxed image, with a wardrobe that looked like it came out of her closet rather than from a costume studio.

Davies also recorded two of country's first feminist concept albums, 1982's *Givin' Herself Away* and 1984's *Where Is a Woman to Go?*—again featuring a combination of original songs and covers. These LPs were way ahead of their time in expressing the woman's side of often difficult issues, and as they drew on a wider repertoire of songwriters, including folk-rocker Joni Mitchell.

In 1985 Davies formed the brief-lived Wild Choir, a country/rock band that showed the influence of British punk-country artists like Nick Lowe and Elvis Costello. After their album went belly up, Davies struggled on as a solo artist, before being hired as one of the first female NEW-COUNTRY producers.

Although Davies was ahead of her time as an artist, many of the new country stars of the nineties continue to cite her work as performer and producer as influential on their sound. Too country to be as successful on the pop charts as Ronstadt, and too pop to be successful on the then more conservative country charts, Davies pointed the way for an entire army of female singers who would address women's issues more honestly. She continues to perform, appearing at Opryland and on country music television and occasionally tours.

Select Discography

Best of Gail Davies, Liberty 94453. Early-eighties recordings originally released on Capitol.

Pretty Words, MCA 42274. 1989 comeback attempt.

◀ DAVIS, DANNY

(born George Nowlan, 1925, Randolph, MA)

In the annals of country music, many names must share the shame of having taken a sharp detour down the road of crass commercialism. At the head of the class stands Danny Davis, who created and directed the Nashville Brass, who contributed to many of the worst excesses of the NASHVILLE SOUND era.

Davis was raised and nurtured on the classics; his mother was an operatic coach, and the family lived in a toney Boston suburb. Young Davis performed classical trumpet, earning a place as a soloist in the Massachusetts All-State Symphony at age fourteen. He entered the New England Conservatory of Music a year later but was lured away from classical music by big-band star Gene Krupa, who offered him a seat in his orchestra. This led to several years of big-band work.

In the fifties, Danny worked as a session musician, eventually working his way up into record producing. He had a solo hit with the pop-ish "Trumpet Cha Cha Cha," which highlighted the melodic, vocally oriented style he had developed. Davis was hired by RCA Records in 1965, where he originally worked with smoky balladeers like Nina Simone. CHET ATKINS, who was head of Nashville A&R (Artists & Repertoire), hired Davis as a producer. With his knowledge of brass instruments, Davis was soon adding ersatz horn sections to RCA's Nashville product. Enjoying the results, he approached Atkins with the idea of turning out some all-instrumental albums featuring brass instruments in the lead.

The result was a series of successful albums credited to the Nashville Brass. These horn-blowin' cowpokes had a hit out of the box with 1969's cover of the HANK WILLIAMS classic "I Saw the Light" followed by "The Wabash Cannonball." A blend of harmless Muzak and all-out drek, the Brass continued to produce hit instrumentals through the seventies, while also earning a seat in kitsch heaven as regular visitors to the lounges of Vegas.

◀ DAVIS, JIMMIE

(born 1902, Beech Springs, LA)

Davis is a country SINGER/SONGWRITER and one-time governor of Louisiana who has had a career that could only happen in country music. He began as a JIMMIE RODGERS imitator, moved into hokum and off-color material, then became a well-known songwriter of sentimental songs ("You Are My Sunshine") and, in a final twist, took up gospel singing.

Davis comes from a rural background, but he is a highly educated man, with B.A. and M.A. degrees and experience working as a college professor in the twenties. Because of his country roots, and his pleasant voice, he was invited in the late twenties by a radio station out of Shreveport to sing old-time songs, which lead to a performing career and recording contract with Victor Records. Davis's first phase of recording, from 1929 to 1934, featured a mix of sentimental "heart" songs and bluesy numbers sung in the manner of Rodgers; he also recorded so-called "hokum" blues (double-entendre songs) such as "Tom Cat and Pussy Blues" and "She's a Hum Dum Dinger," often accompanied by black country blues guitarists, including Oscar Woods.

In 1934 Davis moved to Decca and took on a singing cowboy persona. Davis is said to have cowritten many of his thirties hits, although some of these claims may be exaggerations, but he was certainly the first artist to record many songs that have become country standards, from 1934's "Nobody's Darlin' but Mine" to 1938's "(I Don't Worry 'Cause) It Makes No Difference Now" to 1940's "You Are My Sunshine."

During World War II, Davis moved into politics, serving one term as governor of Louisiana and returning to office in 1960. In between, he became increasingly involved in publishing and business concerns. When he did record, he turned to gospel material, although he had a minor hit with the hokey narrative "Suppertime." His sixties and seventies recordings were almost entirely gospel. In 1969 he married Anna Carter, an alum of the CHUCK WAGON GANG, a well-known country gospel group. Despite failing health, he continued to perform into the eighties.

Select Discography

Rockin' Blues, Bear Family 15125; *Barnyard Stomp*, Bear Family 15285. Two LPs reissuing Davis's early recordings from between 1929 and 1933, particularly focusing on "blue" and risqué material.

Country Music Hall of Fame, MCA 10087. Cross-section of his Decca-label recordings.

◀ DAVIS, MAC

(born 1941, Lubbock, TX)

Davis is a country-pop songwriter and performer who also enjoyed some suc-cess as a television and movie actor. His good-natured personality made him a natural for a mainstream performing career during the seventies boom in easy-listening pop-country music known as COUNTRYPOLITAN.

Born in BUDDY HOLLY's hometown, Davis was raised by his uncle on a ranch and first sang as a member of the church choir. By his teen years, he had been bitten by the rock bug and was performing with friends in local pop-rock groups. In his late teens, he moved to Atlanta, where he worked for the Georgia Board of Probation by day while attending college at night, still performing rock and roll with local amateur groups. He got into the promotion end of the business when he was hired by the Chicago-based R&B label Vee Jay to be their Atlanta repre-sentative in 1962, and then by the country-pop label Liberty in 1965. In 1967 he moved to Liberty's music-publishing arm, Metric Music, based in Los Angeles, where he began working as a song plugger. In this capacity, he began pushing his own songs, placing two with Lou Rawls and GLEN CAMPBELL.

Davis's big break came when he placed his own "A Little Less Conversation" with ELVIS PRESLEY in 1968. The song enjoyed some success, so much so that Presley requested a follow-up, and Davis delivered what would become his first smash pop hit, "In the Ghetto." This began a string of Davis-penned songs that had a gritty reality, mostly recorded by blue-eyed soulsters, including two more songs for Elvis ("Memories" and "Don't Cry Daddy"); two songs for O. C. Smith; the maudlin "Watching Scotty Grow," recorded by Bobby Goldsboro; and KENNY ROGERS and the First Edition's "Something's Burning."

In 1970 Davis decided to promote his own performing career and began to get jobs appearing on TV talk shows and playing in Vegas. He was signed to Columbia Records, producing his first album in 1971. He had a string of hits in the early seventies in what would today be called a middle-of-the-road pop style, from "Be-ginning to Feel the Pain" and "I Believe in Music" in 1971 through 1973's "Ev-erybody Loves a Love Song."

Davis dropped off the pop charts by the mid-seventies but continued to have country hits, including "I Still Love You (You Still Love Me)" and "Picking Up the Pieces of My Life," both in 1977. At the same time, he appeared on a number of televised variety-show specials that drew large ratings, mostly thanks to his affable personality. In 1979 he appeared in the movie *North Dallas Forty*, enjoying some critical success, and it looked like a film career loomed on the horizon.

However, both Davis's music and movie careers fizzled in the eighties. Although a likeable sidekick in films, he was unable to carry a film by himself as a leading man. His appearance with Jackie Gleason in the big-budget flop *The Sting II* effec-tively ended his Hollywood career. Meanwhile, his older-style countrypolitan sound was being displaced by a return-to-roots country; but he still had a few more hits, including 1980's "It's Hard to Be Humble" and "Texas in My Rear View Mir-ror." Although he remains a popular performer, he now rarely cracks the charts.

He made something of a comeback as coauthor, with DOLLY PARTON, of her 1990 hit, "White Limozeen." He also appeared in the early nineties on Broadway as Will Rogers in the popular revue *The Will Rogers Follies*.

Davis showed one way that country music could survive the bleak pop-music landscape of the seventies: by marrying pop's use of glitzy backup singers and middle-of-the-road accompaniments to some of the gritty emotions that always made country music powerful; however, his initial compositions for other artists stood out from other pop songs thanks to their almost menacing realism, while his later songs lapsed into the kind of gooey sentimentality and fear of offending that makes for the worst in mainstream commercial music.

Select Discography

Greatest Hits, Columbia 36317. The mid-seventies hits.

◀ DAVIS, SKEETER

(born Mary Frances Penick, 1931, Dry Ridge, KY)

A sometimes controversial Opry star of the sixties, Davis began her career in ROCKABILLY and became one of the leading purveyors of the NASHVILLE SOUND, often performing the kind of pathetic, tear-soaked numbers that characterized Nashville's view of women in preliberation days.

Davis took her stage name in high school when she performed with a friend named Betty Jack Davis in a vocal duo known as the Davis Sisters. They were discovered after appearing on the *Kentucky Barn Dance* radio show out of Lexington, which led to further radio work in Detroit and Cincinnati and finally a contract with RCA in the early fifties. They scored big with 1953's "I Forgot More than You'll Ever Know," but, in the same year, following a performance they were involved in a severe car crash that took Betty Jack's life and severely injured Skeeter. After her recovery, Skeeter worked for a while with Betty Jack's sister Georgia but then went out on her own.

Skeeter had several early-sixties hits, mostly in the form of the then-popular women's answer song, which responded to hits by male stars. 1960's "(I Can't Help You) I'm Fallin' Too" is, of course, an answer to HANK LOCKLIN's big number "Please Help Me I'm Falling"; and 1961's "My Last Date (with You)" was a reply to FLOYD CRAMER's "Last Date." Both responses were written by Davis. Her biggest hit came in 1962 with "The End of the World," followed by the crossover pop hit "I Can't Stay Mad at You" a year later. In these songs, Skeeter expressed the kind of men-will-ramble-and-women-must-suffer sentiments that make her the first in a line of long-suffering country women who were not exactly role models of liberation.

After a brief flirtation with the pop charts, Davis had a couple more country hits, including duets with BOBBY BARE on 1965's "A Dear John Letter" and 1971's "Your Husband, Your Wife." She also recorded with PORTER WAGONER and GEORGE HAMILTON IV. Always a religious person, she began having her agent write into her contracts that she would not perform where liquor was being served (she didn't want her fans tempted into sin). Meanwhile, she established herself as a Nashville outlaw by touring with the Rolling Stones during the sixties and denouncing the Nashville Police for brutality from the stage of the GRAND OLE OPRY in 1973.

Davis has returned to performing since her marriage to Joey Stampinato, the bass player of roots-rock ensemble NRBQ, with a new emphasis on the harder-rocking side of her personality.

Select Discography

Memories, Bear Family 15722. Two CDs bringing you all sixty recordings made by the Davis sisters along with live cuts, radio appearances, and alternate takes. Includes a lavishly illustrated booklet by Bob Allen and Colin Escott.

Best of Skeeter Davis, Hollywood 206. Cassette-only reissue of her sixties-era recordings.

She Sings, They Play, Rounder 3092. Recorded in 1986 with backup by NRBQ; a rockin' collection of remakes.

◀ DEAN, EDDIE

(born Edgar Dean Glossup, 1907, Posey, TX)

Dean was a minor cowboy star of the forties who is best remembered for coauthoring "I Dreamed of a Hillbilly Heaven," still a kitsch classic.

Dean originally was a gospel singer who worked with a number of popular quartets before he hooked up with his brother Jimmy (not to be confused with the sausage maker) to form a thirties-style brother act. They ended up on the popular *National Barn Dance* show out of Chicago through the thirties, and Eddie even enjoyed a stint on the radio soap opera *Modern Cinderella*, which also originated from the Windy City.

The brothers went to Hollywood in 1937 in search of fame and fortune on the B-film circuit, initially finding work in films with cowboy star GENE AUTRY; Eddie also performed for a while as a member of JUDY CANOVA's radio company. Between 1946 and 1948, Eddie made some twenty films for one of the lesser assembly-line producers of cowpoke dramas.

In the fifties, Dean pursued a singing career with a number of labels, but big hits eluded him. Besides "Hillbilly Heaven," he cowrote "One Has My Name, the Other Has My Heart," and had minor hits with "On the Banks of the Sunny San Juan" and "No Vacancy." Dean was still active through the sixties and seventies on the California country circuit and occasionally issued a record on small, local labels.

◀ DEAN, JIMMY

(born Seth Ward, 1928, near Plainview, TX)

Dean had a series of melodramatic hits in the early sixties and also a successful career on television. He is now more famous for his sausage than his music.

Dean was born to a poor, one-parent household; his father had abandoned his mother, who managed a local barbershop to make ends meet. As a child, Dean worked as a field hand, although he showed an early interest in music, learning in rapid succession piano, GUITAR, accordion, and harmonica. Like many other rural Southerners, the military served as an escape from his impoverished family life. He also discovered he could make a few extra bucks on the side performing in the many small bars and clubs that catered to the military bases. While in the service in the late forties, he formed his first group, the Tennessee Haymakers.

By 1953 Jimmy was located in Arlington, Virginia, performing with a new backup band, the Texas Wildcats. They recorded "Bummin' Around," his first single to gain national attention. Two years later, he was hosting a local television program that caught the eye of the CBS network and in 1957 they launched a morning show hosted by Dean; but the program died due to its lack of a national sponsor.

In 1961 Dean signed with Columbia Records, where he enjoyed his greatest success. His first hit was the self-composed "Big Bad John," a mock-ballad that told the story of a back country hell-raiser. One year later, he scored again with "P.T. 109," a patriotic anthem describing the exploits of John F. Kennedy during World War II.

Dean's good-natured, backwoodsy appeal brought him a second television contract, this time with ABC, where he remained through the mid-sixties. Although he continued to record for various labels through the mid-seventies, his career was increasingly more that of a TV personality rather than a country musician. Lately he's best known for his line of country sausage that he personally promotes through radio and TV ads.

Select Discography

Greatest Hits, Columbia 09285. Cassette-only reissue of his early-sixties platters.

◀ DELMORE BROTHERS, THE

(Alton [guitar, vocals] born 1908, Elkmont, AL; died 1964; Rabon [tenor guitar, vocals] born 1910, Elkmont, AL; died 1952)

One of the greatest of the brother acts of the thirties and forties, the Delmores combined a country-blues approach with innovative GUITAR work. Their thirties recordings were fairly sparse in approach, but in the late forties and early fifties they produced recordings that forecast the ROCKABILLY sound.

The brothers were raised on a farm where their mother, "Aunt" Mollie Delmore, taught them the rudiments of fiddling. They won a fiddlers' contest in 1930 but soon switched to guitars, with Rabon playing the tenor guitar (with four strings tuned like a tenor banjo, this instrument has a smaller body and a sweeter tone than a standard guitar). The brothers began recording for Columbia in 1931 and joined the GRAND OLE OPRY in 1932, remaining there until 1938. Their first recordings already showed great maturity, with their close, uninflected harmonies, great bluesy material (including "Brown's Ferry Blues," "Gonna Lay Down My Old Guitar," and "Nashville Blues"), and Rabon's lead guitar work, which forecast the style of later pickers like DOC WATSON.

In 1944 the brothers began recording in an even bluesier style for King Records out of Cincinnati, often accompanied by electric guitars and string bass. Their 1949 recording of "Blues Stay Away From Me" was a smash country hit, staying on the charts for twenty-three weeks. These recordings were highly influential on the next generation of rockabilly/rockin' country stars, particularly the young CARL PERKINS. The Delmores also worked with MERLE TRAVIS and GRANDPA JONES during this period as the Browns Ferry Four, which concentrated on R&B-influenced music.

In the early fifties, the Delmores based their act in Houston, but the group began to disintegrate after the death of Alton's daughter, Sharon. He never recovered, and he became a heavy drinker. Rabon, meanwhile, developed lung cancer and returned to Alabama to die in 1952. Alton later worked as a traveling salesman and part-time guitar teacher before his death due to alcoholism twelve years later.

The Delmores, like the ALLEN BROTHERS before them, were one of the first country acts to integrate a blues sound in their performances. Unlike other brother acts of the era who emphasized sweetly sentimental material, the Delmores dipped heavily into black traditions. Their powerful twin-guitar work also set them apart from other duos, who mostly played in a more laid-back style (and usually featured a MANDOLIN as the melody or lead instrument). Although their vocals sound almost deadpan today, they have a sly sense of humor that shines through even the most maudlin of their recordings.

Select Discography

Brown's Ferry Blues, County 402. Out-of-print album reissuing their great recordings of 1933 to 1941.

Sand Mountain Blues, County 110. Up-tempo country-boogie recordings originally issued by the King label between 1944 and 1949.

Freight Train Boogie, Ace 455. Their post–World War II King recordings; ha cha!

◀ DEMENT, IRIS

(born 1961, Paragould, AR)

A kind of backwoods NANCI GRIFFITH, DeMent is another folk-styled SINGER/SONGWRITER who has been lumped into the NEW-COUNTRY category.

Born in rural Arkansas to a farm family, DeMent's family moved to Southern California when she was just three. Both parents were deeply religious, performing in the church choir and only allowing gospel music to be played around the house. As DeMent recalled in a magazine interview, "My parents pretty much stuck to gospel music. If JOHNNY CASH did a gospel album, they'd buy that." Her father was also a fiddler, and her older siblings formed a family gospel group called the DeMent Sisters.

DeMent played gospel music on the piano and sang in the church choir like her brothers and sisters until she left home at age twenty-five. Relocating to Kansas City, she began playing the GUITAR and writing songs, many based on her memories of her musical family, including "Mama's Opry," "After They're Gone," and "Our Town." A demo tape of her songs was given to John Prine, who recommended that she come to Nashville. After a few showcase performances, she was signed to Philo/Rounder and recorded her first album with producer JIM ROONEY, who had previously guided Griffith's recording career. DeMent's folk-edged, homespun sound was an immediate hit with critics, and major label Warner Brothers quickly signed her and rereleased the album, beginning a media blitz for the young star.

Select Discography

Infamous Angel, Philo 1138. This album was originally released in 1992 and then reissued by Warners a year later (Warner Bros. 45238).

My Life, Warner Bros. 45493. 1994 release with a star-studded supporting cast.

◀ DENVER, JOHN

(born Henry John Deutschendorf, 1943, Roswell, NM)

Denver is a folk-country SINGER/SONGWRITER who had his greatest success in the mid-seventies with his back-to-nature hymns "Rocky Mountain High" and "Thank God I'm a Country Boy." Denver's bland tenor vocals and golly-gosh manners have made him popular both in films and as a middle-of-the-road popster.

Denver was the son of a career air force pilot. In the early sixties he performed with the Chad Mitchell Trio, one of the more topically oriented of the FOLK-REVIVAL groups. In 1965 he replaced leader Chad Mitchell in the group, continuing to record with them until 1969, when the trio dissolved. Denver was then signed to RCA as a solo artist and recorded his first album, which combined self-penned satirical songs attacking then-president Nixon and the war in Vietnam, along with his sentimental pop songs like "Leaving on a Jet Plane," which had been a hit for Peter, Paul and Mary.

Denver's big break came in 1971 with his recording of "Take Me Home, Country Roads," followed by a string of country-flavored pop hits, including the sappy ballad "Annie's Song" and the enthusiastically uptempo "Thank God I'm a Country Boy." Denver began a film-acting career in 1977, showing himself to be an affable comedian. He continued to record his own material through the mid-eighties with limited success, forming his own label later to promote his country album *Higher Ground* in 1988.

Select Discography

Rocky Mountain High, RCA 5190. The album that started it all.

◀ DESERT ROSE BAND, THE

(Chris Hillman [vocals, guitar, mandolin]; Herb Pederson [vocals, guitar, banjo]; John Jorgenson [vocals, lead guitar]; Bill Bryson [bass]; J. D. Maness [pedal steel guitar]; Steve Duncan [drums])

The latest in a long and distinguished line of California COUNTRY-ROCK bands, Desert Rose is the first to enjoy consistent success on the country charts, demonstrating how much country music has caught up with mainstream rock.

CHRIS HILLMAN, the unofficial leader of the group, is almost a living history of California folk-rock; he was a founding member of both the BYRDS and the FLYING BURRITO BROTHERS. Invited to make a solo album for the country label Sugar Hill in the mid-eighties, Hillman assembled a group of friends, including Jorgenson and Pedersen, to back him up. The album was called Desert Rose, and the name stuck for the band. They were also employed to back up folk-rocker Dan Fogelberg on a mid-eighties tour and album, further cementing their sound.

Their first number-one hit came in 1988 with the country-rocker "He's Back and I'm Blue" followed by another number one with "I Still Believe in You," a mid-tempo love song cowritten by Hillman. However, in the early nineties chart hits eluded the group, which continues to actively record and perform. They have gone through a variety of personnel changes, although the leaders (Hillman, Pedersen, and Jorgenson) have been on hand for most of the recordings.

The band has a light country harmony sound that is not unlike many other pop country bands of the eighties and nineties. This is not too surprising, because many of these younger bands were themselves influenced by California country-rockers like the Byrds, the Burrito Brothers, and the EAGLES. However, there is some irony in the fact that Hillman and company have recently enjoyed only minor success, even as their young imitators top the charts.

Select Discography

One Dozen Roses—Greatest Hits, Curb 77571. Their first hits, originally issued on MCA.

Traditional, Curb 77602. The band playing BLUEGRASS-flavored music joined by fiddler ALISON KRAUSS and EMMYLOU HARRIS.

◀ DEXTER, AL

(born Albert Poindexter, 1902, Jacksonville, TX; died 1984)

Dexter was a popular COWBOY SONG–writer famous for his "Pistol Packin' Mama," an up-tempo forties hit for him and for Bing Crosby, the Andrews Sisters, and Frank Sinatra on the pop charts.

Dexter's music was a blend of the pop side of WESTERN SWING with cowboy and HONKY-TONK motifs. In fact, his "Honky Tonk Blues" from 1936 is thought to be the first song to use the words "honky tonk" in its title or lyrics. However, Dexter's modern-style recording of his "Pistol Packin' Mama"—featuring accordion, steel guitar, and trumpet—brought him his greatest success and influenced the more pop-oriented Nashville recordings of the fifties and sixties.

Besides "Mama," Dexter wrote the words to BOB WILLS's theme song, "Take Me Back to Tulsa," the ever-popular "Rosalita," the bar-room WEEPER "Too Blue to Cry," and the upbeat cowboy number "So Long Pal." His clever blend of country themes and perky, pop lyrics made his songs the ideal bridge between mainstream pop and country.

Dexter spent much of the fifties and early sixties performing at his Dallas-based Bridgeport Club and recording for a number of labels, big and small. He later moved into real estate and retired from music making. His "Too Late to Worry" was covered in the seventies by COUNTRYPOLITAN star RONNIE MILSAP, and his other compositions crop up from time to time in the NEW-COUNTRY music repertory.

◀ Diamond Rio

(Marty Roe [lead vocals]; Jimmy Olander [lead guitar]; Gene Johnson [mandolin, fiddle, vocals]; Dan Truman [keyboards]; Dana Williams [bass, vocals]; Brian Prout [drums])

What happens when a bunch of talented BLUEGRASS musicians, who also can sing up a storm, are cleverly packaged and promoted by a major label? The sad answer is Diamond Rio, an example of how the sum of talented parts can be less than inspiring. Who wants to hear an updated ALABAMA spewing out middle-of-the-road fluff, even if these guys can play the hell out of their instruments?

The group's pedigree may help explain their predicament. The band was born in Opryland USA, the ersatz theme park that has become the home of country music in Nashville. Assembled to play "bluegrass" music (or at least what would sound like bluegrass to the park's visitors), the group grew to include three talented vocalists, with a smooth countryish lead provided by Marty Roe. The group's hot pickers—lead guitarist Jimmy Olander (who worked previously as a session picker with RODNEY CROWELL and FOSTER AND LLOYD), mandolin/fiddle player Gene Johnson (an alum of J. D. CROWE's New South as well as folk-rocker David Bromberg's band), and bassist Dana Williams (who is the nephew of the famous bluegrass pickers the OSBORNE BROTHERS)—are indeed impressive, and the group's harmonies blend a bluegrass sensibility with more pop leanings.

They were signed to Arista Records in 1990 and given their truck-lover's name and a splashy new act and look. Right out of the gate they scored big with the hummable "Meet in the Middle," followed by "Norma Jeanne Riley" and three more top-five songs. Although many of these numbers were enlivened by the group's instrumental work, the result was a bland, middle-of-the-road likability that is the opposite of cutting-edge music making. The band followed up with a second album in 1993, leaning heavily on love ballads (the upbeat "Calling All Hearts" and the weepy "I Was Meant to Be With You" and "In a Week or Two") that garnered them more country-pop radio play. While they sweep up the awards with their clever blend of just enough bluegrass to win over the new traditionalists and more than enough mushy blandness to appeal to Mr. and Mrs. Middle America, one can only hope that this is not a portent of the direction of country music to come.

Select Discography
Diamond Rio, Arista 8673. Their first album (1991).
Love a Little Stronger, Arista 18745. 1994 release featuring the title hit.

◀ Dickens, Hazel

(born 1937, Montcalm, WV)

Country SINGER/SONGWRITER Hazel Dickens gained great popularity among urban folk-music fans in the early seventies, thanks to her partnership with singer/songwriter ALICE GERRARD. With a distinctive, high-pitched mountain voice, reminiscent

of great balladeers like AUNT MOLLY JACKSON, Dickens combined elements of traditional balladry, BLUEGRASS, and HONKY-TONK country in her music.

The eighth of eleven children, Dickens's father operated a small trucking business, practiced fundamental Baptism, and religiously listened to the GRAND OLE
OPRY. Several of her brothers were miners, and many played music. At the age of
nineteen, Hazel followed other family members to Baltimore in search of a better
life. There she met folk-revivalist MIKE SEEGER and became involved with several
local bluegrass bands. She made her first professional recordings with revivalist
Alice Gerrard (who was then known as Alice Foster) in the mid-sixties for Verve/
Folkways. In the early seventies, she continued to work with Gerrard as a duo,
while the pair also performed with the Strange Creek Singers, which featured Gerrard's then-husband Mike Seeger as well as Lamar Grier and Tracy Schwartz.

Dickens has continued to perform and record sporadically through the seventies
and eighties. After two successful duo LPs with Gerrard for Rounder in the early
seventies, she recorded several solo LPs. Her career was given a considerable boost
when she provided the soundtrack for the Oscar-winning documentary *Harlan
County, U.S.A.* Her best-known songs include the traditional-sounding coal miner's
lament, "Black Lung," and an answer song, "Don't Put Her Down, You Helped
Put Her There," written in response to the many songs disparaging honky-tonk
angels. In this song, Dickens combines rough mountain common sense with sentiments borrowed from the urban women's liberation movement, surely one of the
more unusual country pairings.

Select Discography
Hazel and Alice, Rounder 0027; *Hazel Dickens and Alice Gerrard*, Rounder 0054.
Two mid-seventies releases made with her then-partner Alice Gerrard.
A Few Old Memories, Rounder 11529. CD reissue of tracks taken from her late-
eighties albums, mostly with bluegrass band accompaniment.

◀ DICKENS, "LITTLE" JIMMY

(born 1925, Bolt, WV)

"Little" Jimmy is a perennial country hit-maker known for his tiny size, rhinestone-encrusted outfits, and novelty hits, including his big pop crossover, 1965's
"May the Bluebird of Paradise Fly Up Your Nose."

Dickens was the thirteenth child born to a small-time rancher in rural West
Virginia. After attending the small local school, Dickens was accepted into the
University of West Virginia, where he also landed a job as a performer on the local
radio station. After radio stints in Cincinnati and Michigan, the pint-sized crooner,
then billed as Jimmy the Kid, attracted the attention of ROY ACUFF, who invited him
to perform on the GRAND OLE OPRY. By the late forties, he was a permanent member
of the show, a position he still holds today.

Dickens signed to Columbia at the same time, recording a string of novelty hits
in the late forties, including his first top-ten country song, "Take an Old Cold Tater
and Wait," earning him a second nickname, Tater. Other hit novelty numbers

included "I'm Little but I'm Loud," "A-Sleeping at the Foot of the Bed," and "Hillbilly Fever."

In the fifties, Dickens led a hot band called the Country Boys, which featured two lead guitars, PEDAL STEEL GUITAR, and drums. At a time when Nashville recordings were soaked with girly choruses and sentimental strings, this band provided spirited accompaniments to many of his recordings, maintaining a true country sound in the face of considerable pressure to go more mainstream. Many of his recordings from this era share the energy of the best of ROCKABILLY. For this alone, Dickens deserves the seat he earned in the Country Music Hall of Fame in 1983.

After his big pop hit with the silly "Bluebird of Paradise" in 1965, Dickens more or less faded from the charts, but he continues to tour and perform as well as appear on the Opry. Today his appearances have more nostalgia value than anything else, as they maintain a link with country's past.

Select Discography
Straight—From the Heart, Rounder 26. Reissues his better late-forties and early-fifties recordings.

◀ DIFFIE, JOE

(born 1958, Tulsa, OK)
Diffie is another neo–honky-tonker who hopes to cash in on today's craze for barroom-oriented material.

Born in Tulsa, Diffie was raised mostly in rural Duncan, Oklahoma, although his family relocated several times during his early years, moving as far west as Washington state. After attending college briefly, he returned to Duncan to work in an iron foundry, while writing songs at night. His mother sent one of his early compositions to singer HANK THOMPSON, who bought it. After nine years of heavy labor, Diffie was laid off due to tough financial times; with nothing to lose, he headed for Nashville to seek work as a songwriter. In the early eighties, he fell in with a group of other wannabe songwriters, including Lonnie Wilson and Wayne Perry, and the trio wrote HOLLY DUNN's hit "There Goes My Heart Again" in 1984.

For the balance of the eighties, Diffie worked as a demo singer and songwriter. His demos were well-received by the Nashville community, and eventually producer Bob Montgomery at Epic Records signed him, although he waited a few years to release Diffie's first album. He had an immediate hit with 1990's "Home" and has followed it up with some spunky HONKY-TONK numbers, including 1992's "Honky Tonk Attitude" and 1993's "Prop Me Up (Beside the Jukebox If I Die)." He also recorded a duet with popular folk-country star MARY CHAPIN CARPENTER.

However, Diffie unwittingly spoke the hard truth when he told one interviewer "Sometimes I turn on the car radio and for a second I'm not sure if it's me or MARK CHESNUTT or ALAN JACKSON or whoever." This is the problem with many of today's hunks in hats; blindfolded, you can't tell them apart, because they all are cast in the same mold. Diffie lacks the strong personality of Alan Jackson, so his long-term success may be limited.

Select Discography
A Thousand Winding Roads, Epic 46047. 1990 debut album.
Honky Tonk Attitude, Epic 53002.

◀ DILLARDS, THE

(c. 1962–1966; original lineup: Doug Dillard [banjo] born 1937, Salem, MO;
Rodney Dillard [guitar, vocals] born 1942, Salem, MO; Dean Webb [mandolin];
Mitch Jayne [bass])

The Dillards were one of the most commercial and influential BLUEGRASS bands
of the mid-sixties and later evolved into one of the first COUNTRY-ROCK outfits.

The Dillard brothers, sons of an old-time fiddler, grew up surrounded by traditional dance music. In the mid-fifties, a vibrant bluegrass scene developed in metropolitan St. Louis, including the young Dillards along with BANJO-picker JOHN
HARTFORD. After hooking up with local country deejay Mitch Jayne, who became
the group's spokesperson, they made their debut in 1962 performing at Washington
University; soon after, they relocated to California, where they signed with Elektra
Records, then an urban-folk label (and soon to become a folk-rock label). At the
same time, they were hired to portray the Darling family on TV's *Andy Griffith Show*,
giving the band further exposure. Their first two albums were a mix of traditional
country and bluegrass songs along with more contemporary numbers by songwriters like BOB DYLAN.

Because the Dillards were country-born, they brought an authenticity to their
music that other folk-revivalists could only emulate; but, because they were young
and college-educated, they knew how to appeal to a more upscale audience. For
this reason, they became immediately popular on the college circuit, and their
records were marketed primarily to this audience, not to the traditional bluegrass
or country-music consumer.

After recording an influential album of fiddle tunes with guest artist BYRON BER-
LINE, the band split, with Doug leaving to form a folk-rock group with ex-Byrd GENE
CLARK, and Rodney continuing to lead the band with new banjo player Herb Pederson (later a founding member of the DESERT ROSE BAND). Under Rodney's leadership, the Dillards took a more folk-rock direction, recording two concept albums
that featured popular songs by the Beatles and folk artists like Tim Hardin.

The Dillards as a band were dormant through much of the early to middle
seventies but re-emerged with the bluegrass revival of the latter half of the decade.
Rodney and Doug recorded a pair of albums with old friend John Hartford, while
Rodney continued to lead the Dillards, now with Dean Webb, Jeff Gilkinson (vocals, bass, cello), banjoist Billy Ray Latham (who was a member of the influential
KENTUCKY COLONELS, another California-based bluegrass band), and Paul York
(drums). The band continues to record, although they are not as successful or
influential as the first incarnation of the group had been.

Select Discography
There Is a Time, Vanguard 131/32. Classic band recordings originally issued by
Elektra between 1963 and 1970.

Take Me Along for the Ride, Vanguard 79464. A 1992 recording featuring Rodney Dillard.

◀ DINNING SISTERS, THE

(Eugenia ("Gene") and Virginia ("Ginger") Dinning, born 1924; and Lucille ("Lou") Dinning, born 1920, KY)

Country music's answer to the Andrews Sisters, the Dinnings were popular stars of Chicago's *National Barn Dance* in the forties and later had a minor career in musical film shorts and C-grade pictures.

Originally from Kentucky, the sisters were raised primarily on a farm near Enid, Oklahoma, where all eight children were musically inclined. In emulation of the popular Andrews Sisters, identical twins Gene and Ginger and elder sister Lucille formed a harmony group and performed on the local radio station. In 1939 they moved to Chicago, where elder sister Marvis had already begun a career as a big-band singer; two years later, they were hired to perform on the *National Barn Dance* radio show, dubbed the Sweethearts of Sunbonnet Swing. Their mix of down-home sweetness with purling harmonies won them an immediate audience, and soon they had their own radio show, plus an invitation to come to Hollywood to appear in cameo roles in a number of quickie films.

By 1945 they had signed with the fledgling West Coast Capitol label, and they had a couple of hits with remakes of sugary pop numbers like 1947's "My Adobe Hacienda" (written by cowgirl star LOUISE MASSEY) and "Button and Bows" from a year later. They also recorded novelty numbers in a more swinging style reminiscent of the Boswell Sisters, including 1946's "Iggedy Song." Elder sister Lou married country songsmith Don Robertson in 1946 (best known for writing "Please Help Me I'm Falling") and left the act; she was replaced first by Jayne Bundesen and, in 1949, by younger sister Delores Dinning.

The group's career faded in the fifties. Jean later became a songwriter, best known for writing "Teen Angel," the saccharine pop hit of the early sixties. Sister Delores later joined the Nashville Edition, backup singers who appeared regularly on TV's HEE HAW and did session work.

◀ DIXON BROTHERS, THE

(Dorsey [guitar, fiddle, vocals] born 1897, Darlington, SC; died 1968; Howard [guitar, steel guitar, vocals] born 1903, Darlington, SC; died 1968)

The Dixons were cotton-mill workers all their life, but for a brief period in the mid-thirties they recorded a number of classic country numbers, mostly written by elder brother Dorsey.

The entire Dixon family, parents and seven children, worked as mill hands; Dorsey entered the mills when he was twelve years old. From his mother, he learned traditional ballads, play-party songs, and hymns, and as a young teenager he learned to play GUITAR and fiddle. He teamed up with his younger brother, Howard, to perform at local movie theaters as a novelty act between screenings.

By the early thirties, the brothers were working in a mill in East Rockingham, North Carolina, where they met legendary steel guitar player Jimmie Tarleton (of DARBY AND TARLETON fame), who was also working in the mills. Tarleton inspired them to become professional musicians, and also to play more bluesy sounding songs, with Howard taking up the steel guitar in emulation of Tarleton's mastery of the instrument. The duo got their "big break" in 1934 when they appeared on a country radio show out of Charlotte, North Carolina, and two years later were signed to RCA's budget Bluebird label. They recorded sixty numbers over the next two years, including many songs commenting on the hard life in the cotton mills ("Weave Room Blues") and the classic country weeper "I Didn't Hear Nobody Pray," which ROY ACUFF remade into the megahit, "Wreck on the Highway." Although Dorsey wrote both songs, he sold the rights to them to his publisher and never earned a penny from the many recordings of these standards. After 1938 the brothers returned to textile work and abandoned their professional careers.

In the early sixties, Dorsey Dixon was rediscovered by folk revivalists, and he performed at various folk festivals and made a couple of new albums of his own material and traditional country songs. He was asked to record for the Library of Congress in belated recognition of his contributions to country-music history.

Select Discography

Volumes 1–4, Old Homestead 151, 164, 178, 179. Out-of-print LPs reissuing classic material from the brothers (the first two volumes), followed by a collection of their sacred recordings (volume 3) and their novelty and miscellaneous recordings (volume 4).

◀ DOBRO

(Resophonic guitar, c. 1927)

The dobro is a unique American musical instrument that has become central to the sound of modern BLUEGRASS and country music. It is one of the key forerunners of the PEDAL STEEL GUITAR.

The dobro has its roots in the craze for Hawaiian music that swept the country in the twenties. The classical GUITAR was introduced by Portuguese settlers in the islands around the 1830s; eventually, by the century's end, Hawaiian musicians had taken to playing the guitar on their laps, tuning the strings to a full open or partially open chord (known as "slack-key" tuning) and noting the strings with a solid metal bar (hence the name "steel guitar," referring to the bar used to damp the notes, not to the material used in making the guitar itself). Joseph Kekuku is generally cited as the first great Hawaiian player; he toured the United States and Europe at the turn of the century, influencing hundreds of lesser-known vaudeville and tent-show musicians. One of the most popular Hawaiian recording stars of the twenties was Sol Hoopi, whose playing was emulated by both country and blues musicians.

Conventional guitars were modified for Hawaiian playing by being fitted with raised nuts (to increase string height), flush frets (so that the bar could be easily slid across the strings), hollow, square necks (to enable the instrument to sit flat on a player's lap), and stronger and larger body construction (to take the extra tension created by the steel strings used on these instruments, and also to increase volume). However, it was still difficult to produce a conventional guitar with enough power to be heard over an entire band.

One solution was the dobro, invented by a family of Czechoslovakian immigrant instrument makers, the Dopyera brothers (hence the trade name "do-bro" used on some of their instruments). Brother John is generally credited with designing the original resonator used on dobros, a system that employed a primitive non-electric pickup mounted on the bridge of the instrument (like the needle used on early acoustic phonographs), which transmitted the sound down into a chamber that held three megaphonelike cones, facing down (or toward the back of the instrument). Dopyera was awarded a patent for his design in 1927 and a year later began producing instruments with his brothers under the National name. One of their first customers was Hawaiian star Hoopi. These instruments had steel bodies, so are commonly called National steels by today's players. Square-neck models for Hawaiian players and round-neck models for conventional players (highly prized among blues musicians) were both made through the thirties.

In a complex business history, John eventually broke with National in 1929, coming up with a new design for a resonator instrument, the first true dobro. This featured a single cone facing forward, with an elaborate eight-legged "spider" pickup that projected sound down from the bridge to the edges of the cone. In order to make a cheaper instrument than the National steel, the brothers decided to use a plywood body for their new instrument, which they called the dobro.

By the early Depression years, the National and Dobro companies had reunited and were making a wide variety of both steel-bodied and wood-bodied guitars with either the single or tricone resonator. Soon after, a new technology in the form of electric (or amplified) lap guitars cut seriously into the popularity of these earlier so-called resophonic instruments. The dobro probably would have disappeared from the musical scene if it had not been for a couple of influential players. "Bashful Brother Oswald" (aka Pete Kirby) played the instrument in ROY ACUFF's influential band from 1939 through the fifties, appearing weekly on the GRAND OLE OPRY. In bluegrass music, the pioneering FLATT AND SCRUGGS band featured a talented player of the dobro, Uncle Josh (b. Burkett) Graves, who took Earl Scrugg's signature BANJO roll and adapted it to the instrument.

The dobro fell out of popularity in mainstream country music recording circles from the mid-fifties to the mid-eighties, when the whine of the pedal steel guitar dominated recording sessions. The bluegrass revival of the seventies helped bring the instrument back to the fore, with young players like JERRY DOUGLAS showing that the dobro was not just a relic of the past. Douglas has become one of the most in-demand session musicians of the eighties and nineties, and many other players have emulated his versatility on the instrument.

◀ DR. HOOK AND THE MEDICINE SHOW

(Ray Sawyer, aka Dr. Hook [guitar, vocals, percussion]; Dennis Locorriere [guitar, vocals]; Rik Elswit [lead guitar, vocals]; George Cummings [steel guitar, lead guitar]; Billy Francis [keyboards, vocals]; Jance Garfat [bass, vocals]; John David [drums, vocals])

Dr. Hook and the Medicine Show were a silly, novelty country outfit of the late sixties and early seventies, led by eye patch–wearing Sawyer, whose biggest hits were provided by SINGER/SONGWRITER/children's author Shel Silverstein, including the satiric "Cover of the *Rolling Stone*." They later became a mainstream country-pop band, after several personnel changes.

Hook got his zany nickname because of an automobile accident in his youth that left him wearing an eye patch over his left eye. Originally from Chickasaw, Alabama, he began performing in small southern bars at the age of fourteen, taking some time off to pursue an abortive career as a logger before forming a duo with keyboardist Billy Francis. They played up and down the East Coast, one favorite performance spot being Transfer Station, near Union City, New Jersey, where a group of small bars catered to travelers who were often stranded at this bus transfer point for several hours. It was here that Hook met guitarist/vocalist Dennis Locorriere, who originally joined the outfit as a bass player and soon became its co-leader.

After unsuccessfully shopping around demos to New York labels and producers, the band was introduced to Ron Haffkine, who was working as musical director for the film *Who Is Harry Kellerman and Why Is He Saying These Terrible Things About Me?* The film was being scored by Shel Silverstein, who came to Jersey to hear the band and invited them to record the movie's theme song, "Last Morning." They were soon signed to Columbia Records, releasing a series of albums mostly of Silverstein's satiric cowboy-style songs, including "Freakin' at the Freakers Ball," "I Got Stoned (and I Missed It)," and their big FM hit, "Cover of the *Rolling Stone*," which in fact did earn them a cover photo on this prestigious rock journal.

The group broke off from Silverstein in 1972, recording an album of original material that flopped. Meanwhile, the recession of the next few years, plus years of mismanagement, led the group to declare bankruptcy. Trying to dig themselves out of the hole, they self-produced for four hundred dollars the album *Bankrupt*, which was picked up by Capitol Records. The record featured a remake of Sam Cooke's "Only Sixteen" that became the group's next big hit.

The band continued to move in a more country/easy-listening direction through the seventies. Sawyer recorded his first solo album in 1977, scoring a country hit with "If Not You," a syrupy ballad. In 1978 and 1979 they had their biggest hits, including the MOR anthem "When You're in Love with a Beautiful Woman," miles away from their hipper-than-thou image of just a few years earlier. In 1980 they were signed to the disco label Casablanca and had a few more hits before the group fizzled out two years later. Sawyer formed a new Dr. Hook band for touring the revival circuit in 1988.

Select Discography

Doctor Hook and the Medicine Show, Columbia 30898. Rerelease of their first album.
Greatest Hits, Columbia 46620.

◀ DOUGLAS, JERRY

(born c. 1955, Columbus, OH)

One of the great DOBRO players, Douglas has brought this venerable country instrument into NEW COUNTRY by working as a bandleader, session performer, and as a regular on the Nashville Network's *American Music Shop* with MARK O'CONNOR.

Douglas comes from rural Ohio and began his career as a BLUEGRASS player. He performed with the COUNTRY GENTLEMEN in the early seventies, where he met another talented young player, fiddler and mandolinist RICKY SKAGGS. In the late seventies the duo formed a PROGRESSIVE BLUEGRASS ensemble called Boone Creek, to perform more contemporary country material in a bluegrass setting. At the same time, Douglas recorded his first two solo outings for Rounder, *Fluxology* and *Fluxedo* (after his nickname, Flux, which refers to his smooth playing), featuring many contemporary-bluegrass musicians, including Skaggs, TONY RICE, Sam Bush, BELA FLECK, and Russ Barenberg.

Douglas relocated to Nashville in the early eighties and was in immediate demand for session work accompanying the so-called new-country artists, including his old friend Skaggs. He was also signed to MCA's short-lived Instrumental Masters new acoustic music label, where he produced two albums under his own name with many of the same cohorts from his earlier sessions. When Mark O'Connor started the acoustic-oriented *American Music Shop* for TNN, he hired Douglas as a regular musician, and his tasteful dobro and steel GUITAR work can be heard on almost every program.

Although in his own compositions Douglas shows the influence of DAVID GRISSMAN's approach to creating a new-acoustic/jazz-tinged music, most of his session work is limited to traditional-styled fills and melody work. In fact, the demand for the dobro sound is not for cutting-edge work but rather for just the right touch of nostalgia for today's current hip country artists. Douglas fills the bill to a T, because of his ability to perform everything from WESTERN SWING to country WEEPERS.

Select Discography

Everything's Gonna Work Out Fine, Rounder 11535. Compilation culled from tracks on his Rounder solo albums from the early eighties.
Slide Rule, Sugar Hill 3797. 1992 solo recording.

◀ DRAKE, PETE

(born 1932, Atlanta, GA; died 1988)

Premiere Nashville session player on the PEDAL STEEL GUITAR, Drake is also a producer noteworthy for his work for everyone from country crooner JIM REEVES to one-shot country performer Ringo Starr.

Drake was one of the earliest performers to take up the pedal steel guitar, beginning to play when he was nineteen years old. Soon he was leading a band, the Sons of the South, and performing on radio and in small clubs in his native Georgia. He joined the duo WILMA LEE AND STONEY COOPER, coming to Nashville with them in 1959. After a year and a half struggling to find work, Drake caught the ears of ROY DRUSKY and GEORGE HAMILTON IV, two popular country crooners, who invited him to perform on their next sessions. Drake's career as a session player took off; it is said that Drake could be heard on two-thirds of the Billboard's top seventy-five country singles throughout the early sixties. In 1964 he released a solo recording of the pop novelty "Forever," which charted on both pop and country listings.

Drake moved into the studio/production end of the business in the middle to late sixties, soon becoming a powerhouse producer. It was his idea to invite Ringo Starr to make an all-country album after hearing the singer's cover of BUCK OWENS's hit "Act Naturally" (on the Beatles's album). Drake recorded all of the backgrounds and then had Starr overdub vocals; the result was arguably Starr's best solo album, *Beaucoups of Blues*, released in 1970.

Although Drake's production style was less heavy-handed regarding the use of vocal choruses or a heavy beat than many of his Nashville compeers, by the early eighties he was working primarily with older acts, such as B. J. THOMAS and LINDA HARGROVE, who combined pop-sounding accompaniments with country crooning.

◀ DRIFTING COWBOYS, THE

(Don Helms [steel guitar]; Bob McNett [electric guitar]; Jerry Rivers [fiddle]; Hillous Butram [bass])

The backup group that accompanied HANK WILLIAMS on his best-known GRAND OLE OPRY shows and recordings, the Drifting Cowboys became the prototype for hundreds of other HONKY-TONK bands in the fifties and beyond.

The core of the group was steel guitarist Don Helms, who had performed with Williams since 1943 when both were still living in Alabama. With the exception of a brief period when Hank starred on the *Louisiana Hayride* radio show, Helms remained with the singer until his death. On early live Opry shows, the audience went wild every time the steel guitar takes a solo. Helms's playing was always tasteful and discreet; less distinctive a player than pioneers like BOB DUNN, Helms never sought to overwhelm Williams's singing but rather to accompany it.

Guitarist Bob McNett was from Pennsylvania and had originally accompanied cowgirl sweetheart PATSY MONTANA before joining Hank in 1949 when the singer was invited to join the Opry. Fiddler Jerry Rivers, who had previously played as a duo with future BLUEGRASS great Benny Martin, came on board at the same time, as did session bass player Hillous Butram. This core group played on all of Williams's classic MGM recordings from the late forties and early fifties, as well as touring with him and appearing on his regular Opry spots.

Williams's behavior became increasingly erratic as his alcoholism worsened in the early fifties, leading Butram to jump ship to join HANK SNOW in 1952 (he was replaced by Cedric Rainwater, who had worked in bluegrass bands and also as a session musician), and McNett left soon after, to be replaced by Sammy Pruett. When Williams died, the band disintegrated, with individual members continuing to work as session musicians.

In 1977 the group was reunited thanks to Hillous Butram, who was working as a music coordinator for country-themed movies. The group first performed in a Lorne Greene cowflick, *That's Country*, leading to a contract with Epic Records and a hit a year later with a remake of Johnnie Lee Wills's "Ragmop." They continued to perform until 1984, when the group members decided to retire.

◀ DRIFTWOOD, JIMMIE

(born James Corbett Morris, 1917, Mountain View, AK)

Ozark mountain folklorist and song collector, Driftwood is best remembered for his reworking of the traditional fiddle tune "Eighth of January" into the country hit "The Battle of New Orleans."

Raised in the Ozarks, Morris first learned music from his family; his uncle gave him a handmade GUITAR, and he soon mastered fiddle and BANJO as well. Jimmie worked odd jobs through his high school years, occasionally performing on the side at local dances and gatherings, and became a rural school teacher in the late thirties. He taught for ten years while working toward his B.A. degree in education at the state teacher's college in Conway, Arkansas (the town that provided Harold Jenkins with half of his stage name, CONWAY TWITTY).

Contacts with other folklorists in the fifties brought Jimmie into contact with the urban FOLK REVIVAL, and he performed at many festivals and concerts. He was signed to RCA in 1958 as a folk singer and issued an album with the academic name of *Newly Discovered Early American Folk Songs*. On this record, he recorded his version of "The Battle of New Orleans"; country singer JOHNNY HORTON heard it and a year later released his version, which became a massive hit. RCA rushed out a second album plus a single version of Jimmie performing his song. This was followed by "Tennessee Stud," a reworking of the old "Tenbrooks and Molly" story, which was covered by EDDY ARNOLD for a second hit.

Driftwood continued to perform on the folk-revival and country circuits through the early sixties. He remained devoted to the traditional songs and stories of the Ozarks and became well-known for his playing of the mouthbow (sometimes called "diddley bow"), a single-stringed instrument that is played in a similar manner to the Jew's harp (the end of the bow is held up against the player's open jaw, and while strumming vigorously on the string, different notes can be produced by varying the shape of the sound chamber formed by the open mouth).

Driftwood was a founder of the Arkansas Folk Festival in 1963 and later turned his attention to academic folklore work. He has occasionally performed on a local level.

Select Discography

Americana, Bear Family 15470. Three-CD set re-releasing all of his RCA recordings.

◀ DRUSKY, ROY

(born 1930, Atlanta, GA)

Sometimes called the Perry Como of country music (a dubious achievement), Drusky is nonetheless a fine singer and songwriter whose sixties recordings unfortunately suffer from the heavy-handed NASHVILLE SOUND.

Although Drusky's mother was a church pianist who tried to interest him in music, he spent most of his childhood preoccupied with sports. Drusky's interest in country music was born in the navy, where he befriended some shipmates who played together in their own country band. After leaving the service, he enrolled in veterinary school in Atlanta, but by 1951 he had formed his own band, the Southern Ranch Boys. They were hired to play on a small Decatur radio station where Drusky also worked as a deejay. After the band dissolved, Drusky began singing at local clubs and was signed to Starday Records in the early fifties, having a hit with 1953's "Such a Fool." He was invited to join the GRAND OLE OPRY in 1958, where he remained for over two decades as a performer.

By the early sixties, he was working out of Minneapolis as a deejay and had signed to Decca Records. His first hits included the self-penned "Alone with You," "Another," and "Three Hearts in a Tangle," all fine HONKY-TONK ballads, although the recordings were drenched in walls of strings and syrupy vocal choruses. In 1963 he signed with Mercury, producing more hits varying from the novelty of his first Mercury single, "Peel Me a Nanner," through more country heartache songs that had made him famous, like 1969's "Where the Blue and the Lonely Go." He also appeared in two C-grade movies, *The Golden Guitar* and *Forty Acre Feud*. Although he continues to perform on occasion, he is more active today as a songwriter and record producer in Nashville.

◀ DUDLEY, DAVE

(born 1928, Spencer, WI)

If one man can be credited with creating the truck-driving mystique, it would have to be Dave Dudley, whose 1963 recording of "Six Days on the Road" single-handedly created a new genre of country song. He continued to wax odes to the big rigs through the sixties and seventies, adding to the repertoires of bar bands everywhere.

Raised in Stevens Point, Wisconsin, Dudley was given his first GUITAR by his dad when he was just eleven, but baseball was his life throughout his teen years. An arm injury while playing with the Gainesville, Texas, Owls led to his early retirement. He began working as a deejay at a Texas radio station, playing along with the songs, until the station owner encouraged him to perform on his own. He then moved to Iowa and Idaho in the early fifties, where he continued to perform with a number of groups with limited success. Dudley was struck by a hit-and-run driver when he was loading his guitar into his car, further sidetracking his career. His luck changed soon after when he released his ultimate trucker's anthem ("Six

Days") on the tiny Soma label in 1963. The song was a crossover hit on both pop and country charts.

He signed with Mercury in the same year, staying with the label for a dozen years and producing twenty-five country hits. The truck-driving themes continued with odes like "Two Six Packs Away" and "Trucker's Prayer," while he also tried to capture the god, guts, and guns conservative country market with his Vietnam-era waxings of "Mama, Tell Them What We're Fighting For," penned by TOM T. HALL, and KRIS KRISTOFFERSON's "Vietnam Blues." By the early seventies, he was back to the trucking milieu with "Me and My Ole CB," "One AM Alone," and the 1980 hit that listed the contents of every trucker's medicine chest, "Rolaids, Doan's Pills and Preparation H," which he recorded for the revived Sun label. Dudley has been less active in the eighties and nineties.

Dudley's best recordings combined an up-tempo ROCKABILLY accompaniment with his own swaggering vocals. He not only sang about truckers, he embodied the image of the trucker. Just as the cowboy was a symbol of rural defiance and freedom in the thirties and forties, so the trucker became the one-man-against-the-world icon of the sixties and seventies. Dudley was so loved by the truck-driving fraternity that he was awarded a solid gold membership card by the Teamsters.

Select Discography
Truck Drivin' Songs, Intersound 5011.

◀ DUKE OF PADUCAH, THE

(born Benjamin Francis "Whitey" Ford, 1901, DeSoto, MO; died 1986)

Ford was a country comedian and BANJO player who was one of the founding members of the *Renfro Valley Barn Dance*.

Raised by his grandmother in Little Rock, Arkansas, Ford's career is typical of many country musicians of his generation; he moved freely through a variety of styles, from Dixieland Jazz and vaudeville pop to COWBOY SONGS and straight country. At the end of World War I he joined the navy, where he learned the banjo, originally playing the tenor (or four-string) banjo in a jazz style. After touring vaudeville with his own dance band, he hooked up with Otto Gray's Oklahoma Cowboys. In the early thirties, he was hired to host GENE AUTRY's radio program out of WLS in Chicago, where he acquired his comic persona, a new moniker, the Duke of Paducah, and his famous closing line, "I'm going to the wagon, these shoes are killin' me." He moved to Cincinnati's *Plantation Party* radio show in the mid-thirties and then to the new *Renfro Valley* show in 1937.

During the Second World War, Ford toured various army installations as a comedian/musician and joined the GRAND OLE OPRY after the war ended, remaining a regular until 1959. In the fifties and sixties, his homespun humor was so popular that he also developed an inspirational talk, called "You Can Lead a Happy Life," which he delivered to sales conventions and at colleges throughout the country. Although he continued to perform into the seventies, his act, a combination of likable country corn with a few musical numbers, changed little over the years, featuring just enough innovation to carry him along.

◀ DUNCAN, JOHNNY

(born 1938 near Dublin, TX)

Duncan is a country SINGER/SONGWRITER who has had a long and varied career. He achieved his greatest success in the late seventies with a COUNTRYPOLITAN approach and his hunky, he-man looks reminiscent of the young KRIS KRISTOFFERSON.

The cousin of guitarists Jimmy and DAN SEALS, Duncan was raised in a musical household. His mother taught him to play electric lead guitar when he was twelve, and he pictured himself as an instrumentalist in the MERLE TRAVIS tradition. He began performing with his mother and his Uncle Moroney on fiddle, playing local bars and events.

After completing high school, Duncan enrolled at Texas Christian University for a short period but then moved to Clovis, New Mexico, where he began working with legendary producer NORMAN PETTY, who had previously launched the career of another Texan, BUDDY HOLLY. Petty's attempts to turn Duncan into a teen idol went nowhere, despite taking him as far as England to record with what Duncan calls "4,900 violins." He also sang lead with the rockin' instrumental band, Jimmie Gilmore and the Fireballs.

In 1963 Petty gave up trying to promote Duncan, and the singer went to Nashville, where he worked as a deejay. Three years later, he was singing on Ralph Emery's morning radio show, where Columbia A&R (Artists & Repertory) man DON LAW heard him and signed him to the label. He became close friends with CHARLEY PRIDE and toured with the singer, but his initial Columbia recordings were not very successful. In 1972 he was going to leave the label when he decided to make one last try at stardom under the hands of producer BILLY SHERRILL. In 1975 they recorded a number, "Jo and the Cowboy," that Duncan had cowritten with LARRY GATLIN and which prominently featured backup singer JANIE FRICKIE. This led to a series of recordings with Frickie as a duet partner, including a remake of Kris Kristofferson's "Strangers" and number-one hits with "Thinkin' of a Rendezvous" and "It Couldn't Have Been Any Better."

Frickie and Duncan parted company in 1977, and a year later the singer had one more number-one solo hit, with the slightly risqué "She Can Put Her Shoes Under My Bed (Anytime)." The death of his father in 1981 led Duncan to return to Texas and take some time off. He signed with the tiny Pharaoh label in 1986 but has failed to return to the charts, although he remains a popular performer on the country circuit.

Select Discography

Greatest Hits, Columbia 35628. Cassette-only reissue of his sixties and seventies hits.

◀ DUNCAN, TOMMY

(born 1911, Hillsboro, TX; died 1967)

Lead vocalist for BOB WILLS's Texas Playboys, Duncan defined the WESTERN SWING vocal style: smooth, mellow, almost pop-ish, with a Bing Crosby–influenced sound.

He was the natural link between the bluesy vocals of JIMMIE RODGERS and the more modern sound of pop crooners of the forties and after.

Duncan first teamed up with Wills in 1932 as members of the original LIGHT CRUST DOUGHBOYS. When Wills left to form his own band a year later, he took Duncan with him, and the two founded the seminal Texas Playboys. It is Duncan's vocals that are heard on most of Wills's classic recordings, including "San Antonio Rose," "Time Changes Everything," "Mississippi Muddy Water Blues" (adapted from Jimmie Rodgers), and hundreds of others. When Wills left for the West Coast during World War II, Duncan went with him, but the old friends quarreled, and Wills fired Duncan from the band in 1948. Duncan struck out on his own; his early solo recordings were still in a Western swing style but failed to catch on without the Wills name attached to them. In 1961 and 1962, the duo reunited with some triumphant recordings for Liberty. Duncan died of a heart attack in 1967.

Duncan's importance was not only in expanding the repertory of country music to include the pop songs of the day but also in emulating the crooning vocal style of Crosby and others, introducing to country music a smoother, more uptown sound.

◀ DUNN, HOLLY

(born 1957, San Antonio, TX)

Dunn is a SINGER/SONGWRITER who created a flap with her 1991 song "Maybe I Mean Yes," which she withdrew as a single after feminists angrily asserted that the song condoned date rape.

The daughter of a minister, Dunn attended Abilene Christian College, traveling to Nashville after her graduation to join her brother, Chris Waters, who was already a successful songwriter. She took a job as a receptionist at a music publishers' office and soon was singing on demos and writing her own material. Some of her first songs were placed with MARIE OSMOND, LOUISE MANDRELL, and the WHITES.

In 1985 Dunn signed with MTM Records, which tried to market her as a pop singer, with limited success. She talked them into releasing a single of her song "Daddy's Hands," a folk-styled ballad in honor of her father, as a last-ditch attempt to market her. The song was an instant country success, as was the follow-up, a duet with MICHAEL MARTIN MURPHEY called "A Face in the Crowd."

Dunn quickly became known for her strong ballads, most composed by herself, including her late-eighties hits "Strangers Again" and "Someday." She signed with Warner Brothers in 1989, the same year she was invited to join the GRAND OLE OPRY. The minor flap over her 1991 song "Maybe I Mean Yes" brought her publicity in the mainstream press, and she earned some brownie points with more progressive listeners when she asked the label to withdraw the song.

Dunn is a better songwriter and musician than many of her contemporaries; however, her vocals, while strong, don't have much of a country character. She is more of a pop balladeer than a straight country singer.

Select Discography

Milestone: Greatest Hits, Warner Bros. 26630. The hits up to 1991.

◀ DYLAN, BOB

(born Robert Allan Zimmerman, 1941, Duluth, MN)

Although Dylan's major achievements have been in folk, rock, and pop music, he has earned a place in an encyclopedia of country music, and not just because of his two late-sixties LPs, the Western-concept album *John Wesley Harding* and the Nashville excursion *Nashville Skyline*; more important, Dylan is influential because of his breakthroughs as a songwriter, which had a particularly strong impact on country music outlaws like WILLIE NELSON and KRIS KRISTOFFERSON.

Dylan's initial inspiration was SINGER/SONGWRITER WOODY GUTHRIE, whose populist anthems inspired his first social-protest work. The idea that a singer and guitarist who was neither a talented vocalist, pretty face, nor particularly adept instrumentalist could be a "star" performing his own material (which often defied traditional song structures) was radical, to say the least. Dylan also had an annoying habit of creating an image (such as his original, pseudo-folkie stance) and then turning his back on it, even slapping his audience in the face (as in the famous moment at the Newport Folk Festival in 1965 when he "went electric," enraging the assembled folkies).

After his motorcycle accident in 1966, Dylan spent some time holed up in his home in Woodstock, New York, working with the Band in evolving a highly personal, folk-based music that represented the highest flowering of East Coast COUNTRY-ROCK. In their collaborations on *The Basement Tapes*, they felt their way toward this new music, which sounded both rooted in American traditions and also modern. Dylan's influence can be felt most strongly on the Band's first two albums, particularly in songs that reflect American themes while carrying a strong undertow of personal, romantic loss. "The Weight" is one of those cryptic personal songs, while "The Night They Drove Old Dixie Down" is one of the group's strongest American anthems, and an homage to Southern pride.

Dylan's firmest foray into country was 1969's *Nashville Skyline*, recorded with many of the younger musicians who were then gathering in Nashville and who would influence the return-to-roots country music over the next decades. As with much of Dylan's work, it's hard to determine whether this album is an homage to or a satire of Nashville conventions. He radically changed his voice for these recordings, trying hard to remove the raspy, adenoidal quality from his singing, replacing it with a laid-back, crooning style. His duet with JOHNNY CASH on "Girl from the North Country" is the closest the album gets to straight country, although its roots are clearly in folk balladry; most of the other songs, however, continue in the idiomatic Dylan style. The album was enormously influential in pointing other pop/rock performers toward the possibilities of wedding country with rock, although it's a route that Dylan himself did not pursue for long.

From the mid-seventies through the early nineties, Dylan's career has suffered from an often slap-dash approach to recording and his restless search for a new style that will equal the impact of the old. His 1992 release, *Good as I've Been to You*, was widely hailed as a return to his "folk" roots; however, his mostly out-of-tune guitar playing and lackluster singing on this collection of folk standards, plus his failure to credit other performers for arrangements clearly taken note-for-note from their earlier recordings, makes this just another chapter in Dylan's unhappy recent career. A second all-acoustic album, *World Gone Wrong*, appeared in 1993.

As a singer/songwriter writing topical material, and as an expressive, untrained vocalist, Dylan both draws on country traditions and extends them into new areas, pointing the way for other eccentric performers, from Willie Nelson to LYLE LOVETT.

Select Discography

John Wesley Harding, Columbia 09604.

Nashville Skyline, Columbia 09825.

Basement Tapes, Columbia 33682.

E

◀ EAGLES, THE

(1971–1979; original lineup: Don Henley [vocals, drums]; Glenn Frey [guitar, vocals]; Randy Meisner [bass, vocals]; Bernie Leadon [guitar, banjo, vocals]; Don Felder [slide guitar] added 1974; Joe Walsh [lead guitar] added 1976 when Leadon leaves; Timothy B. Schmidt replaces Meisner 1979)

The 1993 release of an all-Eagles tribute album recorded by NEW-COUNTRY artists shows the enduring legacy of this popular seventies group. They were the most successful of COUNTRY-ROCK bands, but only because they crossed out of the genre into being basically a mainstream rock outfit. And their influence on today's country stars is based on the success of their pop-rock songs, not their more country elements.

The original band came out of the Los Angeles folk-rock scene of the late sixties and early seventies. Previous outfits like the BYRDS, FLYING BURRITO BROTHERS, and POCO were all influential on their original sound. The band coalesced around LINDA RONSTADT, who hired them individually to be her backup group. The main country influence on the band came from founding member Bernie Leadon, who had played BLUEGRASS banjo as well as GUITAR in his teenage years and had worked with a later incarnation of the Flying Burritos. Glenn Frey had previously worked in a folk-oriented duo with songwriter J. D. Souther under the name Longbranch Pennywhistle; the two had collaborated on a countryesque song, "Take It Easy," later the first hit for the Eagles. Randy Meisner had been the bass player in one of the first country-rock outfits, RICK NELSON's Stone Canyon Band, while Henley, a Texas native, had previously played with a band of fellow Southerners in a country-rock outfit known as Shiloh.

The first two Eagles albums were solidly in the country-rock tradition of Southern California, although both were recorded in England and produced by rock producer Glyn Johns (who had previously worked with the Beatles, the Who, and Led Zeppelin). The second album was particularly interesting; it was a concept album, telling the story of the Doolin-Dalton gang of outlaws in the Old West, and it yielded the hit "Desperado." A few years later, WILLIE NELSON would make *Red Headed Stranger*, another concept LP rooted in the Old West.

The addition of session guitarist Don Felder in 1974 started the band off in a more pop-rock direction, although they continued to show their folky side in hits like 1975's "Lyin' Eyes," a kind of HONKY-TONK love song for a new age. However, when Leadon left the band in 1976 and was replaced by songwriter/guitarist Joe

Walsh, it was clear that the band was aiming for mainstream pop success, and they achieved it on their 1977 album *Hotel California*, followed by 1979's *The Long Run*. Both established them as megaselling arena rockers, although as the sales increased, so did the tension between the band's primary singers/songwriters, Henley and Frey. Eventually, these tensions led to the band's dissolution, after they released a final, live album.

In 1994, the last incarnation of the band (Henley, Frey, Walsh, Schmidt, and Felder) reunited for the aptly named "Hell Freezes Over" tour (because the band had vowed never to get back together "unless hell freezes over"). A live album followed, as well as a concert broadcast over MTV. The reunited group played a combination of their hits, Henley's solo hits from the eighties (as well as the stray hit from Frey and Walsh), and some new compositions by Henley and Frey. Only Schmidt maintains his boyish looks (and long locks) from the seventies; the rest look like a group of slightly feisty middle-aged men, with Walsh sporting a bleached-blond swept-back hairdo.

The Eagles probably don't belong in this book purely on the merits of their music; but for their influence, they certainly have earned a place. Their pleasant harmonies, memorable melodies, and many songs that extolled an outlaw lifestyle all have been highly influential on New Nashville artists and songwriters. Many of today's Nashville bands—from DIAMOND RIO to LITTLE TEXAS—sound like nothing more than Eagles clones. And performers like TRISHA YEARWOOD and TRAVIS TRITT all sing the praises of the band and perform its material. This leads to the uneasy feeling that the New Nashville is really just the old Hollywood pop-rock in disguise; and there are some who would argue that this, in fact, is really where country music is headed—at least the more commercial variety that is driving out the traditional sounds.

Select Discography
The Eagles, Asylum 5054
Desperado, Asylum 5068
Greatest Hits, Asylum 105.

◀ EARLE, STEVE

(born 1955, San Antonio, TX)

Earle is a country-rocker who has never really lived up to his potential after the release of his now-legendary 1986 album, *Guitar Town*.

Born in Texas, Earle comes from a long tradition of OUTLAW-COUNTRY SINGER/ SONGWRITERS with an attitude. He came to Nashville in 1974, landing a bit part in Robert Altman's film sendup of the country scene, *Nashville*, and began hanging out in local clubs with other displaced Texas singer/songwriters, including TOWNES VAN ZANDT and GUY CLARK. After a brief move to Mexico in 1980, he returned to his native San Antonio and formed his backup band, the Dukes. A year later, he was back with his band in Nashville, working as a songwriter and cutting his first demo recordings in a fifties ROCKABILLY style. He signed with Epic in 1983, releasing five singles, including one minor hit, "Nothin' but You," but these recordings were marred by a derivative Stray Cats sound. After being dropped by the label, he continued to write, and his songs were covered by some of the older outlaws, including JOHNNY CASH and WAYLON JENNINGS.

His 1986 LP, *Guitar Town*, was his first release for MCA, and it seemed to come out of nowhere. Earle combined the people's-poet sensibility of a Bruce Springsteen or John Cougar Mellencamp along with a hard-rocking attitude. The title hit is his best-known song, although the album's slow ballads, including "My Old Friend the Blues" and "Fearless Heart," are perhaps the true high points. Earle's next album, *Exit O*, took him into even harder-rocking territory, at which point many of the more conservative Nashvillians (including NEW-COUNTRY musicians) began to write him off as a rock star wannabe.

Unfortunately, Earle's career since has been spotty. He moved to MCA's pop/rock label Uni in the late eighties and released the half-country, half-rock *Copperhead Road*, which failed to please his core audience or to attract new converts; his follow-up, *The Hard Way*, also fell with a decided thud between two stylistic stools. Critics of the Nashville establishment claim that Earle was too politically left-wing (*Copperhead Road*'s title cut tells the story of a Vietnam vet so traumatized that he lived by himself on a hill growing his own private stash of marijuana to wash away his painful wartime memories). Others countered that his music was too rock-influenced to survive in the country capital. Still others point out that his career's failure to take off may have to do simply with his own inability to produce a follow-up that matches or exceeds the artistic strength of his original breakthrough recording. After a 1990 tour with BOB DYLAN, Earle has for the moment faded from both the country and pop scenes.

Select Discography
Guitar Town, MCA 31305.

◖ EDWARDS, JOHN

(born 1932, Cremorne, Australia; died 1960)
Edwards, an Australian country music fan, compiled the largest private collection of country music recordings from the 1920s, along with memorabilia and related material, which became the heart of the John Edwards Memorial Foundation, the first nonprofit organization dedicated to the study of country music history.

It seems odd that an Australian who never visited the United States would become a country music fan and scholar, but it shows how it could take someone outside of the culture to appreciate the true value of an art form that was often dismissed in the United States as merely "hillbilly music." Edwards died in an automobile accident in 1960, but he left behind a request that his collection be sent to the United States for others to use in the study of country music. American folklorist Eugene W. Earle arranged for the collection to be housed at UCLA and that it be maintained by a new, nonprofit educational organization. Folklorists D. K. Wilgus, Ed Kahn, and Archie Green were among the first officers.

Since its founding, JEMF (as it is commonly known) has built its archive through contributions by other collectors and folklorists. The foundation published one of the first serious scholarly journals on country music (*The JEMF Quarterly*) and reissued early country recordings on record albums, making them accessible to a new generation of scholars and musicians. When the Country Music Foundation was opened in Nashville, a second collection was named for Edwards there, in recognition of the importance of his pioneering archive.

◀ EDWARDS, STONEY

(born 1937, Seminole, OK)

Edwards was performing roots-country before its time, but nonetheless he had some success in the seventies when the COUNTRYPOLITAN sound was dominating the airwaves. Like many other country-soul performers, Edwards had a difficult time finding an audience either on R&B or C&W radio.

Of mixed Indian, African-American, and Irish descent, Edwards was raised in rural Oklahoma, where he was introduced to country music through his mother's brothers, who all played in a country style and who encouraged him to listen to the GRAND OLE OPRY. Stoney learned to play GUITAR, fiddle, and piano by his early teens, playing primarily for his own amusement. His father abandoned the family when Stoney was young, and he had to work at various menial jobs to support the family. In his teens, he moved to Oklahoma City to rejoin his father and then moved to Texas to live with an uncle. By the mid-fifties, he had moved to the West Coast, where he married and began working in Bay Area shipyards.

Stoney worked in the shipyards for fifteen years, until two freak accidents—first carbon monoxide poisoning then a broken back—ended his career as a laborer. He returned to his first love—playing the guitar—and began composing songs in the style of his idols, HANK WILLIAMS and LEFTY FRIZZELL. While performing at a concert to benefit ailing WESTERN SWING star BOB WILLS in 1970, Edwards was spotted by a talent scout for Capitol Records, who signed him to the label. He made his first album in 1971 and two years later had a minor hit with "Hank and Lefty Raised My Soul." His biggest hit came in 1974 with "Daddy Bluegrass," followed a year later by "Mississippi You're on My Mind."

Perhaps because he was an African-American in a predominantly white field, or perhaps because his music was strongly influenced by fifties HONKY-TONK stylings that were yet to be repopularized, Edward's career at Capitol fizzled. He moved to smaller labels in the late seventies, with minor success, and then relocated to Texas, where he has continued to perform locally for the last decade.

◀ ELY, JOE

(born 1947, Amarillo, TX)

Another oddball Texas SINGER/SONGWRITER whose music defies categorization, Ely has enjoyed only sporadic success, much like his friends and one-time band-mates BUTCH HANCOCK and JIMMIE DALE GILMORE.

Born to a nonmusical farming family in Amarillo, Joe began taking violin lessons at age eight, followed a few years later by steel-guitar lessons (taught by a door-to-door salesman/teacher). By his early teens, he had switched to regular guitar and began playing local dates. By his late teens, he was a traveling musician, bouncing back and forth from Los Angeles to Texas, searching for work. He was back in Texas in 1970 and formed a country-folk-rock group called the Flatlanders with Hancock and Gilmore. In 1971 the trio wound up in Nashville, where they recorded what was to become a legendary unreleased album (it finally saw the light of day in 1990). Ely also worked for Joseph Papp, the noted New York City–based theatrical impresario, in the early seventies, providing music for a show that played in New York and then in Europe.

In the mid-seventies a demo tape made by Ely caught the ear of JERRY JEFF WALKER, the elder statesman of Texas singer/songwriters, and Walker recommended him to MCA records. Ely released a couple of albums, most notably 1978's *Honky Tonk Masquerade*, featuring his blend of country, blues, and rock, with elliptical lyrics that were, at best, difficult for both country and rock audiences to follow. At this time country was still mired in COUNTRYPOLITAN and glitzy Vegas-styled acts, while rock was barely recovering from the assault of disco; it's not surprising, then, that Ely's music could not be effectively promoted to either audience. In 1980, in another strange twist in a career filled with them, British punk-rock stars the Clash "discovered" Ely and vigorously promoted his music. He made a few harder-rocking albums, forecasting the sound of rebel rockers like STEVE EARLE by a few years, but again his music bridged so many different styles that it found only cult success.

By the early nineties, Ely had entered the pantheon of legendary Texas outlaws who are venerated as much for their refusal to fit in with the musical mainstream as they are for the music that they produced.

Select Discography

More a Legend Than a Band: The Flatlanders, Rounder 34. This "legendary" album is more famous for its mythic reputation than the quality of the music on it; an interesting document of its time.

Honky Tonk Masquerade, MCA 10220.

Love and Danger, MCA Nashville 10584. 1992 recordings.

◀ EVERLY BROTHERS, THE

(Don [Issac Donald] born 1937, Brownie, KY; Phil [Philip] born 1939, Chicago, IL)

Coming out of a traditional family country-music band, the Everlys revolutionized rock and roll music by introducing the plaintive vocal harmonies heard on classic 1930s brother duo recordings to the late-fifties teen-pop market. From the mid-sixties to their first breakup in 1973, the Everly Brothers recorded some of the first COUNTRY-ROCK songs, and since 1973 as both solo artists and a duo they have continued to honor their country roots.

The boys got their start when Don was eight and Phil was six, touring and performing with their parents, Ike and Margaret, and playing on the family's local radio show. Ike was a fine blues-flavored guitarist who was well-known in the greater Kentucky region (picker MERLE TRAVIS is said to have learned some licks from him). When Phil graduated from high school, the duo hit the road for Nashville, and Don signed up with Acuff-Rose as a songwriter, penning "Thou Shalt Not Steal" for KITTY WELLS in 1954. Two years later they recorded a country single for Columbia called "Keep on Loving Me," produced by CHET ATKINS, but the song went nowhere.

A year later they hooked up with producer/Nashville powerhouse WESLEY ROSE, who brought them to Cadence Records and to country songwriting duo FELICE AND BOUDLEAUX BRYANT. The Everlys struck gold with the pair's "Bye Bye Love." The Bryants' teen-angst lyrics wed with the brothers' sweet country harmonies (reminiscent of the LOUVIN BROTHERS, who were still actively performing in Nashville at this time) gave them chart-busting appeal in both country and pop markets. And although they were marketed as teen popsters, the Everlys never really shed their country identities, recording 1958's classic *Songs Our Daddy Taught Us*, a country tribute album, right in the midst of their more pop-oriented sessions.

In 1960 at the height of their popularity the brothers left Cadence for the big bucks offered by Warner Brothers. Although they lost the services of the Bryants, the Everlys revealed themselves to be adequate writers on their own with "Til I Kissed You" and "When Will I Be Loved," a classic country-rocker later covered by LINDA RONSTADT. Their string of good luck ended in 1963 during a tour of England; although it was reported at the time that Don had suffered from a "nervous breakdown," he now admits that an addiction to prescription pills was the real problem. One year later, the British invasion of American pop charts would push their more folksy sound off of the playlists. They struggled for a new identity throughout the sixties, with their best work issued on *Roots*, a nod to their country childhood that included a fragment of one of the family's radio shows. They also put out a fine country/pop LP, *Pass the Chicken and Listen*, in the early seventies, again produced by Atkins.

In 1973 the duo split up during a performance at Knotts Berry Farm, following an acriminous fight. Don spent most of the next ten years recording country material in the United States for Hickory and other labels, while Phil pursued a more pop-oriented career in Europe, where the brothers always had a strong following. They reunited in 1983 with the country and pop hit "On the Wings of a Nightingale," written for them by Paul McCartney, and continue to record and tour sporadically.

The Everly Brothers brought the brother act tradition into the modern era. The two sides of their personalities—Phil's sunny personality reflected in his high tenor vocals and Don's more brooding pessimism represented by his baritone leads— could be said to represent the tensions in country music itself, between lighthearted commercialism and a darker, more personal style.

Select Discography
Early Recordings, Rhino 70211. Their first recordings made in Nashville in a country style.
Songs Our Daddy Taught Us, Rhino 70212. Reissue of the classic LP.

◖ EXILE

(1980s lineup: J. P. Pennington [guitar, vocals]; Sonny LeMaire [bass, vocals]; Les Taylor [guitar, vocals]; Marlon Hargis [keyboards]; Steve Goetzman [drums])

Exile were a glitzy pop-rock group of the seventies who successfully transformed themselves into a glitzy country-pop group of the eighties, bringing an arena-rock sensibility into the country fold.

The band was founded way back in 1963 as the Exiles, a pop-rock group. One of the original members was J. P. Pennington, who actually has impeccable country credentials: his mother was BANJO/fiddle player LILY MAE LEDFORD, his father was MC of the *Renfro Valley Barn Dance* radio show, and his uncle was RED FOLEY; however, Pennington showed little interest in country music, admitting to one interviewer, "If somebody would have told me in 1972 that I was gonna be in a country band with a number-one record, I would have beat them to death with an Iron Butterfly record." In fact, by 1978 Exile was on the top of the rock charts with the gooey hit "Kiss You All Over." However, they were unable to maintain their lofty position in rock's pantheon, and by the early eighties they were working as a bar band in the Rebel Room, a Lexington, Kentucky, bowling alley.

It was during their period of artistic "exile" that the band began hearing their songs being covered by country artists, including DAVE AND SUGAR, JANIE FRICKIE, and their soon-to-be-rivals ALABAMA. This led their manager to have the band audition in 1983 in Nashville for producer Buddy Killen, who had previously worked with Joe South and other R&B acts as well as mainstream country performers. They scored their first number-one country hit with Pennington's "Woke Up in Love," followed by a string of hits written by Pennington and bandmate Sonny Lemaire. Oddly enough, the band was still creating what in the seventies would have been considered soft-rock or pop songs; but by the mid-eighties this music was called "country." The band also became famous for their lengthy instrumental introductions, as if each song was a mini-drama with its own overture to set the proper mood.

The band began to fall apart in the late eighties, beginning with the defection of keyboardist Marlon Hargis in 1987, followed by Les Taylor a year later. The final blow was the defection of principal vocalist/songwriter Pennington in 1989 (he has since released a solo album for MCA). A new Exile emerged, led by LeMaire and new vocalist Paul Martin (who had replaced Taylor), and they moved to a new label, Arista, scoring another hit with "Yet."

Exile is a group that begs the distinction between pop and country; in fact, they actually show that much of country really is just pop, carefully packaged for a different market. Their influence can be seen in the arena-rock stylings creeping into other country acts.

Select Discography

Keeping It Country, Curb 77295. Late-eighties recordings.

Justice, Arista 8675. The new band, without Pennington, from 1991.

F.

◀ FAIRCHILD, BARBARA

(born 1950, Knoebel, AK)

Fairchild is a pop-country singer best known for her kiddie-themed hits of the mid-seventies, particularly "The Teddy Bear Song." She has since found the Lord and a new career in country-gospel.

Fairchild was raised in rural Arkansas by a small-time trucker and farmer. At an early age she began singing with two aunts in a gospel trio. Her father supported her career from the beginning, taking her to local bars so that she could sing with the bands. When the family relocated to St. Louis in 1962, Fairchild's father became increasingly involved with promoting her talents, arranging for her first recording session in 1965 and, two years later, driving her to Nashville for an audition with Kapp Records. Eighteen-year-old Fairchild had her first hits with the little-tough-gal stance of "Remember the Alimo-ny" and "Breaking in a Brand New Man." These early recordings attracted the attention of Columbia Records, and she soon moved to that label. Fairchild wrote many of her first Columbia releases, including 1970's "A Girl Who'll Satisfy Her Man," reflecting the back-country conservatism that would manifest itself even more strongly in her hit-making years.

In 1973 Fairchild had a big pop and country hit with the sugary-sweet "Teddy Bear Song." The song—which related a young girl's wish that she could be held and cuddled like the Teddy Bear of her youth—led to a spate of similar drivel, including "Kid Stuff," "Baby Doll," and "Little Girl Feeling," that also rocketed up the charts. Fairchild also recorded the 1975 anti–women's lib anthem "I Just Love Being a Woman," guaranteed to keep her off of Betty Friedan's list of best-loved singers. At the same time, more mature material like 1976's "Cheatin' Is," about infidelity, and 1978's "She Can't Give It Away," about the hard life of an aging streetwalker, failed to dent the charts.

By the end of the seventies Fairchild was dropped by CBS, and her second marriage—to a jazz pianist who had inspired her 1978 megadud LP, *This Is Me*, with its light pop arrangements—was on the rocks. She retired to Texas where she was born again and began performing gospel-tinged material. In 1982 she recorded "The Biggest Hurt," an anti-abortion anthem, and two years later she returned to Nashville. She formed Heirloom, a gospel trio with Tanya Goodman and Candy Hemphill, in 1990 and a year later recorded a solo gospel album, featuring the minor hit "Turn Right and Then Go Straight."

Through it all, Fairchild has remained a pleasant-enough pop singer, not so powerful as to blow the tubes out of your stereo, but likeably sincere. Unlike many other gospel performers who send their message home with the subtlety of a sledgehammer, Fairchild lets her material speak for itself, and for this alone she is one of the least annoying of the gospel crooners in performance.

◀ FARGO, DONNA

(born Yvonne Vaughan, 1940, Mount Airy, NC)

Fargo is a mid-seventies chanteuse best known for the perky megahits, "The Happiest Girl in the Whole U.S.A." and "Funny Face."

Born in the heart of mountain-music country (the Mt. Airy/Galax region of Virginia is home to countless old-time and BLUEGRASS musicians), Fargo sang as a youngster but had no ambitions to a musical career. The daughter of a big-time tobacco farmer, she attended college locally, earning a teaching degree, and eventually settled in California to teach. There she met singer/guitarist Stan Silver, who became her biggest booster, manager, and husband; he encouraged her to learn the GUITAR, sing, and write her own material. When she was in her late twenties, she took the stage name of Donna Fargo, recording a single for the Phoenix-based Ramco label. In 1968 she went to Nashville to record the racy (for the time) "Who's Been Sleeping on My Side of the Bed?," which many country stations boycotted, thinking it too suggestive, particularly for a girl singer.

After recording for a number of small labels, Fargo finally hit pay dirt with her "Happiest Girl in the Whole U.S.A.," which was picked up nationally by Dot Records in 1972. The song rocketed to number one on the country charts and earned her a Grammy. The follow-up was another sunshiny anthem, "Funny Face," which cemented Fargo's image as a well-scrubbed, eternal optimist.

Fargo remained with Dot through 1976, when she signed a million-dollar contract with Warner Brothers, which was looking to break into the country market. Her range of material increased, now encompassing the (still perky) rocker "Superman" of 1973 and the slightly feminist "A Song with No Music" (1976) which told of the unhappiness of a woman caught in a difficult relationship. In the late seventies, Fargo moved from recording her own compositions to covering country-pop standards, including "Mockingbird Hill" and "Walk on By." She also landed her own syndicated television show and appeared to be poised for pop-crossover stardom.

In 1978, however, she was tragically afflicted with multiple sclerosis. Although she continued to perform into the eighties, she was increasingly debilitated by her disease. In 1986 she did manage a comeback hit, "Woman of the '80s," which documented the trials and tribulations of five different women struggling with their new roles in a changing world; and while more progressive contentwise than her earlier material, the song still bubbled forth with the sunny attitude that has marked all of her recordings.

Select Discography

The Happiest Girl in the Whole U.S.A., MCA 667. Yikes! This cassette is so cheerful, you'll need to eat a lemon before you listen to it.

◀ FEATHERS, CHARLIE

(born 1932 near Holly Springs, MS)

Fans of fifties ROCKABILLY have long idolized Feathers, who is best known for his fifties recordings, particularly "Tongue-tied Jill" and "Get with It."

Feathers was raised on a farm in rural Mississippi and learned to play GUITAR from a local black sharecropper. He worked for a while for small petroleum companies in Illinois and Texas before settling in Memphis around 1950, working for a box manufacturer until a bout with spinal meningitis left him bedridden for several months. While he was laid up, he listened constantly to the radio, and he made up his mind to become a professional singer.

Legendary Memphis producer SAM PHILLIPS was launching a country label to be called Flip when he met Feathers. He paired him with Bill Cantrell and Quinton Claunch (two local studio musicians who would later start the Hi label, originally a country-oriented company that later recorded Al Green and other classic Memphis soul singers), and the trio recorded the 1955 release "I've Been Deceived," a powerful country WEEPER cut in the style of HANK WILLIAMS. Later in the same year, Feathers worked on demos of songs by Stan Kesler, gaining coauthor credit for the classic country song "I Forgot to Remember to Forget (About You)," which was Elvis's last Sun recording (Feathers later claimed that he taught the King the vocal licks for this number). With Kessler he also cowrote "We're Getting Closer to Being Apart." Feathers cut a second country single, but it went nowhere.

By 1956 Feathers had switched to rockabilly, imitating the vocal hiccups and stutters that were trademarks of this genre. Los Angeles–based Meteor Records issued his single of "Tongue-tied Jill" backed with "Get with It," along with a number of other songs. He then signed with Cincinnati-based King Records, and for a while it looked like Charlie might make it big. He toured with a number of package shows and appeared at Dallas's *Big D Jamboree* before his career fizzled out.

Feathers has spent much of the last twenty-five years recounting for interviewers his days in the limelight, while performing at a variety of small down-and-out bars. A talented country singer, he has also occasionally recorded, most notably in 1991 for Elektra's American Masters series.

Select Discography

Charlie Feathers, Elektra/Nonesuch 61147. 1991 recording featuring a recreation of the classic Sun sound, with fifties-era studio master Roland James on guitar.

◀ FELTS, NARVEL

(born 1938 near Bernie, MO)

Like many country stars of the fifties, Felts went through a period recording teen pop and ROCKABILLY before returning to his country roots.

A farm boy from Missouri, when he was a teenager Felts raised enough money picking cotton to buy a Sears, Roebuck guitar, on which he learned songs off of the GRAND OLE OPRY. Bitten by the rock-and-roll bug, he won his town's high-school talent contest aping CARL PERKINS's "Blue Suede Shoes" and was soon performing on local radio, backing local pop crooner Jerry Mercer.

In his early twenties, Felts showed up at the legendary Sun studios in Memphis, where he backed such stars-to-be as CHARLIE RICH and Harold Jenkins (later CONWAY TWITTY) as well as making some recordings on his own. He recorded for MGM in the late fifties and moved to the tiny Pink label in the early sixties, still searching for that elusive teenage hit. He did have minor success with the sickly sweet "Honey Love."

By the early seventies, he was back in Memphis recording for the Hi label (which began as a country outfit but would become famous for its soulful stars like Al Green) but had little success. He then switched to an even tinier label, Cinnamon, where he had his first country hits, "Drift Away" and "All in the Name of Love" (both from 1973) and "When Your Good Love Was Mine" (1974). Felts's dramatic vocals—smoothly swooping from high falsetto down to low bass notes—combined the excitement of rock and roll with the gentle smoothness that the country audience prized in the mid-seventies. He was signed to ABC in 1975, scoring hits with "I Don't Hurt Anymore" (1977), "One Run for the Roses" (1978), and "Everlasting Love" (1979). Felts continued to record for ABC/MCA into the early eighties but was dropped by the label after his hit-making days ended.

Select Discography

Best of Country, Richmond 2137. Cassette-only reissue of ABC/Dot recordings.

◀ FENDER, FREDDY

(born Baldemar G. Huerta, 1936, San Benito, TX)

Fender is a popular Tex-Mex country star who had a number of mainstream country hits in the mid-seventies. He is the only Hispanic artist who has been able to have country hits while still maintaining his ethnic identity; his sound combines elements of Mexican music (particularly instrumentation and rhythms) with traditional country themes.

Born to a family of migrant farmworkers who roamed throughout the Southwest, Fender took an early interest in the GUITAR, singing along in Spanish. He dropped out of high school at age sixteen to join the marines and returned at age nineteen to play local clubs, taking the name Freddy Fender and performing a combination of ROCKABILLY, R&B, and Tex-Mex standards. He hooked up with club owner Wayne Duncan, and the pair wrote "Wasted Days and Wasted Nights," a local hit released nationally on Imperial.

In 1960 Fender was convicted for possession of marijuana and spent three years in the infamous Angola State Prison in Louisiana (where folksinger Leadbelly had done time earlier). JIMMIE DAVIS, governor of Louisiana and himself an ex–country singer, arranged for Fender's release, with the proviso that he abandon country music as a career! Fender quickly returned to performing, although his recording career was virtually halted.

In 1974 Huey Meaux, a famous Louisiana-based producer of R&B recordings, produced Fender's most successful recordings. His biggest hit was 1975's "Before the Next Teardrop Falls," sung half in English and half in Spanish, along with a remake of "Wasted Days." Meaux's productions emphasized Fender's tear-drenched vocals and an unusual combination of PEDAL STEEL GUITAR, accordion (from Tex-Mex conjunto music), and harpsichord. Fender's first few singles appeared on both country and pop charts, although most of the rest of his hits in the late seventies appealed primarily to a country audience.

Fender spent most of the eighties in relative obscurity. Late in the decade he teamed up with longtime bar-band friends Doug Sahm and Augie Meyers, of the Tex-Mex rock band the Sir Douglas Quintet, and with Flaco Jiminez, one of the masters of Tex-Mex accordion; the four became the supergroup the Texas Torna-dos, which had gained some new success on the country and pop charts.

Select Discography

The Freddy Fender Collection, Reprise 26638. One of many reissues of Fender's mid-seventies hits.

◀ FIDDLE FEVER

(c. 1977–1982: Jay Ungar, Matt Glaser, Evan Stover [fiddles]; Russ Barenberg [guitar]; Molly Mason [bass])

A loose-knit band led by fiddler Jay Ungar, Fiddle Fever performed a wide variety of music, from CAJUN to WESTERN SWING to pure and old-time country. Their unique use of three fiddles, each with a distinct personality, made them one of the more versatile of the old-time revival bands.

Ungar had first gained exposure through performing with folk-blues guitarist David Bromberg in the early seventies, and then cofounded the short-lived Putnam String County Band, along with ex–NEW LOST CITY RAMBLERS member JOHN COHEN. He performed in the mid-seventies as a duo with his then-wife Lynn Hardy for a while before forming Fiddle Fever. Matt Glaser, Evan Stover, and Russ Barenberg had all performed with the various permutations and combinations of progressive bands that grew out of COUNTRY COOKING in the early-to-middle seventies, including Breakfast Special, as well as working as soloists and backup artists.

In the group, Ungar had the more traditional sound; even his own compositions, like "Ashokan Farewell" (which became a major FM-radio hit a decade later when it was used prominently in the PBS *Civil War* series), sounded like roots fiddling. Stover and Glaser, on the other hand, were much more influenced by the jazz styles of Stephane Grappelli and BLUEGRASS players like Kenny Baker. Thus, although the band was fiddle-dominated, it was still able to explore many different styles and moods of music.

By the early eighties, the band had pretty much fizzled out, although it was always pretty informal to begin with. Ungar and Molly Mason were married and performed as a duo sporadically through the next decade, while also running a series of music camps during the summer months in Ashokan, New York. Baren-berg resumed a solo career and has since relocated to Nashville, where he has been performing most recently with ace dobroist JERRY DOUGLAS. Stover was fiddler in the Broadway production of ROGER MILLER's *Big River*, an adaptation of the Huck

Finn story, while continuing to work in a variety of New York bands. Glaser also has continued to appear in the New York area.

Select Discography

Fiddle Fever, Flying Fish 247. Their first and best album, now available only on cassette.

◀ FINK, CATHY

(born 1953, Baltimore, MD)

A FOLK-REVIVAL BANJO player and vocalist, Fink has been active performing both children's music and feminist country material over the last decade.

Raised in suburban Baltimore, Fink first became exposed to old-time country music while a student at Montreal's McGill University. She joined fellow student, guitarist and vocalist "Duck" Donald, and the duo toured Canada through the seventies and released three albums, mostly focusing on old-time duets in the spirit and style of classic thirties duos like the BLUE SKY BOYS. Around 1980 the duo broke up and Fink relocated to Washington, D.C., to pursue a solo career.

Through the early eighties, Fink performed as a soloist and recorded both children's LPs and landmark feminist collections, such as 1985's *The Leading Role*, which featured both BLUEGRASS and country-styled numbers answering age-old stereotypes promulgated through songs more typical to these styles. She also formed a number of loosely knit performing groups, including a duo with Marcy Marxer, another children's performer who had previously played with Boston's all-female Bosom Buddies; and Blue Rose, an all-female country band featuring Marxer, fiddler LAURIE LEWIS and dobroist Sally Van Meter (both of San Francisco's GOOD OL' PERSONS), and Molly Mason (late of FIDDLE FEVER). The Marxer/Fink duo album got some attention on country radio, and they were featured performing on the Nashville Network.

Fink continues to perform as a soloist and as a duo with Marxer. The pair have also produced a number of instructional videos aimed at children interested in playing old-time musical instruments.

Select Discography

Doggone My Time, Sugar Hill 3783. Her old-time songs.
Cathy Fink & Marcy Marxer, Sugar Hill 3775.

◀ FLATT AND SCRUGGS

(Lester Raymond Flatt born 1914, Overton County, TN; died 1979; Earl Eugene Scruggs born 1924, Cleveland County, NC)

Flatt and Scruggs are the two most famous names in BLUEGRASS, thanks to their long association with Columbia Records and the use of their music in the 1967 hit film, *Bonnie and Clyde*. Scruggs single-handedly created bluegrass BANJO picking, and Flatt's smooth lead vocals and creative GUITAR runs have been widely imitated over the last four decades.

Flatt came from a musical family; both of his parents played the banjo in the old-time or frailing style, and he soon picked the instrument up, along with guitar and MANDOLIN. A big fan of BILL and CHARLIE MONROE, Flatt formed an amateur duo, with his wife playing guitar and singing lead while he took the harmony and mandolin parts; at the same time, he worked professionally in a textile mill. By 1939 he had settled around Roanoke, Virginia, where he performed on local radio as a member of the Harmonizers. A few years later, he was also playing with the Happy-Go-Lucky Boys, a group that included fiddler Clyde Moody. Moody was an alum of bands led by both Monroe brothers and introduced Flatt to Charlie Monroe, who hired him and his wife to be members of his group, the Kentucky Pardners, in 1943. Soon tiring of life on the road, Flatt settled in North Carolina, where he worked for a while as a trucker. In 1944 he received a telegram inviting him to join Bill Monroe's new band, the Blue Grass Boys.

Scruggs, the younger of the duo, also came from a musical family. He took up the banjo at an early age and, inspired by the picking of local banjo whiz Snuffy Jenkins, began playing in a three-finger picking style. He quickly developed the capability of playing syncopated melody parts and chord rolls, the rudiments of what would become the bluegrass style. He started performing as early as age six with his brothers and had a radio job with the Carolina Wildcats by the time he was fifteen years old. During World War II, he worked in a textile mill, but by the war's end he had hooked up with "Lost" John Miller, who broadcast out of Nashville. When Miller quit touring, Scruggs was hired to join the Monroe band, just after Flatt had come on board.

The Bill Monroe Blue Grass Boys of 1946 to 1948 is a legendary band, in many ways serving as the archetype of all bluegrass bands that followed. Because mandolinist Monroe had a high, tenor voice, he switched Flatt to singing lead and playing guitar, with Scruggs prominently featured playing his new style of banjo; the group was rounded out by fiddler Chubby Wise and bassist Howard "Cedric Rainwater" Watts. When the band began broadcasting over Nashville's GRAND OLE OPRY, listeners were astonished by their power; many couldn't believe that Scruggs was playing a five-string banjo. Their recordings of Monroe standards like "Blue Moon of Kentucky" and "Molly and Tenbrooks" along with new instrumentals like "Bluegrass Breakdown," which prominently featured Scruggs, were immediate sensations. Monroe preferred high-energy, fast-paced music, often pitching the tunes up a key or two (from D to E, for example) to give them a brighter sound. Flatt, a more laid-back vocalist and guitarist, had trouble keeping up with the rest of the band; it is for this reason, some say, that he developed his characteristic single-note bass runs (as a way to keep up with the frantic pace).

Monroe was a difficult taskmaster who worked his band long and hard hours. In 1948 Flatt and Scruggs quit the band, taking with them bassist Watts and recruiting a young singer/guitarist named MAC WISEMAN along with fiddler Jim Shumate (who was another Monroe alum). They signed a deal with Mercury Records and took the name the Foggy Mountain Boys after the CARTER FAMILY song, "Foggy Mountain Top." Curly Seckler took Wiseman's place almost immediately, playing mandolin (although this instrument was rarely prominently featured in the band's recordings, perhaps because they did not wish to compete with Monroe). Their most famous recording of this period is the 1949 instrumental "Foggy Mountain Breakdown," which was used eighteen years later as the theme for *Bonnie and Clyde*.

The group was signed to a radio job in Bristol, Virginia, where their broadcasts influenced local musicians like the STANLEY BROTHERS and DON RENO to play in the new bluegrass style. They signed with Columbia Records in 1950 (leading Monroe to leave the label, because he felt that they had stolen his sound). One of their first recordings for the new label was "Earl's Breakdown" (1951). By quickly turning the pegs on the banjo, Scruggs was able to drop a note a full pitch after he had struck it. A few years later, he developed special tuners, now known as Scrugg's pegs, to automatically drop or raise a string's pitch.

In 1953 the band signed on with flour maker Martha White, who became their sponsor for many years on radio, television, and tours. They were invited to join the *Grand Ole Opry* in 1955, the same year they launched their first syndicated television program. Through the later fifties, they toured widely on the bluegrass circuit.

In the early sixties, Columbia started to market the group to the FOLK-REVIVAL audience and assigned them a younger producer. They began recording songs by BOB DYLAN and PETE SEEGER, among others, and were hired to perform the theme for *The Beverly Hillbillies* TV program, resulting in their first pop hit, 1962's "Ballad of Jed Clampett." They made guest appearances on the show, further promoting the group. Their big break came in 1967 when several of their songs were used in the film *Bonnie and Clyde*, which attracted a hipper, younger audience. However, as their recordings moved increasingly in a pop direction, Flatt became disillusioned with the new sound. Always a traditionalist, he wanted to return to recording the music that had made them famous. Scruggs, on the other hand, had two young sons who played contemporary music and wanted to broaden his musical horizons. This led to the duo splitting in 1969.

Flatt formed the Nashville Grass with old friends Curly Seckler and Mac Wiseman; Scruggs formed the Earl Scruggs Review with his sons Randy and Gary, along with dobroist Josh Graves. Sadly, Scruggs took a backseat to the other musicians in the Revue, playing less and less of his distinctive banjo, while the material they chose to perform was drawn from the weaker folk-rock songs. By the mid-seventies, the band had pretty much run out of steam, and Scruggs has been almost totally inactive for the last fifteen years. Flatt's Nashville Grass lacked the spark of the original Flatt and Scruggs band of the fifties but was a serviceable bluegrass unit; he introduced a hot young picker named MARTY STUART, who has since broken into the NEW-COUNTRY market. As his health deteriorated through the seventies, the quality of Flatt's lead singing and the band's recordings faltered, although he continued to record and perform until his death in 1979.

Select Discography
The Mercury Sessions, Vols. 1 and 2, Mercury 512644. Reissues all of their Mercury recordings made between 1948 and 1950. Also available on two CDs from Rounder with more complete notes.

Don't Get Above Your Raisin', Rounder 08. Fine early Columbia recordings from the fifties.
Blue Ridge Cabin Home, County 102. More Columbia recordings from the fifties.
1949–1958, Bear Family 15472. Four-CD set of all of their classic fifties recordings.
1959–1963, Bear Family 15559. Five-CD set picking up the chronology from the previous set.
Songs of the Famous Carter Family, Columbia 08464. Recorded in the sixties during the folk revival.

◀ FLECK, BELA

(born 1953, New York, NY)

A progressive BANJO player closely associated with his one-time teacher TONY TRISCHKA, Fleck's career has moved from PROGRESSIVE BLUEGRASS to bebop-flavored jazz to an amalgam of funk and jazz with his latest group, the Flecktones.

Fleck's playing is very much in the style of Tony Trischka in its explorations of the outer limits of five-string banjo technique. Unlike Trischka, he uses silence as a suggestive element in his music (influenced by some of the great jazz improvisers of the fifties and sixties), so that there are often large gaps in his solos, which combine rapid-fire bursts of melody and choppy chords.

Fleck made a series of solo albums for Rounder Records in the late seventies, including some interesting instrumentals that combined a bebop feeling for melody and harmony with traditional bluegrass instrumentation (particularly on his LP *Crossing the Tracks*). A frequent session-mate of these days was Sam Bush, who was also one of the founder/leaders of NEW GRASS REVIVAL; when that band's original banjo player quit in the early eighties, Fleck came on board and performed with the group for several years.

In 1989 he formed his progressive funk-jazz group, the Flecktones, featuring brothers Victor (bass) and Roy (on drumitar, a drum-machine synthesizer in the shape of an electric guitar) Wooten along with Howard Levy (harmonica and keyboards). The group was signed to Warner Brothers and marketed not to the country audience but as a new-acoustic/jazz ensemble. Their music is marred by the often grating, intrusive harmonica playing of Levy, who produces a particularly harsh, nasal whine on the instrument, and the annoying use of drum machine, which tends to reduce all the group's music to a robotic, monotonous funk beat. Fleck's banjo playing, oddly enough, is not heavily featured; he tends to vamp behind the drums or harmonica, and his own solos seem lifeless. In 1993 harmonica/keyboard player Levy quit the band, leaving it a trio.

Select Discography

Crossing the Tracks, Rounder 121.
Daybreak, Rounder 11518; *Places*, Rounder 11522. Two CD compilations drawn from his various Rounder LPs of the eighties.
Bela Fleck and the Flecktones, Warner Bros. 26124. First of three LPs with this jazz-bluegrass fusion group.

◀ FLYING BURRITO BROTHERS, THE

*(1969–1971, sporadically thereafter; original lineup: Gram Parsons [guitar, vocals];
Chris Hillman [guitar, mandolin, vocals]; Chris Ethridge [bass]; "Sneaky" Pete
Kleinow [pedal steel], Jon Corneal [drums])*

The Flying Burrito Brothers were a seminal turn-of-the-decade COUNTRY-ROCK
band, featuring GRAM PARSONS's emotional lead vocals and excellent original songs
(at least until he left the group in 1970). After the demise of their initial lineup,
they remained popular in Europe for years and toured widely there through the
mid-eighties with many personnel changes.

After recording *Sweetheart of the Rodeo*, the BYRDS foray into country-rock, Byrds
founder CHRIS HILLMAN and newcomer Parsons left the band to pursue country-rock
to its logical conclusions. In forming the Flying Burrito Brothers, they were among
the first to incorporate a PEDAL STEEL GUITAR into a pop-rock band (the whining
pedal steel being a hallmark of most country recordings of the era). It's interesting
to note that POCO, formed out of the remnants of Buffalo Springfield in 1969, also
employed a pedal steel player (Rusty Young), while MICHAEL NESMITH's First National Band, another pioneering country-rock outfit, had Red Rhodes on steel.

The original Burritos recorded their classic debut album, *The Gilded Palace of
Sin*, featuring Parsons's updated country HONKY-TONK ballad, "Sin City." The band
announced their nouveau country look with the cover photo, in which bandsmen
were garbed in traditionally lavish Nudie suits (crafted by famous Nashville tailor
Nudie Cohen), although instead of country motifs the suits featured hand-stitched
marijuana leaves as a design element. The album also featured a countrified cover
of the Rolling Stones' "Wild Horses," the ever-popular "Devil in Disguise," cowritten by Hillman and Parsons and covered by numerous PROGRESSIVE BLUEGRASS
bands through the seventies, and "Hot Burrito #2 (I'm Your Boy)," an Ethridge/
Parsons composition.

While the album was being made, drummer Jon Corneal left the group and
was replaced by ex-Byrds drummer Michael Clarke; soon after, Ethridge left, and
was replaced by Hillman on bass (an instrument he had played in the Byrds);
Bernie Leadon was added on guitar and vocals as well (he had previously performed with Doug Dillard and GENE CLARK in their early country-rock band). The
second album was completed and released as *Burrito Deluxe* in 1970, but argu-
ments among Parsons and the rest of the band, due to Parsons's increasing drug
use and unreliability, led to another shakeup, with Parsons embarking on a solo
career and replaced by Rick Roberts. The more-or-less original group released one
more album, but it suffered from Parsons's absence.

Further defections came in mid-1971, when Leadon left to form the EAGLES and
Kleinow retired. Replacements were Al Perkins (pedal steel), Byron Berline (fiddle), Roger Bush (bass), and Kenny Wertz (guitar). This ensemble lasted as a live
touring band until late 1971, when Hillman and Perkins joined ex–Buffalo Springfield leader Stephen Stills to form the short-lived country-rock outfit Manassas. The
balance of the band, without Roberts, became the nucleus of COUNTRY GAZETTE, a

bluegrass-oriented band. Roberts, meanwhile, enlisted yet another group to make a final European tour, before forming the rock group Firefall in 1972.

The legend and legacy of the Burrito Brothers would not die; original members Ethridge and Kleinow revived the name for two mid-seventies Columbia albums, featuring the duo of Gib Guibeau (fiddle) and Gene Parsons (drums) along with bassist Joel Scott-Hill. Ethridge quickly bowed out, replaced by latter-day Byrdsman Skip Battin. The group held on until the mid-eighties with varying personnel, but none of these later "Burrito" recordings were anywhere near as good as their original albums.

Although they enjoyed only marginal success on either pop or country charts during their heyday, the Burritos became a model for almost every country-rock group that followed. Their understanding of the basic affinity between hippie rebellion and country attitudes would finally bear fruit in the mid-eighties when a number of Southern NEW-COUNTRY bands, as well as solo acts, picked up their musical cues. Although the Eagles had greater success (and perhaps more influence on the next generation), it can be said that without the Burrito Brothers to blaze the country-rock trail, there would have been no Eagles.

Select Discography

Last of the Red Hot Burritos, A&M 4343. Reissues their third album.
Farther Along: The Best of the Flying Burrito Brothers, A&M 5216. All the good stuff from their original albums, plus six never-before-released tracks. Includes most of their first album.

◀ FOLEY, RED

(born Clyde Julian Foley, 1910, Blue Lark, KY; died 1968)

Although best-remembered as a smooth-voiced singer of gospel and country ballads, Foley's career took him through a variety of styles, from string-band vocals through R&B, ROCKABILLY, and jump sides to his mainstream Nashville outings. A pioneer performer on radio and television, Foley did much to popularize country sounds for a mainstream audience.

Foley spent most of his high school and college years on the athletic field, winning numerous awards. He won an amateur singing contest at age seventeen and three years later was hired by country radio producer John Lair to be the vocalist with the WLS *Barn Dance* radio program's house band, the Cumberland Ridge Runners. His smooth-voiced vocals on old-time ballads and songs made him an obvious candidate for wider radio exposure; seven years later, Lair built the very popular *Renfro Valley Barn Dance* radio program around Foley. Foley became a big star thanks to this radio exposure, which continued through the forties on WLS, the GRAND OLE OPRY, and finally, from 1954 to 1961, on the early country-music television program, *The Ozark Jubilee*, based in Springfield, Missouri.

In 1941 Decca Records signed Foley to a lifetime contract. His first recordings were in a sentimental vein, including 1945's "Old Shep" (later covered by ELVIS PRESLEY) and 1947's "Foggy River." In the early fifties, he showed an interest in rockabilly and bop, laying down "Sugarfoot Rag" with guitarist Hank Garland. The two would make many other rockabilly-flavored recordings, often accompanied by the sugary ANITA KERR Singers. His bop-style numbers include "Birmingham Bounce" from 1950 and the square-dance favorite "Alabama Jubilee" from one year later. Foley was also interested in R&B, and he recorded covers of "Shake a Hand" (an early ode to integration originally recorded by Faye Adams) and "Hearts of Stone" (originally by the Charms) in the early fifties. Yet his biggest hit was 1951's "Peace in the Valley," a clever combination of country sentimentality with a religious message, and the first gospel song ever to sell a million copies on disc.

Foley spent most of the fifties bouncing between styles, although his gospel recordings were the ones that seemed to do best. Meanwhile, he was increasingly changing his style from that of a jazzy country singer to that of a pop-styled crooner, and the accompaniments on his recordings became knee-deep in the swelling choruses and killer strings that were typical of Nashville at its most grotesque.

In the sixties, Foley continued to be a popular attraction and even appeared for one season on a network TV show, *Mr. Smith Goes to Washington*, costarring with Fess ("Davey Crockett") Parker. One year after being inducted into the Country Music Hall of Fame, he died of a heart attack after a performance. Foley's daughter married teen popster Pat Boone, and they in turn produced white-bread country queen DEBBIE BOONE.

Select Discography
Country Music Hall of Fame, MCA 10084. Selections from his Decca recordings, many sadly featuring atrocious arrangements.

◀ FOLK REVIVAL, THE

(c. 1958–1965)

For a brief period in the late fifties and early sixties, folk music was tremendously successful on the pop music charts. Granted, these hits were mostly produced by professional or at least semiprofessional musicians (not by the "folks" themselves) and were often watered-down versions of true folk styles. Nonetheless, the folk revival had a profound impact on the future direction of pop and country music styles.

There has always been a fascination in the city for the culture of the country. In the nineteenth century, Romantic poets and philosophers idealized country life, and thus encouraged the first folklorists to go into the field to collect the traditional songs, dances, and legends of the ordinary "folk." At the turn of the century, folklorists like Francis James Child of Harvard University and JOHN LOMAX, working out of Texas, published influential collections: Child of literary ballads, and Lomax of the COWBOY SONGS that he collected throughout the Midwest. The recording and radio industries that blossomed in the twenties further spread folk music to the city; it was now possible for a resident of Manhattan to buy a recording of New Orleans jazz or Tennessee string-band music. Traditional folk musicians like WOODY

GUTHRIE and AUNT MOLLY JACKSON were brought to major urban areas to perform, sometimes as curiosities and sometimes to support various political causes.

After World War II, the first folk boom occurred when the Weavers, a group led by banjoist PETE SEEGER, had a massive pop hit with a version of Leadbelly's "Goodnight, Irene," orchestrated by pop producer Gordon Jenkins. The Weavers' success was unexpected but short-lived; because many of its members had been involved in radical political causes in the thirties, the group was effectively silenced during the McCarthy/Communist scare of the early fifties. By the late fifties and early sixties, a new generation of more freshly scrubbed (and less politically adventurous) groups arose to pick up the Weavers' style, beginning with the blandly innocuous Kingston Trio (who had a big hit with the traditional banjo blues number, "Tom Dooley"), the Rooftop Singers, the Chad Mitchell Trio (who specialized in more politically oriented and satirical material), and, of course, Peter, Paul and Mary. More sophisticated groups like the NEW LOST CITY RAMBLERS were able to ride the crest of the popularity of the mainstream groups while never achieving quite the commercial success that these other groups enjoyed.

In this same period, country music also took a turn toward its folk roots. The popularity of the so-called "saga songs," newly composed songs that were written in the manner of traditional ballads, was evidence of this new folk emphasis. JOHNNY CASH's series of albums on folk themes; the renewed popularity of traditional-style performers like Mother Maybelle Carter; some country acts' attempts to cross over into pop-folk (like the BROWNS, who began recording folk-oriented material); and a renewed interest in BLUEGRASS music all showed the effects of the folk revival.

More important to the development of popular and country music in the long run was the emergence of the SINGER/SONGWRITER. Traditionally in pop and country music, professional songwriters wrote songs that were then recorded by trained singers. A songwriter who couldn't "sing" up to professional standards would never have dreamed of recording his or her own material. Nor was the material itself necessarily an expression of personal feelings; it was often written to meet the needs of a specific audience or market. However, in folk circles (and in early country music), artists often wrote and performed their own material; musical ability or the lack thereof (by mainstream standards) was not a deterrent to performing.

Woody Guthrie pointed the way, showing how a singer could be the best interpreter of his own material, despite his rudimentary GUITAR style and nasal voice. BOB DYLAN during the folk-revival days expanded the notion of singer/songwriter, and thousands more arose in his wake. WILLIE NELSON was perhaps the first country songwriter to realize that despite his perceived lack of musical abilities, he too could be the best performer for his own material.

By the mid-sixties, the energy of the folk revival was pretty much absorbed by rock and roll. Interest in folk music reemerged in the mid-seventies, at which time a more sophisticated revival occurred, with various regional musical styles, from WESTERN SWING and CAJUN to old-time string band and Tex-Mex, coming to the fore.

◀ FORD, TENNESSEE ERNIE

(born 1919, Bristol, TN; died 1991)

Finger-snappin', pencil-moustached television star and singer, Ford is best remembered for his (melo)dramatic rendition of MERLE TRAVIS's "Sixteen Tons," a mid-fifties hit. Ford was as much a personality as a country singer, and he became a well-recognized icon of fifties and sixties TV variety shows.

Ford did not have a particularly rural upbringing; he was raised in Bristol, a Southern mill town, where he sang in the high-school choir and played in the school band. When he was eighteen, he got his first job as an announcer at a local radio station and then enrolled in the Cincinnati Conservatory of Music for classical music training. After serving in World War II, he returned to radio work in Pasadena, California, and began working as a vocalist with West Coast cowboy-style bands, most notably with CLIFFIE STONE, a prominent West Coast musician/bandleader/promoter who quickly took Ford under his wing. As an executive of the newly formed Capitol Records, Stone got Ford his recording contract and went on to manage his lengthy career.

Signed to Capitol Records in 1948, Ford had a number of hits with pseudo-Western numbers, beginning in 1949 with "Mule Train," "Smokey Mountain Boogie," and "Anticipation Blues," jazz-flavored renderings of pop tunes written in the style of country blues and COWBOY SONGS. A year later, he scored big with his own composition, "Shotgun Boogie," which lead to his own network radio show.

In 1955 Ford covered Merle Travis's "Sixteen Tons," a song about the life of a coal miner, which Travis had written in the folk style. Ford's rendition became a massive hit, decked out with a crooning chorus and pop-ish instrumental arrangement. Following its success on pop and country charts, Ford had his own TV variety show on NBC, which lasted until 1961, and made regular appearances on a number of other shows, making him a familiar face in American households.

In the early sixties, Ford turned to more conservative material, recording country's first million-selling album, *Hymns* (1963), the first in a series of all-religious recordings. Balancing this with remakes of patriotic material like "America the Beautiful," Ford became a leading conservative voice in the country hierarchy. His smooth-voiced, unthreatening renditions of mostly time-worn material cemented his sixties popularity. He had a chart hit in 1971 with "Happy Songs of Love," but Ford's career had plateaued by that time, although he still performed into the eighties. Ford died in 1991.

Select Discography

Sixteen Tons of Country Boogie, Rhino 70975. Compilation of his better earlier recordings.

A Tribute, Capitol 98953. Hits and more obscure tracks from the Capitol vaults.

Tennessee Ernie Ford, Capitol 95291. Smothered in strings and safe for Middle America, Ford croons his way into your heart.

◀ FORESTER SISTERS, THE

(1984–ongoing; Kathy, June, Kim, and Christy Forester)

Well-scrubbed and perky, the singing Foresters have true country roots and a progressive attitude that has made them consistent chart-toppers since the mid-eighties.

Born in Lookout Mountain, Georgia, to a farmer father and millworker mother, the four children first performed at their local church. In 1978, while Christy and Kim were still in college and June and Kathy were working as grade-school teachers, they formed their first band and played local clubs. A demo tape landed them a contract with Warner Brothers in 1984, and their first hit came a year later, the up-tempo "(That's What You Do) When You're in Love," a traditional stand-by-your-man song but with a twist. (Although the man has cheated on his sweetheart and is forgiven for his transgressions, the lyric implies that perhaps she was doing a little cheatin' too.) They followed this a year later with the play on words of "Lyin' in His Arms Again," the story of a spunky girl who has cheated on her man (a reversal of country's typical gender roles).

The Foresters' first recordings were produced by Wendy Waldman, who had had a career as a folk-rock SINGER/SONGWRITER in the seventies. Waldman supplied them with one of their most moving early hits, 1988's "Letter Home." This simple narrative, about a woman who was homecoming queen, married young and foolishly, and then was deserted by her husband and left to raise the kids, again focuses on issues traditional country songs avoided. While there was always infidelity in country music, the impact of that infidelity on the family—and particularly on the woman left behind—was rarely explored.

The Foresters' early-nineties hits continued to emphasize their spirited, female point of view. Their recordings took on a more jazzy, almost WESTERN SWING approach with 1991's scornful "Men," which sided with their audience of young female boot-wearers, and with the not-quite-over-the-hill older woman's anthem, "I Got a Date" (1992). In its playful video, a newly single mom goes out on her first date since her divorce, reflecting Nashville's recognition of America's changing demographics.

The Foresters' sunny harmonies and golly-gosh-gee personalities make them perfect country performers. While they champion a woman's point of view in their music, they are so wholesome looking that they can hardly be considered threatening to men, who can enjoy the frothy, up-tempo songs without listening too closely to the words.

Select Discography

Greatest Hits, Warner Brothers 26821. Their hits up to 1989.

Talkin' About Men, Warner Bros. 26500. Concept album about the trouble boys create for gals.

◀ FOSTER AND LLOYD

(1987–1990: Radney Foster, born 1959, Del Rio, TX; Bill Lloyd, born 1955, Bowling Green, KY)

Foster and Lloyd brought Beatles-style harmonies and a pop-rock sensibility to NEW-COUNTRY music.

Typical of mid-eighties country acts, this duo brought a myriad of influences to their music, from COUNTRY-ROCK sounds inspired by POCO and the EAGLES to the smooth harmonies of the EVERLY BROTHERS and Beatles John Lennon and Paul McCartney to the HONKY-TONK blues of HANK WILLIAMS. Their biggest hit was their first single, 1987's "Crazy Over You," which combined an intelligent lyric with a solid beat. Their sound was halfway between the cutting edge of NEW COUNTRY and a pleasant, Hall and Oates–style (or perhaps BROOKS-AND-DUNN, although they came later) pop sound.

Radney Foster went solo in 1992, projecting the image of a yuppie country singer with his wire-rim glasses and well-starched suits. His first album featured support from other nouveau country acts, including MARY CHAPIN CARPENTER and JOHN HIATT.

Select Discography

Foster & Lloyd, RCA 6372.
Faster & Llouder, RCA 9587. Their second album.
Del Rio, TX, 1959, Arista 18713. Radney Foster's 1992 solo album, named for the place and year of his birth.
Labor of Love, Arista 18757. 1994 Foster solo outing featuring MARY CHAPIN CARPENTER.

◀ FRAZIER, DALLAS

(born 1939, Spiro, OK)

Frazier is a powerful vocalist and songwriter in pop and country styles who is better known for his songs than his performances.

Born in rural Oklahoma, Frazier and his family made the migration to California, settling like many other Okies in a town called Bakersfield. As a teenager there, he won a talent contest sponsored by FERLIN HUSKY, earning him a place in Husky's road show. He was signed to Capitol Records in the early sixties and moved to Nashville to also work as a songwriter. One of his first hits as a songwriter was the pop novelty "Alley Oop" (based on the antics of the comic-strip hero), recorded by the Hollywood Argyles, but he also had solid country hits as a writer with Husky's recording of "Timber (I'm Fallin')," O. C. Smith's "Son of Hickory Holler," MERLE HAGGARD's "California Cottonfields," CHARLEY PRIDE's "Then Who Am I?" and CHARLIE RICH's "Mohair Sam."

His mid-sixties recordings for Capitol were only somewhat successful; he had a minor hit with his song "Elvira," which was much more successful when covered in 1981 by the OAK RIDGE BOYS. Other contemporary country singers have revived Frazier's material, including EMMYLOU HARRIS, who has recorded his "Beneath Still

Waters." In the early seventies, Frazier recorded for RCA, again with only moderate success, before giving up his performing career.

◀ FRICKIE, JANIE

(born Jane Fricke, 1947, South Whitley, IN)

Frickie is an all-around professional who began her career as a backup singer and had moderate success as a pop-style country vocalist in the late seventies through the mid-eighties.

Inspired by folk revivalists Joan Baez and Judy Collins, Frickie took up playing the GUITAR in her teen years, eventually relocating to Memphis, where she began working as a backup singer for jingles. She then made her way to Nashville, where she worked many country sessions as an uncredited vocalist. She also worked with the Lea Jane Singers, who backed country acts like neo-outlaw JOHNNY RODRIGUEZ. In 1977 Frickie was signed to a solo contract by famed producer BILLY SHERRILL, supposedly because country deejays had sent in letters to Sherrill begging to know the identity of the woman they could hear singing backup on many hit records.

Because of her wide range of experiences singing everything from pop-rock to soda-pop jingles, Sherrill had difficulty deciding what direction to take Frickie's career. Meanwhile, he invited her to overdub a harmony part on CHARLIE RICH's "On My Knees," giving her her first label credit as a backup singer. The song shot to number one, helping to launch Frickie's career. After a few more singles produced by Sherrill, she hooked up with producer Jim Ed Norman, who gave her more upbeat, danceable songs, including her first number-one hit, 1982's "Don't Worry 'Bout Me Baby," with backup vocals by soon-to-be NEW-COUNTRY star RICKY SKAGGS. A third producer, Bob Montgomery, brought her another 1982 hit, "It Ain't Easy Bein' Easy," and her 1983 follow-up hit, "He's a Heartache (Looking for a Place to Happen)." These bubbly numbers, recorded in the ALABAMA/EXILE mode of rock-flavored country, launched Frickie on a glitzy career as a pop singer.

Frickie's success lasted through the mid-eighties. She cut one more session as an overdub singer, accompanying MERLE HAGGARD on 1985's number-one "A Place to Fall Apart," another one of Merle's songs of a relationship gone bad. She signed with new producer Norro Wilson to create a bluesier, gutsier sound, yielding her last number-one hit, 1986's "Always Have, Always Will"; it was at this time that she added the *i* to her last name, because people were always mispronouncing it as "Frick."

With the popularity of new-country stars, Frickie's pop approach sounds decidedly old-fashioned; meanwhile, she has moved into the apparel business, introducing fashions based on her own stagewear designs, with some success.

Select Discography

Celebration, Columbia 40684. Two-cassette set of her hits from 1976 to 1986.

◀ FRIEDMAN, KINKY

(born Richard Friedman, 1944, Palestine, TX)

Friedman and his band, the Texas Jewboys, were popular on the folk, rock, and comedy circuits in the early seventies for their musically literate satires of WESTERN SWING and other popular country forms.

Friedman is an anomaly: a well-educated man of Jewish descent who hails from a small Texas town. His father was a university professor, and Friedman grew up with a sardonic sense of humor. When just out of college, Friedman, along with his close friend Jeff Shelby, formed his first band—a pop-rock send-up known as King Arthur and the Carrotts, specializing in satires of surf music. The two later formed the Texas Jewboys, and by the end of the decade they had a recording contract with the folk-rock label Vanguard.

The Jewboys's biggest hit was 1973's "Sold American," a social-protest song that was later covered by country star GLEN CAMPBELL. Friedman also created a number of tongue-in-cheek Western songs, including "Ride 'Em Jewboy," the unofficial theme song of the band, and the WAYLON JENNINGS–produced "Carryin' the Torch," a satire of the typical country WEEPER, except that the much-put-upon and long-suffering female in this song is the Statue of Liberty. The band folded in 1977, but Friedman continued to perform into the eighties as a solo act. His career took another unusual twist in the mid-eighties when he wrote the first in a number of successful mystery novels, many of which have plots that deal with the ins and outs of the music industry.

Friedman's irreverent look at country clichés helped broaden the audience for the real McCoy, while it also appealed to younger country musicians who hoped to break free from the pop schlock that was dribbling out of Nashville in the sixties and seventies.

◀ FRIZZELL, DAVID

(born 1941, Corsicana, TX)

The much younger brother of legendary HONKY-TONK wailer LEFTY FRIZZELL, David became a COUNTRYPOLITAN star in the early eighties, thanks to his successful duets with SHELLY WEST and a few solo recordings.

Frizzell had a long, arduous climb to success, beginning in the late fifties when he moved to California where his brother Lefty already lived. He was signed by producer Don Law to Columbia in 1958, and released a few singles that barely grazed the bottom of the charts. He then enlisted in the army for a couple of years but was back on Columbia in the late sixties, scoring minor success with 1970's "I Just Can't Help Believing." He toured with BUCK OWENS in the early seventies, signing with Capitol and scoring a few minor hits in 1973 and 1974. He recorded for RSO and MCA, again without much luck, and in 1977 opened his own Concord, California, nightclub, where he began performing with Shelly West, daughter of legendary country chanteuse DOTTIE WEST.

The duo had one release on the disco-oriented Casablanca label before moving to Viva Records, co-owned by actor Clint Eastwood. Their 1981 song, "You're the Reason God Made Oklahoma," was featured in Eastwood's film *Any Which Way You Can* and became a big hit. They continued to record as a duo through 1985, charting hits with "Another Honky Tonk Night on Broadway" in 1983 and "Do Me Right" in 1985. Meanwhile, Frizzell had solo hits with comic novelty "I'm Gonna Hire a Wino to Decorate Our Home" (1982) and "A Million Light Beers Ago" (1983), along with more mainstream countrypolitan numbers like 1985's "Country Music Love Affair."

Frizzell pretty much dropped off the charts after the mid-eighties; his rather melodramatic, pop-oriented style was supplanted by the NEW-COUNTRY movement.

◀ FRIZZELL, LEFTY

(born William Orville Frizzell, 1928, Corsicana, TX; died 1975)

One of the most influential of all the HONKY-TONK singers, Frizzell brought a barroom sensibility into a more mainstream country setting. His vocal mannerisms have been widely imitated, both by traditional country performers such as GEORGE JONES and MERLE HAGGARD, and NEW-COUNTRY stars like GEORGE STRAIT (who recorded "Lefty's Gone" in tribute to the earlier star) and RANDY TRAVIS, to name just a few.

Frizzell was the son of a footloose oil-field worker and gained his nickname thanks to a teenage career as a Golden Gloves boxer. He began performing in Dallas and Waco–area honky-tonks, covering the hits of his two idols, JIMMIE RODGERS and ERNEST TUBB. He had his first hit in 1950 with "If You Got the Money, Honey, I've Got the Time," a classic honky-tonk song noteworthy for its forthright lyrics, Lefty's incomparable vocalisms, and a simple accompaniment (although instead of fiddle or steel guitar, it featured prominent tinkling piano, an early sign of the coming NASHVILLE SOUND). 1951 brought four songs that all made the country top ten at the same time, a feat never since repeated by any artist. Lefty seemed poised to be more popular than HANK WILLIAMS, but then his hits dried up.

In the late fifties, Nashville was swept by a craze for story songs—mini balladlike sagas that told stories of the mythical Old South. Frizzell abandoned his beer-soaked honky-tonk sound to make a number of popular records in this mold, including "Long Black Veil" (1959) and "Saginaw, Michigan" (1964). Sadly, this was his last hurrah as a charting performer; alcohol took its toll on his recordings and live performances, although he continued to perform until his death in 1975. He had been more or less forgotten by mainstream Nashville by then, but his recordings would influence the next generation of country performers.

Select Discography

American Originals, Columbia 45087. His best recordings made between 1950 and 1975.

The Best of Lefty Frizzell, Rhino 71005. Similar to the Columbia set.

Life's Like Poetry, Bear Family 15550. Haul out the checkbook and put a second mortgage on your home; this twelve-CD set gives you 330 songs, including everything Lefty recorded between 1950 and 1975, with a 153-page book by Charles Wolfe.

◀ FRUMHOLZ, STEVE

(born 1945, Temple, TX)

Texas, with its rich individualistic tradition, seems to nurture oddball country stars who combine the sensibility of seventies singer/songwriters with the raucousness of the OUTLAW-COUNTRY movement, including JIMMIE DALE GILMORE, JOE ELY, and LYLE LOVETT. Frumholz is another in this pantheon of musical eccentrics; his combination of rock, BLUEGRASS, country, and God knows what else has made him a legendary performer with a loyal, if small, following.

Enrolling in Texas State University in 1963, Frumholz met future country star MICHAEL MARTIN MURPHEY and the twosome became a duo, later forming the Dallas Country Jug Band. After college and a brief stint in the navy, Frumholz formed a close working relationship with SINGER/SONGWRITER Dan McCrimmon, and the two took the colorful name of Frummox, recording a COUNTRY-ROCK LP for the tiny L.A. label Probe in 1969; two years later, they briefly worked as Stephen Stills's backup band. During this period, Frumholz recorded an album for MIKE NESMITH's Countryside label, but it never saw the light of day.

After struggling for a few more years on the West Coast, Frumholz returned to Austin in 1974, where a vibrant outlaw music scene was brewing. He was befriended by WILLIE NELSON, and appeared on Nelson's *Sound in Your Mind* album as a backup singer; he also provided original material for Nelson to record. In 1976 he finally made an album that was released, aptly called *A Rumour in My Own Time*, featuring many friends, including Nelson, banjoist Doug Dillard, steel guitarist Red Rhodes, and folksinger John Sebastian. Although a cult success, the album was not a commercial one, and Capitol dropped him after he released an even more far-out collection of original material the following year.

By 1979 Nelson had his own label, Lone Star, distributed by Columbia, and invited old friend Frumholz to make an album, titled *Jus' Playin' Along*. This also failed to generate much in the way of sales, and Frumholz has since been one of many "local heroes" who plays regularly in the greater Austin area.

G,

◀ GATLIN BROTHERS, THE

(Larry [guitar, vocals] born 1948, Seminole, TX; Steve [guitar, vocals] born 1951, Olney, TX; Rudy [bass, vocals] born 1952, Olney, TX)

The Gatlins, a popular three-part harmony group of the seventies and eighties, combine Las Vegas glitz with down-home appeal. Although not major chart burners, they have had a steady success rate as a country act on the road and on television.

Larry, the eldest brother, is the group's leader and its main songwriter. All three brothers performed together as children, beginning in church, leading to a stint as a gospel group on Slim Willet's Abilene-based TV show when they were in their teens; they also recorded a religious LP for the tiny Sword & Shield label. Soon after, Larry went into music full-time, working originally with the Imperials, a Las Vegas gospel-harmony outfit that accompanied many major country artists, including ELVIS PRESLEY. DOTTIE WEST encouraged Larry to move to Nashville in 1972, where, a year later, he signed with the Monument label, scoring his first hit in 1976 with his song "Broken Lady."

Meanwhile, brothers Steve and Rudy finished their education at Texas Tech and, along with sister LaDonna and her husband, came to Nashville to audition as backup singers for CHARLEY PRIDE. They eventually worked for TAMMY WYNETTE, leaving her to rejoin their elder brother as a group after his first single hit. Larry continued as a solo act backed by his siblings until 1978, when "I Just Wish You Were Someone I Love" hit number one, credited to Larry Gatlin with Brothers and Friends. Their next single, attributed to the Gatlin Brothers Band, went to number two and by the end of the year the major labels were pounding down their door. They also began appearing on TV variety shows, spreading their appeal well beyond the country audience.

In 1979, for new label Columbia, they scored their next number-one hit, "All the Gold in California," inspired by the bidding war that had ensued among the big-time record execs for the rights to the band. The next three-and-a-half years had their ups and downs as Larry battled alcohol and drug addiction, and the band turned out only a few minor hits. In 1983 they hit number one again with "Houston (Means I'm Closer to You)," although Larry was at a personal low point. The swinging number was an immediate sensation and was followed by another city ode, "Denver." Then Larry checked himself into drug rehab, finally breaking a decade-long pattern of abuse. He became a spokesperson for Members Only, a maker of men's jackets and sponsor of drug-education advertisements. The Gatlins continued to record for Columbia through 1988, scoring hits with "The Lady Takes the Cowboy Every Time" and "Talkin' to the Moon." They signed with the smaller Universe label in 1988, reflecting the fact that their close harmonies and pop arrangements were becoming old hat in the face of the NEW-COUNTRY onslaught.

Still, the Gatlins remain a big draw at Vegas and other lounge venues. Larry scored points as a Broadway star, taking over the lead from MAC DAVIS in *The Will Rogers Follies* in 1992.

Select Discography

Biggest Hits Columbia 44471. Drawn from their mid-eighties recordings.

17 Greatest Hits, Columbia 40187. Cassette-only release featuring their best-known songs recorded between 1974 and 1985.

◀ GAYLE, CRYSTAL

(born Brenda Gail Webb, 1951, Paintsville, KY)

One of the most successful female vocalists of the seventies, Gayle brought an easy-listening sensibility to country music. Gayle's vocal style is the antithesis of the gutsy sound of many of Nashville's most famous women, with a soft sexuality that is decidedly unthreatening. Her image, with her long, straight hair and earth-mother clothing, suggests a seventies post-hippie look, while her vocal style is so middle-of-the-road as to be almost antiseptic.

The youngest sister of country star LORETTA LYNN, Gayle began her career when she was sixteen, backing her sister and CONWAY TWITTY. Lynn gave her her stage name (perhaps inspired, as Lynn tells it, by the country chain of Krystal hamburger stands). Gayle made her first solo recording at age nineteen with her sister's country WEEPER, "I Cried (the Blue Right Out of My Eyes)," but did not crack the country charts again for five years.

Resisting the efforts of Nashville to mold her into a younger Loretta Lynn, Gayle finally hooked up with producer Allen Reynolds, who supplied her 1975 hit, "Wrong Road Again." Three years later, she scored a major pop crossover hit with the bar-lounge favorite, "Don't It Make My Brown Eyes Blue." The tinkling piano prominently featured on this cut, along with Gayle's purring vocals, has earned it a rightful place in MOR heaven. She had a few more pop successes in the late seventies.

In the eighties, Gayle returned to her roots as a country chanteuse and had country hits with a cover of JIMMIE RODGERS's "Miss the Mississippi and You" in 1981 and "Cry" in 1986. However, by the late eighties when NEW COUNTRY was in full swing, Gayle's more relaxed vocal style and the mainstream production values of her recordings made her sound decidedly old-fashioned, even to country listeners. Still, she continues to be a steady concert draw and regular performer.

Select Discography

Hollywood, Tennessee, Liberty 95564. This 1990 reissue of a 1981 album is a classic of the COUNTRYPOLITAN sound, right down to the title.

The Best of Crystal Gayle, Warner Bros. 25622. Her countryesque hits of the eighties.

◀ GENTRY, BOBBIE

(born Roberta Streeter, 1944, Chickasaw County, MS)

Gentry was a slinky-voiced, sultry songstress who had one megahit with 1967's "Ode to Billy Joe."

Raised in the Mississippi delta, Gentry first learned piano by imitating the sounds she heard in church. When the family relocated to Southern California when she was thirteen, she took up a number of other instruments, including GUITAR, BANJO, bass, and vibes. She had always written her own songs, beginning with an ode to the family dog written when she was seven, and continued to write new material through her teen years.

While studying philosophy at UCLA, Gentry began performing an occasional club date. Her love of music led her to enroll at the Los Angeles Conservatory of Music, while she began performing with local acting troupes and made a demo tape of her songs that she circulated among local record labels. LA-based Capitol Records signed her in 1967, and her first single, the self-penned "Ode to Billy Joe," was an immediate sensation on country and pop charts. The mystery of what, exactly, Billy Joe threw off the Tallahatchie Bridge made the song a cult item, while Gentry's smoke-gets-in-your-eyes delivery seemed to put more meaning in the lyrics than perhaps was there. Several albums followed, with several more songs inspired by her backwoods childhood, including "Okohona River Bottom Band" and "Chickasaw County Child" (released as a single in 1968). She recorded an album of duets with GLEN CAMPBELL in 1969, and the duo scored hits with "Let It Be Me" and "All I Have to Do Is Dream," both originally recorded by the EVERLY BROTHERS.

Gentry spent the early seventies performing as a Las Vegas lounge star, while her records disappeared from the charts. Her career revived briefly in 1976 when a film based on her famous song was released, but her marriage to songwriter/performer JIM STAFFORD two years later led to her own retirement as a performer, although she remains active in song publishing.

Select Discography
Greatest Hits, Curb 77387. Late-sixties Capitol recordings.

◀ GERRARD, ALICE

(date and place of birth unknown)

Long active in the Baltimore/Washington country/BLUEGRASS scene, Gerrard has performed as a soloist and in a variety of groups, and is a folklorist and journalist as well.

Gerrard first recorded in the mid-sixties as half of Hazel and Alice, the duo she formed with country/bluegrass SINGER/SONGWRITER HAZEL DICKENS. At the time, she was married to Jeremy Foster and so took the name Alice Foster. Hazel and Alice recorded two albums for Verve/Folkways (although only one was issued at the time) accompanied by a bluegrass band featuring banjoist Lamar Grier and mandolinist DAVID GRISSMAN. In the mid-seventies, the duo reunited, making two albums for Rounder Records, featuring Hazel's original compositions in a feminist vein, including the classic "Don't Put Her Down (You Helped Put Her There)." Meanwhile, Alice had married folklorist/performer MIKE SEEGER, and along with Dickens the two formed the short-lived Strange Creek Singers in 1974 with Seeger's NEW LOST CITY RAMBLERS bandmate Tracy Schwartz and banjoist Grier, performing a mix of old-time and bluegrass music. Gerrard and Seeger also toured as a duo, cutting an album together in the late seventies.

Also in the late seventies, Gerrard hooked up with Jeanie McLerie and Irene Herrman to form the Harmony Sisters, a feminist old-time trio that performed a mix of CAJUN numbers, songs of the CARTER FAMILY, and Alice's own compositions, which often featured working-class women heroes, as in "Payday at the Mill." This informal group lasted until the early eighties. Gerrard also produced the film *Sprout Wings and Fly*, about the life and music of legendary fiddler TOMMY JARRELL.

In 1987 Gerrard relocated to North Carolina, where she founded *The Old Time Herald*, a quarterly magazine that addresses both traditional old-time country music and the second-generation old-time revivalists, often in an outspoken way. She has also formed another band, the Herald Angels, with Gail Gillespie and Hilary Dirlam.

Gerrard's strong voice, along with her affinity for topical material, was an inspiration to many other old-time music revivalists, including musicians like CATHY FINK. She has also been important in the preservation and documentation of many fine traditional musicians.

Select Discography
Harmony Pie, Flying Fish 248; *Second Helping*, Flying Fish 283. Two early-eighties recordings by Gerrard's Harmony Sisters.

◀ GIBSON, DON

(born 1928, Shelby, NC)
Gibson is a deep-voiced SINGER/SONGWRITER who is best remembered for his many hit compositions, including the immortal "I Can't Stop Lovin' You" and "Sweet Dreams."

Gibson was already a fine guitarist during his school days, playing local dances and radio jobs. He signed on with the Tennessee Barn Dance out of Knoxville in 1946 and began recording soon after. His earliest recordings, made with the cowboy band the Sons of the Soil, recalled the style of the popular SONS OF THE PIONEERS, but he soon switched to a HONKY-TONK country style. His mature vocal style really hadn't jelled until he linked up with NASHVILLE SOUND guru CHET ATKINS, who signed him to RCA in 1957. For the next seven years, the pair produced some of the more listenable of the pop-oriented Nashville recordings, with many of the famous session players who helped craft the slick Nashville Sound. Meanwhile, Gibson's career as a songwriter also took off, with the success of KITTY WELLS's cover of "I Can't Stop Lovin' You" in 1957 and the posthumous release of "Sweet Dreams" by PATSY CLINE in 1963.

Gibson's fifties recordings showed the influence both of contemporary country stylings and nascent pop-rock, thus ensuring him a broader audience than many other country artists. His specialty became the tearjerking country ballad, although many of his recordings were so drenched in self-pity that they crossed the line into pure bathos. For this reason, his songs are often better-known in versions covered by other artists.

Gibson's own first hit was the double-sided "Oh Lonesome Me" backed with "I Can't Stop Lovin' You" of 1958. These were followed by further deep-voiced WEEPERS, including "Blue Blue Day," "Give Myself a Party," and "Lonesome Number One." His last big hit was 1961's "Sea of Heartbreak," written by P. Hampton and Hal David, a hanky-wringer that appealed to the pop as well as the country market.

Gibson continued to record through the sixties, as a soloist and in duets with DOTTIE WEST, although an increasing dependence on pills and alcohol slowed his career. After cleaning up his act, he made a comeback in the seventies, most notably as a duet partner with Sue Thompson, scoring a number-one country hit with "Woman (Sensuous Woman)" in 1972. Gibson continues to be an attraction on tour and performs on the GRAND OLE OPRY.

Select Discography
A Legend in My Time, Bear Family 15401. Classic RCA recordings originally made between 1957 and 1964, lovingly remastered, with excellent documentation.
The Singer, The Songwriter, Bear Family 15475/15664. Two megasets (four CDs each) giving you all of Gibson's recordings through 1966.
All-Time Greatest Hits, RCA 2295. Similar to the Bear Family set, although less lavishly produced.

◀ GILL, VINCE

(born 1957, Norman, OK)
Coming out of a pure BLUEGRASS background, Gill has become one of the more traditionally oriented of the NEW-COUNTRY stars.

The son of a judge, Gill began playing GUITAR and BANJO in his early teens, joining the Bluegrass Alliance (forerunners of NEW GRASS REVIVAL) after high school. He then joined with RICKY SKAGGS in the short-lived PROGRESSIVE BLUEGRASS band, Boone Creek. Later he performed with COUNTRY-ROCK outfits, including Sundance and the PURE PRAIRIE LEAGUE, before joining RODNEY CROWELL's backup band, the Cherry Bombs. Although he began recording as a solo artist in 1984, he didn't break through until 1990 with his hit ballad, "When I Call Your Name," leading to his induction into the GRAND OLE OPRY a year later. Gill has maintained his bluegrass roots, performing with MARK O'CONNOR and Skaggs as The New Nashville Cats as well as continuing to record with California bluegrassers BYRON BERLINE, DAVID GRISSMAN, and others for special projects. Gill's wife, Janice, is one-half of the SWEETHEARTS OF THE RODEO.

Besides being a classy tenor vocalist, Gill is an excellent flat-picker on the guitar, a legacy of his bluegrass training. His recordings tend to incorporate bluegrass instrumentation and vocal harmonies into the more progressive productions typical of the new Nashville. He has also remade several country/bluegrass standards, including his hit update of the WESTERN SWING classic "Liza Jane." Of late, his handlers have tried to turn him into a weepy balladeer, but he's at his best on the sprightly up-tempo numbers like "One More Last Chance," a classy revival of the Western Swing sound.

Select Discography

The Best of Vince Gill, RCA 9814. Selections from his first three albums, plus three bonus tracks.

I Still Believe in You, MCA 10630. 1992 collection of romantic hanky soakers.

Vince Gill and Friends, RCA 66432. 1994 release featuring many young Nashville stars.

◀ GILLEY, MICKEY

(born 1936, Natchez, LA)

As owner of Gilley's Bar, Mickey Gilley rode the mechanical bull to country stardom in the late seventies and early eighties, following a long career in ROCK-ABILLY, country, and R&B.

Gilley makes much of his pedigree, and he ought to: His mother, Irene, was the sister of JERRY LEE LEWIS's dad, making Jerry and Mickey first cousins (another first cousin is Jimmy "I Have Sinned" Swaggart). Born in Natchez, Gilley was raised in Lewis's hometown of Ferriday and knew the older songster well. Both were pianists, and Gilley's mature style is, frankly, derivative of his more famous piano-pounding relative. In fact, Gilley didn't try for a musical career until his cousin had a hit with "Crazy Arms" on Sun Records in 1956.

By then, Gilley was living in Houston, and he began recording for a number of small Texas labels, sounding an awful lot like old Jerry Lee. Gilley spent much of the fifties and sixties laboring away as a local favorite, with an occasional moderate hit, primarily limited to Texas radio. By the early seventies, tired of comparisons with Lewis, Gilley gave up playing the piano for a while and tried to create a more countrified persona. He also opened his own club, Gilley's Bar, which eight years later would inspire the "urban cowboy" movement, first mentioned in an article in *Esquire* magazine and then the subject of the 1980 film *Urban Cowboy*.

Gilley's career, meanwhile, had shifted into a higher gear. A local deejay asked him to record a song he had written, "She Calls Me Baby," which Gilley backed with a remake of GEORGE MORGAN's 1949 hit, "Room Full of Roses". This B side, heavy with an echoey steel guitar (supposedly to hide the fact that the steel player was out of tune), became Gilley's first certifiable hit, leading to a contract with Playboy Records. When the record was reissued by Playboy in 1974, it shot to number one. "I Overlooked an Orchid," Gilley's second single and another flower-themed song (with a similar Jerry Lee–style piano introduction), did equally well and was followed by a string of COUNTRYPOLITAN recordings, including 1975's "Roll You Like a Wheel" (a duet with ex-Playmate Barbi Benton), "Don't the Girls All Get Prettier at Closing Time" in 1976, and "Honky Tonk Memories" in 1977.

In 1979 Gilley signed with Epic Records, just in time to cash in on the urban cowboy craze. His remake of the Ben E. King classic "Stand By Me" was featured in the *Urban Cowboy* film, becoming an immediate hit, and was followed by more standard early-eighties country fare, including several number-one hits: "True Love Ways" and "That's All That Matters" (both 1980); "A Headache Tomorrow (or a Heartache Tonight)" (1981) (the song was somewhat controversial because the singer mentions taking "a pill," which Gilley insisted meant aspirin, used as a hangover remedy); "Put Your Dreams Away" (1982); and "Fool for Your Love" (1983).

Gilley faded from the charts in the face of NEW-COUNTRY music, and his club went into a tailspin, a victim of the excesses of the eighties; it closed its doors in 1989, two years after Gilley sued his ex–business partner—although a "new" Gilley's has arisen out of the ashes in the ersatz-country capital, BRANSON, MISSOURI. Gilley himself had one further hit in 1986: "Doo Wah Days," a nostalgic look at fifties rock.

Select Discography
Biggest Hits, Columbia 38320.

◀ GILMORE, JIMMIE DALE

(born 1945, Tulia, TX)

The ultimate "cosmic cowboy," Gilmore is another eccentric SINGER/SONGWRITER out of Texas who has been more legendary than well-known even in the die-hard country circles.

Gilmore came out of Lubbock, Texas, where his first band, the Flatlanders, was financed by BUDDY HOLLY's father. This near-mythic group, featuring JOE ELY (now one of COUNTRY-ROCK's big shakers) and Butch Hancock (another erratic singer/ songwriter), recorded one album in 1971 that went unreleased for nineteen years, finally appearing on Rounder Records. Gilmore spent the mid-seventies on the move, first relocating to Austin, center of Texas's hippie-country music community, and then giving up music altogether to pursue a degree in oriental philosophy at the University of Colorado.

Gilmore returned to Austin in 1980 and recorded two albums for the small Hightone label (usually associated with blues artists) in the mid-eighties, introducing his combination of sophisticated lyrics put to a steady, rocking beat. He managed to hit number seventy-two on the country charts with one of his best-known songs, "White Freight Liner Blues."

Gilmore's career got a boost when he was selected to be part of Elektra records' *American Explorers* series in 1991; these were recordings by lesser-known singer/ songwriters, working in country, ROCKABILLY, and rock styles, who deserved more attention. In 1993 he was signed by Elektra as a regular-label act and embarked on a nationwide tour. Still, Gilmore's music has failed to win a large country audience, while he has also been unable to crack the alternative rock charts.

Select Discography
After Awhile, Elektra/Nonesuch 61148. 1991 "comeback" album.

◄ GIMBLE, JOHNNY

(born 1926, near Tyler, TX)

One of the greatest fiddlers in the WESTERN SWING style, Gimble began his career as a protégé of BOB WILLS and has more recently been a member of WILLIE NELSON's band, as well as guesting with Western swing revival bands like ASLEEP AT THE WHEEL.

Raised in rural Texas, Gimble showed an early facility for music, playing BANJO and MANDOLIN. When in his teens, he joined his brothers' group, the Rose City Hipsters. The band played locally for dances and parties, as well as broadcasted over Tyler's radio station. When he was seventeen, he was hired to play with the Shelton Brothers, which lead to work with JIMMIE DAVIS.

After World War II, Western swing master Bob Wills hired Gimble originally to play mandolin, although soon his talents as a fiddler were made apparent. He remained with Wills through the fifties, and his jazz-influenced fiddling, with its rich tone, became a hallmark of Wills's later recordings. In the sixties and early seventies, Gimble worked as a Nashville studio musician. He rejoined Wills in 1973 for the Texas Playboys reunion LP that was inspired by MERLE HAGGARD's love for Western swing. He then performed through the seventies with several alumni of Wills's band, recording several albums.

In the late seventies, Gimble worked for a while with Willie Nelson's touring band. He has since recorded as a solo artist and sessioned with NEW-COUNTRY stars like GEORGE STRAIT and older traditionalists like Haggard.

Select Discography

Still Fiddlin' Around, MCA 42021. Cassette-only version of this 1988 album; a little overproduced, but nice music nonetheless.

Texas Fiddle Collection, CMH 9027. Mid-seventies recordings with many of the old Texas Playboys on hand.

◄ GIRLS OF THE GOLDEN WEST

(Mildred Fern "Millie" Goad [guitar, vocals] born 1913, Mount Carmel, IL; and Dorothy Laverne "Dolly" Goad [guitar, vocals] born 1915, Mount Carmel, IL; died 1967)

A popular close-harmony Western-style duo of the thirties, the Girls brought an Andrews Sisters sensibility to cowboy-style singing.

Although born in rural Mount Carmel, Illinois, the two Goad sisters were raised primarily in midwestern cities, where their father unsuccessfully tried his hand at a variety of occupations, from storekeeper to insurance salesman and finally to factory worker. Mama Goad was a talented singer of old-time songs, and it was younger sister Dolly who showed the most musical ability, learning to play GUITAR early on from her mother. Dolly was also the most interested in a professional career, dragging her fourteen-year-old sister to an audition for St. Louis's KMOX radio station. They got the job, took the name Girls of the Golden West, and changed their last name from Goad to Good; after a period of radio work in

Kansas and on the Mexican border-radio station XERA, they returned to St. Louis in 1933, where they were discovered by scouts for the Chicago-based *National Barn Dance* show.

They made their first appearance on the Barn Dance in 1934, when they also made their first recordings. The girls were an immediate sensation, with their sweet harmonies, precision harmonized YODELING, and novelty sound effects (such as imitating vocally the sound of a Hawaiian slide guitar). Their first recording was a remake of Belle Starr's risqué hokum number "My Love Is a Rider," cleaned up to fit the Girls' wholesome image, followed by a number of cowboyesque numbers, many written by Millie, including "Two Cowgirls on the Lone Prairie" and "Will There Be Any Yodelers in Heaven?" Lucille Overstake, another popular barn dance performer, wrote their most popular number, "I Want to Be a Real Cowboy Girl," which, like most of their songs, was slightly ahead of its time in its theme (the lyrics implied that a girl could be just as macho as a rootin'-tootin' cowboy).

The girls left Chicago for New York in 1935, and then relocated two years later to Cincinnati's *Midwestern Hayride* program, where they remained into the fifties. Millie eventually retired to raise a family, but Dolly continued to perform on local radio, hosting a children's show and also a pop hit-parade program.

Select Discography
Songs of the West, Old Homestead 143. This out-of-print LP reissues 1930s recordings, plus a 1963 reunion cut with Bradley Kincaid.

◀ GLASER BROTHERS, THE

(Tompall born 1933, Spalding, NE; Chuck born 1936, Spalding, NE; Jim born 1937, Spalding, NE)

The Glasers were a vocal harmony group who recorded both as backup vocalists and on their own without too much success. In the mid-seventies, Tompall became a member of the Texas-based OUTLAW-COUNTRY movement.

Led by eldest brother Tompall, the group first worked as backup singers in Nashville, accompanying MARTY ROBBINS on his hit "El Paso City" in 1959 and four years later worked with JOHNNY CASH on "Ring of Fire." Brother Jim wrote "Woman, Woman," a hit for the pop group Gary Puckett and the Union Gap in the sixties. The Glasers began recording as a group in the mid-sixties, taking a break between 1973 and 1979, after having a minor hit with "Rings" in 1971. They came back in 1981 with "Lovin' Her Was Easier (Than Anything I'll Ever Do)," another minor hit, and also became involved in music publishing.

Brothers Tompall and Jim both pursued solo careers as well, Jim beginning in 1968 and Tompall soon after. Tompall became associated with WAYLON JENNINGS and WILLIE NELSON in the mid-seventies, appearing on the famous *Outlaws* anthology album issued by RCA, giving his career a small boost. He made a couple of LPs for ABC/Dot in the late seventies, but they went nowhere. Jim struggled along trying to make it, finally scoring a number-one hit in 1984 with "You're Gettin' to Me Again" with producer Don Tolle on Tolle's Noble Vision label. Unfortunately, the label folded due to lack of funding, and Glaser ended up working as a backup singer with such COUNTRYPOLITAN stars as RONNIE McDOWELL and SYLVIA.

Select Discography

The Outlaw, Bear Family 15606. Combines two LPs made for ABC/Dot in the late seventies by Tompall Glaser.

The Rogue, Bear Family 15596. Another ABC LP from the late seventies, along with more recent recordings.

◀ GOOD OL' PERSONS

(Kathy Kallick [guitar, vocals]; Laurie Lewis [fiddle, vocals]; Bethany Raines [bass, vocals]; John Reischman [mandolin]; Sally Van Meter [dobro])

The Good Ol' Persons were a mid-eighties San Francisco Bay–area BLUEGRASS/country band with a strong feminist twist, thanks to the sturdy lead vocals and original songs of Kathy Kallick and LAURIE LEWIS.

The name, of course, is a play on "good ol' boys," expanded in politically correct spirit to include women. The cofounders—Kallick and Lewis—were what made this band special; they performed a combination of classic country material by the CARTER FAMILY and the DELMORE BROTHERS, among others, and original songs, which mostly recast traditional country themes. The band was also unusual in that it featured the playing of so many talented female instrumentalists, including Lewis's fine fiddling (she was later replaced by Paul Shelasky and Kevin Wimmer, in succession) and Sally Van Meter's new-acoustic–influenced DOBRO playing.

Even after the band folded in the late eighties, Kallick and Lewis remained closely aligned, recording a duo album in the early nineties. In 1993 Kallick recorded her first solo album, featuring all original material, in an attempt to capture the mainstream country market.

Select Discography

I Can't Stand to Ramble, Kaleidoscope 17. Their first album.

Together, Kaleidoscope 44. Lewis and Kallick's duo album.

Love Chooses You, Flying Fish 487. Lewis's NEW-COUNTRY–style solo album.

◀ GOSDIN, VERN

(born 1934, Woodland, AL)

Gosdin, a country crooner who has had a speckled career, thanks to almost constant label hopping, has a voice that recalls the mournful side of GEORGE JONES.

Raised in rural Alabama, Gosdin performed locally with his brother in a duet act reminiscent of the LOUVIN BROTHERS, who they heard weekly over the GRAND OLE OPRY broadcasts. He also sang in a gospel group over local radio station WWOK. By the mid-sixties, the brothers had relocated to California, where they were members of the Hillmen, a BLUEGRASS band led by CHRIS HILLMAN (who later helped form the BYRDS). In 1966 they recorded an album with GENE CLARK after he left the Byrds, but it went nowhere. The Gosdin Brothers recorded by themselves for Bakersfield International, scoring a hit with "Hangin' On" in 1967, and moved to Capitol a year later for a follow-up, " 'Til the End," which was a minor hit. By 1972 work had dried up, and Vern Gosdin returned to Alabama and abandoned the music business.

Thanks to his Byrds connection, Gosdin had a reputation among seventies country-rockers and was encouraged by EMMYLOU HARRIS to resume his recording career. In 1976 and 1977, he re-recorded the Gosdin Brothers' two earlier hits, which both went top-ten this time, and followed them with a series of recordings through the mid-eighties for a variety of labels. He made a comeback to a major label in the late eighties on Columbia with his LP *Chiseled in Stone*; and while the production is a bit heavy-handed, the title song, along with "Who You Gonna Blame It on This Time," are both fine country WEEPERS, made even more compelling by Gosdin's achy vocals.

Select Discography
The Best of Vern Gosdin, Warner Bros. 25775. Late-seventies recordings that were reissued after Gosdin's success in the late eighties.
Chiseled in Stone, Columbia 40982.

◀ GRAND OLE OPRY

(1925–ongoing)
The *Grand Ole Opry* was not the first country-music radio program, but it became the most popular and the one most closely associated with country-music making. It helped establish Nashville as a center of country music recording and also introduced country music to countless listeners over its long existence.

The Opry's founder was announcer GEORGE D. HAY, nicknamed "The Solemn Old Judge." Hay originally worked for Memphis and Chicago radio stations; he had hosted the *Chicago Barn Dance* in 1924 (later called the *National Barn Dance*), which was the first country-music radio program (it remained on the air until 1960). In 1925 he came to the fledgling WSM station, whose initials stand for "We Shield Millions" (it was run by Nashville's National Life and Accident Insurance Company). A program hosted by Hay featuring elderly fiddler UNCLE JIMMY THOMPSON in November of 1925 proved the popularity of country music, and a few weeks later the *Grand Ole Opry* was launched.

Early stars of the Opry included harmonica playing DOCTOR HUMPHREY BATE and his Possum Hunters string band; the flamboyant banjoist UNCLE DAVE MACON, who often appeared accompanied by SAM AND KIRK McGEE; and the blues-tinged harmonica player DEFORD BAILEY. In the mid-thirties, the Opry launched a booking agency to send its acts on the road. This not only spread the sound of the Opry stars throughout the South and West, it enriched the station, which took a hefty commission on the acts it booked.

The second key figure in the Opry's history was Harry Stone, who was hired to book more modern acts onto the show. In 1931 he brought the Vagabonds, a vocal trio who had previously appeared on Chicago's *National Barn Dance* (which had always been more pop-oriented). Stone would be central in establishing the booking agency, and also in attracting more pop-oriented acts. In the mid-thirties, cowboy-style acts like PEE WEE KING's Golden West Cowboys appeared on the program, and in 1938 a young fiddler/vocalist named ROY ACUFF was invited to join the show, after many years of trying to get on it. Acuff changed the direction of the Opry from being primarily an instrumental broadcast to one focusing on vocals, and his crooning singing helped lay the groundwork for future stars like EDDY ARNOLD. A year later, the Opry joined the NBC radio network, bringing it to a national audience. In the same year, future BLUEGRASS star BILL MONROE joined the cast.

During the thirties and forties, hundreds of similar shows blossomed on local radio stations, giving many country acts their first important exposure. Perhaps the most important radio producer was John Lair, who worked first out of Cincinnati and then, in 1938, created the *Renfro Valley Barn Dance*, both a tourist attraction in the hills of Kentucky and a popular broadcast, featuring a popular young singer/MC RED FOLEY. Lair specialized in packaging bands and singers to fit a specific image, based heavily on a nostalgic (and perhaps exaggerated) sense of what life in the backwoods had been like a century earlier.

In 1940 the Opry cast was invited to appear in a C-grade movie produced by schlock studio Republic pictures. Acuff, young and handsome, was made the lead, but the film also showcased older stars like Uncle Dave Macon. In the same year, Eddy Arnold joined the show's cast as featured singer with Pee Wee King. In the summer of 1940, the first Opry tent show hit the road, and country comic MINNIE PEARL made her debut on the radio program.

For many years, the Opry had moved from various homes, including its original home in a tiny radio studio (that could not accommodate the crowds of listeners who came to see it) through various auditoriums in Nashville. Finally, it found its most famous home in 1943 at the legendary Ryman Auditorium. This would serve as the home for the Opry for thirty years, and is still an important tourist attraction for Opry fans.

In the years following World War II, Nashville blossomed as a country-music center. Although Victor Records had come on a "field trip" to record country stars in the late twenties, no permanent studio opened there until 1947, when WSM engineers opened the Castle Studio. In the same year, an ex-Opry announcer named Jim Bulleit started his Bullet label, and soon after RCA opened its Nashville division, hiring CHET ATKINS to be its staff producer.

Meanwhile, the Opry was bowing to change. In 1943 ERNEST TUBB shocked Opry management when he appeared playing an electric guitar. It took several years for this radical departure, and his HONKY-TONK repertoire, to find a place on the program. A year later, BOB WILLS's Texas Playboys appeared on the air, the first group allowed to use drums in its act (although just a snare drum, and the drummer had to be hidden behind a curtain so the audience wouldn't be shocked). In 1949 a young singing sensation named HANK WILLIAMS brought the steel guitar to the Opry, along with a blues-tinged repertoire. He would remain a popular act until he was fired three years later, due to his unreliable behavior caused by his alcoholism.

George Hay finally retired in 1953, and the Opry spent much of the fifties, sixties, and early seventies becoming a bastion of conservative music-making. While new acts continued to be signed, the show became highly predictable. Meanwhile, the NASHVILLE SOUND that turned mainstream Nashville music recording into a mushy amalgam of purling piano and cooing choruses was also taking its place on the Opry stage. In the sixties and seventies, the Opry had become the voice of conservative America, so much so that when SKEETER DAVIS publicly criticized the Nashville police for brutality from the Opry stage, she created a scandal that derailed her career.

In 1973 the old Ryman was closed and the Opry moved to its current home, the glitzy theme park Opryland USA. Appropriately enough, the new theater was opened by President Nixon, himself a big fan of country music. Its new 4,400-seat auditorium was built to accommodate the large crowds who come to see the show, but it has none of the intimacy of the Ryman. Meanwhile, Opryland blossomed into a major theme park, with rides, hotels, and ancillary attractions, much like Disneyland.

Not surprisingly, the NEW-COUNTRY music of the eighties and nineties has helped revitalize the Opry. Many of these stars looked to performing on the show as a major career validation. Performers still must be invited to join the Opry and must commit to playing a certain number of Saturdays a year on the show, forgoing more lucrative opportunities on the road. But the tradition of Opry membership —with the luster it gives to an act—makes it still one of the most coveted badges of achievement in Nashville.

◀ GREENBRIAR BOYS, THE

(1962–1967; original members: Ralph Rinzler [mandolin, vocals]; Bob Yellin [banjo, vocals]; John Herald [guitar, vocals]; Frank Wakefield [mandolin, vocals] replaced Rinzler from 1965–1967)

One of the most popular of New York's BLUEGRASS revival groups, the Greenbriar Boys did much to popularize bluegrass and country sounds in the early to middle sixties.

Originally formed by guitarist John Herald and BANJO player Eric Weissberg (later famous for his recording of "Duelin' Banjos," which became the theme for the 1973 film *Deliverance*) and other New York–area folkies, the band solidified around 1962 with the addition of Bob Yellin and Ralph Rinzler, who had a more academic bent than the other musicians. The group's first few albums were fairly accurate recreations of traditional bluegrass sounds, much as the NEW LOST CITY RAMBLERS had previously revived old-time country music by studiously recreating earlier recordings. When Rinzler left the group in 1964, he was replaced by Frank Wakefield, who brought a looser style to the group, plus his unique high-tenor vocals. Herald's vocals also straddled the line between traditional bluegrass and HONKY-TONK country.

Rinzler went on to become a noted folklorist and was the head of the Smithsonian Institution's Department of Folklife until his death in 1994. Herald recorded as a solo artist in the early seventies as well as performing with Happy and Artie Traum and other Woodstock-area musicians on the informal *Mud Acres* albums, and then led his own bluegrass band from the mid-seventies through the mid-eighties. Wakefield has recorded sporadically as a solo artist and bandleader; and Yellin is no longer active in the business.

◀ GREENE, JACK

(born 1930, Maryville, TN)

Greene was a successful country crooner of the mid-sixties cast in the pop/ NASHVILLE SOUND mold of his day.

Greene began his career as an instrumentalist, beginning with the GUITAR (which he took up at age eight), and then adding bass and drums to his skills. By the time he completed high school, he was living in Atlanta and playing with a number of cowboy-flavored groups. After a stint in the army in the early fifties, he returned to Atlanta (via Alaska), playing local clubs with a group called the Peachtree Cowboys. It was there that laconic singer ERNEST TUBB discovered Greene in the early '60s, and asked him to join his backup band, the Troubadours.

In the mid-sixties, discovering Greene could sing as well as pick, Tubb invited him to contribute vocals to an album track, "The Last Letter," and soon country deejays were requesting more from the smooth-voiced vocalist. He was signed separately to Decca, and under the hand of veteran producer OWEN BRADLEY he cut his first hit, a cover of DALLAS FRAZIER's "There Goes My Everything," with the cloying JORDANAIRES providing backup harmonies. His next hit, 1967's "All the Time," featured a neoclassical piano break by ace sessionman FLOYD CRAMER and led to Greene's engagement as a regular on the GRAND OLE OPRY.

Greene's hit-making days continued through 1969, with a couple more number-one solo hits and a duet with JEANNIE SEELEY, 1969's "Wish I Didn't Have to Miss You." Seeley remained with Greene's road show through the early eighties. His career steadily declined through the seventies, although he continued to tour and record for Decca/MCA. He later moved to smaller labels in the eighties. In a bizarre twist, Greene, known primarily by the eighties as a touring performer, was victimized by a mysterious impersonator who passed himself off as the country star, amassing huge debts at hotels across the country while bilking investors out of a considerable amount of cash. Finally, this impersonator (who turned out to be a man named Lawrence Irving Taylor) was apprehended in 1988 when he tried to buy a nearly three-quarter-million-dollar horse farm using Greene's name.

Select Discography

Twenty Greatest Hits, Deluxe 7808. Budget cassette-only release.

◀ GREENE, RICHARD

(born 1945, Beverly Hills, CA)

Greene is a far-out fiddler who began his career in BLUEGRASS, moved into contemporary rock, and now plays music that combines classical, jazz, folk, bluegrass, and rock influences.

Raised by a musical family in swanky Beverly Hills, Greene was a classically trained violinist who was named concertmaster of the Beverly Hills Orchestra while still in high school. When he enrolled at the University of California at Berkeley, he was introduced to folk music and soon turned his attention to bluegrass, thanks to his admiration for local fiddler Scotty Stoneman, son of legendary country star ERNEST STONEMAN.

In the mid-sixties, bluegrass legend BILL MONROE hired Greene to play in his band, where Greene met PETER ROWAN, another young musician who had his sights on a new, more progressive style of bluegrass. Greene left Monroe to tour briefly with Jim Kweskin's Jug Band, which featured another Monroe alum, BILL KEITH, and then returned to California to form the rock band Seatrain with Andy Kulberg, formerly of the Blues Project. Rowan later joined the band as vocalist, songwriter, and guitarist.

In 1972, discouraged with the rock world, Greene left Seatrain to work as a pop-rock session musician in Southern California. He performed with Rowan, DAVID GRISSMAN, Keith, and Clarence White in the group MULESKINNER, one of the first PROGRESSIVE BLUEGRASS "bands" (they actually only performed together once, for a television special, and recorded a single album). A year later, he formed with Grissman the short-lived Great American Music Band, which featured blues guitarist Taj Mahal and performed a mixture of different music; and later in the seventies Greene performed in the first incarnation of Grissman's Quintet.

Greene recorded sporadically through the eighties as the leader of various loosely formed groups, including his own Greene String Quartet, which performed everything from classical material to jazz and pop. His integration of bluegrass, rock, and jazz elements into his playing style had great impact on younger progressive bluegrass fiddlers in the seventies and eighties, and he continues to enjoy a small, but loyal, following.

Select Discography
Ramblin', Rounder 0110. Early-eighties release featuring an eclectic mix of jazz, country, and pop.
The String Machine, Virgin 86340. 1991 recording by the Greene String Quartet.
The Greene Fiddler, Sierra 6005. Varied compilation featuring a range of sidemen playing bluegrass, swing, and new-acoustic music.

◀ GREENWOOD, LEE

(born 1942 near Sacramento, CA)

One of the last of the glitzy Nashville singers, smoky-voiced Greenwood had his biggest success in the early to middle eighties with a series of ballads culminating in the patriotic showstopper "God Bless the U.S.A."

Raised by his grandparents on a chicken farm outside of Sacramento, Lee was already playing sax and piano as a youngster in a local band called My Moonbeams. By 1958 he was performing with local country artist Chester Smith and next played for DEL REEVES, with whom he served as a backup musician on GUITAR, BANJO, and bass as well as on sax. In 1962 he formed a pop-oriented band called Apollo, working primarily out of Las Vegas. By 1965 the band had signed with short-lived Paramount Records under a new name, the Lee Greenwood Affair. The band dissolved without making much of a dent on the pop charts, leaving Greenwood working as a card dealer by day and lounge singer by night.

Larry McFadden, who worked as bandleader for MEL TILLIS, heard Greenwood in Vegas in 1979 and urged him to take a more country direction. After a few unsuccessful trips to Nashville to market demos, Greenwood finally landed a contract in 1981, scoring his first big hit with "It Turns Me Inside Out." It's said that his husky voice was caused by years of heavy vocalizing and overusing his vocal cords; he was at first compared with KENNY ROGERS because of his froggy-throated delivery. Soon, though, he got out of Rogers's shadow by scoring a series of hits, mostly in a schmaltzy-ballad mold, including "Ring on Her Finger," "Time On Her Hands," "IOU," "Somebody's Gonna Love You," and "Going, Going Gone." In 1984 he penned "The Wind Beneath My Wings," a big hit in England that later became a chart topper stateside for Bette Midler after it was featured in her film, *Beaches*.

After the 1985 release of "God Bless the U.S.A.," Greenwood concerts became increasingly patriotic, flag-waving affairs, with the overdone anthem a centerpiece of every performance. Still, if your taste runs toward country-pop with a healthy dose of tearful balladry, then Greenwood can deliver the goods like few others.

Select Discography
Greatest Hits, MCA 5582.

◀ GRIFFITH, NANCI

(born 1953 near Austin, TX)

Griffith is a Texas-based chanteuse/songwriter who has made some attempt to crack into the country market. With her quavering voice, quiet and intense stage presence, and confessional repertoire, Griffith would certainly have been classified as a folk or folk-rock artist in the sixties or seventies. Today she is often placed on the country rack for lack of a better category. She is one of those genre-bending artists who have been labeled NEW-COUNTRY, even though she has little in common with the other boot-wearing stars of this category.

Griffith was still working as a schoolteacher when she began issuing her music locally on her own label (B.F. Deal), beginning with *There's a Light Beyond these Woods* in 1978. The folk label Philo picked up her recordings in the early to middle eighties, and Griffith's haunting vocals and combination of original compositions and covers of other singer/songwriters' material made her a popular figure on the folk scene of the day. She was signed to MCA's country division in 1987, where she recorded the LP *Lone Star State of Mind*, including her cover of "From a Distance," the Julie Gold ballad that was to be a hit for Bette Midler a few years later. After a few commercially disappointing LPs aimed at the country market, MCA attempted to market Griffith to a pop audience, moving her to the Los Angeles division of the label. At about this time, ironically, new-country stars KATHY MATTEA and SUZY BOGGUSS had hits covering Griffith's songs, Mattea with "Love at the Five and Dime" and Bogguss with "Outbound Plane." In 1993 Griffith abandoned the pop sheen of her previous two releases to record an entire collection of folk-rock standards, as an homage to the singer/songwriters who had influenced her most.

Griffith has drawn on influences beyond music, including the literature of Southern writers like Flannery O'Connor and Fannie Flagg. Some of her earlier albums were arranged almost like mini novels, with each song forming a "chapter" in the overall story. For this reason, her appeal tends to be strongest among an urban, intellectual audience. This makes her unusual among country artists and may account for her limited success in this category.

Select Discography

There's a Light Beyond These Woods, Philo 1097. Reissue of her first album, recorded live in 1977 and 1978.

Once in a Very Blue Moon, Philo 1096. Her 1984 breakthrough Nashville album produced by country folkie Jim Rooney.

Lone Star State of Mind, MCA 31300. Her 1987 big-label debut.

Other Voices, Other Rooms. Elektra 61464. 1993 LP in homage to her favorite songwriters.

Flyer, Elektra 61681. 1994 album featuring folk-rock accompaniments to her original compositions.

◀ GRISSMAN, DAVID

(born 1945, Hackensack, NJ)

Grissman is a BLUEGRASS MANDOLIN player who has created his own genre of music, which he playfully calls "dawg music," a form of acoustic jazz.

Grissman began his career performing in the New York area both with traditional bluegrass musicians (RED ALLEN and Don Stover) and younger innovators (BILL KEITH). He formed the New York Ramblers in 1965 with banjoist Winnie Winston and Del and Jerry McCoury on GUITAR/vocals and bass, respectively. Although the band did not issue an album during its short period of existence, they achieved a near-legendary status on both the FOLK-REVIVAL and bluegrass circuits. Grissman relocated to California in the late sixties, joining with eccentric guitarist/vocalist/ songwriter PETER ROWAN to form the folk-rock band Earth Opera, and then moved on to the Great American Music Band. In 1973 he was a member of MULESKINNER, a special band put together for a single album of traditional and PROGRESSIVE BLUEGRASS, featuring Rowan, hot guitarist Clarence White, fiddler RICHARD GREENE, and banjoist Bill Keith. He also did session work for many popular mid-seventies singer/ songwriters.

Grissman was invited to record a traditional bluegrass album for Rounder Records in the mid-seventies as a return to his roots. At about the same time, in 1976, he formed his first Quintet, featuring TONY RICE (guitar), Darol Anger (fiddle), Todd Phillips (second mandolin), and Bill Amatneek (bass). The group, which sounded like an updated version of Django Reinhardt's and Stephane Grappelli's thirties-era Quintet of the Hot Club of France, performed Grissman's own jazz-influenced compositions. Their first album on the California-based Kaleidoscope label almost single-handedly launched what is now called "new-acoustic music," and which Grissman christened "dawg" music.

Grissman soon moved to A&M and then to Warner Brothers Records. Later versions of his Quintet have featured mandolinist Mike Marshall and whiz-kid string-bender MARK O'CONNOR (now one of Nashville's premier session players). He has also recorded with his idol, Stephane Grappelli, and his more recent recordings show an even stronger jazz and blues influence than previous work. At the same time, he has continued to perform in traditional bluegrass settings, usually for one-time recording projects, and has also formed an acoustic duo with head Grateful Deadman, Jerry Garcia.

Grissman founded the Acoustic Disc label to issue his own and other acoustic-oriented recordings in the early nineties. The 1994 Grissman quintet features fiddler Joe Craven, flutist Matt Eakle, guitarist Rick Montgomery, and bassist Jim Kirwin. They have more of a light-jazz feel than previous Grissman groups.

Grissman's mandolin playing tends to be light and highly melodic, rather than the guttural, heavy chord chopping often heard in traditional bluegrass work. He also tends to avoid much use of vibrato, another trademark of bluegrass mandolin picking that is often overdone, particularly on slower numbers. Grissman's playing is energetic but not hard-driving like the work of BILL MONROE; instead, the energy of the music comes through complex melodic variations and the excitement generated by this invention.

Select Discography

Quintet, Kaleidoscope 5. This is the album that started it all, defining "Dawg" music and launching one strand of new-acoustic music.

Rounder Album, Rounder 0069. A return to his bluegrass roots.

Here Today, Rounder 0251/0252. 1988 bluegrass sessions with RICKY SKAGGS, DOC WATSON, J. D. CROWE, and others.

Dawgwood, Acoustic Disc 7. His 1993 foray into "dawg" music.

◀ GUITAR

(c. 1850)

The American guitar is a different instrument from its Spanish forebears. Its history has been shaped by a combination of technological advances along with new musical styles.

The common Spanish or so-called "classical" guitar, which dates back to the early nineteenth century, features a wide fingerboard, gut strings, a slotted peghead, and, most important, a fan-shaped bracing system under the instrument's wooden top, which gives it a sweet sound. However, the American guitar has its roots in a group of talented Viennese instrument builders who developed a new way of building guitars. Most notable among these craftsmen was a German immigrant named Christian Friedrich Martin, who began making instruments in 1833 in New York City and moved six years later to Nazareth, Pennsylvania, where his company is still located.

Martin either developed or perfected a new form of bracing called an X-brace. This allowed for greater volume and eventually the introduction of steel strings (fan bracing will not support the increased tension that steel strings create on the face of a guitar). He also redesigned the guitar's body shape, exaggerating the lower bout (or half) of the instrument's body so that it was no longer symmetrical in appearance. By the late 1800s, the Martin style had been copied by mass producers like Lyon and Healy out of Chicago, and guitars were made by the hundreds and were available inexpensively through mail-order catalogs. In major cities, among the middle and upper classes, the instrument became popular with young ladies, and there was a proliferation of instruction books and pieces written for the instrument in a delicate style called "parlor guitar" (so named because the instrument was associated with the formal front room of many middle-class homes).

It is difficult to point to a specific time period or musician who was responsible for introducing the guitar to country music. Certainly the instrument had found its way into the backwoods of American society as early as the 1860s; the image of the guitar-toting cowboy is not entirely a work of fiction. Solo guitarists were soon finding chairs in bands. As the guitar entered the traditional banjo-fiddle ensembles of the South, it flattened out modal melodies (because guitars are oriented toward standard, Western chordal accompaniment) and also gave the music increased power and drive. Early recording guitarists like RILEY PUCKETT and, of course, JIMMIE RODGERS helped popularize the instrument as the ideal accompaniment for the solo vocalist.

The second great technological innovation occurred from the twenties through the forties. As a band instrument, the guitar was hampered by its inability to be heard among the sound of other instruments. Steel strings helped, but they didn't answer the problem entirely. The Martin company developed a new body style it labeled the "Dreadnought," after the World War I battleship class. This squarer and larger-bodied instrument was an immediate success among country and blue-grass musicians. Meanwhile, rival guitar makers like Gibson developed so-called "Jumbo"-bodied guitars, which looked like regular guitars on steroids, and were highly regarded by cowboy stars like GENE AUTRY.

Amplified instruments were the next logical step, although they were slow to win acceptance in country-music circles. The first musicians to use amplification were the players of lap steel guitars in WESTERN SWING bands. They had to be heard over large brass sections and drums, so they had little choice but to turn to amplification. Next, HONKY-HONK singers like ERNEST TUBB began using electric guitars to cut through the noisy atmosphere of these tiny bars. Traditionalists were horrified, but they could do little to stem the tide of the eventual amplification of all country instruments. CHET ATKINS helped popularize the smooth-sounding, jazz-influenced, hollow-bodied electrified guitar by working with the Gretsch company on designing the Country Gentleman model of the early fifties; meanwhile, younger players like BUDDY HOLLY espoused the harder sound of the solid-bodied instruments designed by Leo Fender in the middle years of the decade.

The FOLK REVIVAL of the sixties brought renewed interest in acoustic instruments, and Martin had its best sales year toward the end of the decade thanks to the popularity of folk-derived music. Today, the line between acoustic and electric instruments has been blurred by the prevalence of built-in pickups on acoustic guitars and the increasing use of effects such as reverb or chorusing that used to be limited to electric instruments. But whether acoustic or electric, the guitar remains the primary instrument for all country stars, even if they just carry it as a prop.

◀ GUNTER, ARTHUR "HARDROCK"

(born 1926, Nashville, TN; died 1976)

Gunter was an early performer in what would become known as the ROCKABILLY style, as well as the composer of the COUNTRY-ROCK perennial, "Baby Let's Play House."

After finishing his education, Gunter first entered the music business at age twenty-one as a deejay; soon after, he was recording for a number of small labels. His "Birmingham Bounce," an upbeat country-swing number, was successfully covered on the country charts by RED FOLEY and on the R&B charts by Amos Milburn. Gunter also covered risqué blues numbers like "Sixty Minute Man," anticipating the rockabilly style by nearly half a decade. After serving in the army from 1951 to 1953, he returned to recording for MGM and then for Sun and performed on radio out of Wheeling, West Virginia. He quickly faded into obscurity; however, he reemerged briefly in the early sixties with the Chubby Checker knockoff, "Hillbilly Twist," and then again in the early seventies with a tribute album to HANK WILLIAMS. He died in 1976.

◀ GUTHRIE, WOODY

(born Woodrow Wilson Guthrie, 1912, Okemah, OK; died 1967)

Guthrie was a topical SINGER/SONGWRITER whose songs have become favorites among folk revivalists. Guthrie's songs have become American classics, from "This Land Is Your Land" to "Pastures of Plenty"; he did much to popularize the talking blues; and he even worked as a cowboy singer early in his career, penning one country classic, "Philadelphia Lawyer," later covered by singers from ROSE MADDOX to WILLIE NELSON.

Guthrie's family were pioneers in Oklahoma when it was still part of the unsettled "Indian territory." His father ran a trading post and real-estate office, prospering during the first Oklahoma oil boom. The elder Guthrie was also a part-time guitarist and BANJO picker, and Guthrie's mother, Nora Belle Tanner, was a fine ballad singer. The young Guthrie grew up surrounded by music, including not only his family's singing and playing but also the music of the Native Americans and African-Americans who lived and worked in his hometown.

Guthrie's family life dissolved with the end of the real-estate boom in the mid-twenties, when his father took to heavy drinking and his mother began to show the symptoms of Huntington's Chorea, a disease that would eventually lead to her institutionalization. His sister died in a fire started accidentally by their mother, who was slowly losing her coordination and her mental stability. By his early teens, Woody had quit school and relocated to Texas, where he bummed around taking odd jobs and lived on and off with his father's half-brother in the small town of Pampa. He received a few GUITAR lessons from his relative, and the two played locally. He married Mary Jennings and took up work as a sign painter, while still singing at nights.

In the early thirties, disastrous dust storms caused by years of poor land management swept through upper Texas and Oklahoma. Thousands of family farmers were ruined and took to the road in search of better living conditions. Like many others, Woody abandoned his wife and traveled to California. There he began performing as a cowboy act in a duo with Maxine Crissman, who was known as Lefty Lou. The two had a popular Los Angeles–based radio show on which they performed the kind of Western/cowboy material popular at that time, thanks to the horsy escapades of actor/singers like GENE AUTRY.

Through the mid-thirties, Woody traveled through much of the Southwest as an itinerant painter and singer. He was hired by the WPA to memorialize the building of the Bonneville Dam in Colorado in 1937, writing a series of classic songs including "Roll On Columbia." By the end of the decade, he settled in New York City, where he encountered performers like PETE SEEGER and other young members of the first folk revival. Their leftist political philosophy appealed to Guthrie, who had been radicalized by witnessing firsthand the suffering of rural Americans during the Depression. Guthrie's quick wit appealed to his fellow performers, and his ability to compose a song on almost any topic at the drop of the hat (often by fitting new words to time-honored traditional melodies) made him a favorite performer. At this time, he recorded his famous set of *Dust Bowl Ballads* for RCA, as well as lengthy sessions organized by ALAN LOMAX for the Library of Congress. Although Guthrie's commercial recordings were not terribly successful at the time, they resurfaced in the fifties and early sixties during the next FOLK REVIVAL.

In the early forties, Guthrie performed with a loose-knit group known as the Almanac Singers, along with Seeger, Lee Hays, and Millard Lampell. He supplied the group with many of their popular songs, including "Union Maid," which encouraged workers to fight unfair management practices and unionize.

After serving in World War II, Guthrie settled in Brooklyn, New York, with his new wife, a modern dancer named Marjorie Mazia. However, symptoms of Huntington's Chorea were already manifesting themselves, making his behavior increasingly erratic. Guthrie continued to record and perform until the early fifties, often playing with Cisco Houston, until his health deteriorated to the point that he had to be hospitalized. By the early sixties, when he was a legend among younger singer/songwriters like BOB DYLAN, he was confined to a hospital bed and unable to perform.

Guthrie's contributions to American popular music are immense. He never tried to hide his southwestern roots and always let his nasal twang and Okie accent shine through in his singing (in fact, he may have even intentionally heightened these qualities to try to appeal to an urban audience as an "authentic" folk performer). His simple guitar accompaniments, his appropriation of popular tunes, and his songs that simply and directly addressed topical issues all greatly expanded the possibilities for popular singer/songwriters; the young Bob Dylan was virtually a Guthrie clone. But Guthrie's influence has also been felt on country singer/ songwriters, from the outlaws of the seventies through today's more progressive country writers. Guthrie showed that songs could be both topical and popular, and he also showed that a songwriter could be his own best interpreter, even if his musical skills were not great.

Brother Jack Guthrie (born 1915, Olive, OK; died 1948) was a cowboy-style performer in California who cowrote with Woody the classic song, "Oklahoma Hills"; severely injured in the Second World War, Jack never fully recovered and his career was forgotten in the wake of his older brother's success. Son Arlo (born 1947, New York City) has been a prominent performer on the folk-rock circuit since the late sixties, famous for his half-recited, half-sung comic opus "Alice's Restaurant."

Select Discography

Columbia River Collection, Rounder 1036. Previously unavailable recordings made in the late thirties for the WPA.

Library of Congress Recordings, Rounder 1041/42/43. Three-CD collection of recordings made by Alan Lomax for the Archive of Folksong in 1940.

Struggle, Smithsonian/Folkways 40025. Late-forties, politically themed recordings commissioned by MOSES ASCH.

Sings Folksongs, Smithsonian/Folkways 40007. Forties recordings made with Leadbelly and Cisco Houston.

H,

◀ HAGGARD, MERLE

(born 1937, Bakersfield, CA)

The mythic life of Merle Haggard—born to grinding poverty and fated to a stint in prison, followed by rehabilitation and success wrought from hard work and harder living—is as much responsible for his success as his songs. Like WOODY GUTHRIE, Haggard is an Okie who took his real-life experiences and molded them into his music. Like Guthrie, too, he has been uncompromising in producing records that reflect that experience. Unlike Guthrie, though, Haggard has enjoyed great success on the country charts, nearly ruling the top ten from the mid-sixties through the mid-seventies.

Haggard's parents were displaced Okies from the small town of Checotah (halfway between McAlester and Muskogee); and like many others, they were driven off their land by the ravaging dust storms of the mid-thirties, moving west to California in search of a better way of life. They found living conditions tough there and jobs few; the family was living in a converted boxcar when Haggard was born. They fared better after Merle's father got a job with the Santa Fe Railroad, but this brief period of prosperity ended with his premature death when Merle was nine.

Haggard attributes his troubled teenage years to his father's passing. He became difficult and unruly, constantly running away from home. He ended up serving time in reform school, and then, when he reached age seventeen, served ninety days in prison for stealing. Merle hung with a tough crowd, and when he was released he was soon in trouble again. One night, Haggard and a drunken friend tried to break into a restaurant that they thought was closed; it turned out to be earlier than the boys had thought, and the owner greeted them at the back door just after they had removed the hinges to break in. Haggard spent two and a half years in prison following his arrest. While in prison, he heard JOHNNY CASH perform, which renewed his interest in country music and his desire to write songs that would reflect his own experiences.

Upon his release in early 1960, he was determined to turn his life around. He began working for his brother, an electrician, while performing at night in local bars and clubs. In 1963 he was hired by WYNN STEWART to play in his backup band in Vegas. There, Fuzzy Owen heard Haggard play and signed him to his Tally record label. Haggard had his first solo hit with "Sing Me a Sad Song," followed by a minor duet hit with BONNIE OWENS on "Just Between the Two of Us." (Bonnie was married to BUCK OWENS at the time, although she would soon leave him to marry Haggard and join his road show). 1964 brought his first top-ten hit, "(My Friends Are Gonna Be) Strangers," written by BILL ANDERSON, which also gave Merle the name for his backup band, the Strangers.

Haggard was signed to Capitol Records by producer Ken Nelson, who was in charge of the label's growing country-music and folk rosters. His first hit for the label, "I'm a Lonesome Fugitive," written by Casey and LIZ ANDERSON, defined the classic Haggard stance: that of a man who had been in trouble with the law but now rues his rough-and-rowdy earlier days (although he's still subject to temptation). More prison ballads followed, including Merle's own compositions, "Branded Man" and his first number-one hit, "Sing Me Back Home," the true story of a man about to be executed who asked to hear for one last time a country song to remind him of his long-lost youth. Although this song literally drips with sentiment, Haggard's dry-as-dust delivery and unquestioned tough-guy credentials made it (and many more like it) instantly creditable to his audience. His 1968 hit, "Mama Tried," told of the difficulty his mother had in raising him, and expressed regret for his difficult teenage years.

Unlike many other country artists of the day who were often backed with heavy strings and vocal choruses, Haggard formed a lean, tough backup band he named the Strangers, after his 1964 hit. The original band included Roy Nichols (lead guitar), Norm Hamlet (steel guitar), Bobby Wayne (guitar), Dennis Hormak (bass), and Biff Adam (drums). The band's pared-down sound became a hallmark of Haggard's recordings, and he also wrote songs with its members, including Nichols and drummer Roy Burris (who replaced Adam in 1968).

Haggard gained his greatest notoriety for his 1969 recording of "Okie from Muskogee," a song that enraged hippies and the antiwar movement, while it cemented Haggard's position in mainstream, conservative country circles. Haggard was inspired when drummer Burris spotted a road sign for Muskogee during a tour through Oklahoma; the drummer commented, "I bet the citizens of Muskogee don't smoke marijuana." The song inspired many loony parodies, including Pat Sky's immortal remake (with the ending of the first verse changed to: "Love me, or I'll punch you in the mouth") and the Youngblood's "Hippie from Olema." Haggard feels his message was misinterpreted, although he followed the song with the equally jingoistic "The Fightin' Side of Me," full of old-time American bravado, and began hanging out with President Nixon.

One of Haggard's heroes from his youth was BOB WILLS, who regularly performed in Southern California at the time. So great was his admiration for Wills that Haggard began to rigorously practice the fiddle, seeking to emulate the swinging style of Wills's best lead fiddlers. He paid homage to the master fiddler in 1970 with an album of Wills's standards, recorded with many of Wills's then-retired sidemen, including mandolinist Tiny Moore, who soon joined Haggard's traveling show. It was quite a gutsy move to record this decidedly noncommercial album; it showed the considerable clout Haggard possessed at the height of his career. (Six years later, he had a hit with Wills's "Cherokee Maiden," arranged by Moore.)

By the mid-seventies, Haggard's life and career were in disarray; his marriage to Bonnie Owens was on the rocks, and he broke with his longtime record label, Capitol, in 1977. He took a brief break from the music business, hinting that he would no longer perform, although he quickly reemerged as a performer and recording artist (with ex-wife Bonnie still singing in his show.) He recorded a duet, "The Bull and the Bear," in 1978 with LEONA WILLIAMS (who also cowrote the song); the two were married soon after. (The marriage lasted only until 1983.)

Haggard's recording career was more sporadic in the eighties. He had his greatest recent success in 1983 when he recorded a duo album with WILLIE NELSON, yielding the number-one hit and title track, "Pancho and Lefty" (written by Texan TOWNES VAN ZANDT, the song was introduced to the pair by Haggard's daughter). Since then, he has had occasional chart hits and continues to tour with one of the tightest country revues on the road, stubbornly performing his own brand of country balladry. He has also had a few roles on television and in films, most notably appearing in Clint Eastwood's *Bronco Billy*, yielding the 1980 hit "Bar Room Buddies," a duet with the equally grizzled actor who really made Haggard's day.

Select Discography

Merle Haggard, Capitol 93181. Part of the Capitol Collector's Series, this CD gives a good overview of his career from the early sixties through the seventies.

More of the Best, Rhino 70917. Programmed to complement the Capitol release, this includes rarer tracks from Haggard's oeuvre.

Same Train: Different Time, Bear Family 15740. Reissues Haggard's wonderful tribute to JIMMIE RODGERS, along with some additional tracks not originally included.

Merle Haggard's Greatest Hits, MCA 5386. Budget-priced compilation of eighties-era recordings.

Pancho & Lefty, Epic 37958. Reissue of Haggard's famed duet album with Willie Nelson.

◀ HALL, TOM T.

(born 1936, Olive Hill, KY)

A SINGER/SONGWRITER best known for his narrative songs, Hall wrote the megahit "Harper Valley P.T.A.," recorded by JEANNIE C. RILEY in 1968.

Not surprisingly for a songwriter who loves to tell a story, Hall is a preacher's son who began playing music when he was eight years old on an old Martin GUITAR that his dad gave him. He met an older local musician named Clayton Delaney (immortalized in his 1971 hit "The Year Clayton Delaney Died"), who impressed the young Hall with stories of his successful band and its members, who wore shirts with "puffed sleeves that glowed in the dark," according to Hall. Hall's mother died when he was eleven, and three years later his father was hurt in a gun accident. Hall had to quit school and began working in a local garment factory, a job he held for a year and a half.

Hall began his "professional" career when he was sixteen as an announcer for a small-time local promoter who had a traveling movie theater mounted on the roof of his car! As an added attraction, Hall put together his first band, the Kentucky Travelers, to perform before the movies were shown. They were hired to play on the local radio station out of Morehead, Kentucky, sponsored by the Polar Bear Flour Company, for whom Tom wrote a theme song. After the band broke up, Hall remained at the station as a disc jockey.

In 1957 Hall joined the army and was stationed in Germany, where he performed over the Armed Forces Radio Network and at NCO clubs. He began writing comic songs, including "3,000 Gallons of Beer" and "36 Months of Loneliness," commenting on his experience in the service. In 1961 he was discharged, and he returned to radio work in Morehead, where he opened a small grocery store. He performed briefly with another band, the Technicians, out of Indiana, while moving from station to station as a deejay.

Hall's big break came in 1963 when country singer JIMMY NEWMAN recorded his song "DJ for a Day," which went to number one on the country charts. His song "Mad" was a hit for DAVE DUDLEY the next year, encouraging Hall to relocate to Nashville. Hall was not anxious to record himself but eventually was talked into recording his first single, "I Washed My Face in the Morning Dew," which was a minor 1967 hit.

The songwriter had a banner year in 1968. Jeannie C. Riley's recording of "Harper Valley P.T.A." sold six million copies; Hall compared the experience to "walking down the street and suddenly bending over and finding $100,000." His own recording career soon took off, with hits from 1969's "A Week in the County Jail" to "Old Dogs, Children and Watermelon Wine" and "Ravishing Ruby" from 1973. He recorded an album of BLUEGRASS standards in the mid-seventies, scoring a hit with Tony Hazard's "Fox on the Run," which soon became the most played-to-death number among bluegrass bands, amateur and professional.

Hall's brand of aw-shucks backwoodsy narratives were immensely popular through the mid-seventies, but then his popularity waned. He worked for a while as host of the quiz show *Pop Goes the Country* out of Nashville and made his last significant recordings with banjoist Earl Scruggs in 1982 on the album *The Storyteller and The Banjoman*. Although he had further hits in the mid-eighties with "Everything from Jesus to Jack Daniels" and "Famous in Missouri," Hall has been less innovative and more reliant on his reputation since.

In his best compositions, Hall took the tradition of country balladry to new and contemporary heights. He was unafraid to attack the small-mindedness of traditional country society, and he championed the rights of the "little guy" against the system. Although he also wrote some jingoistic songs in the mid-sixties and early seventies in support of the Vietnam War (including the rabble-rousing "Mama, Tell Them What We're Fighting For"), in general Hall's sympathies are with the downtrodden. In songs like "America the Ugly" and "The Promise and the Dream" he attacks head-on the inadequacy of a country that allows some of its people to go hungry and poor.

Select Discography

Greatest Hits, Vol. 1, Mercury 824143; *Greatest Hits, Vol. 2*, Mercury 824144. Cassette-only, two-volume overview of his Mercury years. (Also packaged on a single cassette as Mercury 810462.)

Ballad of Forty Dollars/Homecoming, Bear Family 15631. His first two Mercury LPs reissued on a single CD.
I Witness Life/100 Children, Bear Family 15658. His third and fourth Mercury LPs.

◀ HAMBLEN, STUART

(born 1908, Kellyville, TX)

Hamblen started out as a thirties-era cowboy singer and film actor, then became a mainstream country songsmith, and finally "saw the light" and became a gospel star, in many ways tracing the increasingly conservative trends of country music over the three decades from the thirties to the sixties.

Raised in rural Texas, Hamblen was naturally introduced to cowboy lore and legend, participating in amateur rodeo events as a teenager. He enrolled in teacher's college in Abilene, planning a career as a schoolmaster, but soon his love of music caused him to switch majors. When he was twenty, he traveled to Camden, New Jersey, where the studios for Victor Records were located, and became one of the first performers to record COWBOY SONGS. Soon after, he headed out to Southern California and began performing on a series of colorful cowboyesque radio programs, including *The Covered Wagon Jubilee*. For a backup band, he formed a swinging ensemble he called the Beverly Hillbillies (a name later used by TV sitcom producers in the sixties). His cowboy compositions included the popular "My Mary" and "Texas Plains," both issued in the mid-thirties.

In the thirties and forties, Hamblen was a popular heavy—that is, bad guy—in many of the low-budget horse flicks that featured white-hat stars ROY ROGERS and GENE AUTRY. He also developed a heavy thirst for liquor, giving himself a bad-boy reputation on screen and off.

After World War II, when the cowboy craze gave way to HONKY-TONK music, Hamblen wrote some of his best-loved songs, including 1949's "But I'll Be Chasin' Women," and "(Remember Me) I'm the One Who Loves You" from 1950, a big hit in a cover version by ERNEST TUBB. 1949 was a banner year in Hamblen's life for another reason: He attended a Billy Graham crusade and was "born again," giving up alcohol and eventually secular-music making as well.

Hamblen's biggest fifties-era hit was the sentimental "This Old House" issued in 1954; Rosemary Clooney successfully covered it in the same year for the pop charts. A year later, HANK SNOW had a hit with Hamblen's "Mainliner." However, Hamblen was soon producing more gospel material, including biblical tunes like "Open Up Your Heart and Let the Sun Shine In," "Be My Shepherd," and the colorfully titled "When the Lord Picks Up the Phone" (let's hope he's not calling collect!).

Hamblen married in the fifties, and he and his wife hosted a Los Angeles–based country-music TV show for a while. He retired from performing during the sixties but returned to radio at the invitation of a local station to begin a gospel hour that was eventually given the colorful title of *The Cowboy Church of the Air*. This show, featuring Hamblen's homespun philosophizing, was syndicated and became quite popular in the seventies. A talented horseman, Hamblen appeared through the seventies in the annual Rose Bowl Parade.

◀ HAMILTON, GEORGE IV

(born 1937, Matthews, NC)

Hamilton has been most successful bringing American country and folk-rock to foreign audiences, particularly in Canada, England, and on the Continent. Like many fifties-era stars, he began recording in the teen-pop mold before moving into country and then contemporary folk.

Born and raised in central North Carolina just outside of the commercial center of Winston-Salem, Hamilton first fell in love with country music thanks to the popular cowboy flicks that were shown at the local movie theaters. He formed a pop-country band in high school and, through producer Orville Campbell, met famous country/rock songwriter JOHN D. LOUDERMILK, who gave him his "A Rose and a Baby Ruth" to record in 1956. The song raced up the pop charts, Hamilton found himself a teenybopper star, and for three years he performed side by side with the likes of the EVERLY BROTHERS, BUDDY HOLLY, and Gene Vincent.

After his pop career fizzled, he relocated to Nashville in 1959, signing up with RCA Records to record mainstream country material. He had a couple of minor hits between 1959 and 1963, including "If You Don't Know, I Ain't Gonna Tell You," "Ft. Worth, Dallas or Houston," and his first number-one country hit, 1963's "Abilene." In the early sixties, he joined the GRAND OLE OPRY, and he remained with that institution throughout the decade.

In 1965, while touring Canada, Hamilton met young SINGER/SONGWRITER Gordon Lightfoot, who introduced him to other new Canadian songwriters, including IAN AND SYLVIA, Leonard Cohen, and Joni Mitchell. Hamilton became a champion of their material, recording several albums devoted to these new-styled folk singers. Although the material did not go down well on the conservative country charts of the day, Hamilton was well-received in Canada and then in England.

In 1971, tiring of the commercialism of Nashville, Hamilton retired from the Opry and moved back to his home state of North Carolina. From there, he began broadcasting a show for Canadian state television, focusing on singers and songwriters from north of the border; this show was syndicated around the world, influencing country music fans in the South Pacific (New Zealand, Australia), the Far East (Hong Kong), and South Africa. Hamilton also continued his peripatetic touring, becoming the first country star to perform behind the Iron Curtain, as well as in many other far-flung corners of the globe.

In the late seventies, Hamilton tried to revive his stateside career, signing with Dot, but he remains primarily known and loved abroad.

◀ HARGROVE, LINDA

(born 1951, Tallahassee, FL)

Hargrove was a country SINGER/SONGWRITER/guitarist of the mid-seventies who was considerably ahead of her time; by the time country caught up with her melding of rock, blues, and country styles, she had been "born again" and retired from music making.

During her Florida childhood, Hargrove was unaware of country music; pop and rock were her first loves, and by her teenage years she was playing guitar and writing her own brand of pop songs. However, BOB DYLAN's *Nashville Skyline* showed her the possibility in country styles, and she traveled to Nashville to try to make it as a songwriter. While cutting a demo session for Epic in the early seventies, she met producer/PEDAL STEEL GUITARist PETE DRAKE, who became her champion and introduced her to many of the more progressive figures of the day in country music and rock, including singer/songwriter MIKE NESMITH, who signed her to his short-lived Countryside label. (The album she recorded was never released after Countryside was dropped by its parent company, Elektra/Asylum.) Other country rockers like Leon Russell recorded her material; her big break came in 1975 when JOHNNY RODRIGUEZ had a hit with her song "Just Get Up and Close the Door." She had a minor solo hit a year later with "Love Was (Just Once Around the Dance Floor)," followed by a couple further singles. In 1978 she was born again and turned her back on secular singing and songwriting to pursue her mission of spreading the gospel.

◀ HARRELL, KELLY

(born Crockett Kelly Harrell, 1899, Drapers Valley, VA; died 1942)

Harrell was a popular old-time vocalist of the twenties who recorded with a subdued string-band accompaniment in the style of his contemporary CHARLIE POOLE.

Harrell was discovered by legendary country producer RALPH PEER when he was living and working as a mill hand in Fries, Virginia. Like VERNON DALHART, he had a semitrained voice with clear enunciation that made him instantly appealing to rural audiences. He began recording in 1924 and continued through the rest of the decade, usually accompanied by fiddle (played by Posey Rorer, who also performed with banjoist Poole), GUITAR, and sometimes BANJO, in the relaxed string-band style of the upper South.

Harrell recorded many traditional songs, including the popular late-nineteenth-century ballad "Charles Guiteau" about the assassin of President Garfield, and composed a few, such as "Away Out on the Mountain," later covered by JIMMIE RODGERS, and "The Story of the Mighty Mississippi," a hit for ERNEST "POP" STONEMAN. Like many other early country artists, Harrell received little in the way of royalties (if anything) from these successes, and his career ended when the Depression knocked the wind out of country-music recording. He returned to mill work in the thirties and died of a heart attack in 1942.

Select Discography

Kelly Harrell and the Virginia Stringband, County 408. Out-of-print LP reissuing classic 78 recordings by Harrell with various accompanists.

◀ HARRIS, EMMYLOU

(born 1949, Birmingham, AL)

A pioneering COUNTRY-ROCK vocalist of the seventies who made a successful transition into pure country in the eighties, Harris has been an influence on many NEW-COUNTRY female vocalists, including KATHY MATTEA, SUZY BOGGUSS, and MARY CHAPIN CARPENTER.

Harris came from a solid, middle-class background. She attended college at the University of North Carolina, forming a folk duo there with a classmate. In 1969 Harris hit the road for Greenwich Village, then the mecca for folk-style singers, and recorded her first solo LP (*Gliding Bird*) on the tiny Jubilee label. In the early seventies, she moved to California and began performing with GRAM PARSONS, the influential country-rocker who had helped transform the BYRDS into a more country-oriented group and who founded the FLYING BURRITO BROTHERS. The two became romantically and musically involved; Harris added harmony vocals to Parsons's solo LPs and performances, her clear, bell-like tones perfectly complementing his lived-in lead vocals.

After Parsons's death due to a drug overdose, Harris became a champion of country-rock, appealing to a primarily urban, college-educated audience. She formed her first backup group, the Angel Band, and had several hits on the country and pop charts through the seventies. Harris's repertoire was heavy on classic country songs of the thirties, forties, and fifties (she was a particular fan of the LOUVIN BROTHERS) and included material by contemporary folk, rock, and country singer/songwriters. Her backup band, renamed the Hot Band in the late seventies, employed many musicians who would later become well-known on their own, including RODNEY CROWELL, RICKY SKAGGS, ALBERT LEE, and VINCE GILL. Skaggs was particularly influential in moving Harris in a pure-country direction, shaping her BLUEGRASS-homage album of 1980, *Roses in the Snow*. (Harris, in turn, encouraged Skaggs to become a solo act.)

In the eighties, Harris focused on the country audience almost exclusively. She created a country song cycle on the 1985 recording *The Ballad of Sally Rose*, her most ambitious project to date as both songwriter and performer. In 1987 she released *Trio* in collaboration with LINDA RONSTADT and DOLLY PARTON, yielding her biggest commercial hits. Into the early nineties, Harris has continued to be active on the country charts, although she has never had the big-selling records that define a marketable star.

Equally as important to the history of country music as her musical output is Harris's image. She is the first successful female country singer to emerge from a country-rock background, and she has done little since to change her style. She has let her hair go naturally gray, dresses simply (although occasionally she wears rhinestone-encrusted cowgirl outfits in homage to country stars of the past), and wears little makeup, in marked contrast to most country female recording stars who often look like exaggerated Barbie dolls. Today's more natural-looking female country singers owes a debt to Harris for her example.

Select Discography

Profile: The Best of Emmylou Harris, Warner Bros. 3258

Profile II: The Best of Emmylou Harris, Warner Bros. 25161

Blue Kentucky Girl, Warner Bros. 3318. One of her better early albums.

Roses in the Snow, Warner Bros. 3422. Her most traditionally oriented album, with arrangements by Ricky Skaggs and picking by Skaggs, JERRY DOUGLAS, TONY RICE, and other progressive bluegrassers.

The Ballad of Sally Rose, Warner Bros. 25205. A song cycle composed by Harris.

◀ HART, FREDDIE

(born Freddie Segrest, 1928, Lochapka, AL)

Freddie Hart's life is one of those rags-to-riches stories—complete with an eighteen-year struggle to make it big—that all country fans love.

Born to a sharecropping family, one of fifteen children, Hart got started on the wrong road early, running away from home when he was twelve, enlisting in the marines (by lying about his age) at fourteen, and serving in the Pacific during World War II. After being released from the service, he took a number of odd jobs on the East Coast, gravitating toward Nashville, even working as a kind of unofficial roadie for HANK WILLIAMS for a while in 1949. Finally, Hart relocated to Los Angeles in 1951 in search of a musical career.

His break came two years later in Phoenix, Arizona, where he was working in a cotton mill. He met legendary honky-tonker LEFTY FRIZZELL, who admired his songwriting abilities and hired him for his backup band as a guitarist, a position Hart held for eleven years. Frizzell also arranged for Hart's debut recording for Capitol Records, 1952's "Butterfly Love," and got him a steady job on the *Town Hall Party* radio show, L.A.'s answer to the GRAND OLE OPRY.

Hart had more success as a songwriter than a performer in the fifties. CARL SMITH covered his "Loose Talk" in 1955 to earn a solid hit; the song has since been covered over fifty times. Two years later, Hart had a minor hit with "Keys in the Mailbox." PATSY CLINE recorded his "Lovin' in Vain" as the flip side to her smash "I Fall to Pieces," GEORGE JONES had a minor 1964 hit with his "My Tears are Overdue," and PORTER WAGONER had a number-three single with "Skid Row Joe" in 1966. Hart's solo career, however, was going downhill, and he moved from label to label through the sixties.

Finally, in 1969, he re-signed with Capitol, delivering a couple of albums. In 1971 the label was ready to drop him when a deejay out of Atlanta, Georgia, began playing one of his album tracks, "Easy Loving," on the radio. The song took off after Capitol had already dropped Hart, but they hastily renewed his contract after the song made number one. The slick production, with parallel GUITAR and steel guitar parts, and slightly racy topic (the song is said to be the first country hit to have the word "sex" in the lyric) made it a natural hit. Hart's vocal style was typical of Nashville's COUNTRYPOLITAN artists: a trace of twang coming through typical pop-style crooning. A follow-up was rushed out, a veritable "Easy Lovin' " clone right down to the guitar/steel guitar riff, called "My Hang-Up Is You."

Hart recorded through the seventies, with hits coming early in the decade (and featuring his backup band, called the Heartbeats, naturally). Many of the songs had a similar sexy undertone, including "If You Can't Feel It (It Ain't There)" (1974) and "The First Time" (1975); and some, like "When Lovers Turn to Strangers" (1977), offered the standard barroom angst.

Capitol dropped Hart in 1979, and he moved on to smaller Sunbird Records, where he had a few saccharine hits. Although he continued to perform in the eighties and turned up on late-night TV ads on the Nashville Network plugging mail-order reissues of his big hits, Hart's hit-making days were over.

◀ HARTFORD, JOHN

(born John Harford, 1937, New York, NY)

John Hartford is an anomaly in country music: a talented instrumentalist (primarily on BANJO but also on GUITAR and fiddle) and songwriter, but also an eccentric performer who has managed to carve out a career—following the path of earlier country stars such as UNCLE DAVE MACON—by writing and performing material that combines earthy humor with social commentary and pointed wit.

The deep-voiced Hartford was born in New York but raised in St. Louis, and he became an active figure in that city's BLUEGRASS scene, performing with artists DOUG DILLARD and BYRON BERLINE. An early love of the Mississippi River led to a brief career working as a deckhand on one of the last great steamboats, while working part-time as a local deejay. In 1965 he moved to Nashville in search of a country-music career.

Hartford signed with RCA records and recorded a series of almost unclassifiable LPs. Although RCA produced him with the typical Nashville backup of the time, his songs were highly personal, ranging from the comic "Old Fashioned Washing Machine" (in which he imitated the sound of an ancient washer on its last legs) to the wordy, anthemic "Gentle on My Mind" and "Natural to Be Gone." Hartford's big break came with the 1967 hit recording of his "Gentle on My Mind" by singer/guitarist GLEN CAMPBELL. He subsequently moved to L.A., where he wrote for both the Smothers Brothers' and Glen Campbell's TV programs and recorded his last record for RCA (*Iron Mountain Depot*), an early stab at COUNTRY-ROCK, which included a cover of the Beatles' "Hey Jude."

In 1970 he returned to Nashville and signed to Warner Brothers, releasing his classic LP, *Aereo-Plain*. For the album Hartford had established a band, bringing together the most talented and progressive of Nashville's musicians, including Tut Taylor (dobro), NORMAN BLAKE (guitar), VASSAR CLEMENTS (fiddle), and Randy Scruggs (bass). The album ranged from Hartford's classic celebration of his steamboat days ("Steamboat Whistle Blues") to an elegy for the original Ryman auditorium, the best-known home of the GRAND OLE OPRY ("They're Gonna Tear Down the Grand Ole Opry").

Hartford soon dissolved his band and spent most of the seventies and eighties touring as a solo musician. Accompanying himself on banjo, guitar, and fiddle, Hartford rigged up a plywood board with a microphone to enable him to clog dance while singing and playing. His love of the Mississippi River emerged again in the concept LP *Mark Twang*, released by Flying Fish Records in 1976, which earned him a Grammy.

In the late eighties, Hartford briefly re-signed to a major record label (MCA) and began performing with his son. He has also been associated with Opryland USA and was instrumental in having an old-time steamboat attraction added to the Opryland theme park. Most recently, he has been issuing his recordings on his own colorfully named label, Small Dog Barking.

Select Discography
Me Oh My, How Time Flies, Flying Fish 70440. Compilation of his mid-seventies through early-eighties recordings.
Mark Twang, Flying Fish 70020. His Grammy-winning solo album.

◀ HAWKINS, HAWKSHAW

(born Harold Franklin Hawkins, 1921, Huntington, WV; died 1963)

The third figure tragically killed in the plane wreck that took the lives of PATSY CLINE and COWBOY COPAS, Hawkins had a spotty career from the mid-forties through the fifties, gaining his greatest success right before his death. Bridging the gap between early HONKY-TONK stars like ERNEST TUBB and the more modern NASHVILLE SOUND, Hawkins was not an innovative artist but served as an important link between the old country and the new.

Having won a talent contest as a teen, Hawkins performed on local radio in his hometown of Huntington until he enlisted in the army in 1942. Four years later, upon his discharge, he returned home and began performing over the popular *Wheeling Jamboree* radio show and recording for the King label out of Cincinnati. Early minor hits included 1949's "I Wasted a Nickel," 1951's "Slow Poke," and the first recording of "Sunny Side of the Mountain," which was to become the theme song for BLUEGRASS singer JIMMY MARTIN.

He was signed to RCA in 1955 and became a member of the GRAND OLE OPRY a year later, but the hits just didn't come. It wasn't until 1963, when he recorded Justin Tubb's "Lonesome 7-7203," that he finally had a number-one country hit; but two days after the song charted, Hawkins was dead.

Select Discography
Hawkshaw Hawkins Volume 1, King 587. CD reissue of 1958 LP that included recordings made from the late forties through the early fifties, including his hit, "Sunny Side of the Mountain."
Hawkshaw Hawkins, Bear Family 15539. His mid-fifties recordings for RCA, which pale in comparison to his earlier King sides.

◀ HAY, GEORGE D.

(born 1895, Attica, IN; died 1968)

Hay was the famous "Solemn Old Judge" who was the founder of and announcer for the GRAND OLE OPRY, country music's best-known radio program.

Hay began his career in real estate, working as a salesman until 1920, when he decided to become a newspaperman. He was hired as a reporter for the Memphis *Commercial Appeal.* The paper branched out into the new field of radio, opening its own station, WMC, where Hay also worked as an editor and announcer. At this station, he began to develop his character, calling himself the Solemn Old Judge and opening his broadcasts by tooting on "Hushpuckena," his name for the steamboat whistle that became his on-air signature. In 1924 Hay was hired away by WLS in Chicago to be the announcer for their popular *National Barn Dance* program. He gained national exposure on this program, and within a year won a popularity poll as the top radio performer in the United States.

In October 1925, the National Life Insurance Company of Nashville opened a small, thousand-watt radio station called WSM (after the company's slogan, "We Shield Millions"). Hay joined the new station as an announcer and newsman. On November 28, 1925, he invited local old-time fiddler UNCLE JIMMY THOMPSON to perform on the station, inaugurating a program Hay called the *WSM Barn Dance.* In January 1926, the show was renamed, following a famous quip by Hay: The radio station carried the Metropolitan Opera, a program they picked up from New York; when his *Barn Dance* program followed an opera broadcast, Hay announced, "You've been up in the clouds with grand opera; now get down to earth with us in a . . . Grand Ole Opry." The name stuck.

Hay was responsible for booking many of the early Opry stars, and he did much to bring the best local talent to the station. He was particularly anxious to book UNCLE DAVE MACON, who was already a well-loved performer in the area. He also introduced to the Opry black harmonica-player DEFORD BAILEY, the McGEE BROTHERS, the DELMORE BROTHERS, and countless other acts.

Hay was central in building WSM into a regional powerhouse. In 1929 the station gained clear-channel status, allowing it to jump to fifty-thousand-watt power by 1932, meaning it could be heard throughout the South and Midwest, and even as far north as Canada. Hay formed the WSM Artists Bureau in the thirties, arranging for tours for many of the radio performers. Through the influence of this powerful booking agency, the station could make or break a performer's career (and also was able to pocket a percentage of the profits performers made on the road).

Although Hay continued to be an Opry presence until his retirement in 1947, he was less than pleased with the new direction country music was taking. He was annoyed when BOB WILLS's band appeared on the program in 1943 with amplified instruments; he had always banned electric instruments from the Opry stage. A staunch traditionalist to the end, Hay was unhappy with the hotter new styles, particularly WESTERN SWING and HONKY-TONK music. Still, Hay's presence on the show through 1947, while diminished, maintained its links to the past, a key element in its continuing success.

◀ HEAD, ROY

(born 1941, Three Rivers, TX)

Head is a Texas rocker who turned to country after his teenybopper years were over.

Born in Three Rivers, Head was raised in the tiny Texas border town of Crystal City in a one-room shack. Initially performing country material with his older brother Donald, he gravitated to R&B and rock in his high-school years, when he formed a local band called the Traits. They had a regional hit in 1958 with "Baby Let Me Kiss You (One More Time)," leading to lots of work throughout the South. In the early sixties, Head came under the influence of legendary pop-rock record producer Huey Meaux, who produced the Traits's biggest pop hit, 1965's "Treat Her Right," making Head something of a legend as an early blue-eyed soulster. Breaking from the rest of the band, Head began touring on his own, although still using the Traits's name; the other members sued him for six-sevenths of all his income, which ended the tour. Soon after, Head developed nodes on his vocal chords, and his career hit the skids.

In the late sixties, Head switched to a country repertoire, encouraged by Houston club owner Lee Savaggio, who gave him a regular place to perform plus a recording contract with his Shannon label. After a couple of regional hits, Head's contract was picked up by ABC/Dot, and he had a top-ten country hit with 1976's "The Door I Used to Close." A year later, Head covered Rod Stewart's "Tonight's the Night" (an unlikely choice) for the cowpoke crowd; in 1979 he moved to Elektra and then, two years later, to smaller Churchill records, scoring moderate success with a combination of revivals of his rockin' hits and more hard-core country material.

Select Discography

Singin' Texas Rhythm and Blues, P-Vine 1610. His sixties-era blue-eyed soul hits, including "Treat Her Right."

◀ HEBB, BOBBY

(born 1941, Nashville, TN)

One of the few black country stars, Hebb is best remembered for his 1966 crossover hit, "Sunny," which made him (for a while, anyway) a favorite lounge act.

When he was twelve, Hebb was discovered by producer ROY ACUFF, who hired him to perform on the GRAND OLE OPRY as a spoons player. Two years later, he made his first recordings for the tiny Rich label, including "Night Train to Memphis." In 1961 he teamed up with Sylvia Shemwell, as the R&B/pop duo Bobby and Sylvia, and performed with her for two years.

In 1966 Hebb was recording again as a solo artist, now for Phillips, and scored a big pop and country hit with "Sunny." He followed this with a cover of "A Satisfied Mind," recorded in more of a country vein, and then disappeared off the charts. By the early seventies he was back to recording for small country labels, scoring a minor hit in 1972 with "Love Love Love." Since then Hebb has specialized in mainstream pop-country.

◀ HEE HAW

(1969–1993; ongoing in reruns)

Hee Haw was originally a network television program featuring country music and humor in a variety-show format. Broadcast for two seasons nationally by CBS, the program was hosted by BUCK OWENS and ROY CLARK, and featured a wide variety of mainstream country performers. The combination of cornball humor and teary-eyed country music dated back to the old-style tent shows that used to tour the South; the quick editing from joke to joke was borrowed from a popular TV series of the day, *Laugh-In*. The network dropped the program after two years, but the producers refused to let it die, taking it into syndication, where it lasted for another two decades. More recently, it has turned up again on TNN in reruns.

Set in "kolorful Kornfield Kounty," *Hee Haw* mixed straightforward musical performances with the kind of rube humor that had been entertaining Southern audiences since the days of the minstrel shows. Add to this a couple of buxom blonds, and you have the surefire formula for long-lasting success. Besides series hosts Clark and Owens, the show featured many regular guests, including BANJO-playing comedians STRINGBEAN and GRANDPA JONES; Roni Stoneman, the big-voiced granddaughter of ERNEST STONEMAN; famed backwoods comedienne/monologuist MINNIE PEARL; and even *Playboy* playmate Barbi Benton. Famed harmonica player CHARLIE MCCOY served as co–musical director for the original program, ensuring that many fine Nashville session players appeared on the show, along with Buck Owens's regular backup band the Buckaroos and NASHVILLE-SOUND vocal groups the Inspirations and Nashville Addition.

Although it was in many ways a throwback to the old stereotype of country music as something produced by dim-witted hayseeds, the show did provide valuable exposure to its stars. In 1992 a last-ditch attempt was made to modernize the show, but it finally died as an original production, although it continues to appear in reruns.

◀ HIATT, JOHN

(born 1952, Indianapolis, IN)

Hiatt is a gravelly voiced SINGER/SONGWRITER who has supplied hits for other artists but has yet to find a niche for his own performances. Combining country, R&B, and rock, Hiatt has created a strong body of highly personal songs for which he is the perfect interpreter, even though chart success has eluded him.

Hiatt first began playing during his high-school years with a local R&B outfit known as the White Ducks; his love for R&B continues to show up in his own songs and performances. In 1970 he moved to Nashville, and by mid-decade he had been signed by Epic Records, where he recorded two LPs, followed by two more for MCA; none sold well, although they helped establish his reputation. Folk-rocker Ry Cooder was looking for material when his manager suggested he listen to Hiatt's records; he liked what he heard and hired Hiatt as his backup guitarist in 1980 (the two would continue to make music together on and off through the next decade). In the mid-eighties, Hiatt recorded a number of albums for Geffen, and his reputation as a songwriter grew. His songs were marked by an often ironic, sometimes cruel portrayal of the foibles of human relationships. However, his increasing dependence on alcohol, plus his own records' poor sales, put an end to his recording career for a while.

Hiatt returned magnificently with 1987's *Bring the Family*, accompanied by Cooder and session drummer Jim Keltner, with British punk-country singer Nick Lowe on bass. Although still sharply focused and humorous, Hiatt's songs and attitude seemed more forgiving than in the past, while the band provided the perfect rocking foil to his music, which combined elements of soul, gospel, country, and ROCKABILLY. Bonnie Raitt scored her first comeback hit with Hiatt's "Thing Called Love" from this album, a bluesy rocker that provided the title for Peter Bogdonavich's 1993 film about a young singer trying to break into Nashville.

Hiatt formed a touring band called the Goners, with whom he produced a follow-up LP, *Slow Turning*, his most "country" in flavor. This featured the Southern-living hymn "Drive South" (a 1993 hit for SUZY BOGGUSS) along with his humorous take on a demented Elvis fan ("Tennessee Plates"), and the HONKY-TONK lament, "Icy Blue Heart," a modernized version of boy-meets-(deadly)-girl-at-the-saloon (covered by EMMYLOU HARRIS).

Although both albums were critically acclaimed, Hiatt was still a slow seller in the stores. An attempt to glitz up his sound with a fuller, pop-rock accompaniment on his next album (*Stolen Moments*, 1991) was a total failure, and it was followed by an odd reunion with Cooder, Lowe, and Keltner, who were now calling themselves Little Village. The album they produced featured songs that were jointly composed by the band, and although Hiatt provided most of the lead vocals (and one suspects the ideas for some of the better songs), the attempt to produce a relaxed, just-a-couple-of-friends-picking-on-the-back-porch sound didn't quite make it.

In 1993 Hiatt released a new solo album, *Perfectly Good Guitar*, on which he attempted to meld his offbeat writing personality with grunge rock, of all things. The album features some excellent songs, the best one of which (not surprisingly) is the most countryesque number, "Buffalo River Home."

Hiatt's vocal style is an endearing mix of R&B and country mannerisms, although his husky singing takes some getting used to, and may account for his lack of popularity among fans of Nashville's more photogenic and smoother-sounding hunks. Hiatt looks as wrinkled and worn as he sounds, the evidence of many years of hard living. But his songs have an authenticity and sense of humor that is both unique and hard-won in a music scene that is often populated by singers who are no more than clever marketing plans packaged in cowboy hats.

Select Discography

Y'All Caught, Geffen 24247. Anthology of his Geffen recordings, made from 1979 to 1985; many are poorly produced, but some good songs are featured nonetheless.

Bring the Family, A&M 5158. 1987 comeback album with great backup by Ry Cooder and company.

Slow Turning, A&M 5206. Hiatt's largely acoustic, most country-oriented recording (of late), with fine songs and backup by his road band, the Goners.

Perfectly Good Guitar, A&M 31454 0135. 1993 grunge-rock/country fusion album.

◀ HIGHWAY 101

(1987–ongoing; original members: Paulette Carlson [vocals]; Curtis Stone; Cactus Moser; Jack Daniels; Carlson was replaced by Nikki Nelson in 1989)

Highway 101 is a hard-rocking country outfit formed originally to accompany smoky-voiced singer Paulette Carlson; but the band has managed to survive her departure.

Carlson has become, deservedly, a new-country star, and recalls the style (musically and fashionwise) of rocker Stevie Nicks. She first came to Nashville in 1978 when she was twenty-four, working on the staff of the OAK RIDGE BOYS' publishing company and backing GAIL DAVIES. Solo recordings for RCA in 1983 and 1984 failed to chart, and she moved back to her native Minnesota in 1985, disappointed with her career progress.

Although Carlson was in semi-retirement, her manager, Chuck Morris, felt that she could be successful if packaged correctly. Noting the increased interest in cowboy-style bands, he enlisted the help of a trio of California COUNTRY-ROCK session musicians to form Highway 101, intended to showcase Carlson in a cowgirl-meets-New-Nashville getup. The group's hits capitalized on her raspy singing and portrayed her as a tough broad who was not to be slighted. Their first charting record, 1987's "The Bed You Made for Me," written by Carlson, was addressed to an ex-boyfriend who had cheated on her; "Whiskey If You Were a Woman," portrays the havoc brought on a marriage by a husband's alcoholism; "All the Reasons Why," from 1988, (cowritten by Carlson) tells of a woman who is unafraid to end an unhappy relationship; and in "Just Say Yes" a woman frankly and unabashedly pursues her man.

Carlson left the band in 1989 to pursue a solo career. Her first solo recording continued the girl-with-an-attitude trend with her minor hit, "Not With My Heart You Don't." Meanwhile, Nikki Nelson, a young, fire-breathing redhead, replaced Carlson as the band's vocalist, singing lead on their up-tempo 1991 hit, "Bing Bang Boom."

Both Carlson and the reconstituted Highway 101 have yet to enjoy as great a success on their own as they had when they were together.

Select Discography

Highway 101, Featuring Paulette Carlson, Warner Bros. 25608. Their debut LP from 1987.

Greatest Hits, Warner Bros. 26253. Best of the original band.

Bing Bang Boom, Warner Bros. 26588. 1991 release with new vocalist Nikki Nelson.

Love Goes On, Liberty 97711. Carlson's 1991 solo debut.

◀ HIGHWOODS STRINGBAND, THE

*(c. 1973–1978: Walt Koken, Bob Potts [fiddles]; Mac Benford [banjo]; Doug
Dorschug [guitar]; Jenny Cleland [bass])*

The Highwoods Stringband was one of the most popular revival string bands of
the seventies. Modeled after Gid Tanner's SKILLET LICKERS, they took a twin-fiddle
sound and high-powered backup and wed it to a humorous approach to fiddle
tunes and old-time songs. They were also inspired by the recordings of traditional
fiddle and BANJO players who were rediscovered in the sixties, particularly fiddler
TOMMY JARRELL.

Originating in the Berkeley, California, old-time music community of the seventies, several members of the band appeared on the seminal anthology *Berkeley
Farms*, recorded by MIKE SEEGER. Group members relocated to Ithaca, New York,
where the final lineup stabilized around 1973. Their first LP, *Fire on the Mountain*
(Rounder), was recorded outdoors, in an attempt to capture the spontaneous
sound of the band; their next two LPs, *Dance All Night* and *Radio Special #3*, were
more professionally recorded. However, none of their albums captured the excitement of hearing the band live. Mac Benford's hoarse vocals, the ragged-but-right
sound of the twin fiddles, and Dorschug's RILEY PUCKETT–influenced guitar runs
made for a sound that was both contemporary and nostalgic. The band influenced
countless other outfits, amateur and professional, particularly the Plank Road
Stringband, The Chicken Chokers, and the Tompkins County Horseflies.

After the band broke up, Benford recorded a solo banjo LP and briefly formed
a new band, the Backwoods Band, in the style of Highwoods; Dorschug went to
work as a record producer for JUNE APPAL Records. The other band members faded
from the performing scene, although Koken re-emerged in 1994, producing a solo
banjo CD.

Select Discography

Fire on the Mountain, Rounder 0023. Their out-of-print debut LP from 1974.

◀ HILLMAN, CHRIS

(born 1944, Los Angeles, CA)

Hillman was a seminal figure in the California COUNTRY-ROCK scene, a founding
member of the BYRDS, the FLYING BURRITO BROTHERS, and the DESERT ROSE BAND.

Born in Southern California, Hillman was raised in the ranch country in the
northern part of the state, where he had his first exposure to country-style music.
His first group was the whimsically titled Scotsdale Squirrel Barkers, a BLUEGRASS
ensemble that became better known in the early sixties as the Hillmen; the band
also featured the Gosdin brothers and Don Parmley. In 1964 Hillman returned to
Southern California to participate in the rich folk music scene in and around L.A.;
there he met ex–folk singers Jim (later Roger) McGuinn and David Crosby. Influenced by the Beatles, they first formed a group called the Jet Set, changing their
names to the very twee Beefeaters, before settling on the Byrds. The group was
one of the most successful folk-rock ensembles of the sixties and collaborated

on the seminal country-rock fusion album *Sweetheart of the Rodeo* with SINGER/ SONGWRITER GRAM PARSONS in 1968.

Hillman and Parsons left the Byrds to pursue country-rock music and in 1969 formed the Flying Burrito Brothers, a band that went through many permutations in its short existence. After the Burritos, Hillman performed with Stephen Stills's short-lived country-rock band, Manassas, and then with singer/songwriters J. D. Souther and Richie Furay in an equally short-lived group. Hillman recorded two solo albums for Asylum records, which fell dead on the charts, before reuniting in the early eighties with McGuinn and GENE CLARK to form an acoustic trio, which had critical if not much commercial success.

A reunion album for the Hillmen and two more solo albums on the country-folk label Sugar Hill followed. In 1985, Hillman and old friend Herb Pedersen were invited to form a backup band for soft-folk star Dan Fogelberg; the band stuck together after the tour was over, to become the Desert Rose Band, and have scored hits on the country charts into the nineties.

Select Discography

The Hillmen, Sugar Hill 3719. Mid-eighties reunion album for this fabled group.
Desert Rose, Sugar Hill 3743. Comeback solo LP from the mid-eighties.

◀ HINOJOSA, TISH

(born 1955, San Antonio, TX)

Hinojosa is another one of those crossover artists who, like statemate NANCI GRIFFITH, straddles various traditions, including seventies SINGER/SONGWRITER, country, and (for Hinojosa) her own take on her Latino heritage.

Raised in a working-class family in the multi-ethnic city of San Antonio, Hinojosa began playing GUITAR in high school, inspired as many others were at the time by the early-seventies soft rock of Joni Mitchell, Judy Collins, James Taylor, and BOB DYLAN. She began writing her own material soon after and recorded a few singles in Spanish for the local market. Relocating to New Mexico, she issued a self-produced cassette, *From Taos to Tennessee*, in 1987, staking out her territory as a NEW-COUNTRY artist with southwestern roots. Soon after, major label A&M picked her up. In 1989 she recorded an album called *Homeland*, produced by Los Lobos sax player Steve Berlin; and a second LP was recorded (under the guiding hand of soulster Booker T. Jones) but not released. In a management shuffle, Hinojosa was dropped from A&M.

Picked up by specialty label Rounder Records, Hinojosa released *Culture Swing*, a mostly acoustic album reflecting Mexican, Spanish, country, and even Caribbean sounds. Strangely enough, the smaller label was able to get her more attention than the conglomerate, and she had a minor hit with her ode to migrant workers, "Something in the Rain." As this is being written, she is recording a new album that is said to have a more sixties pop feel, demonstrating her eclectic musical interests.

In the early seventies, Hinojosa would have been marketed as a singer/songwriter; today, she is considered "country," which shows how broad the category has become.

Select Discography

Taos to Tennessee, Watermelon 1008. Reissue of her first, self-produced LP.
Homeland, A&M 5263.
Culture Swing, Rounder 3122.

◀ HOLCOMB, ROSCOE

(born 1913, Daisy, KY; died 1982)

Holcomb was an intense, high-voiced mountain vocalist and BANJO/GUITAR player who was discovered by folklorist JOHN COHEN in the early sixties and became a central figure in the old-time music revival.

Roscoe lived and worked near Hazard, Kentucky, the center of Kentucky's coal-mining region. His earliest memory was of someone playing the harmonica (which he called the mouth-harp, as many country people do). His brother-in-law gave him a homemade banjo when he was ten, and he was soon playing for local dances. By his late teen years, he was working in the mines and married to a religious woman who thought of music as the devil's work and urged him to give it up. He abandoned playing for a while but soon was back to making music as a sideline to his mining career.

By the late fifties, when John Cohen first heard him play, Holcomb was working odd jobs around his home. Even after he was recorded by Cohen and began appearing at folk festivals, he continued to do hard labor, including paving work on many of the superhighways that were then being put through the mountains. Holcomb never viewed music making as a "profession," although he was deadly serious about maintaining a high level of performance.

Holcomb once said, "If you cut my head off at the throat, I'd go on singing." This is an apt description of his vocal quality, which Cohen described as a "high lonesome sound" (a term that has come to be used to describe much of traditional country and BLUEGRASS vocal music). Holcomb's high-pitched falsetto singing was perfectly suited to his repertory of bluesy songs. He played the banjo in a two-finger, picked style and used a similar style when picking the guitar (achieving a unique, banjolike sound on this instrument). Holcomb's intensity as a performer was legendary; he lived the songs, sometimes crying during performances on stage, even if he was performing a song that he had already sung countless times before.

Holcomb is one of those performers whose recordings truly transcend genre; he is said to have been a favorite musician of everyone from BOB DYLAN to electric blues guitarist Eric Clapton. In the best country music, even music produced by performers who never heard Holcomb, there is a small echo of the intensity that made his performances so breathtaking and pure.

Select Discography

Mountain Music of Kentucky, Folkways 2317. Anthology featuring Holcomb and other musicians from the area.
Roscoe Holcomb/Wade Ward, Folkways 2363.

The High, Lonesome Sound, Folkways 2368. Soundtrack of a film made by Cohen, featuring Holcomb.

Close to Home, Folkways 2374. Holcomb's last album, featuring his unique guitar picking as well as his more familiar banjo work.

◀ HOLLY, BUDDY

(born Clarence Hardin Holley, 1936, Lubbock, TX; died 1959)

One of the founding fathers of COUNTRY-ROCK, Holly's songs and performance style have greatly influenced the growth of country, pop, and rock music since the late fifties.

Holly was exposed to a wide variety of music in Texas, including WESTERN SWING, R&B, and country and western. He formed his first musical group in high school with classmate Bob Montgomery, performing as Buddy and Bob on the local radio station. Montgomery was the songwriter of the duo, mostly writing in ROCKABILLY and straight country styles. (He would later become a leading Nashville writer/producer, penning "Misty Blue," a 1972 hit for Joe Simon, and working with EDDY ARNOLD, B. J. THOMAS, and SLIM WHITMAN.) When FERLIN HUSKY and ELVIS PRESLEY came to town in 1955, the duo was hired as the opening act, leading to Holly's first record contract. He traveled to Nashville to work with legendary country producer OWEN BRADLEY, who turned out to be unsympathetic to Holly's unique blend of rock and country; these first recordings were a failure.

Returning to Lubbock, Holly formed a new group, which he named the Crickets. In 1957 the band hooked up with producer Norman Petty, who operated a studio in Clovis, New Mexico. There, over the next two years, the classic Holly recordings were made, including hits "That'll Be the Day," "Peggy Sue," "Oh Boy," "Words of Love," and "Not Fade Away." Holly split from the Crickets by the end of 1958, settling in New York and recording more pop-oriented tracks accompanied by a thick string section. In 1959 he toured with a new band, featuring bassist WAYLON JENNINGS (whose first single, a cover of the CAJUN classic "Jole Blon," had been produced by Holly), and guitarist Tommy Alsup. It was on this tour that Holly died in the famous plane crash that ended his short career.

It may seem strange to include Holly in an encyclopedia of country music, but his influence was not limited to rock. Many of his songs have been covered by country artists. His hiccupy vocal style is often imitated, and itself can be traced back to the YODELING of country singers like JIMMIE RODGERS or GENE AUTRY. The rockin' sound of Holly's band was a natural outgrowth of earlier rockabilly recordings by other artists, and was in turn influential on the return-to-roots country sounds of the eighties and nineties.

Select Discography

From the Original Master Tapes, MCA 5540. Twenty of his most famous hits.

◀ HOLY MODAL ROUNDERS

(c. 1964–1969: Pete Stampfel [fiddle, banjo, vocals]; Steve Weber [guitar, vocals])

The Holy Modal Rounders were an urban old-time revival duo with a unique sense of humor, and they are best remembered for two LPs they cut for Prestige in the mid-sixties.

Unlike the NEW LOST CITY RAMBLERS and other folk revivalists who were deadly earnest in their attempts to re-create the country music of the twenties and thirties, the Rounders brought a New York, tongue-in-cheek humor to their performances. Their sense that a performer could interact with a culture, rather than just studiously re-create it, was very liberating for an entire generation of revival musicians. Stampfel was the more energetic of the pair, with a high, nasal voice and rough-hewn fiddle style that was perfectly suited to the material; Weber was quieter, playing a blues-influenced GUITAR and providing low harmony vocals.

The Rounders came into contact with New York's growing underground art scene and soon joined forces with the avant-garde rock band the Fugs. Their later albums, with a growing cast of supporting characters, combined avant-garde noise with electrified fiddling, a musical marriage that went nowhere. The group soon disappeared into the haze of late-sixties drug culture. They were reunited in the late seventies by Rounder Records, the folk label named in their honor, although by then Weber was a sad shadow of himself. Stampfel has performed sporadically over the last decade with numerous bands (actually, loose conglomerations of different musicians), sometimes using the name the Holy Modal Rounders and sometimes using other names (such as the Bottlecaps).

Select Discography

Holy Modal Rounders, Fantasy 24711. Reissues their first two (and best) LPs.
Indian War Whoop, ESP 1068. Stampfel and Weber are joined by other musicians on this 1967 album to present psychedelic old-time dance music. Did somebody put something funny in the punch?

◀ HOMER AND JETHRO

(Henry D. Haynes [Homer] [guitar, vocals] born 1920, Knoxville, TN; died 1971; Kenneth C. Burns [Jethro] [mandolin, vocals] born 1920, Knoxville, TN; died 1989)

Homer and Jethro were one of country music's greatest comedy duos, and they also happened to be fine musicians. The pair specialized in satires of country and pop numbers. After Homer's death, Jethro enjoyed a second career as a swing-style MANDOLIN player.

The two players were thrown together accidentally when auditioning for a talent-scouts show for local radio station WNOX in Knoxville. At age twelve, mandolinist Jethro was performing with his brother, while guitarist Homer was playing with a trio. Program director Lowell Blanchard heard both groups jamming together backstage, immediately disqualified them from the talent contest, and hired four out of the six on the spot to be a house band for the station. He named them the String Dusters, and the group specialized in playing the popular swing music of the day. For comic relief, Homer and Jethro worked up a few humorous numbers to perform while the band took a break. Reaction was so positive that four years later they permanently separated from the group to perform strictly as a parody act.

They performed on a variety of radio programs between the late thirties and the mid-fifties, including the *Renfro Valley Barn Dance* and Chicago's *Plantation Party* before the war; Cincinnati's *Midwestern Hayride* from 1945 to 1947 (during which time they made their first recordings for the local King label); Red Foley's program out of Springfield, Missouri; and finally Chicago's prestigious *National Barn Dance* from 1949 to 1958. A year before signing with WLS, they had their first country and pop hit, a satire of "Baby, It's Cold Outside" featuring young June Carter on vocals. In 1953 they had their biggest chart hit with the crossover satire "Hound Dog in the Winter."

Through the fifties, the duo continued to record satirical singles and albums. They graduated from the backwoods circuit to the glitzier Vegas arena in the sixties and also became popular performers on network television. Their 1962 LP, *Playing It Straight*, an all-instrumental homage to the swing music that they both loved to perform, underscored the fact that they were more than just a comedy act. They also got a job promoting Kellogg's Corn Flakes in the mid-sixties.

After Homer's death in 1971, Jethro was inactive for a while. Chicago area SINGER/SONGWRITER Steve Goodman lured him out of retirement to perform on many of the singer's recordings and to tour with him. The BLUEGRASS and new-acoustic music revivals of the mid-seventies brought renewed interest in Jethro's mandolin playing, and he was soon recording solo albums as well as working with jazz instrumentalists like Joe Venuti. Jethro's mandolin style is hardly bluegrass or country influenced at all; he picks up on the techniques of the great thirties jazz guitarists, and, like Tiny Moore (who played five-string electric mandolin with BOB WILLS), takes a highly melodic approach to his playing.

Select Discography

The Best of Homer and Jethro, RCA 61088. Cassette-only reissue of their famous comedy numbers.

Tea for One, Kaleidoscope 14. Solo LP cut by Jethro Burns in the eighties, featuring his wonderful jazz-style mandolin.

◀ HONKY-TONK

(c. 1935–1955)

In the days before the jukebox, the honky-tonk—a small bar often located on the outskirts of town—became a center of musical creation. Employing hundreds of small-time performers (many of whom would later become big-time stars), these local watering holes nurtured a new style of music that would become, in the late forties and early fifties, country music's mainstream voice.

Previously country musicians had performed at local gatherings, often sponsored by schools or churches, and played for a mixed audience including women and children. For this reason, the repertoire tended to emphasize mainstream values: religion, home, faithfulness to wife and mother. This strong moralistic tone reached its apex in the songs of the brother acts of the thirties, who popularized songs like "The Sweetest Gift (A Mother's Smile)" and "Dust on the Bible."

Honky-tonks came to the fore in a response to the lifting of the restrictive liquor laws during the early years of the Depression. However, because Southern towns tended to be conservative, and drinking was still frowned upon, these bars tended to be located either on the outskirts of town or in the no-man's land between towns. Here men could gather after work to enjoy a few beers, play pool, and listen to music. The music was often provided by a lone GUITAR player who often could be barely heard above the racket. For this reason, newly introduced electrified instruments (such as the steel guitar in the thirties and electric guitars and basses in the fifties) along with drums became necessary equipment for the small-time country band, along with microphones to amplify vocals.

Besides this change in presentation, the subject matter of church-mother-home was hardly appropriate for a rough bar atmosphere. Songwriters responded by creating lyrics that reflected the realities of honky-tonk life. Songs about drifting husbands, enticed into sin by the "loose women" who aggregated in bars, and the subsequent lyin', cheatin', and heartbreak created by their "foolin' around," became standard honky-tonk fare, particularly in the late forties. Songs like "Bright Lights, Dim Smoke (and Loud, Loud Music)" celebrate the honky-tonk lifestyle, while at the same time they take a moralistic tone, warning against the allure of cheap drinks and equally cheap women. Typical of the sexist world of country music, the "fallen women" were usually blamed for dragging down their hapless victims, hard-working country men; in songs like "She's More to Be Pitied than Scolded" the moralistic singer reminds his listeners that, after all, it was "the lure of the honky-tonk" that "wrecked" the life of the so-called honky-tonk angel.

In the period from about 1948 to 1955, honky-tonk music became the predominant country form, thanks largely to the contributions of HANK WILLIAMS. In songs like "Honky-Tonkin'," he contributed a more upbeat, less moralistic and dour view of life in the small bars; and his backup combo of crying steel guitar and scratchy fiddle became the model for thousands of honky-tonk bands. The honky-tonk style reached its apex in HANK THOMPSON's 1952 recording of "The Wild Side of Life," another one of those songs that both celebrates and criticizes the honky-tonk life; it inspired the wonderful answer song, "It Wasn't God That Made Honky Tonk Angels," that launched the career of KITTY WELLS.

The coming of the jukebox, which allowed bars to offer music without paying for live performers, pretty much spelled the end of the golden era of the honky-tonk. That and the popularity of younger performers like ELVIS PRESLEY, who launched the brief ROCKABILLY fad (as well as the longer-lasting popularity of white rock and roll), pretty much put honky-tonk music in its grave. Still, the musical style continues to have a strong influence on country-music making today, with the proliferation of local dance halls in some way replacing the original honky-tonks as centers of socializing and music making. Songs like JOE DIFFIE's "Prop Me Up Beside the Jukebox (When I Die)" pay homage to classic honky-tonk themes.

◀ HOOD, ADELYNE

(born 1897, South Carolina; died 1958)

Hood was a fiddler, pianist, and vocalist who originally recorded with VERNON DALHART and CARSON ROBINSON and then made a series of tough-gal recordings. She specialized in semiclassical fiddling and dialect numbers, eventually originating the Aunt Jemima character on radio for Quaker Oats in the late thirties (despite the fact that she was white).

Hood was a classically trained musician from a genteel Southern family when she met popular recording artist Dalhart around 1917. The duo performed together on record and radio before joining with country guitarist Carson Robinson to make the famous Dalhart-Hood-Robinson trio recordings in 1927, primarily of minstrel-era songs. In 1928 Robinson quit, feeling that Dalhart was unfairly milking him of his traditional repertoire, and a year later Hood and Dalhart recorded a series of duets, beginning with their biggest hit, 1929's "Calamity Jane." This highly successful recording led to a series of songs profiling tough, Western women, on which Hood took the lead with support from Dalhart, quite unusual for a female artist of the day. After the stock market crash, Dalhart and Hood split, and she spent several years in London performing in the music halls. When she returned to the United States in 1936, she began broadcasting for the NBC network as a "folk singer," taking the new name of Betsy White. She continued to perform on radio through the mid-forties, often portraying "mammies," when she wed a wealthy Pittsburgh businessman and retired from the business.

Although Hood's country background, like Dalhart's, did not run very deep, she was unmistakably Southern in her accent. Her flair for comic novelty numbers, and her ability to portray different characters through her music, made her tremendously popular in the country market right up to World War II.

◀ HOPKINS, AL, AND THE HILL BILLIES

(c. 1924–1931: Al Hopkins [piano]; Charlie Bowman [fiddle]; Tony Alderman [fiddle]; John Hopkins [guitar]; Frank Wilson [Hawaiian guitar])

Al Hopkins and the Hill Billies were an old-time string band from the North Carolina/Virginia border who popularized the term "hillbilly" as something other than a pejorative name for folks from the backwoods.

The group was groundbreaking in many ways: Although from rural Western Virginia, they were performing in Washington, D.C., over major radio station WRC as early as 1925, which led to auditions with Victor and OKeh records. They were signed by OKeh, and their first session was supervised by legendary producer RALPH PEER. When Peer asked Hopkins for the group's name, he is said to have replied, "Call the band anything you want. We are nothing but a bunch of hillbillies from North Carolina and Virginia anyway." A publicity photo from the time emphasizes this hillbilly image; the band members are decked out in worn coveralls, they wear bandannas and floppy hats (Al Hopkins wears his fashionable Stetson sideways), and they all stand with wide-mouthed grins, emphasizing the country-rube look. However, the strength of their music making and the quality of their recordings also gave new meaning to the word "hillbilly," making it a term of pride as well as scorn (much as in the previous decades Southern black musicians had embraced the term "jazz," which originally also had negative connotations).

The Hill Billies were so popular that they landed a job in New York in 1927, and within the next few years they performed for President Calvin Coolidge and appeared in a early Vitaphone fifteen-minute "soundie" (short film). The band was also unusual in featuring piano accompaniment, played by leader Hopkins, as well as Hawaiian-style slide guitar. However, the Depression brought an end to the group's short ride of fame, and they returned to life in the mountains.

◀ HORTON, JOHNNY

(born 1925, East Los Angeles, CA; died 1960)

Horton was a mid-fifties honky-tonker who single-handedly launched the early-sixties craze for pseudoballads with his hit recording of JIMMIE DRIFTWOOD's "Battle of New Orleans."

Born in rural Texas, Horton's family was from rural Texas and moved back and forth between Texas and California. Horton himself rambled through Texas, California, and the Northwest, going as far north as Alaska. Working in the Northwest's fishing industry and entertaining during his free hours, he gained the stage name of the Singing Fisherman. By the early fifties, he was back in Texas, working local HONKY-TONKS without too much success. It wasn't until he met bass player Tillman Franks, the brains behind the success of several country singers, including DAVID HOUSTON and CLAUDE KING, that his career finally took off.

His first big hit was 1956's "Honky Tonk Man," a song much in the mode of HANK WILLIAMS's style (Horton had married Williams's second wife, Billie Jean, after the elder musician died). He had his first number-one country hit with "When It's Springtime in Alaska" three years later, the first of the so-called saga songs; this one told a Robert Service–like story of tough times in the gold-prospecting days, accompanied by a swelling country-string section. The ever-popular "Battle of New Orleans" followed in the same year, leading to a slew of folky-style "ballads," including 1959's "Johnny Reb" and 1960's "Sink the Bismarck" and "North to Alaska." Toward the end of 1960, Horton was killed in an automobile accident while en route from Texas to Nashville. He continued to be a popular country artist even after his death, and his songs have been covered by everyone from Claude King to DWIGHT YOAKAM.

Select Discography

American Original, Columbia 45071. All your favorite hits on one CD.

1956–60, Bear Family 15470. Four CDs giving you 127 of his Columbia recordings along with demos.

◀ HOT MUD FAMILY

(c. 1972–1982: Dave Edmundson [fiddle, vocals]; Suzanne Edmundson [guitar, vocals]; Rick Good [banjo, vocals]; Tom "Harley" Campbell [bass, vocals])

The Hot Mud Family was an Ohio-based old-time string band active on the FOLK-REVIVAL scene in the seventies.

The original trio—the husband-and-wife team of the Edmundsons along with banjoist Rick Good—performed material in the CARTER FAMILY mold; they viewed themselves as an organic family, if not a blood one, and took their name from a combination of their astrological signs (earth, fire, and water equaling, in their minds, Hot Mud). They were one of the few old-time bands to feature a female in a dominant role as a lead vocalist, and Edmundson played a number of instruments as well, although she most often limited herself to GUITAR on stage. The group recorded a number of albums for JIMMIE SKINNER's Ohio-based Vetco label in the mid-seventies before moving on to the larger Flying Fish label. However, as the old-time revival fizzled out, so did the band (and the Edmundson's marriage), and by 1982 they had all called it quits.

The group's repertoire focused on old-time fare and some straight HONKY-TONK country, thanks to Suzanne's affinity for country WEEPERS. Good was able to re-create the BANJO and vocal style of legendary performer UNCLE DAVE MACON, which became a feature of their stage show. Campbell was a fine bass vocalist, and in the eighties he formed an acoustic-folk trio with fiddler Tom McCreesh and hammer-dulcimer player Walt Michael. He is also the author of the fine bluegrass-gospel number, "The Man in the Middle," which has been covered by a number of eighties-era newgrass bands.

◀ HOT RIZE

(c. 1977–1987: Pete Wernick [banjo]; Tim O'Brien [mandolin, guitar, vocals]; Charles Sawtelle [guitar, vocals], Nick Forster [bass, vocals])

Founded by BLUEGRASS banjoist Pete Wernick, Hot Rize was one of the more traditional of the newgrass bands of the eighties.

Wernick began his career playing second BANJO to TONY TRISCHKA in the all-instrumental, progressive COUNTRY COOKING band from Ithaca, New York, in the mid-seventies. He then moved to Colorado and recorded a solo album, featuring a more traditional bluegrass sound and vocal numbers (although he did play his banjo through a phase shifter, an electronic filtering device that gives the banjo a burbling sound). Shortly thereafter, Hot Rize was formed; its name is taken from a brand of flour made by the Martha White bakeries, FLATT AND SCRUGGS's radio sponsors, and therefore is a nod toward traditional bluegrass. The group recorded several albums through the eighties, drawing on the traditional repertoire of country songs from the thirties and forties, bluegrass standards, as well as their own traditional-style compositions.

Unlike Trischka, whose noodling solos favor melodic improvisation and far-out chord progressions, Wernick has maintained close ties with traditional bluegrass banjo techniques, particularly making the so-called "Scruggs roll" (a method of playing chords in a rapid arpeggio originated by Earl Scruggs) a central element of his technique. O'Brien's high tenor vocals recall a more mellow BILL MONROE, as does his MANDOLIN playing, which tends to be sweetly melodic rather than encompassing the raw power other players have developed. Sawtelle is a fine flat-picker on the GUITAR, somewhere between DOC WATSON and TONY RICE in style.

In the early eighties, Hot Rize introduced a new element to their live show, introducing themselves as another band entirely, called Red Knuckles and the Trailblazers. This parody-country bar band specialized in the HONKY-TONK WEEPERS of the fifties and was both an homage to and a subtle satire of the best (and worst) in this style of music. As an alter-ego band, Red Knuckles made two separate albums, and became almost as popular as the original group.

By the late eighties, O'Brien had moved to Nashville in search of a career as a SINGER/SONGWRITER; he has recorded solo albums of soft-country songs, along with a duo album with his sister Mollie, who sounds like a countrified LINDA RONSTADT, and he has recently been leading an acoustic trio called the Oh Boys, which perform his own compositions plus country standards. Wernick reemerged in 1993 with his second solo album, a collection of bluegrass-style instrumentals along with original compositions recorded with a light-jazz trio (clarinet, vibes, and drums).

Select Discography
Red Knuckles/Hot Rize Live, Flying Fish 70107. CD reissue of two eighties LPs featuring both Hot Rize and their alter-ego band, the Trailblazers.
Take it Home, Sugar Hill 3784. 1990 release.

◀ HOUSTON, DAVID

(born 1937, Bossier City, LA; died 1993)

Houston was a popular country star of the mid-sixties best remembered for his hits "Mountain of Love" and "Almost Persuaded."

Coming from distinguished lineage (his father was a descendant of famous Texan Sam Houston and his mother of Confederate general Robert E. Lee), Houston showed musical talent early on. He was encouraged in his singing career by a family friend, Gene Austin (who was himself a crooning star of the twenties famous for his recording of Irving Berlin's pop classic "My Blue Heaven"). Houston auditioned for the famed *Louisiana Hayride* radio show when he was twelve and was performing as a regular cast member there within a few years. While working on the program, he gained the attention of promoter/musician Tillman Franks, who would play a key role in his career.

After attending college for a few years, Houston returned home to work with his father and brother in their house-building business. Franks called Houston in the early sixties and asked him if he was interested in recording a new song called "Mountain of Love." Franks supervised the recording and took it to Epic Records in Nashville, and Houston was immediately signed to the label. The song was a big 1963 crossover hit, and Houston followed it with even bigger hits, including

1965's "Livin' in the House of Love" and the song most closely associated with him, the Grammy-winning "Almost Persuaded" from 1966, a classic HONKY-TONK tale of a man hovering near the edge of adultery.

A year later, Houston was offered a role in the grade-D country flick, *Cotton-pickin' Chickenpickers*, certainly not one of cinema's finest moments. Meanwhile, he continued to churn out the hits through the early seventies, including two duets with BARBARA MANDRELL, "After Closin' Time" (1970) and "I Love You, I Love You" (1974), plus numerous solo hits. In 1972 he was made a member of the GRAND OLE OPRY, where he performed for twenty-one years until his death.

By the mid-seventies, Houston's career had begun a free-fall from which it never recovered. He bounced from small label to smaller label, scoring a couple of minor hits along the way. Meanwhile, he continued to tour and perform on the lower end of the country circuit, often accompanied by his manager/friend Franks, who played guitar in his backup band.

Select Discography

American Originals, Columbia/Legacy 45074. Recordings made from 1963 to 1970, including all the big hits.

◀ HOWARD, HARLAN

(born 1929, Lexington, KY)

One of Nashville's most prolific and well-loved songwriters, Howard has over four hundred songs to his credit, and many of them have become country standards.

Born in Kentucky, he was raised from the age of two in Detroit, but his Southern family were devoted listeners to WSM's GRAND OLE OPRY, and Howard's first idol was HONKY-TONK singer ERNEST TUBB. He began composing his own songs at age twelve, although he didn't really begin playing GUITAR until after high school graduation, when he was stationed as a paratrooper in Fort Benning, Georgia. There, he made weekly pilgrimages to Nashville on his days off and began aspiring to a country music career.

After serving time in the air force, Howard bummed around the country, eventually ending up in the vibrant music scene in Los Angeles, which centered on the famous *Town Hall Party* radio show. There he met JOHNNY BOND and TEX RITTER, both of whom took an interest in his career and began publishing his songs. He also met and married a young singer named Lulu Grace Johnson (aka JAN HOWARD), who would later have a career on her own. WYNN STEWART was the first person to record a Howard song, "You Took Her Off My Hands," followed by Charlie Waller's classic 1958 recording of "Pick Me Up on Your Way Down," Howard's first certifiable hit. During the late fifties and early sixties, Howard compositions dominated the charts, including 1958's classic WEEPER "Mommy for a Day," recorded by KITTY WELLS; PATSY CLINE's 1961 hit "I Fall to Pieces" (co-written with ex-rocker HANK COCHRAN); 1963's moralistic "Don't Call Me from a Honky Tonk," recorded by Johnny and Jeanie Mosby; "Busted," a hit for JOHNNY CASH on the country charts and RAY CHARLES on the R&B/pop charts in the same year; and

"Streets of Baltimore," co-written with Tompall Glaser of the GLASER BROTHERS, a 1966 hit for BOBBY BARE. In the late sixties, Howard recorded a couple of albums for Monument and smaller labels, although his own performances didn't equal others' interpretations of his songs.

Howard was more active in the business end of the country music industry in the seventies and eighties. His marriage ended in the early seventies. NEW-COUNTRY star RODNEY CROWELL lured him out of retirement to co-write "Somewhere Tonight," a 1987 hit for HIGHWAY 101, but other than that Howard has not been active in writing new material since the early seventies.

◀ HOWARD, JAN

(born Lula Grace Johnson, 1932, West Plains, MO)

Howard was the wife of the famed songwriter HARLAN HOWARD during her biggest hit-making days, although she was most closely associated professionally with the country-pop singer BILL ANDERSON, with whom she recorded many successful duets.

Raised in Missouri, Jan was one of eleven children of a down-and-out farm family. She was exposed early on to country records and radio and began performing locally while still in high school. After two failed marriages, she moved to Los Angeles in the early fifties in search of a musical career, where she met up-and-coming songsmith Harlan Howard, to whom she was soon married. Harlan used her as a demo artist for many of his songs, and soon record execs were as interested in her as an artist as they were in Howard's songs. Also through her husband, she met and befriended JOHNNY CASH and his wife June Carter, and began touring with their road show.

The Howards relocated to Nashville in 1960 to further both of their careers; Jan signed to Challenge Records, cutting a duet with WYNN STEWART on "Yankee Go Home," followed by a successful solo single on "The One You Slip Around With," a wife's teary answer to her husband's wild and reckless ways. She then moved to the Wrangler label, and finally in the mid-sixties she signed to major label Decca, where she was paired with the smooth-voiced baritone of Bill Anderson. Their partnership began with 1966's "I Know You're Married" and continued for five years with a number of top-ten hits, from 1967's "For Loving You" through 1971's "Dissatisfied." Howard also had solo hits, starting with 1966's "Evil on Your Mind" (a number-five hit written by her husband) and her own maudlin composition, "My Son," written in the form of a letter to her son in Vietnam, who was killed two weeks after the song was released in 1968. Other Jan Howard originals include "It's All Over but the Crying," a 1966 hit for KITTY WELLS, and her playfully titled "Marriage Has Ruined More Good Love Affairs" from 1971.

Howard's hits dried up by the mid-seventies when her marriage ended, and she went into semiretirement. She has recorded sporadically since, including briefly for the revived Dot label in 1985, and has toured with the CARTER FAMILY/Johnny Cash road show and TAMMY WYNETTE. By the late eighties she was married again and working in real estate.

◀ HUSKY, FERLIN

(born 1927, Flat River, MO)

Ferlin Husky is two performers in one: country singer Husky and country comic Simon Crum (not to mention his earliest incarnation, honky-tonker Terry Preston).

Husky was raised on a farm in central Missouri, where he first heard country music and learned to play the GUITAR. After serving in the merchant marines, he began working as a country deejay, eventually settling in the vibrant country scene centering around Bakersfield, California. There he was discovered by CLIFFIE STONE, who was working as TENNESSEE ERNIE FORD's manager, and Stone encouraged Husky to begin performing on his own. Thinking his name sounded too rural, Husky took the stage name of Terry Preston on his first recordings. He also took on the comic persona of Simon Crum, a standard backwoods rube character, for his stage act. Initially it was this comic character that attracted record executives, although his first hit, the hanky soaker "A Dear John Letter" from 1953, was recorded under the Preston persona, in duet with JEAN SHEPARD (it inspired their follow-up "I'm Sorry John").

Husky had his first minor hit under his own name with the HANK WILLIAMS tribute "Hank's Song," also from 1953, followed by "I Feel Better All Over" from two years later. In 1957 he remade "(Since You're) Gone," which he had originally cut as Preston five years earlier, and scored another solid hit, followed by "Fallen Star." A year later, alter-ego Crum had a hit with the novelty number "Country Music Is Here to Stay." Husky also made some wonderful satires of ROCKABILLY and early rock-and-roll sounds under the Crum name.

Husky hit a dry spell in the early sixties but returned to the charts during the period of 1967 to 1975 with middle-of-the-road country sounds, beginning with 1967's "Once" through 1975's "Champagne Ladies and Blue Ribbon Babies," co-written with DALLAS FRAZIER. Two years later Husky suffered from a stroke and retired from performing.

Select Discography

Ferlin Husky, Capitol 91629. Overview of his country career.

◀ HUTCHINSON, FRANK

(born 1897, Logan County, WV; died 1945)

Hutchinson was a country-blues vocalist and guitarist who is best remembered for his 1926 recording of "The Train That Carried My Girl from Town." He played the GUITAR using open tunings and a bottleneck slide, in imitation of black blues-guitar styles, and sang in a nasal style reminiscent of blues performers.

Born and raised in the coal belt along the West Virginia–Kentucky border, Hutchinson was exposed early on to blues music thanks to an influx of black laborers who came to the area to lay track for the railroads that serviced the coal mines. One worker who was particularly influential was Henry Vaughn, who, according to Hutchinson-family legend, taught the then-eight-year-old Hutchinson the rudiments of playing slide guitar, using a knife to dampen the strings. Another early influence was Bill Hunt, described by Hutchinson as "a crippled Negro living back in the hills." Hunt was a repository of blues music, ragtime-era novelty songs, ballads, play-party songs, and other items popular in the hills around the turn of the century. Hutchinson absorbed much of this repertory and was performing locally by the early twenties. The tall, red-headed guitarist of Irish stock specialized in performing the blues, quite a novelty for a white musician at the time.

Somehow, OKeh Records of New York heard about Hutchinson and brought him to the big city to record two songs in late 1926: his most famous number, "The Train That Carried My Girl from Town," featuring train-whistle sound effects performed on the guitar, and "Worried Blues." The success of this first recording led to more sessions in 1927, producing a series of blues-tinged recordings, including the traditional bad-man ballad "Stackalee"; a reworking of the black ballad "John Henry" as "K.C. Blues"; a song about the hard times in the coal mines ("Miner's Blues"); and even a half-spoken narrative record based on the sinking of the Titanic ("The Last Scene of the Titanic"). After 1927, Hutchinson recorded sporadically through 1930. He told friends that he would have recorded more blues numbers if OKeh had let him (by the end of his recording career, the company was pushing him to record more mainstream country material for a white market, persuading him to work with a country fiddler). In 1930 the company stopped recording Hutchinson, probably because of the onset of the Depression.

Hutchinson gave up music making, which was always at best an avocation for him, sometime in the thirties. He became a storekeeper and relocated to Columbus, Ohio, where he died in 1945. Hutchinson's recordings, however, had a large impact on performers who followed him. DOC WATSON, for one, recreated his recording of "The Train That Carried My Girl from Town" on one of the first records Watson made after he was discovered during the early days of the FOLK REVIVAL, attesting to the song's popularity some thirty-five years after it was originally released; and in the mid-seventies MIKE SEEGER created a compelling version of the song, accompanied by his own fiddle and harmonica.

Select Discography

Train That Carried My Girl from Town, Rounder 1007. Wonderful reissue of Hutchinson's better 78 recordings, now, sadly, out of print.

I

◀ IAN AND SYLVIA

(Ian Tyson [guitar, vocals]; Sylvia Fricker Tyson [vocals])

Originally a FOLK-REVIVAL duo of the mid-sixties, the Tysons formed one of the first COUNTRY-ROCK bands—Great Speckled Bird, named for the ROY ACUFF classic —and have since been active as country singers.

The duo began performing together in 1961 in their native Canada, moving to New York in search of a more sympathetic audience. They hooked up with folk music's most masterful manager, Albert Grossman, who at the time also handled BOB DYLAN and Peter, Paul and Mary. He got them a contract with Vanguard Records, and they had their first hit with Tyson's multilingual "Four Strong Winds," sung in English and French, a favorite of sensitive, long-haired college girls through the sixties.

The duo were quite popular through the mid-sixties, helping to introduce new Canadian songwriters to the American market, including Gordon Lightfoot and Joni Mitchell. Increasingly interested in blending country music with their own form of folk-pop, they recorded an album entitled *Nashville*, featuring a strange blend of country and improvisational jazz. They then formed a country-rock group called Great Speckled Bird, but the reaction of their fans was hardly enthusiastic; the audience expected to hear sensitive folk-rock and instead were greeted with the unusual (for the time) sound of mainstream country. The group's debut album, produced by seminal rocker Todd Rundgren, went nowhere.

In the seventies, Ian hosted his own Canadian television show, called *Nashville North*, while Sylvia pursued a solo career. More recently, Ian has recorded a couple of albums of Western and COWBOY-flavored songs, both his own compositions and covers of old standards.

Select Discography

Greatest Hits, Vanguard 5/6. Two-CD set compilation of their sixties-era folk-revival recordings.
Cowboyography, Sugar Hill 1021. Ian's 1987 solo album of Western/cowboy numbers.

J.

◄ JACKSON, ALAN

(born 1958, Newnan, GA)

One of the best of the NEW-COUNTRY hunks, Jackson is a talented songwriter and as a performer belongs to the GEORGE JONES school of honky-tonks and heartaches.

Jackson's story is the typical rags-to-riches odyssey that Nashville loves. Marrying young, he worked as a forklift driver while writing songs in his spare time. His wife was his biggest supporter and urged him to relocate to Nashville. His first job was in the mail room with cable's Nashville Network. A chance meeting between his wife and GLEN CAMPBELL at the Nashville airport led to a job as a songwriter with Campbell's publisher (the company later sponsored his first tour). In 1989 he released his first album on Arista, featuring nine of his original songs, including his first hit, "Here in the Real World." 1991 brought his spunky "Don't Rock the Jukebox," a ROCKABILLY-flavored number declaring Jackson's allegiance to traditional country sounds.

Jackson's vocal style owes much to his mentor, George Jones, and the other great fifties HONKY-TONK singers. His recordings are tastefully produced in a NEW-COUNTRY style (plenty of fiddle and twangin' electric guitars, along with occasional DOBRO or PEDAL STEEL GUITAR) and range from old-fashioned WEEPERS to modern dance numbers. His 1993 summer hit, "Chatahootchie," is a perfect example of Jackson's appeal; the video features him water skiing and performing in front of a campfire (for sex appeal), while the song itself is vaguely CAJUN-meets-rockabilly in flavor. Like many new-country hits, it is suited for dancing as well as listening, and the lyrics offer a nostalgic reminiscence of a country adolescence.

Select Discography

Don't Rock the Jukebox, Arista 8681. His second album, from 1991.

◄ JACKSON, AUNT MOLLY

(born Mary Magdalene Garland, 1880, Clay County, KY; died 1960)

Jackson was a union organizer and balladeer who wrote and performed some of the most stirring songs of the thirties. She became a spokesperson for the coal miners and their struggle to obtain better working conditions, particularly among Northern, urban audiences for whom she often performed in the mid-thirties and forties.

The daughter of a coal miner, Jackson was politicized by the many disasters that she witnessed in the small mining communities. As a professional midwife, she worked with many mining families, and her own life was affected by many personal tragedies, including serious injuries to her father and brother and the deaths of another brother, her husband, and her son. She was first jailed for union activities when she was ten years old, and by 1936 she was run out of her mountain home by vigilantes. She was befriended by folklorist ALAN LOMAX and novelist John Steinbeck, who helped organize concerts in New York and Washington to raise money for miners' causes. In the forties, she was recorded by Lomax for the Library of Congress.

Jackson took the powerful vocal style of mountain singing and wed it to topical subjects. Her most famous song is "I Am a Union Woman (Join the CIO)," which became a battle cry for unions in many different industries. Many of her songs were tinged with a bluesy undertone, reflecting not only the many tragedies in her life but also a defiance of fate. Although Jackson was idolized by urban listeners, she recorded only one commercial record and was not well known by country performers. Her sister Sarah Ogden Gunning and brother Jim Garland continued to perform topical songs on the folk circuit through the sixties and seventies.

Select Discography

Library of Congress Recordings, Rounder 1002. Wonderful collection of recordings made by Alan Lomax of the singer in her prime.

◀ JACKSON, CARL

(born 1953, Louisville, KY)

Carl Jackson is a BLUEGRASS BANJO player closely associated in the seventies with GLEN CAMPBELL.

Jackson learned the banjo at age five, performing with his family's band when he was thirteen. He also toured during his teenage years with JIM AND JESSE, as well as recording his first solo album at age eighteen for the local Prize label. One year later, he replaced LARRY McNEELY in Glen Campbell's touring band, beginning an association that would last twelve years.

Jackson's second solo album, produced by Campbell, was released in 1973 and was followed by more traditional outings on the small bluegrass-specialty label, Sugar Hill. In the early eighties he signed with Columbia and scored some minor hits as a NEW-COUNTRY singer, covering LEFTY FRIZZEL's "She's Gone, Gone, Gone" in 1984. Through the later eighties, he worked as a session player and vocalist, often performing with EMMYLOU HARRIS.

Jackson's banjo playing is more traditionally oriented than many of the younger pickers. For this reason, he is more comfortable playing on mainstream country sessions.

Select Discography

Banjo Hits, Sugar Hill 3737. Cassette-only reissue of early solo album with Jesse McReynolds in the backup band.

Song of the South, Sugar Hill 3728. Mid-eighties recording with Emmylou Harris.

◀ JACKSON, STONEWALL

(born 1932, Tabor City, NC)

Stonewall Jackson was a minor country star of the late fifties who had one crossover hit, 1959's "Waterloo."

Jackson came from a poor, rural background. When he was ten, he swapped a beat-up bicycle for a GUITAR and immediately began to play. He served in the navy in the early fifties and then worked as a farmhand until 1956, when he moved to Nashville. He was signed to Acuff-Rose publishing and, thanks to his good looks and pleasant voice, immediately landed television work.

His first country hit was 1958's "Life to Go," followed by his pop crossover, "Waterloo," a novelty song that compared a hapless man's defeat in love to Napoleon's rout. Other early-sixties hits included "A Wound Time Can't Erase," "Don't Be Angry," and the novelty hit "B.J. the D.J." He also had some minor chart hits with his covers of gospel standards "Mary Don't You Weep" and "I Washed My Hands in Muddy Water." Jackson continued to score minor successes through the sixties, with one final burst of chart activity in 1967 with the two-hanky WEEPER "Stomp Out Loneliness." He continued to perform through the seventies with his group, the Minutemen, and made a comeback recording in 1981 without much further success.

Select Discography

American Original, Columbia 45070. Selected recordings cut between 1958 and 1987.

◀ JACKSON, WANDA

(born 1937, Maud, OK)

Wanda Jackson is a country/gospel belter best remembered for her ROCKABILLY hits of the fifties and her spunky delivery.

Jackson was the daughter of a small-town barber who played piano on the side and encouraged her to take up music at an early age. She was a prodigy on GUITAR and piano and was performing on radio as early as age ten. In 1954 she toured with country star HANK THOMPSON, impressing Thompson's bandleader, who recommended her to Decca Records. Her early records were standard-issue WEEPERS, including 1955's "Tears at the Grand Ole Opry." Later that year, however, a tour with ELVIS PRESLEY turned Wanda's musical life around. She signed with Capitol, who packaged her as "the female Gene Vincent," scoring teen-pop hits from "Honey Bop" (1956) and "Fujiyama Mama" (1958) to her biggest number, "Let's Have a Party" (1960). On many of these sides, Wanda was sympathetically backed by the cream of Los Angeles–based country musicians, including guitarists MERLE TRAVIS and JOE MAPHIS and country-boogie pianist Merrill Moore; "Let's Have a Party" featured the piano of R&B superstar Big Al Downing (with whom Jackson toured) and guitarist BUCK OWENS. Like BRENDA LEE, Wanda was one of the few girl singers of the fifties to capture the power of rock and roll.

In the early sixties, Wanda switched back to performing country hanky-soakers, beginning with her own composition, "Right or Wrong" (1961), arranged by her then-bandleader ROY CLARK. She followed this with a second crossover hit, "In the Middle of a Heartache," replete with NASHVILLE SOUND choruses. She was given her own syndicated TV show and continued to churn out sugary hits through the sixties.

In 1973 Wanda made another transition, now devoting herself to gospel material. She left Capitol and recorded for small religious labels, including Word and Myrrh. Although the message changed, the musical arrangements were still heavy-handed.

In the early eighties, Wanda returned to performing rockabilly live, particularly on tours of Europe, where the style was enjoying renewed popularity. She continues to perform a mixture of pop, country, and gospel.

Jackson's best material remains her fifties rockers. With sympathetic backup musicians and her own excellent vocals, Wanda proved that women could rock with the best of them.

Select Discography

Rockin' in the Country: The Best of Wanda Jackson, Rhino 70890. Her greatest rock and country hits.

Rock 'n' Roll Your Blues Away, Varick 025. Live concert recording cut in Sweden in 1984.

◀ JAMES, SONNY

(born James Loden, 1929, Hackleburg, AL)

Raised in a country family, James had his first hits as a teen-pop crooner before reemerging as a country performer in the mid-sixties.

Born into a family of musicians, Sonny appeared with the Loden Family band as early as age four. He took up the fiddle at age seven, and then the GUITAR, becoming proficient enough as a musician to win a job as a staff player on a Birmingham, Alabama, radio station in his teen years. He was drafted into the army during the Korean War, serving for fifteen months, and continued to perform throughout his military service. On his return, he met legendary producer/guitarist CHET ATKINS, who introduced him to Ken Nelson, house producer of Capitol Records. He was signed to Capitol and marketed initially as a teen popster. He scored hits in 1956 and 1957 with "Young Love" and "First Date, First Kiss, First Love," accompanied by thick vocal choruses.

James's career stalled out until 1963, when he returned to the charts with "The Minute You're Gone," followed by a string of mainstream country hits through the mid-seventies. His sixties successes gained him a role in the howlingly bad film, *Hillbilly in a Haunted House*, starring Lon Chaney and Basil Rathbone, a true kitsch classic. His rich baritone voice made him a natural for crossover possibilities, and he drew not only from the country repertoire but also pop, light rock, and even R&B catalogs. Most of his recordings suffered from the NASHVILLE SOUND production values that were prevalent during the heart of his career.

James's career has stalled out since the mid-seventies, although he continues to work in the studio as a musician and singer. He has also occasionally taken a producer's role, most notably on MARIE OSMOND's 1973 recording of "Paper Roses," her first notable country success.

Select Discography
Sonny James, Capitol 91630. His first teen-pop hits along with later country waxings.

◀ JARRELL, TOMMY

(born 1902 near Mt. Airy, NC; died 1987)

Jarrell was one of the great old-time fiddlers and singers, whose rediscovery in the mid-sixties and the recordings, festival appearances, and documentary film that resulted did much to spur on the old-time music revival. His style was much imitated, but, like that of all great musicians, it could never be equaled.

Jarrell came from a musical family; his father, Ben, was a fine fiddler well known in the Galax, Virginia-Mt. Airy, North Carolina, region. Along with BANJO players Da Costa Woltz and Frank Jenkins and child-prodigy musician Price Goodson, Ben recorded as a member of Da Costa Woltz's Southern Broadcasters; they recorded a single session for the Gennett label in 1927. As a youngster, Tommy was fascinated by his father's playing: "Any time he'd take his fiddle out I'd take a strong interest in it. I'd pay close attention to how he'd use his bow arm and I'd watch just exactly how he'd note. I was young, about thirteen, and it would sink in back then." In later life, he could duplicate his father's style, performing the novelty fiddle number "The Drunken Hiccups" in a version remarkably similar to the one his father recorded in 1927. Tommy also learned from older fiddlers in the area, including two Civil War veterans, Pet McKinney and Zack Paine, and banjoist Charlie Lowe, who also performed locally with Jarrell's father.

While many other fiddlers were influenced by more modern styles heard on records and radio, Tommy seems to have learned most of his repertoire in his young days and did not seek to emulate more modern fiddlers. Also unlike more recent players, Tommy used a wealth of different tunings; in fact, he hadn't heard a fiddle tuned to standard tuning, he claims, until he was in his twenties.

Tommy was discovered in the 1960s after years of working as a manual laborer in the mountains and performing locally. When he recorded, he was often paired with Oscar Jenkins, the son of banjoist Frank, who had been recorded with his father. However, Tommy was more sympathetically accompanied by another banjo player, Fred Cockerham, who also appeared on many of his recordings. At times, Tommy would play a simple style of old-time banjo while Fred doubled on fiddle; Fred's fiddling was strongly influenced by more modern players like FIDDLIN' ARTHUR SMITH, and so had a jazzier feel to it.

When the old-time revival blossomed in the seventies, Tommy became a role model to many young aspiring musicians. He opened his home to hundreds of players, appeared regularly at festivals, and recorded widely. Besides his excellent fiddle playing, Tommy was a talented singer, whose expressive vocals added much to his performances. Tommy's son, B.F. (for Benjamin Franklin, named for his grandfather), has performed as a BLUEGRASS fiddler, carrying the family's musical tradition into a third generation.

Select Discography

Rainbow Sign, County 791. Wonderful 1984 recording with Andy Cahan on banjo and Alice Gerrard on guitar.

Tommy and Fred, County 2702. Jarrell's and Cockerham's best duet recordings.

◀ JENKINS, REVEREND ANDREW

(born 1885, Jenkinsburg, GA; died 1956)

Musician, entertainer, and preacher, Jenkins is best known for the many country songs he composed, particularly "The Death of Floyd Collins," a massive hit for country-style songster VERNON DALHART in the twenties.

Born partially blind, little is known of Jenkins's early life, although he apparently mastered a number of musical instruments by his early twenties, including GUITAR, MANDOLIN, BANJO, and harmonica. He became a Holiness Minister in Atlanta in 1910, and nine years later married his second wife, who came from a musically talented family. By this time, he had lost his sight entirely. Jenkins and family became regular performers on Atlanta's WSB from the time it opened in 1922 (they were among the very earliest country performers on radio) and then recorded for a number of years.

Jenkins composed much of their material, including many songs that have entered the country tradition, such as "God Put a Rainbow in the Clouds" and "Billy the Kid." His most popular composition was "The Death of Floyd Collins," which furniture-dealer-turned-talent-scout Polk Brockman (who also discovered FIDDLIN' JOHN CARSON) asked him to write. It was based on the true story of a young man who was exploring the caverns near Georgia's Mammoth Cave in 1925 when he tragically died in a cave-in. The song was sold by Brockman to pioneering record producer FRANK WALKER, who selected it for Dalhart's next recording session. It became one of the most popular of all country 78s, long after the actual event was forgotten.

Jenkins and family performed in the typical parlor style of the day, with subdued instrumentation and pretty harmonies characteristic of family groups such as the CARTER FAMILY. They were the first country family band to record, setting the stage for countless other acts to come.

◀ JENNINGS, WAYLON

(born 1937, Littlefield, TX)

Jennings is a baritone-voiced singer who was a leader of the seventies OUTLAW-COUNTRY movement, a reaction to the stodginess of the NASHVILLE SOUND. Along with singer/songwriters KRIS KRISTOFFERSON and WILLIE NELSON, Jennings expanded the subject matter of country music while returning to a more primal, stripped-down recording sound that honored the roots of the great HONKY-TONK records of the fifties.

Jennings came from a musical family, and he was already performing over local radio when he was twelve years old. He got his first work as a deejay at the radio station in nearby Lubbock, Texas, where he met pop-rocker BUDDY HOLLY. Holly produced Jennings's first single, a cover of Harry Choates's CAJUN classic "Jole Blon," and invited the young singer to be his bass player on what would turn out to be his last tour. Following Holly's death, Jennings continued to work as a deejay and recorded ROCKABILLY for the small Texas label Trend.

In the mid-sixties, Waylon hooked up with CHET ATKINS at RCA Records, where he was initially packaged as a folk singer. Although he had some minor country hits, he was unhappy with the way RCA was handling him and began introducing different material into his recordings. In 1970 he recorded a couple of songs by a then-unknown writer named Kris Kristofferson, including "Sunday Morning Coming Down," and a year later released an album titled *Ladies Love Outlaws* featuring more contemporary songs by HOYT AXTON and Alex Harvey. In 1972 he renegotiated with RCA, gaining artistic freedom over his recordings. The first album made under this new contract was 1973's *Honky Tonk Heroes*, featuring Waylon's road band, the Waylors, on a set of hard-driving songs mostly written by BILLY JOE SHAVER. In 1976 RCA released an anthology album featuring Jennings and his wife JESSI COLTER along with Willie Nelson and TOMPALL GLASER called *Wanted: The Outlaws*, which became the definitive collection for this new style of music. In 1978 he recorded a classic album of duets with Nelson called *Waylon and Willie*.

Although Jennings continued to produce hits well into the eighties, he was starting to sound like a parody of himself. He recorded the theme song for TV's redneck comedy *The Dukes of Hazzard* in the early eighties, followed by a lack-luster album of rock oldies. In the mid-eighties, he reunited with Kristofferson, JOHNNY CASH, and Nelson for a concept LP *The Highwaymen*, which showed how all four of these formally innovative performers had gotten awfully long in the tooth. He left RCA for MCA in the late eighties, but the quality of his recordings continued to drop, although his late-eighties LP *Full Circle* at least showed him reaching for his past glories.

Jennings at his best embodied both physically and aurally the outlaw image. His accompaniment was tough, bass-driven, and reduced to the bare essentials, the perfect complement to his rough baritone. In choosing to perform composi-tions by then-innovative, younger Nashville songwriters, Jennings championed songs that went beyond the pop-schlock posturing that was then being produced by Nashville's establishment. And in relocating to Austin, Texas, with his buddy Willie Nelson in the mid-seventies, he helped establish an alternative center for country music, paving the way for the NEW-COUNTRY revival of a decade later.

Select Discography

The Early Years, RCA 9561. Recordings from 1965 to 1968, interesting for historical, if not great listening, purposes.

Wanted: The Outlaws, RCA 5976. The anthology that started it all.

Only Daddy That'll Walk the Line, RCA 66299. Two-CD set documenting Jennings's recordings from the mid-sixties through the nineties.

Waylon and Willie, RCA 8401. Cassette-only reissue of a classic collaboration.

◀ JIM AND JESSE

(Jim McReynolds [mandolin, vocals] born 1927, Coeburn, VA; Jesse McReynolds [guitar, vocals] born 1929, Coeburn, VA)

Jim and Jesse are something of an anachronism in both the country and BLUE-GRASS worlds. They sound like a typical brother duet of the thirties, right down to their homey harmonies and emphasis on simple MANDOLIN and GUITAR accompaniments. On the other hand, they scored a series of mid-sixties mainstream country hits, and they usually perform accompanied by a full bluegrass band. For this reason, their sound is both nostalgic and contemporary, an amalgam of the thirties, fifties, and nineties.

Their musical pedigree is impressive: Their fiddling grandfather led the Bull Mountain Moonshiners, who recorded in 1927 for RCA (at the same time the CARTER FAMILY made their first recordings). The young boys, Jim on guitar and tenor vocals and Jesse on mandolin and lead vocals, first performed over local radio in 1947 and signed with Capitol in the early fifties. Their career was briefly interrupted when Jesse was drafted to serve in the Korean War, but it picked up steam after his discharge in 1954. They returned to radio work, this time on Knoxville's famous *Tennessee Barn Dance* program, leading their group the Virginia Boys, which featured at this time fiddler VASSAR CLEMENTS and banjoist Bobby Thompson.

After signing with Epic in 1962, they had a series of chart successes, beginning with 1964's "Cotton Mill Man," followed by their biggest chart hit, "Diesel On My Trail." These recordings prominently featured the traditional harmonizing of the brothers, along with Jesse's distinctive mandolin playing, but otherwise were drowned in the then-typical NASHVILLE SOUND. Still, they were the most traditional of any hit-making country act of the era, which was no small achievement. And their recordings were much more funky than those made by the LOUVIN BROTHERS a few years earlier, which were drenched in vocal choruses.

Through the seventies and eighties, Jim and Jesse have ridden the crest of the bluegrass revival, returning to more traditional instrumentation on their recordings and performing at festivals throughout the United States and the world. Jesse's unusual cross-picking style on the mandolin (he strikes the string with the pick moving with up and down strokes, rather than simply using the down stroke as most other players do), along with the brother's homespun harmonies, make them one of the most distinctive of all bluegrass groups.

Select Discography

1952–1955, Bear Family 15635. Fine Capitol recordings, their first for a major label.
Epic Bluegrass Hits, Rounder 20. Recordings cut in a traditional bluegrass style for major label Epic in 1963 to 1964.
Jim & Jesse Story, CMH 8022. Recordings from the seventies.

◀ JOHNNY AND JACK

(John Wright [guitar, vocals] born 1914, Mt. Juliet, TN; Jack Anglin [guitar, vocals] born 1916, Columbia, TN; died 1963)

Johnny and Jack were a popular fifties-era vocal duo who often performed with Johnny's wife, Muriel Deason (aka KITTY WELLS).

Both came from musical families, with Wright descended from a long line of champion musicians, including his fiddling grandfather and BANJO-picking father. He came to Nashville from rural Tennessee when he was nineteen years old, met young singer Muriel Deason, and married her in 1938. Meanwhile, he hooked up with another singer/guitarist named Jack Anglin, and the Johnny and Jack duo was born.

Johnny, Jack, and Kitty toured and performed extensively in the early forties with their backup band, the Tennessee Mountain Boys, performing on radio stations in Greensboro, North Carolina, and Knoxville, Tennessee, among other smaller markets. They joined the GRAND OLE OPRY briefly after World War II but then left to become featured acts on Shreveport, Louisiana's popular *Louisiana Hayride* radio program, before returning to the Opry in 1952. The duo initially cut sides for the Louisiana-based Apollo label, better known for its R&B acts, and then signed to RCA in the late forties.

Johnny and Jack had a string of hits, mostly of the blue-and-lonesome variety and featuring tight-knit harmonies, beginning with "Poison Love" in 1951. They also backed Wells on her breakthrough recording, "It Wasn't God that Made Honky Tonk Angels." Other heart-breakin' hits that they recorded include "Oh Baby Mine (I Get So Lonely)" and "Goodnight, Sweetheart, Goodnight" (both 1954), "Stop the World" (1958), and "Sailor Man" (1959). They had their last hit in 1962 with "Slow Poison."

Jack Anglin died in 1963, ironically, in a car crash on the way to the funeral service for PATSY CLINE. Wright went out on his own, having a hit with the patriotic gut-thumper "Hello Vietnam" in 1965. Son Bobby began performing with Wright and Wells in a family road show in the late sixties, and he recorded a tribute album to Johnny and Jack in 1977 for Starday.

Select Discography

Johnny and Jack and the Tennessee Mountain Boys, Bear Family 1553. Six-CD set featuring all of their recordings made between 1947 and 1962—180 tracks!

◀ JOHNSON MOUNTAIN BOYS, THE

(c. 1982–1988; sporadically thereafter. Dudley Connell [lead vocals, guitar]; David McLaughlin [mandolin]; Eddie Stubbs [fiddle]; Richard Underwood [banjo]; Marshall Wilborn [bass])

There was something eerie about watching this acclaimed mid-eighties retro-BLUEGRASS group perform; decked out in string ties, suit jackets, and white cowboy hats, they looked like a mid-fifties bluegrass ensemble come back to life. While some charged them with the worst type of ersatz recreation of the classic bluegrass sound, they gained a wide audience and helped revive many lesser-known classic songs and instrumentals. As the band matured, they let their own personalities flavor the music more and showed off to good effect their instrumental and vocal virtuosity. Although they officially disbanded in 1988, they have come out of retirement recently to perform again.

Select Discography
Favorites, Rounder 11509. Selections from their Rounder recordings of the eighties.

◀ JONES, GEORGE

(born 1931, Saratoga, TX)

The ultimate HONKY-TONK singer, Jones is the one artist who today's NEW-COUNTRY male vocalists consistently cite as a key influence on their vocal style. Indeed, his distinctive singing style, often jumping from a grumbling bass to a falsetto hiccup within the same measure, is immediately recognizable. Nicknamed the "Possum," Jones is one of those artists whose legend (as a rabble-rousing, hard-drinking, hard-living performer) has more than once threatened to engulf him, yet somehow he survives and maintains his popularity.

Jones began performing honky-tonk material after his discharge from the marines in the early fifties. In 1954 he hooked up with Harold "Pappy" Daily, who served as his manager and also ran Starday Records, which issued his first recordings. His early records showed the deep influence of HANK WILLIAMS, although he also briefly jumped on the ROCKABILLY bandwagon, recording under the names Thumper Jones and Hank Smith and the Nashville Playboys. His first big hits came at United Artists in the early sixties with songs drenched in honky-tonk heartache, including 1962's "She Thinks I Still Care." He also recorded his first duets with Melba Montgomery at this time.

In the mid-sixties, Jones's recordings suffered from the typical girly choruses and echoey guitars that were among the worst excesses of the NASHVILLE SOUND. He married TAMMY WYNETTE in 1969 and moved to her label, Epic, in 1971, hooking up with producer BILLY SHERRILL. There he recorded a series of hugely successful duets with his then-wife, beginning with 1973's "We're Gonna Hold On" and continuing even after their divorce through the seventies. He also recorded a number of solo hits, all custom tailored to his legendary status as a heart-broken, heavy drinker: most notably "If Drinking Don't Kill Me (Her Memory Will)" (1981) and "The One I Loved Back Then" (1986). In the late eighties, Jones branched out to cut a series of duets with unlikely younger partners, from LINDA RONSTADT to Elvis Costello and James Taylor. Through the eighties, Jones had a tendency to coast along on his reputation, both in the choice of his material and in often lackluster (or missed) performances. Of late, he has made yet another comeback (although he's never really gone away) with "I Don't Need Your Rockin' Chair," a good-natured but defiant statement of his determination to stay in the game.

The revival of the honky-tonk sound among today's New Nashville vocalists is largely credited to the influence of Jones. Every time RANDY TRAVIS dramatically drops his voice to a low bass note, he's emulating the style pioneered by Jones.

Although none of the new singers can match his unique vocal style, many try to emulate Jones's image.

Select Discography

The Best of George Jones, Rhino 70531. Recordings made from 1955 to 1987 in a hard-country vein.

Live at Dancetown USA, Ace 156. Wonderful 1965 live recordings with Buddy Emmons on steel guitar. Not great fidelity, but a lot of fun.

I Love Country, Epic 54941. Sixteen tracks from the mid-seventies to early eighties, including remakes of earlier hits.

Greatest Hits, Vols. 1 and 2, Epic 34716/48839. George with Tammy Wynette on their greatest WEEPERS and honky-tonkers.

Walls Can Fall, MCA 10562. 1993 recording reveals that the Possum can still put 'em away like few others.

George Jones Salutes Hank Williams, Mercury 822646. 1994 tribute album, with liner notes by Elvis Costello!

◀ JONES, GRANDPA

(born Louis Marshall Jones, 1913, Niagra, KY)

Jones is a country comedian and BANJO player who has been portraying an eighty-year-old hayseed since he was twenty-two. Jones was a featured performer on the HEE HAW TV show.

Born to a sharecropping family, the youngest of ten children, Jones grew up listening to his father's fiddle and mother's accordion playing. He got his first GUITAR from his brother, and before he was fifteen he was already performing locally for dances and get-togethers.

After moving from farm to farm throughout Jones's early childhood, the family settled in Akron in 1928 where Pop Jones hoped to get a job in a tire plant. Marshall, as he was then known, entered a talent contest at the local Keith-Albee Theatre and won fifty dollars, enough to buy a pretty fancy guitar. He hooked up with harmonica player Joe Troyan and the duo began performing on local radio; Jones was billed as the "Young Singer of Old Songs." From there, they moved to Cleveland, where they were heard by talent scouts for the *Lum and Abner* radio show broadcast out of Boston. They were hired for the corn-pone serial as staff musicians, and there Marshall linked up with country balladeer BRADLEY KINCAID.

Although he was only twenty-two at the time, the gruff-voiced Jones already sounded like an elderly backwoodsman. Seeking to cash in on the image, Kincaid had him outfitted in oversize clothes, old boots, and a comic brush-handle mustache. He renamed him "Grandpa" Jones, and from then on the comedian switched to portraying an energetic old-timer. He even switched to playing the banjo, more often associated with old-time music than the guitar. Jones took UNCLE DAVE MACON as a role model, emulating the older performer's energetic approach to music making.

After touring with Kincaid, Jones had radio jobs on a number of West Virginia–based stations. In 1942 he signed on with the *Boone County Jamboree* broadcast out of Cincinnati, where he met the DELMORE BROTHERS and MERLE TRAVIS; the four formed the Brown's Ferry Four, which sometimes also featured RED FOLEY. Jones also befriended Syd Nathan, a local record-shop owner who later formed King Records, where Jones made his first recordings.

After serving in World War II, Jones returned briefly to Cincinnati, but he felt his talents were not appreciated enough by the radio station there. In 1947 he joined the GRAND OLE OPRY, remaining a favorite performer there for decades. Through the fifties and sixties he toured with Opry package shows, often accompanied by his wife, Ramona. Besides performing traditional mountain songs and energetically playing the banjo, Grandpa and Ramona performed the kind of country comedy dialogues that audiences love. He also made the Lonzo-and-Oscar song "I'm My Own Grandpa" his own theme song.

In 1969 Jones signed on with *Hee Haw*, and his old-time, cornball humor became a permanent feature of this ever-popular program. During the eighties and early nineties, Jones has been less active as a performer.

Select Discography

Grandpa Jones Story, CMH 9007. Cassette-only reissue of seventies-era recordings, with wife Ramona on a couple of cuts.

◀ JORDANAIRES, THE

(Original members: Gordon Stokes [first tenor]; Neal Matthews [second tenor]; Hoyt Hawkins [baritone]; Hugh Jarrett [bass].)

Most famous of all the Nashville vocal groups, the Jordanaires have backed hundreds of country and pop performers. Their greatest fame comes from their association with ELVIS PRESLEY on his first RCA recordings.

Formed in 1948 in their hometown of Springfield, Missouri, the group first sang in pure barbershop style. They came to Nashville in the early fifties, where they emulated the popularity of groups like the Golden Gate Quartet in creating a gospel-harmony hybrid. They began recording spirituals for Decca, backing RED FOLEY on his recording of "Just a Closer Walk with Thee." In 1953 they joined the cast of EDDY ARNOLD's TV show, the first network program to feature Nashville musicians (although it was broadcast from Chicago). They also toured with Arnold, performing at Memphis's Cotton Carnival in 1954, where supposedly a still-green Elvis first heard them.

The Jordanaires were popular at Nashville sessions, and CHET ATKINS, who supervised Elvis's first RCA recordings, undoubtedly brought them in to fatten his sound. They provided everything from pop-sounding "ooh wahs" to sophisticated gospel harmonies and even some doo wop on 1956's "I Was the One" (the B-side to "Heartbreak Hotel"). They went on to record many sides with the King and are an integral part of the sound of his mid-fifties hits, including "All Shook Up," "A Fool Such As I," "Are You Lonesome Tonight," and "It's Now or Never." Their own solo hit, "Sugaree," was a top-ten country song in 1956.

There's hardly a major country artist of the fifties or sixties who was not associated, at least in the studio, with these smooth vocalists. Everyone from PATSY

CLINE to MARTY ROBBINS worked with them (along with popsters like Steve Lawrence and Julie Andrews). They appear on all of RICK NELSON's classic recordings, as well as on JOHNNY HORTON's late-fifties and early-sixties hits. They also are featured on all twenty-eight of Elvis's film soundtracks.

The group continues to work into the nineties with various different personnel.

◀ JUDDS, THE

(Wynonna [guitar, vocals] born Christina Ciminella, 1964, Ashland, KY; Naomi [vocals] born Diana Ellen Judd, 1948, Ashland, KY)

The Judds were a popular mother-daughter duo of the eighties who came out of the NEW-COUNTRY movement but became one of the most successful mainstream acts. Emulating the vocal harmonies of the brother acts of the thirties and forties, they scored many hits combining a repertoire of sexy up-tempo numbers with ballads dripping with nostalgia for "the good old days." Oddly, Naomi seemed to make no attempt to play the role of a country mother; her sex appeal was always much greater than that of her often dour-looking daughter, although Wynonna musically was the heart of the act.

Much has been made of the Judds's story, beginning with Wynonna's birth in rural Kentucky; the family's move to California where Naomi tried unsuccessfully to become a model; their return to Kentucky and a "simple country life" in the mid-seventies, where Wynonna began to show her talent on the GUITAR; Wynonna's "wild teenage years" where only her music would soothe her; their discovery that they could relate to each other through their music; their relocation in 1979 to Nashville where Naomi pursued a nursing degree while the duo recorded demo tapes on a thirty-dollar tape recorder purchased at K-Mart; and their final successful audition, performing the BLUE SKY BOYS' "The Sweetest Gift (A Mother's Smile)" for RCA executives, winning them a recording contract.

The first Judds recordings were very much in the mold of traditional country harmony singing, and the arrangements emphasized acoustic instruments without too much clutter. Their first number-one hit played off their mother-daughter relationship in "Mama He's Crazy." A string of hits came through the eighties, including the sentimental "Grandpa (Tell Me 'Bout the Good Old Days)," the up-tempo "Rockin' with the Rhythm of the Rain," and the anthemic "Love Can Build a Bridge," which showed the talents of Wynonna as a gutsy lead singer, tempered by her mother's sweet harmonies. As their career grew, their recordings became more heavily produced, and their act more elaborate, reflecting country music's tendencies to smother its best acts in glitzy productions.

The Nashville music world was stunned by the announcement of Naomi's retirement from active performing, due to chronic hepatitis, in 1990; the duo undertook a year-long "farewell tour," culminating in a pay-per-view concert at the end of 1991. Wynonna came out from under her mother's shadow with her first solo LP, showing the influence of pop-rock singers, particularly Bonnie Raitt, on her style. In fact, both of her solo LPs show a much more blues-rock orientation than straight country, while her stage show is geared more toward a pop audience.

Without her mother on board to provide sex appeal, Wynonna has been put in the uncomfortable position of being gussied up by her handlers, who have even tried to give her a few dance steps, but she clearly remains most comfortable singing and playing the guitar without having to provide the visual excitement audiences seem to expect in this day of music videos.

Select Discography

Greatest Hits, Vols. 1 and 2, RCA 8318/61018. All their biggies; the first volume takes you to 1987, the second through the rest of their chart-toppers.

The Judds, RCA 8402. Their debut album, and their most traditionally oriented recording.

1983–1990, RCA 66045. Three-CD set for the archives.

Wynonna, MCA 10529. Her 1992 debut solo album.

K.

◀ KARL AND HARTY

(Karl Victor Davis [mandolin, vocals] born 1905 near Mount Vernon, KY; Hartford Connecticut Taylor [guitar, vocals] born 1905 near Mount Vernon, KY)

Karl and Harty, although not related by blood, were an influential duo in the brother-act mold who were members of the cast of Chicago's popular *National Barn Dance* radio show in the thirties, and influenced other acts such as the BLUE SKY BOYS.

Childhood friends from rural Kentucky, Karl and Harty took up music early in life. Karl picked up the MANDOLIN after hearing local mountain songster Doc Hopkins play the (then) exotic instrument, while Harty taught himself to play the GUITAR. Their schoolmaster at least for part of their early teen years was John Lair, who would later go on to be the main force behind the *National Barn Dance* radio show. Lair brought them to Chicago to perform on the show as part of a larger band he assembled, the Cumberland Ridge Runners, which also featured the older Hopkins. They performed on this show, and Lair's related *Renfro Valley Barndance* out of Kentucky, for many years, as well as recording for the budget American Record Corporation (ARC) label in the thirties, and for Capitol after World War II.

Besides playing mandolin, Karl wrote a number of sentimental songs that entered the repertoire of many other country entertainers, beginning with 1934's "I'm Just Here to Get My Baby Out of Jail," later covered by both the Blue Sky Boys and the EVERLY BROTHERS. His 1938 hymn to his home state, "Kentucky," was another favorite for the many brother duos who followed. Karl and Harty's smooth, pop-styled harmonies and relaxed performance style was also widely imitated.

Karl and Harty retired from full-time performing in the early fifties.

Select Discography
Karl & Harty, Old Homestead 137. Out-of-print LP reissuing some of their better material from the thirties.

◀ KAZEE, BUELL

(born 1900, Burton Fork, KY; died 1976)

A college-educated BANJO player and collector of traditional mountain songs, Kazee recorded a number of sides in the late twenties and then again in the early sixties during the FOLK REVIVAL.

Unlike many other mountain musicians, Kazee was well-educated, eventually becoming an ordained minister. His interest in traditional mountain music came more from his status as a folklorist than as a member of the culture. His banjo playing was fairly restrained, as were his vocals, but he did record many classics of the American folk repertoire from 1926 to 1930, including the folk ballad "Wagoner's Lad." He also recorded two series of humorous skits, one recounting a typical backwoods election day and the other, called "A Mountain Boy Makes His First Record," that played up his rural roots. Perhaps because Kazee was more educated, his singing style was fairly simple, without much of the ornamentation or intensity that marked other mountain performers. Kazee's relaxed vocals and clear enunciation were two factors that made his records popular, particularly among other folk-music collectors. An ordained Missionary Baptist minister, Kazee abandoned his "career" as an entertainer when the Depression led his record label, Brunswick, to close down.

Kazee was rediscovered during the folk-revival years, and he made an album for Folkways Records that showed that his style was little changed over the decades. He also occasionally performed at folk festivals.

Select Discography
Buell Kazee, Folkways 3810. Early-sixties recordings.

◀ KEITH, BILL

(born 1942, Brockton, MA)

Keith was one of the first city-born pickers to take up BLUEGRASS-style BANJO, introducing a new, melodically oriented playing style he called chromatic picking.

Born in suburban Boston, Keith first took up tenor banjo to play Dixieland-style music in his high-school years, but he was soon sucked into the Boston area's vibrant FOLK-REVIVAL scene. While attending Amherst College he befriended another young folknik, Jim Rooney, and the pair were soon performing as a duo. He switched to five-string banjo, influenced by PETE SEEGER, and learned to pick in what was then called Scruggs style (after bluegrass banjoist Earl Scruggs), learning the rudiments from Seeger's book. Whereas Scruggs style was centered on playing sequences of chord rolls (quickly played arpeggios, or the grouping of notes from particular chords), Keith developed a style in which he picked out the melody notes of traditional fiddle tunes, such as "Devil's Dream." This style, known as chromatic, became his trademark.

In the early sixties, Keith and Rooney were active figures in the Boston folk-music scene. In 1962 they recorded a locally produced album that was picked up by the national folk/jazz label Prestige a year later. Keith briefly played with bluegrass legend BILL MONROE and band in 1963 (along with young fiddler RICHARD GREENE); Monroe was impressed with his innovative banjo picking and recorded Keith's arrangement of "Sailor's Hornpipe" (although he insisted on calling the young picker "Brad," because, after all, there could only be one Bill in his band). Soon after, Keith gave up bluegrass to play with Jim Kweskin's Jug Band, a sixties folk-revival group, and then took up PEDAL STEEL GUITAR, reuniting with Rooney to record as the Blue Velvet Band, featuring fiddler Greene and banjoist Eric Weiss-berg, on an album of country standards.

Keith returned as a banjo player in 1972 when DAVID GRISSMAN formed the group MULESKINNER to perform on a television program along with Bill Monroe; the band ended up recording an album that was highly influential on the progressive blue-grassers of the seventies. Keith kept a lower profile after that album, recording occasionally with other old folkies such as on the Mud Acres albums (three albums recorded in Woodstock by various local folkies), as well as occasionally issuing a solo bluegrass outing and performing with younger pickers like TONY TRISCHKA. He also issued a couple of solo albums in the eighties and nineties.

Although chromatic-style picking was quite revolutionary when it was new, few have followed Keith's lead in totally eliminating chord work from their playing. As an accompaniment technique, chromatic picking is a dead end, and it seems that there is a limit to the number of fiddle tunes that can be arranged in this style. Still, Keith, with his urban roots, was the first picker to show urban folks that bluegrass wasn't just for cowboy-hat-wearing back-hills boys.

Select Discography
Banjoistics, Rounder 0148.
Fiddle Tunes for Banjo, Rounder 0124. Also includes Tony Trischka and BELA FLECK.
Beating Around the Bush, Green Linnett 2107. 1992 recordings.

◀ KENDALLS, THE

(Royce Kendall born 1934, St. Louis, MO; Jeannie Kendall born 1954,
St. Louis, MO)

The Kendalls are a father-daughter HONKY-TONK harmony duet who were most popular in the late seventies and early eighties.

Royce Kendall was a minor country star of the forties and fifties, performing with his brother, Floyce, as the Austin Brothers. They began playing together when Royce was just five, appearing on local radio. In the fifties, Royce also worked with HANK COCHRAN and CAL SMITH, without too much success. By the sixties, he was running his own barbershop in his native St. Louis.

Royce began singing with his only child, Jeannie, and the pair hit the road for Nashville when she was nineteen. They were signed by producer PETE DRAKE, who produced their first recordings for his own label and employed Jeannie as a backup singer for Ringo Starr's *Beaucoups of Blues* album.

The duo continued to record through the seventies, without too much success. Their first big hit was "Heaven's Just a Sin Away," released by the small Ovation label in 1977. This led to further hits through 1981, including 1978's number-one country hit "Sweet Desire," 1979's "You'd Make an Angel Wanna Cheat," and 1981's "Heart of the Matter." They then moved to Mercury, where they had success with more love-'em-and-leave-'em ditties like "Teach Me How to Cheat." Their last major hit was 1984's "Thank God for the Radio."

Since the mid-eighties, the duo have recorded for various smaller labels. They continue to employ the close-knit harmonies, simple accompaniments, and songs about love affairs gone wrong that have been the heart of their repertoire. It's unusual for a father and daughter to be singing together about boozin', lovin', and losin', but the Kendalls are a hard combination to beat in the heart-wrenching honky-tonk category.

Select Discography
Twenty Greatest Hits, Deluxe 7777.
Heaven's Just a Sin Away, Richmond 2294. Two cassette-only reissues of seventies-era recordings.

◀ KENTUCKY COLONELS, THE

(Clarence White [guitar, vocals]; Roland White [mandolin, vocals]; Billy Ray Latham [banjo, vocals]; Roger Bush [bass])

Thanks to the later success of superpicker Clarence White, the Colonels have become one of the most revered of all the sixties progressive/FOLK-REVIVAL BLUE-GRASS bands, although they performed together only for a few years. White single-handedly transformed the role of the bluegrass guitarist from accompanist (who occasionally played a bass run) to full-fledged soloist, influencing every bluegrass guitarist who came after him.

The White brothers were born in rural Lewiston, Maine, but the family relocated to California in 1954. There, Clarence began performing with his elder brothers Eric and Roland; they even had a local television show, with the group billed as "The Three Little Country Boys." By 1958, banjoist Billy Ray Latham had joined the group, now simply known as the Country Boys. Five years later, the group was known as the Kentucky Colonels, featuring the final lineup of the two Whites, Latham, and Roger Bush, sometimes along with fiddler Bobby Slone; they were now based in the Los Angeles area. Later, Scotty Stoneman (son of the legendary ERNEST STONEMAN, an early country-music star) performed with the band, playing a highly ornamented, flashy, show-style fiddle.

White's life was changed when he heard DOC WATSON perform at a California folk club, The Ash Grove. Watson had developed a unique style of flat-picking fiddle tunes, with his signature piece being a flashy "Black Mountain Rag." White quickly learned the piece, and adapted the flat-picking style to other traditional tunes and ballads. His lightning-fast picking was featured on the Colonel's third album, *Appalachian Swing*, an all-instrumental outing released by the West Coast label, World Pacific. The album quickly went out of print, becoming one of the most collectible of all early bluegrass recordings (it has recently been reissued on CD by Rounder Records).

The group's act was a fascinating mixture of old and new. Billy Ray Latham and bassist Bush performed corny country comedy routines straight out of the hokiest bluegrass stage show, as if they just stepped off a hay wagon at the country fair. The band's repertoire was mostly made up of hoary country and HONKY-TONK classics, along with traditional fiddle tunes. But, thanks to Clarence White's guitar picking, the band earned a well-deserved reputation as a cutting-edge outfit.

The group folded around 1967 or 1968, when Clarence became increasingly interested in COUNTRY-ROCK. He performed on the BYRDS's legendary *Sweetheart of the Rodeo* album and soon after joined the second incarnation of the group, remaining with them through 1972. When mandolinist DAVID GRISSMAN and fiddler RICHARD GREENE were asked to form a bluegrass band to perform on a TV show with BILL MONROE, they enlisted White and singer/guitarist PETER ROWAN to form MULESKINNER. The band recorded one album that was highly influential on the development of new grass later in the decade.

By 1973 White was again performing with his brother Roland in a more traditional bluegrass setting. Sadly, while they were touring, he was struck down by a drunk driver and killed. Roland White soon joined forces with Alan Munde to form COUNTRY GAZETTE, a band that went through many incarnations through the mid-eighties; more recently, he has been performing with the NASHVILLE BLUEGRASS BAND. Billy Ray Latham and Roger Bush performed in a number of folk-rock ensembles, including Dillard and Clark and one of the many later versions of the FLYING BURRITO BROTHERS. Latham joined the latest version of THE DILLARDS in the mid-eighties.

Select Discography

Appalachian Swing!, Rounder 31. Reissue of their classic all-instrumental World Pacific album from 1964, with fiddler Bobby Slone and DOBRO picker Leroy Mack.
Onstage, Rounder 0199. Cassette-only issue of live concert recordings.
Long Journey Home, Vanguard 77004. Live recording from the 1964 Newport Folk Festival, with guests BILL KEITH and Doc Watson.

◀ KENTUCKY HEADHUNTERS, THE

(Original lineup: Richard Young [guitar, vocals]; Greg Martin [lead guitar]; Ricky Lee Phelps [lead vocals]; Doug Phelps [born Calvin Douglas P., bass, vocals]; Fred Young [drums, vocals]; the Phelpses left the band in 1992 and were replaced by Mark Orr [vocals, guitar] and Anthony Kenney [bass])

The Kentucky Headhunters are the closest thing in country music to nineties-era grunge rock. Dressed in suitably ragged clothing, they combine a sound cribbed from the great Southern rockers of the seventies like the Allman Brothers with a true love of traditional country material. Their biggest hit so far is a cover of the TV theme "Davy Crockett."

The Young brothers are from the backwoods town of Glasgow, Kentucky, and along with their statemate guitarist Greg Martin have been playing together since their early teens, often using the name Itchy Brother for the band (named after a cartoon character that Fred Young particularly admired). By the early eighties, Richard Young had located in Nashville, where he was working as a songwriter for Acuff-Rose; his drummer brother was backing up the squeaky-clean vocalist SYLVIA; and guitarist Martin was working for Elvis clone RONNIE McDOWELL. While playing with McDowell, Martin met Doug Phelps, who was bassist in the backup group; he brought his brother Ricky Lee into the nascent Headhunters, and the group's sound was born.

The group's stage act combined seventies arena-rock antics with good-natured backwoods goofiness (the two Young brothers are the visual highlight of the band, with shaggy Fred noteworthy for his near-bald pate and long sideburns, while Richard specializes in the haven't-showered-in-a-year look with long, scraggly locks; Ricky Lee Phelps, with his HONKY-TONK–flavored vocals was the most conventionally handsome in the outfit, bringing some sex appeal to their otherwise anarchic stage show).

The group released two albums, the aptly titled *Pickin' on Nashville* in 1989 (which the band recorded on their own for a total cost of $4,500) and *Electric Barnyard* two years later, the latter spawning their biggest hit with their yuppie-nostalgia recreation of "Davy Crockett." They also covered country tunesmiths like BILL MONROE and DON GIBSON, showing that they had a true understanding of country's roots. The two Phelps brothers, perhaps in search of more mainstream success, left the group in 1992 to strike out on their own as Brother Phelps, recording an amazingly mainstream album that sounds like much of today's blandest pop-country. The Headhunters drew in old friend Mark Orr and another cousin, Anthony Kenney, to fill out the ranks. Although Orr, their new lead vocalist, lacks Phelps's charisma or overall talent, they have soldiered on with their characteristic heavy-duty approach to the country repertoire. Their 1993 hit, "Honky-Tonk Walkin'," draws on the latest craze for country line dances, while at the same time (typically) having its tongue firmly in cheek.

Most recently, the band paid homage to an early idol by recording an album backing pianist Johnnie Johnson, who is most famous for his work on Chuck Berry's classic recordings.

Select Discography

Pickin' on Nashville, Mercury 838744.
Electric Barnyard, Mercury 848054.
Rave On, Mercury 512568. 1993 release with new band members.
Best of The Kentucky Headhunters, Mercury 522710. 1994 compilation.

◀ KERR, ANITA

(born 1927, Memphis, TN)

Anita Kerr was the leader of the syrupy-sweet Anita Kerr Singers, Nashville's answer to a Muzak chorus, who were featured on hundreds of country and pop-rock sessions of the fifties and sixties.

Kerr is a multitalented musician who has worked as a pianist, vocalist, and producer; she was one of the first female record producers in Nashville. She began performing as a child vocalist on her mother's Memphis-based radio show and had her own vocal trio by the time she was in high school. She formed her Anita Kerr Singers in 1949, signing to Decca in 1951, and appeared on the famed *Arthur Godfrey Talent Scouts* TV show in 1956. The Anita Kerr Quartet, with Kerr singing lead, Gil Wright (tenor), Dottie Dillard (alto), and Louis Nunley (baritone) worked on countless Nashville sessions, oohing and aahing behind JIM REEVES, RED FOLEY, the BROWNS, and countless others. As such, they represent the worst excesses of the NASHVILLE SOUND, when plodding pianos and sighing singers drowned legitimate country acts in dreadful audio ooze.

Kerr broke new ground in the sixties as a Nashville producer, working on SKEE-TER DAVIS's *End of the World* LP; women had rarely if ever worked as producers in Nashville before. In the later sixties, she formed a working partnership with "poet" (and I use the term loosely) Rod McKuen for a series of narrated mood albums featuring the Sebastian Strings, as well as leading the "world music" group, the Mexicali Singers.

Anita Kerr deserves much of the credit for the success of mainstream country recordings of the sixties. And for all who love ear candy, there's nothing like an Anita Kerr LP to take you down memory lane. The Anita Kerr singers were also the house vocal group of the *Smothers Brothers* TV show in the late sixties.

Select Discography

Music Is Her Name, Sony Music Special Products 48979. Budget-priced CD featuring Anita Kerr singing with her group.

'Round Midnight, Bainbridge 6228. Cassette-only reissue of a Kerr homage to jazz.

◀ KERSHAW, DOUG

(born 1936, Teil Ridge, LA)

Kershaw is a CAJUN fiddler/vocalist who had a brief period of success on the rock circuit in the early seventies and wrote "Louisiana Man," a well-loved country hit. As well known for his energetic stage antics as he is for his music, Kershaw was one of the first to bring Cajun styles into mainstream country and rock.

Coming from a musical family, Doug was already fiddling at age eight when he made his "professional debut" performing at Lake Arthur's colorfully named Bucket of Blood saloon with his mother, herself a talented singer, guitarist, and fiddler. Four years later, he formed a family band with his brothers Nelson ("Pee Wee") and Russell Lee ("Rusty"), called the Continental Playboys. They performed over local Lake Charles TV and at bars and social clubs. By 1953 the band was down to a brother duo, with Rusty and Doug performing on the prestigious *Louisiana Hayride* radio program and recording for a local label.

In 1956 the duo moved to Nashville, where they were signed to Acuff-Rose's Hickory label. They made recordings in mainstream country, country boogie, early ROCKABILLY, and Cajun styles, scoring their first hit with "Hey Sheriff" in 1958, performed in the close-harmony style of the EVERLY BROTHERS, followed by their biggest successes, 1960's "Louisiana Man" and "Diggy Diggy Lo" the following year.

The brothers' chart success was short-lived, and by 1964 they had split up. Doug continued to work as a session musician through the early seventies, recording with everybody from Earl Scruggs to heavy-metal rockers Grand Funk Railroad. Meanwhile, he had signed with Warner Brothers in 1969, recording several albums that veered from COUNTRY-ROCK fusions to NASHVILLE SOUND productions. His most successful recording was 1976's *Ragin' Cajun*, his most roots-oriented outing. Doug's flamboyant performance style made him a favorite as an opening act on the rock circuit as well as on TV.

Since the mid-seventies, Kershaw has continued to record and tour sporadically, never really breaking into the upper levels of either country or rock charts. He

recently made a comeback recording with Nashville session fiddler MARK O'CON-
NOR, showing that his style has not changed either in intensity or sound.

Select Discography

Legendary Jay Miller Sessions, Flyright 35. Doug with Rusty from the fifties.
Louisiana Man, Sundown 022. Twelve cuts made by Doug with his brother Rusty
in the early sixties for Hickory Records.
The Best of Doug Kershaw, Warner Bros. 25964. Kershaw's later solo recordings.

◀ KILGORE, MERLE

(born Wyatt Merle Kilgore, 1934, Chickasha, OK)

Kilgore was a SINGER/SONGWRITER who later had some success as an actor in
Grade-B Westerns.

Born in Oklahoma, Kilgore was raised in Louisiana and took up the GUITAR at
an early age. He worked as a deejay and guitarist in his late teen years, scoring
his first hit with his own composition, "More, More, More." He was featured guitarist on the *Louisiana Hayride* radio program from 1952 through the end of the
decade. In 1959 he scored a hit on his own with "Dear Mama," while his song
"Johnny Reb" was a massive hit for country balladeer JOHNNY HORTON. His best-
known songs are 1962's "Wolverton Mountain," co-written with CLAUDE KING, whose
recording of the number was a worldwide pop hit, and "Ring of Fire," a megahit
for JOHNNY CASH in 1963, which Kilgore wrote with June Carter. He also wrote the
classics "Seein' Double, Feeling Single" and "It Can't Rain All the Time."

Kilgore himself only managed to score on the lower ends of the country charts,
and by the mid-sixties he was pursuing an acting career in such marginal films as
Nevada Smith and *Five Card Stud*.

Select Discography

Teenager's Holiday, Bear Family 15544. Includes both his early ROCKABILLY and later
straight country recordings.

◀ KINCAID, BRADLEY

(born W. Bradley Kincaid, 1895, Point Leavell, KY; died 1989)

Kincaid is a smooth-voiced singer who was immensely popular in the thirties,
thanks to his radio and personal appearances and recordings, as well as his series
of best-selling songbooks. His repertoire was largely made up of traditional mountain ballads and songs, along with the sentimental songs and hymns that he
learned in his childhood in Kentucky. His singing style, however, was greatly influenced by his advanced schooling and exposure to other forms of classical and
popular music.

Kincaid was born in the backwoods of Kentucky and began playing music as
a young child. His father was a talented singer and musician who traded a hunting
dog for a GUITAR for his young son. Traditional songs, ballads, and hymns were
performed by all the members of his immediate family, and Kincaid can remember
performing the minstrel-show song "Liza Up in the 'Simmon Tree" when he was
just three years old.

Educational opportunities were poor in rural America when Kincaid was young. However, a new school opened in Berea, Kentucky, that was dedicated to educating mountain youth while preserving the traditional arts and crafts of the Appalachians. Kincaid enrolled at the school at age nineteen, entering at the sixth-grade level, and, except for two years during World War I when he served in the army, remained there until he earned his high-school degree. During his Berea years, he met his future wife, who served on the music faculty, and became involved with the Young Men's Christian Association. In the late twenties, he relocated to Chicago to attend the YMCA college.

It was through the YMCA that Kincaid landed his first radio job, as a member of a close-harmony quartet performing on Chicago's largest radio station, WLS. At that time, WLS was also home to the *National Barn Dance*, a leading producer of "old-time" entertainment. When the station manager heard that Kincaid knew many traditional folk songs, he invited him to appear on the program to present his traditional repertoire. Kincaid's appearance was an immediate success, and he became a show regular in 1928.

WLS was owned and operated by Sears, Roebuck Co. (the initials stood for "World's Largest Store," Sears's motto), which was immediately besieged by requests for copies of Kincaid's songs. At Sears's urging, Kincaid compiled a series of songbooks, mostly drawing on his memories of the songs that were popular in his youth. Kincaid's education made him look askance at "composed" or popular songs, although he did include some parlor and sentimental numbers among the traditional ballads and songs. The books were tremendously popular, and many of Kincaid's arrangements were adopted by professional and amateur singers.

At the same time, Sears arranged for his first recording sessions with the Gennett company in the late twenties. These recordings were sold on a variety of licensed labels through Sears, Montgomery Ward, and dime stores, reaching thousands of rural listeners. Kincaid would continue to record for a number of different labels through the late thirties.

From the late twenties through the mid-fifties, Kincaid performed on a variety of radio stations, including Nashville's famous GRAND OLE OPRY program from 1944 to 1949. He also had a touring show, which in the late thirties featured a young country comedian named Marshall Jones, who Bradley renamed "Grandpa." Bowing to the popularity of singing cowboys in the thirties, forties, and fifties, Kincaid took to wearing cowboy attire, although he continued to perform basically the same repertoire of mountain songs.

Kincaid was a tireless performer, even buying his own radio station in 1949 so he could continue performing out of Springfield, Ohio, where he lived at that time. When he "retired" in 1954, he bought a local music store and soon was performing again. He made recordings in the early sixties and seventies and continued to perform until an automobile accident slowed him down in the mid-eighties.

Kincaid's importance was twofold. As a smooth-voiced, accessible singer, he helped introduce a broad audience to the traditional music of the mountains. As a prolific collector and arranger of folk songs, he made available a wide variety of material in arrangements that even a beginning musician could master.

◀ KING, CLAUDE

(born 1935, Shreveport, LA)

A master of the saga song, King had great success through the sixties on the pop and country charts.

Born and raised in Louisiana, King began playing GUITAR in his early teen years but did not intend to be a professional musician; he attended college and business school in the fifties, although at the same time he began to get work performing in local clubs. In 1961 he signed to Columbia Records, right at the beginning of the craze for pseudoballads composed on country themes. King churned out a number of these macho songs of the Old West, beginning with 1961's "Big River, Big Man" and "The Comancheros," scoring his biggest hits with 1962's "Wolverton Mountain," co-written with MERLE KILGORE, and "The Burning of Atlanta." The songs gained considerable success on both pop and country charts, thanks to the vogue for folkish, Western-flavored numbers in the early sixties.

By the mid-sixties, King was recording more straightforward country material, including 1965's "Tiger Woman" and "Friend, Lover, Woman, Wife" from 1969; by the early seventies, his style of music seemed rather passé, although he managed to have a few more hits sporadically through the decade, including his last hit, "Cotton Dan" from 1977.

Select Discography

Wolverton Mountain, Richmond 2231. Cassette-only reissue of 1962 album featuring his biggest hit.

◀ KING, PEE WEE

(born Frank Anthony Kuczynski, 1914, Milwaukee, WI)

Perhaps the only Polish cowboy, King is best remembered for leading the popular Golden West Cowboys and co-writing "The Tennessee Waltz," a 1950 pop hit for Patti Page that has become a country and pop standard.

Many Eastern Europeans settled in the upper Midwest in the late nineteenth century and were quickly absorbed into their communities. Many were musicians, including King's father, who played concertina and fiddle for local dances and parties. There were a wealth of different ethnic groups living in and around Milwaukee, including Poles like the Kuczynski family, but also Germans, Swedes, and Italians, as well as Anglo-Saxons. Like many regional musicians, King's father played a mix of traditional ethnic dance tunes and the country and square-dance tunes that were indigenous to the region. King's parents encouraged him to learn the violin ("not the fiddle," King points out, making the distinction between the classical repertoire performed on violin and folk tunes played on the fiddle). In his high-school years, he bought a secondhand accordion and took the name of Frankie King for local performances; he soon had his own radio show out of Racine, Wisconsin, playing popular tunes.

GENE AUTRY is credited with discovering King, bringing him to Louisville, Kentucky, to accompany him on his radio show in 1935. Autry had always featured an accordion player, and he hired King to fill the shoes of a musician who was leaving his backup group, known then as the Log Cabin Boys. It so happened that the other three musicians in the band were also named Frank; since King was the shortest, he was rechristened Pee Wee, a name he later legally adopted. When Autry packed up his boots for Hollywood, King remained in Louisville, renaming the band the Golden West Cowboys and maintaining the radio program. King soon had his own radio show out of Knoxville, and he joined the GRAND OLE OPRY in 1937, appearing on that program through the early forties. King's group was the first to perform on the Opry with drums, something bitterly opposed by the traditionalists in the audience.

During World War II, King toured with his band (then featuring an unknown singer named EDDY ARNOLD), along with comedian MINNIE PEARL, as part of what was called the Camel Caravan, thanks to its sponsors, the cigarette makers. This outfit toured United States military bases and outposts in Central and South America, performing an increasingly pop-oriented repertoire, including the patriotic tub-thumpers typical of the day and pop-harmony numbers like "Don't Sit Under the Apple Tree," sung sweetly by the Camel cigarette girls.

After the war, Pee Wee resettled in Louisville, where he spent most of the late forties and early fifties. His big hit, "Tennessee Waltz," was cowritten with his new lead vocalist, REDD STEWART, in 1946, but the song didn't appear on the country charts until 1948. It was also covered by COWBOY COPAS; and Patti Page took the song to number one on the pop charts in 1950. In 1965 it was made the state song of Tennessee, and supposedly more than five hundred different versions have been recorded. King continued to record his own compositions, scoring several modest country hits. He also hosted his own syndicated TV program out of Louisville, which was broadcast nationally in the late fifties.

King's activities slowed somewhat in the sixties. He cut out his TV work and cut back on recording, although he still toured extensively through the next decade. His sound and style changed little over the years, a blend of late thirties pop with his trademark bouncy accordion playing and upbeat vocals. In 1969 he retired from performing altogether, to become a promoter, packaging and booking minor country acts on the county-fair circuit.

Select Discography

Rompin', Stompin', Singin', Swingin', Bear Family 15101. Great swinging sides from the mid-forties through the mid-fifties.

◀ KRAUSS, ALISON

(born 1971, Decatur, IL)

Krauss was a whiz-kid fiddler who as a teenager formed her own band, called Union Station, a BLUEGRASS-country unit that has brought a traditional style to the mainstream charts.

Krauss is another in a line of annoying (to those of us who are musically butterfingered) prodigies who begin playing when they are still riding tricycles and begin racking up prizes when most of us are struggling with acne. She won her first fiddle contest at age ten in the traditional Western contest style (i.e., highly ornamented and ornate fiddle solos featuring fleet fingering and fast bow work). She was signed to the bluegrass label Rounder when she was just fourteen and won her first Grammy when she was nineteen.

Her fourth Rounder album saw a change in direction, away from emphasizing her fiddle skills to playing up her country singing. It turns out that Krauss is a good vocalist who combines bluegrass inflections with sounds that owe much to EM-MYLOU HARRIS and many other of the NEW-COUNTRY divas. She had two hits as a singer: "I've Got that Old Feeling" and "Steel Rails." Another innovation was adding Alison Brown to her backup band; this Harvard-educated BANJO player is quickly gaining a reputation as one of today's leading progressive pickers.

Krauss's instrumental skills, well-scrubbed girl-next-door looks, and authentic Midwest twang have made her a role model for many other aspiring bluegrassers and mainstream country acts. In 1993 she was invited to join the GRAND OLE OPRY, the first bluegrass-oriented act in nineteen years to be so honored. Not surprisingly, many more young women are showing up on the Nashville Network, Country Music Television, and on the road grasping a fiddle under their arms.

Select Discography

I've Got That Old Feeling, Rounder 275. 1990 breakthrough album.
Every Time You Say Goodbye, Rounder 285. 1992 album of contemporary and traditional vocals and instrumentals.

◀ KRISTOFFERSON, KRIS

(born 1936, Brownsville, TX)

Kristofferson is a country music SINGER/SONGWRITER who enjoyed a few hits in the early seventies and contributed to the nascent OUTLAW-COUNTRY movement. He came from outside of the Nashville establishment and was never really comfortable as a part of it. Kristofferson eventually abandoned his music career for a successful career in film acting, although he continues to perform music sporadically.

An army brat who is probably the only country star to ever receive a Rhodes Scholarship to attend Oxford University, Kristofferson began performing while living in England, linking up with shameless impresario Larry Parnes, who marketed him as a teen popster under the name Kris Carson. In 1960 he joined the army, and five years later, upon his discharge, he moved to Nashville. He first gained success as a songwriter when ROGER MILLER recorded the original cover of "Me and Bobby McGee" and JOHNNY CASH covered "Sunday Morning Going Down," both in 1969. One year later, SAMMI SMITH had a big hit with his "Help Me Make It Through the Night," a particularly forthright and controversial love song for the time.

Janis Joplin's cover of "Me and Bobby McGee," recorded just before her tragic death in 1971, helped catapult Kristofferson to pop-star status. Two years later, Gladys Knight scored a pop hit with her version of "Help Me Make It Through the Night." In the same year, Kristofferson wed RITA COOLIDGE, a folk-pop warbler. The marriage lasted five years and produced two duo albums.

From the late seventies on, Kristofferson was more or less absorbed with his film career. In the mid-eighties he did record as one of the Highwaymen, a loose-knit group of old friends and fellow outlaws including WILLIE NELSON, Johnny Cash, and WAYLON JENNINGS. He made some solo LPs in the late eighties, which featured somewhat bitter ruminations on the state of contemporary America, but failed to make much of an impact on the charts.

Kristofferson's late-sixties/early-seventies songs helped update traditional Nashville subject matter. "Me and Bobby McGee" brought a hippie sensibility ("Freedom is just another word/for nothing left to lose") to a traditional buddy song, while "Help Me Make It Through the Night" was unusual in its direct invitation for a one-night stand. Kristofferson served as a bridge between folk-rock singer/songwriters, such as BOB DYLAN or James Taylor, and mainstream country.

Select Discography

Me and Bobby McGee, Monument 44351. His breakthrough early-seventies album.
Jesus Was a Capricorn, Monument 47064. Another early album that shows Kristofferson at his best.

L

◀ LANG, K. D.

(born Kathy Dawn Lang, 1961, Consort, Alberta, Canada)

Lang is a gender-bending NEW-COUNTRY star who draws heavily on the sound and repertoire of PATSY CLINE. Lang's audience has been primarily drawn from punk, rock, and even adult pop; her mix of outrageous Western wear, brush-cut hairstyle, and aggressive stage presence made her an anomaly even in the realm of progressive country music. Never totally entrenched in country, Lang has recently recorded an LP of adult pop songs, crossing over into the realm of pop chanteuse as her idol Cline did later in her career.

Lang came to country music thanks to a college dramatic production based on the life of Patsy Cline; in preparing for the role, she fell in love with Cline's music, even believing she was Cline reincarnated. She formed her band, the re-clines, in punning homage to her idol, and recorded a successful album of country covers for the Canadian market in 1984. Two years later, she won a Nashville contract, recording a combination of late-fifties heart-throb ballads and her own often goofy takeoffs on Nashville conventions. Her second Nashville LP, *Shadowland*, was produced by the legendary OWEN BRADLEY, who had also worked with Cline.

Lang's big breakthrough came with 1989's *Absolute Torch and Twang*, which, as the title suggests, weds her twangy country persona with her aspirations to be a pop diva. A mild stir was created a year later when she launched a campaign against meat eating, and two years later when she came out as a lesbian in the gay publication *The Advocate*. Her 1992 recording *Ingenue* took her firmly into the area of femme fatale popster, complete with a video featuring Lang sporting a fifties ballroom-gown while a bubble machine worked in the background.

Lang's big-voiced approach to country music, her combination of reverence and ironic detachment from country traditions, and her willingness to confront her audience all make her the country antistar of the nineties.

Select Discography

Angel with a Lariat, Sire 25441. 1987 debut album.

Shadowland, Sire 25724.

Absolute Torch and Twang, Sire 25877. Her breakthrough album.

Ingenue, Sire 26840. 1992 album in which k.d. goes for the mainstream pop market.

◀ LEDFORD, LILY MAY

(born 1917 near Stanton, KY; died 1985)

Ledford was a fiddler/banjoist who led the Coon Creek Girls, the first all-female country band to be popular in the thirties. She was rediscovered during the seventies old-time music revival.

Born in tiny "Pinch-'Em-Tight Holler" (a name given to her hometown by producer John Lair), Ledford began performing on a homemade BANJO with a groundhog hide for a tone head when she was seven. She took up the fiddle at age eleven, and by the time she was seventeen she was fiddling for tips at the local train station, some eight miles from her home. A local businessman arranged for her to travel north, where she won a talent contest in 1936 and a place on the influential WLS *National Barn Dance*. Producer John Lair encouraged the youngster to switch to banjo, adapt her wardrobe to stereotypical "mountain garb," and perform the older traditional songs of her youth. Ledford commented years later, "Mr. Lair discouraged my buying clothes, curling my hair, going in for make-up or improving my English. 'Stay a mountain girl, just like you were when you came here. Be genuine and plain at all times,' he said."

A year after Ledford came to Chicago, Lair moved to Kentucky to produce the new *Renfro Valley Barn Dance* radio program, taking most of his major performers with him. He had the brainstorm of creating an all-women's band in a backwoods mold. He christened the group the Coon Creek Girls, featuring Ledford on fiddle and banjo, her sister Rosa Charlotte "Rosie" (born 1915; died 1976) on GUITAR, Esther "Violet" Koehler on MANDOLIN, and fiddler/bass player Evelyn "Daisy" Lange. The group was an immediate sensation, one of the most popular acts on the new program. By 1939, Lily's sister Minnie Lena (born 1922; died 1987), known as "Black-Eyed Susan," joined the act, which was now a family trio since Koehler and Lange had both quit, and the group continued to perform with various personnel for another eighteen years.

Ledford was married to Glenn Pennington for twenty-two years, from 1945 to 1967; son J.P. led the pop group EXILE in the seventies, scoring a major hit with 1978's "Kiss You All Over," and then switched to a country sound in the eighties with hits "She's a Miracle" and "Woke Up in Love." Ledford herself returned to performing in the seventies on the old-time music circuit, reintroducing her theme song, the traditional mountain song "Banjo Pickin' Girl."

Select Discography
Banjo Pickin' Girl, Greenhays 712. Late-seventies recordings.

◀ LEE, ALBERT

(born 1943, Leominster, Hertshire, UK)

Although British by birth, Lee has become one of the leading exponents of modern country GUITAR, particularly since his days as a member of EMMYLOU HARRIS's Hot Band. His electric guitar playing shows the influence of earlier country pickers such as CHET ATKINS and MERLE TRAVIS, while it also reflects the styles of

British bluesters like Eric Clapton and folk-rockers like Richard Thompson. Lee's background in rock but sympathy for country makes him the ideal session guitarist for the "new" Nashville.

Lee began his professional career associated with British pop/rocker Chris Farlowe, performing in his backup group, the Thunderbirds, from 1965 to 1967. He joined Joe Cocker's backup band after leaving Farlowe, and then became a member of Country Fever, a British folk-rock ensemble. In 1971 he was a featured member of Head, Hands, and Feet, a band that gained a solid reputation on both sides of the Atlantic for its COUNTRY-ROCK style. After that band folded in 1973, he performed with the re-formed Crickets (BUDDY HOLLY's original backup band), who remained a popular concert draw in the UK, and then he moved to the United States.

From 1976 to 1978, Lee performed with Emmylou Harris on tour and record. His skills on guitar and MANDOLIN made him a popular session player, performing with a wide variety of performers from the rock, blues, and country arenas. In 1979 he released a solo album produced by Harris's then-husband Brian Ahern, and has since sporadically released other solo efforts. In the early eighties, he returned to rock as a member of Eric Clapton's backup band but has since worked primarily on country sessions, backing artists from RICKY SKAGGS to RODNEY CROWELL.

Select Discography
Gagged but Not Bound, MCA 42063; *Speechless*, MCA 5693. Two late-eighties solo outings.

◀ LEE, BRENDA

(born Brenda Mae Tarpley, 1944, Lithonia, GA)
"Little Miss Dyn-a-mite," as she was known in the fifties, Brenda Lee, a big-throated chanteuse, has passed through careers in ROCKABILLY, tearjerkin' country-pop, and cabaret, and then returned to country.

Lee was performing on country radio as early as age seven in and around Atlanta. When she was eleven, RED FOLEY's manager convinced Decca to sign her to a contract, and she had her first hit with "Dynamite" a year later, earning her her nickname. She continued to record in the rockabilly mold through the early sixties, including the novelty Christmas classic, "Rockin' 'Round the Christmas Tree."

In the early sixties, Lee hooked up with producer OWEN BRADLEY, who had been nudging country singers like PATSY CLINE in a more mainstream-pop direction. Together, the duo produced a string of classic country WEEPERS, including "I'm Sorry" (1960), "Dum Dum" and "Fool No. 1" (both 1961), "All Alone Am I" and "Break It to Me Gently" (both 1962), and "Losing You" (1963). Lee wrapped her powerful lungs around the sappy sentiments expressed in these often formulaic songs, managing to find depth in even the tritest lyric. However, by the mid-sixties, although the hits continued to come, Lee's recordings became increasingly predictable.

Following her last country hit in 1966, Lee made an abortive attempt to break into the Las Vegas/cabaret market by recording more mainstream material. However, she returned to the country fold in the early seventies, beginning with "If This Is Our Last Time" in 1971 through 1975's "He's My Rock." She recorded more sporadically from the mid-seventies onward, scoring a minor hit in 1984 with "Hallelujah I Love You So" featuring GEORGE JONES and RAY CHARLES.

Lee's feisty early recordings were undoubtedly her best work. Her powerful singing and rockin' repertoire has been emulated by today's retro-rockabilly artists, including CARLENE CARTER.

Select Discography

Anthology, MCA 10384. Two-CD set that gives a good overview of her career, with a great, illustrated booklet.

◀ LEE, DICKEY

(born Richard Lipscomb, 1931, Memphis, TN)

Moving from rock to teen pop to pure country, Lee's career summarizes about thirty years of American musical history. He has brushed up against success, occasionally scoring a big hit, but then dropped back into obscurity.

Born in the blues-country-rock hotbed of Memphis, Lee formed his first group —a country trio—while still a teenager. Befriended by local radio deejay Dewey Phillips, he was introduced to JACK CLEMENT, who was then working as a recording engineer at the fabled Sun label. Lee cut a couple of country-rock sides for Sun and its affiliated Phillips International label in 1957, including the classic "Good Lovin' " (later a hit for the Young Rascals), before winning a scholarship in wrestling at Memphis State University.

After college, Lee signed to the Smash label as a teen-pop artist, scoring his biggest pop hit with 1962's tear-stained "Patches" as well as other frighteningly bad teen-angst fare such as "I Saw Linda Yesterday" from the same year, the follow-up "Don't Wanna Think About Paula" from 1963, and 1965's "Laurie (Strange Things Happen)."

By the late sixties, Lee's pop career had fizzled, and he signed to RCA as a country artist under veteran producer CHET ATKINS. His first country record was "The Mahogany Pulpit" in 1971, and he hit it big four years later with a remake of the pop hit "Rocky" and 1976's "9,999,999 Tears." Lee left RCA for Mercury soon after, but his career as a performer soon waned. In the early eighties, Lee cowrote a number of hits for NEW-COUNTRY artists, including REBA McENTIRE's second number-one song, "You're the First Time I've Thought About Leaving" (1983), a throwback to earlier HONKY-TONK sounds written in country-waltz time, and GEORGE STRAIT's 1984 hit "Let's Fall to Pieces Together."

◀ LEE, JOHNNIE

(born John Lee Ham, 1946, Texas City, TX)

An "urban cowboy" himself, Lee got a big career boost when his song "Looking for Love" was selected for the popular early-eighties flick *Urban Cowboy*.

Raised in rural Alta Loma, Texas, Lee formed his first band in high school, a country-pop outfit called the Roadrunners. He enlisted in the navy and then worked in California after his discharge, eventually returning to Texas where he hooked up with MICKEY GILLEY, the famous country barkeep, leading Gilley's band at home when Gilley was out on the road. By the mid-seventies, Lee had recorded a number of singles for a variety of small labels and had minor chart hits with "Sometimes," the venerable "Red Sails in the Sunset," and "Country Party."

Gilley's club was selected as the locale for the John Travolta/Debra Winger romance, *Urban Cowboy*, and Lee's baritone warbling on the pop-flavored "Looking for Love" gained him a number-one country hit as well as a top-ten pop single. An album was quickly released, with three more tracks hitting the charts. Lee soon graduated from performing in beer-soaked clubs to playing glitzy venues in Vegas, often performing with Gilley under the name the Urban Cowboy Band. He made tabloid heaven when he married TV-soap star Charlene Tilton of *Dallas* fame in the early eighties, a marriage that lasted through mid-decade. (He even contributed a love ode to his bride called "Lucy's Eyes" after the character she portrayed on the popular melodrama.) After a few more country-pop hits in the early eighties, Lee faded from the charts.

Select Discography
The Best of Johnnie Lee, Curb 77322. Later hits.
Greatest Hits, Warner Bros. 23967. His urban cowboy days.

◀ LEWIS, BOBBY

(born 1946, Hodgenville, KY)

Lewis was a minor country star of the mid-sixties and early seventies best remembered for strumming on a lute instead of a GUITAR.

Bobby started playing the guitar at age nine, when his older brother showed him his first chords. He was soon showing talent as a picker, although he had difficulty handling the jumbo-size guitar that his brother used. Even by high-school he remained small for his age, so he went searching in a local junk shop to find a smaller guitar. What he turned up with was an old lute, which he strung and tuned like a guitar.

When Lewis was eleven, he made his performing debut on the local *Kentucky Barn Dance* radio show out of Lexington, where he continued to perform for three years. He broke into television in the late fifties, and by the early sixties he was appearing regularly on the *Hi-Varieties* show. At the same time, he moved to Nashville, where he recorded an original composition, "Sandra Kay," on a small, local label, gaining him an appearance on the GRAND OLE OPRY and a contract with United Artists Records. His sixties hits included a slew of country WEEPERS, from 1964's "How Long Has It Been" to his biggest hits: "Love Me and Make It Better" (1967), "From Heaven to Heartache" (1968), and the rockin' "Hello Mary Lou" (1970).

Lewis was dropped by United Artists in the early seventies, and moved to the smaller Ace of Hearts label, scoring one more top-twenty hit with "Too Many Memories" in late 1973. The hits pretty much dried up after that, although he did reemerge briefly on the short-lived revived Capricorn label with 1979's "She's Been Keeping Me Up Nights."

◀ LEWIS, HUGH X.

(born 1932, Cumberland, KY)

Hugh X. Lewis was a minor-league recording star and performer of the sixties better known for the hits he wrote for others.

After working as a coal minor and steel-mill foreman through the fifties and early sixties, while strumming the GUITAR in local clubs and bars on the side, Lewis slowly built up a reputation as a talented SINGER/SONGWRITER. He finally gave up his day job in 1963, moving to Nashville, where he had his big break when STONE-WALL JACKSON recorded his novelty song, "B.J. the D.J.," which became a number-one country hit in 1964. The song was quickly covered by KITTY WELLS and CARL SMITH (who later recorded Lewis's "Take My Ring Off Your Finger"), and other big-name Nashville cats had hits with his material, including MAC WISEMAN, who recorded "Heads You Win, Tails I Lose," and GEORGE MORGAN with "One Rose."

Lewis quickly signed a contract with Kapp Records and released the single, "What I Need Most." He stayed with Kapp through the late sixties then moved to GRT with the novelty hit "Blues Sells a Lot of Booze," followed by a stint with a string of smaller labels. He even appeared in the "full-color" film *Forty Acre Feud*, a typical C-grade Western potboiler of the period.

Lewis's songs were a typical mix of novelties, up-tempo HONKY-TONK numbers, and standard you-left-me-and-I'm-blue WEEPERS. Not a particularly distinctive performer, his material was served better when covered by more successful acts.

◀ LEWIS, JERRY LEE

(born 1935, Ferriday, LA)

The "Ferriday Fireball," the original wild man of ROCKABILLY and country, standard biographies of Jerry Lee divide his career into two parts: the era of his original fifties hits, in a rockabilly/pop-rock style, followed by his "comeback" in the sixties, seventies, and eighties as a country star. Actually, Jerry Lee has always recorded country songs, often as B-sides to his original rock hits, and his sensibility is as pure country as you can get.

The Lewis family were farmers in Louisiana. Much is made of the fact that Lewis is related to country crooner MICKEY GILLEY and the fallen TV evangelist Jimmy Swaggart (both are cousins), as if these represent polar sides of Lewis's own personality. His musical influences are diverse, from the WESTERN SWING and jazz piano stylings of MOON MULLICAN to the rocking style of Fats Domino; even the great showman Al Jolson is said to have had an influence on young Lewis. Playing piano since the age of nine, he won a Ted Mack amateur show leading to a gig at the local Natchez radio station. After a brief stint at Bible college, he worked his way to the legendary Sun Studios headed by SAM PHILLIPS.

At Sun, Lewis first worked as a sideman, backing CARL PERKINS. It was at a Perkins session that he encountered ELVIS PRESLEY and JOHNNY CASH in an impromptu jam session consisting primarily of old hymn tunes, which has become known as the "Million Dollar Quartet" session. Lewis's first hit was "Whole Lotta Shakin' Goin' On" from 1957; originally, radio stations were wary of the song, fearing its obscene subtext, but Lewis's wild performance on a Steve Allen TV show catapulted the song—and the star—to fame.

Lewis's rock career came to a grinding halt in 1959 with his scandalous (for the time) third marriage to a thirteen-year-old cousin. He struggled through the sixties, recording in a number of different styles, including his first pure country recordings. In the late sixties and early seventies, he broke through on the country charts with hits in a HONKY-TONK style, including "Another Place, Another Time," "What Made Milwaukee Famous (Has Made a Loser Out of Me)," and "She Even Woke Me Up to Say Goodbye." In 1978 he made yet another country comeback with the humorous "39 and Holding."

The eighties brought continuing personal problems, including tax problems (in 1993, the IRS would seize Lewis's home for back taxes) and the mysterious murder of his fifth wife. Still, Lewis continues to perform regularly, particularly in Europe, drawing on both his rock and country repertoires, while making periodic well-publicized comebacks.

Lewis is important to country music for a number of reasons. His high-voltage personality has made him a legendary performer, although he can be just as unreliable in his stage manner as he is in his lifestyle. His pounding piano style, combining elements of honky-tonk, jazz, R&B, and rock and roll, is as distinctive as his engaged, dynamic vocals. As a country crooner, Lewis has perfectly captured the slightly ironic, world-weary tone of a man down to his last beer (and sinking fast). The melding of his personality with his choice of material makes Lewis, at his best, a pure country performer.

Select Discography

Up Through the Years, 1956–1963, Bear Family 15408. Twenty-four of his greatest Sun sides, including rockabilly, straight rock, and country.

Killer: The Mercury Years, Mercury 935/938/941. Three-volume set covering his sixties-era country, rock, and gospel recordings for Mercury and its subsidiary, Smash.

Milestones, Rhino 71499. Includes his great Sun hits, plus his better later recordings for Mercury.

Rockin' My Life Away, Warner Bros. 26689. Late-seventies sessions originally issued by Elektra; these are fine "comeback" performances primarily in country style, including the hit "39 Years and Holding."

◀ LEWIS, LAURIE

(born 1950, Berkeley, CA)

BLUEGRASS fiddler, vocalist, and songwriter, Lewis is a veteran of several bluegrass bands, including San Francisco's GOOD OL' PERSONS, and is also an accomplished solo artist.

Coming out of the rich Bay Area FOLK-REVIVAL scene, Lewis first got introduced to bluegrass music in 1965 through the early progressive band, THE DILLARDS. In 1973 she formed her first band, the Phantoms of the Opry, playing bass, and later was fiddler for the Good Ol' Persons from 1975 to 1977. Through the rest of the seventies, she worked as a studio musician for a number of Bay Area folkies, including feminist SINGER/SONGWRITER Holly Near, besides running her own instrument-repair shop.

In 1983 Lewis formed a new backup band, the Grant Street Stringband, issuing her first solo album with this group three years later. A number of her original compositions were recorded by new country artists, including "Love Choose You," which was covered by KATHY MATTEA. Legendary cowpuncher PATSY MONTANA recorded her "The Cowgirl's Song," which was selected as the official theme song of the Cowgirl Hall of Fame.

Lewis's albums featured her new-style HONKY-TONK singing on her own country-folk ballads, accompanied by her bluegrass-flavored fiddling. In 1988 she was a member of the all-female Wild Rose band along with CATHY FINK, and she also has continued to perform as a duo with KATHY KALLICK, another Good Ol' Person alum. In the early nineties, Lewis began doing session work in Nashville for a number of new-country acts.

Select Discography

Love Chooses You, Flying Fish 70497. 1989 country-pop recordings.
Singin' My Troubles Away, Flyin' Fish 70515. Recorded with the bluegrass-country group Grant Street.
Together, Kaleidoscope 44. Duet recording with Kathy Kallick.

◀ LIGHT CRUST DOUGHBOYS, THE

(Original lineup, 1931–1932: Bob Wills [fiddle, vocals]; Milton Brown [vocals]; Durwood Brown [banjo]; Herman Arnspiger [guitar]; Clifton "Sleepy" Johnson [steel guitar]; W. Lee "Pappy" O'Daniel [MC])

The Light Crust Doughboys were the first true WESTERN SWING band, introducing two enormous talents: fiddler/vocalist BOB WILLS, who would soon be leading his own Texas Playboys, and vocalist/bandleader MILTON BROWN, who went on to form his Musical Brownies.

Wills had been touring Texas with guitarist Herman Arnspiger when they got a radio job in Fort Worth. They soon hooked up with vocalist Brown, who brought along his brother Durwood, forming a quartet first known as the Wills Fiddle Band and then the Aladdin Laddies (because their radio show was sponsored by the Aladdin Lamp Company). The show was picked up by the Texas Quality Network, a string of radio stations throughout the state. Searching for a sponsor to replace the lamp company, Wills approached PR man W. Lee O'Daniel at the Burrus Mills company, makers of Lightcrust Dough. O'Daniel liked the idea, and the group was renamed the Lightcrust Doughboys, making their home base in Fort Worth. After making a few recordings for Victor, the original group disbanded.

O'Daniel was enthusiastic about continuing the group and soon enlisted his own Doughboys to carry forward the name. They recorded for Vocalion from 1933 to 1935, waxing a mix of up-tempo fiddle tunes, sentimental ditties, and COWBOY SONGS. O'Daniel left the group in 1935 when he formed his own rival Hillbilly Flour Company, hiring his own group of country musicians to work for him. Meanwhile, the Doughboys band continued, led by Western swing legends Eddie Dunn and Cecil Brower, amongst others. They maintained their link with Burrus Mills until 1942; then the Duncan Coffee Company took over their sponsorship, and suddenly they were known as the Coffee Grinders. However, by then the Doughboys name was so well-loved that by the end of World War II they had reverted to using it, even though they were no longer sponsored by the mill. They continued to work on the rodeo/country-fair circuit into the sixties, with varied personnel, including many alums of the great Western swing bands of the thirties, forties, and fifties.

◀ LITTLE TEXAS

(Porter Howell [lead guitar, vocals]; Dwayne O'Brien [guitar, vocals]; Tim Rushlow [lead vocals, guitar, mandolin]; Brady Seals [keyboards, vocals]; Duane Propes [bass, vocals]; Del Gray [drums])

Little Texas is another in a long string of NEW-COUNTRY bands who are heavily influenced by pop-rock bands like the EAGLES, while their vocal harmonies recall mainstream country stars like ALABAMA. While the group is among the few to feature five-part vocal harmonies, their general sound (kick-ass rock and roll moderated with the occasional weepy country ballad) is generic to many bands making their debut in the late eighties and early nineties.

The group originated around the quartet of Tim Rushlow, Dwayne O'Brien, Porter Howell, and Duane Propes. Signed to a "development deal" by major label Warner Brothers, they spent most of the late eighties on the road honing their sound. They also hooked up with keyboardist Brady Seals and drummer Del Gray, completing their transformation into a more pop-oriented group. Finally deemed ready for the recording studio, they produced the album *First Time for Everything* in 1992, yielding five gold singles. This album and their 1993 follow-up, *Big Time*, featured a mix of rough-and-rowdy dance numbers, including the Texasophile's favorite, "God Blessed Texas," that won them the praise of then-governor Ann Richards, along with sentimental ballads like "What Might Have Been," featuring a full orchestral backup. The group scored patriotic brownie points by singing a five-part a cappella version of the national anthem for candidate Bill Clinton, later performing their hit "What Might Have Been" in a show for the president featuring other mainstream artists like easy-listening clarinet tooter Kenny G and pop diva Whitney Houston.

Lead singer Rushlow has said (in all seriousness): "I feel like we're the first country band that was influenced by 'young country.' Sure, we love bands like the Eagles and POCO, but our real influences were Alabama, Restless Heart—country's *new* sound." For better or worse, these spiritual forebears shine through in their every slick note.

Select Discography
First Time for Everything, Warner Bros. 26820. 1992 debut album.

◀ LOCKLIN, HANK

(born Lawrence Hankins Locklin, 1918, McLellan, FL)

A pioneering smooth-voiced country vocalist, Locklin created a pleasant, middle-of-the-road style about a decade before it became the predominant Nashville sound, scoring his biggest hit with 1960's "Please Help Me I'm Falling."

Growing up on a small family farm, Locklin learned GUITAR at an early age, playing for local dances and parties. By the thirties, he was working for the WPA doing road work, while occasionally performing on local radio and still dreaming of being a singing star. His big break came after World War II, when he earned a spot on the prestigious *Louisiana Hayride* radio program; he was signed by Four Star Records and had a minor hit with 1949's "The Same Sweet Girl" (unusual for a HONKY-TONK ballad in that it told of a husband's *devotion* to his wife), followed by a bigger one with 1953's "Let Me Be the One." The success of this second single led to a spot on the GRAND OLE OPRY and a contract with major country label RCA/Victor.

At RCA his mature crooning style came to full flower, and he had a number of hits with pop-ish numbers like 1957's sappy "Geisha Girl," the mushy "Send Me the Pillow You Dream On" and "It's a Little More Like Heaven" both from a year later, and his chart buster "Please Help Me I'm Falling" from 1960, which he rerecorded a decade later with the cloying accompaniment of the Nashville Brass for yet another trip up the charts. (SKEETER DAVIS provided an answer song to this million seller with "[I Can't Help You] I'm Falling Too.") The bathetic "Happy Birthday to Me" followed in 1961. Although he continued to record through the sixties and early seventies, his hits became fewer. He became a popular touring act, known throughout the United States, Canada, and Europe, and for some reason became a big star in Ireland, where his crooner-style vocals won a huge audience.

By the early seventies, Locklin had returned triumphantly to his hometown, buying up his boyhood farm and building a lavish ranch. He was even elected mayor. In the mid-seventies, he was back to performing in the Houston area and recorded with little success in 1975 for the MGM label.

◀ LOGSDON, JIMMY

(born 1922, Panther, KY)

The son of a Bible-thumping minister, Logsdon recorded as a country artist in the fifties but is best remembered for his classic ROCKABILLY side, "I've Got a Rocket in My Pocket" from 1957, issued under the name Jimmy Lloyd.

Logsdon spent much of his childhood moving from town to town while his father pursued the life of an itinerant preacher. The family finally settled in Cincinnati; Logsdon was drafted into the air force soon after, where he was trained in electronics, and after the war he opened an electronics store in nearby Louisville, Kentucky. After hearing HANK WILLIAMS's first recordings, he took up the GUITAR and quickly earned a local following, performing over the radio.

In 1952 he opened for Williams on a local radio show, and the country star was so impressed that he introduced him to Decca producer Paul Cohen. Logsdon recorded a series of Williams-esque numbers, including his best-known country blues recording, "The Death of Hank Williams," backed by the original DRIFTING COWBOYS. A move to the Dot label did little to boost his career, as the Williams HONKY-TONK style was quickly becoming dated. In 1957 he moved to Roulette Records and gained a new persona as Jimmy Lloyd, jumping on the popularity of rockabilly with the classic "Rocket in My Pocket." Although this became a collector's item in later years, it did little for him at the time, and by the early sixties he was back to recording country for the King label. After a few more years of struggling to make it as a country act, Lloyd retired and took a job working for the state of Kentucky.

◀ LOMAX, JOHN AND ALAN

(John born 1875, Goodman, MS; died 1948; Alan born 1915, Austin, TX)

One of the most famous folklorists of our time, John Lomax virtually created the vogue for COWBOY SONGS with his famous 1910 collection *Cowboy Songs and Other Ballads*, as well as conducting pioneering field work throughout the South, often accompanied by his son, Alan.

Raised in the Southwest, Lomax was fascinated with the local songs and legends that he heard from his neighbors, family, and friends. When he entered Harvard, he met folklorist George Lyman Kittredge, a noted collector of folk ballads who, unlike other early collectors who relied on written sources, encouraged his students to conduct what is now known as "field work": to go out among the people and collect their songs. Lomax followed Kittredge's example and published his first collection of what he called "cowboy songs" in 1910, with an introduction by naturalist/politician Teddy Roosevelt. This became the source of material for many so-called "cowboy" recording stars from the thirties on, introducing songs that have become veritable chestnuts, such as "Home on the Range."

After working for a while in banking and as an amateur academic, Lomax took to the road again in 1933, bringing along one of the first portable recording machines (it recorded on discs and was powered by his car battery). His eighteen-year-old son, Alan, accompanied him. One of their most famous stops was to the notorious state prison farm in Angola, Louisiana, where they discovered a convicted murderer and talented guitarist named Huddie Ledbetter, later famous as Leadbelly. Ledbetter became the Lomaxes' driver and was later brought to New York to become one of the stars of the first FOLK REVIVAL.

Meanwhile, the Lomaxes published several more collections, including 1934's *American Ballads and Folk Songs* (1934), *Our Singing Country* (1941), and *Folk Song, U.S.A.* (1947). The two became codirectors of the Library of Congress's Archive of American Folksong in 1937; Alan Lomax also produced radio programs and recordings of traditional folk musicians beginning in the late forties. The elder

Lomax starred in his own radio series, called *The Ballad Hunter*, shortly before his death.

In the late fifties, Alan was among the first to take stereo equipment into the field, producing two large series of recordings of traditional country and blues music from the South, issued by Atlantic and Prestige records. From the mid-sixties on, Alan became increasingly involved in the study of what he called "cantometrics," an attempt to study the links between traditional musics from around the world. Working out of Columbia University, he became more active in the academic field than in popular music. Recently he produced a series of programs on world music and dance for public television, and he has also written *The Land Where the Blues Began*, his memoirs of recording blues musicians in the South in the thirties, forties, and fifties.

Select Discography

John Lomax Sings American Folksongs, Folkways 3508. John Lomax recorded these songs in the late forties; although he was not a great performer, they are of some historical interest.

Sounds of the South, Atlantic 82496. Reissue of Alan Lomax's field recordings made in 1959, featuring many fine blues and country performers. Features a booklet illustrated with Lomax's photos.

◀ LONZO AND OSCAR

(Lloyd George [aka Ken Marvin; aka Lonzo] [guitar, vocals]; Rollin Sullivan [Oscar] [mandolin, vocals])

Lonzo and Oscar were a classic country-comedy duo who had their biggest hit in 1947 with "I'm My Own Grandpa," later a theme song for comedian GRANDPA JONES.

The duo got their start as members of EDDY ARNOLD's backup band, where Sullivan played rhythm guitar and George (who took the stage name of Ken Marvin) played bass. Arnold asked them to perform a standard country cut-up act for his stage show, because he was uncomfortable handling comic material himself. Originally they were known as Cicero and Oscar, but Marvin was uncomfortable with the high-falutin' Greek name and wanted to switch it to something a little more authentically backwoodsy. It is said that an exasperated hotel clerk, on seeing Marvin haul his laundry down through the main lobby of his hotel, berated him by calling him "Lonzo" (an insulting name for a backwoodsman), and the name stuck. The duo hit pay dirt with their recording of "I'm My Own Grandpa" in 1947 and broke away from Arnold to become GRAND OLE OPRY stars on their own.

When Marvin tired of the comic routine, he was replaced by Sullivan's older brother John as a new "Lonzo"; they continued to perform together until John's death in 1967, recording for Victor, Columbia, and the BLUEGRASS Starday label, continuing the act in its corn-pone style nearly unchanged for almost twenty years. Dave Hooten was brought on board as the third Lonzo in 1968, and the duo continued to perform into the seventies, carrying the tradition of hayseed comedy into a new era.

◀ LOUDERMILK, JOHN D.

(born 1934, Durham, NC)

One of the most famous country songwriters of the fifties and sixties, Loudermilk supplied hundreds of songs to Nashville's establishment, while also recording his own material mostly in a folksy manner.

The son of a carpenter who had worked on the Duke University chapel, Loudermilk began his musical career in church, becoming a member of the local Salvation Army band in his teens, and quickly mastered a number of instruments. When he was twelve, he won a Capitol Records–sponsored talent contest run by a Durham radio station and hosted by country music legend TEX RITTER. As a teen, he was employed by the local radio station, where he worked as a bass player for the noon-hour band and did odd jobs around the office. Influenced by the popularity of rhythm and blues and teen pop, he wrote a song called "A Rose and a Baby Ruth," premiering it on the station. A local producer heard the song and had his protégé, GEORGE HAMILTON IV from nearby Winston-Salem, record it. The record became a 1956 million-seller, launching Hamilton's and Loudermilk's careers.

Loudermilk still hadn't settled on music as a career; hedging his bets, he entered college, while at the same time releasing his first recording of his own material, "Sitting in the Balcony," under the nom de disc of Johnny Dee. In 1957 rocker Eddie Cochran covered the song, for another big hit. By the late fifties, Loudermilk had moved to Nashville, where he hooked up first with Cedarwood Music and then the country powerhouse Acuff-Rose. One of his first country hits was the saga song "Waterloo," recorded by STONEWALL JACKSON. In 1959 Loudermilk made another solo recording, now taking the name Tommy Dee, on the minor hit "Three Stars," a bathetic attempt to cash in on the death of BUDDY HOLLY. Loudermilk penned another big teen-pop number, "Ebony Eyes," a 1961 hit for the EVERLY BROTHERS.

Meanwhile, Loudermilk was blossoming as a country tunesmith. He supplied SUE THOMPSON with her big 1961 hit "Sad Movies (Make Me Cry)," followed a year later by his song "Norman." He began recording on his own in the folk-pop style that was then coming into vogue, and had minor hits with "The Language of Love" and "Thou Shalt Not Steal" (both 1961) and "Road Hog" (1962). When George Hamilton's teen-pop career faded, he also turned to country, and he naturally asked old friend Loudermilk to supply him with some material; the results were the hits "Abilene" (1963) and "Break My Mind" (1967). "Tobacco Road," one of Loudermilk's most realistic and moving portrayals of the tough times faced by rural folks, was a hit for the British country/rock outfit the Nashville Teens in 1964. By the late sixties, he had turned his attention more to record production, working as producer on the first album by Southern rockers the Allman Brothers. In 1971 he had his last major pop hit with "Indian Reservation," recorded by Paul Revere and the Raiders.

In the early seventies, Loudermilk became interested in academic ethnomusicology, or the study of folk and traditional musics. Since that time, he has been

more or less inactive in the country music scene as a songwriter, although he has
served on the boards of various country music organizations, and his songs continue to be covered by new Nashville artists.

◀ LOUVIN BROTHERS, THE

*(Ira and Charlie Louvin; Ira born 1924, Rainesville, AL; died 1965; Charlie born
1927, Jefferson City, MO)*

Influenced by the popular brother acts of the thirties, the Louvins became big
stars on the GRAND OLE OPRY from the mid-fifties through the early sixties with their
brand of gospel-influenced harmonies and songs.

Raised in Henegger, Georgia, the duo began singing from an early age and were
particularly influenced by traditional balladry, old-time gospel, and the sounds
heard over the radio and on record, especially acts like the MONROE BROTHERS, the
DELMORE BROTHERS and the BLUE SKY BOYS. Their big break came in 1943 when they
won a position on early-morning radio in Chattanooga, Tennessee, thanks to a
local talent show. By the late forties, they moved to WNOX in Knoxville and the
popular *Midday Merry-Go-Round* program. They recorded briefly for MGM and
Decca in the late forties and then signed to Capitol in 1951 under the management
of FRED ROSE.

Their hits began in the mid-fifties with "I Don't Believe You've Met My Baby"
and "You're Running Wild," leading to a regular spot on the *Grand Ole Opry*. At
the same time, they issued a theme album, *Tragic Songs of Life*, a combination of
traditional ballads and modern sentimental songs with sparse, primarily acoustic
backup, which Capitol issued with a strange cover that resembled the tacky art on
pulp fiction of the day. Still, this remains one of their finest recordings, for its fine
singing, tasteful accompaniments, and sympathetic production values; their later
fifties and early-sixties sessions were marred by the heavy-handed NASHVILLE SOUND,
although their tasteful and distinctive singing shines through the acoustic sludge.
About half of their albums were all-gospel recordings, and they also paid homage
to their roots on a tribute album to the Delmore Brothers.

The brothers had an increasingly stormy relationship, and Charlie finally broke
with his brother in 1963 to pursue a solo career, beginning with the hit "I Don't
Love You Anymore." Ira continued to appear with his wife, Florence, who performed under the stage name of Anne Young; both were killed in an automobile
accident in 1965. In 1970 and 1971, Charlie formed a partnership with minor-league
country vocalist Melba Moore, who had previously recorded with Gene Pitney and
GEORGE JONES and continued as a solo artist on the Opry and the road through the
nineties.

Charlie and Ira together are credited with writing some four hundred songs,
including the perennial standard "When I Stop Dreaming" (covered by EMMYLOU
HARRIS, among many others). Their trademark high-vocal harmonies, with a plaintive sound reminiscent of backwoods gospel music, makes almost all of their recordings worth hearing, even when they are awash in crooning background

choruses. They were one of the few modern country duos to be able to preserve a true country sound into the early sixties.

Select Discography

Close Harmony, Bear Family 15561. Eight CDs offering 220 songs cut between 1947 and 1965 for Capitol and MGM. Great notes (by Charles Wolfe) and rare pictures accompany these classic sides, some of which suffer from Nashville Sound production.

Greatest Hits, Capitol 57222. Nine hits of the fifties and sixties on this cassette-only release.

Radio Favorites, 1951–1957, Country Music Foundation 009. Air checks from the fifties.

Fifty Years of Makin' Music, Playback 4505. Charlie Louvin joined by country stars WILLIE NELSON, WAYLON JENNINGS, CHARLIE DANIELS, TANYA TUCKER, GEORGE JONES, and more.

◀ LOVELESS, PATTY

(born Patricia Ramey, 1957, Pikesville, KY)

Loveless is a big-throated, HONKY-TONK–style singer who became a major star in the late eighties. She is a fine singer who recalls performers like PATSY MONTANA, ROSE MADDOX, and LORETTA LYNN (who, incidentally, is her cousin), to name just a few, while still having a contemporary edge.

Born in rural Kentucky, the daughter of a coal miner, Loveless was first introduced to country music through her older brother, Roger, who later managed her career. She began performing as a duo with him at age twelve. He took her to Nashville two years later, where she was hired to replace cousin Loretta in the WILBURN BROTHERS summer touring show. She toured for several summers with them, eventually wedding their drummer, Terry Lovelace. After her wedding, she went into semiretirement (although she continued to sing rock and pop music locally), leading the life of a housewife in North Carolina.

After her marriage failed, she returned to Nashville in the mid-eighties, changing her stage name to Loveless because it was easier to pronounce and also because she didn't want to be associated with soft-core porn star Linda Lovelace. Her brother got her an introduction to MCA Records and producer Emory Gordy, Jr., with whom she has been associated ever since. From her debut LP, she has recorded a mix of NEW-COUNTRY styles by leading singer/songwriters of the Nashville scene. Some of her early hits included the ballad "I Did" from her first LP and up-tempo numbers like "Timber I'm Falling in Love" and "I'm That Kind of Girl" (both with a rocking edge). Vocal troubles waylaid her career in the early nineties, but she returned triumphantly in 1993 with her hit single, "Blame It on Your Heart," an up-tempo but mild rocker, and a country swing hit, "Mister Man in the Moon."

Loveless's recordings have always featured the finest traditional musicians (such as fiddler Stuart Duncan of the NASHVILLE BLUEGRASS BAND, guitarist ALBERT LEE, and multi-instrumentalist MARK O'CONNOR) wed with a contemporary big drum sound to make it palatable to pop radio. Her voice is unaffected country; she manages to honor the stylings of the greatest country singers without aping them shamelessly. In other words, she is a unique vocalist who is mindful of tradition while continuing to create her own personal style.

Select Discography

Patty Loveless, MCA 5915. 1987 debut LP.

Up Against My Heart, MCA 10336.

Only What I Feel, Epic 53236. 1993 album, her first for a new label, and a return to honky-tonk roots.

When Fallen Angels Fly, Epic 64188. 1994 release marred by a weak selection of songs.

◀ LOVETT, LYLE

(born 1956, Klein, TX)

Lovett is a Texas-bred songster as well known for his tall hairdo and craggy features as he is for his music, which is just quirky enough to draw attention on both pop and country charts.

Born and raised in the small town of Klein, Lovett's musical tastes were melded by a mixture of Texas HONKY-TONK, BOB WILLS's classic WESTERN SWING, and the neo-hipster attitude of pop singers like Tom Waits. His own career was slow getting off the ground, so he worked a while as an assistant to his mother, who taught courses on motivational training for businesspeople, while he pursued his musical career at local clubs at night. Finally, he raised enough carfare to come to Nashville, where he landed in the early eighties, looking for a recording contract.

Lovett's half-spoken vocals, wordy songs, and wacky looks got him some initial attention, including a recording contract with Curb Records (an MCA affiliate), producing his first single "Farther Down the Line," drawing on and skewing the classic image of the rodeo cowboy. This was followed by further Western-flavored numbers, including his only top-ten hit, "Cowboy Man." Who else but Lovett would have the audacity to title a song "An Acceptable Level of Ecstasy," addressing issues of upper-class racism?

Lovett hit his stride with his third album, titled *Lyle Lovett and His Large Band*, melding Western swing and jazz influences. Oddly enough, the minor hit off this record was an acoustic cut, "Nobody Knows Me (Like My Baby)," a tender, offbeat love song, rich with the kind of hip wordplay that makes Lovett's best compositions so intriguing to his fans.

Lovett fits in with the other great Texas country songwriters—ranging from WILLIE NELSON and BILLY JOE SHAVER to JERRY JEFF WALKER and NANCI GRIFFITH—in his literate, witty lyrics, offbeat melodies, and myriad influences, from Dylanesque poetry to HANK WILLIAMS and Bob Wills–style arrangements. Like the other Texans, too, he is something of an anomaly in an industry that prizes more predictable product. For this reason he is destined to have a strong cult following while widespread commercial success will probably elude him.

Lovett's career got an odd boost in 1993 with his surprise marriage to Hollywood actress Julia Roberts, which splashed his droopy jowls across supermarket tabloids as the world's seemingly most unlikely husband for the troubled starlet. (Ironically, he had a minor hit in 1992 with his swing-band version of "That's No Lady [That's My Wife]"). However, after the rumor-mill dust settles, his career will probably continue on its own self-made path. He also has had a number of small parts in some of Robert Altman's recent films. If only because he remains true to his personal vision, Lovett is an artist worthy of attention, even if his music sometimes fails to find its audience.

Select Discography

Lyle Lovett, MCA 5748. 1986 debut album.

Pontiac, MCA 42028.

Lyle Lovett and His Large Band, MCA 42263. His 1989 release, with a Western swing feel.

Joshua Judges Ruth, MCA 10475. From 1992.

◀ LULU BELLE AND SCOTTY

(born Myrtle Eleanor Cooper, 1913, Boone, NC; Scott "Skyland Scotty" Wiseman born 1909; died 1981)

Country duos were immensely popular in the thirties, thanks to the proliferation of brother acts. Husband and wife Lulu Belle and Scotty added a down-home, family image to the mix, while they introduced several songs written by Scotty that have become country standards, including the sentimental "Remember Me" and "Have I Told You Lately That I Love You?" (Scotty also coauthored with BASCOM LAMAR LUNSFORD the perennial favorite comedy number, "Mountain Dew.") Their smooth vocal harmonies helped move country music toward a more mainstream, pop orientation.

Lulu Belle began performing as a soloist in her teen years and successfully auditioned for a role with the popular *National Barn Dance* radio show out of Chicago when she was nineteen. She first performed country comedy bits (playing a backwoods hayseed in the manner of MINNIE PEARL) with popular entertainer RED FOLEY until the station paired her with another newcomer, Scott Wiseman, nicknamed "Skyland Scotty." Their radio partnership blossomed into a romance, and the duo married. They became one of the most popular acts on the *Barn Dance*, and, thanks to their considerable exposure, recorded prolifically for many different labels. They performed a mix of traditional and more recent compositions, leaning toward sentimental and heart songs, many composed by Wiseman to suit the duo's romantic image. Their early recordings featured spare accompaniments, with solo GUITAR augmented with second guitar and BANJO and sometimes harmonica and fiddle; the emphasis is on their beautiful harmony singing, and justly so. From the late forties through their retirement from performing in 1958, they augmented their radio work by hosting a local, Chicago-area musical-variety television program.

In the late fifties, sensing the onslaught of rock and roll, the duo retired to North Carolina, where Lulu Belle became a successful local politician and Scotty took up teaching.

Select Discography

Sweethearts of Country Music, Hollywood/IMG 289. Cassette-only issue of recordings of unknown vintage.

◖ LUMAN, BOB

(born 1937, Nacogdoches, TX; died 1978)

A ROCKABILLY-turned-country star of the fifties and sixties, Luman's career traces the many changes in country music during this era.

The son of a talented old-time fiddler, guitarist, and harmonica player, Luman got early exposure to country music and was playing GUITAR by the time he was in high school. After playing local clubs and winning a slew of talent contests, he was hired to replace JOHNNY CASH on the popular *Louisiana Hayride* radio program, taking on a more teen-pop sound. In the mid-fifties, he recorded in a rockabilly style on small Texas labels, including with one band led by legendary string-bender JAMES BURTON. Luman's "A Pink Cadillac and a Black Mustache" is a legendary recording among fans of classic rockabilly, although it did little on the charts at the time.

In the late fifties, the EVERLY BROTHERS took an interest in his career, encouraging their new label, Warner Brothers, to sign him in 1959. In 1960 he had his one and only pop hit, Boudleaux Bryant's "Let's Think About Living," which also charted on the country listings. Lesser pop hits followed, including "Why Why Bye Bye" from the same year and 1961's "The Great Snowman." His pop career was cut short when he was drafted into the military; by the time he returned in 1963, the British Invasion was beginning to sweep older American acts off the radio, and he turned to country.

In 1964 he signed with Hickory, the label run by Nashville starmakers ROY ACUFF and WESLEY ROSE, scoring a minor country hit with "The File" in the same year. He moved to Epic in 1966 and had a slew of hits in the NASHVILLE SOUND–style of the day, beginning with 1968's "Ain't Got Time to Be Unhappy" through 1974's "Still Loving You." He moved to Polydor in 1977 and under the guidance of Johnny Cash had one last hit with "The Pay Phone." Ironically, his last album was called *Alive and Well*; a year after its release, in 1978, Luman died of pneumonia in a Nashville hospital.

Select Discography

American Originals, Columbia 45078. Cassette-only issue of Epic recordings from the early seventies.

◖ LUNN, ROBERT

(born 1912, Franklin, TN; died 1966)

An ex-vaudevillian who worked on the GRAND OLE OPRY stage for over twenty years, Lunn's claim to fame was the "talking blues," a long, often comic, spoken narrative accompanied by simple blues chord patterns played on the GUITAR.

Lunn joined the Opry in 1930 and remained with the show for twenty-eight years (with a break for service in World War II). Despite the popularity of his act, he rarely recorded, perhaps because most of his material was fairly similar. However, his regular radio appearances were quite influential on other country performers, most notably WOODY GUTHRIE, who transformed the talking blues into an effective form of often ironic commentary on social conditions during the Depression and World War II years.

◀ LUNSFORD, BASCOM LAMAR

(born 1882, Mars Hill, NC; died 1973)

Lunsford was one of the few folklorists to actually grow up within the mountain culture. Founder of the Asheville Folk Festival in 1928, he was also a fine BANJO player, singer, and teller of traditional mountain stories.

Although he learned to play banjo and fiddle as a child, Lunsford did not initially pursue a career in music. His first job was as a rural fruit-tree salesman, and he traveled throughout the Appalachians selling his product to the landlocked mountain farmers. Along the way, he became interested in the traditional songs, dances, and tales that he heard. He returned to school to study folklore and law, eventually becoming a full-time lawyer and an amateur folklorist. In 1928 he was instrumental in starting what was officially known as the Mountain Dance and Folk Festival in Asheville, a community on the edge of the Appalachians where the Rockefellers had a palatial summer estate. He also made a few commercial recordings in the twenties but, like BUELL KAZEE, never pursued a professional performing career.

In the thirties, Lunsford became a close friend of Scotty Wiseman, one half of the famous mountain-music team of LULU BELLE AND SCOTTY. He wrote the original lyrics for the pseudofolk song "Good Old Mountain Dew," which Scotty set to music. This has since become a favorite of the FOLK REVIVAL. Also in the thirties he began recording for the Library of Congress, becoming an important informant for folklorists JOHN AND ALAN LOMAX. He also helped found the National Folk Festival.

After World War II, Lunsford recorded sporadically for folk-revival labels and continued to perform in the Asheville area. He possessed a clear-as-a-bell singing voice; like other Carolina singers DOC WATSON and JEAN RITCHIE, he sang in a relaxed style, unlike the intense vocalizing of deep mountain singers like ROSCOE HOLCOMB, making his music much more accessible to an urban audience. He used the banjo as a simple but effective accompaniment to his repertoire, which was made up mostly of traditional ballads, nineteenth-century play-party and folk songs, and more recently composed compositions.

Select Discography

Music from South Turkey, Rounder 0065. Also includes George Pegram and Red Parham.

Smokey Mountain Ballads, Folkways 2040. 1947 recordings.

◀ LUTHER, FRANK

(born Frank Luther Crow, 1905, Larkin, KS)

Luther was an early city entertainer who entered the country music field, primarily working with CARSON J. ROBINSON, and later became a popular performer of children's music.

Educated in music in college, Luther performed with several local popular vocal quartets of the mid-twenties, including the DeReszke Singers (for whom he provided piano accompaniment) and the Revellers, who were minor midwestern radio stars. He came to New York in 1928, where he hooked up with fellow Kansas native Robinson, and the duo recorded many pop, novelty, and countrified songs for the urban market, often under the names of Bud and Joe Billings. Ethel Park Richardson, a New York radio hostess who specialized in presenting so-called "country" music for city dwellers, used them regularly on her popular radio broadcasts. With Robinson, Luther took songwriting credit for adaptations of traditional humorous and COWBOY SONGS, including "Barnacle Bill the Sailor" and "Home on the Range," both of which existed long before the duo "wrote" them. Luther also recorded as a solo artist, picking up on the cowboy fad in the thirties.

In the mid-thirties, he formed a radio trio with his wife, Zora Layman, a fiddler who had previously worked with Carson Robinson replacing ADELYNE HOOD on his recordings. The duo were sometimes accompanied by RAY WHITLEY (a singing cowboy star of the era). By the decade's end, he was writing and performing children's material with wife Zora, and the two became the most popular children's artists on record; although they divorced in 1940, they continued to perform together for another eight years. In the fifties, he moved into record production before finally retiring from the music business.

◀ LYNN, LORETTA

(born Loretta Webb, 1935, Butcher Hollow, KY)

One of country music's pioneering female performers and songwriters, Lynn has a classic country voice that is perfectly suited for her to-the-point lyrics with their uniquely woman's point of view. Perhaps the only country singer who has taken on a wide variety of issues, from birth control to the Vietnam war to wife abuse, Lynn has made an important contribution to widening the subject matter and audience for country music.

Lynn was born in a small coal-mining community, as she emphasized in her biography, *Coal Miner's Daughter* (1976, later a feature film). When she was thirteen, she married Oliver "Mooney" Lynn, who later became her manager. The couple relocated to Washington State, where Lynn raised four children while she began performing her own material. Her first single, "I'm A Honky Tonk Girl," released in 1960 on the tiny Zero label, was in the classic barroom mold. This brought her to the attention of OWEN BRADLEY, the legendary producer who had worked with PATSY CLINE, who had befriended the younger singer.

Her early-sixties recordings showed the influence of KITTY WELLS in their brash lyrics of lovin' and losin'. Soon, however, her vocal style softened, while her original material turned to unusual (for the time) topics, including "Don't Come Home A-Drinkin' (With Lovin' on Your Mind)," "You Ain't Woman Enough," and "The Pill," a song in support of birth control. All of the songs were written from a woman's point of view; although their sound was classic HONKY-TONK, their message was unusually liberated for the country audience of the mid-sixties and early seventies. It is also noteworthy that Lynn wrote her songs from the point-of-view of a wife, a figure not often encountered on the honky-tonk landscape (primarily peopled by wayward husbands and "honky-tonk angels," the unattached women who lured them to their dooms). This heavy dose of reality in a medium that seemed to thrive on fantasy pointed the direction for many of the more progressive songwriters of the seventies and eighties. Her autobiographical song, "Coal Miner's Daughter" from 1970, expressed the pride and anguish of growing up dirt poor in the mountains.

The early seventies saw her teamed up with CONWAY TWITTY on a series of successful duets, including "After the Fire Is Gone" and "Louisiana Woman, Mississippi Man." Her autobiography, published in the mid-seventies, was instrumental not only in cementing her image as a "true country woman," but in reasserting country music's roots at a time when many acts were trying to cross over onto the pop and rock charts.

Sadly, the success inspired by her autobiography and the subsequent film of her life seems to have encouraged Lynn in the eighties and early nineties to move in a more mainstream direction. She less frequently writes her own material, and the material selected for her is weak. Her live show leans heavily on her early hits, and her many fans seem content to hear her perform the same repertory of well-known numbers. Although Lynn paved the way for today's more assertive female singers, she has not joined their company in continuing to produce significant music.

Select Discography
Coal Miner's Daughter, MCA 936. Reissued to cash in on the success of the movie.
Country Music Hall of Fame, MCA 10083. Comprehensive anthology of Lynn's best recordings.
Greatest Hits, Vols. 1 and 2, MCA 31234, 932. CD reissues of the big hits.
I Remember Patsy, MCA 31325. CD reissue of Patsy Cline tribute album.

◀ LYNNE, SHELBY

(born Shelby Lynn Moorer, AL, 1969)
Lynne is a torchy balladeer in the K. D. LANG mold who, like Lang, has tried to cross over into pop vocalizing.

Lynne's life has not been an easy one. Her father was a violent ex-marine who beat his wife and two daughters. His wife left him to protect her children, and she even dreamed of forming a JUDDS-like duo with her elder daughter Shelby. However, that dream died when her husband tracked down the family to Mobile in 1986 and killed his ex-wife, then committed suicide.

Still recovering from this terrible family tragedy, Shelby got her big break on the cable program *Nashville Now* just a year later. She was immediately signed to a recording contract and began touring as an opening act for RANDY TRAVIS. She specialized in love-gone-wrong songs, including her first hits "The Hurtin' Side" and "I Love You So Much It Hurts," as well as tearjerking classics like "Heartbreak Hotel" and "I Can't Stop Lovin' You."

Her 1992 album, *Temptation*, found her dipping even further into middle-of-the-road heartbreakers, although the WESTERN SWING–influenced accompaniment is unusual for a NEW-COUNTRY artist. Although she sounds somewhat uncomfortable singing the more upbeat numbers, her big voice and gutsy delivery is perfectly suited to the more bluesy ones.

Select Discography

Sunrise, Epic 44260. 1989 debut album.

Temptation, Morgan Creek 20018. Western swing–style recording from 1993.

M.

◀ MAC AND BOB

(Lester McFarland [mandolin, vocals]; Robert Alexander Gardner [guitar, vocals])

Blind performers Mac and Bob are famous for creating the vocal duet accompanied by MANDOLIN and GUITAR; if they were not the first to perform in this style, they were certainly the first to record in it, beginning in 1926 and continuing on radio through the early fifties. As such, they were influential on many of the so-called brother acts that followed, from the BLUE SKY BOYS to the MONROE BROTHERS and the DELMORE BROTHERS.

McFarland, a Kentucky native, and Gardner, from Tennessee, met at the Kentucky School for the Blind where they were both enrolled in their teens. They began performing together immediately, gaining local popularity. They began broadcasting over Knoxville's KNOX in 1925 and were signed to Brunswick records a year later. They got their widest exposure through a number of stints on the popular *National Barn Dance* program out of Chicago (from 1931 to 1934 and again from 1939 to 1950). Their records were issued and reissued throughout the period on a number of bargain labels, and marketed through mail-order outlets like Sears and Montgomery Ward, making them highly influential throughout the South.

The Mac and Bob style was greatly influenced by the light popular parlor music that they heard as youths. Their biggest hits were sentimental songs, including "When the Roses Bloom Again" and "Tis Sweet to Be Remembered"; they even recorded the 1890s-era college hit, "I'm Forever Blowing Bubbles." They did manage to wax a few more traditional numbers, including the ever-popular hymn "This Little Light of Mine," but their repertoire was primarily drawn from what was then called "old-time" music, i.e., the popular hits of the Victorian era and the early twentieth century.

Bob retired in 1951, while Mac continued as a solo artist for another two years.

◀ MACK, WARNER

(born Warner McPherson, 1938, Nashville, TN)

Mack is a minor-league country SINGER/SONGWRITER who had a decade's success beginning in the mid-sixties.

Born in Nashville, Mack was raised in Vicksberg, Mississippi, where he began his performing career in high school. In the late fifties, he was a regular on the famous *Louisiana Hayride* radio show, also working on RED FOLEY's *Ozark Jubilee.*

His first record, a minor teen-pop hit from 1957 called "Is It Wrong?," was issued under the name Warner Mack, and the nickname stuck.

Mack came to Nashville in search of a new career in the early sixties, first charting in 1964 with the moderately successful "Surely." A year later, he produced the big seller "The Bridge Washed Out," followed by lesser hits through the decade's end, including 1966's "Talkin' to the Wall" and "How Long Will It Take?" from a year later. Mack's popularity faded in the early seventies, and his last charting single was 1977's "These Crazy Thoughts" issued by the tiny Pageboy label. He has since taken to the barroom and country-fair circuit.

◀ MACON, UNCLE DAVE

(born 1870, Smart Station, TN; died 1952)

Uncle Dave Macon was one of the most colorful and often-recorded of all the stars of Nashville's GRAND OLE OPRY. He appeared on the Opry's stage from its opening days into the early 1950s, when he was in his early eighties, performing a combination of traditional BANJO songs, sentimental songs, and his own compositions, often commenting on contemporary trends.

Macon began playing banjo as a youth, mastering both the traditional clawhammer (sometimes called frailing) style, in which the performer brushes across the strings with the back of his playing hand while catching the fifth or drone string with his thumb, as well as the more modern two-fingered picking style. Although he performed occasionally in medicine shows and for local entertainment, Macon remained a small-time farmer and operator of a hauling business until his fifties. When the *Grand Ole Opry* radio program was first started, host GEORGE D. HAY was anxious to book Macon for the program, having heard of the local celebrity's good-humored singing and banjo playing. Macon was soon the show's biggest star, remaining a crowd-pleasing performer for nearly three decades.

Macon's hearty vocals, good humor, and energetic banjo playing influenced an entire generation of musicians, including STRINGBEAN and GRANDPA JONES. He recorded hundreds of 78s, often accompanied by the talented McGee Brothers. In the forties and early fifties, he was often accompanied by his son, Dorris, in Opry appearances.

Macon's repertoire, like that of other early country performers, was made up of a mix of traditional songs and dance tunes, sentimental and popular songs of the late nineteenth and early twentieth centuries, and his own offbeat adaptations of these songs along with original compositions. Macon's presentation of his material showed the influence of years of performing on the tent-show circuit; his recordings often began and ended with a lusty shout of "Hot dog!" Macon's biting social commentary is illustrated in songs like "In and Around Nashville," in which he criticizes, among other things, women who chew gum and wear "knee-high" skirts. In his "Tennessee Gravy Train," Macon commented on a contemporary scandal that led to the failure of several local banks. A dedicated mule-driver, Macon sang several songs praising this more reliable means of transportation (and source of his livelihood) over the newly introduced automobile. One of his popular songs,

"The Cumberland Mountain Deer Chase," describing a deer hunt back in the mountains, was transformed in the fifties by PETE SEEGER into a long story-song for children that he called "The Cumberland Mountain Bear Hunt."

Select Discography
Go Along Mule, Country 545. Among the many Uncle Dave reissues on LP, this has the best selection and sound.
Country Music Hall of Fame, MCA 10546. Late-twenties recordings featuring the McGee Brothers.

◀ MADDOX, ROSE

(born Rosea Arbana Brogdon, 1925, Boaz, AL)

Maddox was a HONKY-TONK singer of the late forties and early fifties who performed with her family band as the Maddox Brothers and Rose, and then switched to recording in a traditional BLUEGRASS setting. She was one of the earliest powerhouse female vocalists, setting the stage for the success of KITTY WELLS a few years later.

Rose's family, like many other southerners and westerners who had previously worked on farms, emigrated to Southern California in search of a better way of life in the early thirties. Her five older brothers had a band in a Western/cowboy style, which performed at local rodeos and parties. In 1937 the group was approached by a Modesto radio station to put on a cowboy music show, with the stipulation that they have a female singer. Twelve-year-old Rose was enlisted, and the Maddox Brothers and Rose was born.

The band temporarily broke up due to World War II but returned with a vengeance in the late forties, signing with Southern California's Four Star label and producing a series of hilarious, high-energy recordings melding WESTERN SWING with early honky-tonk. Rose's big-throated vocals were ably accompanied by the band, along with her brothers' good-natured horseplay (they provided many shouted asides, jokes, and other interjections, particularly on the up-tempo numbers). The group's biggest hit was a 1946 cover of WOODY GUTHRIE's "Philadelphia Lawyer," introducing the song to the country repertoire. They also recorded a range of music from boogie-woogie and jazz-influenced numbers like "Milk Cow Blues" to sacred songs like "Gathering Flowers for the Master's Bouquet" to country WEEPERS like "Tramp on the Street" and "Blue Eyes Crying in the Rain."

In 1951 the group was signed to Columbia, still maintaining their high-energy style. However, the label saw more potential in Rose's more serious side and began playing down their antics on the recordings. The band was featured on the popular *Louisiana Hayride* radio program in the early fifties and continued to record and perform through 1957; one of their last hits featured Rose's brother Don on vocals on "The Death of Rock and Roll," one of country's first reactions to the latest trend in pop music.

Rose switched to Capitol Records in 1959 as a solo artist and continued to have hits through the early sixties with her gutsy recordings of "Down, Down, Down," "Sing a Little Song of Heartache," and duets with BUCK OWENS, another Southern

California–based Capitol star, on "We're the Talk of the Town," "Loose Talk," and the classic "Mental Cruelty." In 1963 bluegrass star BILL MONROE suggested to Capitol that Rose's style was perfectly suited to his style of music, and since the FOLK REVIVAL was in full swing, the label decided to release an album of Rose singing bluegrass standards accompanied by Monroe and RENO AND SMILEY. This album was way ahead of its time, becoming a collector's item a decade later during the bluegrass revival and launching an entirely new career for Maddox. After a period of inactivity from the mid-sixties through the mid-seventies, she returned as a blue-grass vocalist, recording a number of records for folk-revival labels and performing on the bluegrass circuit. Maddox's strong vocals set her leagues apart from even younger female bluegrass singers.

Maddox was important in pointing women in country music in a new direction: They could be gutsy and strong, while at the same time remaining acceptable to a predominantly male (and conservative) audience. She also was a pioneering woman in bluegrass, at a time when women in the field were few and far between. As such, she served as an inspiration to later female bluegrass/country stars, such as ALISON KRAUSS.

Select Discography

America's Most Colorful Hillbilly Band, Arhoolie 391. Reissues wonderful Maddox Brothers and Rose recordings cut between 1946 and 1951; good clean fun. Origi-nally reissued on two Arhoolie LPs in the mid-seventies.

◖ MAINER, J. E.

(born 1898, Joseph Emmett Mainer, Weaversville, NC; died 1971)

Mainer was an old-time country fiddler and bandleader who led a variety of groups under the name of Mainer's Mountaineers from the thirties through the sixties. Mainer's group enjoyed popularity during the FOLK REVIVAL, thanks to re-cordings made in the late fifties by folklorist ALAN LOMAX.

Mainer and his younger brother, BANJO player Wade (born 1907) were both cotton-mill workers who began working semiprofessionally as musicians in the late twenties. In 1934 they were hired by WBT out of Charlotte, North Carolina, and formed their first band, a quartet originally known as the Crazy Mountaineers, featuring yodeler/guitarist "Daddy" John Lowe and mandolinist/guitarist Zeke Mor-ris (one-half of the Morris Brothers duo). A year later they were signed to Bluebird and made their first recordings, including their 1936 hit, "Maple on the Hill." The group's sound was fairly primitive even for this time, recalling the earlier string bands of the twenties, although Lowe's YODELING and COWBOY-SONG repertoire looked forward to the nascent singing-cowboy craze.

The Mountaineers existed in various forms through the thirties. At times, Wade and J.E. would split, each leading his own Mountaineers, while at other times they came back together. Wade formed his own group, the Sons of the Mountain-eers, in 1937, taking Zeke Morris with him along with fiddler Clyde Moody and scoring a hit with "Sparkling Blue Eyes" two years later, one of the last songs featuring string band accompaniment to make the country charts. His recordings were a little more modern sounding, particularly in his duets with Zeke Morris, which were patterned after the very successful mid-thirties recordings of the BLUE SKY BOYS.

After a period of inactivity during World War II, both brothers turned up again in the late forties as recording stars on the King label. Their stage show and recordings were a hodgepodge of old-time string-band music, recreations of minstrel and medicine-show material, and sentimental and heart songs of the turn of the century. Toward the end of the decade, folklorist Alan Lomax discovered Mainer's band and recorded them for two large projects he was producing at that time, *The Sounds of the South* series (issued by Atlantic Records in the late fifties) and a similar series for the Prestige label. This led to renewed interest in the group and some bookings on the folk-revival and BLUEGRASS circuits. Later in the sixties, Wade led a more bluegrass-oriented outfit, while J.E. was in semiretirement, working repairing fiddles.

Select Discography
J. E. Mainer's Crazy Mountaineers, Old Timey 106/107. Two out-of-print LPs reissuing early recordings by Mainer's band.

◀ MANDOLIN

The mandolin, originally of Neapolitan origin, has become a key voice in BLUE-GRASS and country music. Its odyssey into country music is a typical American story of experimentation and innovation.

The eight-stringed instrument, tuned like a fiddle, originally was made with a bowl-shaped back, like a lute. In the late nineteenth century, American musical instrument designer Orville Gibson came up with a new idea: a carved-body instrument, to emulate the design of the great violins. The back of his instruments had a slight arch but sat more comfortably against the player's body than the old bowl-shaped design. Gibson came up with two basic designs: one a pear-shaped instrument with a sweet sound that he called his "A" model, and the other a more fancy design with scrolls and points that he called the "Florentine" or "F" model. Gibson sold his design to a consortium of Michigan-based businessmen in 1902, and soon they were mass-producing these instruments. Mandolin clubs sprang up on college campuses and in small towns, many organized by the Gibson company, while just after World War I the company introduced an inexpensive "Army and Navy" model specifically for sale at military bases. Other makers—notably mass-marketers Lyon and Healy—entered the fray, and soon inexpensive instruments were readily available.

The mandolin first became popular among the brother acts of the thirties, although there had been a couple of mandolin players in earlier string bands. The sweet-voiced instrument, perfect for playing short melodic fills, became a favorite after it was popularized by duos like the BLUE SKY BOYS. Then, in the mid-thirties, a new brother act with a much more high-powered sound hit the radio: the Monroe Brothers. BILL MONROE played a Gibson F-5, the fanciest of the Florentine models introduced in the twenties, which had a biting sound; his melodic parts were intricate, passionate, and flashy. After the brothers broke up, Bill formed his first Blue Grass Boys and became the pioneer of bluegrass-style mandolin. In fact, most bluegrass pickers prefer the F-series Gibson instrument because it is the one most closely associated with Monroe, and dozens of companies have copied the design.

The mandolin enjoyed a further resurgence in popularity in the seventies when a group of ex-bluegrass players took the instrument into the realm of a blend of new-acoustic and jazz music. DAVID GRISSMAN pioneered what he called "Dawg music," performing in a quintet with two mandolins; soon others were forming similar outfits. Earlier pickers like Tiny Moore (who had played for BOB WILLS) and Jethro Burns (one half of the famed HOMER AND JETHRO comedy act) gained new popularity as masters of a jazz-flavored style of picking. The instrument, which was rarely heard on country recordings outside of bluegrass records, enjoyed new popularity thanks to session work by Grissman and others. Most recently, Sam Bush (an original member of NEW GRASS REVIVAL) has been Nashville's most busy session picker; he also works regularly in EMMYLOU HARRIS's backup band.

◀ MANDRELL, BARBARA

(born 1948, Houston, TX)
Mandrell is a country queen of the mid-seventies and early eighties whose glitzy act hides her real talents as an instrumentalist and vocalist.

Mandrell came from a musical family, born in Texas but raised in Southern California. She began playing with the family band at a young age and was adept at a number of instruments, particularly the difficult-to-master PEDAL STEEL GUITAR. When Mandrell was eleven, she was already playing the instrument in Las Vegas shows, and two years later she toured with JOHNNY CASH performing for military shows in Vietnam and Korea.

After a minor hit as a vocalist with the song "Queen for a Day," released by the small Mosrite label, Mandrell and family moved to Nashville, where she was signed by Columbia in 1969. Her first success was covering R&B standards, beginning with "I've Been Loving You Too Long," originally recorded by Otis Redding, followed by such chestnuts as "Do Right Woman—Do Right Man" through 1973's "Midnight Oil." In mid-decade, she signed with ABC/Dot and had her first period of wide popularity, with hits including 1977's "Married (but Not to Each Other)" and the 1978 number-one country single, the cleverly titled "Sleeping Single in a Double Bed."

Mandrell continued to be a major star in the early eighties, thanks to increased exposure hosting a network variety program with her sisters, Irlene and Louise. A combination of HEE HAW and the *Bell Telephone Hour*, the show offered the girls' sweet harmonies and musical talents, as well as decidedly low-brow comedy routines. Mandrell continued to put out solo hits, including 1981's "I Was Country When Country Wasn't Cool," 1983's "One of a Kind Pair of Fools," and 1984's duet with LEE GREENWOOD, "To Me."

Barbara's life and career were dealt a severe blow in 1984 when she was involved in a head-on collision with another car, leading to a long period of hospitalization and some doubts about her ability to recover. She came back full steam a year later, with the hit "Angel in Your Arms," although her popularity on the country charts was already eroding due to the influx of NEW-COUNTRY stars. Mandrell can still pack 'em in at Vegas (or BRANSON, MISSOURI) like few other stars, but her chart-topping days appear to be over, perhaps because her older style of country-meets-pop seems somewhat dated in today's return-to-roots renaissance.

Select Discography
The Best of Barbara Mandrell, MCA 31107. Her best mid-seventies recordings.
Keys in the Mailbox, Liberty 95794. 1991 return to country form.

◀ MANDRELL, LOUISE

(born 1954, Corpus Christi, TX)
Fiddle-and-bass-playing sister of pop chanteuse BARBARA MANDRELL, Louise enjoyed some spillover popularity in the early eighties thanks to her exposure on her big sister's television program.

Originally a member of the Mandrell family band, the Do-Rites, playing bass, Louise graduated to playing with Nashville crooner Stu Phillips in the early seventies, followed by a stint as the girl singer in MERLE HAGGARD's Strangers. In 1978 she signed as a solo act to Epic and a year later married country singer R. C. BANNON, with whom she had her first major hit, the duet "Reunited." The pair signed to RCA in 1981, and Louise continued to have solo hits with "Where There's Smoke There's Fire." Beginning in 1983, she appeared with Barbara and sister Irlene on network TV, spawning hits with "Save Me" and "Too Hot to Sleep," followed by her last major charting song, 1984's "I'm Not Through Loving You Yet."

Louise's career slowed after the Mandrell sisters' TV show was canceled. Although she has a perky personality and is a talented musician like her sister, she failed to cross over into the lucrative middle-of-the-road pop market that embraced Barbara. Lacking as much musical personality as her elder sister, Louise's music also suffered from its pop leanings, which went out of mode in the late-eighties return-to-roots music that swept the country charts.

Select Discography
The Best of Louise Mandrell, RCA 6714. Cassette-only reissue of her early-eighties hits.

◀ MANN, LORENE

(born 1937, Huntland, TN)
Mann was a popular SINGER/SONGWRITER of the mid-sixties who penned some unusual country songs.

Born on a farm near the Alabama/Tennessee border, Mann began playing GUITAR at age twelve, learning the instrument from her older brothers. She came to Nashville at age nineteen in search of a career as a songwriter. She began performing in the mid-sixties, dueting with Justin Tubb (Ernest's son) and Archie

Campbell. Her solo recordings include the unusual "Don't Put Your Hands on Me," in which she tells off a two-timer, and, perhaps most radical of all, "Hide My Sin," about a woman's mixed feelings after having an abortion (certainly the only Nashville-produced recording that features the famous back-up singers the JORDAN-AIRES, spelling out "A-B-O-R-T-I-O-N"). After these mid-sixties successes, Mann faded from the music scene.

◀ MAPHIS, JOE

(born 1921, Suffolk, VA; died 1986)

Multi-instrumentalist most famous for his lightning-fast GUITAR picking, Maphis revolutionized country and pop guitar playing through his creative acoustic and electric picking.

Raised in Cumberland, Maryland, Joe began performing with his father in the family band, the Railsplitters, in 1932. Not content to simply play chord accompaniments to the band's up-tempo readings of traditional square-dance tunes, Maphis developed his unique approach to finger-picking the melody. When he was seventeen, Maphis went professional, eventually performing on country radio shows such as Chicago's *National Barn Dance*. He took up the newly introduced electric guitar in 1947 and in the same year hooked up with vocalist Rose Lee (born 1922, Baltimore, Maryland), who was to become his musical partner and, five years later, his wife. The duo wrote the HONKY-TONK classic, "Dim Lights, Thick Smoke (and Loud, Loud Music)," still one of the favorites of this genre. In 1952 they were invited to star on the *Town Hall Party* television program, where Joe helped launch the career of junior string-bender Larry Collins of the COLLINS KIDS.

In 1954 Maphis became one of the first performers in any musical style to play a twin-necked guitar, recording "Fire on the Strings," his adaptation of the country fiddle classic, "Fire on the Mountain." He also began performing as a session musician on MANDOLIN and BANJO as well as guitar, and recorded and performed with the other great country guitar ace of the day, MERLE TRAVIS. Maphis's distinctive picking can be heard on the early pop hits of RICKY NELSON, as well as on such classic bits of yuppie nostalgia as the theme songs for TV's *Bonanza* and *The FBI*.

Maphis and his wife continued to record through the sixties, seventies, and eighties, first for mainstream Capitol Records and later for BLUEGRASS (Starday) and gospel (World) labels. He also encouraged his young niece, BARBARA MANDRELL, another multi-instrumental talent, to enter country music as a profession (Mandrell returned the favor by featuring Maphis and buddy Travis on one episode of her TV variety show in the early eighties). Always a heavy smoker, Maphis succumbed to lung cancer in 1986. Sons Dale and Jody have carried forward his sound as Nashville sessionmen.

Select Discography

Flat Picking Spectacular, CMH 9030. Cassette-only reissue of seventies-era recordings.

◀ MARTIN, GRADY

(born 1929, Chappel Hill, TN)

Martin is one of the best-known studio guitarists in Nashville, appearing on thousands of recordings cut in the fifties, sixties, and seventies.

Martin played fiddle and GUITAR as a youngster; in fact, he debuted on the GRAND OLE OPRY as a fiddler at age seventeen, not on the guitar, two years after moving to Nashville from his small hometown. He cut the jazzy guitar instrumental "Chattanooga Shoeshine Boy" on his own in the late forties and then moved into a steady stream of session work, beginning with HANK WILLIAMS and continuing with most of the big-name country acts of the fifties and sixties. Martin was a member of the group of studio musicians who worked under the guidance of producer CHET ATKINS, including tinkling pianist FLOYD CRAMER; and like Cramer he developed a pleasant, adaptable, middle-of-the-road style. In 1979 he joined WILLIE NELSON's road band. Martin is also the author of the country/pop hit "Snap Your Fingers," recorded by DICK CURLESS, DON GIBSON, pop crooner Dean Martin, and, more recently, RONNIE MILSAP.

◀ MARTIN, JANIS

(born 1940 near Richmond, VA)

Martin was one of the few fifties-era female ROCKABILLY stars. She was promoted by record label RCA as a clean-cut teenager with a decidedly sexy delivery.

Already appearing on Richmond radio as a diminutive country star in 1954, Janis was, like many teens of the time, an avid fan of R&B. At age fifteen, she made a demo cover version of "Will You Willyum" that was heard by RCA's director of A&R (Artists & Repertory), Steve Sholes. She was brought to Nashville to record under the guiding hand of CHET ATKINS, producing a series of minor rockabilly hits, including 1956's "My Boy Elvis" and "Let's Elope Baby," 1957's "Cracker Jack" and a cover of the old folk chestnut "Billy Boy Billy Boy" (rocked up for the teen-pop market), and her last hit, 1958's "Bang Bang" (recently covered by NEW-COUNTRY artist KELLY WILLIS). Already married at age fifteen (a fact that RCA's PR department kept carefully under wraps), Martin's career was ended when she became pregnant in 1958; she made an attempted comeback on the smaller Palette label in 1960, with little success. After her second marriage ended in 1970, she returned to touring sporadically, reviving her trademark "female Elvis" persona.

Select Discography

The Female Elvis, 1956–1960, Bear Family 15406. All of her recordings for RCA and Palette.

◄ MARTIN, JIMMY

(born 1927, Sneedville, TN)

Jimmy Martin is a country vocalist who wed the sensibilities of BLUEGRASS and mainstream country to make a series of classic recordings in the fifties and sixties. His vocals combine the smoothness of a pop crooner with characteristic YODELING vocal breaks that are pure traditional country, making him one of the most easily recognized vocalists in all of country music.

Martin's career began on the radio in 1948; a year later, he was invited to join BILL MONROE's Blue Grass Boys as lead vocalist to replace MAC WISEMAN. He performed with Monroe on classic recordings until 1953 and was probably Monroe's second greatest lead vocalist (Lester Flatt would have to take the highest honors). In 1951 and 1952, he briefly broke from Monroe to record with country MANDOLIN picker Bobby Osborne, making a series of classic vocal-duo recordings.

In 1954 Martin, Bobby Osborne, and his BANJO-playing brother Sonny performed as the OSBORNE BROTHERS band for a year; two years later, Martin formed the first of his Sunny Mountain Boys, performing on both the GRAND OLE OPRY and the *Louisiana Hayride* radio programs. Martin was the first of the pure bluegrass stars to cross over, attempting to create what he called "good 'n' country music," a kind of less hard-driving, more vocally oriented bluegrass music. This led to mid-sixties country hits with songs like "Widow Maker" and "Sunny Side of the Mountain," which became his theme song. He also began performing novelty numbers, chasing the elusive chart hit.

Martin nurtured many talents in his band, including banjoists J. D. CROWE, Bill Emerson, and Alan Munde, and mandolinists Paul Williams and Doyle Lawson. His career was given a gigantic boost when he was invited to perform on the NITTY GRITTY DIRT BAND's landmark 1971 recording, *Will the Circle Be Unbroken;* he contributed fine vocals on his upbeat reading of HANK WILLIAMS's classic "I Saw the Light" and his own "Sunny Side of the Mountain." Despite the introduction to a rock audience, Martin continued to perform on the country and bluegrass circuit where he felt most at home.

Select Discography

You Don't Know My Mind, Rounder 21. Great fifties-era recordings in a bluegrass style.

Twenty Greatest Hits, Deluxe 7863. 1970s-era recordings from the Gusto label.

Jimmy Martin and the Sunny Mountain Boys, Bear Family 15705. Five-CD boxed set covering his entire career, from 1954 to 1974. Includes 146 cuts (!) featuring many celebrated sidemen. For the deep-of-pocket Martin fan.

◀ MASSEY, LOUISE, AND THE WESTERNERS

(born Victoria Louise Massey, 1908, Texas; died 1983)

Louise Massey was the motivating force behind her family band of Western-style musicians. She is famous for composing the country-pop hit "My Adobe Hacienda."

The family originally hailed from Texas but relocated when Massey's father purchased a farm in the then–sparsely populated recent state of New Mexico in 1914. The entire family of father, mother, and eight children were musically inclined, with dad playing old-style Western fiddle and daughter Louise a talented pianist and vocalist. Louise married bass player Milt Mabie in 1919, and he quickly became a member of the group. They began performing on the local vaudeville circuit in the early twenties and then began longer tours across the United States and Canada, with the elder Massey finally retiring because of the rigors of life on the road. The rest of the band settled into a five-year stint on KMBC radio out of Kansas City, which led to a broadcast on the station's parent network, CBS. In 1933 a talent scout for the WLS *Barn Dance* out of Chicago heard the group and signed them to this influential show.

The center of attention of the band was the glamorous Louise, who besides providing lead vocals was also something of a fashion plate, wearing Spanish-style costumes for their South-of-the-Border numbers and pioneering sequined cowboy suits for herself and members of the band, while she wore satin boots. The group, now known as Louise Massey and the Westerners, moved east to broadcast out of New York for a couple of years, before returning to Chicago and then going to Hollywood to appear in the C-grade flick *Where the Buffalo Roam*, starring TEX RITTER.

Like most of the cowboy bands of the day, the group played a wide range of material, mostly filtered through a soft, pop sound. Besides the obligatory cowboy and sentimental numbers, they could play dance music from fiddle tunes to Eastern European polkas, waltzes, and schottisches; novelty numbers, ragtime, and light jazz; and even an occasionally jazzed-up traditional mountain song. Louise wrote many of the group's hits, including their early 1934 disc, "When the White Azaleas Start Blooming," featuring her honey-voiced vocals; 1939's "South of the Border (Down Mexico Way)" and "I Only Want a Buddy (Not a Sweatheart)," a typical, tough-girl I-don't-need-no-man ditty; and their biggest number, 1941's "My Adobe Hacienda," which became a crossover pop hit after the war.

In 1948 Louise and husband Milt retired to New Mexico. Brother Curt went to Hollywood, where he would gain fame as the writer of two of the most memorable TV themes of all times: for *The Beverly Hillbillies* and its spinoff series, *Petticoat Junction* (that's him singing on that one).

◀ MATTEA, KATHY

(born 1959, Cross Lanes, VA)

Originally a BLUEGRASS singer/guitarist, Mattea has become one of the most successful of the new traditional artists, without selling out either to slick commercialism or to upscale, Las Vegas country-pop.

Mattea began playing music in her teens and joined her first bluegrass band, Pensboro, while a college student. She left college to move to Nashville, where she got a job as a tour guide at the Country Music Hall of Fame and occasional work as a backup and demo vocalist, working most notably on sessions for Bobby "Honey, I Miss You" Goldsboro.

New-country producer Allen Reynolds signed her to Mercury in 1983, but she failed to produce any hits until three years later, when she scored big with a cover of NANCI GRIFFITH's "Love at the Five and Dime." The hits, as they say, just kept coming through the eighties, including the modern-day TRUCK-DRIVING SONG "Eighteen Wheels and a Dozen Roses" from 1988, "Come from the Heart" and "Burnin' Old Memories" from a year later, and "She Came from Fort Worth" in 1990. Mattea suffered from vocal chord problems in 1992, but she came through surgery and returned to the charts a year later.

Mattea's music strikes a balance between mainstream country and her own traditional roots. Possessed of a powerful voice, with just a hint of country flavoring, Mattea is just pop enough to appeal to a mass audience. Mattea is best defined by what she is not: She's not a pure folkie like NANCI GRIFFITH, or a Southern cutie like SUZY BOGGUSS; she's also not a glitzy, ready-for-Vegas belter like LORRIE MORGAN. Mattea just simply puts the music out there, with a minimum of fuss, and for that she deserves plenty of kudos.

Part of the dilemma she faces is illustrated by her 1991 experiment with a melding of Scottish folk influences and contemporary country on her album *Time Passes By*; a courageous career step, in that it went against the grain of the slicker Nashville productions of the time, the album ultimately did not sell very well; Mattea was chagrined to find her own *A Collection of Hits* LP outstripping it in sales. In 1992 she returned with a more mainstream album, in an attempt to balance her own artistic goals with the necessity of maintaining a mainstream career.

Select Discography

A Collection of Hits, Mercury 84230. The hits up to 1990.
Time Passes By, Mercury 846975. Concept album based on folk-flavored influences.
Lonesome Standard Time, Mercury 512567. 1992 return to mainstream country.

◀ McAULIFFE, LEON

(born William Leon McAuliffe, 1917, Houston, TX; died 1988)

One of the pioneers of the steel guitar, McAuliffe is best known for his "Steel Guitar Rag," which he first recorded as a member of BOB WILLS'S TEXAS PLAYBOYS.

McAuliffe was a protégé of BOB DUNN, the steel guitarist who is most famous for his jagged-edged solos with MILTON BROWN. Leon joined the LIGHT CRUST DOUGHBOYS in 1933 and moved on to Wills's band two years later. He recorded "Steel Guitar Rag" (an adaptation of Sylvester Weaver's country-blues recording, "Guitar Rag") in 1936. His electrified steel guitar lines, often in duet with electric guitarist Eldron Shamblin, helped mold the Wills's sound through the thirties. McAuliffe also sang lead vocals on many of the more bluesy numbers. Wills's joyful shouts of "Take it away, Leon!" are heard on many of these classic recordings.

McAuliffe spent the World War II years in the navy but returned in 1946 to form his own band, known as the Cimarron Boys. His 1949 recording of "Panhandle Rag," also his own composition, became a much-imitated standard in the WESTERN SWING repertoire. He stayed with Columbia through the fifties and then recorded for a variety of smaller labels in the sixties, including his own Cimarron label. By the late sixties, he owned two small radio stations around Rogers, Arkansas, but the mid-seventies Western swing revival brought him out of retirement as a leader of the Original Texas Playboys, featuring many players from the various incarnations of Wills's bands. The band was active for about a decade, until age and ill-health caught up with many of the members. McAuliffe died of heart disease in 1988.

McAuliffe was one of the first to play an electrified lap steel guitar. Unlike his mentor Bob Dunn, whose playing was noted for its sharp, almost abrasive sound, McAuliffe developed a sweeter, more flowing and lyrical style. Still, he managed to pack considerable punch, and his sliding chords often propelled Wills's band. He was also an important composer, with "Blacksmith Blues" and "Cozy Inn" to his credit along with his more-famous instrumentals.

◀ McBRIDE AND THE RIDE

(Terry McBride [vocals, guitar]; Ray Herndon [vocals, guitar]; Billy Thomas [bass, vocals])

McBride and the Ride are one of many eighties-era groups that were put together to serve a specific market niche; their style is a kind of update of the vocal harmonies of groups like ALABAMA, spiffed up a bit to fit in a contemporary sound.

As a group of studio musicians, Terry McBride and Ray Herndon were brought together by MCA producer Tony Brown, who had a mission: to create a new band. Thomas, who had background in COUNTRY-ROCK from his work in RICK NELSON'S Stone Canyon Band and then in the backup bands for EMMYLOU HARRIS and VINCE GILL, was brought along to fill out the sound. Their pleasing vocals were married to an upbeat, neo–HONKY-TONK sound (perfect for NEW-COUNTRY radio), and they had a hit out of the gate with "Can I Count on You." Although they have not been consistent hit makers, they remain a popular group on the road and on country music television. Like many other Nashville-manufactured bands, they are competent if not exciting, making music that sounds more crafted than heartfelt.

Select Discography

Sacred Ground, MCA 10540. 1992 album.

◀ McCALL, C. W.

(born 1929, William Fries, Audubon, IA)

McCall is an ex–advertising executive turned monologuist and country star who rode the mid-seventies craze for TRUCK-DRIVING SONGS. His biggest hit, 1975's "Convoy," was made into a popular film by blood-and-guts director Sam Peckinpah three years later.

Fries was a fine arts major at the University of Iowa who went into advertising. In the early seventies, he created the character of C. W. McCall for an ad campaign for a local bakery. His spoken monologues on behalf of the goodness of old-time baked products soon were drawing lots of attention on local radio; in 1974 he adapted the routine successfully to his first record, "The Old Home Filler-Up and Keep on A-Truckin' Cafe," also his first commercial hit. Follow-up monologues included "Wolf Creek Pass," "Classified," "Black Bear Road," and his biggest hit, "Convoy." McCall continued to churn out minor hits, including 1976's "There Won't Be No Country Music (There Won't Be No Rock 'n' Roll)" and the comic novelty "Crispy Critters," followed a year later by "Roses for Mama." In 1982 he was elected mayor of the small Colorado town of Ouray and retired from both advertising and music making, although he attempted a comeback in 1990 that went nowhere.

Select Discography
Greatest Hits, Polydor 825793. Cassette-only reissue of mid-seventies and early-eighties recordings.

◀ McCLAIN, CHARLY

(born Charlotte Denise McClain, 1956, Memphis, TN)

McClain is a middle-of-the-road country-pop chirper who had her greatest success in the early to middle eighties.

Born in the rhythm-and-blues capital of the South, McClain began performing early, playing bass in her brother's COUNTRY-ROCK band from the age of nine and becoming a regular performer on the Memphis-based *Mid-South Jamboree* radio show in her teen years. She hooked up with the local pop-rock band, Shylo, and their producer Larry Rogers made a demo tape of her singing, which he passed along to famed country producer BILLY SHERRILL. This led to a contract with Epic in 1976 and her first single, "Lay Down," followed by her first hits two years later, "Let Me Be Your Baby" and "That's What You Do To Me."

McClain formed her own country-pop backup band, Bluff City, and became a popular touring attraction in the early eighties. Chart toppers included the suggestive "Who's Cheatin' Who" from 1980 and 1981's "Surround Me with Love" and "Sleepin' with the Radio On." She also cut duets with JOHNNY RODRIQUEZ ("I Hate the Way I Love It," from 1979), MICKEY GILLEY ("Paradise Tonight" from 1983 and "Candy Man" from the next year), and Wayne Massey ("With Just One Look in Your Eyes," from 1984, and "You Are My Music, You Are My Song" from a year later), who became her husband in 1984.

The NEW-COUNTRY boom pretty much ended the popularity of pop-oriented artists like McClain, although she continued to record through the eighties.

Select Discography
Biggest Hits, Epic 40186.

◀ McCLINTON, O. B.

(born Obie Burnett McClinton, 1942, Senatobia, MS; died 1987)

McClinton is perhaps best known in pop circles for the many R&B hits that he penned, including James Carr's "You Got My Mind Messed Up" and Otis Redding's "Keep Your Arms Around Me." But his first love was HANK WILLIAMS–style country music, and this is the type of music that he recorded on his own, showing once again the cross-fertilization between black and white cultures that occurred in the South.

The son of an African-American land-owning reverend in rural Mississippi, O.B. was exposed early on to country radio, particularly favoring the bluesy sounds of Hank Williams. At seventeen, he ran away from home and landed in Memphis, where he got his first GUITAR. After working odd jobs in the big city, he returned to Mississippi to attend Rust College on a choral scholarship, performing with the A Cappella Choir there. In 1966, after graduation, he returned to Memphis and worked as a deejay for a while, before enrolling in the air force at the end of the year. He appeared in several talent shows, where he was discovered by the owner of Memphis's Goldwax records, Quinton Claunch. His songs became popular among many Memphis-based soul artists, and in the early seventies he attracted the attention of Stax Records executive Al Bell, who signed McClinton to Stax's country label, Enterprise.

O.B.'s first hit was 1972's "Don't Let the Green Grass Fool You," followed by a cover of the MERLE HAGGARD classic "Okie from Muskogee" remade as "Obie from Senatobia." He had a 1974 hit with "Something Better," and, a year later after Stax folded, moved to several other labels before landing at Epic, where he was produced by Buddy Killen, who had discovered Joe Tex. O.B.'s Epic hits include the 1978 single "Hello, This is Anna." He moved to the smaller Sunbird label in the early eighties and then to the even smaller Moonshine label, for which he had a minor hit in 1984 with "Honky Tonk Tan," before being diagnosed with cancer. The disease took his life in 1987.

◀ McCOY, CHARLIE

(born 1941, Oak Ridge, WV)

McCoy is the best-known session harmonica player of the sixties and seventies; his style virtually defined how the instrument would be used on mainstream country releases.

Born in rural West Virginia, he began playing the harmonica at age eight and had some music training in his teen years as both a vocalist and arranger. In the late fifties, he began performing on both rock and country circuits as a backup artist. MEL TILLIS heard him playing at one local gig and introduced him to his Nashville agent, who brought the musician to the country capital, where he began working sessions, tours, and the GRAND OLE OPRY radio show. He gained a great deal of exposure working in country star STONEWALL JACKSON's touring band.

In the early sixties, McCoy began performing as a solo vocalist, without much success, although he did have a minor hit in 1961 with "Cherry Berry Wine" issued on the small Cadence label. He was much in demand as a studio musician through the sixties, impressing folk-rocker BOB DYLAN, who used him on his *Blonde on Blonde* and *Nashville Skyline* sessions. This led to work with other pop stars interested in the country sound, including Ringo Starr, Joan Baez, and ELVIS PRESLEY. He joined with the Nashville-based supergroup AREA CODE 615, and his harmonica playing was featured on their instrumental hit, "Stone Fox Chase."

In 1972 his solo recording of "Today I Started Loving You Again," originally recorded as an album track four years earlier, started getting airplay on country radio, and it was followed by a series of covers, including HANK WILLIAMS's "I'm So Lonesome I Could Cry" and the perennial BLUEGRASS fiddle-festival favorite, "Orange Blossom Special." He recorded "Boogie Woogie" with Barefoot Jerry in 1974, and in the early eighties he formed a performing partnership with Laney Hicks, which produced the minor hits "Until the Night" (1981) and "The State of Our Union" (1983). McCoy served as musical director for the country comedy show HEE HAW from 1977 through the early eighties.

Select Discography

The Fastest Harp in the South, Monument 44354. Reissue of sixties-era recordings.

◀ McDANIEL, MEL

(born 1942, Checotah, OK)

McDaniel is a country SINGER/SONGWRITER who had his biggest success in the early eighties with a number of pop-country hits.

The Oklahoma native took a while to establish himself, beginning as a fifties-era rocker and then relocating to Nashville. After failing to make a dent on the country scene he moved to Alaska, where he worked as a lounge singer, but finally returned to Nashville, where he performed in the Holiday Inn while pushing his songwriting career. His big break came in 1976 when his comic novelty "Roll Your Own" was covered by COMMANDER CODY AND HIS LOST PLANET AIRMEN, as well as by HOYT AXTON and ARLO GUTHRIE. This led to a contract with Capitol and a minor hit with a cover version of "Have a Dream on Me" in 1976, followed by a couple more minor successes through the late seventies.

In the early eighties, McDaniel's luck took a turn for the better. His 1981 releases, "Louisiana Saturday Night" and "Right in the Palm of Your Hand," were major successes, followed by a number of top-twenty hits through the mid-eighties. He was made a member of the GRAND OLE OPRY in 1986, but after that the hits dried up. He remains a performer on the second-string road circuit where old country stars may go on forever.

Select Discography
Greatest Hits, Liberty 46867. Reissues seventies Capitol-label recordings.

◀ McDONALD, SKEETS

(born Enos William McDonald, 1915, near Greenaway, AK; died 1968)

McDonald was an early cowboy star who is best remembered for his self-penned 1952 hit "Don't Let the Stars Get in Your Eyes."

Raised on a small farm, in 1932 he and his family moved to Michigan, where he formed his first band, the Lonesome Cowboys, a high-energy outfit specializing in a blend of country, pop, and jazz. They performed on Michigan radio through the early forties, until McDonald was drafted in the army in 1943. He revived the band in 1946 and made a couple of solo recordings, including the hanky soaker "Please Daddy Don't Go to War" in 1950. He was hired as lead singer for Michigan-based Johnny White and His Rhythm Riders soon after, returning to an up-tempo country-boogie sound with a couple of minor hits, including "Mean and Evil Blues" and "The Tattooed Lady." By 1952 he was living in Los Angeles and signed to Capitol, where he had his big hit with the schmaltzy "Stars."

By the mid-fifties, McDonald had jumped on the ROCKABILLY bandwagon, with some early recordings that are much prized among collectors of this genre of music, including "You Ought to See Grandma Rock and Roll." He was signed as a country act to Columbia in the early sixties, having minor hits in the mid-sixties with "Call Me Mr. Brown" and "You Took Her Off My Hands," both in the then-prevalent pop-country style. He died of a heart attack in 1968.

◀ McDOWELL, RONNIE

(born 1951, Portland, TN)

McDowell is a small-time country star who boosted his career by crooning over poor old ELVIS PRESLEY's bones with the 1977 hit WEEPER "The King Is Dead."

Raised on a farm, McDowell enlisted in the navy, where he had his first experience as a performer. In 1969, on his discharge, he formed his first band, the Nashville Road, which became popular on the bar circuit through the South. He struggled through the early seventies in search of a record contract, with little success. After the death of Elvis, McDowell was moved to write "The King Is Dead"; his demo tape of the song was picked up by tiny Scorpion Records, who rushed it out to cash in on the Elvis mania. He had a couple of follow-up hits on Scorpion and also provided Elvis sound-alike vocals for the 1979 ABC television documentary on the Memphis hip shaker.

His 1979 recording of his original composition "He's a Cowboy from Texas" announced a new countrified direction for his career, and he left Scorpion soon after it charted for Epic, where he quickly produced another self-penned hit, "World's Most Perfect Woman." He hooked up with soulful producer Buddy Killen, and the duo cowrote "Lovin' and Livin'," his first hit of 1980. In 1981 he had two hits with songs written by young songwriter Jamie O'Hara (later of the O'KANES), and he followed these with the 1983 tongue-in-cheek number-one hit "You're Gonna Ruin My Bad Reputation." The hits slowed up in the mid-eighties, and by 1987 he had moved to the Curb label, where he had his last hit, a remake of CONWAY TWITTY's "It's Only Make Believe." Since then, McDowell has taken his Elvis show on the road, reverting to lip-curlin' imitations of the King.

Select Discography

Older Women and Other Greatest Hits, Epic 40643. Early-eighties recordings, including his best-known hits.

The Best of Ronnie McDowell, Curb 77254. Late-eighties and early-nineties recordings.

◀ McENERY, RED RIVER DAVE

(born 1914, San Antonio, TX)

McEnery rode the COWBOY-SONG wave in the thirties to become a permanent fixture in country music circles, best known for his story songs based on people in the news.

After performing through the South on a variety of small radio stations, McEnery hit it big when he hooked up with New York City's WHN in 1938, where he remained for three years. Before returning to his native Texas, he released his recording of "Amelia Earhart's Last Flight" in 1941, the first in a long string of topical songs based on current events. After returning to San Antonio, Dave began performing on a string of the Tex-Mex border stations; these unregulated stations could be picked up throughout much of the United States, further spreading his fame. After the war, he appeared in a couple of C-grade Westerns, including 1948's *Swing in the Saddle*.

Dave's career went into an eclipse in the fifties, but he came back with a vengeance in the early sixties with "The Ballad of Francis Gary Powers," recounting the story of the shooting down of the famous U-2 pilot over Russia. He followed this with such perishable topical numbers as "The Flight of Apollo Eleven" and even "The Ballad of Patty Hearst." In his later years, Dave was more of a personality than a performer, well-known for his long white hair and pointy goatee, gold-colored boots, and glittering, Nudie-style cowboy duds.

◀ McENTIRE, REBA

(born 1955 near Kiowa, OK)

This ropin'-and-ridin' sweetheart began her career very much in a NEW-COUNTRY/cowgirl mold but has since veered increasingly—and very successfully—into being the ultimate country diva and an industry power broker.

McEntire comes from an authentic rodeo family; her grandfather was a celebrity on the national rodeo circuit, and her father a talented roper. Her brother, Pake, and two sisters, Alice and Susie, all performed in rodeos, as did young Reba, and the four formed a family singing group, scoring a local hit in 1971 with a ballad memorializing their grandfather, "The Ballad of John McEntire." Country star RED

STEAGALL heard Reba belt out the national anthem at the National Rodeo Finals in Oklahoma City in 1974 and invited her to come to Nashville to make a demo. Reba, her mother, and brother Pake all ended up in Music City, and both brother and sister made their first albums in late 1975.

Reba's first recordings were in a traditional style, and although they forecast the new country trends of the next decade, they failed to find much chart action. Meanwhile, she married bulldogger (champion steer wrestler) Charlie Battles and got her teaching certificate just in case her singing career failed to take off. In the late seventies and early eighties she finally began to see some chart action, covering PATSY CLINE's "Sweet Dreams" and "A Poor Man's Roses." Her first number-one record came in 1983 with "Can't Even Get the Blues." McEntire's producer insisted she record the song, although she resisted cutting yet another ballad, preferring to try some more up-tempo material.

But it was as a balladeer that Reba reached her greatest popularity in the mid-eighties. Her highly emotional, charged vocals were perfectly suited to the often melodramatic material she recorded. She did, however, maintain a country-influenced technique, using bends, twirls, trills, and even a slight yodel—all found in traditional mountain singing—to give her vocals added depth and authenticity. Meanwhile, her image was constantly being pushed upscale by her handlers, who were steering her in the direction of becoming a Vegas-style diva.

In 1987 McEntire divorced her first husband and two years later wed her steel guitarist/road manager, Narvel Blackstock. The duo began building McEntire's empire, taking over the responsibility of managing and booking her act, working with the record company and producers to shape her image, and even becoming involved in the nuts and bolts of song publishing and transporting equipment for tours. Although McEntire took a more active hand in her career, there was not much change in the music that she produced; she continued to turn out finely crafted pop ballads, with the occasional more spirited number thrown in for variety. She also began to pursue an acting career, landing some minor roles in TV miniseries and movies, but her best acting remained in her videos, in which she continued to project a feisty, if down-home and loveable, personality.

Select Discography
Greatest Hits, MCA 5979. The hits through 1987.
Whoever's in New England, MCA 31304. One of her better eighties-era recordings.
The Best of Reba McEntire, Mercury 824342. Latter-day recordings.

◀ McEUEN, JOHN

(born 1945, Long Beach, CA)

McEuen was a founding member of the folk-rock country group the NITTY GRITTY DIRT BAND, and he has since had some success as a solo artist.

Growing up in suburban Long Beach, John was first exposed to rock and roll and R&B via his older brother Bill, who was a local deejay and concert promoter. While still in high school, John formed a folk band with a couple of friends, originally taking the name the Illegitimate Jug Band (because they didn't have a jug player). This group evolved into the Nitty Gritty Dirt Band, and brother Bill soon became their manager. McEuen primarily played BLUEGRASS-style BANJO in the group, although he also played GUITAR, MANDOLIN, and sometimes even fiddle.

After leaving the Dirt Band in the late eighties, McEuen signed as a solo artist to Vanguard Records. He has produced a couple of solo albums in a style that melds bluegrass with Irish traditional music, old-time country, and jazz, similar to other performers working in the PROGRESSIVE BLUEGRASS/newgrass styles, such as TONY TRISCHKA. He also produced and hosted a special on the music of the Old West for TNN.

Select Discography

String Wizards, Vanguard 79462. His first 1991 solo album, with contributions by VASSAR CLEMENTS, BYRON BERLINE, JERRY DOUGLAS, and Earl Scruggs.

◀ McGEE, SAM

(born 1894, Franklin, TN; died 1975)

Sam McGee was a country guitarist with blues influences who worked for many years with his brother, Kirk, and as an accompanist for UNCLE DAVE MACON and FIDDLIN' ARTHUR SMITH.

McGee came from a musical farming family; his father was a fiddler and the McGee boys were playing music early on in the family band. Both Sam and Kirk also remember being greatly influenced by the playing of local black musicians; Sam said that the sound of traditional blues would "just ring in my head." The brothers were discovered by Uncle Dave Macon in 1924; Sam was thirty years old at the time and working as a blacksmith. Soon, the two brothers were touring with the flamboyant banjoist, with Sam playing GUITAR and Kirk playing fiddle. They became members of the GRAND OLE OPRY in 1926 and at that time made their first solo recordings, including Sam's unusual finger-picked guitar instrumental, "Franklin Blues," showing the influence of black blues guitarists. Macon and the McGees were joined by fiddler Mazy Todd, and for a 1927 recording session the quartet billed themselves as the Fruit Jar Drinkers and recorded some of the most high-spirited string-band music of the era.

Although both McGees would continue to perform with Uncle Dave through the thirties, they also hooked up with a more modern performer, Fiddlin' Arthur Smith, early in the decade to form the Dixieliners. Kirk switched to BANJO in this group, which featured both Smith's more modern, jazz-influenced fiddling and his smooth vocals. The group disbanded by the decade's end but would reunite in the sixties to record and perform at folk festivals.

In the forties, the McGee Brothers hooked up with BILL MONROE's new band, the Blue Grass Boys, joining Monroe's traveling tent shows. During the fifties, they continued to perform on the Opry, often as members of a revived Fruit Jar Drinkers featuring various other Opry old-timers. The sixties FOLK REVIVAL brought them an entirely new audience of young, urban pickers; MIKE SEEGER produced two albums of the McGees with Arthur Smith as well as a solo album by Sam in the early seventies.

Sam McGee continued to perform on the Opry until his death in a farming accident in 1975. At that time, his brother Kirk also retired from playing for the most part. All in all, they had nearly fifty years of Opry membership and were among the last early cast members to still perform on the program.

McGee's unique guitar style influenced a generation of pickers. His syncopated instrumentals, including the oft-copied "Buck Dancer's Choice," became test pieces for any would-be finger picker. The McGees brought an authentic appreciation for syncopated music into the country repertoire and were a key link between black and white country traditions.

Select Discography

Fiddlin' Arthur Smith and His Dixieliners, Vols 1 and 2, Country 546/547. Two out-of-print LPs reissuing thirties recordings by Smith and the McGees.

McGee Brothers and Arthur Smith, Folkways 2379. Early-sixties recordings of the reunited trio, made by Mike Seeger.

Milk 'Em in the Evening Blues, Folkways 31007. Late-sixties recordings by the brothers with Smith.

◀ MILLER, BOB

(born 1895, Memphis, TN; died 1955)

Miller was a country songwriter and record producer who began his career producing topical material that was covered by many early country artists.

Raised in Memphis, a melting pot of black jazz and blues and white country music, Miller got his first job as a pianist working on a riverboat on the Mississippi. This led to an early career in jazz and pop music as a conductor, arranger, and music publisher. He joined the staff of Irving Berlin's publishing company in New York in 1928 and soon after founded his own Bob Miller music company, becoming a major force in New York's Tin Pan Alley.

In 1931 producer ART SATHERLEY hired Miller to work with him for the American Recording Company (ARC) label. ARC specialized in producing material for catalogs like Montgomery Ward and Sears, Roebuck, along with various discount labels sold through dime stores. As such, they had a vibrant line of "hillbilly" recording artists, including VERNON DALHART and CARSON ROBINSON. Miller began writing material for them, ranging from topical laments like "Eleven Cent Cotton, Forty Cent Meat" (focusing on the squeeze that farmers felt in trying to make a living) to more sentimental numbers like "Rockin' Alone (In an Old Rockin' Chair)." In the mid-forties, he produced his biggest hit, the patriotic "There's a Star Spangled Banner Waving Somewhere," a major hit for ELTON BRITT.

In the postwar years, Miller spent most of his time administering his various copyrights and living off royalties from his songs, until his death in 1955.

◀ MILLER, JODY

(born 1941, Phoenix, AZ)

Jody Miller is a minor-league country artist who began her career in folk-pop, had a fluke crossover hit in the mid-sixties and became a mainstream country artist in the seventies.

The daughter of an old-time fiddler, Miller was born in Arizona but raised in Oklahoma, where she developed an early love of horseback riding. She formed a pop vocal trio while still in high school, and after graduation she headed for California in search of a career. However, soon after, she broke her neck in a riding accident and returned home to recuperate. It was during this period of recovery that she began performing on the local coffeehouse circuit. She befriended folksinger/songwriter Tom Paxton, appearing on his syndicated television program, along with actor Dale Robertson, who gave her demo tape to Capitol. The label signed her as a young "folk singer" in 1963.

Two years later, Miller had a fluke pop and country hit with her cover of Mary Taylor's "Queen of the House," a pre–women's liberation answer song to ROGER MILLER's famous "King of the Road." This led to several albums of country covers, but Miller was unable to duplicate her initial hit and was dropped by the label in 1968.

Miller dropped out of the music industry for two years but then returned to performing when she was signed to Epic in 1970, working with legendary COUNTRYPOLITAN producer BILLY SHERRILL. He provided her with a hit straight out of the gate, "Look at Mine," and followed it with other sprightly hits through 1972. Miller also recorded a duet with JOHNNY PAYCHECK, "Let's All Go Down the River," which was a moderate hit in 1972.

Miller continued to record through the seventies for smaller labels, achieving less success as her perky style began to wear thin. She still occasionally performs, although she has more or less retired to pursue horse farming in her native Oklahoma.

◀ MILLER, ROGER

(born 1936, Fort Worth, TX; died 1992)

Roger Miller was a fine SINGER/SONGWRITER best known for his string of mid-sixties pop and country hits, including the novelty songs "Dang Me" and "Chug-a-Lug" and the classic trucker's anthem, "King of the Road."

Although born in a city, Miller grew up in tiny Erick, Oklahoma. His father died when he was an infant, and Miller was raised by his aunt and uncle, who had a small cotton-and-chicken farm there. Like many other future country stars, Miller was exposed to the music through the radio. His in-law, country comic SHEB WOOLEY, also encouraged him to perform.

After completing the eighth grade, Miller worked as a ranch hand and small-time rodeo star for several years before enlisting in the army during the Korean war. By this time, he was an adept guitarist and could play the fiddle, BANJO, piano, and drums as well. After the war, while stationed in South Carolina, Miller served with a sergeant whose brother was Jethro of the famous HOMER AND JETHRO comedy act. He encouraged Miller to go to Nashville and arranged for an audition for him at RCA Records. Although Miller's initial audition was not successful, he did eventually get session and band work, playing the fiddle for comedian MINNIE PEARL and joining FARON YOUNG's backup band as a drummer.

In the late fifties, Miller began achieving success as a songwriter, first with "Invitation to the Blues," covered by both RAY PRICE (with whom Miller played as a backup musician) and later pop singer Patti Page. Further hits included "Half a Mind" for ERNEST TUBB and "Billy Bayou" for JIM REEVES. Miller had his first hit as a performer with 1961's "When Two Worlds Collide," which he cowrote with BILL ANDERSON.

Miller was still frustrated, however, with Nashville's failure to take him seriously as a solo act, so in 1963 he relocated to Hollywood, where he signed with the MGM subsidiary, Smash Records. It was at this label that he had his biggest success, including his first two novelty songs, 1964's "Chug-a-Lug" and the perennial favorite "Dang Me." His most productive year was 1965, which saw, besides the monster hit "King of the Road," "Engine Engine No. 9" and "Kansas City Star." Smash, a label more oriented toward the pop scene than country, successfully marketed Miller as a pop star, and, oddly enough, his songs reached number one on the pop charts but only settled in the top ten on the country listings. In 1966, mellow-voiced Andy Williams had a big hit with Miller's "In the Summertime," leading him to invite the country performer to appear on his high-rated television show.

Miller was a talented comic vocalist whose gentle twang betrayed his country roots but whose vocal styles were subdued enough to win a mainstream audience. Although Nashville executives found his voice "unusual," it was the perfect vehicle for expressing his often ironic, slightly skewed vision of the world. His success as a crossover artist on the pop charts was mainly thanks to his easygoing vocals and amusing songs. And, unlike other acts who were buried by the NASHVILLE SOUND of the sixties, Miller's best records were made in Hollywood and had the same stripped-down sound favored by BUCK OWENS and other California country stars.

Miller's career from the late sixties through the mid-eighties was spotty at best. He mostly lived off of his big hits, while he continued to record erratically. His big comeback came in the mid-eighties with the Broadway hit, *Big River*, a musical based on Mark Twain's *Huckleberry Finn*, which he scored. Miller's good-humored countryesque songs were a perfect fit for this informal musical, and his success on the Broadway stage brought renewed interest in his country-music career. Sadly, Miller died soon after, although his classic recordings continue to sell into the nineties.

Select Discography
The Best of Roger Miller, Vols. 1 and 2, Mercury 848977/512646. His Smash label recordings of the sixties, with the first volume focusing more on country styles and the second on his pop hits, including "King of the Road."

◀ MILSAP, RONNIE

(born 1944, Robbinsville, NC)

Milsap is a pop country singer who was most popular from the late seventies through the mid-eighties. With a voice similar in timbre to James Taylor's, Milsap's performances share with the pop singer a similar sugarcoated romanticism.

Blind from birth, Milsap was a musical prodigy, proficient on several instruments by the time he was ten years old. In high school, he formed his first rock group, and, after an abortive attempt at college, decided to pursue music-making full time. He performed with blues rocker J. J. Cale before going out on his own, recording his first singles for the Sceptre label in an R&B style. Through the sixties, Milsap toured and performed with other R&B performers.

In 1969 he settled in Nashville and began writing and performing in a mainstream country style. Although he had some minor hits, his career didn't really take off until he signed with RCA in 1973. His recordings were given the standard-for-the-day COUNTRYPOLITAN production, making them immediately popular not only on the country but also the mainstream pop charts. From 1975's "Day Dreams About Night Things," Milsap scored chartbusters through the mid-eighties, primarily recording smooth ballads. Perhaps his biggest crossover pop/country hits were 1981's "(There's) No Gettin' Over Me" and "I Wouldn't Have Missed it For the World," and his 1982 remake of Chuck Jackson's 1962 hit, "Any Day Now." His stage act became increasingly glitzy, and he became a fixture on country and pop television shows.

Milsap's career pretty much petered out when the NEW-COUNTRY movement made his brand of sentimental love songs sound increasingly passé, although he continues to be a strong concert draw.

Select Discography

Greatest Hits, Vols. 1–3, RCA 8504/75425/66048. The first two volumes take you through 1985, by which time most of the hits had occurred.

◀ MONROE, BILL

(born 1911, Rosine, KY)

Justifiably known as the "Father of BLUEGRASS Music," mandolinist Bill Monroe has been a member of the GRAND OLE OPRY since 1939 and a highly influential composer, vocalist, and instrumentalist.

Monroe was the youngest in a family of farmers and musicians: Elder brother CHARLIE MONROE played GUITAR and Birch the fiddle. The family farmed 655 acres of prime Kentucky land, and Bill was raised working the land. Because he was the youngest by a wide gap (Charlie, the next in line, was eight years older), and also because of poor eyesight, Monroe grew up a shy loner who sought refuge in his music. He has often cited two important musical influences from his youth. One was his mother's brother, known as "Uncle Pen" (Pendleton Vandiver), who was a champion fiddler. Young Monroe often accompanied him to play at local dances, and absorbed his repertoire of traditional fiddle tunes. The second influence was black blues guitarist Arnold Shultz; although unrecorded, Monroe claims that Shultz was a fine interpreter of the blues, and it's undoubtedly from him that he picked up his own blue and lonesome sound. Young Monroe also heard recordings of traditional country performers, including JIMMIE RODGERS and CHARLIE POOLE.

Charlie and Birch left home searching for employment in the North in the mid-twenties, settling in East Chicago, Indiana. Bill joined them there when he was eighteen years old, staying for five years. They worked in the local oil refineries by day while playing music at nights and on weekends. In 1934 Chicago radio station WLS offered them full-time employment. Birch quit the group, but Charlie and Bill continued as the Monroe Brothers. They relocated to the Carolinas in 1935, performing on radio out of Greenville and Charlotte sponsored by Texas Crystals, a popular if somewhat dubious over-the-counter home remedy.

In 1936 Bluebird Records (a division of RCA Victor) made the brothers' first recordings. Although these were in the style of the popular brother duets of the era, one could already hear the difference in Bill's intense singing and lightning-fast MANDOLIN playing. They recorded traditional songs and hymns, including their first hit, "What Would You Give (in Exchange for Your Soul)." Their recording of the folk standard "Nine Pound Hammer (Roll on Buddy)" was widely imitated and shows how they could take a traditional song and modernize and energize it. Charlie's laconic delivery was a good foil for his brother's highly charged tenor vocals, and their records and radio appearances were very successful.

The brothers split up in 1938, with Bill relocating to Arkansas and forming his first band, the Kentuckians. He was then hired by an Atlanta station, forming his first group, known as the Blue Grass Boys. In 1939 he auditioned for legendary *Grand Ole Opry* announcer GEORGE D. HAY, who hired him on the spot; Monroe's first performance on the Opry was of the Jimmie Rodgers classic "Mule Skinner Blues," which he made his own.

In the early forties, Monroe was still searching for a sound. He hired BANJO player Dave Akeman (aka STRINGBEAN) primarily to provide comic relief for his stage act; the banjo is barely heard on the group's recordings. He also hired fiddler Chubby Wise and accordionist Sally Ann Forrester (fiddler Howdy Forrester's wife); Monroe's mother had played the accordion, and it was a popular instrument in WESTERN SWING bands of the day. Monroe's early Blue Grass Boys was a swinging outfit, although still rooted deeply in country sounds.

In 1945 and 1946, Monroe's greatest band was assembled, featuring Wise on fiddle, Lester Flatt on guitar and lead vocals, Earl Scruggs on banjo, and Cedric Rainwater (born Harold Watts) on bass and vocals. This lineup would become the classic bluegrass ensemble. The group recorded some of Monroe's first compositions, including the classic "Blue Moon of Kentucky" and "Will You Be Loving Another Man?" They also recorded fine instrumentals, with "Bluegrass Breakdown" introducing Earl Scruggs's new banjo style, the model for all bluegrass banjo playing to come. The group also recorded as a gospel quartet, with Scruggs taking the bass vocal part and playing guitar, on some absolutely stunning country gospel numbers that combined the modern sound of bluegrass with the ancient modalities of SHAPE-NOTE SINGING. Flatt's laconic lead vocals (like Charlie Monroe's before him) were a perfect foil to Monroe's intense high tenor, and the band had the power of twice to three times the number of pieces. Their Columbia recordings made between 1946 and 1948 along with their appearances on the Opry and on the road made them legends in their own time.

FLATT AND SCRUGGS left the band to form their own group in 1948, and Monroe would never again feature the banjo as prominently as he did before, perhaps an indication that he realized Scruggs could not be replaced, perhaps out of anger with his sidemen who had deserted him. In the early fifties, he signed on lead guitarist/vocalist JIMMIE MARTIN, along with a number of different banjo players, including young SONNY OSBORNE, and fiddlers VASSAR CLEMENTS and Buddy Spicher. He composed a series of high-powered instrumentals featuring his mandolin playing, including "Rawhide" and "Roanoke." He also composed an homage to his fiddling uncle, "Uncle Pen," which has become a bluegrass standard. By the middle to late fifties, Monroe was experimenting with a twin-fiddle sound, composing the instrumental "Scotland" using one fiddle as a drone to try to capture the modal sound of the traditional music that was at the roots of his Appalachian heritage (the original recording featured fiddlers Kenny Baker and Bobby Hicks).

In the early sixties, Monroe linked up with Ralph Rinzler, a young mandolinist who became his connection to the FOLK-REVIVAL world. Rinzler encouraged Monroe's label, Decca, to reissue his fifties recordings on LP (many had previously been available only on hard-to-find 45s), giving them the careful annotation that they deserved; he also acted as Monroe's agent, booking him into many prestigious folk festivals. Most importantly, Rinzler introduced Monroe to younger musicians, who were invited to join his band, including fiddler RICHARD GREENE, innovative banjoist BILL KEITH, and SINGER/SONGWRITER PETER ROWAN, with whom Monroe wrote "The Walls of Time." Keith was particularly important; his melodic banjo playing, in which single notes were picked with no chord accompaniments, was prominently featured on Monroe's instrumental recordings, including his famous rendition of "Sailor's Hornpipe." This was the first time since Scruggs was in the band that Monroe had featured the banjo; typically, he refused to call the younger picker "Bill" (there was only room for one Bill in his band), so he nicknamed him Brad, after Keith's middle name, Bradford.

By the late sixties and early seventies, Monroe was an established legend in the bluegrass and country worlds. Fiddler Kenny Baker, who had originally played with Monroe in the late fifties and early sixties, became a fixture in the band from 1967 through the early eighties, and his sympathy for traditional fiddle styles, along with a more modern swing, made him the perfect fiddler for Monroe's band. Son James Monroe, born in 1941, was often featured in the band on bass and vocals, although he also formed his own group, the Midnight Ramblers. New-country star RICKY SKAGGS, who got his start in bluegrass, did much to revive Monroe's songs for a new audience, as well as featuring the older picker in his music video for "Country Boy" and on his recordings. While Monroe had more recognition thanks to the bluegrass revival, his bands became less innovative, and, particularly in the eighties and nineties as he got older, his playing became less energized and his singing flatter. Still, Monroe remains one of the legends of the music, who will probably perform up to the day he dies.

Monroe's contribution to bluegrass music is so great it is difficult to summarize: He formed the first great bluegrass band, which became a model for all others; his mandolin playing includes melody picking with a chopping chord style that produces accompaniment helping to propel the beat forward; he possesses a distinctive high-tenor voice, immediately recognizable on his recordings, and which may explain why he tends to pitch his music up a key or two (giving it a brighter sound); and his compositions, both instrumental and vocal, have become the standards both as tests for young pickers and as the backbone of the bluegrass repertoire.

Select Discography

Feast Here Tonight, RCA 5510. Out-of-print two-LP set reissue of the great Monroe Brothers recordings cut for Bluebird in the thirties.

Bill Monroe and His Blue Grass Boys, County 104, 105. Late-forties recordings with Flatt and Scruggs.

In the Pines, Rebel Canada 853. Decca recordings from the early fifties, when Monroe was at the height of his powers.

Off the Record, 1945–1969, Smithsonian/Folkways 40063. Live tracks lovingly assembled by Monroe protégé/manager Ralph Rinzler.

Live Duet Recordings, 1963–1980, Smithsonian/Folkways 40064. Monroe had a special relationship with blind guitarist DOC WATSON, who performed with him several times over the year to recreate the classic Monroe Brothers sound.

1945–1949, Columbia 52478. All of his Columbia sides, although some are alternate takes, featuring Flatt and Scruggs.

1950–1958, Bear Family 15423. Four CDs reissuing everything Monroe recorded for Decca in this era, with notes by Charles Wolfe and Neil Rosenberg.

1959–1969, Bear Family 15529. All of his Decca recordings, including Bill Keith and Peter Rowan.

1970–1979, Bear Family 15606. All of his MCA recordings from this era, including the classic sessions that produced the *Uncle Pen* album.

Music of Bill Monroe, MCA 11048. Four-CD set with 98 songs, mostly from his Decca/MCA recordings of 1950–1994, with a wonderful illustrated booklet.

◀ MONROE, CHARLIE

(born 1903, Rosine, KY; died 1975)

Elder brother of BILL MONROE and one-half of the Monroe Brothers duo, Charlie went on to have a minor career leading older-style bands through the late fifties.

A more low-keyed guitarist and singer than his very highly energized brother, Charlie split from Bill in 1938, leading first a trio known as the Monroe Boys and then a band called the Kentucky Pardners. Alumni of his band include many well-known names in BLUEGRASS and country music, including Lester Flatt (who was hired away by his brother, Bill), Ira Louvin of the LOUVIN BROTHERS, and fiddler

Curly Sechler. The band recorded for Victor from the mid-forties through early fifties when they switched to Decca, also home to brother Bill.

Charlie ended the band in 1957, although he continued to make personal appearances and a few recordings into the early sixties for the small Rem label. After a decade of working for Otis Elevator and Howard Johnson's in Indiana and Tennessee, he was lured out of retirement by JIMMY MARTIN in 1972 to perform at a bluegrass festival. For the following three years until his death, Monroe returned to performing primarily on the festival circuit.

◀ MONTANA, PATSY

(born Rubye Blevins, 1914, Hot Springs, AK)

The first female country vocalist to have a million-seller, Montana lay the groundwork for women to enter country music in a big way after World War II.

A talented fiddler, vocalist, and yodeler, Montana originally partnered JIMMIE DAVIS in the early thirties before joining the Prairie Ramblers, a four-piece Western band featured on Chicago's WLS *Barn Dance* program, the main rival to the famous WSM GRAND OLE OPRY. Their 1935 recording of "I Wanna Be a Cowboy's Sweetheart" was Montana's million-selling breakthrough, setting the stage for a series of Western-themed novelty numbers (including a nod to big-band sounds on "Swing Time Cowgirl"). She remained with the Ramblers through 1941, recording sporadically through the forties as a soloist and appearing on radio, on the ABC network program *Wake Up and Smile*, right after World War II. She retired in the fifties and returned to occasional performing in the seventies.

Montana's gutsy, powerful lead vocals and strident YODELING flew in the face of the stereotype that women should be demure and limit their activities to the kitchen. Recording executives may have feared that featuring a female in a country band or as a soloist would offend listeners, who were basically conservative. Montana's big hit had her asserting that she wanted to "rope and ride" just like her cowboy sweetheart, so it was as assertive in its message as its delivery. Her success paved the way for other big-throated women, particularly fifties stars KITTY WELLS and PATSY CLINE.

Select Discography

The Cowboy's Sweetheart, Flying Fish 90459. Cassette-only reissue of seventies-era recordings.

◀ MONTGOMERY, MELBA

(born 1938, Iron City, TN)

Montgomery is best known as a duet partner for other country artists, including GEORGE JONES and Charlie Louvin (of the LOUVIN BROTHERS).

Born in Tennessee but raised in rural Alabama, Montgomery was introduced to music as a young girl by her father, who taught singing at her home town's Methodist church, and played fiddle and GUITAR at local parties. Along with her brothers, she formed a family harmony band, performing at fairs, talent contests, and local charity events.

In the late fifties, Montgomery relocated to Nashville in search of a singing career and won a 1958 talent contest sponsored by WSM, the home station of the GRAND OLE OPRY. One of the judges was ROY ACUFF, who added her to his road show. In 1962 she broke with Acuff and a year later was linked with George Jones for a series of successful duets, beginning with "We Must Have Been Out of Our Minds" and followed in 1964 by "Let's Invite Them Over." She continued to record and perform with Jones until 1967, although she also made solo recordings with some success, including 1963's "Hall of Shame," as well as duets with other pop and country stars, including Gene Pitney in 1966.

In the early seventies, Montgomery moved to Capitol Records, where she was paired with producer PETE DRAKE and singing partner Charlie Louvin. When Drake was invited to start a country division for the folk/rock label Elektra in 1973, he took Montgomery with him, and she scored her biggest solo hits under his hand, including the 1974 number-one cover of HARLAN HOWARD's "No Change," a drippy sentimental recitation record. By 1977 the hits had dried up, but Montgomery continued to record for smaller labels into the early eighties, scoring only sporadic success. She reunited with Louvin for some lackluster recordings in the early nineties.

Montgomery is the ideal partner for a stronger, male vocalist; her solo recordings, however, lack enough power and presence to make them memorable.

Select Discography

Do You Know Where Your Man Is? Playback 4508. 1992 recordings cut with Charlie Louvin.

◀ MOODY, CLYDE

(born 1915, Cherokee, NC)

Moody, a vocalist best known for his work with the original Blue Grass Boys under BILL MONROE, gained popularity after World War II as a sentimental country crooner.

Moody got his start when he was twenty-one performing with country bandleader J. E. MAINER, with whom he performed from 1936 to about 1938. He then performed with a more modern radio outfit, the Happy-Go-Lucky Boys with singer Jay Hugh Hall, before joining with Bill Monroe to handle lead vocal chores with the first incarnation of the Blue Grass Boys in the early forties. Moody contributed the fiddle ballad "Six White Horses" to Monroe's repertoire but left the band to work briefly with GRAND OLE OPRY star ROY ACUFF before striking out on his own. He scored hits with the fledgling King label, beginning with "Shenandoah Waltz," literally dripping with sentimental goo, followed by similar tearful numbers, including "Carolina Waltz," "Next Sunday Darling Is My Birthday" (later covered by the STANLEY BROTHERS), and "I Know What It Means to Be Lonesome." He spent the late forties through early fifties in the Washington, D.C., area before returning to his native North Carolina, where he continues to perform and record occasionally.

Moody's repertoire has changed little since his hit-making days of the forties, and a little of his crooning goes a long way. Still, he remains an entertaining performer.

Select Discography
White House Blues, Rebel 1672. Recent recordings by this country stalwart.

◀ MOONSHINE KATE

(born Rosa Lee Carson, 1909, Atlanta, GA)

BANJO and GUITAR player Rosa Lee "Moonshine Kate" Carson is best known as the accompanist to her father, FIDDLIN' JOHN CARSON. Serving as a foil to her father on a number of classic country-comedy recordings, Kate established the character of the sassy, wise-cracking mountain woman who could hold her own against her lazy, heavy-drinking father, setting the stage for the next generation of female country comics. Additionally, Kate made some excellent solo recordings from 1924 to 1935, with her slow, drawling, blues-influenced vocals anticipating the HONKY-TONK gals of the fifties. Her best-known recording was of the topical ballad "Little Mary Phagan," which retold the story of the 1913 murder of an innocent factory girl, supposedly at the hands of her employer, Leo Frank. She also recorded the melodramatic "heart songs" that were a favorite part of many singers' repertoires, including "The Poor Girl's Story" and "The Lone Child." She even covered JIMMIE RODGER's "T for Texas," complete with YODELING and fancy guitar licks, forecasting the popularity of the yodeling cowgirls of the mid-thirties and forties.

Select Discography
The Old Hen Cackled, Rounder 1003. Recordings cut with her father.

◀ MORGAN, GEORGE

(born 1925, Waverly, TN; died 1975)

Morgan was a smooth-voiced country crooner and songwriter in the EDDY ARNOLD style who had his greatest successes in the late forties.

Morgan spent his high-school years in rural Ohio. On completing his schooling, he worked part-time as a performer while holding day jobs in truck driving and sales. After World War II, he was hired as a regular vocalist on Wheeling, West Virginia's WWVA *Jamboree* radio program, which won him the attention of Columbia Records. In 1947 they released his first recording, his self-penned schmaltz classic, "Candy Kisses," which raced to number one. He became a member of the GRAND OLE OPRY in 1949 and had a few lesser follow-up hits with the equally sentimental "Rainbow in My Heart," "Room Full of Roses," and "Cry-Baby Heart."

Although he continued to be popular on radio and in personal appearances, Morgan never equaled his early hit-making days. By the mid-sixties, Columbia had dropped him, and he moved to Starday, where his recordings suffered from the day's pop-style accompaniments. By the early seventies, he was moving from label to label, scoring a minor hit with 1973's "Red Rose from the Blue Side of Town" on MCA. In 1975, while working on the roof of his house, he suffered a heart attack and died soon after.

His daughter, LORRIE MORGAN, who performed with her father from her early years on the Opry, is now a successful NEW-COUNTRY balladeer.

Select Discography
American Originals, Columbia 45076. Budget-priced anthology of his best recordings cut between 1949 and 1963.

◀ MORGAN, LORRIE

(born Loretta Lynn Morgan, 1959, Nashville, TN)

Blond bombshell Morgan is a true daughter of Nashville (her father was country crooner GEORGE MORGAN), whose trials and tribulations in life are themselves the stuff of country music legend. A belter of big-throated ballads and jumpy up-tempo numbers, Morgan is in danger of becoming the kind of glitzy lounge singer who ends up performing in Vegas.

A tumultuous adolescence led quickly to a singing career, first as a backup singer for GEORGE JONES's traveling company. She briefly married Ron Gaddis, who played steel guitar for Jones, and the two had a daughter in 1979. She found life on the road with the hard-drinkin', high-livin' Jones tough and temporarily retired from performing. In 1984 she joined the GRAND OLE OPRY, where she had sung as a child, and in 1987 she met NEW-COUNTRY singer KEITH WHITLEY, who was to become her second husband. Whitley was a heavy drinker, and he died of alcohol poisoning two years later. Ironically, his death propelled Morgan to country stardom; her WEEPER "Dear Me," which in retrospect seemed to reflect her own turbulent life," became a hit shortly after. She has become a consistent hit maker in the early nineties.

While Morgan's close-cropped bleached hair and aggressive performance style align her with the more progressive elements in new country, her repertoire is pretty much standard country fare. Although the lyrics to the snappy "Watch Me" tell of a brassy girl who is quite prepared to leave her two-timing boyfriend, the video for the song ends with Morgan melting in the arms of the snake. Her biggest hit is the lushly romantic "Something in Red," the kind of classic chanteuse number that plants her squarely in the tradition of middle-of-the-road country queens like PATSY CLINE. And although Morgan prefers leather to gingham skirts, she sells a traditional Nashville feminity for a new generation of good ol' boys.

Select Discography
Something in Red, RCA 3021. 1991 album featuring the title ballad.
Watch Me, RCA 66047. 1992 album with the title hit, featuring more ballads and up-tempo numbers produced in a glitzy style.

◀ MORRIS, GARY

(born 1948, Fort Worth, TX)

Morris was a hunky country star of the early eighties who has also had success as a stage and television actor.

Classically trained as an opera singer, Morris got his musical start in the church choir before forming a pop-country trio in high school. After graduation, the threesome successfully auditioned for a job in a Denver country music club, where they performed for several years. Morris returned to Texas in the early seventies, where he hooked up with pop tunesmith Lawton Williams (he wrote Bobby Helms's hit "Fraulein"), who actively promoted the singer's career. Williams was active in the presidential campaign of Jimmy Carter and arranged for the singer to perform at Carter rallies; this led to a performance at the White House in 1978, followed by some demo recordings for MCA, and finally a contract with Warner Brothers in 1980 under the hands of producer Norro Wilson.

Morris's greatest success came in the early eighties, beginning with 1981's COUNTRYPOLITAN ditty "Headed for a Heartache," through 1983's "Velvet Chains," and then a string of number-one country hits beginning with "Baby Bye Bye" in 1985 and its follow-up, the R&B-flavored "I'll Never Stop Loving You." In 1984 Morris appeared off-Broadway costarring with LINDA RONSTADT in an updated version of Puccini's *La Bohème*. He asked Ronstadt to record "Makin' Up for Lost Time," a song he cowrote with Dave Loggins, as a duet with him, but since she was signed to another label, the record was eventually made with his labelmate CRYSTAL GAYLE, producing a 1986 number-one hit. Although Gayle had recorded her part separately from Morris and had never met the singer, the success of this song led to them recording an entire album of duets a year later.

Morris's TV career blossomed in 1986 when he was hired to portray a blind country singer in several episodes of ABC's soap-sudsy *Dynasty II: The Colbys*; he premiered on the show his last number-one single, 1987's "Leave Me Lonely" from his album *Plain Brown Wrapper*, a more simplified, roots-oriented effort than his earlier Nashville-pop work. Later that year, he appeared in the Broadway production of *Les Miserables*. Although he continues to perform on the GRAND OLE OPRY and to record and tour, his country recording career fizzled out in the late eighties.

Select Discography
Plain Brown Wrapper, Warner Bros. 25438.

◀ MULESKINNER

(1973: David Grissman [mandolin, vocals]; Peter Rowan [guitar, vocals];
Clarence White [guitar]; Richard Greene [fiddle]; Bill Keith [banjo])

One of the first revival BLUEGRASS supergroups, Muleskinner lasted only long enough to appear on a single TV special and make one album, but the band was quite influential on the growth of PROGRESSIVE BLUEGRASS.

All of the group's members had originally performed in bluegrass bands: PETER ROWAN, RICHARD GREENE, and BILL KEITH were early-sixties alumni of BILL MONROE's band, Clarence White had been a founding member of the KENTUCKY COLONELS, and DAVID GRISSMAN was a founding member of the New York Ramblers, who had also performed with RED ALLEN and Del McCoury. In the mid-to-late sixties and early seventies, they had all pursued different musical directions, with Keith joining Jim Kweskin's Jug Band and another one-off project, the Blue Velvet Band (a country ensemble led by Boston folkie Jim Rooney); White playing lead guitar for the BYRDS; Greene fiddling with the rock band Seatrain; and Grissman and Rowan forming the progressive rock band Earth Opera. Muleskinner was their first "return" to their bluegrass roots.

The band was formed at the invitation of a California public television station that had booked Bill Monroe's Blue Grass Boys and wanted to have a young band as a second act to provide a "fathers and sons" angle to the show. Their perform-ance was so successful that they were given a one-record deal with Warner Broth-ers; this album was reissued several times through the seventies and eighties, influencing subsequent generations of bluegrass pickers. Besides reworkings of traditional material, it featured the first appearance on record of a David Grissman original as well as Rowan's unique songs. (Rowan's "Blue Mule" is a retelling of the traditional "Molly and Tenbrooks" story, this time with Molly beating her op-ponent by flying up into outer space.) The album also introduced Clarence White's excellent acoustic-guitar picking to an entire new generation (his earlier bluegrass recordings were virtually unavailable at the time).

Although the band never toured, band members (with the exception of White, who was tragically killed in a hit-and-run accident soon after) have reunited from time to time. The record set the stage for eighties and nineties bluegrass super-groups featuring various different members of Muleskinner, as well as forecasting the blend of rock, jazz, and bluegrass that would become known as progressive bluegrass (or "newgrass").

Select Discography

Live: Original Television Soundtrack, Sierra 6001. Not the album that made them famous but the actual soundtrack off the local public television program that was the impetus for forming the band.

◀ MULLICAN, MOON

(born Aubrey Mullican, 1909, near Corrigan, TX; died 1967)

Mullican was one of the first great HONKY-TONK songsters and pianists, whose swinging style influenced an entire generation of keyboard ticklers, particularly the Ferriday Fireball, JERRY LEE LEWIS.

Raised in a religious household, Mullican began his keyboard career playing on the family's pump organ, although his secular bluesy style was not pleasing to his fundamentalist family. Around age twenty-one, he worked his way up to the Houston area, where he performed as a pianist in several unsavory nightspots, earning the nickname "Moon" because he worked all night and slept all day. He soon was leading his own band, performing throughout the Louisiana/Texas re-gion, and by the end of the thirties was also working with several prominent

WESTERN SWING ensembles, most notably one led by swinging fiddler Cliff Bruner, as well as performing on radio out of Beaumont. In 1939 he made his way to Hollywood to appear in the "classic" film *Village Barn Dance*, and he began performing in the Los Angeles area.

Returning to Texas in the forties, Mullican continued to perform while he opened his own nightclubs in Beaumont and Port Arthur. His big break on the country charts came in 1947 with his cover of the CAJUN classic "Jole Blon," renamed "New Jolie Blon," on the King label. He had a series of hits on King with folk and jazz-influenced numbers, including a cover of Leadbelly's "Goodnight Irene" (popularized by the FOLK-REVIVAL group the Weavers on mainstream radio) and his own "Cherokee Boogie," cowritten with W. C. Redbird.

Mullican stayed with King through 1956, although the hits pretty much dried up in the early fifties; still, his recordings featured many of the greatest hillbilly jazz pickers, including steel guitarist SPEEDY WEST and fiddler Jimmy Bryant, running the gamut from hanky-soaking WEEPERS to upbeat country to full-fledged rock and roll. When he signed with Decca and came under the hand of producer OWEN BRADLEY, the quality of his recordings suffered greatly, because Bradley tried to mold him into just another mainstream Nashville act (Bradley later admitted that he just didn't know what to do with Mullican). Mullican continued to broadcast and perform through the sixties until he died of a heart attack in 1967.

Although there had been other, earlier Western swing pianists who blended blues and jazz influences into the country mix, Mullican combined a bluesy vocal style and a great command of piano styles into his playing, plus a unique performing personality. He was the first pianist to really stand out from the pack, and as such was highly influential on the next generation of performers.

Select Discography

Moonshine Jamboree, Ace 458. His great King recordings, some previously unissued.

Moon Mullican Sings His All-Time Hits, King 555. More recordings from the King archives.

◀ MURPHEY, MICHAEL MARTIN

(born 1945, Dallas, TX)

SINGER/SONGWRITER Murphey has always showed a strong affinity for COWBOY SONGS and, since 1990, has primarily recorded traditional and newly composed songs celebrating life on the range.

Born in urban Texas, Murphey was educated at UCLA and quickly became part of the burgeoning California folk-rock scene. He was a member of the COUNTRY-ROCK band the Lewis and Clark Expedition, scoring minor success on the pop charts, while his songs were recorded by a diverse range of Southern California groups, including the NITTY GRITTY DIRT BAND and TV's the Monkees. Returning to Texas in 1971, Murphey scored his first hit in 1972 with "Geronimo's Cadillac," a Native American rights anthem. Four years later, he had his biggest successes on the pop-rock charts with "Wildfire" and "Carolina in the Pines," followed by country hits with "Cherokee Fiddle" and "A Mansion on the Hill" in 1977. In 1978, he settled on a ranch in Taos, New Mexico, furthering his interest in songs of the West.

In the eighties, Murphey primarily charted as a country singer/songwriter, beginning with 1982's "What's Forever For" through a number of other love-gone-wrong hits, including "Will It Be Love by Morning," "I'm Gonna Miss You, Girl," and "Talkin' to the Wrong Man." Unlike the other Texas outlaws, Murphey's songs were fairly accessible, not delving into the deep metaphysics of JIMMIE DALE GILMORE or the hard rock of STEVE EARLE.

In 1990 Murphey recorded his first all-COWBOY-SONG album, including such venerable old chestnuts as "Home on the Range," "When the Work's All Done This Fall," and "Old Chisholm Trail," combined with newer hippie-cowboy anthems like Ian Tyson's "Cowboy Pride." This album was the first in a trilogy of releases for Murphey all in the cowboy vein. The albums have become increasingly bombastic; while still including old chestnuts from the cowboy songbook, Murphey has introduced his own epic-length songs, including a seven-minute retelling of the life of Belle Starr. A recent album also features an annoying tribute to MARTY ROBBINS, featuring a "duet" with Robbins on "Big Iron" (his 1960 pseudo-cowboy hit) created through the miracle of overdubbing (Robbins has moved on to the great cow palace in the sky).

For fans of the myth of the West as much as the starker reality, Murphey offers a nostalgic recreation of the old days when men were men and cows were cows. If you drive a Jeep Wrangler but live in Scarsdale, you should keep a Murphey tape handy when you hit the ol' Chisholm trail.

Select Discography

Best of Country, Curb 77336. His early- to mid-seventies hits.
Cowboy Songs, Warner Bros. 26308. 1990 album of horsy favorites.

◖ MURPHY, JIMMY

(born 1925, Republic, AL; died 1981)

Murphy was a country-blues and ROCKABILLY SINGER/SONGWRITER whose unique GUITAR style and often tongue-in-cheek songs are some of the most unusual in postwar country music. Despite a lack of commercial success, Murphy's recordings have become prized collectors items, and his 1978 comeback LP is one of the best of the country music revival.

Murphy was the son of a coal miner, who was exposed early on to the music of the GRAND OLE OPRY and classic blues performers like Blind Boy Fuller and Leadbelly through 78 recordings. He learned to play the guitar from local musician Bee Coleman, who showed him an open E tuning that was ideally suited to the blues (Coleman's father recorded country blues under the name Dutch Coleman in the late twenties and returned to recording in the fifties, focusing on gospel material). Murphy first performed on radio in Birmingham and then, after finishing school, joined his father as an apprentice bricklayer. Sometime around 1950, he arrived in Knoxville, where he eventually ended up as a featured performer on the *Midday Merry-Go-Round* on a local radio station. About the same time, he was introduced to CHET ATKINS, who arranged for his first recordings for RCA.

Murphy's recordings were unique among postwar records in that they just featured his bluesy guitar with the accompaniment of Anita Carter on bass and background vocals. They also were made up of his own compositions, which had unusual themes (aging, wayward children) and imagery. For instance, his song "Electricity" is a fast-moving blues with lyrics that compare the power of God's love to the invisible force of electrification.

The recordings Murphy made from 1951 to 1952 for RCA were unsuccessful, and he did not return to the studio until 1955, when he recorded some new compositions in a rockabilly style for Columbia, including his take on the classic "Sixteen Tons," renamed "Sixteen Tons Rock and Roll" (with the immortal chorus, "Go, cats, go, dig that coal!") These records also failed in the marketplace, and although Murphy continued to perform on radio and in local appearances, his recordings were more sporadic through the late fifties and sixties.

Musicologist Richard K. Spottswood rediscovered Murphy in 1976 when he was assembling a set of recordings for the Smithsonian in honor of the U.S. bicentennial. He arranged for the recordings, issued by bluegrass-revival label Sugar Hill in 1978, that brought Murphy back into the limelight. These sensitively handled sessions (produced by RICKY SKAGGS) introduced a new generation to Murphy's dry vocals, hot guitar licks, and unique songs.

Characteristically, Murphy disappeared again after making his comeback, preferring to forsake even the margins of the mainstream musical world for a life of day labor and part-time music making. His recordings remain a provocative indication of the direction postwar country could have taken had the Nashville A&R men stuck closer to the roots of the country sound.

Select Discography

Electricity, Sugar Hill 3702. Out-of-print, fine 1978 album.

◀ MURRAY, ANNE

(born 1946, Spring Hill, Nova Scotia)

Canada's gift to Nashville pop, Murray is one of those smooth-voiced crooners who combines good-girl looks with golly-gosh material, making her a consistent country as well as pop hit maker.

Murray was raised in the coal mining/fishing village of Spring Hill, where country music was fairly typical radio fare, although her mother and father preferred the light pop of Perry Como and Rosemary Clooney, perhaps explaining her later affinity for similar music. She began singing pop and folk music in high school, although she didn't really intend to pursue a musical career; instead, she enrolled in teacher's college, majoring in physical education. However, she continued to perform in local clubs and auditioned for local television programs, including the popular folk-pop show *Sing Along Jubilee*. Although her initial audition in 1964 was a failure, producer and cohost William Langstroth was sufficiently impressed to invite her to audition again two years later, when she finally made the mark. She remained with the show for four years.

Another producer associated with the show, Brian Ahern (who would later produce EMMYLOU HARRIS's successful seventies recordings) encouraged her to pursue a full-time musical career and produced her first album for the Canadian Arc label in 1968. Canadian Capitol was impressed and signed her to a contract in 1969. Its U.S. sister label picked up her single, "Snowbird," which became a U.S. gold record in 1970.

Capitol immediately brought her to Los Angeles and vigorously promoted and showcased her as a pop recording star. But the hits dried up for a while, and Murray felt somewhat lost in the big California city. In 1973 she finally returned to the pop charts with a cover of Kenny Loggins's "Danny's Song," and a year later she had her first country hit, again produced by Ahern, a cover of DICKEY LEE's "He Thinks I Still Care" (originally a 1962 hit for GEORGE JONES). Murray had learned this song during her *Sing Along Jubilee* days and recorded it as something of an afterthought; it established her as a country star.

In the mid-seventies, Murray tired of the endless touring and decided to wed longtime friend William Langstroth and retire for a while. Although Capitol had plenty of material in the can, Murray actually did little recording until she returned from her self-imposed exile in 1978. She made a big splash on pop and country charts with the cloyingly sentimental "You Needed Me," following it with a number-one country hit, a cover of "I Just Fall in Love Again." Now working with mainstream country producer Jim Ed Norman, Murray churned out the hits in the late seventies and early eighties, including 1980's "Could I Have This Dance?" featured in the film *Urban Cowboy*. Murray became one of the most popular of the early-eighties divas, even though her musical output was no more "country" than it was "easy listening." She gained further attention with her 1983 hit "A Little Good News," which pleased such political conservatives as then–vice president Bush, who quoted from its lyrics during campaign speeches.

In 1986 Murray decided to move into a more pop-oriented direction, working with new producer David Foster (known for his middle-of-the-road pop production style). Despite this attempt to storm up the pop charts, Murray scored another country number one with "Now and Forever (You and Me)" from these sessions. A follow-up album continued this new emphasis on mainstream pop, but Murray only managed to alienate her core country audience while failing to cross over into the more lucrative mainstream market. Since the late eighties, when the NEW-COUNTRY style swept away the popularity of performers like Murray, she has mostly worked the Vegas-show circuit.

Select Discography

Country Hits, Liberty 46487. Capitol recordings showcasing the songs that made the country charts.

A Little Good News, Liberty 46629. With the title song that got Vice President Bush's foot tapping! A typical, early-eighties countrypolitan outing for the singer.

There's a Hippo in My Tub, Liberty 16233. Cassette-only reissue of one of Murray's more colorfully titled albums.

N,

◀ NASHVILLE BLUEGRASS BAND

(c. 1985–ongoing: Pat Enright [guitar, vocals]; Alan O'Bryant [banjo, vocals]; Stuart Duncan [fiddle, vocals]; Roland White [mandolin, vocals]; Mark Embree [bass])

The Nashville Bluegrass Band is one of the better new bands to come to life in the eighties, combining seasoned veterans with talented newcomers. Although they have not pioneered a new sound, they have gone a long way toward reviving and restoring mainstream BLUEGRASS styles.

The core of the band is centered on guitarist Pat Enright and banjo player Alan O'Bryant, both seasoned hands on the bluegrass scene. Young fiddle-whiz Stuart Duncan, who has made a career as a session man on countless NEW-COUNTRY recordings, fleshed out the lineup. Roland White, a legendary bluegrass revivalist who headed the KENTUCKY COLONELS with his brother Clarence and then cofounded COUNTRY GAZETTE with banjo player Alan Munde, replaced the original mandolin player in the early nineties, filling out the band's sound.

The group specializes in original compositions that recall earlier bluegrass sounds, particularly country gospel. Their quartet singing is particularly effective and one of the highlights of their shows. They do not emphasize instrumental flash, like many of the younger progressive bluegrass bands, but rather provide workmanlike backups to the songs. In fact, the instrumental solos are downplayed and modest, and many songs are taken at a moderate pace, unlike other bluegrass bands who often sound like they've just overdosed on caffeine.

Select Discography
Waitin' for the Hard Times to Go, Sugar Hill 3809. 1993 recording.

◀ NASHVILLE SOUND, THE

(c. 1954–1970)

In an attempt to "broaden" the appeal of country music, several producers—mostly notably CHET ATKINS and OWEN BRADLEY—developed a more pop-oriented style of recording that almost completely eliminated traditional country instrumentation and led the careers of singers away from country or HONKY-TONK toward a more bland, middle-of-the-road repertoire of pop ballads (for men) and tearjerkers (for women).

In the early fifties, younger Nashville-based musicians felt some embarrassment about the "old-fashioned" musical styles and hillbilly routines employed by older acts. They thought the clichéd image of the fiddle-sawing, BANJO-whomping backwoodsman was holding back country music; many were more interested in playing jazz, which they felt was a more "progressive" musical style. A leader of this movement was Chet Atkins, whose elder brother was a talented jazz guitarist and who himself had a great love for the chamber-style jazz that was popular in the fifties. At the Carousel Club in Nashville, an informal group of musicians began jamming with Atkins to play this melding of Nat King Cole and Dave Brubeck–style jazz, including pianist FLOYD CRAMER, sax master BOOTS RANDOLPH, Bob Moore on bass, and Buddy Harman on drums. Because Atkins was working as assistant head of A&R at RCA (he became head of the country division in 1957), the leading Nashville studio, he was in a position to hire these musicians for session work. Cramer was particularly popular, playing piano on hundreds of sessions, including those for ELVIS PRESLEY on classics like "Heartbreak Hotel." Along with this "modern," light jazz–style instrumentation, Atkins introduced vocal choruses, particularly the JORDANAIRES and the (dreadful) ANITA KERR Singers, again to soften the rough edges of country recordings.

In a similar move, producer Owen Bradley worked through the fifties at Decca to change country music into a more popular style. His biggest achievement was in molding the career of singer PATSY CLINE, who started out as a big-lunged honky-tonker but was transformed into the kind of dreamy, pop chanteuse that makes middle-aged men's hearts go pitty-pat. Cline hated the more pop-oriented material that Bradley asked her to record, but her cold-as-ice, gliding vocals became the model for hundreds of country singers to come, who gave up the old mountain dew for the bubbly champagne of mainstream pop.

Nashville had become a professional music-making center by the early sixties. Slews of session musicians prided themselves on their ability to accompany anybody, and thus to sound like nobody. Although some developed a distinctive style (such as Cramer's "slip-note" piano playing), the emphasis was on a homogenized, one-sound-fits-all style of playing that was bound to take the character out of the music. Plus, with the advent of large music publishing houses (beginning with Acuff-Rose), Nashville became the last bastion of professional songwriting, a Tin Pan Alley of the South. Unlike in folk and rock, where songwriters were beginning to perform their own material (and becoming stars), in country the music was still dominated by "professionals" who carefully molded the music to fit the often conservative audience.

Naturally, as country instrumentation was eliminated, the repertoire was watered down until country acts were covering the same kind of lame, mainstream pop that dominated the white-bread charts of the fifties and early sixties. Pretty soon, you couldn't tell JIM REEVES from Perry Como, and if you could, who cared? When the BROWNS hit the country charts singing the Edith Piaf remake "Les Trois Cloches (The Three Bells)," the spirit of HANK WILLIAMS was surely grieving in his grave. Although Atkins always argued that the Nashville Sound was a compromise, a way of preserving country music during a time when its popularity was in decline, it is undoubtedly his greatest sin against the music. It was up to a select band of pioneers—like BILL MONROE in bluegrass or the renegade ROCKABILLY stars like CARL PERKINS or JERRY LEE LEWIS—to keep the true spirit of country alive during the dark days of the Nashville Sound.

The Nashville Sound naturally matured into the seventies phenomenon known as COUNTRYPOLITAN, where middle-of-the-road pop music flooded the country charts.

◀ NELSON, RICK(Y)

(born Eric Hilliard Nelson, 1940, Teaneck, NJ; died 1985)

The son of well-known bandleader Ozzie and singer Harriet Nelson, who later created a successful family comedy on radio and television, Rick Nelson was originally a teen-pop star in the late fifties who became an innovative performer of COUNTRY-ROCK before the music reached its greatest popularity.

Nelson got his start when his girlfriend admitted that she had a heavy-duty crush on ELVIS PRESLEY; stating that he could also play the GUITAR, Ricky found himself in the role of teen idol thanks to his frequent appearances on the family's TV show. Many of his early pop recordings had a fine, stripped-down flavor, thanks to the dazzling string work of JAMES BURTON, who would continue to work with Nelson after he made a career switch to country. In the mid-sixties, after his career as a teen idol had fizzled, Nelson began recording country music, featuring the work of the most progressive young songwriters, including WILLIE NELSON, with James Burton playing guitar and DOBRO in his backup band. To mark this change, he altered his name from the juvenile "Ricky" to the more mature "Rick."

After hearing BOB DYLAN's crossover country LP, *Nashville Skyline*, Nelson formed the Stone Canyon Band in late 1969, probably the first country-rock band in Los Angeles, if not the entire country. Joining him was ex-POCO bassist Randy Meisner (who later formed the EAGLES) as well as other floating members, including TOM BRUMLEY, a steel guitarist who had previously worked with BUCK OWENS's Buckaroos. They recorded and performed a mix of covers of SINGER/SONGWRITER material by Dylan, Tim Hardin, and Randy Newman, as well as Nelson's own compositions.

Nelson's career got a shot in the arm in 1973 when he had a hit with his ironic "Garden Party," a song commenting on his audience's unwillingness to let him escape his teen-idol past (it was inspired by an experience he had performing in an oldies show at Madison Square Garden). Oddly enough, Nelson would embrace his earlier hits by the end of the decade, even referring to himself once again as "Ricky Nelson." Remaining a solid road act, Nelson died en route to a gig in 1985.

Select Discography

Best of Rick Nelson, MCA 10098. His more "mature" recordings cut after the teen-pop years were over between 1963 and 1975.

In Concert: The Troubadour, 1969, MCA 25983. Reissue of important Decca LP that showed Nelson in the early phases of his country-rock career; features Randy Meisner and Tom Brumley.

All My Best, MCA 6163. Originally released in 1985 by Rick on his own Silver Eagle label and hawked on late-night television, this is a nice collection of remakes featuring the JORDANAIRES on backup vocals.

◀ NELSON, WILLIE

(born 1933, William Hugh Nelson, Abbot, TX)

Willie Nelson was one of the most influential country songwriters (in the early sixties) and performers (from the mid-seventies to the mid-eighties). A leader of the so-called OUTLAW movement, Nelson abandoned the slick Nashville sound of the sixties to forge his own unique style, laying the groundwork for the explosion of NEW COUNTRY in the eighties. His reedy, sun-beaten voice and bluesy songs reflecting romantic love gone awry have become an integral part of American popular culture, well beyond the confines of strictly country music.

Nelson, the son of a rural farmer, began performing while still in high school. He served in the air force until 1952 and worked in Texas and briefly in Vancouver, Washington, as both a performer and country deejay. After publishing his first song, he moved to Nashville, where he hooked up with RAY PRICE, working as bassist in his backup band, the Cherokee Cowboys. His first success was as a songwriter, penning such number-one country classics as "Crazy" for PATSY CLINE and "Hello Walls" for FARON YOUNG, both in 1961.

He signed to Liberty and then to RCA Records in the sixties as a solo artist, but his unique style was ill-suited to the heavy-handed productions typical of the day. When his house burned down in 1970, he returned to Austin, Texas, turning his back on the country music community. Influenced by younger performers who were also weary of the NASHVILLE SOUND, including KRIS KRISTOFFERSON and WAYLON JENNINGS, Nelson began to experiment with writing song cycles, or groups of related songs, that would be issued on a series of seminal LPs, including 1973's *Shotgun Willie*, 1974's *Phases and Stages* (telling the story of the breakup of a relationship from both the man's and woman's perspective), and 1975's landmark *Red Headed Stranger*, a romantic story set in the nineteenth-century West. He was given artistic control over his recordings and often pared down his sound to just his own vocals and guitars, as on his first hit, 1975's cover of FRED ROSE's "Blue Eyes Crying in the Rain" from the *Stranger* concept LP.

The outlaw movement was given a strong push by RCA when they released the compilation album *Wanted: The Outlaws* in 1976, featuring Willie, Jennings, JESSI COLTER (then Jennings's wife), and TOMPALL GLASER. In typical contrary fashion, Willie followed this success with an album of covers of thirties and forties pop standards, *Stardust*. He proved what country audiences long knew; that there was a strong following for these pop songs among country-music fans, as well as among the rock and yuppie audiences who were attracted to Willie's straight-ahead approach to music.

Through the late seventies and early eighties, Willie performed as a soloist and in duets with Jennings, Leon Russell, MERLE HAGGARD, and in the informal group, the Highwaymen, with JOHNNY CASH, Kristofferson, and Jennings. He even cut a duet with Spanish crooner Julio Iglesias on the saccharine "To All the Girls I Loved

Before." A brief movie career also developed, including a 1980 remake of the venerable tearjerker *Impromptu* (about a classical musician's love affair with his student) improbably reset in the world of country music as *Honeysuckle Rose* (yielding the hit "On the Road Again," which has become a theme song for Nelson), and a TV version of *Red Headed Stranger* (1987).

Tax problems with the IRS led to one of the most unusual deals in music history: Willie recorded two solo LPs on which he performs his old songs accompanied only by his guitar; the albums were then marketed directly through late-night TV ads, with the proceeds used to pay off back taxes. He returned to more mainstream recording on his sixtieth birthday with a new album produced by pop producer Don Was and a TV special.

Nelson's success in broadening the country market in the seventies and early eighties opened up the field to influences such as COUNTRY-ROCK, WESTERN SWING, and HONKY-TONK. He proved, along with BOB DYLAN, that a songwriter could be the most expressive performer of his own material, even if his vocals were not as "polished" as those of more commercially oriented performers (although Nelson, unlike Dylan, is a talented guitarist). In a culture oriented toward youth, Nelson's well-lined face and laid-back performances show that artistry can overcome imagery.

Select Discography

Nite Life, Rhino 70987. Early, hard-to-find tracks.

Best of Willie Nelson, RCA 56335. Variable collection of his RCA recordings.

Phases and Stages, Atlantic 82192. Legendary concept album produced by Jerry Wexler in Muscle Shoals.

Red Headed Stranger, Columbia 33482. The famous concept album.

Stardust, Columbia 35305. Old standards crooned by Willie.

To Lefty from Willie, Columbia 34695. Wonderful 1977 tribute album featuring songs associated with LEFTY FRIZZELL.

Who'll Buy My Memories, Sony Special Product 52981. Two-CD set with just Willie and his guitar, issued to help pay off his tax bills.

◀ NESMITH, MICHAEL

(born 1942, Dallas, TX)

One of the original "pre-Fab Four," a member of TV's Monkees, Nesmith was nonetheless a creative SINGER/SONGWRITER who was one of the founders of COUNTRY-ROCK.

The son of a secretary who invented Liquid Paper, and thus earned a small fortune, Nesmith learned to play the GUITAR after serving a stint in the air force in the early sixties. After a successful audition, he gained a position as the only star of *The Monkees* TV show who actually played his instrument and wrote songs. Although Nesmith continued to provide country-rock originals for the group, he was dismayed by the hype surrounding them and left soon after the TV show was canceled.

Nesmith's fame as a songwriter steadily grew in the late sixties. His "Different

Drum" was a 1967 hit for LINDA RONSTADT, as a member of the Stone Poneys; the NITTY GRITTY DIRT BAND had a minor hit with his "Some of Shelley's Blues"; and MOR-meister Andy Williams had a big hit with his early-seventies composition "Joanne."

Meanwhile, Nesmith formed a series of loose-knit country-rock bands, called the First (or Second) National Band, often in cahoots with steel guitarist Red Rhodes, recording an eccentric mix of Nesmith's own compositions and psychedelized adaptions of country standards. In the early seventies, Elektra invited him to form the Countryside label to record Los Angeles's burgeoning country-rock scene, but the label was short-lived due to a change in management of the parent company.

In the mid-seventies, Nesmith became increasingly interested in experimentation with video, suggesting the original idea for MTV and becoming one of the first and most inventive creators of music videos through his company, Pacific Arts. He more or less retired as a performer, although he continues to occasionally produce new material in a style that is distinctly his own.

Select Discography

The Older Stuff, Rhino 70763. His great country-rock sessions from 1970 to 1973.
The Newer Stuff, Rhino 70168. On which our hero ventures out into territories only he would explore.

◀ NEW COUNTRY

(also new traditionalism; nouveau country; roots country)

In the mid-eighties, a group of country performers proved that a return to a more pure country sound could be successful, thus reinvigorating the music and launching the country music revival of the next decade.

In the seventies, country had gone mainstream, with acts like KENNY ROGERS performing in what was called the COUNTRYPOLITAN style. This mixture of easy-listening blandness with mainstream-pop sensibilities (and just a hint of country twang) had transformed the country charts into a pale imitation of middle-of-the-road pop. While successful with the Vegas crowd, the music was far removed from country's roots.

Younger musicians who were attracted to country music were not fans of this watered-down music. Some, like GRAM PARSONS, came out of the folk-rock tradition. Parsons was a fan of fifties HONKY-TONK country, and he began performing this earlier material in his concerts as well as writing songs that reflected this sensibility. Other musicians entered the country arena through performing BLUEGRASS music. RICKY SKAGGS was a high school–age MANDOLIN player when he joined RALPH STANLEY's traditional bluegrass band; Stanley's repertoire also drew on earlier country songs, particularly postwar honky-tonk tunes and WEEPERS, as well as a smattering of traditional folk songs and hymns.

The two strands—COUNTRY-ROCK and PROGRESSIVE BLUEGRASS—came together in EMMYLOU HARRIS's backup band in the late seventies. Harris had been Parsons's musical partner, and she inherited his backup band (which she renamed the Hot

Band) after his untimely death in 1973. By the late seventies, Ricky Skaggs had become musical director of the band, and Harris recorded a bluegrass homage album (*Roses in the Snow*) drawing on Skaggs's repertoire and arrangements. While Harris moved more toward bluegrass, Skaggs himself began adopting her folk-rock sound, recording an album of bluegrass and country standards with a folk-pop backup for the specialty Sugar Hill label.

Skaggs was the first new-country star to break through to mainstream success. In the early eighties, he signed with Columbia's Epic label and had a series of hits, most notably 1984's "Country Boy" (the video for which features veteran bluegrass mandolin player BILL MONROE performing a buck dance on a New York City subway train!). Recording executives were surprised by the success of this music, which was much more country sounding than the work of leading hit makers of the day like Kenny Rogers or BARBARA MANDRELL.

The new-country movement really took off in 1987, when first-time recording artist RANDY TRAVIS scored a megahit with his debut album, *Storms of Life*. Travis was an unabashed fan of earlier honky-tonk heroes like GEORGE JONES; his first hit, "Digging Up Bones," featured the kind of sly humor that made the great honky-tonk songs of the fifties so memorable. Travis's deep-baritone voice was richly ornamented with the kinds of swirls, trills, and yodels that make classic country instantly recognizable. Plus, his backup band featured a simple, pared-down, bar-band sound.

Like every movement that begins with a relatively pure agenda, new country has been expanded and exploited by the recording industry and the artists themselves to a point where the term has become almost meaningless. Under the new-country tent you can find singer/songwriters like MARY CHAPIN CARPENTER and NANCI GRIFFITH; country-rockers like the KENTUCKY HEADHUNTERS; the pleasant-voiced hunks in hats, like MARK CHESTNUTT and ALAN JACKSON; babes in boots, the female equivalent of the hunky he-men who trade on their youthful looks as much as their music, such as MICHELLE WRIGHT and LARI WHITE; mainstream pop stars like GARTH BROOKS, who combines arena rock, a SINGER/SONGWRITER stance, country, and middle-of-the-road pop in his act; and on and on. Almost any music that has strong lyrical and melodic content with a semiacoustic backup is lumped in the new-country category, and today's country fans are as likely to drive BMWs as pickup trucks.

◀ NEW GRASS REVIVAL

(c. 1972–1990: Sam Bush [fiddle]; Curtis Burch [guitar, dobro, 1972–1981]; Pat Flynn [guitar, vocals, 1981–1990]; Courtney Johnson [banjo, 1972–1981]; Bela Fleck [banjo, 1981–1990]; Ebo Walker [bass, 1972–1973]; Joel Cowan [bass, vocals])

One of the most influential of the PROGRESSIVE BLUEGRASS groups, the New Grass Revival was born out of an earlier group known as the Bluegrass Alliance, featuring hot guitarist Dan Crary as its leader. When Crary left the band in 1970, he took the name with him; he was replaced by Sam Bush, who along with Courtney Johnson,

Curtis Burch, and Ebo Walker brought a rock-and-roll sensibility to their performance of traditional instrumentals and songs. Walker was soon replaced by powerful
singer Joel Cowan, who had previously performed in a rock-and-roll band exclusively. This first version of the band, which lasted through the early eighties, helped
popularize the newgrass sound. Their stage act and performance style were geared
to appeal to young listeners who grew up on rock, while they still drew on the
traditional bluegrass repertoire to some extent.

Burch and Johnson tired of the endless touring that is the life of a bluegrass
outfit and were replaced by progressive banjoist BELA FLECK and singer/guitarist Pat
Flynn. Fleck brought a more jazz-influenced sound, particularly in his approach to
harmonies and his sparse, melodic improvisations. The band scored their greatest
success with 1988's *Hold to a Dream*, their sole LP to have much action on the
country charts. However, they were quite a successful performing band, touring
on the bluegrass, college-campus, and to some extent traditional country circuit.

The band fizzled out in the early nineties. Bush continues to be a much-in-
demand session musician (and currently works in EMMYLOU HARRIS's backup band),
while Fleck formed a jazz-country fusion band, the Flecktones, who have had some
success both on the pop and country charts.

Select Discography

Fly Through the Country, Flying Fish 70032. Reissues two classic seventies albums
by this influential group.

On the Boulevard, Sugar Hill 7745. The later incarnation of the band with Bela
Fleck.

◀ NEW LOST CITY RAMBLERS, THE

*(1958–c. 1970; sporadically thereafter: Mike Seeger [fiddle, banjo, guitar,
harmonica, mandolin, vocals]; Tom Paley [banjo, guitar, vocals, 1958–1963];
John Cohen [banjo, guitar, mandolin, vocals]; Tracy Schwartz [fiddle, banjo,
guitar, mandolin, vocals, 1964–thereafter])*

The first and perhaps greatest of the old-time string-band revivalists, the Ramblers introduced to a new, urban audience the classic sounds of CHARLIE POOLE,
the SKILLET LICKERS, DOCK BOGGS, and many other recording artists of the twenties
and thirties. Taking an almost academic approach (perhaps as an antidote to the
slick commercialism of FOLK-REVIVAL groups like the Kingston Trio), they repro-
duced the sound of these early recordings almost note for note. As the years went
by, the group loosened up somewhat, taking a more interpretative role in their
recreations.

MIKE SEEGER, the son of folklorist Charles Seeger and half-brother of folk revivalist
PETE SEEGER, was enamored of BLUEGRASS and country music in the Washington,
D.C., area where he grew up. Yale-educated John Cohen was active in the New
York folk scene in the fifties, while Tom Paley, a mathematician, was from the
Boston area. The trio's academic background is reflected in their approach to the
music, particularly on their first few albums released by Folkways in the late fifties
and early sixties. They often focused on a single theme—such as Prohibition or

Songs of the Depression—and presented the music with meticulous documentation, including information on their sources. Their appearance at the 1959 Newport Folk Festival introduced them to the folk-revival audience and led to many years of popularity on the college and small folk-club circuit.

Paley left the group in 1963 to form another short-lived old-time band, the Old Reliable String Band, with New York–based musician Arnie Rose; he then relocated to England, where he recorded a duet album with Mike Seeger's sister Peggy. In the late sixties, he formed the New Deal String Band with British musicians Janet Kerr on fiddle and Joe Locker on BANJO, and in the late seventies he recorded a solo album.

To replace Paley, Seeger brought in his friend Tracy Schwartz, who brought a more modern sound to the group. Schwartz's background in bluegrass widened the group's repertoire to include recreations of fifties-era country recordings as well as the older styles they had previously performed. The band recorded an all-instrumental album, perhaps the first to emphasize this side of the old-time music tradition, as well as accompanied legendary country performer COUSIN EMMY on a 1967 recording. 1968's concept album, *Modern Times*, was perhaps one of their best recordings; while still centering on a general theme (country folks' reaction to the changes in their lives brought about by industrialization), the band took a freer approach to the music, putting their own personal stamp on it.

By the early seventies, the Ramblers were performing together only sporadically. Seeger was pursuing a solo career and also performing with his then-wife ALICE GERRARD as a duo and in the bluegrass/country band, the Strange Creek Singers, which also featured Tracy Schwartz. Cohen formed the Putnam String County Band with fiddler Jay Ungar, guitarist/vocalist Lynn Ungar, and cellist Abby Newton, one of the more innovative revival bands of the early-seventies. Schwartz performed with Seeger in the Strange Creek Singers for a while and then began performing with his wife, Eloise, and eventually his children as well, while pursuing an interest in CAJUN music.

Although the Ramblers never officially disbanded, for the last two decades they have only performed together on and off, mostly for special occasions such as reunions or at festivals.

Select Discography

The Early Years, Smithsonian/Folkways 40036. Selections from their albums cut between 1958 and 1962 with Tom Paley.

The Later Years, Smithsonian/Folkways 40040. The band's best recordings from 1963 to 1973.

◀ NEW RIDERS OF THE PURPLE SAGE

(c. 1971–1978; primary lineup: Dave Torbert [guitar, vocals]; Buddy Cage [steel guitar]; Skip Battin [bass]; Spencer Dryden [drums])

In the wake of the Grateful Dead's two successful COUNTRY-ROCK albums of the early seventies, the New Riders of the Purple Sage (they took their name from a Zane Grey dime-store Western novel) were formed as a spinoff band so lead Deadhead Jerry Garcia could pursue his interest in making country music and playing the PEDAL STEEL GUITAR. The original band members included other Deadsmen Mickey Hart (drums) and Phil Lesh (bass) along with the husband-and-wife team of Keith (keyboards) and Donna (vocals) Godchaux; this same aggregation also toured in the mid-seventies under the name of the Jerry Garcia Band.

New steel guitarist Buddy Cage came on board after Garcia's interest waned, and along with guitarist/vocalist Dave Torbert, he led the group through most of its recordings. They recorded two fairly decent country-rock albums for Columbia in 1972 and then disbanded for a while. By the mid-seventies, they were back as a true band, now joined by ex-BYRDS bassist Skip Battin and ex–Jefferson Airplane drummer Spencer Dryden. However, their later recordings were fairly lame blends of pop and rock, and the band fizzled out by the decade's end.

Select Discography

New Riders of the Purple Sage, Columbia 30888.

The Adventures of Panama Red, Columbia 32450. Their two early-seventies albums for Columbia.

Before Time Began, Relix 2024. Attention Deadheads! Here's Jerry and crew kickin' up the sawdust on early, previously unreleased recordings.

◀ NEWBURY, MICKEY

(born Milton Newbury, 1940, Houston, TX)

Better known as a songwriter than performer, Newbury has written solid hits for country, pop, and R&B artists.

After graduating from high school, Newbury bummed around for a while in the Houston/South Texas/Gulf Coast region, playing piano in small bars and clubs. He joined the air force, where he discovered a skill for songwriting, and began seriously working on songs when he was twenty-four. He moved to Nashville in the mid-sixties and had his first hit when DON GIBSON covered his "Funny Familiar Forgotten Feeling." He then hit the pop charts with KENNY ROGERS and the First Edition's smash version of "I Just Dropped In (to See What Condition My Condition Was In)." He had another hit with the country WEEPER "She Even Woke Me Up to Say Goodbye," recorded by JERRY LEE LEWIS in his mid-sixties country phase, and R&B hits for Bobby Bland ("You've Always Got the Blues") and Solomon Burke ("Time Is a Thief").

In the early seventies, Newbury was signed to Elektra's new country division. His biggest solo hit was 1972's "American Trilogy," based on three traditional Civil War songs, which did even better when it was covered by ELVIS PRESLEY. Newbury's recording career quickly died, although he continued to write highly literate country hits through the seventies.

Select Discography

The Best of Mickey Newbury, Curb 77455.

◀ NEWMAN, JIMMY "C"

(born 1927, Big Mamou, LA)

Newman brought CAJUN sounds to the country charts in the late fifties and early sixties and has continued to be one of the few artists who can perform successfully in either style.

An authentic French-Louisianian, Newman began playing in the Lake Charles area, already performing the mix of country and traditional Cajun dance numbers that would become his trademark. Beginning in 1949 he recorded for several small local labels and quickly gained a strong regional following. Hired for the popular *Louisiana Hayride* radio program, he was quickly signed to Dot, where he had a rockin' country hit with "Cry, Cry, Cry" (1954). He was invited to join the GRAND OLE OPRY in 1956 and had his biggest country-pop hit a year later with "A Fallen Star."

After a couple of lackluster years at MGM, Newman returned to the country charts under the hands of producer OWEN BRADLEY at Decca Records, beginning with 1961's "Alligator Man" (playing off his Cajun heritage) and the half-spoken record "Bayou Talk." Although Bradley managed to cover Newman's distinctive style in the same schlocky instrumentation he employed on all of his NASHVILLE SOUND sessions, the essential regional character of Newman's music was not lost. In 1962 he recorded *Folk Songs of the Bayou Country* to appeal to the nascent FOLK-REVIVAL crowd; the album featured many songs sung in his native Cajun French and wonderful instrumentation by noted Cajun fiddler Rufus Thibedeaux and "Shorty" LeBlanc on accordion. Unfortunately, most of Newman's later Decca recordings were pitched at the mainstream country audience, and much of his Cajun heritage was lost.

In the mid-seventies, Newman returned to his roots with a new band called Cajun Country. Although no longer a strong chart presence, he continues to record and perform locally, mostly focusing on traditional material.

Select Discography

Cajun and Country Too, Swallow 6052. Cassette-only reissue of mid-seventies recordings.

◀ NEWTON, JUICE

(born Judy Kay Newton, 1952, Lakehurst, NJ)

Newton was a country-rock-pop star of the late seventies and early eighties, best remembered for her cover of the sixties soft-pop hit, "Angel of the Morning."

Born in New Jersey, Newton was raised in Virginia, where she began performing folk songs as a teenager. After attending college in North Carolina and working in local coffeehouses, she moved to California where she met guitarist Otha Young. The two formed a light folk-rock band called Dixie Peach that evolved into Silver Spur. The group stayed together for about two years, recording a couple of albums and scoring a minor hit with 1976's "Love Is a Word."

Newton went solo in the late seventies, signing with Capitol in 1981 and scoring immediately on the pop charts with her remake of "Angel of the Morning" followed by "Queen of Hearts." From 1982 to 1987, she was marketed as a country act, although little about her sound had changed. Her first country hit went straight to number one; it was "The Sweetest Thing (I've Ever Known)," which was written by her longtime associate, Otha Young, and had originally been recorded by Silver Spur in 1975. She had a final pop hit with "Love's Been a Little Hard on Me," followed by her countrified cover of BRENDA LEE's "Break it To Me Gently." A remake of the Little Anthony and the Imperials' hit "Hurt" was a big country hit for her in 1986, as was a duet with EDDIE RABBITT on "Both to Each Other (Friends & Lovers)."

In 1986 Newton broke with her longtime boyfriend Young and wed a polo player. As if in reaction to this life change, she moved from recording country-pop to an attempt at more glitzy, mainstream material, with little success. She has since become a staple of the Vegas circuit.

Select Discography
The Early Years, RCA 61142. Reissue of recordings originally made by Silver Spur, featuring Newton as lead vocalist.
Greatest Country Hits, Curb 77367.

◀ NITTY GRITTY DIRT BAND, THE

(c. 1965–ongoing: Jeff Hanna [guitar, vocals]; John McEuen [banjo, mandolin, 1965–1986]; Jimmy Ibbotson [guitar, vocals, 1971–ongoing]; Jimmy Fadden [drums], Lee Thompson [mandolin, 1965–1975]; Bob Carpenter [keyboards, 1984–ongoing])

The Nitty Gritty Dirt Band is a California COUNTRY-ROCK group that crossed over into being a pure country outfit in the mid-seventies.

Formed from the California folk-rock community, they initially scored hits with the late-sixties pop song "Buy for Me the Rain" and a remake of the twenties standard "The Teddy Bear's Picnic." They disbanded in the late sixties only to reform in the early seventies, scoring their biggest pop hits with country-rock versions of "Mr. Bojangles" and MIKE NESMITH's "Some of Shelly's Blues."

In 1971 the band organized sessions in Nashville that brought together traditional country stars (Earl Scruggs, Maybelle Carter, JIMMY MARTIN, MERLE TRAVIS, and DOC WATSON) to perform a set of country standards. The result was the landmark three-LP set, *Will the Circle Be Unbroken*, which helped popularize these country stars among rock audiences and elevated the band to hero status in both the country and rock communities.

By the mid-seventies, the group was performing country-rock material under the name the Dirt Band. They were down to a quartet (Lee Thompson had left the group), but they continued to try to appeal to both their rock and country constituencies. In the mid-seventies, going by the name Toots Uncommons, they backed the comic novelty "King Tut," recorded by Steve Martin (who, incidentally, was managed by JOHN MCEUEN's brother, Bill, who had handled the band since its inception). They also scraped near the bottom of the top ten with their 1979 recording of "An American Dream."

By the eighties, the "Nitty Gritty" was back in their name, and they were recording as a pure, NEW-COUNTRY act. They scored a number of hits performing a combination of original songs and Nashville songwriters' products, with just a hint of traditional flavorings. In 1984 they had their first country number one with RODNEY CROWELL's "Long Hard Road (The Sharecropper's Dream)." In 1985 and 1986, in time for their twentieth anniversary, they hit number one again with "Modern Day Romance," a pure new-country song cowritten by Kix Brooks (later of BROOKS AND DUNN). Founder-member McEuen left after the band's anniversary year to pursue a career as a solo BANJO performer, leaving a quartet of Jimmy Ibbotson, Jeff Hanna, Jimmy Fadden, and country/rock keyboardist Bob Carpenter, further pulling the band in the new-country direction. A follow-up to the famous *Will the Circle Be Unbroken* was released in 1989, with a cast drawing on more contemporary country figures (ROSANNE CASH, JOHN HIATT, and so on), although it was not as much of a landmark effort as the first set. That same year, the band produced a streak of top-ten country singles, solidifying their position as more consistent hit makers than in the past.

The Dirt Band is one of the few survivors of the Southern California country-rock scene. Although they have gone through many stages—with the best material and lineup coming in the early seventies—they continue to produce a strong vocal blend combined with fine musicianship. It is true that they have come to sound like many other generic country outfits, but they have a more eclectic repertoire and a deeper understanding of country roots than many more-modern bands.

Select Discography

Twenty Years of Dirt, Warner Bros. 25382. Best-of collection covering recordings from 1966 to 1986.

Will the Circle Be Unbroken, EMI 46589. Reissue of the famous three-LP set on two CDs.

Will the Circle Be Unbroken, Vol. 2, Universal 12500. Less exciting follow-up to the original cut in 1989.

Not Fade Away, Liberty 98564. The 1992-era band, including "special guest," SUZY BOGGUSS.

◀ NOACK, EDDIE

(born Armond A. Noak, Jr., 1930, Houston, TX; died 1978)

Noack was an active recording artist from the late forties through 1960—moving between country, HONKY-TONK, and ROCKABILLY—as well as a country songsmith who is best remembered for providing HANK SNOW's mid-fifties hit, "These Hands."

Born in Houston, Noack received a college degree in English and journalism from Baylor University. An amateur musician, he won a talent contest in 1947 at the Texas Theatre, leading to local radio work and, two years later, to a contract with the local Gold Star label. His first hit was a cover of the pop hit "Gentlemen Prefer Blondes." He soon was label hopping, scoring his biggest country hit in

1951 with "Too Hot to Handle" on the TNT label; this led to a contract with the Nashville-based Starday label that ran through the mid-fifties. In 1958 he moved to Pappy Dailey's "D" label, recording rockabilly and teen pop under the pseudonym of Tommy Wood and having another minor country success under his own name with "Have Blues Will Travel." He soon became active in Dailey's music-publishing operation and retired from performing in the early sixties to focus on the business side of Nashville.

During the fifties, following Hank Snow's success with "These Hands," Noack's songs were covered by many mainstream country acts, including honky-tonkers ERNEST TUBB and GEORGE JONES. Jones covered many of Noack's songs in the early sixties, including "Barbara Joy," "No Blues Is Good News," and "For Better or Worse."

Noack made several abortive comeback attempts as a recording artist from the late sixties to his death. Perhaps his most interesting recording was *Remembering Jimmie Rodgers*, which featured sparse, acoustic instrumentation (unusual for the time) in a program of material that had all been made famous by the Yodelin' Brakeman. His recordings were issued by a variety of tiny labels, here and abroad, but with little success. Ironically, after Noack's death, his earlier recordings were rediscovered, particularly among COUNTRY-ROCK and rockabilly fans.

◀ NORMA JEAN

(born Norma Jean Beasler, 1938, Wellstown, OK)

Norma Jean was a popular country singer of the sixties who is best known as PORTER WAGONER's duet partner (until she was replaced by young DOLLY PARTON in 1967) and for her series of solo recordings celebrating the life of the working poor.

Influenced by KITTY WELLS, who she heard performing on the GRAND OLE OPRY as a child, Beasler began singing on the radio when she was thirteen years old and was touring as a vocalist with various WESTERN SWING bands two years later. She made her way to Nashville, where she hooked up, emotionally and professionally, with Wagoner, who molded her "just folks" image. She recorded a number of brassy songs, including her first hit, 1964's suggestive "Let's Go All the Way." 1967 brought her first working-class anthem, "Heaven Help the Working Girl (in a World That's Run By Men)." After parting with Wagoner, she recorded the concept LP, *I Guess That Comes from Being Poor*, featuring hokey crowd-pleasers like "The Lord Must Have Loved the Poor Folks (He Made So Many of Them)."

After her marriage to a fellow Oklahoman, Norma Jean retired from the music business from 1974 to 1984, when she returned to Nashville and began performing her old hits as a nostalgia act.

O,

◀ OAK RIDGE BOYS THE

(c. mid-sixties–ongoing; best-known lineup: Duane Allen [lead vocals, guitar]; Joe Bonsall [tenor vocals]; William Lee Golden [baritone vocals]; Richard Sterban [bass vocals])

Originally a country-gospel quartet, the Oak Ridge Boys gained their greatest success in the late seventies and early eighties as a pop-vocal group, scoring a crossover hit with 1981's "Elvira." Tracing their roots to a gospel quartet that performed in and around the Oak Ridge, Tennessee, nuclear facility, the group has gone through many personnel changes from its founding in the late forties to today.

Original founder Walter Fowler was a member of the Georgia Clodhoppers, a country-gospel quartet based in Oak Ridge, Tennessee, in the late forties. Inspired by the success of EDDY ARNOLD, Fowler recorded as a soloist for Decca and King, writing and performing such sentimental country favorites as "I'm Sending You Red Roses" and "That's How Much I Love You Baby." The Clodhoppers eventually took the more elegant Oak Ridge Quartet name, but Fowler left the band by the early fifties to become a gospel music promoter.

The Oak Ridge personnel soldiered on through the sixties, and the lineup stabilized in the mid-seventies. All of the group's members were educated musicians, and they all had long histories in other gospel or pop-vocal groups. Lead singer and guitarist Duane Allen, who joined in 1966, had a music degree from East Texas State and had previously sung baritone in the popular group, the Southernaires. Tenor Joe Bonsall, a native of Philadelphia and an Oak Ridge Boy since 1973, performed with many local street-corner harmony groups, as well as dancing regularly on Dick Clark's *American Bandstand* television show. Baritone Bill Golden, who joined in 1964, had performed with his sister as a country duo in his native Alabama and had also worked in a paper mill. Distinctive bass Richard Sterban, a New Jersey native who came to the group in 1972, had performed with the gospel groups the Keystone Quartet and the Stamps (who recorded and toured with ELVIS PRESLEY).

The Oak Ridge Quartet, as they were known in their gospel incarnation, were successful recording artists and performers by the mid-seventies. However, their iconoclastic attitude, including their long hair and beards and use of drums and electrified instruments in the backup band, was upsetting to some of the more traditional members of the gospel audience. Meanwhile, they longed to cross over to the more lucrative pop market. Their first break came when they were invited to provide vocal backups on Paul Simon's mid-seventies hit "Slip Slidin' Away." They were then signed to ABC in 1977 and also began performing at upscale venues in Vegas, opening for ROY CLARK.

Mainstream hits came through the early eighties, along with dozens of TV appearances on variety shows as well as dramatic parts on country-oriented shows like *The Dukes of Hazzard*. Among their better-known wax is 1981's zillion-selling "Elvira" (with the distinctive "oom-papa-mow-mow" bass line borrowed from the early-sixties teen-pop hit), the patriotic "American Made" from 1983 (picked up as a jingle by Miller Beer), 1985's cover of the Staple Singers' gospel favorite "Touch a Hand, Make a Friend," and 1988's "Gonna Take a Lot of River," featuring new lead singer Steve Sanders (William Lee Golden had been forced out of the band in 1987 and subsequently, unsuccessfully, sued the group for forty million dollars).

The Oak Ridge Boys' combination of traditional gospel harmonies with doo-wop and early rock influences, plus their dramatic stage presentation, were highly influential on the new country-harmony groups that followed, including ALABAMA.

Select Discography
Greatest Hits, Vols. 1–3, MCA 5150/5496/42294.
The Long Haul, RCA 66004. 1992 release showing that the Oaks are still . . . well, the Oaks.

◀ O'CONNOR, MARK

(born 1962, Seattle, WA)

A child virtuoso on a number of instruments, O'Connor was a championship fiddler in the seventies who became, in the mid-eighties, the most in-demand session musician in Nashville. He has recorded with hundreds of artists in country and pop, besides his own solo albums.

O'Connor showed jaw-dropping capabilities on a number of musical instruments by the age of eleven; he first started playing classical GUITAR at age six, winning a flamenco competition four years later. He soon turned his attentions to country music, quickly mastering BLUEGRASS guitar, MANDOLIN, BANJO, and DOBRO. But his true capabilities were first revealed when he picked up the fiddle at age eleven (he was inspired to take up the instrument after seeing DOUG KERSHAW performing on JOHNNY CASH's television show); eighteen months after his first violin lesson, he won the Junior division of the National Old-Time Fiddler's Contest in Wesier, Idaho.

O'Connor was signed to Rounder Records, a bluegrass label, soon after and released his first album at age twelve; he recorded five more albums for the label in the seventies, including a solo guitar record that showed his capabilities as a flatpicker. Over the next decade, he won every major U.S. fiddle championship, winning the open competition at the National Festival four times before retiring undefeated.

Like many other contest winners, Mark's original style was very flashy, designed to bring a crowd to its feet. However, in his late teen years, he came under the influence of progressive bluegrassers and acoustic-jazz musicians like DAVID

GRISSMAN, whose group he joined in the early eighties (as a guitarist). His fiddling began to pick up a sweeter tone and a sophistication and subtlety that is not usually heard in championship fiddling circles. After a year with Grissman, O'Connor played briefly with the Dregs, the original country/grunge-rock fusion group, and also toured with Merle and DOC WATSON, PETER ROWAN, and JERRY DOUGLAS. In 1983 he relocated to Nashville, where he soon was working as a studio musician.

O'Connor's dexterity on a number of instruments, and his ability to quickly fashion an appropriate style for an accompaniment, led him to be a major session player, recording with country stars as well as pop-rock singers like James Taylor and Paul Simon. In the late eighties, he signed with Warner Brothers as a solo artist, producing the *New Nashville Cats* LP as an homage to his bluegrass roots with popular country stars RICKY SKAGGS, VINCE GILL, and STEVE WARINER as his informal bandmates. In 1989 he was named the musical director of *American Music Shop*, an acoustic-music concert series on cable's Nashville Network; he composed the theme song for the program and leads the band, which also includes dobroist Jerry Douglas.

As O'Connor's fame has grown, so have his musical ambitions, although he has been less successful outside of the pure country realm. He composed a violin concerto that was premiered by the Sante Fe and Nashville Symphony Orchestras in 1993, taking the solo chair himself. His 1993 album, a series of duets with his many musical mentors, includes everyone from CHARLIE DANIELS to jazz bow-bender Stephane Grappelli, classical star Pinchas Zuckerman, and Indian jazz-rock violinist L. Shankar. Such eclectic musical tastes are to be admired, although the result tends to be a homogenized music that is neither country, jazz, classical, or rock.

Select Discography

The Championship Years, Country Music Foundation 015. Mark as a young fiddle-burner performing in various contests.

National Junior Fiddle Champ, Rounder 0046. Cassette-only reissue of his first album, cut when he was twelve.

Retrospective, Rounder 11507. Best of his many Rounder albums.

New Nashville Cats, Warner Bros. 26509. Fine bluegrass/HONKY-TONK country outing with Skaggs and Gill.

◀ O'DAY, MOLLY

(born LaVerne Williamson, 1923, Kentucky; died 1987)

O'Day was a gutsy HONKY-TONK wailer who abandoned her career to take up evangelical preaching.

O'Day was the daughter of a Kentucky coal miner. All the members of her family were musically talented, and Molly listened to the *National Barn Dance* radio program out of Chicago as a child, particularly admiring the singing of PATSY MONTANA and TEXAS RUBY, two cowgirl stars. In 1939 her older brother Skeets got a radio job in West Virginia and invited his then-sixteen-year-old sister to be his vocalist, under the stage name of Mountain Fern. In 1940 she broke with her brother and joined Lynn Davis's group, the Forty-Niners, and a year later married Davis. The two spent the World War II years working radio in West Virginia, Alabama, and Kentucky; it was during their last job, in Louisville, that Williamson gained the stage name of Molly O'Day. She also met a young singer/guitarist, HANK WILLIAMS, who impressed her with his sincerity and powerful songs.

The husband-and-wife duo's greatest success came in 1945 when they joined Knoxville's WNOX. A year later, Molly was signed to Columbia and had hits with "Tramp on the Street," her best-loved song; the honky-tonk anthem "I Don't Care If Tomorrow Never Comes" (which she learned from Hank Williams); and the tearjerking ballad, "The Drunken Driver." Molly's music was also spread through her songbooks, which she sold through her radio show and personal appearances throughout the South and Midwest.

As her career progressed, O'Day showed a growing propensity for religious material, particularly songs that emphasized man's failures and his need to seek solace in God. In 1949 she was hospitalized, apparently following an emotional breakdown, and, following her release, she and her husband entered the Church of God. Although she continued to record through 1951, she was no longer interested in being an entertainer. In 1954 Lynn was ordained a minister, and for the next three decades the duo preached in the small West Virginia coal-mining towns of their childhoods. Although O'Day made some religious recordings for small labels in the sixties, she never again returned to commercial country music. She died of cancer in 1987.

O'Day could have become a major star in the fifties; her powerful singing, linked with a highly emotional delivery, set the stage for the next generation of female country stars on the honky-tonk side of the aisle.

Select Discography
Molly O'Day and the Cumberland Mountain Folks, Bear Family 15565. Two CDs of O'Day's Columbia recordings made between 1946 and 1951. Includes duets with husband Lynn Davis.

◀ O'KANES, THE

(1986–1990: Kieran Kane [guitar, vocals]; Jamie O'Hara [mandolin, vocals])

Popular vocal duo of the mid-eighties, the O'Kanes performed a roots-oriented music with a unique twist on traditional country harmony.

The duo were both songwriters for Nashville's Tree Music when they began performing together. O'Hara had written many hits for mainstream country acts, most notably "Grandpa (Tell Me 'Bout the Good Ol' Days)" for the JUDDS, while Kane had written "Let's Have a Party," a hit for ALABAMA. Kane brought a more rock-oriented sound to the group, having grown up in Queens, New York, while O'Hara had a soft-country orientation, coming from a rural Ohio home.

The duo were most noteworthy for their unorthodox approach to harmony; they often traded harmony and lead parts several times in a single song, while each vocal line maintained its own special quality (because each singer had a very distinctive voice). They also used spare, almost minimalistic accompaniments, shunning the arena-rock or glitzy-pop styles of many of their country contempo-raries. Kane played MANDOLIN from his BLUEGRASS days, while O'Hara played simple GUITAR, and their accompanists often included accordion, fiddle, subtle electric guitar, and bass, recalling bluegrass instrumentation without using these acoustic instruments in a bluegrass style. Their unusual sound can be heard from their first hits, including their only number-one country disc, 1987's "Can't Stop My Heart from Lovin' You." They had a couple more hits later in 1987 and in 1988, but their laid-back, acoustic style was not as popular as that of more up-tempo groups.

After their successful debut in 1986, the duo lost steam with each successive release and finally called it quits in 1990. Three years later, O'Hara released his first solo effort, reflecting a continuation of the O'Kanes' philosophy of soft-country sounds presented in sparse settings. Kane followed with his own solo release in 1994.

◀ OLD AND IN THE WAY

(c. 1976: Jerry Garcia [banjo, vocals]; David Grissman [mandolin, vocals]; Peter Rowan [guitar, vocals]; Vassar Clements [fiddle], John Kahn [bass])

In the beginning, before God created the Grateful Dead, there was a young, BLUEGRASS BANJO picker named Jerry Garcia working around San Francisco in a jug band. Garcia's love for bluegrass music did not end after he became the ultimate hippie rocker, and he formed the informal group Old and in the Way in 1976 as a means to express his love for this music (the name comes from the words of a sentimental old-time song). He joined forces with a then-obscure West Coast ses-sion player named DAVID GRISSMAN on MANDOLIN and PETER ROWAN, both of whom had previously played together in another one-off group, MULESKINNER. Fiddler VAS-SAR CLEMENTS was an alum of JOHN HARTFORD's early-seventies band and had played with many other folk revivalists, including David Bromberg. They recorded one album, released by the Dead's own Round record label, featuring many Rowan originals that have since become newgrass standards: "Panama Red" and "Land of the Navajo," two of his mythic Western ballads being the best known. Garcia has since revived the band from time to time with various different personnel; he teamed up again with Grissman in 1993 to record an acoustic duo album for children.

Select Discography

Old and in the Way, Sugar Hill 3746. Reissue of their first album.

◀ ORBISON, ROY

(born 1936, Vernon, TX; died 1989)

Orbison exists in that mythical region somewhere between country and rock; indeed, though he has recorded and been successful in both genres, he is most famous for a series of early-sixties pop ballads that exist in their own special world, propelled by his operatic, unearthly singing voice.

Orbison began performing as a teenager, leading the country band the Wink Westeners, who performed on his tiny hometown radio station. After finishing high school, he enrolled at North Texas State, where he encountered soon-to-be-teen-popster Pat Boone, who encouraged him to adapt to the new sound of rock and roll. In the mid-fifties Roy formed the Tune Wranglers, attracting the attention of JOHNNY CASH, who recommended that he send a demo tape to SAM PHILLIPS's Sun Records.

At Sun, Roy hit it big in 1956 with the novelty "Ooby Dooby," a teen rocker written specifically with that audience in mind. A year later, Orbison was working in Nashville as a songwriter for legendary promoter WESLEY ROSE. He penned "Claudette" (named for his then-wife) for the EVERLY BROTHERS, which became another big pop hit.

In 1959 Rose arranged for Orbison to record for Monument Records, where he had his greatest success with a series of balladic pop tunes that defy categorization. These include 1961's "Cryin'," 1962's "Dream Baby," "Blue Bayou" and "In Dreams" from 1963, and the classic 1964 recording of "Oh, Pretty Woman" featuring Roy's trademark growl. Orbison became a huge success, not only in the United States but in England, where he was revered by British Invaders like the Beatles and the Rolling Stones. Orbison, whose vision was terribly limited since childhood, forgot to bring his regular glasses to a show in England and so was forced to wear his prescription sunglasses. These dark glasses, along with his jet black hair and black suit, became trademarks for the singer. Ironically, the success of British acts on the U.S. pop charts from 1964 on did much to end Orbison's popularity at home.

In the mid-sixties, in search of broader horizons as an actor as well as a singer, Orbison signed with MGM, which had both a record label and major film studio. He appeared in the lame B-grade film *Fastest Guitar Alive* and also provided the soundtrack. Tragedy struck with the death of his wife in a 1965 motorcycle accident and, two years later, a freak fire at his home that killed two of his children. However, Roy continued to perform, although by the early seventies his career was just about over. LINDA RONSTADT scored a huge success in 1977 with her cover of Roy's "Blue Bayou." This brought the singer out of retirement and back in the studio for two albums, although neither was particularly successful.

The eighties saw a continued interest in Roy's music, and he made a series of duet recordings, including one with EMMYLOU HARRIS on "That Loving You Feel Again" and an intense duet with Canadian punk-country star K. D. LANG on his "Crying." Roy's biggest triumph came at the end of his life when he was invited to join the loose-knit pop band the Traveling Wilburys, comprised also of George Harrison, Jeff Lynne, BOB DYLAN, and Tom Petty. Lynne produced a comeback solo LP, featuring the upbeat "You Got It" and dramatic "Mystery Girl," which was released just after Orbison's death due to a heart attack.

Although Orbison was not a pure country star by any means, his impact was felt in country as well as pop music. His unique musical personality inspired countless others to follow their own musical inspiration.

Select Discography

The Sun Years, Rhino 70916. Includes previously unreleased material.

For the Lonely, Rhino 71493. Great recordings cut between 1956 and 1965, Orbison's primo years.

The Legendary Roy Orbison, Sony Music Special Productions 46809. The ultimate gift for your friends in dark glasses; four CDs covering thirty years of recordings from 1955 to 1985 with an illustrated booklet.

◀ OSBORNE BROTHERS, THE

(Robert born 1931, Hyden, KY; Sonny born 1937, Hyden, KY)

The Osborne Brothers are PROGRESSIVE BLUEGRASS/country musicians who have pioneered the use of amplified instruments, as well as drums and steel guitars, in BLUEGRASS, and are noted for their innovative harmonies and high-powered recordings.

The two brothers performed together from childhood and were already working professionally in the early fifties when Bobby was drafted to serve in the Korean war. Young Sonny was an accomplished BANJO player at age fourteen (1952), so good that he was invited to join bluegrass legend BILL MONROE's band for touring and recording during that summer. When Bobby returned from Korea, the brothers began performing together as a duo in 1953 over local Knoxville radio. In 1954 they relocated to Michigan to perform and record with JIMMY MARTIN, another Monroe alumnus, and among the classic sides the trio cut were "Chalk Up Another One" and "20/20 Vision."

A year later, they were in Dayton, Ohio, where they hooked up with another bluegrass legend, RED ALLEN, who was at the beginning of his career. The group signed to MGM records in 1956, scoring with their cover of COUSIN EMMY's classic reworking of "Reuben/Train 45," renamed "Ruby." Their dramatic harmonies—Red on lead, Bobby, with his distinctive high tenor, and Sonny on baritone—highlighted on the a cappella introduction, made the single a standout. The use of drums on these recordings made them controversial among pure bluegrass fans, although they clearly fit in with the high-energy music that the brothers created. They also pioneered the use of twin harmony banjos, an innovation later copied by progressive bands like COUNTRY COOKING.

After Allen left the group, the brothers began performing over the WWVA *Jamboree* radio program in Wheeling. In 1959 Sonny Birchfield took over the lead vocal chores. A year later, the band was booked into Antioch College in Yellow Springs, Ohio, where they introduced bluegrass music to a young, educated audience. They were soon in demand on the college and folk-festival circuit, while they still maintained strong ties to country music. In 1964 they were invited to join the GRAND OLE OPRY, one of the few bluegrass groups at that time on the Opry stage, and signed with Decca. Their mid-sixties recordings broke further barriers in instrumentation, including their use of piano on "Up This Hill and Down," electric bass on "The Kind of Woman I Got," and PEDAL STEEL GUITAR on their big

1967 hit, "Rocky Top," which has become perhaps the most overplayed song in all of bluegrass.

In 1976 the Osbornes left Decca for the more traditional bluegrass label, CMH, and then began recording for Sugar Hill in the early eighties. Their music remains as high-powered as ever, although in today's world of progressive bluegrass and newgrass, they hardly sound as controversial as they did some thirty years ago.

Select Discography

Osborne Brothers and Red Allen, Rounder 03. Wonderful cassette-only reissue of their fine fifties-era recordings with lead singer Allen.

Osborne Brothers, Rounder 04. Late-fifties recordings by the duo.

The Best of the Osborne Brothers, MCA 4086. Two cassettes featuring their sixties-era Decca recordings.

Once More, Sugar Hill 2203. CD reissue of remakes of their favorite bluegrass numbers originally issued on two LPs in 1985 and 1986.

◀ OSLIN, K. T.

(born Kay Toinette Oslin, 1942, Crosett, AK)

Oslin is a SINGER/SONGWRITER with a feminist slant who had her first success in the late eighties when she was already in her forties after a career that spanned folk, theatrical music, and recording TV jingles.

Although born in rural Arkansas, Oslin relocated with her family first to Mobile and then to the Houston area. In 1962 she formed a folk trio with singer/songwriter GUY CLARK and local radio producer Chuck Jones. She moved to Los Angeles soon after, joining forces with another folksinger, Frank Davis, and together they issued an LP that went nowhere. She switched to theatrical singing, touring with the road company of *Hello Dolly!*, and ended up in New York City in 1966.

After a few more bit parts on Broadway and off, as well as work cutting commercial jingles, Oslin began experimenting with songwriting. By 1978 she had built up an impressive portfolio and attracted the attention of Nashville publishing executive Dianne Petty. However, Nashville didn't seem ready for her more liberated themes, although she did briefly record under the name Kay T. Oslin for Elektra in 1981 and 1982. She then returned to New York for more commercial work.

Finally, in 1987, Oslin signed with RCA in Nashville, scoring a hit with her own " '80s Ladies," an ode to her generation of women who had "burned our bras and burned our dinners." A series of spunky country chart-toppers followed, including "Didn't Expect It to Go Down This Way" (and its immortal couplet "I'm overworked and overweight/I can't remember when I last had a date") and her 1990 number-one hit, "Come Next Monday."

Oslin's Broadway background is evident in her big-voiced approach to ballads, the mainstay of her repertoire. Although her message is liberated, her style is middle-of-the-road and fairly old-fashioned.

Select Discography

'80s Ladies, RCA 2193. 1987 album featuring the title hit.

◀ OSMOND, MARIE

(born 1959, Ogden, UT)

The only female member of the Osmond-family clan, Marie represents the apotheosis of the sickly sweet, primly neat girl singer who appeals to the most conservative elements in the country audience. A marginally talented singer, she trades off on her wholesome image and made-for-TV personality.

The Osmonds are one of those pop phenomena that defy explanation or even description. Whiz producer MIKE CURB had shaped pop careers for brothers Donny and Little Jimmy; in search of another star, he turned to the Osmond matriarch and asked her if thirteen-year-old Marie had any talent. Mom assured him she did, although she liked country music best, not the cloying teen pop that her brothers performed. Curb hooked her up with veteran ex–ROCKABILLY star SONNY JAMES, who produced her first number-one success, a cover of the 1960 "classic" by Anita Bryant, "Paper Roses," which Osmond cut in 1973; not only was it a number-one country hit, but it hit number five on the pop charts, proving once and for all that you can't account for America's musical taste. As a teen, Marie joined with brother Donny performing pop-flavored material on the Vegas/club-lounge circuit. The duo were paired from 1976 to 1979 on a variety TV show, which opened with good-girl Marie sweetly singing "I'm a little bit country," while leather-pants-wearing, pseudo-tough-guy Donnie thrilled preadolescent America by chiming in "I'm a little bit rock 'n' roll." By country, it seems that her handlers meant she was the less threatening of an already sugarcoated duo; Marie's career has been built on this all-American image.

Fortunately for fans of true country, Osmond's career faded after the TV show went off the air, although she made a comeback in the mid-eighties both as a soloist with the cloying "There's No Stopping Your Heart" (written by Michael Brook, aka Bonagura, who would later form the group Baillie and the Boys) and in duets with popsters DAN SEALS and Paul Davis. Neither her vocal style (which is a mixture of mid-seventies rock, pop, and schlock) nor her accompaniments are particularly country, but that's okay with her audience, which prizes her primarily because of their memories of her teenage success.

Select Discography
The Best of Marie Osmond, Curb 77263. All the hits that you can bear.

◀ OUTLAW COUNTRY

(c. 1975–1985)

The so-called outlaws—led by WILLIE NELSON and WAYLON JENNINGS—were frustrated by how NASHVILLE SOUND and COUNTRYPOLITAN productions transformed country music into light, mainstream pop. Influenced by traditional country sounds, particularly WESTERN SWING and Texas HONKY-TONK, as well as the breakthroughs of singer/songwriters like BOB DYLAN who proved that pop songs could have a message, the outlaws made a highly personal music that helped revive interest in true country sounds.

The movement took its name from a 1975 RCA anthology called *Wanted: The Outlaws* that featured recordings by Jennings and Nelson. However, the movement dates back to Nelson's frustration with working as a songwriter and performer in mid-sixties Nashville. Although he had provided major hits for other artists, Nelson felt that Nashville's producers didn't understand his own approach to making music. Influenced by Bob Dylan and other sixties singer/songwriters, Nelson was beginning to write more personal music that he felt only he could perform. Yet Nashville's producers were burying his music in the same hyperslick commercial production that they applied to all country acts. Fed up with his inability to make music his own way, Nelson left Nashville to live in Austin, Texas, in 1968.

Texas is a breeding ground for an unusual crop of country SINGER/SONGWRITER. With its strong streak of independence, its musical mix of honky-tonk, Mexican, Western swing, and COWBOY-SONG traditions, Texas has been fertile ground for innovative musicians. Already a number of songwriters were gathering in Austin, including JERRY JEFF WALKER, JOE ELY, and JIMMIE DALE GILMORE. Nelson's arrival on the scene helped further invigorate it; he began sponsoring an annual picnic/festival that brought younger Nashville songwriters and performers like KRIS KRISTOFFERSON and Waylon Jennings to the region.

The outlaw musicians appealed not only to a core country audience but also to fans of COUNTRY-ROCK and singer/songwriters. Nelson left RCA to record for Atlantic, a company more famous for its jazz releases than for pure country, then moved to Columbia; these labels promoted his music in the college, FM market as well as to country enthusiasts. Nelson's success making music in his own way had a profound influence on Nashville. For one thing, it showed that returning to roots-country sounds, rather than simply pandering to the latest pop styles, could be a way for country music to survive. For another, it showed that the strong tradition of eccentric, highly individual musicians who had created country music needed to be honored and developed if the music was to grow. This led directly to the revolution that has come to be known as NEW COUNTRY.

Select Discography

Wanted: The Outlaws, RCA 5976. The compilation album that gave the movement its name.

◀ OVERSTREET, PAUL

(born 1955, Van Cleave, MS)

Overstreet is a SINGER/SONGWRITER who is better known for providing hits for other folks—particularly nouveau-country hunk RANDY TRAVIS—than for his own recordings.

He originally came to Nashville in 1973, but it took him about ten years of struggle to get to the top of the heap. By the early eighties, he was producing a string of hits, including several for Randy Travis, such as his first biggie, "Diggin' Up Bones" (a clever, honky-tonkesque song about a man's old true loves who return to haunt him), "On the Other Hand" (an on-the-edge-of-cheating song), "Forever and Ever Amen," and "Deeper than the Holler"; the JUDDS' sappy "Love

Can Build a Bridge"; GEORGE JONES's hit "Same Ole Me"; TANYA TUCKER's bad girl song "My Arms Stay Open All Night"; "Houston Solution" for RONNIE MILSAP; and the list goes on and on.

As a performer, Overstreet first worked with Thom Schulyer and Fred Knobloch, two fellow songwriters who longed to get in front of the mike, and they formed S.K.O. The trio had a few 1987 hits, including the number-one "Baby's Got a Brand New Band." Overstreet left the group to pursue a solo career, having his biggest hit in 1990 with "Daddy's Come Around." In the meantime, he had found God, a particularly fatal event in the career of a good ol' honky-tonker, and since the early nineties he has forsaken his mainstream career to perform religious material.

Select Discography
Sowin' Love, RCA 9717. 1989 debut solo album.

◀ OVERSTREET, TOMMY

(born 1936, Oklahoma City, OK)

Overstreet was a minor-league country performer of the early seventies who is best known for his work on TV's HEE HAW.

Born in urban Oklahoma City, Tommy was raised in Houston and became interested in a musical career thanks to his parents, who bought him a GUITAR when he was fourteen, and a cousin, Gene Austin, who had been a successful pop crooner in the twenties, famous for his hit recording of Irving Berlin's "My Blue Heaven." In high school, Tommy performed in a teen-pop style on the local radio station and then, when his family moved to Abilene, began performing as Tommy Dean of Abilene, again in a pop-rock style.

He moved to Nashville in 1967 in search of a country career and was hired to manage the country label Dot. He himself signed to Dot in 1969, scoring his first country number one with 1971's "Gwen (Congratulations)" and continuing to hit the top twenty of the country charts through 1977. His recordings were the typical COUNTRYPOLITAN fare of the day, as much influenced by Neil Diamond and other pop-schlock acts as they were by any country roots. In fact, Overstreet admits that he was hardly a country-music fan, although he saw country as an area that would support his watered-down mainstream pop style in the early seventies. In 1979 he signed with Elektra/Asylum, which made a brief attempt at starting a country division, and then recorded for A&M and smaller labels in the early eighties. Since then, Overstreet has mostly stuck to the country-fair and rodeo circuit.

Select Discography
Greatest Hits, Hollywood 390.

◀ OWENS, BONNIE

(born Bonnie Campbell, 1933, Blanchard, OK)

Bonnie Owens is a fine country-style vocalist in the female-WEEPER mold who has been overshadowed by her association with two of country's megastars, first husband BUCK OWENS and second husband MERLE HAGGARD.

Originally from a dirt-poor Oklahoma family, Owens worked as a child picking cotton to help her family survive. The family relocated to Arizona when she was a young teenager, and things looked up for a while. She got her first job in Mesa, Arizona, working on the *Buck and Britt* radio show, where she met future husband Buck Owens. The twosome worked for a while in a touring country band, eventually making their way in the mid-fifties to new country mecca Bakersfield, California, where Bonnie was hired to sing by Herb Hensen on his locally broadcast *Trading Post* TV show. The Owenses' marriage soon dissolved, and Bonnie's mother came West to care for her two children while Bonnie began building her career as a solo artist. She had her first local hit with the early-sixties "Dear John Letter," released on the tiny Marvel label, and a following hit with her tribute song to PATSY CLINE, "Missing on a Mountain."

In the early sixties, she befriended an up-and-coming country singer named Merle Haggard, and the two began making demo recordings together, attracting the attention of local producer/record label owner Fuzzy Owen. Owen signed Bonnie and Merle to his Tally label, and Bonnie had solo hits with 1963's "Daddy Doesn't Live Here Anymore," a classic WEEPER, and the more feisty "Don't Take Advantage of Me" from a year later. In 1964, Bonnie teamed with Merle, and the duo scored a big hit with "Just Between the Two of Us," leading to a contract with Capitol Records for them both. They were married in 1965.

Bonnie had a couple more hits through the sixties as a solo artist but retired from performing in 1970, at least on her own. Although she divorced Haggard in 1975, by the early eighties she was back in his band, working as a singer and managing his business affairs.

One of Bonnie's sons from her marriage to Buck Owens is Buddy Alan, who has had some success as a solo country performer as well as performing with his dad in the early seventies.

◀ OWENS, BUCK

(born Alvis Edgar Owens, 1929, Sherman, TX)

One of the creators of the Southern California country sound, Buck Owens is best known for his early-sixties hits, including his first number-one country tune, "Act Naturally," later covered by the Beatles.

Originally from Texas, Buck, the son of a sharecropper, was born in relative poverty. The family moved to Arizona in search of a better standard of living, but to little avail, and Buck had to leave school after the ninth grade to help support his family. Already a talented musician playing both MANDOLIN and GUITAR, he was performing on local radio out of Mesa, Arizona, when he was just sixteen. He met future wife BONNIE (Campbell) OWENS there and married her a year later.

In 1951 he relocated to Bakersfield, California, which was a center of California's country-music community in the fifties, thanks to its booming oil industry. He formed his first band, the Schoolhouse Playboys, a swingin' ensemble in which he played sax and trumpet, all the while working as a guitarist on numerous country and pop-rock sessions. He also recorded some ROCKABILLY tunes under the name of Corky Jones. Local country star TOMMY COLLINS gave Owens his first big break in the mid-fifties when he hired him to be lead guitarist in his band and featured him on many of his early hits. Owens formed his own band, the Buckaroos, in the late fifties, and was signed to Capitol as a solo performer. The Buckaroos helped define the "modern" country-band sound; rather than featuring acoustic guitars and mandolins, the band featured stinging electric-guitar leads played by Don Rich on the newly introduced Fender Telecaster (Rich also provided wonderful harmony vocals), along with "crying" steel guitar licks played by TOM BRUMLEY. Both of these elements would become standard on country recordings of the sixties.

Owens's first hit was "Second Fiddle," followed by "Under Your Spell Again" from 1959, "Excuse Me, I Think I've Got a Heartache" from a year later, and 1961's "Fooling Around." From the first, Owens established himself as a purveyor of upbeat, HONKY-TONK–flavored material, with a distinctive vocal style that showed the influence of Western cowboy yodelers as well as the beer-soaked honky-tonk vocalizing of HANK WILLIAMS. Owens was rarely off the charts in the '60s, with wonderful hits such as 1963's "Act Naturally," "I've Got a Tiger by the Tail" and "Buckaroo" from 1965, "Waitin' in the Welfare Line" from a year later, and 1969's "Tall Dark Stranger." He also made some fine duet recordings in the early sixties with WESTERN SWING–turned–BLUEGRASS vocalist ROSE MADDOX.

After his sixties hits, Owens hooked up with a new country music TV show called HEE HAW. The success of the show made Buck one of the most instantly identifiable of all country stars, despite the fact that the quality of his recordings had declined. His career hit a nadir in 1974 when he issued the junky novelty number "Monster's Holiday." By the early eighties, he was focusing on his business interests and had practically retired from music making. Then, in the mid-eighties, nouveau-country star DWIGHT YOAKAM took Owens's characteristic sixties sound and reintroduced it to a new generation of listeners. Owens's rerecorded "Act Naturally" as a duet with Ringo Starr (who popularized the song with the Beatles), cut a duet with Yoakam, and returned to performing on the road.

Select Discography

The Buck Owens Collection (1959–1990), Rhino 71016. Three CDs covering Owens's entire career; great sound and seventy-six-page, illustrated booklet by country authority Rich Kienzle.

The Very Best of Buck Owens, Rhino 71816. Sixteen of his biggest hits, drawn from the three-CD set.

At Carnegie Hall, Country Music Foundation CMF 012. Live 1966 concert that presents Buck and his band at their peak, originally issued as Capitol 2556.

◀ OXFORD, VERNON

(born 1941, Benton County, AK)

Oxford is a traditional-style, HONKY-TONK vocalist who has been more popular in Europe than in the United States, although he was reintroduced to the American audience through a series of albums for the bluegrass label Rounder in the early eighties.

The son of a fiddle player, Oxford was raised amidst music making, both at home and in church. After the family moved to Kansas, he took up the fiddle and became a state champion, forming his own band and touring through the West. He eventually made it to Nashville in the mid-sixties and was briefly signed by RCA at the height of the NASHVILLE SOUND era. Oxford's sound was far too traditional for the times, and he was dropped by the label. He began touring Europe, where his popularity was so great that RCA re-signed him in the mid-seventies, and he had one big hit with 1976's "Redneck." Soon after, he moved to the more traditionally oriented Rounder label, which heavily promoted his recordings as examples of the true country sound. Unfortunately, the NEW-COUNTRY movement was yet to take root, and these recordings again proved more popular abroad than at home.

Select Discography

Keepin' It Country, Rounder 156. Cassette-only reissue of early-eighties recordings.

P.

◀ PARKER, LINDA

(born Genevieve Elizabeth Meunich, 1912, Covington, KY; died 1935)

Linda Parker was an early star of WLS's popular *National Barn Dance*, specializing in sentimental ballads sung in a clear, professionally trained voice.

Parker was born across the river from Cincinnati and raised in urban Gary, Indiana, where she began performing as a teenager on radio and in clubs, where John Lair, the enterprising producer of Chicago's *National Barn Dance* radio show, discovered her. He gave her her new name, little-girl sweetheart image, and a country repertoire. She was made the featured singer of the show's house band, the Cumberland Ridge Runners, and given the cutesy nickname "the Little Sunbonnet Girl" (she was pictured in publicity photos wearing a gingham sunbonnet and dress; backwoods dress became the standard uniform for female country performers after her). Although she was often pictured holding a BANJO or GUITAR, Parker did not play either instrument; again, the publicity machinery molded her image to include the accouterments that fans expected to see.

From 1932 to her death from appendicitis three years later, Parker was a favorite act, dividing her repertoire between nineteenth-century WEEPERS like "I'll Be All Smiles Tonight" and the occasional brassy traditional song like "Single Girl." She sang in a clear, soothing style that reflected her pop music roots and became a model for country radio stars through the thirties. Her death at age twenty-three cemented her appeal to Depression-era listeners; in her honor, WLS stars KARL AND HARTY rewrote the old standard "Bury Me Beneath the Willow" to become "We Buried Her Beneath the Willow."

◀ PARNELL, LEE ROY

(born 1956, Abilene, TX)

Parnell serves up a heaping portion of good-time Texas-style musical stew, including a dash of BUDDY HOLLY rock, a hearty dose of BOB WILLS WESTERN SWING, and the zest of R&B and Tex-Mex music.

Performing since his teen years, Parnell formed his first band at age nineteen, playing in and around his hometown of Abilene. He came to Nashville at age twenty-one and was one of many young singers showcased and discovered at Nashville's Bluebird Cafe, where he first performed in 1987. Signed to Arista in 1988, he produced his first album a year later, scoring immediately with his tough-minded blend of country, rock, and soul. His first success was the rockin' "Oughta Be a Law," followed by the country-gospel of "The Rock," and his own song, "Road Scholar." Unlike many of the other hunks in hats, Parnell brings a true understanding of country's various styles and some authentically strong material to the plate. For this he is to be watched.

Select Discography

Lee Roy Parnell, Arista 8625. 1990 debut album.
Love without Mercy, Arista 18684. 1992 second album.

◀ PARSONS, GRAM

(born Cecil Connor, 1946, Winterhaven, FL; died 1973)

A seminal figure in the birth of COUNTRY-ROCK, Parsons's fast-lane lifestyle led to his premature death, but not before he influenced a generation of new country singers.

Parsons was born in Florida but raised in Georgia, the son of country SINGER/ SONGWRITER "Coon Dog" Connor, who took his own life when his son was thirteen. An early love for the GUITAR led Parsons in 1962 to form his first professional band, the FOLK-REVIVAL trio the Shilohs (which also included JIM STAFFORD, who later had country hits including 1973's "Spiders and Snakes," and Kent LaVoie, who later formed the pop band Lobo and had hits with bubblegum anthems like 1971's "Me and You and a Dog Named Boo").

Parsons was admitted to Harvard's Theological Seminary in 1966, and while in the Boston area he formed the short-lived International Submarine Band. This group is generally credited with being the first to record what would become country-rock music. He then joined the folk-rock group the BYRDS and participated in their seminal country album, *Sweetheart of the Rodeo*. Parsons's original "Hickory Wind" is one of the high points of the album, which includes many country standards.

Parsons and Byrds's bass player CHRIS HILLMAN formed the FLYING BURRITO BROTHERS in 1969, along with ex-Byrds drummer Michael Clarke, "Sneaky" Pete Kleinow on steel guitar, and bassist Chris Ethridge. Their first album, *The Gilded Palace of Sin*, featured the Parsons's classic "Sin City," a country song for a new generation of hippie-country singers. In 1970 banjoist Bernie Leadon joined the group (he would later be a founding member of the EAGLES), and a second album followed, featuring a cover of Mick Jaggers's and Keith Richards's "Wild Horses." Parsons left the group soon after to pursue a solo career.

Parsons introduced a new singer as a member of his backup band on his first solo album: Her name was EMMYLOU HARRIS. The duo recorded some of the most compelling country-rock, particularly on Parsons's second solo disc, *Grievous Angel* from 1974, featuring a remake of FELICE AND BOUDLEAUX BRYANT's "Love Hurts." JAMES BURTON, a guitarist who had previously recorded with ELVIS PRESLEY and RICKY NELSON, and whose trebley sound was a defining one in country-rock, also performed with Parsons.

Years of drug and alcohol abuse caught up with Parsons, and he died soon

after the release of his second solo album. In a bizarre move, his manager kid-
naped the singer's corpse from the funeral parlor, in order to carry out Parsons's
last request to be cremated. Since his death, numerous tapes (including early
recordings from the Shilohs and live concert material and outtakes) have been
issued, furthering his legend. Emmylou Harris has made it a point to credit Parsons
for her own career and to keep at least his name current whenever she is asked
about the roots of her music.

Parsons's influence was great: He took country themes and modernized them,
so that a younger audience could sympathize with the material. He showed how
the nostalgic sadness of country music could be wed to the power of rock and
roll. Incidentally, he introduced country instrumentation—BANJOS, fiddles, PEDAL
STEEL GUITARS—into the world of rock, paving the way not only for countless other
rock bands (from POCO to the Eagles) but also for rockin' country bands (such as
SAWYER BROWN).

Select Discography

Warm Evenings, Pale Mornings, Bottled Blues, Raven 24. Covers Parsons's entire
career, from the Shilohs through the Byrds to his solo work.
GP/Grievous Angel, Reprise 26108. CD reissue of both of Parsons's early-seventies
albums on one disc.
Live 1973, Sierra 6003. With Emmylou Harris.

◀ PARTON, DOLLY

(born 1946, Locust Ridge, TN)

Actress, country and pop star, and businesswoman, Dolly Parton is hardly the
aw-shucks, country-bred, dumb-blonde personality that she often projects. A talented singer and songwriter, she has shown a unique ability to market herself and
mold an image while at the same time produce unique, personal music that continues the great traditions of previous generations of singer/songwriters.

The fourth of twelve children raised in poverty in rural Tennessee, Dolly's first
recordings were made in 1959 for Goldband; in 1964 she traveled to Nashville,
signing with Monument Records and scoring her first hit with "Dumb Blonde" in
1967. The same year she joined forces with country legend PORTER WAGONER, a
savvy businessman who ran a large country revue. He recorded a string of duets
with the younger singer, beginning with a cover of Tom Paxton's "Last Thing on
My Mind," which helped launch her career.

Dolly's solo recordings from RCA in the late sixties and early seventies established her as a sensitive SINGER/SONGWRITER who could reflect on her own rural
heritage. In songs like 1971's "Coat of Many Colors," she honored the memory of
her mother, who had made her a patchwork coat out of fabric remnants. Many of
her songs were based on childhood memories, presenting in a straightforward,
unembarrassed way the often hard times that she endured as a child. In 1974
Parton permanently split from Wagoner, who was bitterly jealous of his younger
rival's talent and success, and her songs began to be covered by folk-rock artists
from LINDA RONSTADT ("I Will Always Love You," later also a number-one hit for

pop singer Whitney Houston in 1992 through 1993) and Maria Muldaur ("My Tennessee Mountain Home"). This encouraged Parton to attempt her own cross-over recordings for the pop charts, beginning with the bouncy 1977 hit, "Here You Come Again."

In 1980 Parton's everywoman personality was perfectly exploited in the working class/feminist movie *9 to 5*. This depiction of the revenge a group of secretaries exact on their domineering and sexist boss appealed to working women and helped cement Parton's image as just another gal. Her title composition for the film was a pop and country hit. This success led to a decade of minor and major film roles, plus continued recordings in a pop-country vein. Longtime friendships with singers Linda Ronstadt and EMMYLOU HARRIS resulted in the 1987 LP *Trio*, a rather subdued folk-country outing that produced a minor hit with their cover of Phil Spector's "To Know Him Is to Love Him." In 1989, in an attempt to return to her roots, she recorded a more country-oriented LP called *White Limozeen*, produced by NEW-COUNTRY star RICKY SKAGGS, for an artistic if not a great commercial success.

Parton also showed savvy as a businesswoman, opening her own theme park, Dollywood, to celebrate Tennessee mountain crafts and culture. This somewhat ersatz recreation of an idealized mountain life has proved to be quite successful, helping the economic revitalization of her childhood region and, not incidentally, also making a good deal of money for the singer.

Dolly's sister Stella (born 1949) had some minor country hits in the mid-seventies, including 1975's "Ode to Olivia," in which she defended Olivia Newton-John against her country music critics.

Select Discography

The World of Dolly Parton, Vols 1. and 2, Monument 44361/44362. Her first, mid-sixties solo recordings, including the hit "Dumb Blonde"; of interest to Partonophiles.

The RCA Years, 1967–1986, RCA 66127. Two-CD set featuring thirty tracks, taking her from her early recordings to her COUNTRYPOLITAN heyday.

Trio, Warner Bros. 25491. With Ronstadt and Harris; pleasant, if understated.

White Limozeen, Columbia 44384. Nice 1989 album produced by Ricky Skaggs.

Heartsongs, Columbia 66123. 1994 all-acoustic effort featuring the cream of young bluegrass-inspired pickers, including JERRY DOUGLAS on DOBRO, Carl Jackson on BANJO, and ALISON KRAUSS on fiddle and harmony vocals. A fine return to form.

◀ PAUL, LES

(born Lester William Polfus, 1915, Waukeseha, WI)

One of the pioneers of electric-GUITAR playing and design, Paul is best remembered for his sugary pop hits of the fifties, accompanying his then-wife Mary Ford.

From his earliest days, Paul was an amateur inventor, tinkering with radio sets and early forms of amplified guitars. He took up harmonica and piano when he was nine, followed soon after by guitar. He began performing as a guitarist/country comedian under the name of "Hot Rod Red, the Wizard of Waukesha," appearing before local Lions clubs and playing over local radio. He then moved to Chicago to perform with the Western group Rube Tronson and His Texas Cowboys over WLS, now taking the stage name of Rhubarb Red. By the mid-thirties, he was broadcasting as Rhubarb Red, performing country music in the mornings, and then switched to jazz picking under his new stage name, Les Paul, in the afternoons. He had a hit record with a countrified cover of "Just Because" that was released on the dime-store Montgomery Ward label.

In 1936 he formed a light-jazz trio with second guitarist Jim Atkins (half-brother of CHET ATKINS) and bassist Ernie Newton; they were hired to tour with the popular Fred Waring Pennsylvanians dance band. In 1939 he returned to Chicago and two years later perfected a solid-body electric guitar design, the first of its kind, the same year he relocated to Los Angeles.

After serving in the army, Paul returned to civilian life performing as a duo with girl singer/guitarist Colleen Summers, who had previously played with cowboy star JIMMY WAKELY; she took the stage name of Mary Ford by the late forties. The new duo began recording together the jazzy pop songs that would make them famous. Meanwhile, Paul's fascination with electronics led him to experiment with multiple overdubbings of the guitar and vocal parts, creating some of the earliest over-tracked recordings. Their fifties pop hits included jazzy versions of "How High the Moon," "Nola," "Lover," and "The World Is Waiting for the Sunrise."

In 1952 the Gibson company issued the first "Les Paul" guitar, an electric, solid-body instrument based on his earlier designs. This has remained one of the most popular of all electric guitars, although it has been somewhat overshadowed by Leo Fender's fifties guitar designs, including the Telecaster and Stratocaster models that are favored by rock musicians.

Paul and Ford divorced in 1962, and Paul retired from performing. However, interest in his recordings and his phenomenal guitar technique led him to return to performing in the seventies. His album of duets with Chet Atkins (*Chester and Lester*), released in 1976, brought out the best in both guitarists.

Select Discography
The Best of Capitol Masters, Capitol 99617. Reissues late-forties and early-fifties pop hits with Mary Ford.
The Fabulous Les Paul and Mary Ford, Columbia 11133. Their later fifties hits.
Masters of the Guitar Together, Pair 1230. With Chet Atkins.

◀ PAYCHECK, JOHNNY

(born Donald Eugene Lytle, 1941, Greenfield, OH)

One of the orneriest of the outlaws, Paycheck had a megahit in 1977 with the worker's anthem "Take This Job and Shove It."

Exposed to country music from his youth in Ohio, Paycheck began playing GUITAR and bass as a teenager, as well as writing countrified songs. He began working as a bass player in PORTER WAGONER's Wagonmasters backup band in the late fifties, followed by stints with FARON YOUNG, GEORGE JONES, and RAY PRICE, taking up steel guitar as well. In the late fifties, he cut some ROCKABILLY–style sides under the name of Donny Young and had a minor hit with "Shakin' the Blues."

In the early sixties, he returned to performing and writing country material and was signed to Mercury in 1965, when he took his new stage name of Johnny Paycheck. (The original Paycheck was a little-known boxer who unsuccessfully bouted with Joe Louis in 1940.) He had a couple of modest hits in the mid-sixties, including 1965's "A-11" and "Heartbreak Tennessee" from a year later, and wrote hits for TAMMY WYNETTE ("Apartment No. 9") and RAY PRICE ("Touch My Heart"). In 1966 Paycheck cofounded the Little Darlin' record label, scoring a hit with his own "The Lovin' Machine." However, by the late sixties his career was derailed by his increasing dependence on alcohol and drugs.

Famed producer BILLY SHERRILL gave Johnny a chance at making a comeback in the early seventies, and he scored a couple of hits with the Sherrill-produced "Song and Dance Man" from 1974 and "I Don't Love Her Anymore" from a year later. But Johnny's bad-boy ways caught up with him again in 1976, when he declared bankruptcy after several questionable business dealings went sour. However, a year later he was back on the charts with the appropriately titled "I'm the Only Hell (Mama Ever Raised)" and the DAVID ALLAN COE–penned "Take This Job (And Shove It)," his sole number-one country hit. Paycheck continued in the humorous vein in 1978 with the self-mocking "Me and the IRS" and the gushy "Friend, Lover, Wife" that he cowrote with producer Sherrill.

Paycheck teamed up with his old boss George Jones in 1979 for a series of successful duets, beginning with a countrified cover of Chuck Berry's classic, "Maybelline." The duo produced a rockin' album with the tongue-in-cheek title of *Double Trouble*. Next, he teamed with another country legend, MERLE HAGGARD, with the appropriately titled duet "I Can't Hold Myself in Line," a 1981 hit. However, Paycheck's rough and rowdy ways got the better of him again, and by 1983 he had moved to the tiny AMI label; two years later, he was convicted on an aggravated assault charge following a barroom brawl in his native Ohio and sentenced to a nine-and-a-half year prison sentence. His sentence was overturned on appeal in 1987, and he returned to recording, now for Mercury, producing some of the best music of his career, although the hit from these sessions, "Old Violin," was a tearjerker of the first order. Paycheck faded from the scene soon after.

Select Discography
Biggest Hits, Columbia 38322.
Take This Job and Shove It, Richmond 2300. Reissue of his most famous album, with the big hit title cut.

◀ PAYNE, LEON

(born 1917, Alba, TX; died 1969)

A blind multi-instrumentalist and singer, Payne is most famous for his compositions, including "Lost Highway," a major hit for HANK WILLIAMS.

Payne was born blind and, like many blind children of the day, was encouraged by his teachers at the Texas School for the Blind to take up music as a means of

supporting himself. It turned out that he had unusual musical capabilities, and by
his early teens he had mastered a number of instruments from GUITAR to piano
and drums, to name a few. He also had a pleasant, smooth voice, reminiscent of
successful pop crooners like Bing Crosby.

By the mid-thirties, he was working with a number of the popular WESTERN SWING
bands of the day, including a couple of gigs with the legendary band led by BOB
WILLS. After World War II, he was a member of Jack Rhodes's Rhythm Boys, and
in 1949 he formed his own band, the Lone Star Buddies. In that same year, he
had his only hit as a performer with the sentimental valentine "I Love You Because," which he wrote for his wife.

From the late forties through the fifties, numerous artists had hits covering
Payne's material. Some of his better-known songs include "Lost Highway," "Blue
Side of Lonesome," "They'll Never Take Her Love from Me," and "You'll Still Have
a Place in My Heart." Meanwhile, Payne continued to record as a solo artist, for
labels big and small, until a first heart attack in 1965 led him to cut back on his
performing activities; four years later, a second attack took his life.

◀ PEARL, MINNIE

(born Sarah Ophelia Colley, 1912, Centreville, TN)

Minnie Pearl is probably the best known and one of the greatest of all country
comedians; her time-honed, cornball humor has appealed to generations of country music fans.

Like many other rural comedians who played hayseed parts, Pearl is not as
dumb as she acts. In fact, Pearl was raised in an educated family, exposed to
classical music and literature (and only vaguely aware of the country music
around her). Her mother, known as "Aunt Fannie" Colley, led a book circle and
played organ at the local church. The young Colley aspired to be an actress and
attended the tony Ward-Belmont College, a high-class finishing school in Nashville,
where she also showed talent as a dancer.

After graduation and teaching dance locally, Pearl was hired to be a dramatic
coach for a small Atlanta company that specialized in sending directors out into
small Southern towns to mount amateur productions. She worked at this job for
five years. While working in the tiny town of Baileyton, Alabama, she was put up
by a local family; the family's grande dame was a great teller of tales and became
the model for Colley's new creation, Minnie Pearl. She began performing monologues based on this backwoods character as a way of raising interest in the plays
that she was directing.

In the late thirties, Pearl's father died and she returned to her hometown to
take care of her ailing mother. Asked to entertain a local bankers' meeting, she
revived her hayseed character, taking as her hometown the nearby railroad
crossing named Grinder's Switch. One of the bankers recommended that she audition for the GRAND OLE OPRY, where her act was appreciated though not without
concerns that some of the rural listeners might be offended by it. So Minnie's first
broadcast was scheduled for 11:05 P.M., well after the prime listening time. It turns

out their fears were groundless, because Pearl soon became one of the Opry's most popular attractions. Made a permanent member in 1940, she continues to perform today, although of late her advancing age has led her to cut back on her performance schedule.

The Pearl persona—with the flowered hat with a price tag hanging off of it, the thrift-store cotton-print dress, and her signature greeting of "How-dee"—is instantly recognizable even by people who rarely listen to country music. Her typical monologue is made up of a string of corny old jokes set as "true events" from the little town of Grinder's Switch; this trick of incorporating hoary old jokes into what purports to be real stories was appropriated by latter-day monologuist Garrison Keillor, whose monologues are set as "news" from his fictional hometown of Lake Wobegon.

◀ PEDAL STEEL GUITAR

(c. 1950)

What would a classic country recording of the late fifties and early sixties be without the sound of a crying pedal steel guitar? The instrument has become an integral part of country music-making, and its sound defines for many people a country recording.

The steel guitar has its roots in the lap-played Hawaiian styles of the twenties. It's called a *steel* guitar because the player uses a steel bar to note the strings (not because the body of the instrument is made of steel, although some do feature metal bodies). Originally, standard guitars were adapted for lap playing by raising the nut (which raised the strings) and lowering the frets. However, because the sound hole was facing up rather than out, it was difficult to produce an instrument that could be easily heard, particularly in a band setting.

In a search for greater volume, instrument builders like the Dopyera brothers introduced models with built-in resonators, marketed as National steel guitars and later as DOBROS. In the mid-thirties, electric amplification came in, and players like BOB DUNN in WESTERN SWING ensembles began playing electrified instruments, for greater volume and a cutting, hard-edged sound. In the late forties, the amplified steel guitar became a part of HONKY-TONK ensembles, thanks to the radio appearances and recordings of HANK WILLIAMS, whose backup band featured the instrument. The bluesy sounds that could be created on the instrument were a perfect accompaniment to the sad-and-lonesome music that Williams made.

With amplification, there was no longer a necessity for the guitar to have a large and bulky body that had to be balanced on the player's lap. One of the first innovations was the electrified instrument nicknamed the "frypan"; this tiny-bodied instrument was easily transportable and sat comfortably on a player's lap but still had all the power that amplification offered. Later, musicians began mounting these instruments on legs. Because lap players work with open tunings, it is often necessary to retune their instruments many times during a performance, a time-consuming annoyance. Someone came up with the idea of mounting two separate necks on a stand, each tuned to a common, but different, open chord, to alleviate this problem. More strings were added, again to expand the range of the instrument. Eventually, ancillary pedals and levers were added to the instrument, giving the player greater control over volume, retuning individual notes, and other special effects.

One of the first country musicians to embrace the new so-called pedal steel was SPEEDY WEST, who began using the instrument in 1948. His wide-ranging session work on the West Coast helped popularize the instrument among other players. In the mid-fifties, BUDDY EMMONS began playing with popular singer LITTLE JIMMY DICKENS, and he also became a leading innovator in instrument design and manufacture when he founded the Sho-Bud company. By the early sixties, the pedal steel was firmly established on all of Nashville's recordings, despite the fact that more traditional instruments like the fiddle and BANJO had been eliminated by producers working in the confines of the new NASHVILLE SOUND.

When COUNTRY-ROCK groups were first formed in the late sixties, the pedal steel was eagerly embraced by a new generation. GRAM PARSONS's first country-rock outfit, the International Submarine Band, featured a young steel player named J. D. Maness, whose style was widely copied. POCO centered on steel player Rusty Young, the FLYING BURRITO BROTHERS featured "Sneaky" Pete Kleinow, and MIKE NESMITH's First National Band had Red Rhodes. These groups eliminated the excesses of the Nashville Sound but kept the pedal steel as a vital link to country's past.

The seventies saw a revival of interest in the pedal steel's ancestors, including the dobro and earlier electrified steel instruments. But the pedal steel continues to be found in most major country stars' backup bands, while individual players have evolved diverse styles that take the instrument far beyond the clichéd, trademark whining sound that used to be its limits.

◀ PEER, RALPH

(born 1892, Kansas City, MO; died 1960)

Peer was one of the first great producers of country music as well as the founder of Peer-Southern Music, among the first publishers of country songs.

Peer was born to the music business; his father sold phonographs and had a link with the Columbia company, for whom Peer worked in his native Kansas City from 1911 to 1919. He was hired by a rival firm, the General Phonograph Company, in 1920 to run their OKeh division. His first job was to oversee the recordings of blues singer Mamie Smith, recording her "Crazy Blues" in 1920, said to be the first blues recording by a black singer. In 1923 he was contacted by an Atlanta furniture dealer who wanted him to record a local fiddler named FIDDLIN' JOHN CARSON. The resulting record—Carson's rendition of "The Little Old Log Cabin in the Lane" backed with "The Old Hen Cackled"—is generally credited as the first country-music recording.

In 1925 Peer moved to Victor Records, where he was offered a unique arrangement: Instead of paying him a salary, they offered him the publishing rights to any of the material that he recorded. Because there were no publishing rights for traditional songs or tunes, Peer began to encourage his artists to write their own material. In 1928 Victor and Peer co-founded Southern Music, which became a leading publisher of blues and country material.

In the summer of 1927, Peer made a field trip to Bristol, Tennessee, that would become legendary in recording circles. At this session he discovered both JIMMIE RODGERS and the CARTER FAMILY, and he oversaw their first recordings. His music-publishing arm would naturally become the outlet for both of these acts' prolific compositions.

In 1932, forseeing the change in musical tastes, Peer branched out in his publishing business to sign popular songsmiths like Hoagy Carmichael, while he also explored the international market. He was central in the founding of Broadcast Music International (or BMI) in 1940, which challenged the more conservative ASCAP (American Society of Composers, Artists, and Performers) in its dominance of the music-licensing field.

In the forties and fifties, Peer left the day-to-day operations of his company increasingly to his son, while he pursued a lifelong interest in horticulture, becoming a world-renowned authority on camellias.

◀ PENNY, HANK

(born 1918, Birmingham, AL; died 1992)

Penny was a WESTERN SWING–style bandleader who turned to upbeat country and HONKY-TONK in the fifties.

Inspired by pioneering bandleaders BOB WILLS and MILTON BROWN, Penny formed the Radio Cowboys, gaining fame over station WWL in New York as well as a number of stations in the South. He first recorded for Vocalion in the late thirties under the direction of ace producer ART SATHERLEY. At that time, his band featured fiddler BOUDLEAUX BRYANT (who later became one of country's and rock's greatest songwriters), as well as master musicians Noel Boggs and Eddie Duncan.

Penny relocated to the West Coast after the war, and his greatest recordings were made in the postwar years from 1945 to 1950 for the Cincinnati-based King label. By then, Penny's band featured hot string-bender MERLE TRAVIS, along with Boggs, ace steel guitarist SPEEDY WEST, and chanteuse Jaye P. Morgan. Their instrumental work was outstanding, reflecting the influence of the new chamber jazz that was coming out of the West Coast, although they also began recording novelty numbers that would increasingly form the backbone of Penny's repertoire.

In the fifties, Penny moved to RCA and Decca, but the quality of his work suffered at the hands of unsympathetic producers. By decade's end, he was working out of Las Vegas with a new band, featuring young hotpicker ROY CLARK as well as steel guitar legend Curly Chalker. Penny spent most of the sixties performing as a country comedian and retired in the early seventies in Los Angeles.

◀ PERKINS, CARL

(born 1932, Tiptenville, TN)

One of the greats of early rock and roll, Perkins's career has crisscrossed genres from ROCKABILLY to country and back to jazzy rock. He is well remembered for his fifties compositions, most notably "Blue Suede Shoes," the first song to top the country, R&B, and pop charts, establishing rock and roll as a dominant pop style.

Born to a poor farming family, Perkins was exposed to music from youth. His father was an avid fan of the GRAND OLE OPRY, and it was one of the few radio shows he would allow to be played on the family's radio. A second important influence was black sharecropper "Uncle" John Westbrook, who played GUITAR in a rural, finger-picking blues style.

After World War II, the family relocated to Bemis, Tennessee, where Carl's uncles were working in a cotton mill. They settled in their first home with electricity, and soon Carl was practicing on a second-hand electric Harmony guitar in the attic. He cites as inspirations for his single-string guitar lead work Opry artists like ARTHUR "GUITAR BOOGIE" SMITH, whose big hit that earned him his nickname was released in 1946, along with Butterball Page, who played lead in ERNEST TUBB's backup band in the forties.

In the early fifties, Carl talked his brothers Jay and Clayton into forming a country trio, and they began performing in local HONKY-TONKS as the Perkins Brothers. After a while, it became clear to Carl that the group would need drums if they were to provide a danceable beat for their customers. After a trial drummer joined in 1953, Clayton brought on board schoolmate W. S. "Fluke" Holland, who had a keen appreciation for R&B music as well as country. Carl, meanwhile, was moving the music in an up-tempo direction to suit dancing, thus forming the seeds of rockabilly. At the same time they were playing honky-tonks at night, the brothers worked by day in Jackson's Colonial Bakery.

In 1954 Perkins heard ELVIS PRESLEY's recording of "Blue Moon of Kentucky" on the radio and realized that someone else was experimenting with up-tempo country music. He took his brothers to Memphis in search of Sun Records, where Presley recorded, and met legendary producer SAM PHILLIPS. In October, Phillips recorded Perkins's first song, a country honky-tonk ballad called "Turn Around." A second session yielded another HANK WILLIAMS–style number, "Let the Jukebox Keep on Playing," complete with crying steel guitar and fiddle. But the flip side revealed another side of Perkins's personality; the song "Gone, Gone, Gone" had only muted steel guitar and no fiddle, with Perkins right up front in the mix, featuring a rocking beat along with scat vocals. This was his first recording in his new R&B-influenced style.

In late 1955, Perkins returned to the studio to record two boppin' numbers and two more standard country WEEPERS. Although in the past Phillips had issued the country songs as the A-sides, keeping the up-tempo material for the less-often played flip sides, he decided to issue the two rockabilly numbers on one single, "Blue Suede Shoes" backed with "Honey Don't." "Blue Suede Shoes" would establish Perkins's reputation; it also saved Phillips from bankruptcy and made Perkins an instant star.

Sad to say, Perkins's new success was short-lived. While on the road to New York for a taping of the *Perry Como* television show in early 1956, his manager fell asleep at the wheel, and all three Perkins brothers were injured. Carl lost key national exposure and momentum; another hillbilly rocker, Elvis Presley, would soon be grabbing the spotlight. Perkins's next releases came out in summer 1956; both were country-flavored numbers, "Boppin' the Blues" followed by "Dixie Fried." The latter is one of Perkins's best songs, although its Southern-oriented lyric limited its mass-market appeal.

In late 1956, Perkins returned to Sun Studios for another session. This time young session pianist JERRY LEE LEWIS was on hand, and Elvis Presley showed up at the studio to say hello to his old friends. Later in the session, another newcomer, JOHNNY CASH, stopped by. Phillips happily recorded the jam session that resulted, and the collection of old country tunes and hymns has since been released credited to the Million Dollar Quartet.

By 1957 Perkins was a has-been at Sun. Newer artists Johnny Cash and Jerry Lee Lewis were successful on the country and rock charts, respectively, and Perkins was pretty much ignored by Phillips. Producer Don Law from Columbia Records signed the frustrated singer in 1957 and the following year began issuing teen-oriented pop with him, including "Pink Pedal Pushers" and "Pop Let Me Have the Car." However, Perkins sounded somewhat uncomfortable in the role of teen idol.

In the next years, tragedy beset his life: his brother Jay died of a brain tumor in 1958; Perkins and his other brother both became alcoholics (Clayton eventually died of alcoholism); drummer W. S. Holland quit the group in early 1959.

In the early sixties, Perkins was disillusioned with the music business; dropped by Columbia in 1963, he recorded country material briefly for Decca before being dropped again. He went into retirement for a while, until early 1964 when he was approached to tour England with another rock and roll legend, Chuck Berry. Perkins was surprised to discover that he was venerated in England, particularly by a young guitarist named George Harrison, who had learned many licks off of Perkins's recordings. The Beatles' recordings of Perkins's songs—including "Honey Don't," "Matchbox," and "Everybody Wants to Be My Baby"—revitalized the singer's career in Europe, where he quickly became a favorite touring artist.

In the late sixties, Perkins was a featured artist in Johnny Cash's touring group. For Cash he wrote the nostalgic 1968 country hit "Daddy Sang Bass," about a backwoods country band. He recorded a comeback album with the rock revivalists NRBQ in 1979, producing a minor hit with "Restless," and then recorded sporadically through the eighties, primarily in Europe, waxing a mix of country and early rock. In 1986 he reunited with Cash and ROY ORBISON for the *Class of '55* album, an attempt to recapture the glory days of Memphis.

Perkins brought a country sensibility to rhythm and blues. His combination of soulful vocals, hot guitar picking, and a powerful band set the stage for countless other acts in rockabilly, mainstream rock and roll, and NEW COUNTRY. His influence can be heard throughout American popular music.

Select Discography

Honky Tonk Gal, Rounder 27. Sun era recordings, including some previously unreleased tracks.

Jive After Five, Rhino 70958. His best cuts from between 1958 and 1978, after the Sun years.

Restless, Columbia/Legacy 48986. Mostly teen-pop material from Columbia cut in the late fifties and early sixties, although it also includes tracks from late-seventies sessions with NRBQ.

◀ PHILLIPS, SAM

(born Samuel Cornelius Phillips, 1923, near Florence, AL)

The legendary recording engineer/owner of Sun Records, Phillips discovered, among others, ELVIS PRESLEY and made him a star.

Phillips's father owned a large tenant farm on the Tennessee River just outside of Florence, Alabama, and was fairly well-to-do until the stock market crash decimated his savings. In 1941 his father died, and Phillips left high school, taking jobs at a grocery store and then a funeral parlor to help support his mother. Meanwhile, he studied engineering through a correspondence course and got his first chance to work on radio at WLAY in Muscle Shoals. After marriage and further radio jobs in Decatur and Nashville, Phillips settled in Memphis to work for WREC in 1945, where his brother Jud was already working in a singing group. Five years later, he opened his Memphis Recording Service as a means of supplementing his income.

Originally, Phillips recorded local R&B performers, including Howlin' Wolf, B. B. King, and Jackie Brentson, licensing the recordings to established companies like Chess out of Chicago or Modern out of Los Angeles. In 1952 he began Sun Records, scoring his first hit with his own rewriting of the popular Big Mama Thornton song "Hound Dog," entitled "Bear Cat," which was recorded by local deejay Rufus Thomas. Other R&B acts, along with the doo-wop group the Prisonnaires (the novelty was that all of the members were real prisoners), were quickly added to Sun's roster.

In 1953 a local boy came into the studios to make a birthday present recording for his mother; his name was Elvis Presley. Some time over the next year, the young singer made an impression on Phillips who was said to be looking for a white singer who could sound black (Phillips recognized the popularity of R&B music among white teenagers but realized that a white singer would be more acceptable to radio programmers, parents, and the teens themselves). Phillips teamed Elvis with guitarist Scotty Moore and bassist Bill Black and shaped his first recording, the blues standard "That's All Right" learned from Big Boy Crudup, backed with BILL MONROE's "Blue Moon of Kentucky."

The great success of Elvis swamped the tiny Sun label, and within a year Phillips sold his contract with the hip-shaker to RCA for a then-enormous sum of $35,000. Attempts to mold CARL PERKINS, JOHNNY CASH, and JERRY LEE LEWIS into the "next Elvis" were only partially successful; Perkins's career was dogged by bad luck, Cash had little sympathy for the teenie-bop material that Phillips had him record, and Lewis made the mistake of marrying his thirteen-year-old cousin. Besides these country rockers, Phillips also recorded some pure country acts (usually issued on the Phillips International label rather than Sun), but by the early sixties the label had pretty much run out of steam. The Sun masters were sold to country producer SHELBY SINGLETON in 1969, and since that time Phillips has been active primarily in other business interests, including radio stations and Holiday Inns.

Select Discography

The Sun Story, Rhino 75884. Two-CD set featuring R&B and country acts originally recorded by Phillips.

◀ PICKARD FAMILY, THE

(c. 1924–c. 1950s; original lineup: Obed "Dad," Leila May [Wilson], Ruthie, and Ann Pickard [vocals])

The Pickards, early vocal stars on the GRAND OLE OPRY, specialized in sentimental songs of family and home.

Led by multi-instrumentalist Obed "Dad" Pickard and his wife, Leila May, the group began broadcasting over the Opry in 1926 and then moved to more than forty other radio stations in a long history of performing. Dad specialized in the sentimental ballads of the late nineteenth century that had been popular in sub-urban parlors and then spread to the country, such as "Poor Kitty Wells," evergreen classics like "She'll Be Comin' 'Round the Mountain," and standard COWBOY SONGS like "Bury Me Not on the Lone Prairie." The group eventually worked in major cities like Detroit, New York, and Philadelphia, spreading the country music style into urban areas, and published many popular songbooks that became the basis for many artists' performing repertoires. The group recorded about forty sides from 1927 to 1930, during the height of the country music craze. By the late thirties, the Pickards (like the CARTER FAMILY) were broadcasting over the famous border radio stations out of Mexico. In 1940 the family moved to California, making a few appearances in C-grade films, and then starring on a live television variety program out of Los Angeles from 1949 to 1954.

◀ PIERCE, WEBB

(born 1926, West Monroe, LA)

Pierce was one of the most successful and popular of the HONKY-TONK singers of the fifties and sixties, second only to EDDY ARNOLD in placing chart hits during that period.

Born in rural Louisiana, Pierce began playing GUITAR as a teenager and got his first radio job after World War II, in Monroe. He went to Shreveport, then the center of country-music making in the state, thanks to the popular *Louisiana Hayride* radio program that originated there. After a couple of unsuccessful years, during which he was reduced to working at the local Sears, Pierce finally attracted the attention of Horace Logan, the program's producer, and was hired to join its cast in the early fifties.

Webb had made recordings as a vocalist with Tillman Frank's band (including the minor hit "Hayride Boogie") for the local Pacemaker label and then was signed on his own to Four Star. His band at the time featured future big names in country circles, including pianist FLOYD CRAMER and guitarist FARON YOUNG. In 1952 he was signed to Decca, where he had his first hit, "Wondering," followed quickly by the number-one record "Back Street Affair." Between 1952 and 1958, all of his releases made the country top ten; in 1954, he left the *Hayride* to join the more prestigious GRAND OLE OPRY. Some of Pierce's best-known recordings include classic barroom numbers such as 1953's "I'm Walking the Dog," "That's Me Without You," and the beer-soaked "There Stands the Glass"; 1954's up-tempo "More and More" and the classic "Slowly" (featuring a Bud Isaac weeping steel guitar solo that helped popularize the instrument in country circles); 1956's "Teenage Boogie" (a remake of his first recording, "Hayride Boogie"), a cover of the EVERLY BROTHERS's "Bye Bye Love" and "Honky Tonk Song," both from 1957; and two songs cowritten with MEL TILLIS, 1958's "Tupelo County Jail" and "A Thousand Miles Ago" from the following year.

Although he was no longer dominating the charts, Pierce continued to produce solid hits through the mid-sixties, including "Sweet Lips" (1961), "Crazy Wild Desire" (1962), also cowritten with Tillis, and his last major hit, "Memory Number 1" (1964). In the mid-sixties, Pierce switched his attention to the business end of publishing and promoting and became a symbol of country-music excess when he had the first custom-made guitar-shaped swimming pool installed at his home and began cruising around Nashville in a Cadillac encrusted with silver dollars. Although he continued to record for Decca/MCA through the mid-seventies, Pierce's hits became fewer and fewer after the mid-sixties. In 1977 he moved to the tiny Plantation label and then semiretired, although he was lured out of retirement for a duet session with country outlaw WILLIE NELSON in a 1982 remake of his 1955 recording of "In the Jailhouse Now."

Select Discography

The One and Only, King 648. Late-forties recordings.

Greatest Hits, MCA 120. Cassette-only reissue of recordings from the fifties and sixties.

King of the Honky Tonk, Country Music Foundation. Eighteen classic recordings.

◄ POCO

(1968–1982; original lineup: Richie Furay [guitar, vocals]; Jim Messina [guitar, vocals]; Rusty Young [steel guitar]; Randy Meisner [bass, vocals]; George Grantham [drums, vocals])

Poco was among the first COUNTRY-ROCK bands. They never achieved much popular success, but several band members would be influential in the next generation of country-rock and mainstream pop.

Richie Furay and Jim Messina had met as members of the last incarnation of the Buffalo Springfield, which had fallen apart early in 1968. Determined to pursue a more countrified sound, they formed a new group originally called Pogo, after the popular comic strip; however, when the owners of the strip objected, the group changed its name to Poco. The band emphasized soft folk-rock harmonies with just a dash of countrified flavor, particularly emphasized by Rusty Young's tasteful steel guitar work, a novelty for a rock-and-roll ensemble.

The group seemed to be in a constant state of flux when it came to its personnel. Bassist Randy Meisner was the first to go after about a year, joining RICK NELSON's seminal country-rock outfit, the Stone Canyon Band, and then cofounding the EAGLES; he was replaced by Timothy B. Schmidt. Messina left in the early seventies to pursue a career as a record producer; he ended up producing a new SINGER/SONGWRITER named Kenny Loggins and soon returned to performing in the very popular seventies duo of Loggins and Messina. Messina was replaced on GUITAR, by Paul Cotten who had previously played with the country-rock ensemble the Illinois Speed Press. Furay left to form a country-rock trio with CHRIS HILLMAN (previously of the BYRDS and the FLYING BURRITO BROTHERS) and singer/songwriter J. D. Souther. He was not replaced.

The band soldiered on through the seventies, led by original member Rusty Young, and scored some minor chart successes. Schmidt left in 1977 to replace Meisner in the Eagles, and Grantham also left at the same time; they were replaced by Charlie Harrison on bass and Steve Chapman on drums, with the addition of keyboardist Kim Bullard. This group lasted until about 1982, when they finally bit the dust. The original members have reunited from time to time, first in 1984 to make a comeback album and then again in 1991, with little success.

Select Discography

Poco, Epic 26522. Budget CD reissue of their first, 1969 album.

The Forgotten Trail, Epic 46162. Two-CD set of recordings from 1969 to 1974, with historical booklet.

Crazy Loving, MCA 42333. Hits from 1975 to 1982 by the later incarnations of the band.

◄ POOLE, CHARLIE

(born 1892, Alamance County, NC; died 1931)

Influential North Carolina banjoist/vocalist/bandleader, Poole had a short but extremely prolific career as a recording artist. He is the Buster Keaton of traditional music; he even looked like Buster, with his large, flat face and bulging ears. If Buster Keaton had sung, he would undoubtedly have sounded like Charlie Poole, whose slightly droll but deadpan vocal style is immediately recognizable.

Born in rural North Carolina, Poole developed a unique BANJO style based on the traditional styles around him. Unlike banjoists from the deeper South, who brush against the strings in a style known as "frailing," Carolina pickers have tended to pick the strings using two or three fingers; eventually, this style evolved into what is now called BLUEGRASS banjo picking, developed by two Carolinians, "Snuffy" Jenkins and Earl Scruggs. Poole also credited as an influence ragtime banjoist Fred Van Epps, who made hundreds of recordings in the first decades of this century; the Carolina picker even made a few instrumental recordings in emulation of the ragtime banjoist's style. There were also stories that Poole had damaged his right (picking) hand in a childhood accident playing baseball, leading to the creation of his unique style; in any case, as an adult, he picked the banjo with his thumb and two fingers.

Poole worked most of his life in the textile mills, as did many other contemporary country musicians. He was working in the small textile town of Spray, North Carolina, when he began his performing career. He first formed a duo with fiddler Posey Rorer, originally a coal miner from Tennessee who was injured in a mining accident and so had taken to working in the mills. They were joined by guitarist Norman Woodlieff to form the first version of what would become the North Carolina Ramblers. In 1925 the trio went north to jobs in Passaic, New Jersey, working for a car manufacturer. Poole went to New York and arranged for them to record for Columbia Records, where in 1925 they made their first recordings, which were immediately successful. The first record issued by the Ramblers was "Don't Let Your Deal Go Down," a blues-influenced song that remained in print for years and became Poole's signature number.

The band had a unique style, centering around Poole's wry, uninflected vocal style and intricate, chordal work on the banjo. Poole sang a combination of sentimental heart songs and comic novelty numbers, many originating in the late nineteenth and early twentieth centuries. Although his vocal style was not highly ornamented like other Southern singers, he did possess a deadpan humor, jazzy phrasing, and, most important for early recordings, clear pronunciation, which made these discs extremely popular. Unlike other string bands, the North Carolina Ramblers were a subdued group, focusing on Poole's banjo and vocals accompanied by discreet GUITAR and fiddle. Poole's versions of many songs, including "Jay Gould's Daughter," "Ramblin' Blues," "Hungry Hash House," and "If I Lose (Let Me Lose)," have become standards in the old-time country repertoire. Poole made jazz-influenced recordings of old-time numbers, such as his "Goodbye Liza Jane," which would indirectly influence such artists as WESTERN SWING fiddler BOB WILLS, who also adopted old-time fiddle tunes to a new, jazz- and blues-influenced style.

The band went through several personnel changes in its short life; West Virginia guitarist Roy Harvey replaced Woodlieff on their second Columbia session in 1926, and fiddler Rorer left the band in 1928, to be replaced by Lonnie Austin and, two years later, by Odell Smith. Like many recording units of the day, the band was not a fixed ensemble but probably had a set of floating members who would come together for specific recording dates or local jobs.

In 1929 Poole decided to enlarge the Ramblers to include many of the other musicians who had been performing with them. However, producer FRANK WALKER at Columbia was unwilling to change the successful Ramblers formula. Instead, the group went to the budget Paramount label, recording under the name of the Highlanders. This group featured a much richer ensemble sound, including piano played by Roy Harvey's sister, Lucy Terry, and the twin fiddles of Austin and Smith. They also made a series of comic-novelty dialogue recordings, entitled "A Trip to New York," perhaps to answer the popularity of the SKILLET LICKERS' series of playlets.

In 1931 Poole was so popular that he was invited to come to Hollywood to provide background music for the movies. However, he died of a massive heart attack before he could make the trip West. Although he hardly looked the part, Poole was the first in a line of high-living country stars, whose life was tragically cut short due to his love of heavy drinking. His recordings sold very well throughout the South and continued to sell after his death, so that the influence of Poole was deeply felt for decades later. When County Records, a New York old-time revival label of the seventies, began reissuing these sides, they found a new and enthusiastic audience (and eventually they released four LPs of Poole's classic recordings).

After Poole's death, many of the other musicians associated with him continued to record, often in bands formed to mimic the sound of the original group; Roy Harvey even formed his own North Carolina Ramblers in the early thirties with fiddler Posey Rorer and Bob Hoke, followed by a second Poolelike group.

Select Discography
Charlie Poole, County 110. Poole's classic sides in clean, remastered sound.

◀ PRAIRIE RAMBLERS

(c. 1930–1956; original members: Chuck Hurt [mandolin, banjo]; Floyd "Salty" Holmes [guitar, harmonica, jug]; Tex Atchison [fiddle], Jack Taylor [bass])

The Prairie Ramblers were an influential cowboy WESTERN SWING ensemble of the early thirties that broadcast over WLS's powerful *National Barn Dance* radio program out of Chicago.

Originally a traditional string band influenced by the jazz craze, the three members came from rural Kentucky and called themselves the Kentucky Ramblers. They got their first radio job in the early thirties out of Davenport, Iowa, where they were heard by talent scouts for WLS's *National Barn Dance*. They joined the *Barn Dance* in 1932 and remained there for nearly two and a half decades. At first they accompanied popular cowgirl vocalist PATSY MONTANA, but they soon began recording on their own, originally for the budget ARC label. Their repertoire became increasingly urbanized and pop; they even recorded hokum double-entendre blues numbers under the pseudonym of the Sweet Violet Boys.

The band went through many personnel changes, beginning in 1937 when Tex Atchison jumped ship to head West, where he appeared in C-grade Westerns as well as fronting many of the popular California cowboy bands. He had several replacements. Floyd "Salty" Holmes came and went from the band through its long existence, performing for a while on the GRAND OLE OPRY with his wife, Maddie (whose sister was the popular country vocalist MARTHA CARSON), as the duo of Salty and Maddie. Taylor and Hurt somehow stuck it out through the band's entire twenty-four-year run; after the band ended, they were absorbed lock, stock, and barrel into Stan Wallowick's Polka Chips dance band, where they continued to play into the sixties.

The Prairie Ramblers Western-jive style has been often copied, most recently by the popular neo-cowboy ensemble, RIDERS IN THE SKY.

◀ PRESLEY, ELVIS

(born 1935, Tupelo, MS; died 1977)

Although best remembered as a teen idol and rock star, Presley maintained a strong connection with country music throughout his career, and his singing style, repertoire, and myth had as large an impact on country music as it did on pop in general. It is a rare artist whose music transcends categorization, and an even rarer one who remains influential more than a decade after his death; Presley is such a performer, becoming more legendary as the years go by.

Born the son of a white sharecropper, Presley's earliest musical influences were the white church and black field hands. He was undoubtedly exposed to country radio, which at the time was a mix of white "mainstream" country (including JIMMIE RODGERS–style country blues and HANK WILLIAMS–style HONKY-TONK) and the nascent R&B music (including jive, blues, and swing recordings, along with early "rockin'" sides). His family relocated to Memphis, where Elvis was somewhat of a loner in high school. After completing his education, he worked as a truck driver, while he also made a few amateur recordings at SAM PHILLIPS's legendary Sun Studios. It was here that he was to make his first commercial recording, launching an entirely new sound.

Sam Phillips's genius was in recognizing that Elvis could mimic the bluesy phrasing of popular black singers, while (thanks to his skin color) he would be acceptable to a mainstream white audience. On his first recording, Elvis bridged the gap between R&B and country by recording on the A-side "That's All Right Mama," originated by bluesman Big Boy (Arthur) Crudup, but backing it up with the bluegrass standard "Blue Moon of Kentucky" by BILL MONROE. Elvis's Sun recordings were marketed as "hillbilly bop" rather than rock, and Elvis was booked onto *The Louisiana Hayride*, a popular country radio program. His first tours were pretty much limited to the South, and his primary market was country/ROCKABILLY.

When Elvis hooked up with Colonel Tom Parker, who had previously successfully marketed country legend HANK SNOW, he made the first step into mainstream acceptance. Parker arranged for Presley to record for RCA, a label better equipped than Sun to market him to the nascent teen-pop crowd. At RCA, Elvis's initial recordings were produced by CHET ATKINS and were glossed up with production values similar to those that Atkins brought to his other NASHVILLE SOUND recordings. The JORDANAIRES, a popular white gospel harmony group, were employed as backup singers, providing the "bop-bops" on "Don't Be Cruel" and countless other Presley recordings. Although Presley was marketed (and successful) as a teen popster, the sound of his recordings was not much different than RCA's other Nashville output of the day.

Elvis's fifties career ended with his induction into the army, and some believe that his first (and last) golden age ended at this time as well. He spent much of the early to mid-sixties after his return from service in Hollywood, producing lack-luster recordings and starring in C- to D-grade films. However, in 1968, a rock comeback was staged as an NBC-TV special; this was followed by some classic recordings made in Memphis with a tougher, COUNTRY-ROCK sound, producing hits like "In the Ghetto" (penned by MAC DAVIS), and "Suspicious Minds," which has become a country standard. Unfortunately, the seventies would find Elvis mostly working in Vegas, where his weight and dependence on drugs increased while his talent drained away. He died of heart failure due to drug abuse in 1977.

Elvis maintained a lifelong love of gospel music, another link with his country roots. In 1956 Elvis stopped by at Sun Studios to visit CARL PERKINS during a recording session; an impromptu jam, which was joined by JERRY LEE LEWIS and JOHNNY CASH, ensued. Not surprisingly, the session was almost entirely gospel favorites that the so-called "Million Dollar Quartet" knew from their youth in church. Elvis recorded several gospel LPs, which sold primarily in the country market.

It would be impossible to find a performer in any type of popular music uninfluenced by Elvis today. His energetic stage performances (proving, definitively, that white men *can* dance), his sneering demeanor, and his intense vocals that combined sweet crooning with blues inflections and a gospel fervor all have found their place in country music.

Select Discography

Million Dollar Quartet, RCA 2023. The legendary sessions with Perkins, Cash, and Lewis. This is mostly a program of standards, particularly hymns, and many tracks last a minute or less. Great notes by Colin Escott.

Twenty Great Performances, RCA 2277. Just about everything you'd like to have.

The King of Rock and Roll: Complete '50s Masters, RCA 66050. Five CDs and lavish booklet (with excellent documentation by Peter Guralnick) including all of the lip-curler's classic recordings.

◀ PRICE, KENNY

(born 1937, Florence, KY; died 1987)

Known affectionately as "the round mound of sound," Price gained his greatest popularity through his appearances on the HEE HAW TV program in the late sixties and early seventies.

Raised in rural Kentucky, he got his first guitar from the Sears, Roebuck catalog and began playing for local functions. After service in the Korean War, he returned home to study music seriously at Cincinnati's Conservatory of Music. In 1954 he joined WLW out of Cincinnati as a regular performer on their *Midwestern Hayride* radio show, serving as lead singer with his band, the Hometowners. On the *Hayride* he met Bobby Bobo, who would later move to Nashville and open Boone Records, Price's first label. In the mid-sixties, Price followed Bobo to Nashville and signed with Boone, recording a couple of hits, including 1966's "Walking on New Grass" and "Happy Tracks," both written by Ray Pennington, LILY MAE LEDFORD's husband and the father of J. P. Pennington of the country-pop group EXILE.

A couple more hits followed, and in 1969 Price was signed to RCA, where he had hits in 1970 with "Biloxi" and "Sheriff of Boone County." At about this time, he also joined *Hee Haw*, where his likable personality and smooth singing style fit in perfectly with the show's upbeat tone. Leaving RCA in 1974, Price recorded for the smaller MRC and Dimension labels through the early eighties, without achieving much success, although he continued to be a popular performer on the country-fair and rodeo circuit. He died in his hometown in 1987.

◀ PRICE, RAY

(born 1926, Perryville, TX)

Ray Price has had a long career in country music, beginning as a HONKY-TONK singer in the HANK WILLIAMS mold in the early fifties and transforming himself into a histrionic crooner at the height of the NASHVILLE SOUND in the sixties. Still, Price was always somewhat controversial, pushing the envelope of country music, although sometimes in a decidedly pop-schlock direction. Along the way, he nurtured the careers of many younger country innovators, including WILLIE NELSON and KRIS KRISTOFFERSON.

Born in rural eastern Texas, Price was raised on a small farm. As a youngster, he developed a lifelong love for animals (and a passion for raising fine horses) and began to play the GUITAR. When Price was a teenager the family relocated to urban Dallas, where he began performing locally. Intending to be a veterinarian, he went to Abilene to enter college, but his college career was interrupted by a four-year stint in the marines during World War II. On his return, he began performing on Abilene radio, taking the name of the "Cherokee Cowboy."

In 1949 Price was invited to join Dallas's prestigious *Big D Jamboree* radio show, which was broadcast both locally and, in part, nationally by CBS radio. This led to a contract with the Bullet label, where Price recorded his first weepy, HONKY-TONK numbers, in a style very reminiscent of his then-idol Hank Williams. Coming to Nashville in 1951, he met his idol, with whom he briefly lived and toured, often standing in for the older singer when he was too drunk to perform. At the same time, he signed to Columbia, achieving his first hit with 1952's "Talk to Your Heart."

After Williams's death, Price began performing with the DRIFTING COWBOYS, Hank's old backup band, which by the mid-fifties he enlarged into a new group, which he called the Cherokee Cowboys; alums would include Willie Nelson and steel guitarist Buddy Emmons. Price created a stir in Nashville by including a drummer in his group. (For years, drums were forbidden on the GRAND OLE OPRY's stage.) In these early recordings, Price used the drummer and rhythm section to create what is now known as the shuffle beat, which became a standard for country music recording (most recently revived by young country stars like GEORGE STRAIT).

Price's first big hits were 1954's "I'll Be There" and his signature tune, "Release Me," which has become a country classic. From that point on, he was rarely off the charts. A list of Price's fifties and sixties hits reads like an encyclopedia of country standards, including 1956's "Crazy Arms," "City Lights" from 1958, 1959's "Heartaches by the Number," 1963's "Make the World Go Away," "The Other Woman" in 1965, 1970's "For the Good Times" (written by the then relatively unknown Kristofferson), and 1973's "You're the Best Thing That Ever Happened to Me," all released by Columbia. As Price matured, his tear-in-the-throat style changed to a smoother, pop-crooner style. He also challenged country fans by introducing full string sections on his sixties recordings, a revolutionary move for the time, and abandoned his stage cowboy suit for a suit and tie, emphasizing his ambitions to become a mainstream star.

Price continued to record through the seventies, although he took considerable time off to pursue his first love, horse farming. Many of his recordings were marred by excessive, heavy-handed orchestrations and Price's own increasing pretensions to being a pop warbler. One of his best later works was 1980's *San Antonio Rose*, reuniting him with Willie Nelson and bringing forth a hit with their cover of BOB WILLS's classic "Faded Love." More recently, Price has recorded for the Step One label, usually in his all-out pop mode, although occasionally with more tasteful acoustic instrumentation, returning to Columbia in 1992 for the album *Sometimes a Rose*.

Select Discography

The Essential, Columbia Legacy 48532. His best recordings cut between 1952 and 1961, before he went nuts with the string sections.

The Honky Tonk Years, Rounder 22. Cassette-only reissue of his earliest recordings (1951 to 1956) showing the greatest influence of Hank Williams (which is not surprising, considering that Hank's band, the Drifting Cowboys, are on hand on many cuts).

San Antonio Rose, Columbia 36476. With Willie Nelson.

Sometimes a Rose, Columbia 48980. Heavily produced 1992 album.

◀ PRIDE, CHARLEY

(born 1938, Sledge, MS)

One of the best-selling country artists of the sixties and seventies, Pride is noteworthy for being one of the few black performers to break through to true country stardom. Pride's interest in country music reflects the fact that in the rural South traditional country (and blues) audiences crossed racial lines; and his success reflects both the slickness of Pride's recordings and the smooth-as-silk quality of his vocals.

Pride was born one of eleven children to poor tenant farmers. Like many other black families in rural Mississippi, they made their living picking cotton, for which they were paid three dollars for every hundred pounds picked. Early on, Pride became a fan of country radio, particularly emulating the bluesy sounds of HANK WILLIAMS, and he taught himself the GUITAR. At the same time, an early talent for athletics manifested itself, and he began playing baseball in the old Negro league in the late fifties.

After serving in the military, Pride was hired to play for a minor-league team in Helena, Montana. He continued to perform in local bars in his free time, while he also worked off-season for Anaconda Mining as a smelter. In 1963, RED SORVINE was passing through the region and heard Pride perform; he encouraged Pride to come to Nashville to audition for RCA. Pride stalled for a year, while pursuing his dreams of big-league baseball as a member of the New York Mets farm team. In 1964 he traveled to Nashville to audition for famed country producer CHET ATKINS, who signed him to RCA.

Pride's recording career was blessed with early success. His first single, "Snakes Crawl at Night," was an immediate top-ten country hit and was followed by another hit, "Just Between You and Me." Within a year of the release of his first single, he was invited to join the GRAND OLE OPRY, where he became immediately one of the most popular performers. Atkins smothered Pride's vocals in the blend of echoey guitars and girly choruses that Nashville was becoming (in)famous for, and the country audience ate it up. RCA placed little emphasis on Pride's racial identity, and no one in the audience seemed to mind that he was a lone black star among a white (and relatively conservative) group of musicians.

Pride enjoyed his greatest success in the late sixties and early seventies, winning numerous Grammy, CMA, and gold record awards. In addition to the standard songs of lovin' and losin', Pride was also a popular gospel recording artist, bringing the same smooth, pop delivery to his gospel recordings that he did to his songs of heartache.

A longtime resident of Dallas, Pride retired from performing in the eighties, although he continues to record sporadically, issuing a couple of albums late in the decade for the small 16th Avenue label. His 1993 comeback single, "Just for the Love of It" is typical sixties Nashville in its conservative message, and Pride's voice still sounds smooth as silk, even though the backing is simpler than on his earlier recordings, reflecting the influence of NEW COUNTRY.

Select Discography
The Best of Charley Pride, RCA 5968.

◀ PROGRESSIVE BLUEGRASS

(c. 1975–ongoing)

The mid-seventies BLUEGRASS revival spawned a number of groups that used traditional bluegrass instrumentation but were influenced by other types of music, from swing and jazz to rock and progressive music. Known at the time as either "progressive" or "newgrass" bands (the newgrass name coming from the popular group NEW GRASS REVIVAL), these bands were met with some hostility from traditionalists while they greatly helped expand the bluegrass style and the market for bluegrass music. Many of the newgrass pioneers have returned to playing more traditional bluegrass styles in later years.

Undoubtedly the most important group to the growth of progressive bluegrass was the New Grass Revival. While there had been groups in the sixties that sought to stretch the bluegrass repertoire (the COUNTRY GENTLEMEN, the GREENBRIAR BOYS, and the Charles River Valley Boys, to name a few) by drawing on a wider range of musical influences, the New Grass Revival was the first to try to introduce the energy of rock and roll as well as pop and rock songs into their repertoire. Their use of electric bass and electrified BANJO and fiddle was distressing to bluegrass traditionalists.

Another important early progressive band was COUNTRY COOKING. The original instrumentals by band members TONY TRISCHKA and Peter Wernick were based on jazz harmonies and unusual rhythms. Trischka also produced a number of even more far-out solo albums in the seventies, beginning with his *Bluegrass Light*, which took the banjo far beyond the usual bluegrass repertoire. The music was so experimental that some people mockingly called it "spacegrass," a name that stuck.

In the mid-seventies, mandolinist DAVID GRISSMAN expanded progressive bluegrass to encompass acoustic jazz. This hybrid form of music—which he called Dawg music—was often played in small ensembles featuring just MANDOLINS, fiddle, and guitar, but mainstream bluegrass bands were also inspired by Grissman's work to venture into jazz and swing territories. This movement was called by some "jazzgrass," although it didn't really last very long. Soon, Grissman's lighter, swinging style of picking the mandolin was simply incorporated into mainstream progressive bluegrass, although he continues to produce his own quirky brand of music into the nineties.

Like most progressive music, the best elements of progressive bluegrass—advanced harmonies and rhythms, electrified instruments, a broader range of songs—have all been incorporated more or less into mainstream bands today. Meanwhile, artists like Sam Bush (originally of New Grass Revival) and Trischka have returned to playing more traditionally oriented music, so that progressive and traditional bluegrass have met on a new common ground. While progressive bluegrass was undoubtedly an important trend in the expansion of bluegrass both as a style and in reaching a broader audience, it has not survived as a separate genre.

◀ PRUETT, JEANNE

(born Norma Jean Bowman, 1937, Pell City, AL)

Pruett was one of the most popular singer/songwriters of the seventies, scoring a string of hits beginning with 1973's "Satin Sheets."

Music was an integral part of the Bowman household, whether it was at church or at local playparties. Norma Jean, one of ten children, began playing piano and GUITAR at an early age, and soon was well-known locally for her talents. In the early fifties she married guitarist Jack Pruett, who brought her to Nashville in 1956 when he was hired to be MARTY ROBBINS's guitarist, a position he held until 1970.

At first she remained a housewife, caring for her children and singing only socially. However, Robbins urged her to turn professional and arranged for her first, not terribly successful, recordings for RCA in 1963 and 1964. He did, however, give a big boost to her career in 1966 when he had a hit record with her song "Count Me Out"; in the same year, Pruett was made a member of the GRAND OLE OPRY.

In 1969, Decca signed Pruett. Unlike many other artists of the day, Pruett shunned the NASHVILLE SOUND, relying on a simpler production style featuring tasteful guitar, bass, and her own double-tracked harmony vocals. Her first minor hit was 1971's "Hold On to My Unchanging Love," but she really made it big in 1973 with "Satin Sheets." This was followed by "I'm Your Woman," her first in a string of stand-by-your-man-type ditties. (She eventually took a more liberated outlook in her 1983 hit, "Eighties Ladies").

Pruett continued to score hits through the seventies, but her career slowed when she left MCA in 1981 for the smaller Paid label. She began turning her attention to her love of cooking, opening a successful restaurant and limiting her performing and touring. In 1986 she was instrumental in establishing the first ever segment of the *Grand Ole Opry* program dedicated solely to female musicians, a milestone in the history of this rather conservative institution.

◀ PUCKETT, RILEY

(born George Riley Puckett, 1884, Alpharetta, GA; died 1946)

One of the first great country singers, Riley Puckett was also a member of the legendary SKILLET LICKERS string band. His smooth vocal style, coupled with his innovative although sometimes erratic GUITAR playing, made him highly influential on BLUEGRASS and mainstream country artists who followed.

Puckett was born with sight, but when he was three months old, a mistreated eye ailment led to almost total blindness. Trained at the Macon School for the Blind, he first took up the BANJO and then switched to the guitar, quickly evolving an unusual style featuring bass-note runs as bridges between chord changes. While doubtless other guitarists used bass runs previously, Puckett's runs were more elaborate and fully worked out than others who were recording at the time or immediately after.

When Georgia fiddler James "Gideon" Tanner was invited to record for Columbia Records in 1924, he took along Puckett as his accompanist to the New York sessions. Soon after, when Columbia urged Tanner to form a string band to cash in on the popularity of that format, Puckett and Tanner formed the Skillet Lickers. Puckett's vocals were an integral part of the band's popularity during its heyday from the mid-twenties through the mid-thirties. His fine baritone voice, with just a slight country inflection, made him immediately appealing not only to a country audience but also to the broader pop market. He made many solo recordings at the same time as working with Tanner's band, including the 1924 recording of "Rock All Our Babies to Sleep," which finds Puckett YODELING and is thought to be the first country recording featuring this vocal style.

Puckett's repertoire, typical of the mountain musicians of his day, was made up of traditional songs and dance tunes, along with songs from the minstrel tradition, blues, topical songs, and recent popular and sentimental songs. Puckett was not a distinctive singer, in that he did not imbue his vocals with deep feelings, but rather took a straightforward approach to telling the story of the song.

From 1934, when the Skillet Lickers folded, through 1941, Puckett primarily recorded for RCA Victor (he also briefly recorded for Decca in 1937), while performing on radio stations in Georgia and bordering states. His vocal style became increasingly smooth, showing the influence of pop crooners like Bing Crosby.

During the string-band revival of the seventies, the Skillet Lickers' early recordings were rediscovered, renewing interest in Puckett's solo recordings as well. His guitar playing—with its intricate bass runs that were sometimes executed with a quirky sense of rhythm—led to some discussion among revivalists and scholars alike as to whether Puckett intentionally played arhythmically or whether he simply lacked the technique to execute his advanced ideas. Needless to say, his unique playing style was never duplicated.

Select Discography

Red Sails in the Sunset, Bear Family 15280. Bluebird recordings from 1939 to 1941, featuring mostly pop numbers remade in Puckett's signature style.

◀ PURE PRAIRIE LEAGUE

(c. 1972; original lineup: Craig Fuller [lead vocals, guitar]; George Powell [guitars, vocals]; John David Call [guitar, vocals]; Jim Caughlin [bass]; Jimmy Lanham [drums])

Pure Prairie League was a popular Western-flavored COUNTRY-ROCK outfit of the seventies and early eighties that has had varied personnel through a long and tumultuous life. Never really storming the charts, the group did establish a strong regional following.

Originally from Ohio, the group first performed in Columbus, centering on songwriter/guitarist George Powell and lead singer Craig Fuller. After recording a single LP for RCA, they recruited local drummer Billy Hinds to take the place of Jimmy Lanham, who had already left the group. Hinds would bring his friends Michael Connor on keyboards (in 1972) and soon after Mike Reilly on bass (to replace Jim Caughlin). The band recorded a second album (with a studio bassist, not Reilly), but, like the first, it saw little action and RCA threatened to drop the group. However, in late 1973, the song "Amy," from the group's first album, started to get regional airplay. It eventually hit the national charts, leading RCA to rerelease the second album, and the group had a second hit, Powell's "Leave My Heart Alone."

Just as it looked like the group would break through to bigger success, Fuller got into trouble on a draft-evasion charge. It took the band eighteen months to regroup, hiring Cincinnati-based singer Larry Goshorn to take over for Fuller. Goshorn brought his brother, Timmy, to replace John David Call. Both brothers brought a love of BLUEGRASS, the music of the EVERLY BROTHERS, and early rock and roll to the group. This new lineup remained stable through 1977, producing a series of successful albums.

At the end of the summer in 1977, Powell left the group along with the Go-shorns; the brothers and a third sibling formed a family band that was more country-oriented, while Powell decided to leave the grueling life of a touring musician to spend more time with his family. Now based in Los Angeles, the band recruited two new members, SINGER/SONGWRITER and multi-instrumentalist VINCE GILL, who came from a traditional bluegrass background, and singer/songwriter/reedsman Patrick Bolin, who had a rock background. This band lasted from 1979 through 1980, having hits with both Bolin's and Gill's compositions. Then, Bolin was replaced with singer/guitarist Jeff Wilson, and the band moved to Casablanca Records from their original label.

Throughout these many personnel changes, the basic sound of the band, re-markably enough, remained pretty much the same: an amalgam of soft rock, tinged with countryish influences. In fact, it seems that the new members were melded into the band, rather than remolding its sound. Never achieving great success, the band faded away in the late eighties.

Select Discography

Mementos, Rushmore 07001. Overview of their career from 1971 to 1987, repre-senting everyone who passed through the band.

R.

◀ RABBITT, EDDIE

(born 1944, Brooklyn, NY)

Rabbitt was a hunky, ersatz country star of the mid-seventies and early eighties who personified the COUNTRYPOLITAN sound of easy-listening, pop-ish hits.

Rabbitt was born in Brooklyn to an Irish fiddler father. His family relocated to East Orange, New Jersey, where Eddie learned to play the guitar from his scoutmaster, Tony Schwickrath, who had a minor career performing as Bob Randall. Rabbitt won an amateur contest while still a high-school student, landing him a radio job broadcasting live from a Paterson bar. This led to further work in local clubs in the New York City/North Jersey area.

Rabbitt relocated to Nashville in search of a career as a performer. He immediately placed his song "Working My Way Up to the Bottom" with ROY DRUSKY and was soon a staff writer at Hill & Range. His "Kentucky Rain" was covered by ELVIS PRESLEY, earning the old hip-shaker his fiftieth gold record. This was followed by RONNIE MILSAP cutting his "Pure Love" in 1973; one year later, Eddie got his own recording contract with Elektra records.

Eddie had a couple of hits in the mid-seventies, mostly written or cowritten by him, and mostly in a neo-HONKY-TONK vein ("Drinking My Baby Off My Mind," "Two Dollars in the Jukebox," "We Can't Go on Living Like This"). In 1979 he was asked to perform the title song for Clint Eastwood's comic western *Every Which Way But Loose*. This led to another movie job, singing the theme song for *Roadie* in 1980, called "Driving My Life Away"; this was Rabbitt's first crossover hit.

In the early eighties, the good-looking, smooth-singing star was rarely off the pop and country charts. He had a series of hits with the pop-rock songs "I Love a Rainy Night," "Step by Step," and "Someone Could Lose a Heart Tonight," all in 1981. All of these songs were produced in a manner not too different from typical mainstream pop recordings of the era; in fact, there is little to distinguish Rabbitt from his pop counterparts.

From the mid-eighties on, Rabbitt's career as pop crooner faded, while he continued to tour and perform for his loyal country fans.

Select Discography

All-Time Greatest Hits, Warner Bros. 26467.

The Best Years of My Life, Liberty 94152. Two-CD set culled from Rabbitt's recordings made between 1968 and 1990.

◀ RAILROAD SONGS

The railroad played a key role in opening up rural America to outside influences between the mid-nineteenth century and first decades of the twentieth century. It also became the subject of many country songs, as did the workers who manned the trains.

In the early days of railroading, when time tables were at best approximations and even time zones were not clearly established, train accidents caused by two trains being on the same track at the same time (but heading toward each other) were frighteningly common. In the sentimental literature of the day, as well as song, the "honest trainman" who stayed with his train even as it hurtled into another locomotive became a hero, like the captain who bravely goes down with his ship. One of the most popular of these sentimental stories was retold in "The Wreck of the Old 97," which was recorded by VERNON DALHART and became country music's first million-selling hit.

The image of the trainman was so beloved in country culture that one of the first great country stars, JIMMIE RODGERS, was promoted as the "singing brakeman." Rodgers had indeed worked on the trains, but when he originally began performing, he dressed in natty clothes and horn-rimmed glasses, looking very much like a well-scrubbed, urban college graduate. However, once he was signed to Victor Records, one of the first publicity shots that was released by the company showed him in full railroader's regalia, including striped overalls and hat. It was important for the PR folks at the label to establish Rodgers as "one of the folks," and clearly fancy duds would not do the trick. Rodgers's railroad image was emulated by other performers, just as the cowboy image would become standard for country performers a decade later.

The train had a more subtle influence on rural music. The "high, lonesome sound" of the train whistle, echoing across the mountains, has been celebrated in many country songs. The whistle came to be a symbol for the life beyond the small rural communities, and the train a symbol of escape and freedom. Where once rural folks were condemned to a life of hard labor on small, often isolated farms, now they could travel to the big cities in search of higher paying jobs, and more social freedom. BILL MONROE was just one of many southerners who escaped the backwoods of Kentucky by taking a train to East Chicago, Indiana, joining his brothers as a laborer in the oil industry. One of his most famous songs celebrates the feeling he got as a youth when he heard the train whistle: "When I hear that whistle blow/I want to pack my suitcase and go!"

Train sound effects were often imitated by master instrumentalists, who could make a career out of reproducing the various sounds of the chugging locomotives. One of the first GRAND OLE OPRY stars, harmonica player DEFORD BAILEY, specialized in recreating these sounds in his very popular showpiece, "Pan American Blues," named after the famous long-distance train. In the thirties, the Rouse Brothers created a classic train number, "Orange Blossom Special," featuring imitations of train whistles played on the fiddle, which has since become one of the most imitated and overplayed pieces in BLUEGRASS and country music.

Eventually, the automobile (and later still the airplane) would replace the train as the popular means of transportation. And the truck driver would replace the trainman as the hero of many country songs.

◄ RAINWATER, MARVIN

(born Marvin Karlton Percy, 1925, Wichita, KS)

Rainwater is a SINGER/SONGWRITER of Indian descent who had his greatest success with country and ROCKABILLY recordings in the late fifties.

Raised in Kansas, Rainwater was actually named Marvin Percy (Rainwater was his mother's maiden name); he grew up in a fairly well-to-do family and originally trained to be a veterinarian. After serving in the navy in World War II, he took up a career in music, getting his first break in 1946 when he was hired by RED FOLEY to perform on his popular *Ozark Jubilee* radio show. Taking his "Indian" name, Rainwater was an immediate success, leading to early-fifties recordings on the small Four Star and Coral labels. His second break came in 1955 when he appeared on the popular *Talent Scouts* TV show, hosted by the affable, ukulele teasin' Arthur Godfrey. This led to a contract with MGM records.

MGM cranked up the publicity machine, promoting Rainwater as a "full-blooded Cherokee brave" and having him appear in full Indian regalia, including headdress! Meanwhile, his recordings were a mix of country and rockabilly, beginning with his first hit, 1957's "Gonna Find Me a Bluebird," which he also wrote. His biggest record was "Whole Lotta Woman," a rockabilly classic that oddly enough was too racy for pop radio (programmers thought the lyrics were "too suggestive") but was acceptable to the normally more conservative country stations. His last hit was a cover of JOHN D. LOUDERMILK's "Half Breed" in 1959.

Rainwater label-hopped through the sixties, without much success. In the mid-sixties, he had to have throat surgery and was out of commission for about four years, until his comeback in 1971. He has remained popular in Europe, where fans of vintage country and rockabilly continue to come out in droves to see his concerts.

Select Discography

Classic Records, Bear Family 15600. Four CDs with illustrated booklet including all of his MGM, Brave, UA, and Warner Bros. recordings.

◄ RANCH ROMANCE

(1987–ongoing: Jo Miller [guitar, vocals]; Barbara Lamb [fiddle, vocals]; Lisa Theo [mandolin, vocals]; Nancy Katz [bass, vocals])

It had to happen: an all-female cowboy quartet! If the novelty of Doug Green's RIDERS IN THE SKY is wearing thin, how about giving this Seattle-based quartet of neo-cowgirls a try?

The group was formed in 1987 as "an all-star cowgirl revue" by Jo Miller as something of a lark. They were featured on the Nashville Network a year later and released their first record on their own label soon after. A soon-to-be-out-of-the-closet K. D. LANG invited them to perform as her opening act on her 1989 tour (while she was still in her own cowgirl phase), and the band was signed to Sugar Hill Records, where they issued their first album in 1991.

Essentially a novelty band, Ranch Romance faces the same problem as their male cowpoke counterparts; within the limits of the hokey cowboy style, how far can a band go? Once one's recorded "Back in the Saddle Again" as a kind of sophisticated homage to (at the same time a satire of) country-western conventions, there's a limit to what one can achieve. Still, bands like these make for pleasant entertainment at least for the occasional listener.

Select Discography

Blue Blazes, Sugar Hill 3794. Their first album for Sugar Hill.

◀ RANDOLPH, "BOOTS"

(born Homer Louis Randolph III, c. 1927, Paducah, KY)

Randolph is one of the most popular of Nashville's session musicians—perhaps the "world's only hillbilly saxophone player," as he claims—who has had a number of crossover hits, beginning with 1963's classic "Yakety Sax."

Born in rural Kentucky, Boots came from a musical family. As soon as he could hold the instrument he began playing ukulele in the family band, which included his fiddler father, GUITAR-playing mother, older brothers Earl (BANJO) and Bob (MANDOLIN), and bass-playing sister Dorothy. The group was quite active in the mid-thirties, when farm and industrial work were hard to find, thanks to the Depression. The family settled in Cadiz, Kentucky, where Boots entered elementary school. His father traded an old revolver for a trombone, which he gave to Boots when he was ready to enter high school, and Boots played in his high-school band in his new home town of Evansville, Indiana. He switched to saxophone, because he tired of carrying the cumbersome trombone in the school's marching band, and with his brother Bob soon formed a combo that was popular playing on local army bases in the early years of World War II.

After serving in the army from 1945 to 1946, he returned to Evanston, where work was hard to find. By the early fifties, he was playing in a bar out of Decatur, Illinois, where he was heard by the country comedy duo, HOMER AND JETHRO. They recommended Randolph to country producer CHET ATKINS, who invited him to come to Nashville to work as a sessionman and solo artist. He recorded with many of RCA's country acts, as well as popsters like Perry Como, folk singer Burl Ives, and even ELVIS PRESLEY. Randolph was hired by OWEN BRADLEY to play on BRENDA LEE's early rockin' sessions, where his jazzy stylings were an immediate sensation.

In the early sixties, RCA dropped Randolph as a solo artist, and he signed with Monument. In 1963 he had his big pop hit with "Yakety Sax," an instrumental he had composed almost a decade earlier with another member of his combo, James Rich. This was followed by "Mr. Sax Man" a year later, and then by schlocky versions of current pop hits, including 1966's "Shadow of Your Smile." Randolph continued to churn out the easy-listening material through the seventies and eighties.

Select Discography

Country Boots, Monument 44358. 1974 album featuring contributions from Mother Maybelle Carter, Atkins, Josh Graves, and other premiere Nashville session pickers. *Yakety Sax*, Monument 44356. Featuring his big hit.

◀ RAUSCH, LEON

(born Edgar Leon Rausch, 1927, Springfield, MO)

Rausch is a Texas vocalist best known for his association with BOB WILLS from 1958 until the veteran fiddler's death.

Born in Missouri, Rausch played several instruments from an early age and beginning at age eleven performed with his father at local dances and fairs. After a stint in the navy in World War II, he returned to Springfield, where he continued performing locally. He then relocated to Tulsa, Oklahoma, in 1955 in search of more work as a singer. In 1958 he was hired as lead vocalist for Bob Wills's Texas Playboys, the first permanent vocalist in the band since TOMMY DUNCAN had been fired a decade earlier. He worked with Wills through the sixties, as well as for his younger brother Johnnie Lee Wills from 1962 to 1964. After Wills semiretired in the late sixties, Rausch formed his own New Texas Playboys, who had some success on the regional Long Horn label. When Wills was coaxed out of retirement for his "last sessions" in 1973, Rausch came on board again as lead vocalist and then continued to perform with the revived Texas Playboys through the seventies after Wills's death. In the eighties, he made two excellent LPs for the Southland label, with a swinging ensemble molded after the Playboys.

◀ RAVEN, EDDY

(born Edward Garvin Futch, 1944, Lafayette, LA)

Raven has had a long and winding career, beginning in the fifties in teen-pop. He returned to country music in the early seventies, when he began writing and recording music with a distinct CAJUN/R&B flavor. He was not much of a success as a country performer, however, until the eighties, when he scored a series of hits.

Raven's father was a truck driver and sometime country guitarist who encouraged his son's musical inclinations. By the time Eddie was a teenager, the family was living in Georgia, where he took his stage name and recorded his first discs in a teen-rock style for the tiny Cosmo label. Returning to Louisiana, Eddie met local record producer/performer Bobby Charles (who is best remembered for his hit recording of the peppy "See You Later, Alligator"), who scored a local hit with his recording of Raven's "Big Boys Cry." Raven continued to perform as a rocker, working for a while with the young, up-and-coming brothers Johnnie and Edgar Winter out of Texas.

By the late sixties, though, Raven's rock career was in a shambles and he was at loose ends. Old friend and fellow Cajun Jimmy C. Newman introduced him to his contacts at Acuff-Rose publishers, and Raven was soon churning out country hits, beginning with "Country Green" and "Touch the Morning" for DON GIBSON and "Good Morning, Country Rain," a hit for JEANNIE C. RILEY. A showcase performance at Nashville's King of the Road Motor Inn (these names just aren't made up, you know) led to a recording contract with ABC in 1974 and a minor hit in the same year with "The Last of the Sunshine Cowboys." Raven continued to supply songs for other country acts, including ROY ACUFF's 1974 late-career smash, "Back in the Country," while he began appearing at more upscale venues, including Las Vegas.

In the late seventies, he signed with Monument and then, in the early eighties, Elektra, scoring some minor hits. But when he signed with RCA in 1984 he really started churning out the number-one records, including "I Got Mexico" (which he cowrote with Paul Worley), the R&B-style "Shine, Shine, Shine" (introduced on the syndicated *Dance Fever* TV show in 1987), the Cajun-flavored 1988 hit "I'm Gonna Get You," the calypso-esque "Joe Knows How to Live" from later in that year, and "In a Letter to You" and the semiautobiographical "Bayou Boys," both from 1989. Raven explained that he was trying to meld country, R&B, calypso, and Cajun, certainly an unusual and unique marriage. However, after these successes, he dropped off the charts again in the nineties, although he continues to perform and has recently recorded for Liberty.

Select Discography

The Best of Eddy Raven, RCA 6815. Hits from 1984 to 1988.

◀ RAYE, SUSAN

(born 1944, Eugene, OR)

Raye is a pleasant singer who had some late-sixties and early-seventies hits thanks to her association with her mentor, BUCK OWENS.

Born in Eugene but raised in the nearby small town of Forest Grove, Raye began performing as a teenager on local radio, both as a singer and deejay. By the mid-sixties, she was a featured performer on Portland's *Hoedown* television show, as well as performing at clubs through the Northwest, where Buck Owens's manager, Jack McFadden, heard her and decided to bring the singer to audition for the Bakersfield star. Owens hired her for a stint in his backup band in 1965 and then again in 1968. A year later, he arranged for her to record her first single for Capitol, "Maybe If I Closed My Eyes," which he also wrote for her. This led to a series of hits through to the mid-seventies, including the syrupy "Pitty, Pitty, Patter (I've Got a Happy Heart)" (1971), aorta-pumpin' platters "My Heart Has a Mind of Its Own" and "Love Sure Feels Good in My Heart" (both 1972), and a turn away from her good-girl image with "Cheatin' Game" (1973) and the scolding "Whatcha Gonna Do with a Dog Like That" (1974). Raye also continued to record duets with Buck, including the minor 1975 hit, "Love Is Strange." Raye's solo career dried up after that, although she continues to record occasionally, including a 1984 Westexas release, "Put Another Notch in Your Belt," which was a minor chart success.

◀ RED CLAY RAMBLERS, THE

(c. 1973–ongoing; mid-seventies lineup: Tommy Thompson [banjo, vocals]; Jim Watson [mandolin, vocals]; Bill Hicks [fiddle, vocals]; Mike Craver [piano, vocals]; Jack Herrick [trumpet, bass, vocals])

The Red Clay Ramblers, one of the most innovative of the seventies string-band revival groups, melded traditional dance tunes and songs with swing, early jazz, country-gospel, and their own unique compositions.

The members of the band, founded in Chapel Hill, North Carolina, in 1973, were interested in pursuing the vocal-music side of the old-time tradition; other local bands, like the Fuzzy Mountain Stringband (of which Hicks had been a member) and the Hollow Rock Stringband (of which Thompson had been a member), were instrumentally oriented. The group recorded their first album with guest artist Fiddlin' Al McCandless, who is more BLUEGRASS-oriented in his style than the rest of the band. While finishing these recordings, pianist Mike Craver joined the group, and they experimented with added ragtime and blues to the mix. With the addition of trumpeter Jack Herrick in 1975, the group's best lineup was completed.

The Ramblers made a series of innovative records from the mid-seventies through the early eighties. Thompson and Craver wrote some amusing novelty songs in the manner of country-jazz, including "The Ace," which tells of a blind date gone seriously wrong, and "Merchant's Lunch," which plays off the country clichés of roadside diners and big-rig truckers. Vocalists Thompson, Craver, and Watson also did much to revive the repertoire of the CARTER FAMILY, recording a trio album in homage to the earlier group. Even when the group recorded a traditional dance tune—like "Forked Deer"—they jazzed it up considerably, adding a ragtime-piano part or muted trumpet. Thompson's comic bass vocals, Watson's gritty country tenor, and Craver's ethereal boy alto combined to make a distinctive group-harmony sound, with a strong nod toward the roots of country harmony (particularly old-time church harmonies).

In the eighties, the band went through several personnel changes, while also working with playwright/filmmaker Sam Shepherd, scoring his play *A Lie of the Mind* and the film *Far North*. Most recently, they worked with comic mimes Bill Irwin and David Shiner in their Broadway production of *Fool Moon*. Only Thompson and Herrick remain of the seventies band.

Select Discography
Twisted Laurel/Merchant's Lunch, Flying Fish 77055. CD reissue of two fine albums from the mid-eighties.
Rambler, Sugar Hill 3798. 1992 album with a later incarnation of the band.

◀ REED, BLIND ALFRED

(born 1880, Floyd, VA; died 1956)

Reed was one of the greatest topical songwriters of the twenties. He contributed to the old-time music repertoire such classics as the social-protest song "How Can a Poor Man Stand Such Times and Live" and the humorous "Why Do You Bob Your Hair Girls (You Know That It's a Sin)."

The West Virginia coal miner and fiddler was discovered by RALPH PEER at his legendary 1927 sessions held in Bristol, Virginia, which also produced the CARTER FAMILY'S and JIMMIE RODGERS'S first recordings. Reed recorded prolifically for Victor, playing fairly simple fiddle parts to accompany his own clearly sung vocals, usually performed with discreet GUITAR accompaniment. Reed had a clear, powerful voice, and his songs often tackled topical issues in a humorous way, making them immediately popular.

Many of his songs commented on the troubles that women bring to men, although it's not always clear just how serious the fiddler is being in songs like "We Just Got to Have Them, That's All," which traces all the way back to the Garden of Eden the problems women have created for their mates. Reed capitalized on his biggest hit, "Why Do You Bob Your Hair Girls," a semiserious indictment of the craze for short hair, with a second number ("Bob Hair Number 2") in which he continues to take a fundamentalist approach to the question of coiffure ("Short hair belongs to men," the song warns).

Perhaps Reed's greatest song is the poignant "How Can a Poor Man Stand Such Times and Live?" In a straightforward style, Reed outlines how rural Americans are exploited by middlemen and entrepreneurs, while they benefit little from their labor. The repeated chorus line (and title of the song) says it all; Reed does not embellish or force the message but lets the song speak for itself. Perhaps only FIDDLIN' JOHN CARSON's "Taxes on the Farmer Feeds Them All" comes close in its simple eloquence as a great social-protest song of the era.

Select Discography

How Can a Poor Man Stand Such Times and Live?, Rounder 1001. Great collection of Reed's original 78s beautifully remastered and documented.

◀ REED, JERRY

(born Jerry Hubbard, 1937, Atlanta, GA)

Affable country songwriter/singer/guitarist, Jerry Reed has had equal success as a session player, solo artist, and as a country-fried actor.

Coming from a mill-working family in Atlanta, Georgia, Reed took up the GUITAR as a youngster and was a talented picker by the time he reached his teenage years. A friend of the family introduced him to publisher/producer Bill Lowery in 1955, when Jerry was just sixteen, and he was signed to a recording contract with the Los Angeles–based Capitol label. His biggest success, however, came as a songwriter when teen rocker Gene Vincent had a hit in 1956 with his song "Crazy Legs."

After serving for two years in the army, Reed settled in Nashville, signing to Columbia and having minor hits with the instrumental "Hully Gully Guitars" and a cover of Leadbelly's perennial folk classic, "Goodnight Irene." However, Reed's real success came as a session player, backing country and pop acts. CHET ATKINS, another talented guitar player, signed him to RCA in 1965, and he had his first major hit two years later with "Guitar Man," which was quickly covered by another RCA act, ELVIS PRESLEY (Presley also covered Reed's semicomic song "U.S. Male"). Reed continued to score hits through the early seventies, most notably with his unique blend of CAJUN, rock, and country on 1970's "Amos Moses," his first number-one country hit and a significant pop hit as well.

Reed's work through the seventies became increasingly erratic, vacillating between powerful, rockin' country recordings and the kind of gooey, let's-all-sing-together records that bring to mind the ANITA KERR Singers at their worst. His last solid country hit was 1971's cover of the HANK SNOW classic, "I'm Movin' On." His best work continued to be as an instrumentalist, particularly on several duet albums with Chet Atkins.

Reed pursued an acting career beginning in 1974 with Burt Reynolds's country flick *W. W. and the Dixie Dance Kings*; he continued to work with Reynolds in many of his light comedies, including the popular *Smokey and the Bandit* pictures. Meanwhile, his recording career continued to suffer, and he was reduced to waxing such comic novelties as "She Got the Goldmine (I Got the Shaft)" in the early eighties (although the song did go to number one). Reed made several abortive comebacks in the middle to late eighties, with little success, although he continues to be a popular act on the road.

Select Discography

Rockin' with the Guitarman, Revival 3017. Fifties-era recordings featuring Jerry in his rockin' hillbilly phase.

The Best of Jerry Reed, RCA 54109. His mid-sixties through early-seventies work.

◀ REEVES, DEL

(born Franklin Delano Reeves, 1933, Sparta, NC)

Dubbed the "Dean Martin of country music," thanks to his smooth-voiced sixties hits, Del began his career in an old-style harmony duet, then recorded HANK WILLIAMS–style HONKY-TONK and teen rock before moving onto a successful country career.

Born in North Carolina, a true son of the Depression (he was even named for the new president who promised to pull the country out of the economic doldrums), Reeves began performing country music almost as soon as he could walk; he had his own local radio show when he was just twelve. After a stint at college and in the air force, Del settled in Southern California, where a vibrant country community was busy creating what would become known as the BAKERSFIELD SOUND.

He hooked up with mandolinist Chester Smith, who had his own country-music television show, and the two recorded some charming old-style harmony duets for Capitol in 1957. Then Del went solo, and Capitol producer Ken Nelson (who had previously scored big molding the career of Gene Vincent) tried to turn him into a teen popster; Del did his best but was not very comfortable with the material. At about this time, he met his future wife, Ellen Schiell, and the two began writing country songs, placing hits with mainstream artists from CARL SMITH to SHEB WOOLEY.

Del's first success as a country artist came in 1961 with "Be Quiet Mind," released by Decca Records; he then moved to Reprise (the first country artist to record for Frank Sinatra's label) and Columbia but failed to achieve much success until 1965, when he hit it big on United Artists with his song "Girl on the Billboard." This began a string of hits through the early seventies, including "Women Do Funny Things to Me" (released in 1966, the same year Del joined the GRAND OLE OPRY), "Looking at the World Through a Windshield" (1968), and baseball anthem "The Philadelphia Fillies" (1971). Del's mature style was solidly in the pop-country mold, with a laid-back vocal style reminiscent of singers like Dean Martin, to whom he was often compared.

By the late seventies, Del had left United Artists to record for a variety of small labels. He scored little chart action until his fluke 1987 hit, "Dear Dr. Ruth," addressed to the diminutive sex therapist from New York. The record was considered "shocking" for a country audience and got him a little bit of press in his declining years.

Select Discography
His Greatest Hits, Razor & Tie 2046.

◀ REEVES, GOEBEL

(born 1899, Sherman, TX; died 1959)
Although from a solidly middle-class background (his father was a Texas state legislator), Reeves became famous as the "Texas Drifter," a hobo performer who wrote the well-known "Hobo's Lullaby," which became a signature tune for WOODY GUTHRIE.

Reeves served in World War I, a stint that apparently politicized him, for when he returned to the United States he took to a life of rambling, eventually joining the fledgling union movement, particularly the International Workers of the World. He recorded for OKeh and Brunswick in the twenties and thirties and claimed to have written, in addition to "Hobo's Lullaby," such classic Western and RAILROAD SONGS as "Hobo and the Cop," "Railroad Boomer," "Bright Sherman Valley," and "Cowboy's Prayer." He also performed narrations, spinning tall tales about the life he had lived across the United States. A fine singer and yodeler, Reeves suffered from a pretty large ego; he even claimed to have taught JIMMIE RODGERS to yodel, one of those apocryphal stories that is impossible to disprove. He died in California in 1959 after being inactive on the music scene for many years.

◀ REEVES, JIM

(born 1923, Galloway, TX; died 1964)
Jim Reeves was a smooth-voiced country balladeer who continued to produce hits even after his untimely death in an airplane crash. Although his early recordings had a fine HONKY-TONK style, at least in their accompaniment, later recordings were mainstream pop productions in the spirit of the NASHVILLE SOUND of the era.

Jim came from a single-parent household, where his mother worked as a field hand after the death of his father. He showed an early interest in music and was given a GUITAR by a construction worker friend of the family when he was five years old. He made his first radio broadcast at age nine out of Shreveport.

He developed an interest in baseball during his high-school years and was signed to the St. Louis Cardinals because of his pitching skills. However, he injured his ankle in 1947, which ended his baseball career. Meanwhile, he had continued to play music on the side while studying elocution in college. At about the same time as his injury, he met his future wife, Mary White, who was a schoolteacher who further encouraged him to seek a career in music. Jim landed a job as an announcer at a local radio station, thanks to a baritone voice that carried well over the air. In 1949 he made a few recordings for a small Houston-based label, and by 1951 and 1952 he was announcing for KWKH, the Shreveport, Louisiana, station that hosted the well-known country radio program, *The Louisiana Hayride*. It was while performing on the Hayride that he was heard by Fabor Robinson of Abbott Records, who immediately signed him.

Reeves's first country hit came out in 1953 with "Mexican Joe." In 1955 he moved to the GRAND OLE OPRY and signed with RCA, hitting immediately with "Yonder Comes a Sucker." In 1957 he scored his first crossover hit with "Four Walls," which led to many television appearances. His 1959 recording of "He'll Have to Go" is typical of the direction Reeves's music was taking; while the accompaniment and subject matter harks back to the honky-tonk tradition, his smooth vocals already forecast the middle-of-the-road direction his career would take in the early sixties.

Indeed, from 1960 to his untimely death in 1964, Reeves was rarely off the charts, beginning with "I'm Getting Better" from 1960 through 1962's "Adios Amigo," 1963's "Is This Me?," to his last single released while he was still alive, "Welcome to My World." His style was by now unabashedly romantic, with sighing choruses washing over his baritone burblings.

Apparently, Reeves left enough recordings in the can to stock an entire second career, and he continued to have hits on the country charts right through the early seventies. His wife, Mary, cannily packaged this unissued material, and his popularity grew from the first posthumous single, 1964's "I Guess I'm Crazy," through 1970's "Angels Don't Lie" to 1979's "How I Miss You Tonight." Through the miracle of electronic overdubbing, the deceased Reeves was even able to "perform" an entire album's worth of duets with the equally cold-in-the-ground country star PATSY CLINE.

Select Discography

Welcome to My World, RCA 66125. Two-CD set, including early recordings (pre–Nashville Sound) as well as the obligatory later, softer, pop-schlock stuff.

Live at the Opry, Marble Arch 144. Great collection of live recordings made between 1953 and 1960. Unlike his studio work, this features tight honky-tonk–style backups. This same set was issued on LP by the Country Music Foundation.

◀ REMINGTON, HERB

(born c. 1920, Mishawaka, IN)

One of the pioneers of the steel guitar, Remington helped put the instrument on the map thanks to his postwar recordings with BOB WILLS.

Remington began playing Hawaiian-style guitar as a boy in his Indiana home. As a teenager he moved to California in search of work as a musician. He played briefly with RAY WHITELY's WESTERN SWING band before being drafted in 1944 and serving in the army for two years. On his return, he auditioned for Bob Wills's younger, drummer brother Luke, who had his own band. The elder Wills, seeing a talented musician, swapped steel players with his brother. In the days immediately following the war, Wills's band was considerably smaller than his prewar outfits, which had featured a full complement of horns; Remington became a key part of this pared-down band, which also featured electric guitarist Eldon Shamblin and mandolinist "Tiny" Moore. Remington wrote and played lead with Wills on a number of classic instrumentals, including "Boot Heel Drag," "Playboy Chimes," and "Hometown Stomp." His best-known instrumental was recorded just after he left Wills's band and had joined HANK PENNY's COWBOY-SONG outfit; called "Remington Ride," it's even been covered by blues guitarist Freddie King.

After his marriage, Remington relocated to the Houston area where he appeared on the early-sixties recordings of GEORGE JONES and WILLIE NELSON. He continues to record and perform, often with his son Mark on vocals.

◀ RENO, DON

(born c. 1924, Spartanburg, SC; died 1984)

Reno was one of the first and greatest BLUEGRASS BANJO players, who is best known for the recordings he made with guitarist Red Smiley and the Tennessee Cutups from the early fifties to the late sixties.

While playing banjo with the Morris Brothers, Reno was almost hired by BILL MONROE to take the banjo spot in his Blue Grass Boys band in 1943; unfortunately, Reno was drafted and Earl Scruggs got the job. However, when Scruggs left the band with Lester Flatt to form their own group, Reno came on board, performing with Monroe in 1948 for about a year; he then met guitarist/vocalist Red Smiley, and the two performed with a couple of other bands before forming their own group in 1951. His unique banjo style, including picking single-string melodies in the style of tenor banjo players of the thirties, made him an immediate standout. In 1955 Reno joined ARTHUR "GUITAR BOOGIE" SMITH in recording the original version of what was then called "Feuding Banjos" (and is now better-known as "Dueling Banjos"), with Smith playing tenor and Reno playing five-string.

The Reno and Smiley Tennessee Cutups was one of the most respected in bluegrass, slightly more progressive than Monroe and FLATT AND SCRUGGS in their outlook and certainly very prolific. However, Smiley's health began to deteriorate in the early sixties, and by 1968 he had to leave the band (he died in 1972); Reno then formed a new Cutups with vocalist/guitarist Bill Harrell, and they worked together until 1978. Reno continued to perform until his death in 1984, often accompanied by his sons Ronnie on GUITAR, Dale on MANDOLIN, and Don Wayne on banjo. Ronnie currently hosts *Reno's Old-Time Music Festival*, a program devoted to acoustic and bluegrass country music, on the Americana cable network. The elder Reno's banjo picking was quite influential on the next generation of players, such as Eddie Adcock of the COUNTRY GENTLEMEN.

Select Discography

Collector's Box Set, Starday 7001. Four CDs giving you 115 classic Reno and Smiley tracks cut between 1951 and 1959.

A Variety of Country Songs, King 646. More fifties-era recordings.

Family and Friends, Kaleidoscope 34. Cassette-only reissue of early-eighties album by Reno accompanied by his sons and other notable bluegrass names.

◀ RESTLESS HEART

(c. 1983–ongoing; best-known lineup [1987–1990]: Larry Stewart [vocals]; Greg Jennings [guitar, vocals]; Dave Innis [keyboards]; Paul Gregg [bass, vocals]; John Dittrich [drums])

A manufactured mid-eighties group whose members were assembled by producer Tim DuBois (who later guided DIAMOND RIO to fast fame), Restless Heart is another in the string of EXILE–style country popsters who produce a highly professional, if soulless, country-pop music.

The group had its roots in DuBois's desire to find an outlet for his unusual songs, which were too rock to be country but too country to appeal to mainstream rock. DuBois knew Greg Jennings from his days as a student at Oklahoma State University in the mid-seventies, as well as Scott Hendricks, who would work as coproducer on the band's early hits. Hendricks brought into the fold bassist Paul Gregg, and the remainder of the band—all Okies with the exception of drummer John Dittrich—was assembled from the ranks of studio and club players around Nashville in early 1983.

After recording demos of DuBois's songs, they were signed to RCA and had their first hit in 1986 with the pop-flavored "That Rock Won't Roll." Original lead singer Verlon Thompson remained with the group through their first single and then was replaced by Larry Stewart, whose smooth pop vocalizing came to define the group's sound. Their biggest hit came in 1988 with "Wheels," the title song of a concept album that celebrated life on the road. Stewart left the band in 1990, and the group soldiered on now led by Jennings, Dittrich, and Gregg as lead singers and songwriters. No longer under the guiding hand of DuBois, and sounding somewhat dated in the face of the NEW-COUNTRY movement, Restless Heart still manages to appeal to the pop fringes of the country audience.

Select Discography

The Best of Restless Heart, RCA 61041. The hits through 1990.

◀ RICE, TONY

(born 1945, Los Angeles, CA)

A talented guitarist and vocalist, Rice got his start in PROGRESSIVE BLUEGRASS and then moved into more jazz-oriented instrumental music while also performing SINGER/SONGWRITER and folk-country material.

Rice began as a guitarist and vocalist in the BLUEGRASS ALLIANCE and banjoist J. D. CROWE's influential early-seventies progressive band, the New South. Rice's guitar work was heavily influenced by DOC WATSON and Clarence White, although his skills soon outstripped those of his mentors. He recorded progressive bluegrass with DAVID GRISSMAN on his 1975 *Rounder Album* and then joined in the formation of Grissman's first quintet, dedicated to performing the mandolinist's jazz-influenced compositions. Rice soon struck out on his own, forming his Tony Rice Unit to perform progressive string music of his own composition.

In the eighties, he alternated between recording instrumental and vocal LPs. His vocal LPs tended to feature material from singer/songwriters from both folk-rock and NEW-COUNTRY movements, such as BOB DYLAN, RODNEY CROWELL, Gordon Lightfoot, NORMAN BLAKE, MARY CHAPIN CARPENTER, and James Taylor. He also recorded an LP of duets with RICKY SKAGGS in 1980, in the manner of the brother acts of the thirties and forties. Rice's pleasant tenor voice, along with his considerable talents as a guitarist, make all of his vocal albums pleasant listening, although his new acoustic/jazz LPs can border on the pretentious and repetitious.

Select Discography

Tony Rice, Rounder 0085. His debut solo album, with BLUEGRASS and jazz-tinged material.

Devlin, Rounder 11531. Compilation of his various new-acoustic/instrumental albums for Rounder.

California Autumn, Rebel 1549. 1990 soft-country set.

◀ RICH, CHARLIE

(born 1932, Colt, AK)

One of the great wasted talents of country music, Rich gained his greatest successes from his weakest recordings. Prematurely gray and thus nicknamed the "Silver Fox," Rich was an exceptionally talented pianist, vocalist, and songwriter who never really reached his full potential.

The son of a heavy-drinking dirt farmer and a fundamentalist mother, Rich was greatly influenced by jazz and blues as a young musician. Unlike many other country performers, he studied music in college at the University of Arkansas. He joined the air force and was stationed in Oklahoma, where he formed his first semiprofessional combo, the Velvetones, a jazz/blues combo in the Stan Kenton mold. Future wife Margaret was the group's lead vocalist. After leaving the air force, Rich returned to West Memphis, Arkansas, to help his father work his cotton farm. While performing with Bill Justis's band there, Rich was invited to come to audition with legendary producer SAM PHILLIPS at Sun Records.

Still playing in a jazzy style, Rich was initially dismissed by Phillips, who invited him instead to listen to early JERRY LEE LEWIS recordings and come back when he had absorbed Lewis's frantic keyboard pounding. Rich would session on many late-fifties Sun recordings, backing ROCKABILLY talents like Billy Lee Riley, Ray Smith, and Warren Smith. He scored his first hit with 1959's "Lonely Weekends," a song very much influenced by the sound of early ELVIS PRESLEY, although the girly choruses almost drown his mournful vocals.

Rich struggled in the early to mid-sixties to find his sound, moving from the boogie-woogie of "Big Boss Man" of 1963 to the country-novelty of "Mohair Sam," even recording a straight country/HONKY-TONK LP for Memphis's Hi Records, a label later better known for its soul acts. In 1968 he hooked up with Epic Records and producer BILLY SHERRILL, who was instrumental in launching the COUNTRYPOLITAN sound.

It took five years for Rich and Sherrill to hit a winning formula, but they hit it big from 1973 to 1975 with songs like "Behind Closed Doors," "The Most Beautiful Girl in the World," "A Very Special Love Song," and "Every Time You Touch Me." Rich won numerous country awards, while at the same time, thanks to their slick production, his songs found a new audience among middle-of-the-road radio listeners. Rich became the epitome of countrypolitan, and many other artists soon jumped on the bandwagon (creating the backlash that would be known as OUTLAW music by WILLIE NELSON and his coterie). Sadly, though, Rich soon lapsed into predictable formula, even waxing a schmaltzy version of "America the Beautiful" for the bicentennial. The late seventies and early eighties were spent label hopping. Although Rich continued to have hits, most notably 1979's "I'll Wake You Up When I Get Home," his days of chart-topping success were over.

Music critics like Peter Guralnick have lamented that despite his bluesy phrasing, jazz-tinged piano, and smoky, world-weary vocals, Rich never reached the level of artistic success that he deserved, although he achieved some commercial popularity in the early seventies. In fact, it seems that his more commercial recordings, which tended to sanitize Rich's musical and vocal delivery, did much to destroy his talent, rather than encourage it.

Select Discography

Complete Smash Sessions, Mercury 643. Mid-sixties recordings, including the 1965 hit "Mohair Sam." Halfway between rock and country.

American Originals, Columbia 45073. Drawn from his years with Epic from the late sixties through his mid-seventies hits.

Pictures and Paintings, Blue Horizon 26730. 1992 comeback recording.

◀ RIDDLE, ALMEDA

(born Almeda James, 1898, lower Cleburne County, AR; died 1980)

Riddle was one of the finest singers of traditional ballads and gospel songs, with a clear, powerful delivery that represented mountain singing at its finest.

Born and raised in rural Arkansas, where she spent her entire life, Riddle learned a rich repertory of traditional ballads, children's songs, and religious songs from her family, particularly her father, J. L. James, a descendant of the famous outlaw James brothers, and a timber merchant of Irish descent who worked as an amateur singing teacher as well as playing the fiddle. Almeda could remember him singing every morning and evening from his large collection of songbooks; because he could read music, he would often form small singing classes, teaching a ten-day class in sightsinging. Almeda began collecting what she called "ballets" from a young age, including her father's version of the classic English ballad, "The House Carpenter." Her mother's brother, Uncle John Wilkerson, was also a strong influence, although he sang many "silly songs" that Almeda's mother objected to, including "Froggie Went a-Courtin'," with its unusual nonsense-word chorus, which Almeda performed for the rest of her life.

Almeda married H. P. Riddle in 1916, who was himself a fine singer. The two would often sing together after supper. They lived together happily for a decade in Heber Springs, Arkansas, until a cyclone hit the town, taking the life of Almeda's husband and youngest child and seriously injuring the other children. Almeda spent four months in the hospital recovering and then returned to live on her father's farm with the surviving members of her family.

Riddle was never a professional performer and probably would have lived and died unknown if she had not been discovered by folklorist ALAN LOMAX when he was amassing a series of albums for Atlantic Records in the late fifties, issued as the Southern Folk Heritage Series. Riddle's clear-as-a-bell singing and wide repertory of unusual versions of well-known songs made her the hit of this series, leading to a solo album issued by Vanguard Records in 1966 along with appearances at folk festivals. In the seventies, she recorded two albums for Rounder Records, as well as a few recordings for smaller labels. Her chilling version of "The Old Churchyard" is one of the greatest recordings of solo singing on record.

Although not from the deep South, Riddle was one of the finest ballad singers in the tight-throated style that is prevalent throughout the lower Southern Appalachians. She sang with great expression and intensity, fully inhabiting each song in order to tell the story clearly to her audience.

Select Discography

Ballads and Hymns from the Ozarks/More Ballads and Hymns, Rounder 0017/0083. Two great albums from the seventies, now out of print.

◀ RIDERS IN THE SKY

(1985–ongoing: Ranger Doug [born Douglas B. Green, guitar, vocals]; Woody Paul [born Paul Woodrow Chisman, fiddle, vocals]; Too Slim [born Fred LaBour, bass, vocals])

The Riders is a cowboy comedy act that pays homage to the classic stars of COWBOY SONG while satirizing the conventions of cowboy films and radio of the forties and fifties.

They are certainly an unlikely comedy group. Douglas B. Green, the band's leader, was formerly the aural historian at the Country Music Foundation and a leading scholar who has written widely on the history of country music. Woody

Paul was a nuclear engineer with a degree from MIT before he took up cowboy fiddling. The band began its life in 1985 as a genuine attempt to revive both the hokiness and the goofy charm of early cowboy acts; the threesome appear in the classic rhinestone-encrusted cowboy wear, and their stage show recreates the gimmickry of past cowboy troupes.

However, as they have continued to perform, the Riders have become a parody of a parody, with their humor increasingly wearing thin. Their original compositions have increasingly relied on silly titles ("Concerto for Violin and Longhorns") while their recreations have taken on the air of cowboy schtick. Still, they remain popular as performers, with their own radio program, *Riders Radio Theater*, broadcast over National Public Radio, and even briefly had their own network Saturday-morning kiddie show. They appear regularly on the GRAND OLE OPRY and the Nashville Network, although it has become hard to tell if the audience is laughing at them or with them or both.

Select Discography

The Best of the West, Vols. 1 and 2, Rounder 11517/11524. Compilation CDs of their first albums cut for Rounder.

Riders Radio Theater, MCA 42180. 1988 album recreating the classic cowboy radio shows of the thirties and forties.

Cowboys in Love, Columbia 64268. 1994 recordings.

◀ RILEY, JEANNIE C.

(born Jeanne Caroline Stephenson, 1945, Anson, TX)

Riley is a country one-hit wonder who scored big with her cover of TOM T. HALL's "Harper Valley P.T.A." in 1968. She is probably most responsible for bringing a hipper look to country music, including miniskirts and boots, which for the time was certainly daring stage wear for a country artist.

Riley grew up in a small town in Texas, where her father worked as an auto mechanic and her mother was a fundamentalist Christian. She began singing locally while still a teenager and married a gas-station attendant, Mickey Riley, when she was seventeen. In 1966 they moved from Texas to Nashville, where she worked as a secretary in the music industry while making demo recordings on the side. She was hired by famed producer SHELBY SINGLETON to launch his new country label, Plantation, and scored a megaselling hit right out of the box with "Harper Valley."

With her sexy stage presence and smooth vocals, Riley scored a couple of minor follow-up hits, including 1968's "The Girl Most Likely" (the tale of a sexy, small-town girl who always got into trouble, playing up Riley's risque image), 1969's "There Never Was a Time," 1970's "Country Girl," and 1971's "Good Enough to Be Your Wife" (in which the heroine of the song refuses to have an affair with the barfly who is making moves on her, because she's too good to simply be a one-night fling), before moving to MGM and lesser stardom. She broke up with her husband in 1970 and continued to record occasionally through the mid-seventies, when she became a born-again Christian and gave up secular music (and incidentally reunited with husband Mickey). She continues to record and perform as a gospel artist but will only play dates where alcohol sales are strictly banned.

Select Discography

Here's Jeannie, Playback 4502. 1991 release of recordings of unknown origin.

◀ RITCHIE, JEAN

(born 1922, Viper, KY)

If one person can be credited with reviving interest in the Appalachian dulcimer, it would have to be folk-revivalist Jean Ritchie. Thanks to her series of successful recordings in the early to middle sixties, and her instruction book for the instrument, she introduced thousands of players to the dulcimer. Her quavery-voiced renditions of English ballads—many of which had been in her family for generations—were also quite influential on younger folkniks like Judy Collins and Joan Baez, to name just two.

The Ritchie family were among the first settlers in the Cumberland Mountain region in the late 1700s. Many were known locally as fine ballad singers and musicians, including Ritchie's parents, Balis, a school teacher, and her mother, Abigail Hall. The relatives would all gather together and play various instruments, including fiddle, BANJO, GUITAR, and the three-stringed dulcimer, which became Ritchie's favorite. As a youngster, she became deeply interested in the traditional songs passed along by her family, beginning a lifetime of collecting.

Unlike other mountain children, Ritchie was fortunate enough to be able to attend college at the University of Kentucky, completing a B.A. degree in the mid-forties. After graduation, she won a Fulbright Scholarship to study British balladry in England. On her return to Kentucky in the mid-fifties, she became active in the beginnings of the FOLK REVIVAL and began to publish a collection of songbooks based on her family's song repertoire.

Unlike some other mountain singers who sing in a harsh, nasal twang that is jarring to urban ears, Ritchie sings in a relaxed style that is similar to that of DOC WATSON, who hails from nearby Deep Gap, North Carolina. This full-voiced singing style is prevalent throughout the upper South and, along with the region's softer accent, makes singers from this region more easily understood by audiences used to the trained voices of pop crooners. Because she is an educated folklorist, Ritchie was able to present her material to an urban audience in such a way that they could appreciate and understand it.

Ritchie was most popular in the late fifties and early sixties, when she recorded for mainstream labels like Riverside and Elektra as well as Folkways Records. She appeared at the Newport Folk Festival for several years, as well as most other major festivals. After the folk boom died down in the late sixties, Ritchie switched her emphasis to her own material, including topical songs addressing the damage done to the Kentucky landscape by strip mining. She continued to record sporadically for larger labels, often saddled with unsympathetic accompanists who played in a soft-rock style, clearly not suited to her back-home presentation.

In the early eighties, along with husband George Pickow, Ritchie formed the

Greenhays label to issue her own recordings along with other folk revivalists. By the end of the decade, however, she was little heard or seen on the folk circuit.

Select Discography

Live at Folk City, Smithsonian/Folkways 40005. Reissue of early-sixties concert with Doc Watson.

The Most Dulcimer, Greenhays 70714. 1985 recording emphasizing her skills on this instrument.

◀ RITTER, TEX

(born Woodward Maurice Ritter, 1905, Nederland, TX; died 1973)

Ritter was a singing cowboy and country star of the forties through the sixties as noted for his acting in horse operas as his recordings.

Ritter was raised on a farm that was first settled by his great-grandfather in 1830, a four-hundred-acre spread in South Texas that was originally part of Mexico. He was a true cowboy, raised amid cattle roundups and ranch hands, not just a cowboy-come-lately like other performers. Ritter was introduced to COWBOY SONGS at the University of Texas, JOHN LOMAX's alma mater, where folklorist J. Frank Dobie was still collecting and teaching the material. He began performing this material on radio in Houston in 1929 and traveled to New York in 1931 to appear as an actor in the play *Green Grow the Lilacs*. During scene changes, he performed his cowboy ballads, becoming an immediate sensation. He remained on the East Coast for five years, performing on New York radio stations and giving lecture-concerts in which he introduced "authentic" cowboy material to his audiences. He made his first records for budget-label ARC in 1934. Also during his stay in New York, he worked on the original *Lone Ranger* radio series as both a writer and actor.

In 1936 he traveled to Hollywood to cash in on the singing-cowboy craze in the movies. Although his films suffered from low, low budgets, they often featured good music, including 1940's *Take Me Back to Oklahoma*, featuring WESTERN SWING veteran BOB WILLS as the second lead. After 1943, JOHNNY BOND became his bandleader on film, often appearing with him. All in all, between 1936 and 1945 he made over sixty horse flicks for one-horse operations including Grand National and Monogram as well as more established B studios like Universal and Columbia. In 1942, after unsuccessfully recording for ARC and Decca, Ritter was signed to the fledgling Capitol label as their first country act and recorded a combination of traditional folk songs ("Boll Weevil," "Rye Whiskey"), sentimental ditties ("There's a Moon Over My Shoulder"), and patriotic numbers ("Gold Star in the Window").

Ritter's biggest break came in 1953 when he recorded the theme song for the high-class Western *High Noon*. Although he didn't appear in the film, it gave a considerable boost to his career. Along with his friend Johnny Bond, he served as host of the popular *Town Hall Party* television program, which featured guitar wizard JOE MAPHIS, furthering Ritter's exposure to a country audience. By the late fifties and early sixties, he was working as a straight-country act, scoring his biggest hit with 1961's unabashedly sentimental "I Dreamed of a Hillbilly Heaven." Following in the footsteps of MARTY ROBBINS and JOHNNIE HORTON, who were enjoying success with their narrative songs newly composed in the style of traditional folk songs, Ritter recorded a gory collection of pseudo-cowboy numbers in 1960 called *Blood on the Saddle*, named after the gruesome cowboy standard. In 1965 he gained belated admittance to the GRAND OLE OPRY.

In the late sixties, Ritter attempted to cross over into politics, running without success for senator and governor of Tennessee. He served as narrator for the 1971 *Thank You, Mr. President* album, featuring various conservative country performers crooning in honor of then-president Richard Nixon. His son, John Ritter, gained great popularity in the seventies for his starring role in the TV series, *Three's Company* and, more recently, *Hearts Afire*.

Select Discography

Tex Ritter, Capitol 95036. His better-known recordings for this label.

◀ ROBBINS, MARTY

(born Martin David Robinson, 1925, Glendale, AZ; died 1982)

A cowboy-style SINGER/SONGWRITER, Robbins was both a country and pop star in the late fifties but is best remembered for his long string of country successes from the early fifties through his death in 1982.

Like many in his generation, Robbins was bitten early by the cowboy bug. Raised in the small town of Glendale, Arizona, he was particularly close to his grandfather, a retired medicine-show performer known as "Texas" Bob Heckle. Heckle was immersed in cowboy lore, much of which he shared with his young grandson. Saturday matinees featuring GENE AUTRY filled out Robbins's cowboy education, and he soon was playing a secondhand GUITAR given to him by his older sister.

When he was twelve, the Robinson family relocated to urban Phoenix, where Marty attended high school and began getting into scrapes with the authorities. He enlisted in the navy in 1944 and was stationed in the Pacific, where he began to write original songs and perform them for his fellow soldiers. On his return to Phoenix after the war, Robbins drifted from job to job while beginning to perform locally in clubs and bars at night. He took the name Marty Robbins because it sounded a little more Western than his real name, and also because he feared his parents would disapprove of his aspirations to be a professional singer.

By the early fifties, Marty was performing on local radio station KPHO, hosting his own *Western Caravan* show. LITTLE JIMMY DICKENS was a guest on the show and was so impressed that he recommended that his label, Columbia, sign the artist. In 1952 Robbins released his first single for Columbia, "Love Me or Leave Me Alone," and a year later joined the GRAND OLE OPRY, where he remained a member for twenty-nine years until his death. Two months after his first Opry appearance, Robbins scored his first top-ten country hit, "I'll Go on Alone"; but for the next two years, Robbins struggled to place his songs on the country charts.

His big break came in 1956 with "Singing the Blues," followed a year later by

"Knee Deep in the Blues," "The Story of My Life," and his own teenie-bop classic, "A White Sport Coat (and a Pink Carnation)." These jazzy-style country numbers, with Marty's peppy, smooth vocals, not only scored big on the country charts but also helped him break through into the pop charts. He continued in this pop-influenced vein through the fifties, turning out 1958's "She Was Only Seventeen" and "Stairway of Love."

Robbins's career took a Western swing with his appearance in the 1958 film *Buffalo Gun*, along with other country stars WEBB PIERCE and CARL SMITH. He recorded his classic album of Western story-songs, *Gunfighter Ballads and Trail Songs*, a year later, which produced several hits, including "The Hanging Tree" and "El Paso," a song that would become closely associated with him. Propelled by sessionman Grady Martin's Spanish-style lead guitar, the song ran over four minutes, an amazingly long number for a hit single on radio of the day. It topped both country and pop charts, gaining the first Grammy award ever given to a country song. Robbins followed it with another pseudofolk number, "Big Iron" (based on the story of a Texas Ranger, which Robbins learned in his youth from his grandfather), as well as "Battle of the Alamo."

Robbins continued to be a force on the country charts through the sixties, although, like many other Nashville recording artists, his recordings were increasingly buried in murmuring choruses. While he continued to produce hits with his own and other's compositions, and toured extensively throughout the United States and Canada, the hits started to thin out by the end of the decade, with his most distinctive recording being 1968's "I Walk Alone," another blues-tinged number in the vein of his earlier hits. In 1969 he suffered the first in a series of massive heart attacks; he claimed to have had a vision of Christ while he was on the operating table, which helped him to a speedy recovery and his first hit of the next decade, the schmaltzy "My Woman, My Woman, My Wife," which introduced the COUNTRYPOLITAN era.

Robbins pretty much coasted along on his reputation through the seventies, although he did turn out a few further hits, mostly under the hand of seasoned producer BILLY SHERRILL. "El Paso City," a 1976 release, was a follow-up to his earlier hit, filled with references to his best-loved song, and, along with "Among My Souvenirs," was one of his last two number-one country hits. In the seventies, Robbins suffered many injuries pursuing his hobby of stock-car racing. In 1981 he suffered a second heart attack but recovered to make a comeback a year later with his last release, "Some Memories Just Won't Die," before a final major heart attack killed him in 1982.

Select Discography

1951–1958, Bear Family 15570. Five-CD set covering 136 numbers cut from Robbins's first session in 1951 through 1958; these are his teen-pop tracks.

The Essential, Columbia/Legacy 48537. Two-CD set covering his career from 1951 to 1982.

Gunfighter Ballads and Trail Songs, Columbia 00116. Reissue of his early-sixties Western-flavored hits.

◀ ROBERTSON, UNCLE ECK

(born Alexander Campbell Robertson, 1887, Amarillo, TX; died 1975)

Robertson was a flashy Texas-style fiddler who is generally credited with making the first recording of an old-time fiddle tune, "Sally Goodin," in 1922. Although he was the first to record, Robertson was a fairly modern-style fiddler, playing many variations on the tunes that he recorded, using tricks such as double-stops, syncopations, flattened "blue" notes, and drones, which have all become hallmarks of the Texas school of championship fiddling.

Raised in the farm country of West Texas, Robertson began fiddling as a youngster, playing for socials and dances locally. By the time he reached his teenage years, he was already traveling around the state, competing in fiddler's conventions. He is said to have dressed in full cowboy gear and later claimed to be the first country performer to adopt this outfit. In 1922 Robertson and a local fiddler, Henry Gilliland, who was thirty-nine years his senior, traveled to Virginia to appear at a Civil War veterans' reunion. They eventually worked their way up to New York City, where they made some recordings for Victor, including Robertson's legendary solo recording of "Sally Goodin." Robertson returned to Texas soon after and made only one further recording in 1930, when country producer RALPH PEER recorded him along with members of his family.

Through the thirties and forties, Robertson performed locally in Texas, both on radio and at fiddlers' conventions. The old-time music revival brought new attention to his early recordings, beginning with Harry Smith's legendary reissue of early recordings on his *Anthology of American Folk Music*, a six-record set issued by Folkways Records in the early fifties (and kept in print for over thirty years later), featuring Robertson's "Brilliancy Medley," which has become a staple for BLUEGRASS bands. In the early sixties, RCA reissued "Sally Goodin" on an anthology of old-time music, which further spread the word about Robertson and his playing. Robertson was rediscovered in the early sixties and appeared at a number of folk festivals and made some final recordings for folklorist MIKE SEEGER, revealing that he was still a fine musician in the Texas style.

Almost every Texas contest-style fiddler since Robertson is indebted to him. His ringing tone, clean noting, and talent for improvisation all have become hallmarks for contestants at fiddlers' conventions.

◀ ROBINSON, CARSON J.

(born 1890, Oswego, KS; died 1957)

Robinson is a songwriter and guitarist noted for his association with pioneering recording star VERNON DALHART, but who then made hundreds of recordings on his own.

Robinson began his career performing country songs in his native Oswego, eventually moving on to Kansas City, where he worked on local radio. In 1924 he made his first recordings for Victor, as a novelty whistler. In the same year, he became Dalhart's accompanist and occasional accompanying vocalist. Robinson

provided Dalhart with some of his hit songs, beginning with compositions addressing the day's hot topics, such as the Scopes Trial. After breaking with Dalhart in
1927, Robinson joined forces with another city-bred vocalist, FRANK LUTHER, and
later led a series of Western-oriented bands in the thirties and forties.

Robinson wrote hundreds of songs, including the country-nostalgia numbers
"Blue Ridge Mountain Home" and "Left My Gal in the Mountains"; the ever-
popular comic novelty "Life Gets Tee-Jus, Don't It" (as well as the sequel "More
and More Tee-Jus, Ain't It" and another humorous monologue, "Settin' By
the Fire"); and the oft-covered slightly blue "Barnacle Bill the Sailor," to name
just a few.

In his later career, Robinson kept up with changing trends, recording with
backup by his own Pleasant Valley Boys in a (for then) modern-country style.
During the World War II years, he churned out patriotic tub-thumpers with unfor-
tunate names like "We're Gonna Have to Slap the Dirty Little Jap." He took the
pseudonym "The Kansas Jayhawk," and right before his death even dabbled in
the nascent ROCKABILLY style with his humorous "Rockin' and Rollin' with
Grandmaw."

◀ ROCKABILLY

(c. 1954–1959)

Literally the wedding of rock and roll with "hillbilly" or country music, rockabilly is a limited style but one that was highly influential in the mid-fifties. ELVIS
PRESLEY's first Sun recordings are firmly in the rockabilly style; indeed, it was Elvis's
success that helped nail down rockabilly's basic sound: jazzy riffs from a single
GUITAR, a heavy, slapped bass, and frantic, pounding drums. Countless country
stars jumped on the rockabilly bandwagon, some producing one or two classic
sides while others fading into obscurity. The most successful were the Burnette
brothers, Johnny and Dorsey, who led the Rockabilly Trio.

Perhaps the greatest rockabilly star was CARL PERKINS. His blend of high-energy
country sounds with R&B and blues made him an innovative composer and performer. From the sassy attitude of "Blue Suede Shoes" to his cover of Blind Lemon
Jefferson's classic "Matchbox," Perkins defined the rockabilly sound and attitude.
While some would also place JERRY LEE LEWIS in the style, his music mixed many
other elements into the stew, including the jazz tinges of WESTERN SWING piano and
the intensity of country gospel.

Not surprisingly, the success of rockabilly led many other country acts to join
in on the craze, sometimes for one-off recordings, sometimes for a few years of
ceaseless searching for hits. The style was dismissed by older country performers,
who felt it represented a sellout to teen-pop trends. Country comedian FERLIN HUSKY
took on the pseudonym of Simon Crum to record some humorous satires of rockabilly's excesses.

Rockabilly's stripped-down sensibility—including simple instrumentation, basic
riffs, and primal lyrics—appealed strongly to the post-punk crowd in the middle
to late seventies, particularly in Europe, when the style was revived and many

pioneering figures returned to the stage. Meanwhile, groups like the Stray Cats from Long Island picked up on a rockabilly sensibility, enjoying some success in the early eighties, but, like so many others, they eventually found the style rather limiting. Today, elements of the rockabilly sound can be heard in NEW-COUNTRY music, particularly the heavy backbeat and slapped bass, but no star centers his or her act solely on the rockabilly style.

◄ RODGERS, JIMMIE

(born 1897, Meridian, MS; died 1933)

Perhaps the most influential country singer of all time, Jimmie Rodgers in his short career wed black blues and jazz with the traditional country repertoire to form a truly unique type of music that has influenced generations of country performers. Like many country stars, Rodgers had a gimmick: he yodeled. While undoubtedly his YODELING was a crowd pleaser, Rodgers managed to make it an integral part of his music, so that it would be impossible to think of such standards at "T.B. Blues," "Peach Pickin' Time in Georgia," "Waitin' for a Train," "Muleskinner Blues," or "Blue Yodel Number 1 (T for Texas)" without the yodeling at the end of each verse. Neither a terrific guitarist nor a particularly wide-ranging vocalist, Rodgers, like many other country performers, made a virtue out of his limitations, giving a wonderfully expressive, and often slyly humorous, reading to his songs.

The son of a railroad man, Rodgers worked as a brakeman until tuberculosis cut short his career in 1924. Determined to become a professional performer, he worked the medicine-show circuit of the South performing in black face. He also performed more pop-oriented material with his backup band, the Teneva Ramblers, who would subsequently record without him. He gained an audition with noted producer RALPH PEER in 1927 and was signed to Victor records at the same time as the CARTER FAMILY. In his short, six-year career, he made over 110 sides, with backings as various as small jazz bands (including Louis Armstrong on trumpet), Hawaiian-flavored groups, and both white and black string bands. Ironically, some of his most moving performances featured just his simple, strummed GUITAR accompaniments. Victor successfully marketed his recordings by promoting Rodgers as the "Singing Brakeman" (the name of a short motion picture in which Rodgers appeared in 1929) and "America's Blue Yodeler."

Rodgers's recordings enjoyed immediate success; his first "Blue Yodel" sold a million copies, and many of his recordings have remained in print, in one form or another, for the last six decades. Thanks to the tireless promotion of his wife and daughter, Meridian, Mississippi, has had an annual Jimmie Rodgers day for the last four decades; the star was the first musician inducted into the Country Music Hall of Fame, in 1961; and his complete recordings have recently been reissued in this country on seven CDs on the Rounder label.

Rodgers's recordings were primarily made up of blues-influenced numbers, along with Tin Pan Alley standards, jazzy numbers, and the sentimental heart songs that had been popular in the mountains since the 1890s. Rodgers promoted the image of an urbane country performer; he was often pictured wearing a straw hat set jauntily on the back of his head, a polka-dot tie, and a natty suit. Unlike other contemporary acts, he did not try to act like a "backwoodsman." However, his music still reflected the lonesome sound of mountain ballads, embodying the yearnings of white and black southerners in their longing for a better life.

Plagued by TB, Rodgers performed and toured as widely as possible but made his greatest impact through his recordings. He made his last recordings in New York in 1933; two days after this final session, he died in his New York hotel room. The death of Jimmie Rodgers only added to his legendary status; like HANK WILLIAMS and ELVIS PRESLEY after him, Rodgers became a larger-than-life performer after his death, with record sales continuing unabated for six decades.

Select Discography

Singing Brakeman, Bear Family 15540. Lavishly produced six-CD set with notes by Nolan Porterfield; all of his Victor recordings, 145 songs in all. The same material was issued on seven individual CDs by Rounder (1056–1062), without the lavish booklet.

◀ RODRIGUEZ, JOHNNY

(born Juan Raoul Davis Rodriguez, 1951, Sabinal, TX)

Although of a Tex-Mex background, Rodriguez was a mainstream country star of the seventies and eighties with a slight OUTLAW image thanks to his association with singer TOM T. HALL.

The eighth son of a Chicano family, Rodriguez began playing GUITAR at age seven, performing in a local band during his high-school years. He made some demo recordings in San Antonio in 1969, but they went nowhere. Meanwhile, Rodriguez began attracting the attention of the local authorities for various minor infractions; he eventually served prison time for the heinous crime of stealing and barbecuing a goat. In prison he became well-known for his singing, and one of the guards introduced Rodriguez to the owner of a country music bar in Bracketville when he was paroled in 1970. It was while performing there that he was first heard by Tom T. Hall and BOBBY BARE, both of whom encouraged him to pursue a country music career.

In late 1971, Rodriguez came to Nashville to work as guitarist in Hall's band, the Storytellers, and also auditioned as a solo act for Mercury Records. His first single, "Pass Me By," from 1972, went to number nine on the charts, and in the following year he had his first number-one records with "You Always Come Back (to Hurtin' Me)," which he cowrote with Tom T. Hall, and his self-penned "Ridin' My Thumb to Mexico." He followed this with two covers in 1974, the traditional country WEEPER "That's the Way Love Goes," written by LEFTY FRIZZELL with Sanger D. Shafer, and the Beatles' "Something," an unusual move for a country artist. The hits kept coming through the late seventies, when his increasing use of drugs sidetracked his career, although he did manage to make a comeback in 1983 with two recordings featuring backup vocals by LYNN ANDERSON: "Foolin'" and "How Could I Love Her So Much." In 1987 he made a second abortive comeback, this time scoring a minor hit with "I Didn't (Every Chance I Had)" before fading back into obscurity.

Select Discography

Greatest Hits, Mercury 826271. Cassette-only collection of his seventies hits.

◀ ROGERS, KENNY

(born 1937, Houston, TX)

The king of mid-seventies COUNTRYPOLITAN, Rogers did more to drag country music into the pop domain than any other singer of his generation. For this, he is to be either glorified or vilified, or perhaps both, but in any case his gruff vocals and washed-in-the-water-of-Vegas stage show have made him a perennial country favorite even now, when his pop-charting days are over.

Rogers was born to relative poverty in Houston; the lingering effects of the Depression plus his father's alcoholism and thus unreliability as a worker joined to make the family's life even worse. He had his first exposure to music in the church choir and then took up the GUITAR, teaching himself to play chords. He often got together with another neighborhood kid, pianist MICKEY GILLEY, to perform the latest pop hits.

In high school, Kenny formed the Scholars, a ROCKABILLY outfit, and signed as a soloist with the local Carlton label. He recorded an album in 1959 titled *One Dozen Goldies* (despite the fact that none of his previous singles had earned anywhere near gold-record status). After a brief college try at the University of Houston, he joined a light-jazz trio led by Bobby Doyle, who recorded for Columbia in 1962, followed by a stint with Kirby Stone's pop-jazz group. He relocated to Los Angeles in 1966, hooking up with the folk group the New Christy Minstrels and made some recordings as a soloist for Mercury in 1966.

Along with fellow Minstrel Mike Settle, he formed the folk-tinged pop vocal group the First Edition, scoring a major pop hit with 1967's "Just Dropped In (to See What Condition My Condition Was In)." Other hits, in a more country vein, followed, including "Ruby (Don't Take Your Love to Town)" and the folk anthem "Reuben James." The group remained together under Rogers's leadership until 1975, when he embarked on a solo career.

The late seventies were golden years for Rogers, beginning in 1977 with his monster hit "Lucille," establishing him as a star on both country and pop charts. He followed it with a hit 1978 duet with DOTTIE WEST on "Every Time Two Fools Collide," solidifying his position as a country-music star. Later that same year, he scored on his own with Don Schlitz's "The Gambler," which has become his best-loved country-flavored song (and also inspired a made-for-TV movie two years later).

Guided by mastermind promoter Ken Kragen, Rogers's career veered into mainstream mush in 1979 with hits like the hopelessly saccharine "You Decorated My Life," a duet with popster Kim Carnes on "Don't Fall in Love with a Dreamer" a year later, and his breathy reading of Lionel Richie's "Lady," establishing him firmly as a mainstream pop star.

After scaling the heights of mainstream pop, Rogers spent most of the eighties returning to performing for country audiences, although his rhinestone-studded collection of shirts (left open to the navel) still firmly places him in the Vegas camp. He has also taken to acting, mostly in made-for-TV movies, and primarily in parts that are tailor made for his personality. Meanwhile, he is often in the tabloids and has been interviewed by Barbara Walters on prime-time television, a sure sign that Rogers has made it as a mainstream artist, and not by carrying the smaller country torch.

Select Discography
The Early Years, Special Music 4801. Reissue of his hits leading the First Edition.
The Gambler, EMI 48404.
Greatest Country Hits, Curb 77358.

◀ ROGERS, ROY

(born Leonard Franklin Slye, 1911, Duck Run, OH)
An influential singing cowboy and movie star, Rogers founded the Western group the SONS OF THE PIONEERS, who served as his backup band from 1934 until 1948. This smooth-harmony vocal group did much to modernize the cowboy sound and style.

The son of migrant farm workers, Leonard Slye came to California in 1930 to work as a fruit picker. He began performing with a number of Western bands, founding his own group, the Sons of the Pioneers, in 1934. Their big break came supporting GENE AUTRY in his 1935 epic, *Tumbling Tumbleweeds*. Slye decided he could be a singing cowboy, too, and took the names Dick Weston and then Roy Rogers (perhaps in homage to country legend, JIMMIE RODGERS). He began starring in B-grade Westerns in 1938 and, four years later when Autry went off to fight in World War II, became the country's leading cowboy star.

In 1947 he wed Dale Evans (born Frances Smith, 1912, Uvalde, TX), a pop chanteuse who had appeared in many of his Westerns and would continue to work with him through the rest of his career. From the fifties to today, the pair has worked in radio, films, and TV, and Roy has also pursued business interests, including a franchise of fast-food joints. His best-known song is his theme song, "Happy Trails." The duo founded their own museum in their hometown of Victorville, California, where one can visit the stuffed remains of Roy's favorite ride, Trigger (1932 to 1965).

Select Discography
The Best of Roy Rogers, Curb 77392. Fifties and sixties recordings.

◀ RONSTADT, LINDA

(born 1948, Tucson, AZ)
Ronstadt is a pop vocalist who was one of the first COUNTRY-ROCK stars whose records scored on both country and pop charts. Ronstadt's combination of the songs and sensibilities of HANK WILLIAMS and BUDDY HOLLY pointed the way for a

new marriage of country and rock, while reviving sales of the original recordings of both of these performers.

Ronstadt was born to a middle-class family in urban Tucson, where her father, a Mexican-American, operated a hardware store. As a teenager, she was a fan of both ELVIS PRESLEY and Hank Williams and even enjoyed her father's taste for traditional Mexican mariachi music. After one year of college in her native state, she packed her bags for the bustling California folk-rock scene.

In Los Angeles, she hooked up with Kenny Edwards and Bob Kimmel to form the Peter-Paul-and-Maryish trio, the Stone Poneys. Their big hit was 1967's "Different Drum," a country-rock ballad penned by MIKE NESMITH. The band soon dissolved, and Ronstadt recorded two straight-country LPs, one including a cover of "Silver Threads and Golden Needles," which would remain popular with her fans through the seventies.

In 1974 she teamed up with pop producer Peter Asher (who was originally one half of Peter and Gordon, England's answer to the EVERLY BROTHERS) to record a series of hugely successful albums. Each featured songs in a pop-rock/country vein, including her hit covers of Buddy Holly's "That'll Be the Day," Hank Williams's "I Can't Help It if I'm Still in Love with You," ROY ORBISON's "Blue Bayou," DOLLY PARTON's "I Will Always Love You" (later a hit for soulster Whitney Houston), NEIL YOUNG's "Love Is a Rose," and WILLIE NELSON's "Crazy." She even recorded the traditional "I Never Will Marry" as a duet with Dolly Parton, one of the country singer/songwriters whom Ronstadt admires the most.

The eighties found Ronstadt searching for a new musical style. She passed through new wave to Gilbert and Sullivan then formed an alliance with arranger Nelson Riddle to cover forties pop. She finally went whole hog for the Mexican mariachi music that she loved from her childhood, sung in Spanish (Ronstadt even adapted the full Mexican performer's regalia, making her look in some critics' minds like an escaped waitress from Taco Bell). In 1987 she rejoined with old friends EMMYLOU HARRIS and Dolly Parton to release *Trio*, a simple and rather low-keyed homage to their country roots.

Ronstadt's strong vocals, sassy image, and mainstream acceptability brought country music to a new level of sophistication. She proved that classic country performed in a simple, reverent fashion could be successful on today's country and pop charts, leading the way for the NEW-COUNTRY revival of the mid-eighties and early nineties. Her independence as a woman and her promotion of the work of female songwriters also set the stage for the rebirth of women as movers and shakers in the country world.

Select Discography

Heart Like a Wheel, Capitol 46073. Ronstadt combines folk, rock, and country influences on this fine 1974 outing.

◀ ROSE, FRED AND WESLEY

(Fred born 1897, Evansville, IN; died 1954; Wesley born 1918, Chicago, IL)

Fred Rose was a pioneering publisher, songwriter, and producer in country music, while his son Wesley built on his father's empire (in partnership with ROY ACUFF) to make it one of the powerhouses of the Nashville music establishment.

The elder Rose began his career as a Chicago-area pianist, initially recording jazz for the Brunswick record label and piano rolls for QRS. In Chicago, he wrote many songs for the big-throated chanteuse Sophie Tucker, including her signature tune, "Red Hot Mama," as well as "Deed I Do," and "Honestly and Truly." After working in Paul Whiteman's band for a while, he joined CBS radio as a house producer in Chicago and then relocated to the West Coast, where he hooked up with up-and-coming cowpoke star GENE AUTRY, composing his megahit, "Be Honest with Me." Recognizing the market for country music, he moved to Nashville where he was hired as staff pianist for WSM, home of the GRAND OLE OPRY, and quickly befriended a young fiddler/singer named Roy Acuff. Acknowledging the value of the acts that he was managing and producing, he joined with Acuff in 1942 to form Acuff-Rose music publishing and helped found Broadcast Music International (BMI) as an alternative to the more conservative ASCAP (American Society of Composers, Authors, and Publishers), which was uninterested in representing country or blues composers.

Son Wesley was trained as an accountant and worked for Standard Oil before joining the family business in 1945. Fred left the business to take a more active hand in managing his last great discovery, HANK WILLIAMS, for whom he composed "Kaw-Liga." Other popular Rose compositions include "Blue Eyes Crying in the Rain" (revived by WILLIE NELSON), "Tears on My Pillow," "A Mansion on the Hill," and "Settin' the Woods on Fire." After his father's death, Wesley discovered and helped build the career of acts like the EVERLY BROTHERS. In the late fifties, he founded with Acuff the Hickory record label, which became the home for many important country acts in the early sixties.

◀ ROSENBAUM, ART

(born c. 1945, New York, NY)

A folk-revivalist and record producer, Rosenbaum did much to popularize traditional BANJO styles through his recordings and instruction books.

Rosenbaum is one of those rare urban artists who does not merely imitate traditional styles; he seems to be able to get to the heart and soul of the sound, so that his performances are both recreations and new creative works, extensions of the folk traditions into new territory. His high, reedy voice perfectly captures the high, lonesome sound of mountain singing, without sounding at all condescending like some other revival singers do.

Rosenbaum first made an impact on the revival scene in the mid-sixties when his roots-oriented banjo playing was featured on an Elektra Records anthology of banjo music. Because this label catered to city folks (and even folk-rockers), these recordings helped introduce old-time banjo playing to a new audience. He also recorded and produced a fine collection called *Fine Times at Our House* for Folkways Records, featuring fiddler John "Dick" Summers, that became a favorite among young old-time revivalists. In 1968 he authored a banjo instruction book that emphasized mountain styles.

In the early seventies, Rosenbaum relocated to Iowa where he taught painting. With BLUEGRASS-style fiddler Al Murphy he recorded a duo album that was released by the tiny Meadowlands label, followed by two solo albums for the folk-instructional label, Kicking Mule. In the late seventies, he relocated again, to Athens, Georgia, where he began recording blues, religious music, and old-time string-band music. These field recordings were issued by Flyright Records (a German label) and Folkways. He also authored a book on Georgia's traditional music, illustrated with his own drawings and paintings of musicians along with his wife's photographs.

Although Rosenbaum does not perform often, his recordings were quite influential, particularly on the old-time string-band revival of the seventies. His combination of scholarship and creativity make him one of the most listenable, and enjoyable, of all of the urban revivalists.

Select Discography

Art of the Old Time Banjo, Kicking Mule 519. Cassette-only reissue of mid-seventies album.

◀ ROWAN, PETER

(born 1942, Wayland, MA)

One of the pioneers of newgrass and its more spacey offshoots, Rowan is an energetic vocalist/guitarist/MANDOLIN player/songwriter whose sensibility combines traditional BLUEGRASS with Tex-Mex and cowboy themes.

Rowan was a product of the teeming folk-rock movement of the greater Boston area. Boston hosted a crowd of nascent rockers and social-protest singers but also had a strong tradition of supporting bluegrass and country acts. Rowan was impressed with the energy of bluegrass and relocated to Nashville to meet the father of the music, BILL MONROE. By the mid-sixties, he was writing with Monroe (the classic "Walls of Time") and recording as a member of the Blue Grass Boys, along with young fiddler RICHARD GREENE. Rowan ultimately was frustrated by Monroe's strict traditionalist approach, and he returned to the Boston area to form the eclectic rock band Earth Opera, with mandolinist DAVID GRISSMAN, also an ex-bluegrasser.

In the late sixties, Greene invited Rowan to join the progressive California rock band, Seatrain, and so he relocated to California. After Seatrain reorganized without Rowan in 1972, Rowan formed several short-lived traditional bluegrass bands, including 1972's MULESKINNER (with Greene, Grissman, banjoist BILL KEITH, and guitarist Clarence White) and OLD AND IN THE WAY, with Grissman, Jerry Garcia (banjo), and VASSAR CLEMENTS (fiddle). Both bands performed traditional bluegrass numbers and Rowan's bluegrass-style original songs, including "Blue Mule" (which took the story of *Tenbrooks and Molly*, a Monroe classic, into outer space) and a classic update of the badman ballad "Panama Red." In the mid-seventies, he hooked up with his two brothers, calling themselves the Rowans, and for Asylum they recorded two folk-rock albums, which gained the group a cult following if not great commercial success.

By the end of the seventies, Rowan was performing as a soloist leading his own Green Grass Gringos band, whose floating membership included traditional bluegrass fiddler Tex Logan, progressive fiddler Richard Greene, and Tex-Mex accordion whiz Flaco Jiminez. Rowan's intense and expressive high-tenor lead vocals were perfectly suited to his songs that wed New Age sensibilities to classic stories of the Southwest to create a new mythical interpretation of America's cowboy past.

Select Discography

Peter Rowan, Flying Fish 70071. Reissue of late-seventies solo album.
The Walls of Time, Sugar Hill 3722. 1991 bluegrass album with RICKY SKAGGS, Eddie Adcock, and Sam Bush.

S.

◀ SATHERLEY, ART

(born 1889, Bristol, UK; died 1986)

One of the pioneering producers of traditional country recordings, Satherley worked for early labels Paramount, Plaza, ARC (American Record Company), and finally Columbia, overseeing the sessions of country bluesmen and what was then called hillbilly music.

Born in England, Satherley came to America when he was twenty-four, initially working in a lumber mill owned by the Wisconsin Chair Company. Like many other furniture manufacturers, the company expanded into producing phonographs and then into making records on its house label, Paramount. Satherley worked his way up the ranks, producing landmark recordings for the company's "race" series, beginning with the Norfolk Jubilee Quartet's 1923 recording of "My Lord's Gonna Move This Wicked Race." Focusing on the black market, he took ads in newspapers that catered to it, and developed the careers of bluesmen Blind Lemon Jefferson and Blind Blake and cabaret blues star Ma Rainey.

In 1929 Satherley took a position with the Plaza label, which mostly sold through Sears, Roebuck and other catalog sources. Soon after, the label, combined with other dime-store outfits, was renamed American Record Company, or ARC. Satherley became the firm's Southern-music producer, traveling through the South setting up makeshift sessions to record whatever talent he could unearth. Among his country-music finds were ROY ACUFF, BOB WILLS, and GENE AUTRY; he produced Autry's 1931 recording of "That Silver-Haired Daddy of Mine," a breakthrough hit for the cowboy star, which also brought the company much-needed capital during the depths of the Depression.

In 1938 Columbia Records acquired ARC, and Satherley remained with the parent label until 1952. He established Columbia's presence in the new country-music recording capital, Nashville, overseeing sessions by SPADE COOLEY, ROSE MADDOX, BILL MONROE, and RAY PRICE, to name a few. His assistant, Don Law, was to become a leading country producer in the late fifties and sixties.

◀ SAWYER BROWN

(c. 1984–ongoing: Mark Miller [lead vocals]; Bobby Randall [guitar]; Gregg "Hobie" Hubbard [keyboards]; Jim Schloten [bass]; "Curley" Joe Smyth [drums]; Randell left in 1993 and was replaced by Cameron Duncan)

A COUNTRY-ROCK band discovered by Ed McMahon on TV's *Star Search*, Sawyer Brown has progressively become more oriented toward country and less toward rock, although they still have the flavor of a mid-seventies arena-rock band.

The band came together as backup musicians for singer Don King; vocalist Mark Miller and keyboard player Gregg Hubbard were friends from high school in Florida, while guitarist Bobby Randall and bassist Jim Schloten were from Michigan; drummer Joe Smyth had previously played percussion with the Maine Symphony. While working for King, they were impressed by the commercial success of ALABAMA and, after leaving King's employ, formed the original band, giving it a similar name (Savannah) in hopes of attracting similar success.

The group soon took the name of Sawyer Brown from an intersection in Nashville and got their first break in 1984 when they won first prize on *Star Search*. The prize was a recording contract, and the boys immediately scored with 1985's "Step That Step," written by Miller, their second single and a number-one hit. They followed with more fluffy upbeat numbers, including the too-cute "Betty's Bein' Bad" and a remake of GEORGE JONES's "The Race Is On." Their road show featured smoke bombs, twirling lights, and jazzy costumes, reflecting their arena-rock leanings and paving the way for similar theatrics from more straight-country acts like GARTH BROOKS.

In the early nineties, recognizing that NEW COUNTRY was making their meld of Alabama and EXILE rock sound passé, the group remade itself in the boot-scootin' mode of a good-time, HONKY-TONK band. It turned out that they could produce watered-down WESTERN SWING in an attractive manner. Miller continues his Mick Jagger-esque stage antics, particularly in their video for "The Boys and Me," an unabashed retro-rocker. All in all, if not exactly a weighty group, they do provide high-energy entertainment for the masses.

Select Discography

Greatest Hits, Curb 77578. The hits up to 1990.

Cafe on the Corner, Curb 77574. 1992 album, more of the same "we're rowdy and ready" music.

◀ SCHNEIDER, JOHN

(born 1954, Mount Kisco, NY)

Famous for portraying Bo Duke in the country-corn television show *The Dukes of Hazzard*, Schneider parlayed his acting role into a brief career on the Nashville charts, beginning with his ELVIS PRESLEY cover "It's Now or Never" from 1981.

Schneider is an actor who was raised in suburban New York until he was twelve, when his parents divorced and he moved with his mother to Atlanta, Georgia. After working high-school, summer stock, and amateur productions, he landed the role of the youngest and not-brightest Duke on the popular TV series when he was twenty-four. Three years later, he signed with the Scotti Brothers label, having his hit with "It's Now or Never," but he was unable to follow it up.

Then from 1984 to 1987, Schneider produced a string of hits, beginning with "I've Been Around Enough to Know," all cut by whiz-bang Nashville producer Jimmy Bowen. With his hunky good looks and a voice reminiscent of GEORGE STRAIT, Schneider had a brief run as a NEW-COUNTRY star. Then his thespian ambitions got the best of him, and he returned to TV and Broadway, appearing in the musical *Grand Hotel*.

Select Discography
Greatest Hits, MCA 42033. A more appropriate title would be "greatest hit"; lots of eighties-style mainstream country songs.

◀ SEALS, DAN

(born 1948, McCamey, TX)

Seals is a seventies popster most famous for the song "I'd Really Like to See You Tonight," which he recorded (as "England Dan" Seals) with John Ford Coley. Following the duo's demise, Seals had some success in the mid-eighties as a country artist.

Seals comes from a musical Texas family; his father played with ERNEST TUBB and led a family band that featured older brother Jimmy (who later achieved fame with Dash Crofts, first as a member of the Champs, famous for their early sixties rock instrumental hit, "Tequila," and then for their late-sixties, early-seventies hippie folk hits, including "One Toke Over the Line") as well as young Dan on bass. Dan heard only country music until he was ten, when the family relocated to Dallas and some R&B and pop sounds began creeping into the mix. He formed his first band as a teenager, playing country for Lions clubs and rock and roll for teenage dance parties. In 1967 he formed his first recorded group, Southwest F.O.B. (Freight on Board) with friend John Ford Coley, and they scored a freak hit with 1968's flower-child pop song "Smell of Incense."

Like many other pop bands of the sixties, the band was unable to produce a follow-up, and Seals and Coley relocated to California to perform as a folk duo. There, Seals took the stage name of England Dan, and the twosome began to record, scoring a hit record in Japan in 1973. Three years later, they hit the jackpot with the song "I'd Really Love to See You Tonight," a soft-rock hit that Seals correctly states would be classified as "country" in today's market. The duo produced a number of follow-up songs, mostly sounding like watered-down clones of their initial hit, all without success.

Seals retired to Hendersonville, Tennessee, where he reverted to his initial love of country music. He released his first country single in 1984, the self-penned "God Must Be a Cowboy," and had a hit right out of the gate. His biggest year was 1986, when he recorded a duet with MARIE OSMOND on "Meet Me in Montana." Followups were 1988's "Bop," a kind of techno-pop dance number with vague country feeling, the rock-tinged "Addicted," and the weepy ballad "You Still Move Me."

Seals's success in soft rock/folk/country-pop shows how these styles are in a sense interchangeable; today's country is, in the hands of artists like Seals, really just an extension of seventies folk-rock. On the continuum that exists between folk-pop-country, Seals falls firmly into the middle, creating pop songs with a hint of country feeling.

Select Discography

The Classic Collection, Vols. 1 and 2, Liberty 95952/96384.
Songwriter, Liberty 98481. 1992 recording.

◀ SEEGER, MIKE

(born 1933, Washington, D.C.)

Folk-revivalist, multi-instrumentalist, folklorist, and record producer, Seeger has played a seminal role in the preservation and popularization of old-time country music. Son of ethnomusicologist Charles and composer Ruth Crawford Seeger, and half-brother of folk revivalist PETE SEEGER, Mike has been active on the folk scene for nearly forty years.

Seeger began performing as a BLUEGRASS–style BANJO player in the Washington, D.C. area in the mid-fifties. In 1957 he produced for Folkways Records one of the first albums of bluegrass music, an important anthology because Folkways catered to a northern, urban audience that was unfamiliar (at that time) with the diversity of bluegrass styles. About the same time, with Tom Paley and JOHN COHEN, he formed the NEW LOST CITY RAMBLERS, a band dedicated to performing the old-time music of the twenties and thirties in almost literal, note-for-note recreations.

Seeger made his first solo LP in 1962 (*Old-Time Country Music*, Folkways). By using an Ampex multitrack tape machine, he was able to play all of the parts, creating in effect his own string band. The sound of the album was not much different from the style of the Ramblers at that time. Perhaps most interesting was his recreation of both Monroe Brothers on the tune "Rollin' On."

In this same period, he began making a series of field trips to the South. One of the first artists he discovered was blues guitarist Elizabeth "Libba" Cotten, who had worked as a maid for the Seeger family. It turned out that she was a talented GUITAR player in the country-blues style, as well as a skilled songwriter. (Her "Freight Train" became one of the hits of the FOLK REVIVAL.) Seeger also sought out performers of the twenties and thirties who had stopped recording; one of his most important finds was banjoist DOC BOGGS. He was also a champion of the autoharp, introducing the country picking of Maybelle Carter and other important autoharp players to a new audience. His anthology *Mountain Music on the Autoharp* introduced several fine players, including Kilby Snow.

Seeger recorded a second solo album in 1965 for Vanguard, a more low-keyed affair than his first, while continuing to perform with the Ramblers through 1968. Although the Ramblers never officially disbanded, they were less active from 1968 onward. Seeger made two excellent solo albums for Mercury in the mid-seventies, *Music from True Vine*, featuring the charming autoharp song "I Rambled This Country from Early to Late," and *The Second Annual Farewell Reunion*, which featured

Seeger playing with traditional performers and revivalists. The most interesting cut on the latter album was his re-creation of "The Train That Carried My Girl from Town," by FRANK HUTCHINSON, featuring Seeger on fiddle, harmonica, and vocals along with the slide guitar of Ry Cooder.

In the early seventies, Seeger formed with Ramblers bandsmate TRACY SCHWARTZ, then-wife ALICE GERRARD, HAZEL DICKENS, and bluegrass banjo player LAMAR GRIER a bluegrass-country group called the Strange Creek Singers. This short-lived band played an amalgam of country and bluegrass sounds. Seeger also performed as a duo with Alice Gerrard (the pair recorded an album for Greenhays Records), and with his sister Peggy Seeger. (The two made a 1968 duo recording for British Argo Records and also recorded for Rounder selections from their mother's collections of children's songs.)

Through the eighties and early nineties, Seeger continued to perform as a soloist and sometime member of the New Lost City Ramblers. He also was the main force behind the old-time music "exercise" record, *A-Robics and the Exertions* (Flying Fish). He continues his fieldwork; in the late eighties he produced the videotape *Talkin' Feet*, a documentary on traditional flat-foot dancing of the upper South.

Select Discography

Fresh Old-Time Stringband Music, Rounder 0262. 1988 release with various young and innovative string bands accompanying Seeger.

American Folk Songs for Children, Rounder 0268/0269. Two-CD set of songs collected by Ruth Crawford Seeger and performed by Mike with sisters Peggy and Penny.

◖ SEEGER, PETE

(born 1919, New York, NY)

Son of musicologist Charles Seeger and half-brother of country-folk musicians Peggy and MIKE SEEGER, Pete Seeger has done more to popularize the five-string BANJO than perhaps any other performer besides Earl Scruggs. He developed a simplified version of clawhammer-style banjo playing (the traditional banjo strum) that gave just about every folk revivalist of the fifties, sixties, and seventies their first exposure to the instrument, while he revived traditional mountain folk songs in his performances from the late forties through today.

After attending Harvard for a couple of semesters, Seeger left school in 1938 to accompany folklorist ALAN LOMAX on a field trip to the South. It was there he heard banjoist Pete Steele, who impressed him not only with his energetic banjo playing but also his repertoire of traditional songs about coal mining and his own compositions, including "Pay Day at Coal Creek." He settled in New York in 1940, forming the Almanac Singers, one of the first FOLK-REVIVAL groups, with singers Lee Hays and Millard Lampell. WOODY GUTHRIE joined the fold in 1941. They recorded topical songs on unionism and pacifism (before the United States entered World War II), and antifascist anthems (while the U.S. was at war with Germany). Seeger enlisted in the army during the war and the group disbanded.

After the war, Seeger again became involved with progressive musicians in the

New York area, helping to found People's Songs, a booking agency for left-wing singers, as well as the folk journal *Sing Out!* In 1949, along with Hays, Fred Hellerman, and Ronnie Gilbert, he formed the Weavers. They attracted the attention of Decca Records with their energetic reworkings of world folk songs and had major pop hits with their arrangements of the African folk song "Wimoweh" (featuring Seeger's high-tenor vocals and strummed banjo) and Leadbelly's "Goodnight Irene." The Weavers were the model for all of the folk-revival groups of the early sixties, including the Kingston Trio, the Tarriers, Peter, Paul and Mary, and dozens more. Despite their great success on the charts, the band's members were attacked by anti-Communist politicians and groups who were suspicious of their earlier leftist activities. Unable to get work, the group folded in 1952 but then reunited triumphantly in 1955. Seeger left permanently in 1958.

During the fifties, Seeger began recording for the small specialty label Folkways. His first solo album, *Darling Corey*, featured mountain folk songs that Seeger had learned during his field trip with Lomax and from other traditional sources. He also recorded in the mid-fifties the seminal *Goofing Off Suite*, in which he adapted classical, jazz, and pop tunes to the five-string banjo. This record was highly influential on other banjo players who hoped to expand the repertoire of the instrument. He recorded numerous children's albums, resetting UNCLE DAVE MACON's song "The Cumberland Mountain Deer Chase" into a story song that he called "The Cumberland Mountain Bear Hunt." (In the early sixties, he encouraged Folkways to reissue an album of Macon's recordings from the twenties and thirties.) Toward the end of the fifties, he recorded a series of folk ballads (*America's Favorite Ballads*, five albums) as well as traditional industrial ballads. Also in the fifties, Seeger self-published the first edition of his book, *How to Play the Five-String Banjo*, which not only gave detailed instruction in his distinctive frailing style but also introduced BLUEGRASS picking to urban players, highlighting the contributions of Earl Scruggs.

In the early sixties, Seeger became increasingly involved with political causes and began performing more contemporary material. He also began writing his own songs. (He had previously written the folk classic "If I Had a Hammer" in the early fifties with his Weavers mate, Lee Hays.) In the sixties, he set the words of Ecclesiastes to music, producing a hit for the BYRDS with "Turn! Turn! Turn!"; he also wrote the hits "Where Have All the Flowers Gone?" and "Bells of Rhymney." His song "Waist Deep in the Big Muddy" got him into trouble again with the censors, because it critized Lyndon Johnson's war efforts in Vietnam. He was invited to perform the song on the *Smothers Brothers* television show (incidentally the first time he was invited on network television since he was blacklisted in the fifties), but the song was cut from the program; only after considerable protest was he invited back to perform it on another occasion.

By the late sixties, Seeger more often played the twelve-string GUITAR rather than the banjo, emulating the style of Leadbelly. Although he continued to perform in the seventies (often in partnership with Arlo Guthrie), eighties, and through today, his more recent performances have lacked the enthusiasm and power that he had as a young player. Increasing hearing problems have limited his performance in the past few years. In 1994 he was honored by the Kennedy Center.

Select Discography

American Industrial Ballads, Smithsonian/Folkways 40058. Reissue of an album originally recorded in the late fifties.

Darling Corey/Goofin' Off Suite, Smithsonian/Folkways 40018. Two of Seeger's more innovative fifties recordings, the first dedicated to traditional banjo songs, the second to instrumental versions of everything from fiddle tunes to classical music and pop songs.

We Shall Overcome, Columbia 45312. Two-CD set drawn from a Carnegie Hall concert in 1963, during the height of Seeger's involvement in civil rights and other contemporary issues.

◀ SEELEY, JEANNIE

(born 1940, Townville, PA)

Seeley is a smoldering country vocalist best known for her mid-sixties hits and her association with songwriter HANK COCHRAN, who was her husband at the time.

The daughter of a steelworker and sometime farmer, Seeley was performing by age eleven, when she appeared on local radio; five years later, she was regularly featured on a country television show out of Erie. After graduating high school, she enrolled in night school for banking while working as a secretary by day. With three friends, she left Pennsylvania to cross the country in 1961, ending up in Beverly Hills, where she worked briefly in a bank before taking a job as secretary at Liberty Records, where she met a young country guitarist named Hank Cochran. She began writing songs (soulster Irma Thomas had a hit with her "Anyone Who Knows What Love Is" in 1964), worked as a deejay, and recorded for the tiny Challenge label. Cochran urged her to follow him to Nashville for a career in country music.

Arriving in Nashville in 1965, Seeley went into the studio with Cochran, who wrote and produced her first big hit, "Don't Touch Me," a sultry, backroom ballad that was a 1966 Grammy Award winner. The couple married, and Seeley continued to produce hits between 1966 and 1969, as well as appearing on the GRAND OLE OPRY, causing somewhat of a stir because she refused to appear in the frilly, gingham look of a backwoods girl, instead wearing miniskirts. In the late sixties, she performed several hit duets with singer Jack Greene, including "I Wish I Didn't Have to Miss You," and appeared in his road show.

In the early seventies, Seeley returned to the charts, thanks to her association with country outlaw WILLIE NELSON and friends. She had hits with her reworking of traditional folk ballads, changing "Can I Sleep in Your Barn Tonight Mister?" into the definitely racier "Can I Sleep in Your Arms," while the Southern lament "Come All You Fair and Tender Ladies" was transformed into the bouncy "Lucky Ladies." By the late seventies, she was even recording the spicy "Take Me to Bed," showing how far mores had changed in country music.

Seeley dropped off the country charts in the eighties, turning her attention to roles in regional theater productions of popular musicals and to publishing a volume of her saucy aphorisms, while still appearing on the Opry.

◀ SELDOM SCENE

(c. 1971–1980, sporadically thereafter: Mike Auldridge [dobro]; John Duffey [mandolin, vocals]; Ben Eldridge [banjo, vocals]; John Starling [guitar, vocals]; Tom Gray [bass, vocals])

The Seldom Scene was a Washington, D.C.–based PROGRESSIVE BLUEGRASS band of the seventies whose popularity transcended the traditional BLUEGRASS field to include pop fans like LINDA RONSTADT and Jonathan Edwards, both of whom recorded with the band.

The group was born out of the remnants of one of Washington's longest-lived and most popular outfits, the COUNTRY GENTLEMEN, which had centered primarily on high-tenor vocalist and MANDOLIN whiz John Duffey. With the smooth lead vocals of John Starling, the new band focused more on contemporary country and folk-rock songs than traditional bluegrass fare. Named the Seldom Scene because they began their lives as an informal band playing at Washington's legendary Red Fox Inn, by the mid-seventies they had amassed a huge following, particularly among younger bluegrass fans.

The group was not only progressive in its song selection, but it featured some of the finest bluegrass players around. Auldridge was the first of many second-generation DOBRO players who transformed the instrument from primarily a background instrument used for special effects to one capable of taking blazing lead solos. (Country trivia fans note: Auldridge's uncle was Ellsworth T. Cozzens, who played Hawaiian guitar on many of JIMMIE RODGERS's classic country 78s.) Similarly, Starling was an energetic lead guitarist, whose single-note leads influenced the next generation of new-acoustic pickers.

The band began to run out of steam in the late seventies, with Starling making an abortive attempt at a career as a soloist in the early eighties; he was replaced for a while by SINGER/SONGWRITER Phil Rosenthal. They have repeatedly reunited, and currently continue to perform, with bassist Tom Gray replaced by T. Michael Coleman on electric bass (he had previously worked with Merle and DOC WATSON), giving them an even more contemporary sound.

Select Discography

The Best of the Seldom Scene, Rebel 1101. Drawn from their first three Rebel albums.

Old Train, Rebel 1536. Late-seventies recording with guests Linda Ronstadt and RICKY SKAGGS.

At the Scene, Sugar Hill 3736. 1983 edition of the band with singer Phil Rosenthal filling John Starling's shoes.

◀ SHAPE-NOTE SINGING

Shape-note singing refers to a method of teaching music to non–musically literate singers, employed in the late eighteenth century by traveling "singing masters." Originally in New England, and then spreading to the South and West, these
itinerant teachers came to towns, mostly at the invitation of the local church, to
teach the local choirs how to sing. They employed special songbooks that drew
on a repertoire of well-known folk and hymn tunes that the congregation would
know. The parts were notated using different shapes for the various scale tones
(triangles, squares, diamonds, etc.), and were often limited to a five-note (penta-
tonic) scale, common in folk and hymn tunes. The harmonies were also simplified,
based on common intervals such as fourths and fifths, giving the music a distinct,
archaic sound. By singing the tones associated with the shapes, the congregation
could quickly learn new songs and new harmonies.

Although shape-note singing soon died out in northern cities, where more sophisticated congregations learned to read music "properly," it lingered in the rural
South. Annual conventions would be held with the purpose of singing an entire
songbook in a single day and evening (this was accomplished by rapidly "reading"
each verse and chorus and then moving onto the next song, singing only one verse
of each hymn). These events would also involve communal socializing, and often
a large communally prepared meal would be served at the halfway point.

Even in churches that did not employ shape-note singing, the harmonies from
these hymnals could be heard in their choirs, so that an older style of singing was
unintentionally preserved. When BLUEGRASS groups began incorporating gospel music into their repertoires, they naturally drew on the rich shape-note singing tradition. Many bluegrass singers were raised singing in church choirs, and so their
vocal styles and harmonies often recall the tonalities of shape-note singing. This
is particularly true of more traditionally oriented groups, such as the STANLEY
BROTHERS.

◀ SHAVER, BILLY JOE

(born 1941, Corsicana, TX)

The outlaw's OUTLAW, Shaver is best known for writing all of the songs for WAY-
LON JENNINGS's first great LP, 1973's *Honky Tonk Heroes*. His ballads celebrating
hard-as-nails characters, along with his own impeccable Texas heritage, have made
Shaver one of the unsung heroes of roots-country music.

Shaver's own career has been spotty at best. His parents split up before he was
born, so he was raised by his grandmother. He left school after the eighth grade
to work for various uncles on their farms and then took odd jobs in everything
from the navy to bronco busting to sawmill work (where he lost parts of all four
fingers of his right hand). In the late sixties, he began making trips to Nashville to
try to sell his songs, eventually hooking up with singer/song publisher BOBBY BARE,
who put him on retainer and began promoting his material to the first generation
of country outlaws.

Shaver's big break came in 1971 when KRIS KRISTOFFERSON covered his "Good Christian Soldier," followed by TOM T. HALL tackling "Old Five and Dimers Like Me." But Shaver's outlaw credentials were solidified when Waylon Jennings decided to record a theme album of his ballads called *Honky Tonk Heroes*, launching Shaver's songwriting career into full swing as well as elevating Jennings to star status. Meanwhile, Shaver had begun recording as a solo artist, first for MGM and then Monument, the later album being produced by his friend Kristofferson and featuring many of the so-called outlaw musicians. Some of his popular songs from the seventies include "I Been to Georgia on a Fast Train" and "Ain't No God in Mexico."

Shaver also managed to place a few songs with Southern rock groups, including the Allman Brothers, who covered his "Sweet Mama"; this association led to a contract with Capricorn Records in the mid-seventies and some abortive attempts to crack into the rock charts. After the label folded, Shaver went unrecorded for a few years until he signed with Columbia in 1980, recording an album issued in 1981. The title cut, "I'm an Old Chunk of Coal . . . ," was immediately covered by JOHN ANDERSON, who had a hit with it.

Through most of the eighties and the NEW-COUNTRY revival, Shaver was without a record label, although his songs continued to crop up here and there. In 1993, for the small Zoo-Praxis label, he made a comeback album featuring old friend Waylon Jennings, Shaver's son Eddy, who is a fine rock and country-style guitarist, and even musty old rock-and-rollers like Al Kooper. Undeterred by the move toward arena rock that has propelled new country into the pop mainstream, for this album Shaver continued to create mythic songs that seem to resonate through the entire history of country music. Particularly moving is the title cut, "Tramp on Your Street," which tells of the ten-mile pilgrimage he made as a young boy to hear the legendary HANK WILLIAMS.

Select Discography

Tramp on Your Street, Zoo Praxis 72445-11063. 1993 comeback recording.

◀ SHELTON, RICKY VAN

(born 1952, Grit, VA)

The country-cover king, Ricky Van Shelton has a ROCKABILLY-flavored style and a million-dollar smile that has made him a favorite on the country circuit.

Born in rural Virginia, Shelton was first more interested in rock and roll than country music, although he did sing in the small church choir where he was raised. Brother Ronnie played MANDOLIN and had his own BLUEGRASS/country band, and he encouraged his younger sibling to take up country music. Shelton remained in his hometown into his early twenties, working as a pipefitter by day and a musician at night. Then his wife got a job as a corporate personnel director in Nashville, and the two moved to the country-music capitol.

Shelton worked on demos in his basement while performing nights in a small club called the Nashville Palace, where he met another country hopeful who was working washing dishes (RANDY TRAVIS). His wife befriended the wife of a *Nashville*

Tennessean reporter, who brought one of Shelton's tapes to Columbia producer Steve Buckingham, who signed the artist in 1986. A year later, he had his first hit with his first of many covers, "Somebody Lied," originally recorded by CONWAY TWITTY two years previously. His follow-up hits came from even further back in the country music songbook, including HARLAN HOWARD's "Life Turned Her that Way" (a hit for MEL TILLIS in the sixties), "Statue of a Fool" (a pop song recorded by Jack Greene in 1969), and 1989's "From a Jack to a King," which was originally written and recorded by Ned Miller in 1963. In the early nineties, he had a hit covering Elvis's "Ring Around My Neck," which was featured in the film *Honeymoon in Vegas.*

Shelton has a pleasant-enough voice, and his recordings are tastefully produced in a light rockabilly style. However, it is his hunk-of-the-month looks that have won him the legions of female fans that keep him on the charts. Neither an innovative nor a retrogressive figure, he produces the closest thing to mainstream country one can find on today's charts.

Select Discography

Living Proof, Columbia 44221. Nice 1988 album.
Don't Overlook Salvation, Columbia 46854. 1992 country-gospel album.
Greatest Hits Plus, Columbia 52753. The hits to 1992.

◀ SHENANDOAH

(c. 1988–ongoing: Marty Raybon [lead vocals]; Jim Seales [guitar]; Stan Thorn [keyboards]; Ralph Ezell [bass]; Mike McGuire [drums])

Shenandoah was one of the first late-eighties bands to turn away from the glitz-country of ALABAMA, EXILE, and other pop-oriented groups to return to a roots-country sound. With each album that they've produced, they've turned increasingly toward a more hard-country sound.

The group originated as the informal house band of Muscle Shoals's MGM Club, where they all worked as session musicians and songwriters. Leader Marty Raybon worked a day job as a bricklayer with his father, with whom he also played together in a family BLUEGRASS band. Raybon began hunting for a record deal, finally hooking up with CBS's Robert Byrne, who offered to hire Raybon if he brought along his backup group. Byrne also gave them the name Shenandoah.

Their first album was a decided dud, as Byrne tried to mold their sound into mainstream country-pop; but they came back with a more roots-oriented second disc, which produced their first hits, "The Church on Cumberland Road" and "Sunday in the South." However, their breakthrough into widespread popularity brought legal difficulties in 1991, as three other bands—from Kentucky, Nevada, and Massachusetts—sued the group, claiming that they had prior rights to the Shenandoah name. The lawsuit bankrupt the band by the end of the year, and they were dropped by CBS.

In 1992 they had settled the various lawsuits (making the argument that, after all, they had not chosen the name, but it was given to them by CBS so therefore they couldn't be accused of stealing it). Moving to RCA, the group scored new hits with the country-honk numbers "Rock My Baby" and "(Your Leavin's Been) a Long Time Comin'." The band began 1993 with the dance-oriented hit "If Bubba Can Dance" and the humorous "Janie Baker's Love Slave."

All in all, the band is a good antidote to the hopeless pop-schlock produced by the hit makers of the eighties. The influence of their success also pushed some of these older glitz-bands, like SAWYER BROWN, into producing more country-oriented material, and for that alone they deserve praise.

Select Discography
Greatest Hits, Columbia 44885. Their Columbia hits (up to 1992).
Long Time Comin', RCA 66001. 1992 album, their first for a new label.

◀ SHEPARD, JEAN

(born 1933, Paul's Valley, OK)

A no-frills, fifties-style, teardropping balladeer, Shepard was one of the first female country vocalists to break through, although it took a while for her career to develop.

Born to an Okie family that relocated to the Bakersfield, California, area in search of a better life, Shepard began her career as a bass player in the all-female Melody Ranch Girls band in 1948. A few years later, she was discovered by HANK THOMPSON, who recommended her to his producer, Ken Nelson, at Capitol Records. Her first hits were duets with FERLIN HUSKY ("A Dear John Letter" followed by "Forgive Me John") recorded in 1953. She toured with Husky in the following year and appeared with RED FOLEY on his radio show. In 1956 she was invited to join the GRAND OLE OPRY thanks to her solo hits "Satisfied Mind" and "Beautiful Lies." At this time, she made what is probably the first country-music concept LP, *Songs of a Love Affair*, in which the twelve-song cycle, all penned by Sheppard, tells a wet-hanky story of the breakup and final reconciliation of two lovers.

Her career languished after her marriage to HAWKSHAW HAWKINS, and she remained off the charts until 1964, one year after Hawkins's death in the same airplane accident that took the life of PATSY CLINE. Her 1964 recording of "Second Fiddle (to an Old Guitar)" launched a series of hits with equally colorful titles, from 1966's "Happy Hangovers to You" through 1967's "Your Forevers (Don't Last Very Long)" to "Slippin' Away" in 1973, her biggest chartbuster ever. She continued to record through the late seventies and early eighties for a variety of small labels, with little success.

Shepard created controversy in country-music circles in the seventies with her outspoken opposition to the COUNTRYPOLITAN movement. She resented the encroachment of pop music into country's terrain, preferring to hold onto the sweet, suffering image that made her famous, as well as her stripped-down HONKY-TONK sound.

Select Discography
The Best of Country, Richmond 2143. Cassette-only reissue of her hits.

◖ SHEPPARD, T. G.

(born William Browder, 1942, Humboldt, TN)

A soulful singer/instrumentalist, Sheppard rode the urban cowboy craze of the late seventies and early eighties to a long string of country successes.

Originally from Tennessee, Browder grew up in a musical household (his mother was a piano teacher and gave her son his first lessons on that instrument). Browder mastered GUITAR and saxophone by his teen years and formed his first group, a rockin' R&B band called the Royal Tones. He then set out for the R&B mecca of Memphis, Tennessee, when he was sixteen. He was hired by producer/ guitarist Travis Wammack to play in his band, and even made some rockin' recordings on his own, singing lead on the Embers' minor hit "The Girl Next Door," and taking the nom de disc of Brian Stacey to produce one minor chart-topper, "High School Days." He then worked in the promo department of RCA Records out of Memphis.

After leaving RCA, Browder formed his own promotional company called Umbrella Productions. One of his clients was songwriter Bobby David, who had written "Devil in the Bottle." Unable to place it with any acts, Browder cut it himself in 1974 for Motown's short-lived country division, Melodyland, taking the name T. G. Sheppard to avoid any conflict of interest with his management business (backup vocals were provided by a young up-and-comer named JANIE FRICKIE). The song was an instant hit, and Sheppard continued to produce successful records for Motown until they closed their country division in 1976.

A year later, he signed with Warner Brothers and began a long, fruitful relationship with producer Buddy Killen. Together, they produced a string of hits: 1979's "Last Cheater's Waltz"; the pseudo-autobiographical "I'll Be Coming Back for More" (with its spoken first verse), and "Do You Wanna Go to Heaven" from 1980; 1981's "I Feel Like Lovin' You Again" (originally titled "I Feel You Coming Back Again," but the songwriters worried that "I feel you coming" might be misinterpreted), "I Loved 'Em Every One" (T.G.'s first pop crossover hit), and "Party Time" (written by Bruce Channel, famous for his pop hit "Hey, Baby!"); and 1982's "Only One You," "Finally," the patriotic "War Is Hell (on the Home Front Too)," and a duet with KAREN BROOKS, "Faking Love." In 1983 he switched to producer Jim Ed Norman, and the hits slowed, although he did produce the silly "Make My Day" based on the famous Clint Eastwood line (and featuring Eastwood on the record).

Then, in 1985, Sheppard teamed with legendary R&B producer Rick Hall and had another string of hits, including 1986's "Strong Heart" and 1987's "One for the Money." Since then, Sheppard has turned his attention increasingly to his business interests, including a racing team, a Smoky Mountain bed-and-breakfast and a nearby Mexican restaurant, and Kansas City's Guitars & Cadillacs nightclub.

Select Discography

The Best of T. G. Sheppard, Curb 77545.

Biggest Hits, Columbia 44307. R&B-tinged recordings from 1985 to 1987.

◀ SHERRILL, BILLY

(born Phil Campbell, c. 1938, Alabama)

Sherrill is a legendary Nashville producer who nurtured the careers of CHARLIE RICH, TANYA TUCKER, JOHNNY PAYCHECK, TAMMY WYNETTE, and countless others as an A&R (Artists & Repertoire) man at Epic Records from the mid-sixties on. He also was responsible for the COUNTRYPOLITAN sound of the late sixties and early seventies, bringing a more pop-oriented sound to Nashville recordings, downplaying traditional instruments and adding layers of strings and vocal choruses.

The son of an evangelist, Sherrill first took up the piano to accompany the hymns that were part of his parents' revival meetings. As a teenager, he switched to saxophone and led a jumping band performing jazz-flavored instrumentals. After a brief career as a solo artist in the late fifties and early sixties, he hooked up with legendary producer SAM PHILLIPS, who hired him to operate his Nashville studios. After Phillips's label collapsed, Sherrill joined Epic Records, where he has remained ever since.

From the start, Sherrill worked not only molding an artist's sound but also selecting and often coauthoring their material and carefully honing their image. Among his classic productions are "Stand By Your Man," Tammy Wynette's famous ode to marital fidelity, which he cowrote with her; all of Tanya Tucker's early hits; and Charlie Rich's megahit, "Behind Closed Doors." Wynette's recordings represent the highest achievement of the Sherrill style; her powerful vocals, recalling the conviction of the great gospel singers, are set in a lush musical backdrop, transforming her songs into miniature anthems.

While Sherrill was the seventies' most successful producer, the NEW-COUNTRY movement of the eighties made his style seem overblown and tired. Since then he has focused more on administrative duties, although he continues to work occasionally as a producer. One of his last and most interesting projects was a collaboration with British musician Elvis Costello on his country-homage album, *Almost Blue*.

◀ SHOCKED, MICHELLE

(born c. 1962, Texas)

Another eccentric Texan, Shocked is a SINGER/SONGWRITER of some power who has adapted WESTERN SWING and old-time fiddle music to her own unique personality.

Shocked reveals little about her life; even her real name is unknown, although she admits to being raised by a strict Mormon family. She went to Europe when she was a teenager to perform but returned to Texas by her early twenties. In 1987 she was singing at an informal session at the Kerrville Folk Festival when English record producer Pete Lawrence heard her perform; he issued recordings made informally at the festival as *The Texas Campfire Tapes* in the same year. This led to a major-label signing and her first studio album, *Short Sharp Shocked*, a year later, which primarily showcased her talents as a singer/songwriter. *Captain Swing* was an attempt to modernize Western swing for a new audience; this produced the minor hit "The Greener Side" (the video for the song featured hunks in skimpy swimsuits dancing around Shocked, perhaps as a none-too-subtle reaction to music video's propensity to feature male rock stars surrounded by adoring, scantily clad women). Her 1992 album, *Arkansas Traveler*, took as its theme the unusual idea of writing new lyrics for traditional fiddle tunes, featuring many fine acoustic pickers, with mixed results.

Shocked has had at best only a cult following and can be considered as much a rock (or punk) performer as a country artist. But her attempts to wed country influences with modern, literary lyrics certainly deserve recognition if only for their sense of commitment, daring, and fun.

Select Discography

The Texas Campfire Tapes, Mercury 834581.
Short Sharp Shocked, Mercury 834924.
Captain Swing, Mercury 838878.
Arkansas Traveler, Mercury 512101.

◀ SHOLES, STEVE

(born 1911, Washington, D.C.; died 1968)

A longtime A&R (Artists & Repertoire) man at RCA Records, Sholes had a lasting impact on country music through his production work in the postwar years.

Joining the original Victor label in 1929, he remained with the label until his death nearly forty years later. After World War II, he became an A&R man working out of the company's new Nashville offices, signing a host of artists including country legends JIM REEVES, HANK SNOW, SKEETER DAVIS, and CHET ATKINS (he also used Atkins as a producer on scores of recordings in the fifties and made him his assistant in 1962) and legendary rocker ELVIS PRESLEY. He was one of the key forces behind the establishment of a Country Music Hall of Fame in 1961, and he helped raise funds for its permanent museum. He died of a heart attack while driving to the Nashville airport in 1968.

◀ SINGER/SONGWRITER

It is so common today for pop artists to perform their own material that it's easy to forget that just a few decades ago this was the exception rather than the rule. The revolution that brought forth the singer/songwriter began in the early sixties and came to its full flowering in the following decade.

In the early days of American popular music, from the mid-nineteenth through the mid-twentieth centuries, songwriters were professionals who worked to create hit songs; singers were also professionals, who specialized in performing them. Although there were occasionally songwriters who gained success singing their own material (Fats Waller and Hoagy Carmichael are two examples from the pop world), they were the exception rather than the rule. In country music, of course, songs were often "written" by the performer, but this had a different meaning than in the pop world; often a singer would take a common folk song, ballad, or blues and reshape it to fit his or her own personality. Many of the songs "written" by A. P. Carter of the CARTER FAMILY, for example, were simply reworkings of traditional folk songs. However, there were many noteworthy songwriters among country and folk recording artists, including the great WOODY GUTHRIE, who would inspire the folk revivalists of the sixties.

A young singer/songwriter from Hibbing, Minnesota, named Robert Zimmerman was a great fan of Guthrie's, and he came to New York hoping to meet his idol. When he arrived, he had already transformed himself into BOB DYLAN and he began writing and performing a string of social-protest songs that were unique in their vivid imagery and the power of their expression. Dylan's lyrics became increasingly imagistic in the mid-sixties, thanks to the influence of poets like Allen Ginsberg, and he adopted the instrumentation of a rock band for his backup group after hearing the BYRDS successfully perform his songs (they had a hit with his "Mr. Tambourine Man" among others). The fact that Dylan was—at best—a marginal vocalist and only a fair performer on the GUITAR was inspirational to thousands of other wannabe stars; suddenly, it became clear that a songwriter even of limited performing capabilities could make it big (and also could be an effective performer; despite his so-called "deficiencies," Dylan's performances were often far superior to the many cover versions by more conventional singers).

A slew of singer/songwriters appeared on the pop charts in the late sixties and early seventies. James Taylor had a hit with his countryesque *Sweet Baby James* album, particularly the autobiographical song "Fire and Rain"; Carole King set new sales records with her *Tapestry* album, featuring the hit "You've Got A Friend"; and Joni Mitchell was creating and performing her best-known songs (for the album *Blue*). Often, these performers were accompanied by a soft-rock backup band—acoustic guitar with electric bass, drums, and sometimes piano or synthesizer—and the overall sound was pleasantly middle-of-the-road (what today is called adult-contemporary music).

The singer/songwriter movement was eclipsed in the middle to late seventies by the emergence of punk and new-wave music. Its influence, however, was strong on young country stars of the eighties and nineties, most notably GARTH BROOKS, who proclaimed himself a fan of James Taylor (naming his firstborn daughter Taylor in honor of the earlier star). Many of today's "country" stars—notably MARY CHAPIN CARPENTER, NANCI GRIFFITH, LYLE LOVETT, and Brooks—draw on the singer/songwriter tradition, performing their own material with a soft-rock accompaniment. In fact, if Griffith and Carpenter had recorded in the seventies instead of the nineties, they would have been classified as singer/songwriters, not country artists. (Griffith has suffered an identity crisis throughout her career, first recording on a folk label, Philo, then signing to MCA's country division, and finally being transferred within the label to its pop division after her "country" recordings failed to chart. She now records for Elektra, a pop label.)

◀ SINGLETON, SHELBY

(born 1931, Waskom, TX)

Singleton is a legendary rock, R&B, and country producer who was most active from the mid-fifties through the late sixties.

Singleton was originally hired in the mid-fifties by Mercury, where he worked with legendary soul acts such as Clyde McPhatter. In 1962 he was made director of the Smash label, a Mercury subsidiary, which also produced the company's country output. He signed ex-rocker JERRY LEE LEWIS (and oversaw his country sessions) along with TOM T. HALL and CHARLIE RICH. In 1966 he formed a slew of his own labels: Silver Fox and SSS International to concentrate on soul music and Plantation for the country market. His first discovery was JEANNIE C. RILEY, whose monster hit, "Harper Valley P.T.A.," he produced. He also promoted LINDA MARTELL. At the same time, he established his own music publishing operation.

In 1969 Singleton purchased the Sun Records catalog from SAM PHILLIPS and from that point on has focused more of his attention on the business side of licensing recordings and songs rather than on producing new material.

◀ SKAGGS, RICKY

(born 1954 near Cordell, KY)

Hailing from a musical family, Ricky Skaggs is one of the few artists who has successfully crossed over from traditional BLUEGRASS to mainstream country while still maintaining his basic sound and style. He was one of the first NEW-COUNTRY stars of the early eighties who led the return to country's roots in repertoire and style. Although he has not been as consistently popular as some of the more flashy acts who have followed his lead, Skaggs remains an important force in country music today.

A multi-instrumentalist, Skaggs began his career while still in high school, with his friend KEITH WHITLEY, performing duets for MANDOLIN and GUITAR in a traditional style derived from country's brother acts. The duo was particularly enamored of the STANLEY BROTHERS' sound, and they soon found themselves performing as members of Ralph Stanley's band. Poor pay and a grueling touring schedule led to Skaggs's retirement and brief employment as an electric-company worker in a suburban Washington, D.C., power plant. There, he began performing with a later version of the progressive bluegrass band, the COUNTRY GENTLEMEN.

In the early '70s, he joined briefly with J. D. CROWE's groundbreaking bluegrass ensemble, the New South, along with ace guitarist/vocalist TONY RICE. Determined to modernize and popularize the bluegrass sound, he formed his own progressive band, Boone Creek, with DOBRO player JERRY DOUGLAS, who has appeared on many of Skaggs's recordings, and singer/guitarist Terry Baucom. By the late seventies, he was working as a backup musician for EMMYLOU HARRIS, helping mold her new traditional approach on landmark albums such as *Roses in the Snow*.

Blessed with a unique, high-tenor voice, Skaggs recorded his first solo album in a contemporary country vein for the bluegrass label, Sugar Hill, while at the same time he made a duet album with Rice featuring just their guitar and mandolin and vocal harmonies in an homage to the thirties country sound. He was quickly signed to CBS and had a string of hits in the early eighties with his unique adaptations of bluegrass and country standards of the fifties. In fact, his cover of BILL MONROE's "Uncle Pen" in 1984 was the first bluegrass song to hit number one on the country charts since 1949! He also was one of the first new-country artists to tour Europe, scoring great success in England, where he performed with a diversity of artists from Elvis Costello to Nick Lowe.

The mid-eighties found Skaggs teetering on the edge of a more pop-country sound, but basically he has stuck close to his country roots in choice of material and performance. He married country vocalist Sharon White of the WHITES and produced some of their successful recordings in the eighties. While Skaggs's more recent recordings have not hit as big on the country charts, he continues to be influential as an instrumentalist and producer. He returned to his bluegrass/country-swing roots as a member of MARK O'CONNOR's New Nashville Cats, which featured another crossover artist from bluegrass, VINCE GILL. Skaggs continues to represent bluegrass music on awards programs, often performing with such veterans as Bill Monroe and his old mentor, Ralph Stanley.

Select Discography

Family and Friends, Rounder 0151. Charming album with Skaggs's parents and longtime associates playing traditional country and bluegrass material.
Sweet Temptation, Sugar Hill 3709. Skaggs's first attempt to break into the mainstream country market.
Skaggs and Rice, Sugar Hill 3711. Duet album featuring popular numbers of the thirties and forties.
Waitin' for the Sun to Shine, Epic 37193. His 1981 LP that helped introduce the new-country revival movement.
My Father's Son, Epic 47389. 1991 album featuring mostly mainstream country, with a little gospel.

◀ SKILLET LICKERS, THE

(c. 1925–1931: Gid Tanner [fiddle, vocals] born James Gideon Tanner, 1885; died 1960; Clayton McMichen [fiddle, vocals] born 1900; died 1970; Riley Puckett [guitar, vocals]; Land Norris [banjo])

Perhaps the greatest of the classic old-time string bands, the Skillet Lickers was one of the most influential, thanks to the outfit's energetic recordings of dance tunes, sentimental and humorous songs, and a famous series of country-humor skits depicting a group of backwoods moonshiners.

Tanner was the elder statesman of the band, a famous solo performer on his own who made fiddle recordings for Columbia in 1924 accompanied by blind guitarist/vocalist RILEY PUCKETT. Tanner sang in a comic, high falsetto voice, and his fiddle playing was in the rough, often loose rhythmic style typical of his generation of Georgia fiddlers (including his major rival in fiddle contests, FIDDLIN' JOHN CARSON). The Columbia label urged Tanner to form a band because of the increasing popularity of string bands, and so he invited younger Georgia fiddler Clayton McMichen to join with him and Puckett, along with banjoist Land Norris (who can just barely be heard on their recordings).

McMichen looked down his nose at the stage antics and crude style of Tanner. Influenced by the jazz and pop music of the twenties, he was intent on making the Skillet Lickers a more modern band. As the band gained in popularity, Tanner's role was often reduced to just occasional falsetto vocals; McMichen took the fiddle lead, and introduced a second fiddler, another young Georgian named Lowe Stokes, to play harmony. Sometimes McMichen, Stokes, and Tanner all played simultaneously, anticipating the harmony fiddles of later BLUEGRASS recordings. Unlike in other string bands, the BANJO was always kept discreetly in the background, perhaps reflecting McMichen's feeling that the instrument was old-fashioned and not suited to his more modern, hard-driving music.

Puckett was the lead vocalist of the band; his rich baritone voice was perfectly suited to the sentimental and old-time dance songs that the group performed. Plus, his voice was smoother than that of most country singers of the day, and it carried well on the primitive recording technology used at the time. He was also famous in his day as a guitarist, introducing sometimes wildly erratic bass runs to his playing style, which caught on with guitarists from Maybelle Carter to DOC WATSON. Puckett went on to be a minor solo star and is said to have been the first country vocalist to yodel on a record, although he never made it his trademark as did JIMMIE RODGERS.

The high energy of the Skillet Lickers was in marked contrast to Columbia's other big successful string band, the North Carolina Ramblers led by banjoist CHARLIE POOLE. Their sedate, almost deadpan style was the exact opposite of the exuberant, hell-fire energy of the Georgia band. The Skillet Lickers' sound was emulated by many of the old-time revivalists of the seventies, including the HIGHWOODS STRINGBAND as well as the Plank Road Stringband and many others.

McMichen left the band in the early thirties and the great days of the original Skillet Lickers ended. Tanner continued to use the name with various supporting musicians, including his son Gordon on fiddle. McMichen formed his Georgia Wildcats, a band that recorded pop and jazz as well as country, forecasting the WESTERN SWING movement of later in the decade. He relocated to Kentucky, where he continued to perform until the early fifties when he retired from music making, although he made one appearance at the Newport Folk Festival during the FOLK-REVIVAL days of the sixties.

◀ SKINNER, JIMMIE

(born c. 1920 near Berea, KY; died 1979)

Skinner was a well-known country tunesmith who also ran a mail-order country music record business and several small labels out of Cincinnati, Ohio, his home in the middle to late seventies.

Working as a deejay through the forties and early fifties, Skinner had some minor success as a songwriter, beginning with 1941's "Doin' My Time." By the early fifties, he was working out of Knoxville, Tennessee, and his songs were becoming increasingly popular, particularly among BLUEGRASS and more traditional country musicians. JIMMY MARTIN had a mid-fifties hit with Skinner's HONKY-TONK classic "You Don't Know My Mind." At the same time, Skinner signed with Mercury Records and had his sole top-ten hits as a performer in 1957 with "I Found My Girl in the U.S.A." and "Dark Hollow," which has become a bluegrass standard. Although he continued to record through the seventies for various labels from Decca to Starday and King to his own Vetco label, he had little success as a performer. He formed Jimmie Skinner Music in the early seventies, selling his own and other traditional country records by mail order, and then gave up his business to relocate to the Nashville area. However, he died soon after in 1979, suffering a heart attack in his Hendersonville, Tennessee, home.

Select Discography
Twenty-two Greatest Hits, Deluxe 7814. Cassette-only reissue of Starday/King recordings.

◀ SKYLINE

(c. 1983–1990: Tony Trischka [banjo]; Dede Wyland [guitar, vocals]; Danny Weiss [guitar, vocals]; Barry Mitterhoff [mandolin, vocals]; Larry Cohen [electric bass, vocals])

Skyline was an early-eighties New York–based BLUEGRASS band led by BANJO whiz TONY TRISCHKA and his then-wife Wyland. They combined progressive instrumentals with often sappy folkish country songs, making for an odd musical marriage.

Both Weiss and Wyland were smooth vocalists who combined folky leanings with a love for the newer countryesque songs created in the seventies and eighties. Trischka, ever the spacey banjo noodler, and Barry Mitterhoff (a founding member of New Jersey's Bottle Hill Boys), were both enmeshed in progressive, far-out picking, so that the group's accompaniments were often skittish and disjointed, seemingly at odds with the pop-country flavorings of the songs. Larry Cohen's electric bass playing was often innovative, and he was responsible for many of the group's farout arrangements. But on the whole, it must be said that this conglomeration should have either gone one way or the other, becoming a COUNTRY-ROCK band with drums and synthesizers to accommodate the vocalists, or become a spacey newgrass outfit, to accommodate the banjo and MANDOLIN parts.

After Wyland and Trischka split, another female vocalist came on briefly to finish out the band's jobs. The group broke up in the early nineties.

Select Discography
Fire of Grace, Flying Fish 70479. Their last album from 1990, the only one on CD.

◀ SMECK, ROY

(born 1900, Reading, PA; died 1994)

Smeck was a fleet-fingered multi-instrumentalist who recorded a slew of novelty instrumentals in the twenties and thirties as well as backing country and pop artists. He was particularly well-known for his GUITAR instruction books and his Hawaiian style of playing, which influenced many country steel-guitar players.

Smeck was a New York City–raised musician who showed an early talent on a plethora of stringed instruments. He worked on the RKO (Radio Keith Orpheum) circuit in the city, as well as appearing in early Vitaphone shorts produced by Warner Brothers to promote the idea of talking pictures. He melded a number of influences in his playing, including the jazz single-note picking of guitarist Eddie Lang, the Hawaiian slide work of early recording star Sol Hoopi, and the high-energy tenor BANJO work of jazz/novelty musician Harry Reiser.

Besides his solo recordings, Smeck worked as an accompanist on slide and regular guitar for country performers VERNON DALHART and CARSON ROBINSON as well as sessioning with jazz and dance bands. He led his own group, the Vita Trio, through the thirties, usually playing slide guitar on instrumental versions of pop numbers. Smeck also issued a seemingly endless stream of instruction books, so-called five-minute methods for guitar, Hawaiian-style playing, ukulele, and tenor banjo, which were sold through mail-order houses and music shops, reaching countless musicians.

Smeck continued to make recordings into the sixties, often playing ukulele on heavily produced sessions for Kapp, ABC-Paramount, and other labels. In the mid-seventies, blues reissue label Yazoo inspired a new round of Smeckomania by reissuing some of his classic 78 recordings, wowing another generation of BLUE-GRASS, blues, and jazz pickers.

Although much of Smeck's work is marred by a hot-shot, novelty approach, his truly awesome picking powers still befuddle fledgling string-benders today. His masterful handling of the slide guitar, cleanly picking out notes and chords, helped popularize the instrument beyond the strict Hawaiian repertoire featured on many other recordings. He showed how the instrument could be used to take a lead melody part on pop songs, undoubtedly influencing the great WESTERN SWING steel guitarists like BOB DUNN and LEON McAULIFFE.

Select Discography

Plays Hawaiian Guitar, Banjo, Ukulele and Guitar, 1926–1949, Yazoo 1052. CD re-issue of great early sides emphasizing his string wizardry.

◀ SMITH, ARTHUR "GUITAR BOOGIE"

(born 1921, Clinton, SC)

Smith was an influential guitarist who was himself inspired by the single-string jazz work of the legendary French gypsy musician, Django Reinhardt. His nick-name is drawn from his most famous composition, and distinguishes him from FIDDLIN' ARTHUR SMITH.

An adept player on BANJO, MANDOLIN, and GUITAR, Smith began performing as a teenager in South Carolina, landing his own radio show out of Spartanburg before World War II. While serving in the navy during the war, he was stationed near Washington, D.C., where he developed his famous instrumental "Guitar Boogie," first issued on the tiny Super Disc label in 1946. The song became a nationwide hit after it was acquired by MGM in 1947. Recorded on an acoustic guitar with just bass and rhythm guitar accompaniment, the piece was widely influential on country pickers and the nascent ROCKABILLY players; it was covered twelve years later by the Virtues as "Guitar Boogie Shuffle."

In the fifties, Smith had his own television program out of Charlotte, North Carolina, where he broadcast for over a decade. He made some excellent jazz-flavored recordings on guitar and mandolin for MGM. As a novelty, he cut a self-composed piece called "Feudin' Banjos," which featured alternating parts for four-string (or tenor banjo, played on the recording by Smith) and five-string banjo (played by DON RENO). This piece was later covered in the early seventies as "Duelin' Banjos" (now with banjo and guitar) by Eric Weissberg and became a massive hit after it was used in the film *Deliverance*. Smith had to fight in court to be given composer's credit (and royalties) for this later recording.

Smith's sixties recordings suffered from a clutter of strings, vocal choruses, and even burbling organ. He more or less retired by the end of the decade and was working in the early eighties organizing fishing shows in North Carolina.

◀ SMITH, CAL

(born Calvin Grant Shofner, 1932, Gans, OK)

An alumnus of the ERNEST TUBB band, Smith had some success in the late sixties through the mid-seventies, but his career has declined since then.

Born in Oklahoma, Smith was raised in suburban San Francisco, California, getting his first regular exposure as a performer on the San Jose–based *California Hayride* program early in the fifties. He worked sporadically through the decade as a deejay and performer, finally hooking up with Ernest Tubb in the early sixties and playing with the famous Texas Troubadours as a vocalist and rhythm guitarist. Thanks to Tubbs's recommendation, Smith was signed to Kapp Records, for whom he scored a minor hit in 1967 with "Drinking Champagne," and began working as an opening act for bigger-name stars on the road. From 1972 to 1975, he had several big country hits, including "I've Found Someone of My Own," the number-one "The Lord Knows I'm Drinking," and a cover of Don Wayne's comic number "Country Bumpkin." His last charting hit was "I Just Came Home to Count the Memories" in 1977. Soon after, he was dropped by MCA (which had taken over the Kapp/Decca catalog in the early seventies) and occasionally recorded for smaller labels, including remakes of his early hits. He has been less visible since.

Select Discography

Country Bumpkin, MCA 424. Cassette-only reissue of his early-seventies hits.

◀ SMITH, CARL

(born 1927, Maynardsville, TN)

Carl Smith was an influential country singer of the fifties and sixties who modernized the HONKY-TONK sound of HANK WILLIAMS for a new generation.

Smith came from the same town that gave country music ROY ACUFF, and his sound was originally heavily influenced by the elder musician, as well as by EDDY ARNOLD. He got his first break on radio station WROL in Knoxville after World War II and then was hired for the WSM morning show in Nashville in 1950. This led to a contract with Columbia Records and his first hit with 1951's "Let's Live a Little." Through the fifties, he produced myriad hits, mostly beer-soaked classics like "Loose Talk," "Hey Joe," "Kisses Don't Lie," and "If Teardrops Were Pennies." His mid-fifties band, known as the Tunesmiths, was a classic honky-tonk unit, featuring the bass-twangy guitar of Sammy Pruett (who had previously played with Hank Williams's Drifting Cowboys). Smith was also one of the first bandleaders to feature drums, which were still controversial in country music; his drummer Buddy Harman later became a leading Nashville sessionman.

Smith combined a honky-tonker's attitude with flashy Western garb, and even borrowed a few choice songs from the Western repertoire, including BOB WILLS's classic "Time Changes Everything." In the mid-fifties, Smith wed June Carter and performed with the Carter Sisters and their famous mother, Maybelle. The two produced a daughter, Carlene, who is now a well-known country-rocker (performing under the name CARLENE CARTER).

By the late fifties, Smith jumped on another big country bandwagon, capitalizing on the popularity of pseudofolk songs sung in a melodramatic style with his last big hit, 1959's "Ten Thousands Drums," telling a revolutionary war story in all its guts and glory. In 1957 he married his second wife, Goldie Hill (who also had a minor career as a country singer), and settled down on a large horse farm. Although he continued to record for Columbia through 1974, and then made some more recordings for the smaller Hickory label in the mid-seventies, he never achieved the same chart success he had had in the fifties, and eventually he gave up performing to focus on his home life.

Select Discography
The Essential, 1950–1956, Columbia/Legacy 47996. His best recordings.

◀ SMITH, CONNIE

(born Constance June Meadot, 1941, Elkhart, IN)

Connie Smith was one of the great throbbin', sobbin' singers of the sixties who gave it all up for Jesus, her personal heartache mirrored in her choice of material.

Born to an abusive father in a large household (she was one of thirteen siblings), Smith had a troubled youth, culminating in a nervous breakdown at the end of her teenage years. By 1963 she had settled into being a rural housewife when she won a talent contest in Ohio, attracting the attention of Opry star BILL

ANDERSON, who recommended her to RCA. She made her first recordings under the guidance of CHET ATKINS in 1964, including her first hit "Once a Day," an Anderson-crafted WEEPER.

Through the sixties and early seventies, Smith was idolized as a pretty-as-a-picture "young lady" who had the ability to pour her heart out through her vocal chords. She made a specialty of singing songs of loneliness and desolation, scoring hits from 1966's "The Hurtin's All Over (Me)" through 1972's "Just for What I Am." She also toured widely with many other country stars and appeared in a couple of the hilariously bad country flicks of the day, including *Road to Nashville, Las Vegas Hillbillies*, and *Second Fiddle to a Steel Guitar*.

Two failed marriages and a general dissatisfaction with the marketing of female country stars (who were paraded at conventions before audiences of usually all-male deejays and music executives for their "enjoyment") led Smith to become increasingly unhappy with her career. In 1972 she wed for a third time and began incorporating more gospel into her act. She and her husband became evangelists, and by the turn of the decade Smith had retired from performing, except for her weekly spot on the GRAND OLE OPRY, where she continued to share her gospel fervor.

She made an abortive attempt to recapture her secular career in the mid-eighties but primarily has hewed the gospel line. She now lends her heart-rending vocals to words of sin and redemption, rather than heartbreak and hurtin'.

Select Discography
The Best of Connie Smith, Dominion 574.

◀ SMITH, FIDDLIN' ARTHUR

(born 1898, Humphreys County, TN; died 1971)

Not to be confused with his younger, guitar-picking namesake, Fiddlin' Arthur Smith was one of the first modern-style fiddlers to bring jazz and swing influences to traditional country playing. He was also a smooth vocalist, and his recordings were well-loved and widely imitated throughout the old-time music community of the South.

Smith was a railroad worker who hooked up in the early thirties with the McGEE BROTHERS, early GRAND OLE OPRY stars who had previously worked with UNCLE DAVE MACON. They formed the Dixieliners Trio, recording throughout the thirties and performing over Nashville's powerful WSM. Smith's supersmooth fiddling and crooning vocals made the band immediately popular. One of the Trio's best-selling recordings is the oft-covered "More Pretty Girls Than One" issued in 1936.

In the early forties, Smith worked as fiddler with the DELMORE BROTHERS. After World War II, he relocated to the West Coast, where he worked in various low-grade Westerns and accompanied many country artists on tour and record. In the early sixties, thanks to the FOLK REVIVAL, the McGee Brothers were rediscovered and recorded again with Smith, issuing two albums produced by MIKE SEEGER for the Folkways label. They also appeared at folk and BLUEGRASS festivals.

Smith transformed old-time fiddling, using standard violin tuning (many old-timers used unusual, modal tunings), smoothing out the melody lines and incorporating elements drawn directly from jazz (such as blue notes and syncopation). He had an enormous effect on contest or show fiddling, particularly as practiced in Texas and the West; he was perhaps the first fiddler to add clean playing, speed, and flash to his instrumental recordings. His vocal style was similarly modern, again encouraging a move away from the "backwoods and hollers" sound of older country stars.

◀ SMITH, SAMMI

(born 1943, Orange, CA)

Sammi Smith is a soulful, smoky-voiced singer best known for her (at the time shocking) cover of "Help Me Make It Through the Night" in 1971.

Although born in California, Smith was raised in Oklahoma, where she began performing in local clubs when she was twelve years old. As a teen, she was heard by Marshall Grant, who was then working as bassist for JOHNNY CASH in his famous Tennessee Three group. Grant recommended that she come to Nashville, where he introduced her to Cash's label, Columbia, which signed her in the mid-sixties.

After scoring some minor hits for Columbia, including "So Long, Charlie Brown" in 1968 and "Brownsville Lumberyard" a year later, she was dropped by the big label and signed by smaller Mega Records. Her first single, "He's Everywhere," was a moderate hit, but it was her second release, a cover of KRIS KRISTOFFERSON's controversial "Help Me Make It Through the Night," that really set her career ablaze. At the time, the thought of a woman inviting her lover to spend the night (particularly in country music circles) was shockingly risqué, but the risk paid off in huge sales.

Smith spent the seventies label-hopping, scoring minor successes with a number of new songs and covers, mostly sung in the backroom, R&B-colored style that she had perfected. Most memorable was her 1975 recording of "Today I Started Loving You Again." 1979 brought her last chart hit, "What a Lie." Although her recordings were good, none got higher than the top twenty, and by the early eighties she was without a label and more or less forgotten by the Music City establishment.

Select Discography

Help Me Make It Through the Night, Richmond 2261. Cassette-only reissue of her biggest hit and other recordings from the late sixties and early seventies.

◀ SNOW, HANK

(born Clarence Eugene Snow, 1914, Liverpool, Nova Scotia, Canada)

Canada's greatest country singer, who was bitten early on by the country-music bug after hearing the recordings of JIMMIE RODGERS, Snow composed some classic country songs, while his smooth and clean vocalizing helped popularize the music for a wide audience.

Snow left home when he was twelve to take a job as a cabin boy on a freighter.

An early love of Jimmie Rodgers and American cowboy legends led him to take up the GUITAR, and he was soon a proficient performer, getting his first break at age nineteen when he was hired by the local radio station. He was signed to RCA in Canada in 1934, recording two of his own songs that were closely modeled after Rodgers's recordings. He nicknamed himself the "Yodeling Ranger," combining Rodgers's famous YODELING persona with that of the heroic Canadian mounted police. Later he changed his nickname to the "Singing Ranger" in recognition of the end of the yodeling fad. Through the thirties, he continued to work in Canada, gaining the attention of American country performers who passed through the local clubs.

One of these performers, ERNEST TUBB, recommended Snow to the management of the WWVA *Jamboree* in the mid-forties and eventually convinced the GRAND OLE OPRY to hire him in 1950. Meanwhile, his 1949 recording of the sentimental "Marriage Vows" was a minor hit; his follow-ups, the classic "I'm Movin' On" and "Golden Rocket" in 1950, both million-sellers, established his career. Snow produced many hits through the fifties for RCA, including "Rhumba Boogie," "I Don't Hurt Anymore," "A Fool Such as I" (covered in an up-tempo version by ELVIS PRESLEY), "Ninety Miles an Hour (Down a Deadend Street)," and many more. Snow's recordings were remarkably simple productions, highlighting his fine singing voice that had equal appeal to mainstream and country audiences. In 1953 he was a prime mover behind establishing a Jimmie Rodgers Memorial Day in the singer's hometown of Meridian, Mississippi, acknowledging his considerable debt to the earlier singer. Toward the end of the decade, he began recording theme albums, particularly of RAILROAD SONGS (again reflecting his love of the songs of Jimmie Rodgers), although many of these recordings were marred by the typical NASHVILLE SOUND productions of the era.

Although Snow continued to work through the sixties, seventies, and eighties, his last big hit was 1962's "I've Been Everywhere," a novelty song featuring a jawbreaking list of towns in which Snow has traveled; and he last made the charts in 1973 with "Hello Love" (later the theme song of *A Prairie Home Companion*'s Garrison Keillor). A staunch traditionalist, Snow became increasingly conservative as time went by, taking to wearing rhinestone-encrusted suits and becoming somewhat of a country cliché. Even in the fifties he had recorded some teeth-gnashing solo recitation discs, usually telling stories of Old Doc Brown or some other crusty character, complete with choruses swelling gently in the background. Still, he remained a popular performer on the Opry and on tour, despite his lack of recording success. Snow also became involved in raising money for abused children, a cause close to his heart because he had been abused as a youth.

In 1984 RCA dropped the singer from its roster after a distinguished fifty-year recording career, reflecting the bottom-line mentality of today's recording executives and their lack of understanding or appreciation for country's history. Snow was understandably enraged by RCA's moves, and RCA, in retaliation, kept his recordings unavailable domestically for many years, although by the late eighties they had relented and made a few skimpy reissues available.

Snow's son, appropriately named Jimmie Rodgers Snow, had a few minor country hits of his own before becoming a full-time evangelist.

Select Discography

Snow Country, Pair 1314. Twenty RCA cuts representing a good cross-section of his
work.

The Singing Ranger, Vols. 1–4, Bear Family 15246, 15502, 15587. Megasets of all of
Snow's RCA recordings from the thirties through the sixties, all with lavishly illustrated booklets with notes by Charles Wolfe.

◀ SONS OF THE PIONEERS

*(c. 1934–ongoing; original members: Leonard Slye [aka Roy Rogers], Bob Nolan,
Tim Spencer, Karl and Hugo Farr, and Lloyd Perryman)*

One of the most famous Western/COWBOY-SONG vocal groups, the Sons of the
Pioneers have soldiered on for six decades with varying personnel, with their most
influential recordings coming in the late thirties through the early fifties. They
virtually invented the Hollywood image of the cowboy singer, who roamed the
prairies with a song never far from his lips.

Originally formed as the Pioneer Trio with Leonard Slye, Bob Nolan, and Tim
Spencer, they became the Sons of the Pioneers around 1934 in Southern California
with the addition of the talented Farr Brothers on GUITAR and violin. With a swinging, jazzy sound, and pop-flavored three-part harmonies, the Pioneers were an
immediate sensation on stage and screen. Lead vocalist Slye became better known
as ROY ROGERS and went solo by 1937 as a recording artist and actor. The core
group of Nolan, Spencer, and the Farrs stuck together through the early fifties with
various additional members. Nolan was a virtual one-man hit-making machine,
creating such classic cowboy tonsil-twisters as "Cool Water," the band's unofficial
theme song; "Tumbling Tumbleweeds"; and the immortal "A Cowboy Has to
Sing." Spencer was also no laggard in the song-making department, turning out
"Cigarettes, Whiskey, and Wild Women," "Careless Kisses," and "Roomful of
Roses." The Sons combined a sanitized Western image, with wide smiles and even
wider-brimmed hats, and silky smooth harmonies that were straight from the Rainbow Room. They also popularized smooth, harmonized YODELING, and performed
cowboyesque rope tricks and other novelties in their stage show.

The group originally recorded for Decca and Columbia before World War II
and then began a long association with RCA Victor from the early forties through
the late sixties. During their early RCA years, they recorded with many famous
Nashville sidemen, including guitarist CHET ATKINS, who produced many of their
sessions, and legendary steel guitarists Joaquin Murphey and Noel Boggs, along
with the talented Farrs. By the early fifties, RCA was covering their bases by having
the Sons record with such pop singers as Perry Como, the Fontaine Sisters, and
the Three Sons; on a handful of sides, they even accompanied opera superstar
Ezio Pinza for some of the most surreal arias under the Western skies.

By the mid-fifties, the powerhouse vocal/songwriting team of Nolan and Spencer was gone, but by then the group had a life of its own. By adding new vocalists and musicians as the years have gone by, the Sons have carefully recreated their past hits in a patented style. Unlike their early fifties recordings in which RCA sought to modernize their style, their later recordings through the end of the sixties pretty much emphasized the pure cowboy-meets-cocktail-lounge style, slicked up a bit but none the worst for wear. Spencer died in 1974 and Nolan died six years later, but the Pioneers have gone on, performing in winters in Las Vegas and summers in Branson, Missouri, as recently as the late eighties.

Select Discography

Country Music Hall of Fame, MCA 10090. Covers their best recordings from 1934 to 1954.

Columbia Historic Edition, Columbia 37439. Drawn from a single 1937 session for the budget ARC label, but a very fine one.

◀ SONS OF THE SAN JOAQUIN

(c. 1988–onging: Joe, Jack, and Lon Hannah)

These Sons are nouveau COWBOY-SONG harmonizers who tip their ten-gallon hats in the direction of the original SONS OF THE PIONEERS, whose style and repertoire they have inherited.

During the Depression, the Hannah family, who were Missouri farmers, headed West for better job opportunities in the foothills of the Sierra Nevadas. Jack and Joe's dad settled the family on a cattle ranch and, after hours, would sing with his sons his favorite music, the slick Western cowboy songs of the hit groups of the day, including the Sons of the Pioneers. Eventually the trio performed locally to some success, although Jack and Joe didn't think of making music a career. Instead, both ended up as schoolteachers, although they continued to sing on an amateur basis in local musical theater and opera productions, as well as in church.

Meanwhile, Joe settled down and had his own family, including a son named Lon who also showed an interest in vocalizing. Although he also became a schoolteacher by trade, Lon too performed locally on an amateur level, as well as in the Bennett Consort, a jazzy scat-singing group modeled after the popular Manhattan Transfer.

In the mid-eighties, Joe and Jack decided to return to performing the cowboy music of their youth and invited Lon to join their group. By 1989 they had won the attention of nouveau country cowfellow MICHAEL MARTIN MURPHEY, who asked them to provide backup vocals on his album *Cowboy Songs*; he also produced their debut album for Warner Western Records. By 1992 all three were able to retire from teaching to take up singing full-time. Their second album, *Songs of the Silver Screen*, is a pure homage to the great cowboy acts of the thirties, forties, and fifties.

Like their fellow cowboy revivalists RIDERS IN THE SKY this group's carbon-copy of old-style cowboy music is a little bit eerie. The line between homage and parody can be dangerously razor-thin. One wonders also if the audience comes to admire the music or laugh at it, particularly when one considers that commercial cowboy music, even in its original incarnation, was itself a kitschy reflection of the real music of the West. Still, in these times of endless nostalgia, there is room for groups like this one that seamlessly reproduce a past musical style.

Select Discography
A Cowboy Has to Sing, Warner Bros 26935.

◖ SOVINE, RED

(born Woodrow Wilson Sovine, 1918, Charleston, WV; died 1980)

Sovine was a fifties-era honky-tonker who later gained fame thanks to his "touching" country recitations, culminating in the million-seller "Teddy Bear," which should win an award as an all-time hanky soaker.

Raised in West Virginia, Red had his first professional job on his hometown radio station, playing with Jim Pike's Carolina Tar Heels in the mid-thirties; later he performed on radio out of Wheeling. After World War II, he formed his first band, the Echo Valley Boys. They were hired in 1949 to replace HANK WILLIAMS on the prestigious *Louisiana Hayride* program (Williams was booted out because of his drinking problems), where they remained until 1954. Red also took over Hank's duties as the "Old Syrup Sopper," promoting Johnny Fair Syrup on a daily fifteen-minute show for the same Shreveport radio station.

In Shreveport, Sovine hooked up with WEBB PIERCE, and the two began writing and performing together. Moving to the GRAND OLE OPRY in 1954, they made their first duet recordings with a hit cover of GEORGE JONES's "Why Baby Why" followed by Sovine's first recitation record, "Little Rosa," featuring an "authentic" Italian accent by Sovine that will set your teeth on edge. (Despite its hokey text and horrendous Italianesque delivery, the record hit number five on the charts.)

Sovine's recording career took a dip in the late fifties and early sixties, although he continued to perform. He reemerged in 1964 on the Starday label with two number-one hits: "Dream House for Sale" and "Giddyup Go." The second record was the first in a new series of recitation records, this one on the theme of the lonely life of truck drivers, including 1967's hit "Phantom 309." Another period of semi-obscurity followed, with Sovine hitting the performing road but not recording much. About a decade later, when the CB craze swept the land, Sovine scored his biggest hit ever with "Teddy Bear," which tells the "touching" story of a crippled youth who communicates with truckers via his CB radio, using as the handle (you guessed it) "Teddy Bear." It's the kind of sappy sentiment that brings tears to the eyes!

Sovine last hit the charts in 1980 with "It'll Come Back." In the same year, he died—appropriately for a singer who celebrated life on the road—after suffering a heart attack while driving in Nashville. After his death, his fans demanded that "Teddy Bear" be rereleased, and the disc sold another half-million copies, proving beyond a shadow of a doubt that you can't keep a good tearjerker down.

Select Discography
The Best of Red Sovine, Deluxe 7828. Reissue of his better Starday recordings.

◀ SPEARS, BILLY JO

(born 1938, Beaumont, TX)

Spears is a blues-influenced belter who has had a spotty career on the country charts.

Born in Beaumont, she appeared on the popular *Louisiana Hayride* radio program when she was just a teenager, already singing sultry material (she debuted with the slightly risqué "Too Old for Toys, Too Young for Boys"). After graduating high school, she worked at a local carhop while still pursuing a singing career at night. She was discovered by country songsmith Jack Rhodes, who brought her to Nashville to audition for United Artists Records, to which she signed, but these recordings went nowhere. She switched to Capitol Records and had her first hits, including 1969's "He's Got More Love in His Little Finger" and the number-four country song "Mr. Walker, It's All Over." From the start, Spears sounded more like a cocktail-lounge torch singer than a country queen, even though her recordings were mainly marketed to a country audience.

Spears was unable to maintain the momentum of her initial hits and so dropped off the charts. In the mid-seventies, she returned as a countrified disco queen, recording the racy "Blanket on the Ground," a number-one hit in 1975, followed by a couple more chart busters, including her 1979 remake of the Gloria Gaynor bass-heavy disco hit "I Will Survive" and a duet with DEL REEVES on "On the Rebound."

In the early eighties, she moved to smaller labels with less success. She remains a popular figure in the European market, although less well known in America.

◀ SPEER FAMILY, THE

(1920–1967; original members: George Thomas ["Dad"] and Lena Brock ["Mom"] Speer; Pearl and Logan Claborn)

One of the first and longest-lived gospel singing families, the Speers performed from the mid-twenties to the mid-sixties in a style that harked back to traditional SHAPE-NOTE SINGING. Their greatest popularity came after World War II when they became leaders of the new Nashville gospel movement, modernizing their sound to fit in better with country's increasingly middle-of-the-road orientation.

The Speers, a religious family, got their start when bass vocalist George Thomas Speer wed the talented pianist and singer Lena Brock in 1920. Enlisting the help of his sister and brother-in-law, Pearl and Logan Claborn, to sing alto and tenor, George formed a family gospel quartet. The group made their living selling songbooks in rural churches throughout the mid-South, performing the material so that their audience could hear it and hopefully be inspired to buy the books.

By the late twenties, the arduous life of traveling musicians began to wear on the Claborns, and, meanwhile, the Speers themselves were beginning to produce talented, singing offspring. The children were gradually brought on board to replace their aunt and uncle; the Speer lineup eventually included eldest brother

Brock, Ben, Rosa Nell, and Mary Tom. By the late thirties, Rosa Nell was showing talent on the piano, so her mother switched to the accordion.

After World War II, with the growth of interest in gospel music in the country-music field, the Speer family settled down in Nashville. Their postwar recordings were highly influential, particularly noteworthy for the powerful vocals of Mother Speer on her signature song "I'm Building a Bridge." In the early fifties, the Speer daughters were settling down to form families, so Brock's wife was brought on board, as well as the first non-Speer members, who became honorary "Speer sisters." In 1954 the family landed a local TV gospel show, gaining further exposure, and by the late fifties their recordings were awash in the echoey harmonies that were typical of mainstream country. Up until her death in 1967, Mom Speer remained the motivating force behind the group. Her powerful vocals, with just a hint of jazzy syncopation, gave the group its characteristic sound.

◀ SPRAGUE, CARL T.

(born 1895 near Alvin, TX)

Sprague was one of the first singing cowboys, whose 1925 Victor recording of "When the Work's All Done This Fall" helped start the cowboy music craze.

Raised on a ranch in South Texas, Sprague learned most of his COWBOY SONGS from a singing uncle. However, he did not intend to pursue a musical career; instead, he attended Texas A&M, studying physical education. Hearing VERNON DALHART's successful recordings of folk songs for Victor, he realized a similar market might exist for the songs he learned as a youth. He traveled to New York and had three sessions for Victor in 1925, 1926, and 1927, recording many songs that would later enter the repertoire of the singing cowboys of the thirties. However, Sprague never performed as a professional; instead, he pursued singing as a hobby while working as an athletics coach at Texas A&M.

During the FOLK REVIVAL of the sixties, Sprague was rediscovered and again performed his cowboy material, recording an album of Western songs for the German Bear Family label in 1972.

◀ STAMPLEY, JOE

(born 1943, Springhill, LA)

Best known as one-half of the comic country duo of Moe and Joe (with singer MOE BANDY), Stampley's career moved from rock and pop in the fifties and sixties, to COUNTRYPOLITAN in the seventies and finally to hard-edged HONKY-TONK in the eighties.

Raised in a northern Louisiana town near the Texas and Arkansas borders, Stampley heard country music from his early days, particularly the recordings of his father's favorite star, HANK WILLIAMS. He started playing the piano when he was eight and was already performing locally as a teenager when he caught the attention of a local deejay, MERLE KILGORE. Kilgore arranged for Stampley's first recordings in a teen-pop mold for Imperial Records, cut in 1957 and 1958, but they made little impact. A second session for the Chicago blues label Chess in 1961 was also unsuccessful.

Influenced by the success of ELVIS PRESLEY and JERRY LEE LEWIS, and loving the music of R&B vocal groups like the Miracles and the Impalas, Stampley formed the Uniques, who had a regional hit with the R&B flavored "Not Too Long Ago" in 1966, which was cowritten by Stampley with Kilgore. After this success, the band faded into obscurity.

In the early seventies, Stampley began writing country songs, which he submitted to Al Gallico of Nashville's Algee Music. Gallico signed on as his manager and arranged for a contract with Paramount Records. Stampley's first minor country hit was 1971's "Take Time to Know Her," followed by the top-ten "If You Touch Me (You've Got to Love Me)." Stampley continued to have hits with his country-soul recordings through the mid-seventies, including 1973's "Soul Song" and "I'm Still Loving You" from a year later. A switch to Epic Records brought hits in a similar vein, including 1975's "Roll on Big Mama," and the first of his more honky-tonk–style material, 1975's "She's Helping Me Get Over You" and 1976's "Whiskey Talkin'."

In 1978 ace producer BILLY SHERRILL took over Stampley's recording career and moved him in a more solid countrified direction. A year later, Stampley formed his partnership with Moe Bandy, releasing the number-one hit, "Just Good Ole Boys," which set the pattern for a series of successful tongue-in-cheek numbers, their most famous being 1981's "Hey Joe (Hey Moe)." Stampley's solo successes included 1980's "Put Your Clothes Back On" and "Haven't I Loved You Somewhere Before," and the boozy hits, 1981's "Whiskey Chasin'," 1982's "Back Slidin'," and 1983's "Double Shot of My Baby's Love."

After the mid-eighties, Stampley's chart success pretty much dried up, but he remains a popular attraction on the club and barroom circuit.

◀ STANLEY, ROBA

(born 1910, Gwinnett County, GA; died 1986)

Roba Stanley was an early country guitarist and vocalist who made a handful of recordings in her teen years before retiring from the musical scene. Her records were rediscovered in the seventies by old-time music enthusiasts, and she was belatedly recognized as one of the pioneers of old-time country music.

The daughter of country fiddler Rob Stanley (born c. 1859; died c. 1935), Roba was raised on a farm in northern Georgia. She showed an early talent as a guitarist, borrowing her older brother's instrument while he worked in the fields. Her father soon invited her to accompany him at square dances. Their local performances drew the attention of Atlanta's radio station, WSB, where the two debuted in early 1924. The novelty of a young, female guitarist performing and singing traditional dance songs led to an offer to record from OKeh records.

Roba made a series of recordings in 1924 and again in 1925. On her later date, she was accompanied by HENRY WHITTIER, one of the pioneering country fiddlers.

Impulsively marrying at age fifteen, Roba settled with her new husband in Florida; discouraged from performing, she retired from the music business.

Roba was the first in a line of spunky teenagers who sang slightly racy material. In this way, she forecast the novelty and popularity of girl singers who were "old beyond their years" such as TANYA TUCKER.

◀ STANLEY BROTHERS, THE

(Carter Glen Stanley [vocals, guitar] born 1925, McClure, VA; died 1966; Ralph Edmond Stanley [vocals, banjo] born 1927, McClure, VA)

The most traditional-sounding of BLUEGRASS bands, the Stanley Brothers with their group the Clinch Mountain Boys brought the high, lonesome mountain singing style to the new bluegrass style.

The Stanleys were raised in rural western Virginia, where their mother was an old-time BANJO player. Both sons began playing the banjo, learning traditional songs like "Little Birdie" in the drop-thumb or clawhammer style. Carter switched to GUITAR after Ralph became proficient on banjo, and the duo began performing locally. Their first professional work came after World War II with Roy Sykes and the Blue Ridge Boys in 1946; one year later, they left the band, along with mandolinist "Pee Wee" (Darrell) Lambert, to form the Clinch Mountain Boys. It was about this time that they heard the legendary performances of BILL MONROE's Blue Grass Boys, and Ralph adopted the finger-picking style of Earl Scruggs to his banjo playing. The Stanley's band was hired to perform over the radio in Bristol, Tennessee, and made its first recordings for the tiny Rich-R-Tone label out of Johnson City.

In 1949 they relocated to take a radio job in Raleigh, North Carolina, where they were heard by Columbia talent scout ART SLATHERLEY, who signed them to that label. (Supposedly, Monroe left the label because he was angered by Columbia's decision to hire another bluegrass group; he signed to Decca in 1950.) The Stanleys recorded for Columbia for three years, featuring their breathtaking traditional harmonies on traditional mountain ballads and Carter Stanley's compositions in a traditional vein, including the classic "White Dove" and "A Vision of Mother." In 1952 the group added guitarist/vocalist George Shuffler, a talented flatpicker who would be featured prominently as a soloist in the band for the next decade.

Carter took a job as lead vocalist for Bill Monroe's band briefly in 1952, recording the lead vocals on the HONKY-TONK song, "Sugar Coated Love." The brothers reunited in 1953, signing to Mercury, and remaining with the label through 1958, then recording for King/Starday through to Carter's death. By this time, they had solidified their sound around lead guitar and banjo, with Ralph's licks limited to a fairly small repertoire. Carter's expressive lead vocals were perfectly complemented either by Ralph's unearthly high mountain tenor or Shuffler's more modern-sounding harmonies.

In the late fifties and early sixties, the market for bluegrass music was fairly small, so the Stanleys relocated to Florida for the winters, hosting a radio program as well as recording for smaller local labels. The FOLK REVIVAL of the sixties helped revive the Stanleys' popularity, and they toured the revival circuit and in Europe. Carter's life was cut short by alcoholism in 1966, and for a while it seemed as if the band would fold.

However, Ralph emerged as an important band leader by the decade's end. To fill Carter's shoes he first enlisted vocalist Larry Sparks (he went on to be one of the seventies' most important PROGRESSIVE BLUEGRASS performers) and then the more traditionally oriented Roy Lee Centers, who sounded eerily like Carter. The band signed with Rebel Records and were popular both on the revival and traditional bluegrass circuits. Centers's murder in 1974 was another blow to Stanley, but Ralph soon lined up two high-school-age musicians he had discovered, mandolinist RICKY SKAGGS and guitarist KEITH WHITLEY, helping to launch their careers in bluegrass and later the new traditional Nashville music.

The Stanley band has centered for the last two decades on Ralph's banjo, the showy fiddling of Curly Ray Cline, and the bass playing of Jack Cooke, usually augmented by a young guitarist/vocalist and mandolinist. Despite the variability in the talents of the lead vocalists, the sound of Stanley's music remains pretty much unchanged. Ralph Stanley's contribution and influence on Nashville's NEW-COUNTRY stars was finally acknowledged by the 1993 release of a two-CD set on which he performs with Ricky Skaggs, VINCE GILL, and other new Nashvillians.

The Stanley repertoire has also remained fairly constant since the late fifties. Their theme song is the "Clinch Mountain Backstep," an instrumental that combines the modality of old-time mountain banjo tunes with the energy and sheen of bluegrass picking. Their repertoire has always combined traditional mountain ballads, including Ralph's powerful vocals on songs like "Man of Constant Sorrow," along with more modern honky-tonk classics, such as "She's More to Be Pitied than Scolded." Drawing on their experience singing in small local churches, the Stanleys have always included both traditional and contemporary gospel songs in their repertoire and have recorded some of the most memorable gospel LPs in the bluegrass canon.

Select Discography

Bluegrass, Vols. 1 and 2, Rounder 09/10. LP reissues of their earliest recordings.
The Stanley Brothers and the Clinch Mountain Boys, Bear Family 15564. All of their classic recordings from 1949 to 1952. Ralph knew about two licks on the banjo (and he uses them in every song), but these are still classic recordings.
The Stanley Brothers and the Clinch Mountain Boys, King 615. One of many LPs that King records assembled from various fifties-era sessions.
Hymns and Sacred Songs, King 645. Reissue of wonderful gospel LP originally pressed in 1959.
Long Journey Home, Rebel 1110. Reissue of Wango-label recordings from the early sixties featuring guitar wizard George Shuffler.
Saturday Night and Sunday Morning, Freeland 9001. 1993 two-CD set featuring secular ("Saturday night") and sacred ("Sunday morning") numbers performed with a slew of new-country and bluegrass talents.

◀ STARR, KAY

(born Katheryn LaVern Starks, 1922, Dougherty, OK)

Starr was a bluesy, big-throated singer who achieved great success in the late forties and early fifties, paving the way for vocalists like PATSY CLINE.

Born on an Indian Reservation, Starr was raised in Dallas, where at age nine she already had her own fifteen-minute daily radio show. Her prematurely husky voice won her many fans, and she began performing as a teenager with the popular WESTERN SWING bands of the day, including BILL BOYD's Cowboy Ramblers and one of the later incarnations of the LIGHT CRUST DOUGHBOYS. In the late thirties, her family moved to Memphis, where Starr again found a big audience for her powerful delivery.

Starr spent the war years traveling to different army bases to perform; she came down with a severe case of laryngitis due to the overuse of her voice and exposure to cold on army transport planes. The result was an even sexier, growling delivery that made her a postwar sensation. She first hit it big in 1950 with ''Bonaparte's Retreat,'' written for her by WYNN STEWART and PEE WEE KING, followed in the same year by her duet with TENNESSEE ERNIE FORD on ''I'll Never Be Free.'' She crossed over onto the pop charts with her big-throated delivery of 1952's ''Wheel of Fortune'' and ''Side By Side'' from a year later, one of the first recordings to feature a double-tracked vocal. After a few hitless years, she came back big time on the country charts with 1961's ''Foolin' Around'' and ''Four Walls'' from the following year. She continued to record country material through the seventies.

Select Discography

Capitol Collectors Series, Capitol 94080. Her fifties-era hits in their original recordings.

◀ STATLER BROTHERS, THE

(1963–today; original members: Lew DeWitt [tenor vocals]; Philip Balsley [baritone vocals], Harold Reid [bass vocals]; Don Reid [lead vocals]; DeWitt was replaced by Jimmy Fortune in 1982)

Not really brothers or named Statler, the Statler Brothers have been one of the most popular of the smooth-harmony vocal groups in country music for over thirty years.

Originally forming in 1955 as a church-based trio in Staunton, Virginia, around Lew DeWitt, Phil Balsley, and Harold Reid, the group was first called the Kingsmen (not of ''Louie Louie'' fame; that's another story). In 1960 Harold's younger brother Don joined as lead vocalist, and the group signed on with JOHNNY CASH's road show; they're featured on Cash's recording of CARL PERKINS's classic ''Daddy Sang Bass.'' Soon after, they changed their name to the Statler Brothers, taking their surname from a Massachusetts-based manufacturer of tissues (appropriately enough, they would later record some classic hanky soakers).

In 1964 they signed with Columbia Records (Cash's label) and had their first hit with the DeWitt-penned "Flowers on the Wall" a year later. Follow-up hits included 1967's "Ruthless" and the corny "You Can't Have Your Kate and Edith Too," although Columbia didn't do much to promote their career. In 1970 they switched to Mercury and had their first solid hit with the crossover success of "Bed of Roses." Many of their seventies hits were written by the brothers Reid, including 1972's nostalgic "Class of '57," the sentimental tearjerkers "I'll Go to My Grave Loving You" from 1975 and their first number-one single, "Do You Know You Are My Sunshine," from 1978, and the humorous "How to Be a Country Star" from 1979. Recalling their roots as a gospel quartet, they also recorded all-religious albums, including two albums based on the Old and New Testaments released in 1975.

In the early eighties, cofounder Lew DeWitt was forced to retire due to continuing problems from Crohn's disease; he died in 1990. His replacement was Jimmy Fortune, who contributed many of the brothers eighties hits, including "Elizabeth" (a paean to movie actress Elizabeth Taylor) from 1984, and "My Only Love" and "Too Much on My Heart" from a year later.

Although the Statlers have fallen off the charts, they remain immensely popular in places like Nashville and Branson, Missouri, as well as many places in between. They have hosted for many years their own variety show on TNN, which was the top-rated show on the fledgling cable network when it first began. Their brand of smooth, church-oriented harmonies and mixture of sentimental and humorous material has always made them one of the most popular—and lasting—of all country quartets.

Select Discography

The Best of the Statler Brothers, Vol. 1, Mercury 822524. Their biggest hits from the early to middle seventies.

◀ STEAGALL, RED

(born Russell Steagall, c. 1942, Gainsville, TX)

Steagall had some popularity in the mid-seventies with his brand of Texas-style WESTERN SWING and HONKY-TONK.

Raised in Gainsville, Texas, Steagall suffered from polio in his early teen years and used the time during his recuperation to master GUITAR and MANDOLIN. He enrolled in West Texas State University to study animal husbandry at the same time that he formed his first country band to work nights and weekends. After graduation, he worked for a while as a soil chemist before being hired by United Artists' West Coast office to work in A&R (Artists & Repertory). His first big break came when RAY CHARLES covered his song "Here We Go Again" and had a modest R&B and country hit in 1967.

Steagall formed his own band, the Coleman County Cowboys, and began touring the rodeo circuit, where he has always enjoyed his greatest popularity. He recorded as a solo artist for Dot and Capitol in the early seventies, scoring modest hits beginning with 1972's "Party Dolls and Wine" and "Somewhere My Love"; his biggest hit came in 1976 with his homage to Western swing, "Lone Star Beer and Bob Wills Music." After that, his recording career slowed, although he continues to be a big attraction on the rodeo trail.

Select Discography
For All Our Cowboy Friends, MCA 680. Budget cassette featuring typical Western numbers.

◀ STEVENS, RAY

(born Ray Ragsdale, 1939, Clarkdale, GA)

Stevens is a purveyor of the kind of cutesy country comedy that either makes you laugh hysterically or gag on a spoon, as well as the equally nauseating "heartfelt" number like his 1970 hit, "Everything Is Beautiful."

Trained in classical piano, Stevens formed an R&B dance band in high school, performing material drawn from favorite groups like the Coasters and Drifters. He also worked as a weekend deejay. In 1956 his family relocated to Atlanta, and a year later Ray made his recording debut, without much success, on Capitol. He then enrolled at Georgia State, majoring in classical piano and music theory.

After graduation, he moved to Nashville, where he scored his first novelty comedy hit with 1962's "Jeremiah Peabody's Polyunsaturated Quick Dissolving Fast Acting Pleasant Tasting Green and Purple Pills" followed by the equally "amusing" "Ahab the Arab." After a stint in the mid-sixties in record production, Ray really came to the fore with a slew of novelty hits beginning with 1969's "Guitarzan" and "Along Came Jones." In 1970 he turned out the feel-good song, "Everything Is Beautiful." He also appeared on many popular TV variety shows, including the *Ed Sullivan* and *Andy Williams* shows.

Ray moved more into the country music camp in the seventies, beginning with "Sunday Morning Coming Down" and "Nashville." He had another pop-novelty hit in 1974 with "The Streak," commenting on the then-popular fad of streaking, or running naked in a public place. He moved to Warner Brothers in the mid-seventies, having hits with covers of pop classics like "Misty" and "Indian Love Call" for the country market. In 1979 he had a hit with another tongue-in-cheek ditty, "I Need Your Help, Barry Manilow."

The eighties saw Stevens returning to the kind of country corn that made him famous, including 1980's "Shriners Convention," 1984's "Mississippi Squirrel Revival," and "It's Me Again, Margaret" from a year later. He continues to be a popular live attraction at glitzy venues from Vegas to Branson, Missouri, and his recordings and videos are regularly hawked on late-night TV for insomniacs in need of a good old country belly laugh.

Select Discography
Ahab the Arab, Polygram 169. Early comic novelty recordings.
Greatest Hits, Curb 77464. Country and comedy numbers.
Ray Stevens, RCA 56344. Early-seventies recordings.

◀ STEWART, GARY

(born 1944, Letcher County, KY)

Pianist/songwriter Stewart combines country, rock, HONKY-TONK, and R&B into a unique package that has made him a cult figure on the fringes of the Nashville establishment.

Born one of nine children to a coal-mining family, Stewart's family moved to Florida when he was twelve, and he was performing at local clubs by his midteens. His first recording, which went nowhere, was the rockin' "I Love You Truly" released in 1964 on the small Cory label. In the mid-sixties, country star MEL TILLIS caught his act and urged him to come to Nashville to work as a songwriter.

In 1967 Stewart teamed up with an ex-rocker named Bill Eldridge, and the duo wrote a number of hit songs for mainstream country acts, beginning with 1969's "Sweet Thang and Cisco" covered by NAT STUCKEY. Meanwhile, Stewart made some unsuccessful solo recordings for Kapp, and by the mid-seventies, discouraged, he returned to his Florida home after cutting a demo tape of Motown-style material.

His demo caught the attention of Roy Dea, who signed Stewart to RCA in the early seventies, where he had his first hit in 1974 with "Drinkin' Thing." This was followed by a couple of years of hit making, including his sole number-one country song, the cleverly titled "She's Acting Single (I'm Drinking Doubles)." By 1978, however, Stewart's hit-making days had ended.

In the early eighties, Stewart found a new songwriting partner in Dean Dillon and the two had minor hits with 1982's "Brotherly Love" and "Smokin' in the Rockies" from a year later. Dillon was able to make the transition into more mainstream songwriting, but Stewart stuck resolutely to his blend of honky-tonk and R&B. In 1988 he cut a comeback album for the blues-oriented label Hightone, but it was only marginally successful; he has continued to turn out recordings for this label. Stewart has won praise among progressive rock critics as well as straight-country minions, but his music has never really clicked with a broad public.

Select Discography

Gary's Greatest, Hightone 8030. Traces his career from the seventies through 1991.

◀ STEWART, REDD

(born Henry Redd Stewart, 1921, Ashland City, TN)

Stewart is a country crooner best known for his long association with PEE WEE KING, with whom he cowrote the ever-popular "Tennessee Waltz."

Born in Tennessee, Stewart wrote his first song when he was fourteen for a local car dealership. He formed several country bands working out of Louisville, Kentucky, where, in 1937, he met ace accordion-squeezer Pee Wee King. King hired Stewart as a musician, but he took a vocal role with the band when singer EDDY ARNOLD left to pursue a solo career. During World War II, Stewart served in the South Pacific, and his experiences there led him to write "A Soldier's Last Letter," later a megahit for ERNEST TUBB.

Stewart's greatest success came with the postwar King band. The duo first produced 1946's reworking of the traditional fiddle tune, "Bonaparte's Retreat," the hit that launched the career of KAY STARR, followed by their most famous song, 1948's "Tennessee Waltz," not only a massive country hit but a top-charting pop number for singer Patti Page in 1950; "Slow Poke" from 1951; and "You Belong to Me," a 1952 pop hit for Jo Stafford.

Stewart remained with King until the mid-sixties. He also cut solo recordings for a variety of labels, although none were as successful as his performances with the King band.

◀ STEWART, WYNN

(born Wynford Lindsey Stewart, 1934, Morrisville, MO; died 1985)

Along with BUCK OWENS, one of the pioneers of the HONKY-TONK, BAKERSFIELD SOUND was Wynn Stewart, whose career never quite reached the heights it deserved.

Performing in church from an early age, Wynn landed a local radio show out of nearby Springfield, Missouri, when he was thirteen. A year later, his family relocated to Los Angeles, where he lost no time in forming a band and beginning to perform and record, at first for the tiny Intro label in 1950. In 1953 he formed his first classic country band, featuring ace steel guitarist Ralph Mooney, bassist/singer Bobby Austin, and guitarist Roy Nichols. They recorded his composition "Strollin'," which led to a contract with Capitol and his first hits, including 1955's "Keeper of the Keys." By the late fifties, he had moved to the Jackpot division of the Challenge label, owned by his friend, producer Joe Johnson, and scored with the ROCKABILLY-style "Come On" in 1958. Johnson teamed him with Harlan Howard's wife JAN HOWARD for a series of rather tepid duets between 1959 and 1961. In 1961 he scored a regional hit with "Big, Big Love," which was covered nationally by friend Buck Owens.

In the early sixties, Stewart became resident musician at the country-music haven the Nashville Nevada Club in Las Vegas; he also worked as a deejay and hosted his own local television show. Capitol producer Ken Nelson heard him performing there and re-signed him to the label in 1963, although nothing much happened until 1967's "It's Such a Pretty World Today" hit the charts and stayed for twenty-two weeks in a row. Similarly upbeat titles followed through 1970, with Stewart's normally aggressively honky-tonk personality somewhat toned down by the choice of kissy-poo material.

In the seventies, Stewart label hopped from RCA to Atlantic to Playboy, scoring one comeback hit in 1976 with "After the Storm." After that, he turned to producing his recordings himself for his own Win label as well as various smaller outfits. In the early eighties, his earlier recordings were reissued by the German Bear Family label, renewing interest in him as a pioneering honky-tonk and rockabilly star. A revival tour was planned for 1985, but Stewart died of a heart attack before it began.

◀ STONE, CLIFFIE

(born Clifford Gilpin Snyder, 1917, Burbank, CA)

Instrumentalist/bandleader Stone became one of the pioneering country music promoters, producers, and songwriters, who engineered the successful career of mainstream country acts like TENNESSEE ERNIE FORD.

The son of a comedian/BANJO player who performed professionally as Herman the Hermit, Stone showed an early interest in jazz and pop music, taking up the bass and forming his first dance band while in high school. After finishing school, he played bass with well-known period orchestras led by Anson Weeks and Freddy Slack. However, his interest turned to the blossoming Southern California country-music scene, and in 1935 he got his first job as a country deejay. By the late thirties and into the forties, he became one of the most influential deejays in the area, hosting numerous shows, including the CBS network's *Hollywood Barn Dance* and the early-morning *Wake Up Ranch*.

After World War II, Stone signed up with the fledgling Capitol label both to serve as head of their new country-and-western division and as a recording artist. He recorded from the late forties through the mid-sixties for the label in a swinging Western style, having hits with "When My Blue Moon Turns to Gold Again" (now a BLUEGRASS standard), "Blue Canadian Rockies" (later covered by GRAM PARSONS while a member of the BYRDS), and "Blues Stay Away from Me." Working with younger musicians like MERLE TRAVIS and Eddie Kirk, Stone coauthored such classic country tunes as "Divorce Me, C.O.D.," "Sweet Temptation," and "So Round, So Firm, So Fully Packed."

In 1947 Stone took a Pasadena-based deejay named Ernie Ford and molded him into Capitol's first big country star, "Tennessee" Ernie Ford. Ford's likable personality made him a popular figure on early country television, including Stone's own *Hometown Jamboree* broadcast out of Los Angeles. Stone was also an early champion of the careers of HANK THOMPSON and Merle Travis; it was Travis's song "Sixteen Tons" that provided Ford with his biggest hit.

In the sixties and seventies, Stone was more active behind the scenes than as a recording artist. Besides running a couple of music-publishing firms, he continued to produce recordings, forming his own Granite label in 1976, and has served on several industry panels. He also became a prominent promoter of bluegrass concerts in the Southern California area into the early eighties.

◀ STONE, DOUG

(born 1956, Newnan, GA)

Another one of the early-nineties hunks of the month, Stone is a solid country crooner whose style is reminiscent of MERLE HAGGARD.

Raised in rural Georgia, Stone was inspired to go into music by his mother, who had aspirations to be a country singer. He formed his first band when he was fifteen and continued to perform in the Newnan area while working in a variety of factory jobs. In 1987 he was discovered by country agent Phyllis Bennett while performing at the VFW hall in his hometown; she arranged for his demo tape to be heard by Epic Records' director of country music, and he was signed to the label.

His first hit was 1990's "I'd Be Better Off (in a Pine Box)," with a hard-edged HONKY-TONK sound akin to the early-sixties recordings of Merle Haggard. His next single—"Fourteen Minutes Old"—went to number one, cementing his position as a solid contender in the NEW-COUNTRY arena. He followed with the easy shot of "A Jukebox with a Country Song," which trumpets typical redneck values, and "Warning Labels," a more clever sendup of honky-tonk values.

Stone's career was slowed somewhat in 1992 when his hard-livin', good-ol'-boy diet of grits, grease, and gravy led to quadruple-bypass surgery.

Select Discography

Doug Stone, Epic 45303. His first album.

◀ STONEMAN, ERNEST "POP"

(born 1893, Monorat, VA; died 1968)

One of the first country artists to record, Ernest Stoneman was also one of the longest to remain on the scene, returning as the leader of the Stoneman Family Band in the fifties and sixties until his death.

Hailing from a musical family in Western Virginia, Stoneman was a carpenter by trade and a musician by avocation. By his twenties, he could play the GUITAR, autoharp, mouth harp (or harmonica), and Jew's harp. He contacted OKeh recording executive and pioneering country music producer RALPH PEER in 1924 and made some test recordings that were eventually released early the next year, including the first recording of "The Sinking of the Titanic." Stoneman continued to record through the twenties for numerous labels, both as a soloist and as leader of a string band, the Blue Ridge Corn Shuckers, featuring fiddler Uncle Eck Dunford.

Like many other early stars of country music who actually came from a rural background, Stoneman was not the most "intensely" traditional in his approach to music making; i.e., instead of singing in a highly ornamented style, he sang in a relaxed, almost spoken manner, with clear pronunciation. His string-band recordings were also more genteel than the rough-and-rowdy style preferred by deep South bands like the SKILLET LICKERS.

With the coming of the Depression, the recording industry was severely crippled and Stoneman's initial career ended. He worked in a munitions factory through World War II, settling outside of Washington, D.C., and did not return to active performing until the first FOLK REVIVAL of the early fifties. Stoneman had thirteen children, many talented musically, and so he formed a family band that began performing in the Washington area, with sons Scotty (fiddle), Jim (bass), and Van (guitar), and daughters Donna (MANDOLIN) and Roni (BANJO), plus Pop leading the brood on guitar and autoharp. They recorded for various labels, but their most important and influential album came out in 1957 on the Folkways label, introducing their sound to the urban folk-revival audience. In 1962 they were made

members of the GRAND OLE OPRY and continued to perform through the sixties for
both country and folk-revival audiences. They also appeared on diverse television
programs, from *Shindig* to *Hootenany* to the *Jimmy Dean Show*.

After Pop Stoneman's death, the group moved in a more BLUEGRASS-oriented
direction. Son Scotty left the band first and won fame on the West Coast as a
bluegrass fiddler, particularly for his work with the PROGRESSIVE BLUEGRASS band the
KENTUCKY COLONELS in the early sixties. Daughter Roni became a talented comedian, appearing as a regular on the ever-popular HEE HAW TV program.

Select Discography

Ernest "Pop" Stoneman and his Dixie Mountaineers, 1927–1928, Biograph 8004.
Out-of-print LP reissuing early recordings.
First Family of Country Music, CMH 9029. Cassette-only reissue of seventies-era in-
carnation of the family band.

◀ STRAIT, GEORGE

(born 1952, Pearsall, TX)

Strait is one of the great HONKY-TONK/WESTERN SWING revivalists, and one of the
few NEW-COUNTRY acts who, so far at least, hasn't strayed too far into pop-rock. His
recordings have done much to revive the best of the Southwest sound, right down
to the trademark twin harmony fiddles (often featuring veteran swing fiddler
JOHNNY GIMBLE).

The son of a junior-high-school teacher who also raised cattle on the side, Strait
began, as most of his generation did, playing rock and pop music. He eloped with
his high-school sweetheart and soon after joined the army. The army sent him to
Hawaii, where, oddly enough, he began performing country music, perhaps to
remind himself of home. Returning to the family farm, he began performing locally
with the group Aces in the Hole and recorded for the tiny D label out of Dallas.
He hit Nashville in the late seventies but failed to find a contract until 1981, when
he signed with MCA.

From his first album, Strait established his signature southwestern sound, scoring
a number-six hit with his first single, "Unwound." His sound recalled the best of
the early-fifties honky tonkers, including HANK THOMPSON, RAY PRICE, and FARON
YOUNG, before they became buried in the NASHVILLE SOUND of the late fifties and
early sixties. Strait continued to hit it big through the eighties, covering BOB WILLS's
classic "Right or Wrong" and Whitey Shafer's "Does Fort Worth Ever Cross Your
Mind?" His novelty hit, "All My Ex's Live in Texas," even got some pop radio play.

Although George has more recently recorded more slick, "urban" country material, such as "Ocean Front Property," his vocal style and arrangements continue
to have enough pure country in them to win over the most rabid of traditionalists.
He gave an unaffected, straightforward acting performance in the 1992 film *Pure
Country*, which garnered him minor critical praise. Strait continues to make his
home on a ranch in Texas, staying close to his southwestern roots.

Select Discography
Does Fort Worth Ever Cross Your Mind?, MCA 31032. Strait's fourth LP from 1984, and his first classic one, with stripped-down production and a definite HONKY-TONK slant.
Greatest Hits, MCA 5567. The hits up to 1985.
Greatest Hits, Vol. 2, MCA 42304. The hits from 1985 to 1988.
Beyond the Blue Neon, MCA 42266. Another classic LP from 1989.
Pure Country, MCA 10651. 1992 soundtrack album from the film that tried to turn Strait into a celluloid star.

◄ STREET, MEL

(born King Malachi Street, 1933, Grundy, WV; died 1978)
   One of the first new HONKY-TONK singers, Street's life and career ended tragically before the new traditionalist movement of the eighties, which undoubtedly would have brought him wider fame.
   Beginning his musical career as a sideline by performing on local radio, Street worked for many years in the construction and auto paint and repair businesses. By the late sixties, he had his own television show out of rural Bluefield, West Virginia, and in 1970 made his first recording for the tiny Tandem label. The B-side of this single, "Borrowed Angel," his own composition, slowly gained momentum on the charts, finally hitting the top ten when it was reissued by Royal American Records in 1972. Despite the success of this hit, and the follow-up, "Lovin' on Back Streets," Street was ignored by the major labels until four years later, when he signed with Polydor. Polydor had the clout to properly promote him, and he had several more hits over the next two years, including 1978's top-ten "If I Had a Cheatin' Heart." However, the stress of success was too much for the singer, and he committed suicide on his birthday in the same year.
   Street's emphasis on the traditional honky-tonk sound was undoubtedly ahead of his time. He was one of the first younger artists to appreciate the achievements of GEORGE JONES and other somewhat forgotten stars of the fifties and early sixties. He also was among the first to record songs by younger artists like EDDIE RABBITT and EARL THOMAS CONLEY, who would later become hit makers on their own.
   Select Discography
Greatest Hits, Deluxe 7824. Cassette-only reissue of hits.

◄ STRINGBEAN

(born David Akeman, 1915, Annville, KY; died 1973)
   Stringbean was a country comedian and BANJO player who briefly performed with BILL MONROE's original Blue Grass Boys.
   David Akeman's father was a traditional banjo player, and his son followed in his footsteps when he made his own first instrument at age twelve. He began performing in the Lexington, Kentucky, area, landing a radio job when he was

eighteen as a member of Cy Roger's Lonesome Pine Fiddlers. Like most country groups at the time, the Fiddlers prominently featured a country-rube comedian as part of their act; the gangly, six-foot-two-inch banjo player seemed a perfect candidate to take this role. Akeman was given the nickname Stringbean because of his long, lean build.

In the late thirties, he hooked up with Charlie Monroe's band, again taking the comic role. At about the same time, Bill Monroe was forming his first Blue Grass Boys, and hired Stringbean away from his brother to be the comedian and banjo player in his new outfit. Stringbean's main role was as a stage comedian; his old-fashioned frailed banjo style did not fit in with even this early version of the Blue Grass Boys, which was a swinging outfit propelled by Monroe's high-powered MANDOLIN playing. (His banjo playing can barely be heard on Monroe's recordings.) Stringbean would be replaced in the mid-forties by innovative banjoist Earl Scruggs.

In the late forties, Stringbean embarked on a solo career as a comic and banjo player in the tradition of UNCLE DAVE MACON (he later recorded a tribute album to the elder banjo player). He was a well-loved member of the GRAND OLE OPRY for over twenty-five years. His career was given a boost in the late sixties when the popular television show HEE HAW was first broadcast; he was an original cast member, whose style fit in perfectly with the hayseed humor of the program. Stringbean was murdered along with his wife when the pair encountered a burglar robbing their home after a performance at the Opry in 1973.

Select Discography
A Salute to Uncle Dave Macon, Hollywood 309.

◀ STUART, MARTY

(born 1958, Philadelphia, MS)

Stuart was a child prodigy MANDOLIN and GUITAR player who performed with Lester Flatt and other traditional bluegrassers before become a hip-wiggling NEW-COUNTRY star. Stuart's Nashville-based recordings of the late eighties and early nineties show a strong ROCKABILLY influence, including the twangy guitar sound that is a trademark of early rock.

Beginning as a hot, young string-bender, Stuart began performing professionally at the age of twelve as a member of Lester Flatt's Nashville Grass. After Flatt's death, he worked with JOHNNY CASH and BOB DYLAN, recording his first solo album for Sugar Hill, a bluegrass label, in 1982. He jumped on the new-country bandwagon in 1986, signing with Columbia, but didn't achieve immediate success until his breakthrough single of 1991, "That's Country," and its follow-up, a duet with TRAVIS TRITT on Stuart's self-penned "This One's Gonna Hurt You," very much in the tradition of HONKY-TONK WEEPERS.

Stuart has gone straight for the glitz in his stage dress, a kind of Nudie-suit-meets-Elvis style. But, despite his considerable talents as a guitarist and songwriter, his vocal range is limited and rather thin.

Select Discography

Once Upon a Time, CMH 8000. From the mid-seventies, Lester Flatt and the Nashville Grass recordings, featuring young Marty Stuart when he was an adolescent string wizard.

Busy Bee Cafe, Sugar Hill 3726. 1982 recording, his first toe in the water of contemporary country.

This One's Gonna Hurt You, MCA 10596. 1992 LP featuring most of his hits.

◀ STUCKEY, NAT

(born Nathan Wright Stuckey, II, 1938, Cass County, TX)

Stuckey is a minor-league country performer of the sixties who never quite made it; he is best remembered for composing the BUCK OWENS's hit "Waitin' in the Welfare Line."

Trained as a radio announcer and deejay, Stuckey worked in a jazz group in the late fifties before forming his first country band, called the Corn Huskers, performing on the popular *Louisiana Hayride* radio program. He was signed to the Shreveport-based Paula label, having a hit in 1966 with "Sweet Thang," the same year Owens scored with his "Waitin' in the Welfare Line." He switched to RCA in 1968, scoring minor hits with the novelty "Plastic Saddle" from the same year and a cover of Gary Stewart's "Sweet Thang and Cisco" a year later. He recorded for MCA in the mid-seventies to critical acclaim but little commercial success and has since disappeared from the country scene.

◀ SWEETHEARTS OF THE RODEO

(c. 1986–ongoing; Janice Oliver Gill [guitar, vocals]; Kristine Oliver Arnold [guitar, vocals])

Taking their name from the BYRDS' COUNTRY-ROCK album, the Sweethearts are a sister act who have taken California-style country to its next logical evolution.

Born in Torrance, they were raised in Manhattan Beach, not exactly a country-music capital (California's country scene was centered in Bakersfield, a dusty inland town northwest of the beach scene). However, they came of age just as the California country-rock scene was beginning to blossom; groups like the Byrds were flirting on the edges of country, and new bands like the FLYING BURRITO BROTHERS and POCO formed in the early seventies were dedicated to the country-rock fusion. The girls began playing country and BLUEGRASS in high school and were soon booked in clubs up and down the coast. In one of these clubs, Janice met future husband VINCE GILL, who was also part of Southern California's bluegrass scene.

When Gill relocated to Nashville, he took his by-then-retired wife with him. The sisters soon reunited and began performing again and won a national talent contest sponsored by Western-wear makers Wrangler jeans, which led to a contract with Columbia Records. The label emphasized their tough-girl image, emphasizing their sisterly harmony primarily on remakes of fifties ("Hey, Doll Baby") and sixties

("I Feel Fine") rock, recast in a countryesque vein. Although their records won critical praise, they were not traditional enough for die-hard country fans or mainstream enough to win over a pop audience, so that by 1992 Columbia dropped the act. Meanwhile, Gill's megasuccess has overshadowed his wife and sister-in-law's more modest achievements. The Sweethearts have recently signed with the traditional-bluegrass label, Sugar Hill, and not surprisingly, their 1994 album for the new label is in a more traditional vein.

Select Discography

One Time, One Night, Columbia 40614. Their second album from 1988, featuring guests MARK O'CONNOR and Augie Meyers.

Sisters, Columbia 47358. 1992 album, their last for a major label.

◀ SYLVIA

(born Sylvia Kirby, 1956, Kokomo, IN)

In the early eighties, CRYSTAL GAYLE had serious competition in the soulful-long-haired-beauty department from one-name wonder Sylvia. Like Crystal, Sylvia, too, was a minor-league vocalist whose good looks and canny pop productions hid her meager talents.

Born and raised in suburban Indiana, Sylvia came to Nashville when she was nineteen years old looking for a secretarial position. She found one with PiGem music, where she worked not only as a typist but also as a demo singer. She went on the road with JANIE FRICKIE in 1977 just as that singer was breaking out as a solo act, and later in that year she auditioned unsuccessfully to join DAVE AND SUGAR as a Sugar replacement, showing her pop leanings. RCA was impressed enough with her audition that she was given a solo contract, and the label sent her out on the road to open for CHARLEY PRIDE.

Sylvia first hit it big in 1981 with "Drifter," a song that put a Western theme to a disco beat (if you can believe it). After a second hit in 1982 with "Nobody," the singer continued to produce charting singles through 1985, when she retired from active performing because she was tired of the stress of being a star. It was a good thing, too, because her middle-of-the-road country pop would soon go out of vogue, thanks to the resurgence of more traditional country sounds.

Select Discography

Greatest Hits, RCA 5618. Calling all Sylvia fans: Here's the collection that will fill your eyes with tears (come to think of it, anyone would cry to hear these numbers).

T.

◀ TALLEY, JAMES

(born 1943, Mehan, OK)

Talley is a cult-favorite SINGER/SONGWRITER who melds country with social-protest, blues, and R&B styles. He has a strongly devoted, if small, audience.

Born near Tulsa and raised in Albuquerque, New Mexico, Talley was educated at UCLA and the University of New Mexico, studying American culture. After graduation, he worked as a social worker among inner-city Hispanics and then moved to Nashville, where he worked with urban blacks. In the early seventies, he self-financed an album of songs based on his experiences growing up in rural Oklahoma, called *Got No Bread, No Honey, but We Sure Got Love*, which was licensed by Capitol Records and became a classic. A second album, *Trying Like the Devil*, took a more political bent. His albums had little commercial success, although he did earn an invitation to perform at Jimmy Carter's inauguration. After dropping out of sight for a few years, he returned on the German Bear Family label in 1985 for another fine session. He has since gone underground again.

Select Discography
Got No Bread, No Honey, but We Sure Got Love/Tryin' Like the Devil, Bear Family 15433. Both of his classic albums on one CD.
The Road to Torreon, Bear Family 15633. Mid-eighties recordings are presented along with a photo booklet by Cavalliere Ketchum.

◀ TAYLOR, TUT

(born Robert Taylor, 1923, Milledgeville, GA)

Taylor is an influential DOBRO player and instrument maker, best known for his early-seventies association with JOHN HARTFORD.

A talented musician who could play a variety of instruments by his early teens, Taylor began his career as an instrument builder. During the sixties FOLK REVIVAL, he toured as a dobro player with a number of semipopular folk bands, including the Folkswingers and the more BLUEGRASS-oriented Dixie Gentlemen. He hooked up with fiddler VASSAR CLEMENTS, and the duo became the nucleus of John Hartford's backup band in 1969, remaining with him for a couple of years. His tasteful playing with Hartford helped reintroduce the dobro to a new generation of pickers. He recorded two solo albums for Rounder Records in 1973 and 1977 and became a popular figure on the bluegrass circuit. In the eighties, he turned his back on performing to focus on instrument building and repair; his music shop has become a mecca for traditional musicians in the Nashville area.

◖ TEXAS RUBY

(born Ruby Agnes Owen, 1908, Wise County, TX; died 1963)

Texas Ruby was a cowgirl vocalist of the thirties who became one of the earliest HONKY-TONK wailers of the fifties. Big-voiced, and larger-than-life in character, Ruby was known for her tough temper and equally tough vocals.

Born to a real cowboy family, Ruby was raised in the wilds of Texas, performing from an early age with her brothers and sisters (brother Tex would later compose the cowboy standard, "Cattle Call," a hit for EDDY ARNOLD). She began performing on her own in her teen years, working her way by 1933 to Cincinnati, where she hooked up with cowboy bandleader ZEKE CLEMENTS, with whom she performed through the thirties. They performed over WHO out of Des Moines, Iowa, in the middle of the decade, where Ruby had one of her famous fits when she got mad at the young announcer who introduced them, a greenhorn named Ronald Reagan.

In 1936 the couple were booked into New York City's Village Barn, a Greenwich Village nightclub known for its hokey Western decor where urban rustlers could get a country fix. This led to work in Texas and Ruby's first recordings, made with Clements's band the Bronco Busters, for Decca. Ruby and Zeke went from Texas to California, where Ruby's continued ill temper and heavy drinking took its toll on the act; by 1939, they had split up, with Ruby linking up with another beau, trick fiddler Curly Fox, who was to become her husband.

Ruby and Fox performed on the GRAND OLE OPRY from 1944 to 1948, during which time they recorded for Columbia and King. Ruby switched from her earlier cowgirl YODELING act to a more contemporary, honky-tonk persona for these records, including classic he-done-me-wrong songs like "Ain't You Sorry That You Lied," "You've Been Cheating on Me," and "Have You Got Somebody Else on the String." In 1948 the duo relocated to Houston, where they performed for the next decade, and then moved to Los Angeles briefly in 1960 to appear on the popular *Town Hall Party* television program. By mid-1962, they had returned to Nashville, recording a comeback album in March 1963. That same month, Curly came home to their trailer after an Opry performance to discover it engulfed in flames; Ruby apparently had fallen asleep while smoking a cigarette and died in the blaze.

Ruby was one of the first tough mamas of country music, earning the nickname the "Sophie Tucker of Country" for good reason. Besides her gruff vocals and equally gruff onstage personality, she pointed the direction for an entire generation of honky-tonk gals. Although her backup bands still recalled the saddle-sore country outfits of the thirties, the themes of her forties and fifties recordings were modern, particularly in her "I-don't-have-to-take-anymore-of-your-cheatin' " attitude.

◀ TEXAS TORNADOS

(c. 1989–ongoing: Doug Sahm [guitar, vocals]; Augie Meyers [organ, vocals]; Freddie Fender [guitar, vocals]; Flaco Jimenez [accordion, vocals])

The Texas Tornados is made up of COUNTRY-ROCK survivors from the sixties who have formed the ultimate superstar bar band and perform a mix of traditional Tex-Mex and modern country compositions.

Doug Sahm and Augie Meyers were legendary members of the pop-rock group the Sir Douglas Quintet, which had a hit with the R&B-flavored 1965 recording "She's About a Mover." After the band splintered, the duo continued to perform together sporadically. Sahm relocated to California, where he scored a hit with the 1969 hippie-love ode "Mendocino," introducing Tex-Mex sounds and instrumentation to the psychedelic rock audience. Through the seventies and eighties, Sahm and Meyers continued to record and perform together and separately, gaining a large cult audience.

FREDDIE FENDER was another musician to come out of the rich traditions of southwestern music; born Baldemar G. Huerta, he originally recorded in Spanish before scoring his mid-seventies country hits. Like both Sahm and Meyers, he was living off of his past reputation as a hit maker by the late eighties, when the Texas Tornados came together.

The final band member is legendary southwestern accordionist Flaco Jimenez, who comes from a line of talented players of traditional Spanish dance music (his father was a well-known and oft-recorded accordionist, as is his brother). Flaco had sessioned and toured with Ry Cooder for his legendary *Chicken Skin Music* LP, as well as with other country-pop stars.

The group itself is nothing more than a glorified bar band, although these musicians are some of the greatest to ever have played on a beer-soaked stage. Still, they have primarily been performing either the past hits of individual band members or a mix of folk-influenced and NEW-COUNTRY material in a loose-as-a-goose style that reveals years of experience but also shows an underlying refusal to work hard at their music. Their recordings have scored minor success on the country charts.

Select Discography
Zone of Our Own, Reprise 26683. Their third album, and probably their best.

◀ THOMAS, B. J.

(born Billy Joe Thomas, 1942, Houston, TX)

Thomas is a country-pop vocalist best known for his sweet crooning on the 1969 recording of Burt Bacharach's saccharine sixties anthem "Raindrops Keep Falling on My Head," featured in the film *Butch Cassidy and the Sundance Kid* and a major hit on both country and pop charts.

In the late fifties, Thomas was already rockin' and rollin' as a member of the Houston-based Triumphs, remaining with the group into the mid-sixties. A locally released cover version of HANK WILLIAMS's "I'm So Lonesome I Could Cry" was picked up by the national Scepter label, giving the group their first hit in 1966. Thanks to its success, Thomas left the group and began recording in a soft-pop vein, having minor hits with 1968's "Eyes of a New York Woman" and "Hooked-on a Feeling." His big break came with the perennial middle-of-the-road classic "Raindrops," which continues to be performed wherever tinkling lounge pianists reign.

Thomas continued to record in a pop-rock vein through the early seventies and then switched to country music, scoring a hit in 1975 with "(Hey Won't You Play) Another Somebody Done Somebody Wrong Song," recorded in the classic Nashville style, complete with tinkling keyboards and girly choruses. In 1976 he became a born-again Christian and through the early eighties recorded gospel-tinged pop material, winning a Grammy in the gospel category for his 1977 album *Home Where I Belong* on the religious Myrrh label.

Thomas returned to his secular roots in the mid-eighties, continuing to record a mix of pop and country through the early nineties, periodically making a comeback without making much of a dent on the charts. His Vegas-size histrionics, married to a voice that reeks with pop schmaltz, makes him at best a minor figure in contemporary country, although fans continue to flock to hear him perform live.

Select Discography
Greatest Hits, Rhino 70752. All the biggies in chronological order with decent, if skimpy, notes.

◀ THOMPSON, HANK

(born Henry William Thompson, 1925, Waco, TX)

Thompson is a Texas singer/guitarist who helped carry on the WESTERN SWING sound for a new generation of honky-tonkers.

Thompson began as a teenage performer on local radio as Hank the Hired Hand, as well as recording for the tiny, local Globe label. These sides were so successful that they led TEX RITTER to recommend him to California-based Capitol Records, to which Thompson was signed in 1948 and where he remained for eighteen years. His backup band, the Brazos Valley Boys, provided the drive of a good Western swing outfit; on record and tours, they were often augmented by legendary Capitol session guitarist MERLE TRAVIS. While the band was a swinging one, Thompson's song choice focused on women, booze, and heartbreak, classic HONKY-TONK themes.

Thompson's first big hit was "Humpty Dumpty Heart" from 1948; he followed this with many classics, including 1952's honky-tonk theme song, "Wild Side of Life." In the mid-fifties, he helped promote singer WANDA JACKSON by featuring her in his live shows and in recordings.

In the early sixties, impressed by the success of big-band vocalist Louis Prima in performing for the Vegas crowd, Thompson hit the trail for the gamblers' capital, recording a fine live LP there in 1961. After leaving Capitol in 1966, Thompson roamed among labels for a while and began performing mostly with anonymous session musicians. His 1970s recordings are marred by a generic, mainstream Nashville sound. Thompson continues to record and perform and is most active around Fort Worth, his current home.

Select Discography
Capitol Collectors Series, Capitol 92124. His best sides from 1947 to 1960.
Country Music Hall of Fame, MCA 10545. His Dot and ABC recordings from the sixties and seventies.

◀ THOMPSON, SUE

(born Eva Sue McKee, 1926, Nevada, MO)

Thompson was a pop-country chanteuse of the sixties famous for her little-girl vocal style.

Thompson was a precocious performer, playing GUITAR and singing on stage from age seven. Her family relocated to California, where she won a San Jose–based talent contest, gaining the attention of Dude Martin, who ran San Francisco's *Hometown Hayride* television show. The two married, and Thompson became a featured performer on the show, as well as recording with Martin's Round-up Gang backup band. She broke up with Martin and then married country singer HANK PENNY, performing with him in Las Vegas until that marriage, too, dissolved in the late fifties. Through the fifties, she made unsuccessful recordings for a number of labels.

By the early sixties, she was living in the Los Angeles area and signed with the new Hickory label, led by WESLEY ROSE. She had her first hits on the pop charts with 1961's "Sad Movies (Make Me Cry)" and "Norman," and then moved to countrified material. Her career wound down by the late sixties, although she returned to the charts in the mid-seventies with the twosome "Big Mable Murphy" and "Never Naughty Rosie." She continues to perform in her native Southwest.

Select Discography
Greatest Hits, Curb 77462.

◀ THOMPSON, UNCLE JIMMY

(born 1848, Smith County, TN; died 1931)

Old-time fiddler Thompson was the first musician to appear on the premier broadcast of WSM's *Saturday Night Barn Dance* on November 28, 1925, accompanied by his niece Mrs. Eva Thompson Jones on the piano. The show quickly became famous as the GRAND OLE OPRY. Thompson played for the full hour on the first *Barn Dance* broadcast and continued to be the featured artist for at least a month afterward. When word spread that old-time music was being performed on the air, the show's producer/host GEORGE D. HAY was flooded with similar acts but continued to employ Thompson until 1928; his traditional backwoods fiddle style strongly appealed to the rural audience that the program was aimed at. Although he worked most of his life as a farmer, Thompson also performed locally at dances and fiddlers' contests and conventions. He recorded for Columbia in 1926 and again for Vocalion in 1930, before dying of pneumonia at the age of eighty-three in 1931.

◀ THREE LITTLE MAIDS, THE

(c. 1932–1935: Evelyn, Eva, and Lucille Overstake)

This clean-cut vocal trio were the darlings of WLS's *National Barn Dance* radio program; all three went on to further careers in country music.

Hailing from Decatur, Illinois, the girls originally sang together as a group at home, influenced by their religious upbringing and the family's association with the Salvation Army; a song that became closely associated with them was "I Ain't Gonna Study War No More" (originally a hymn, and then an antiwar anthem during the fifties and sixties FOLK REVIVAL).

Eldest sister Evelyn provided the trio's distinctive baritone voice; when the group dissolved in 1935, she continued to perform on the *Barn Dance* for another twenty years. Middle sister Lucille was the musical brains behind the trio; she played the GUITAR, the only one of the three to play an instrument, and probably worked out the group's vocal arrangements. After the group had disbanded, she turned to performing slightly "blue" material under the name Lucille Lee, recording with the Sweet Violet Boys, a pseudonym used by PATSY MONTANA's backup band, the Prairie Ramblers, for this racy material. She wrote a number of suggestive titles, including "I Love My Fruit," about the pleasures of eating in bed. In the forties, with the cowboy/girl phase in full blossom, Lucille transformed herself into Jenny Lou Carson, recording for Decca and writing classics like "Jealous Heart" and "Let Me Go, Lover" and patriotic numbers like "Dear God, Watch Over Joe" and "When the Boys Come Marching Home." She switched to recording in the cowgirl/folk vein for Mercury Records in the fifties. Youngest sister Eva began performing with the group when she was just thirteen; she attracted the attention of WLS star RED FOLEY, who married her in 1935, ending the group. Her daughter, Shirley Foley, wed Pat Boone and became his performing sidekick in the fifties; Shirley and Pat, in turn, gave the world DEBBIE "You Light Up My Life" BOONE. Eva's life ended tragically when she committed suicide after learning that husband Red was cheating on her with another (younger) singer.

◀ TILLIS, MEL

(born 1932, Tampa, FL)

A fine songwriter and performer, Tillis hit his stride in the late fifties as a writer and in the late sixties as a performer.

Born in Tampa, Tillis was raised in the small town of Pahokee, where he learned to play the GUITAR. After serving in the air force in the early fifties and spending two years in college, Tillis went to Nashville in search of a career as a singer. WEBB PIERCE liked his material and recorded Tillis's "I'm Tired" in 1957. The duo cowrote

"I Ain't Never" soon after and also recorded a duet together in 1963 on the humorous "How Come Your Dog Don't Bite Nobody but Me." Tillis was signed to Columbia Records, which didn't really know what to do with him, and he scored only minor hits beginning with 1958's sentimental "The Violet and the Rose."

Tillis's next big break came in 1963 when BOBBY BARE had a monster hit with his "Detroit City." He signed with Kapp Records and had his first hit on his own with 1965's "Stateside," which became the name of his backup band, followed two years later by a monster hit with Howard Harlan's classic WEEPER "Life Turned Her That Way" (covered by RICKY VAN SHELTON in 1987). As a songwriter, Tillis had another hit with KENNY ROGERS and the First Edition's cover of his "Ruby (Don't Take Your Love to Town)."

Tillis began the seventies on MGM, recording a fine combination of HONKY-TONK songs and weepers, including 1971's "The Arms of a Fool" and "Brand New Mister Me," a remake of "Sawmill" in 1973 (which he had originally cut for Columbia in 1959), "Midnight Me and the Blues" from 1974, and "The Woman in the Back of My Mind" in 1975. He then switched to MCA, where his recordings took a decided turn toward pop-schlock after one last fine honky-tonk number, "Good Woman Blues" in 1976. Tillis hit his nadir in 1978 with the maudlin "I Believe in You."

Tillis switched to Elektra in 1980, recorded an album of duets with that boots-wearin' gal Nancy Sinatra in 1981, and then returned to MCA for a couple of minor hits, including 1983's "In the Middle of the Night" and 1984's "New Patches." Although falling off the charts in the early eighties, Mel has remained a popular performer on the road and on TV. Daughter PAM TILLIS is one of NEW-COUNTRY's finest singers.

Select Discography
Greatest Hits, Curb 77482. Recordings from the late seventies and early eighties of varying quality.

◀ TILLIS, PAM

(born 1957, Nashville, TN)

NEW-COUNTRY star and daughter of SINGER/SONGWRITER MEL TILLIS, Pam broke through on the country charts in the early nineties with her combination of sassy love songs and humorous takes on country-music conventions.

Tillis is typical of Nashville's new-country performers in that her musical education, while rooted deeply in country traditions, took her through a variety of styles. She performed, sang, and composed in rock, free-jazz, top-forty, disco, forties jazz/pop, and even new-wave styles through the mid-eighties. Although these efforts met with limited commercial success, they helped build an eclectic base for her later musical explorations.

In 1986, Tillis formed Twang Night, a mock-country revue that both celebrated Nashville's HONKY-TONK glories and built her reputation as a new-country songwriter. In the late eighties, her songs were covered by the trio of DOLLY PARTON, LINDA RONSTADT, and EMMYLOU HARRIS ("Those Memories"), HIGHWAY 101 ("Someone Else's Troubles Now"), and Judy Rodman ("Goin' to Work"). Tillis recorded on her own for Warner Brothers, but she didn't chart until switching to Arista in 1990.

Recent Tillis hits include 1991's steamy, romantic love ballad "Maybe It Was Memphis," 1992's sensual "Shake the Sugartree," and her 1993 tongue-in-cheek "Cleopatra (Queen of Denial)," in which Tillis has created the ultimate suffering country female.

Tillis is an energetic performer, with strong, assertive vocals that show her background in rock and R&B. Still, she has an identifiably country sound, grounding her music in the traditions of Nashville's great women vocalists of the fifties and sixties.

Select Discography

Put Yourself in My Shoes, Arista 8642. Her 1991 breakthrough album.
Homeward Looking Angel, Arista 18649. Fine 1992 album.

◀ TILLMAN, FLOYD

(born 1914, Ryan, OK)

Tillman is a legendary HONKY-TONK SINGER/SONGWRITER who was also a pioneer performer on the electric guitar. In the words of the *Faber Encyclopedia of Popular Music*, "What JIMMIE RODGERS did for railroads in country music, Tillman did for adultery" with his most famous composition, 1949's "Slipping Around."

Tillman was a multitalented instrumentalist who performed with many of the Southwest's best WESTERN SWING bands in the thirties, beginning with the band led by German immigrant Adolph Hofner, and eventually hooking up with legendary fiddler Cliff Bruner. In 1938 Bruner recorded Tillman's song "It Makes No Difference Now," which has become a country classic, thanks primarily to a cover recording by JIMMIE DAVIS, who acquired a half-interest in the song from Tillman. Its success led to a solo contract for Tillman with Decca in the early forties, and he scored hits with his self-penned "They Took the Stars out of Heaven" in 1942, followed a year later with "Each Night at Nine."

After the war, Tillman enjoyed his greatest success as a recording artist with Columbia, with hard-hitting honky-tonk anthems, beginning with 1946's "Drivin' Nails in My Coffin," "I Love You So Much It Hurts" from the next year, and the immortal "Slipping Around" (with the answer song "I'll Never Slip Around Again," rushed out to capitalize on the original song's success). His jazzy vocal style, influenced by his years of performing Western swing, would in turn inspire a new generation of singer/songwriters, particularly a young Texan, WILLIE NELSON. Tillman continued to record sporadically through the fifties and sixties, scoring one more hit in 1960 with "It Just Tore Me Up." He has since lived primarily off of the income from his early successful songs, which continue to be performed by both old and new country artists.

Select Discography

Country Music Hall of Fame, MCA 10189. Early Decca-label recordings.

◀ TIPPIN, AARON

(born 1958, Pensacola, FL)

A hunky hit maker of the early eighties, Tippin celebrates the ordinary, working man in much of his material, appealing to the core country audience.

Although born in Florida, Tippin was raised in rural South Carolina, where he dreamed of becoming a commercial pilot. He obtained his pilot's license when he was fifteen and began studying so he could be certified to fly large commercial jets. Music was strictly a sideline at this time, but when the early eighties brought the energy crisis and recession, Tippin realized that his future as a pilot was limited. Discouraged further by the failure of his marriage, he took a job in a cotton mill and temporarily abandoned music.

However, in 1985, he moved to Nashville and was hired as a staff writer by Acuff-Rose. After recording demos and writing songs, he was signed by RCA in 1990, producing an immediate sensation with his first single, "You've Got to Stand for Something," released in the wake of the Gulf War. This patriotic gut-thumper set the stage for future Tippin hits celebrating the ordinary man, including "Trim Yourself to Fit the World" and "Working Man's Ph.D." Because Tippin writes his own material, it tends to reflect his own concerns; for example, the hit "There Ain't Nothin' Wrong with the Radio" answers critics of country and pop music who think music is leading young listeners astray.

A pleasant enough SINGER/SONGWRITER, it is undoubtedly Tippin's he-man looks and mainstream values that endear him to his audience.

Select Discography

You've Got to Stand for Something, RCA 2374. 1991 debut album.

◀ TRAVIS, MERLE

(born 1918, Ebenezer, KY; died 1983)

One of the most innovative and influential country guitarists, Travis was also a fine songwriter whose songs have the lasting quality of mountain ballads with more than a nod to the sounds of the HONKY-TONK.

Travis's father was a BANJO player and taught him to play the instrument in a two-finger picked style that was common in the upper South in the twenties and thirties. When the youngster switched to the GUITAR, he adapted this picking style to the new instrument, playing the bass strings with his thumb while using a flat pick on the upper strings. He dampened the strings with the heel of his hand as he strummed, giving a choked sound to his music. This technique has come to be known as "Travis picking," and it was highly influential on the next generation of country guitarmen, including CHET ATKINS, DOC WATSON, and scores of others.

Travis hooked up briefly with Clayton McMichen's jazzy band the Georgia Wildcats in the mid-thirties and was soon after hired by Cincinnati's *Boone County Jamboree*, a popular radio program, where he worked for a decade as a soloist and accompanist, performing with GRANDPA JONES and the DELMORE BROTHERS in the informal group known as the Brown's Ferry Four (named after the Brothers' big hit, "Brown's Ferry Blues"). The group recorded in various configurations for the fledgling Cincinnati-based King label, which would in the early fifties become a leader in country and R&B recordings.

During the last two years of World War II, Travis served in the military, returning to civilian life and settling in Southern California, where he worked with several of the transplanted WESTERN SWING bands that were based there. He was signed to another new label, Capitol, and had his first solo hits (all coauthored with CLIFF STONE), the honky-tonkin' "Divorce Me C.O.D.," "So, Round, So Firm, So Fully Packed," "Sweet Temptation," and the tongue-in-cheek "Smoke, Smoke, Smoke That Cigarette," which was written for and recorded by TEX WILLIAMS. In 1947, he cut an album called *Folksongs from the Hills*, which included his own compositions in a folk style based on his memories of the tough life of the coal miners in his native Kentucky. Two of these songs, "Dark as a Dungeon" and "Sixteen Tons," have become standards in the folk and country repertoires, the latter thanks to TENNESSEE ERNIE FORD's finger-snappin' 1955 cover version.

In the fifties, Travis experimented with developing a solid-body electric guitar; instrument makers Paul Bigsby and Leo Fender both worked on Travis's design, which eventually led to the mass production of the instruments that would become the lead voice in rock-and-roll ensembles. The electric instrument that Travis often played suited his picking style, which emphasized a percussive, rhythmic chop while downplaying the natural ringing sound of the acoustic instrument.

Through the fifties and sixties, Travis worked both as a soloist and session artist, although he never regained the popularity of his late-forties recordings. He was invited to participate in the NITTY GRITTY DIRT BAND's all-star country tribute album, *Will the Circle Be Unbroken*, in 1971, which helped to revive his career as a performer. After that recording, he made a few more albums with Chet Atkins and JOE MAPHIS, as well as returning to his Western swing roots on an album featuring many alumni of BOB WILLS's bands.

Select Discography

Folksongs of the Hills, Bear Family 15636. The great late-forties folk sessions cut for Capitol and a lesser-known return to the folk style in 1963.
The Best of Merle Travis, Rhino 70993. All the hits from the original sessions.

◀ TRAVIS, RANDY

(born Randy Traywick, 1962, Marshville, NC)

Randy Travis is among the most successful of the NEW-COUNTRY performers, because his music at once pays homage to the country past while it often seems to be gently poking fun at its conventions. Although he has become a more conservative performer as his success has deepened, Travis is still able to wring that authentic lonesome sound from his deep baritone vocals and well-chosen, well-crafted country songs.

Born to a poor North Carolina family, Travis was exposed early to the classic country recordings of HANK WILLIAMS, LEFTY FRIZZELL, GEORGE JONES, MERLE TRAVIS, and ERNEST TUBB, all of whom were idolized by his father. He began playing GUITAR at age eight and was performing as a duo with his brother six years later at local clubs. When he was sixteen, he ran away from home and won a talent contest in Charlotte, which led to his discovery by local bar owner Lib Hatcher, the Svengali manager who would support his career for seven years before he hit it big (the duo later married).

Performing under the name Randy Ray, Travis came to Nashville with Hatcher at the age of twenty-three. He was quickly signed to Warner Brothers records and recorded the classic *Storms of Life* LP. Randy's hits off this first album have the sly edge of the best of country music: "On the Other Hand" tells the story of a married man wavering on the edge of an affair but who keeps being reminded of his marital status by the ring he wears "on the other hand"; "Digging Up Bones" tells of a man who keeps "digging up the bones" of his failed relationship; the humor is perfectly paired with Randy's deadpan delivery.

Randy has scored countless hits since his first successes, but most have retreated from the adventuresome quality of his first recordings. His next big hit, "Forever and Ever Amen," is a touching piece of country corn, but it takes itself a bit too seriously. Similarly, more recent numbers echo the country clichés of love that runs "deeper than the hollers, higher than the mountains."

Still, Randy's quavering bass vocals, earnest awkwardness as a performer, and even his rudimentary guitar picking make him almost the archetypical country singer. He manages to put forward with conviction even the sappiest sentiments and never seems to be stooping for a hit even as his accountants deposit his latest royalty checks.

Select Discography

Storms of Life, Warner Bros. 25435. 1986 debut LP, still a classic.
Greatest Hits, Vols. 1 and 2, Warner Bros. 45044/45045.

◀ TRISCHKA, TONY

(born 1948, Syracuse, NY)

If one person can be praised (or blamed) for the noodling, spacey BANJO playing that was an integral part of PROGRESSIVE BLUEGRASS bands of the seventies, it would have to be Tony Trischka, the man who launched a thousand notes.

Trischka originally reached prominence as a member of COUNTRY COOKING, an all-instrumental band that was famous for the twin banjos of Trischka and Peter Wernick. When the band dissolved in the early seventies, Trischka released his first solo album, *Bluegrass Light*, a kind of Sun-Ra-meets-Earl Scruggs outing. Although not exactly easy listening, the album opened up the potential for playing a wider melodic and harmonic range on BLUEGRASS-style banjo. During this same period, Trischka also performed with the eclectic band Breakfast Special, a more spacey incarnation of the earlier Country Cooking.

After a few more avant-garde solo albums, Trischka returned to the fold on the half-traditional, half-modern album *Banjoland* from the late seventies. He even played (gasp!) in traditional Scruggs style, announcing that far-out cats like himself were not adverse to honoring bluegrass's roots. In the early eighties, he formed the band SKYLINE, which featured an odd wedding of contemporary country songs with his own toned-down original instrumentals.

After Skyline's demise in the mid-eighties, Trischka performed as a solo artist and as part of the Rounder Records banjo tours, featuring BELA FLECK, BILL KEITH, and other bluegrass pickers. While his picking still reflects the influences of jazz, avant-garde, and rock-and-roll styles, his repertoire hews closer to traditional sources, and even his own compositions stick close to bluegrass roots. Of late, he has presented "History of the Banjo" concerts, in which he plays everything from minstrel-era pieces to his own progressive instrumentals.

Select Discography

Dust on the Needle, Rounder 11508. Compilation of his many Rounder albums.
Solo Banjo Works, Rounder 0247. Solos by Trischka and Bela Fleck.

◀ TRITT, TRAVIS

(born 1963, Marietta, GA)

Tritt, one of the more distinctive of the NEW-COUNTRY vocalists and performers, has a knack for performing and writing interesting material that both honors and extends country traditions. Although like many other successful country acts he is in danger of lapsing into glitzy showmanship, Tritt seems rooted enough to last for the long run.

From his first recording, Tritt showed an understanding and appreciation of traditional country genres, particularly HONKY-TONK laments, that set him apart from other crooning wannabes. His vocal style has a healthy quaver to it that recalls mountain singers as well as previous stars like HANK WILLIAMS and GEORGE JONES. Plus many of his better songs, like 1993's hit "T-R-O-U-B-L-E," recall, perhaps unintentionally, classic country genres (in this case, songs like "S-A-V-E-D" by the BLUE SKY BOYS and "D-I-V-O-R-C-E" by TAMMY WYNNETTE, although it certainly takes a much different slant than either the Bible-thumping of the Boys or Wynette's "let's-not-tell-the-children" theme).

Coming from a rural middle-class background, Tritt had his first exposure to music in the church choir. He taught himself GUITAR when he was eight and wrote his first song at age fourteen. Like many other of today's country artists, he was as equally influenced by mid-seventies folk-rock as he was by pure country, learning songs by groups like the EAGLES (he participated in a 1993 fund-raising album of Eagles songs released by new-country artists).

After high school, Tritt worked for four years on a loading dock, working his way up to a manager's position while still performing part-time in local clubs. He was heard by Danny Davenport, a Georgia-based talent scout for Warner Brothers records, who was as much interested in his songwriting abilities as his performing skills. They worked together for two years crafting demo tapes for the label, leading to the release of his first album, 1990's *Country Club*, which yielded four hit singles, including the number-one country hit "Help Me Hold On." Mega–music manager Ken Kragen, of "We Are the World" fame, came on board to handle Tritt's career, undoubtedly helping to vault him into the upper stratospheres of country stardom.

Tritt's career really took off with his second album, released in 1991. This yielded the barroom anthems "Here's a Quarter (Call Someone Who Cares)" and "The Whiskey Ain't Working Anymore" (the latter a duet with new-country hunk MARTY STUART). Fans took to throwing quarters at Tritt while he performed, which made him quickly drop his signature song from his concerts for fear of suffering injuries from the flying change!

In 1992 Tritt was inducted into the GRAND OLE OPRY and remains the youngest member of this venerable institution. He toured with Stuart while at the same time gaining exposure thanks to Kragen through the placement of his songs in movies, including the theme song for *My Cousin Vinnie* ("Bible Belt," a collaboration with the country-rockers Little Feat) and a cover of ELVIS PRESLEY's "Burnin' Love" for *Honeymoon in Vegas*. In 1993 he appeared with another Kragen client, grizzled country crooner KENNY ROGERS, in a TV movie, *Rio Diablo*.

Tritt's 1993 successes include the topical "Lord Have Mercy on the Working Man," with a clever video showing how the "honest, ordinary citizen" is ignored by the media and politicians; and the bar-hopper's anthem "T-R-O-U-B-L-E," which gave his third album its title tune. In the video for this honky-tonk rev up, Tritt appears in tight leather pants, wriggling his way through the number. This is somewhat ironic in light of his criticism of BILLY RAY CYRUS for reducing country music to he-man attitudes, but, as they say, there's no arguing with success.

Select Discography
Country Club, Warner Bros. 26094. 1990 debut album.
T-R-O-U-B-L-E, Warner Bros. 45048. Get out those hip-huggin' leather pants and your wide-brimmed cowboy hat and boogie on down to the Tritt bar and grill for some boot-scootin' fun!

◀ TRUCK-DRIVING SONGS

There are three subjects that have become the leading stereotypes of country songwriting: mother, prison, and trucks. The image of the lone trucker blazing a path through the wilderness has replaced the cowboy in American folklore as the last hero of the blacktop frontier. An explosion of songwriting in the early sixties through the CB craze of the seventies helped fuel this myth into an entire subgenre of country music.

MOON MULLICAN's recording of "Truck Driver Blues" from 1939 is generally credited with being the first trucking ode on wax. However, the song that spurred the movement was DAVE DUDLEY's 1963 megahit, "Six Days on the Road." JIMMY MARTIN leapt on the trucking bandwagon with his "Widow Maker" from 1964; DICK CURLESS followed with his 1965 hit, "Tombstone Every Mile"; and traditional bluegrassers JIM AND JESSE scored a surprise 1967 hit with "Diesel on My Trail." Roger Miller's "King of the Road" was a country hit in 1964 and crossed over to the pop charts in 1967. And, of course, there is the infamous "Truck Drivin' Man," the best-loved and most often parodied song of the open road. Two small BLUEGRASS/country labels, Starday and King, fueled the truck-driving mania, releasing several albums with colorful names like *Super Slab Hits, Truckin' On, Forty Miles of Bad Road*, and

Diesel Smoke, Dangerous Curves with equally colorful covers shot "on location" at truckstops, showing big rigs, bad dudes, and the gals that they love.

Many of these songs incorporated the sentimentality of earlier country odes celebrating the railroad engineer. The engineer who bravely piloted his train (even staying at his post through a gruesome train wreck) was replaced in the new trucker's songs by the image of the brave, honest truck driver, who sometimes had to give his own life to save another. A subgenre of trucking recitations, stories supposedly told by the rigmasters themselves about the difficulties of life on the road, reached their nadir in the classic "The Man Behind the Wheel," a recording that falls squarely into the so-bad-it's-good genre of schlock classics.

The seventies brought a new wrinkle to the truck rage: the CB (citizens band) radio, with its own special jargon. The biggest song to celebrate the new wave of CB outlaws was C. W. McCALL's hit "Convoy." More recently, ALABAMA has had hits with "Roll On (Eighteen Wheeler)," and the trucker has been turned into a romantic softie in KATHY MATTEA's 1988 hit "Eighteen Wheels and a Dozen Roses."

A footnote from the hippie culture was the popularity of the Grateful Dead's "Truckin'" from their early-seventies COUNTRY-ROCK LP *American Beauty*. The expression "Keep on Truckin'," with its sexual overtones (and reference to the popular thirties dance style), originated in the world of swing jazz; the Dead melded this groovy image with the traditional country notion of the truck driver as his own man. Lowell George of the blues-rock band Little Feat wrote two of the most memorable hippie truck-driving anthems, "Willin'" (oft-covered by seventies-era GUITAR strummers) and an answer song to "Truck Driving Man" called "Truck Driving Girl." R. Crumb, comic-book artist and amateur musician who formed his own country-swing group, the Cheap Suit Serenaders, in the seventies, took the motto "Keep on Truckin'" for his comic-book hero, a figure who often appeared painted on the sides of everything from the hippie truck—the VW bus—to big rigs themselves.

◀ TUBB, ERNEST

(born 1914, Crisp, TX; died 1984)

For those only familiar with Tubb's later performances and recordings, when he was suffering from an ongoing battle with emphysema, it's difficult to remember how important and groundbreaking an artist he was. Tubb introduced electric lead guitar to country music as early as 1941, and was the first member of the GRAND OLE OPRY to perform with amplified instruments. He was also one of the greatest performers of HONKY-TONK songs, legitimizing the genre for a broader audience. His slightly off-pitch, relaxed vocals were perfectly suited to the rough-and-tumble honky-tonks where he had his musical training.

Tubb had no ambitions to be a country singer until he heard the recordings of JIMMIE RODGERS. So determined was he to emulate Rodgers's style that he sought out the singer's widow, who gave him her blessings to perform the blue yodeler's material. From the mid-thirties through the early forties, Tubb honed his style, beginning as a pure Jimmie Rodgers imitator but slowly transforming himself into a more modern, honky-tonk singer. Undoubtedly, his experience performing in many small barrooms across Texas helped shape his newer sound; he had to rely on amplified instruments to cut through the noise, and he chose songs that expressed classic barroom sentiments.

The real change came with his signing to Decca Records in 1940 and his enormous hit, one year later, with the loping "Walking the Floor Over You," the quintessential honky-tonk anthem that was to become his lifelong theme song, and perhaps the first country recording to feature electric-guitar lead. Tubb's bone-dry delivery wed with the chunky rhythm of the backup band made this recording a country classic. During the World War II years, Tubb migrated to Hollywood, where he appeared in several B-grade horse operas and even recorded with pop music's Andrews Sisters.

Tubb made his most influential recordings and radio appearances in the late forties and early to middle fifties with his band, the Texas Troubadors, always featuring electric lead guitar. He nurtured the talents of several guitarists, including Fay "Fatty" Smith, Eddie Tudor, Jimmie Short, and, later, Billy Byrd and Leon Rhodes, as well as steel guitarists Buddy Charlton and the legendary Buddy Emmons. Tubb introduced the electric guitar to the Opry when he became a member in 1943; four years later, he opened his Record Store around the corner from the Ryman Auditorium, and for many years hosted WSM's *Midnight Jamboree* radio show, broadcast immediately following the Opry, from his store. (When Opryland USA opened, a replica of his store was opened in the park to simulate the original.)

From the early sixties onward, Tubb coasted on his living legend status. His stripped-down sound was augmented on recordings with heavy-handed choruses while the quality of his singing suffered due to the illness. Although he continued to perform until his death in 1984, his recording career pretty much ended in 1970.

Tubb has been followed on the Opry by his son, SINGER/SONGWRITER Justin (born 1935, San Antonio, Texas). Best known as the author of "Lonesome 7-7203," a 1963 hit for HAWKSHAW HAWKINS, Justin has also been active as a recording star and member of the Opry since 1955. While his father was an innovator, Justin has taken a conservative tack, fighting for the pure honky-tonk sound during the 1970s when COUNTRYPOLITAN ruled the airwaves. While he continues to appear on the Opry, the younger Tubb has made few recordings over the last twenty years.

Select Discography
Country Music Hall of Fame, MCA 10086. Great cuts from 1941 to 1965, all the Tubb you'll probably need.

Let's Say Goodbye Like We Said Hello, Bear Family 15498. Every studio cut from 1947 to 1953 that Tubb made, 114 in all.

Yellow Rose of Texas, Bear Family 15688. Five CDs give you 150 Tubb thumpers, pickin' up where the last collection ended.

Live 1965, Rhino 70902. One of a thousand nights on the road for Ernest and the boys; although he's a little past his prime, this is a fine document of a country road show.

◀ TUCKER, TANYA

(born 1958, Seminole, TX)

Country music has an unending appetite for "bad little good girls," girls who are both sexy and slightly dangerous but somehow also wholesome. Tanya Tucker literally began her career as a little girl who was "wise beyond her years," and she has continued to walk the fine line between HONKY-TONK heroine and the girl next door.

Born in Texas and raised in Phoenix, Arizona, Tucker was raised by a father who was a star-struck, country-music fan determined to make his daughter a hit. He pushed the youngster on stage whenever a country act came into town. When she reached nine years old, convinced he had star material on his hands, he financed a trip to Nashville. After several unsuccessful attempts, her demo tape landed in the hands of ace country producer BILLY SHERRILL, who signed her at age thirteen to Columbia. She immediately hit with the slightly suggestive "Delta Dawn" and "Would You Lay with Me (in a Field of Stone)." Tucker was instantly successful at playing up her sexy-but-sweet image.

By the end of the seventies, as she reached her late teen years, Tucker's career took a detour into an ill-advised attempt to cross over into pop/rock with the album *T.N.T.* (she appeared on the cover decked out in leather, in an attempt to give her a more "mature" image). The early eighties brought duets with her then-beau GLEN CAMPBELL in a more mainstream country fashion. After struggling to find a style, she returned in the mid-eighties to traditional country and honky-tonk sounds.

While Tucker continues to record in a variety of styles, from sentimental ballads to hard-edged country-rock, her best material continues to play on her image of a good-girl-gone-(slightly)-bad. Her 1992 hit, "It's a Little Too Late," is a classic honky-tonk number, which also caters to the latest craze for country dances. Tucker is one of the few female country stars who could get away with singing this type of song, which would more typically be given to a male artist because of its implicit sexuality. She is able to communicate a nonthreatening good humor to her audience that allows her to cross the line just a little bit beyond what might be otherwise acceptable for a country "lady."

Select Discography

Greatest Hits, Columbia 33355. The Billy Sherrill–produced sides through 1975 that made Tanya the "good girl gone bad."

Greatest Country Hits, Curb 77429. Draws on her recordings from 1986 onward.

Can't Run from Yourself, Liberty 98987. 1992 LP, typical of her latest work, in which Tucker tackles big-throated ballads and ballsy barroom numbers.

◀ TURNER, ZEB

(born William Grishaw, c. 1915; died 1978)

Turner was a pioneering guitarist in the country-boogie style as well as a prolific songwriter, although he remained in the shadows of country-music history through most of his career.

He first performed as a member of the Hi Neighbor Boys, who recorded for the budget American Record Company (ARC) label in 1938. His stage name came from his signature tune, the flashy "Zeb Turner Stomp"; brother James Grishaw took the name Zeke Turner at about this same time.

After World War II, Turner was signed to the tiny Bullet label out of Nashville, recording "Mountain Boogie," one of the first so-called "country-boogie" instrumentals (i.e., it blended the bouncy feel of boogie-woogie with countryesque guitar licks). The Grishaw brothers worked as studio musicians on recordings by HANK WILLIAMS and RED FOLEY, and in 1947 EDDY ARNOLD had a hit with "It's a Sin," a HONKY-TONK WEEPER written by Zeb. He also wrote the WESTERN SWING standard "Texas in My Soul."

By the early fifties, Turner had moved East and was working out of the Baltimore/Washington, D.C., area, when he made some excellent recordings in a number of different styles, from R&B to country weepers, for the Cincinnati-based King label. Sometime thereafter, he moved to New Jersey and then, finally, to Montreal, where he last performed as a folksinger before his death in 1978.

◀ TWAIN, SHANIA

(born c. 1958, Timmins, Ontario, Canada)

Twain is an impossibly perky Canadian songstress who had a hit out of the box with the impossibly perky "What Made You Say That?"

Of mixed parentage (her father was an Ojibway Indian), Shania grew up in relative poverty in the backwoods of Ontario. She has been singing since the age of three, winning talent shows from the age of eight, and performing locally and on national television from her early teen years. She trained as a Broadway-style singer/dancer/performer. Professionally trained in Toronto, she began performing at the resort town of Deerhurst after both of her parents were tragically killed in an automobile accident. From glitzy Vegas-style material, she decided to jump on the country bandwagon, coming to Nashville in 1991. She was quickly signed to Mercury Records, hitting it big with her sexy video presence on her first single, "What Made You Say That?"

The singer cites as her "two biggest influences . . . Gladys Knight and Karen Carpenter." That about sums up her style: just a little soul mixed with a lot of middle-of-the-road pizzazz. Like many other Canadian exports (MICHELLE WRIGHT, for example), Twain is best viewed as a sexy stage presence first and a singer second.

Select Discography

Shania Twain, Mercury 514 422. 1993 debut album.

◀ TWITTY, CONWAY

(born Harold Jenkins, 1933, Friars Point, MS; died 1993)

Conway Twitty's career was typical of many country singers of his generation. Although born in the backwoods and bred on country and blues, his first success was in pop-flavored ROCKABILLY, in the wake of ELVIS PRESLEY's enormous popularity. After the British invasion, when rockabilly fell out of favor, he hewed out a successful career as a country vocalist, enjoying his greatest success in the seventies on his own and in duets with LORETTA LYNN.

Twitty's father was a ferryboat captain who operated the tug between Friars Point, Mississippi, and Helena, Arkansas. His father gave him his first rudimentary GUITAR lessons, and young Jenkins had his own country band performing on Helena radio by the time he was ten years old. He cited two important influences from his earliest years: the playing of the jukebox at the local HONKY-TONK, and the singing at the "little Negro church" across the cotton fields from his home. "I would sit on the ditch bank and listen to them sing for two or three hours," he recalled, and "I'd be singing right along." Like many of his contemporaries, Twitty would wed black and white musical influences in his mature works.

As a teenager, Jenkins dreamed of being a professional baseball player; he was talented enough to get an invitation to join the Philadelphia Phillies. He also contemplated a career as a minister. Both plans were put aside when he received his draft notice in the mid-fifties. While he was in the army, he continued to perform country music. Meanwhile, another country artist, Elvis Presley, was recording his first big hits in a new style: rockabilly.

On Jenkins's return from service, he heard the first Elvis recordings and, inspired by Elvis's success, decided to adapt to the new rockabilly sound. He decided that if he was going to be a rock star he needed a rock star's name. Looking on a map, he hit on the names of two local towns: Twitty, Texas, and Conway, Arkansas. He called his band the Twitty Birds. (Later, when he achieved success as a country star, he made his home into a theme park. Its name? Why, Twitty City, of course!)

His first big hit came in 1958 with "It's Only Make Believe," which he cowrote, a million-seller on the pop chart. A number of rockabilly/teen-pop singles followed on MGM, including 1960's hit "Lonely Blue Boy." His success won him the attention of Hollywood, and, like Elvis, he appeared in a number of forgettable B flicks performing his music and "acting." (These films, like the best country songs, are most memorable for their titles, including *Sex Kittens Go to College* and *Platinum High*.) After the Beatles broke through the charts in 1964, however, Conway's pop career fizzled.

After an abortive attempt to be a mainstream, pop crooner, he relocated to Oklahoma City and formed a new, country-oriented band, the Lonely Blue Boys. Legendary Decca producer OWEN BRADLEY signed him to the label, where he remained for many years. After appearing on his own local TV show, Twitty relocated to Nashville, where, by the end of the sixties, he was a major star. His first big country hit came in 1970 with "Hello Darlin' " and was followed by further charting singles through the decade. Most of his best songs were on the subjects of lovin', leavin', and being lonely, classic country concerns, from the humorous ("Tight Fittin' Jeans") to the cloyingly sentimental ("After All the Good Is Gone").

At the same time, he began a successful collaboration with singer LORETTA LYNN. Their duets included sexually suggestive numbers that initially upset mainstream country deejays. Their first hit, 1971's "After the Fire Is Gone," reflected a typical Twittyesque concern: a relationship on the skids. Other numbers celebrated regional identity ("Louisiana Woman, Mississippi Man") and down-home humor ("You're the Reason Our Kids Are Ugly").

Twitty's distinctive baritone voice had some of the same earthiness of JOHNNY CASH, with its hint of hard living that is more typical of the country blues. His gruff, almost conversational style made a perfect foil for the more polished performances of Lynn, making for a believable and realistic male-female dialogue.

Twitty became a yeoman performer in the eighties and early nineties. Though rarely charting as he did in the past, he continued to perform most months of the year, while his home became a kind of landmark shrine for country-music fans. He had just finished a date in NEW-COUNTRY mecca, BRANSON, MISSOURI, in the spring of 1993 when he collapsed from a ruptured blood vessel. He died soon after.

Select Discography

The Best of Conway Twitty, Mercury 574. Reissues his fifties-era hard rockers.
Greatest Hits, Vols. 1 and 2, MCA 31239/31240. His country recordings from the mid-sixties through the mid-seventies.
Final Touches, MCA 10882. 1993 posthumous album shows that Twitty was still in fine form up to his death.

◀ TYLER, T. TEXAS

(born David Luke Myrick, 1916, Mena, AK; died 1972)

One of the creators of the country narrative record, Tyler had a string of hits beginning with 1948's "A Deck of Cards."

Tyler was born in Arkansas but raised in Texas, where he began performing as a singer/guitarist as a teenager. He went East after high school, appearing on the popular radio show *Major Bowes Amateur Hour*, which led to further work on radio out of Newport, Rhode Island. By the late thirties, he had moved to Los Angeles, where he played with a couple of the popular cowboy-type bands of the day. In 1942 he was appearing on the popular *Louisiana Hayride* radio program but was then drafted into the war.

After serving in the army in World War II, he returned to Hollywood. He formed his own band and signed with the small Four Star label, where producer/owner Don Pierce helped shape his initial hits. Pierce supplied Tyler's first hit, "A Deck of Cards," a sentimental, half-spoken number that described a World War II soldier whose deck of cards helped see him through the tough days of war. This was followed by a Tyler/Pierce composition, "Dad Gave the Dog Away," "Remember Me" (which became Tyler's theme song), "Bumming Around" from 1953, and "Courting in the Rain" from a year later.

After appearing in the B-grade horse opera *Horseman of the Sierras* in 1949,

Tyler hosted his own country TV show, Los Angeles's well-loved *Range Round Up*, beginning in 1950. He continued to record from the mid-fifties through the mid-sixties, following Pierce to his new label, Starday, and also cutting sides for King, Pickwick, and Capitol, without producing any hits. By the mid-sixties, Tyler gave up his secular career to pursue a new career as a minister. He died of cancer in 1972.

Select Discography
The Great Texan, King 689.
T. Texas Tyler, King 721. Reissues of his King label recordings.

V

◀ VAGABONDS, THE

(Herald Goodman [vocals]; Curt Poulton [vocals, guitar]; Dean Upson [vocals])

The Vagabonds were the first "professional" group to appear on the GRAND OLE OPRY, signaling a turn toward more commercial, pop-oriented music on the show in the thirties.

Hired by GEORGE D. HAY's assistant Harry Stone, the group were not southerners nor were they primarily musicians. Instead, they were a vocal trio, with professional music training, who specialized in sentimental novelties like "When It's Lamp Lighting Time in the Valley." The group was originally formed by Dean Upson and worked out of Chicago's WLS in 1925; three years later, Curt Poulton joined, and then, in 1930, Herald Goodman completed the outfit, now working out of St. Louis. They were hired by the Opry in 1931 and stayed there for seven years, while also recording for the budget Bluebird label.

The group disbanded in 1938, with Upson and Poulton staying at WSM; Upson eventually joined the station's management staff and Poulton continued to work as an announcer and guitarist, while Goodman took his talents to KVOO out of Tulsa, where he headed up the new *Saddle Mountain Roundup.*

◀ VAN DYKE, LEROY

(born 1929, Spring Fork, MO)

Van Dyke was a two-hit wonder of the late fifties and early sixties, most famous for his comic novelty, 1956's "The Auctioneer."

Trained in agricultural science, Van Dyke worked as a real-life auctioneer after serving in the Korean War. He developed his "Auctioneer" song based on the high-speed patter used at livestock auctions, performing it at a talent contest in 1955 that won him a contract with Dot Records. A year later, the song was a massive country and pop hit, and he was invited to join RED FOLEY's *Ozark Jubilee.*

In the early sixties, Van Dyke had his second surge of popularity with "Walk on By," a 1961 pop and country hit issued by Mercury. This was followed by two more charting songs, "Big Man in a Big House" and "If a Woman Answers," both from a year later. However, his hits soon dried up again, and he was dropped by the label in 1965. Two years later, he appeared in the film *What Am I Bid?*, reviving his auctioneer routine.

Van Dyke continued to record for various labels, big and small, through the seventies and eighties with little success.

Select Discography
Twenty Greatest Hits, Playback 12334. Cassette-only reissue.

◀ VAN ZANDT, TOWNES

(born early 1940s, Fort Worth, TX)

Van Zandt is a moody Texas SINGER/SONGWRITER, part of the seventies OUTLAW COUNTRY/HONKY-TONK revival in Texas that included his contemporaries and friends JERRY JEFF WALKER and GUY CLARK. Van Zandt's material is somewhat darker and more ominous than the others', and his unique delivery makes it difficult for other artists to cover it.

Van Zandt was a native Texan, but his father was an oil worker who moved from state to state, so the young singer was raised in various Western states. He briefly attended the University of Colorado but dropped out to become, in his own words, "a folksinger." He returned to Texas in 1966, playing a variety of small clubs. Van Zandt signed with Poppy Records in 1969, producing a series of albums over the next few years.

Van Zandt's songs have a heavy blues influence, enhanced by his strained, emotional vocals. Like his fellow Texans, he was equally influenced by the honky-tonk traditions of lonesome balladry and the self-confessional music of singer/songwriters like BOB DYLAN. Often, his songs tell stories, with an undercurrent that indicates that something more is going on below the surface. His best-known song is "Poncho and Lefty," covered by WILLIE NELSON and WAYLON JENNINGS on their duet album of the same title, as well as by HOYT AXTON and EMMYLOU HARRIS. Other story songs from the singer include "Mr. Gold and Mr. Mud" and "Tecumesah Valley."

In 1976 he finally moved to Nashville at the insistence of his manager and signed to Tomato Records to produce a few more albums before again dropping into obscurity. After almost a decade of inactivity on record, Van Zandt returned to the studio in 1987 for the specialty BLUEGRASS label Sugar Hill.

Select Discography
At My Window, Sugar Hill 1020.
Live and Obscure, Sugar Hill 1026.
Rain on a Conga Drum, Hypnotic 713561006. Early-nineties live recording from Germany featuring many of his seventies hits and a couple of new songs.

W

◀ WAGONER, PORTER

(born 1930 near West Plains, MO)

Wagoner is a smooth-voiced country SINGER/SONGWRITER who hosted a pioneering syndicated country-music program and boosted the career of DOLLY PARTON. He represented the apex of the NASHVILLE SOUND in the sixties and seventies, maintaining just enough country twang in his vocals to separate him from mainstream crooners.

The son of a midwestern farmer, Wagoner was exposed to country radio from an early age and soon was singing and playing along with his favorite songs. When he was fourteen, he was hired as a clerk at a West Plains market, where he often entertained customers with his music. The store owner decided that Wagoner's music was good for business so he sponsored him on a fifteen-minute radio show on the local station. By the late forties, Wagoner's show was attracting regional attention, and in 1951 he was booked to perform on the radio station in the capital city of Springfield.

Coincidentally, RED FOLEY was establishing his *Ozark Jamboree* television program at about this time, which originated from Springfield. He took Wagoner under his wing and by the mid-fifties made him a star of the program. This led to a recording contract with RCA and Wagoner's first hit, "Satisfied Mind," in 1955. His first gospel recording, "What Would You Do (If Jesus Came to Your House)," followed a year later. In 1957 he was invited to join the GRAND OLE OPRY and relocated to Nashville. Soon after, Porter formed his backup band, known as the Wagonmasters.

Wagoner's career would continue to alternate crooning ballads and pop-gospel for over twenty years. His biggest hit was 1965's "Green Green Grass of Home," which also made a major dent on the pop charts. The swelling choruses and saccharine accompaniment of this recording, along with Wagoner's melodramatic vocals, were typical of the grandiose Nashville productions of the day. Other notable Wagoner outings include "I've Enjoyed as Much of This as I Can Stand" from 1963, "Skid Row Joe" of 1966, and 1968's "Be Proud of Your Man," all expressing typical good-old-boy sentiments.

In 1960 Wagoner began his syndicated television program out of Nashville. Starting with just eighteen stations, the program grew to be one of the most popular in syndication, with over a hundred outlets in the early seventies. Wagoner introduced girl singer NORMA JEAN in the early sixties as his partner, and then, in 1967, gave Dolly Parton her first career exposure. The pair charted with the duet "Last Thing on My Mind," a Tom Paxton FOLK-REVIVAL standard, and continued to work and record together through 1975. Wagoner felt that he deserved the credit for Parton's later success and resented her attempts to establish herself as a solo act in the early seventies. Parton, on her side, felt stifled by Wagoner's old-fashioned musical ideas and eventually was forced to break off from him. A series of lawsuits followed, and Wagoner's career faded while Parton made the crossover into mainstream pop and movie-star status.

Although Wagoner continued to produce minor hits into the early eighties, his crooning vocal style was something of an anachronism in the new Nashville. RCA dug in the vaults to find unissued Porter-and-Dolly material, and this along with his more recent solo recordings kept the fans reasonably happy. Like many country performers before him, Wagoner discovered his core fans were slow to abandon him, so he has been able to continue touring and performing while his recordings continue to sell.

Select Discography

The Thin Man from West Plains, Bear Family 15499. Four CDs gives you a decade's worth of Wagoner's RCA recordings, beginning with his first session in 1952 when he sounds very much like a Hank Williams wannabe, through the birth of his distinctive sound.

Pure Gold, Pair 1991. Ten sixties-era RCA recordings, not exactly golden but surely no dross.

Sweet Harmony, Pair 1013. Two-CD set featuring Dolly Parton.

◀ WAKELY, JIMMY

(born James Clarence Wakely, 1914, Mineola, AK; died 1982)

Wakely was one of the postwar era's most popular singing cowboys, who started the vogue for cheating songs with his megahit duet, "Slippin' Around," recorded with pop singer Margaret Whiting.

Born in a small Arkansas town, Wakely was raised in Oklahoma. After finishing his education, he held a series of low-level jobs, eventually working his way up to being a local journalist. Meanwhile, he formed his own cowboy trio with Johnny Bond and Scotty Harrell, and they landed a job on Oklahoma City radio in 1937. Three years later, GENE AUTRY guested on their program, liked what he heard, and hired the group on the spot for his popular nationally broadcast *Melody Ranch* radio show.

Wakely's exposure on Autry's show catapulted him to cowguy fame; within two years, he had formed his own band, nurturing the career of such West Coast master musicians as steel guitarist SPADE COOLEY, bassist CLIFFIE STONE, and guitarist MERLE TRAVIS. During the war, he began appearing in a slew of D-grade Westerns, making him nearly as popular as Autry on the silver screen.

In 1948 Wakely had his first major hit with "One Has My Name, The Other Has My Heart," the first in a string of cheating songs that would virtually create the genre. This was followed a year later by his duet with Margaret Whiting, "Slippin'

Around" and, soon after, the answer song, "I'll Never Slip Around Again." Meanwhile, he piled on the solo hits with 1949's "I Love You So Much It Hurts," 1950's "My Heart Cries for You," and 1951's "Beautiful Brown Eyes." In 1949, he began his own CBS radio show, which lasted for nine years.

Beginning in the mid-fifties, Wakeley's career began to slow down. His recordings began to suffer the same fate of other country artists, with syrupy productions featuring mewing choirs. In the mid-sixties, he formed his own record label, Shasta, but by the seventies he was reduced to playing the ersatz cowboy circuit, appearing in Vegas along with his children, Johnny and Linda Lee. He died in 1982.

Select Discography
Beautiful Brown Eyes, Richmond 2183. Cassette-only reissue of recordings of unknown vintage.

◀ WALKER, BILLY

(born 1929, Ralls, TX)

Walker was a solid hit-maker in the sixties who began his career with the gimmick of appearing in disguise, gaining the appellation the Masked Singer.

Born in Texas, Walker was raised in New Mexico, where he picked up music making at an early age. He won a local talent contest when he was fifteen years old; the prize was his own fifteen-minute radio show broadcast out of Clovis, New Mexico. Five years later, he was hired to perform on the popular Dallas-based *Big D Jamboree* show, where he took on the persona of the Masked Singer. He was signed to Columbia soon after.

Although active as a performer and recording artist through the fifties, Walker didn't have his first hit until his country chart-topper "Charlie's Shoes" appeared in 1962. He was quickly invited to join the GRAND OLE OPRY, and had a string of hits through the sixties, including remakes of jazz-pop songs ("Willie the Weeper" from 1962), Western-themed outings ("Cross the Brazos at Waco," 1964), and more traditional, country WEEPERS ("Bear with Me a Little Longer" [1966], "Anything Your Heart Desires" [1967], and "Thinking About You Baby" [1969]).

In the seventies, Walker continued to have hits in the then-prevalent COUNTRY-POLITAN style, including his 1970 cover of the R&B classic "When a Man Loves a Woman" and "I'm Gonna Keep On Lovin' You" from a year later. After a few more mid-seventies hits, he turned increasingly toward gospel material, returning to mainstream country in the mid-eighties for a series of duets with BARBARA FAIRCHILD, including 1986's "Answer Game."

Select Discography
The Best of Billy Walker, Deluxe 7825. Cassette-only reissue of unknown vintage.

◀ WALKER, CHARLIE

(born 1926, Collins County, TX)

Walker is best known for his 1958 hit, "Pick Me Up on Your Way Down," written by ace tunesmith HARLAN HOWARD.

Born and raised in Texas, he began his career as a vocalist in BILL BOYD's Cowboy Ramblers, joining the group in 1943. In the late forties and early fifties, he retired briefly from performing to work as a country music deejay. Signed to Columbia in the mid-fifties, he had a megahit in 1958 with "Pick Me Up on Your Way Down," a song turned down by his labelmate RAY PRICE. He continued to record for Columbia and its subsidiary Epic through the early seventies, including his HONKY-TONK trilogy "Close All the Honky Tonks" (1964), "Honky Tonk Season" (1969), and even a cover of the Rolling Stones' "Honky Tonk Women" (1970). He had a novelty hit with 1967's "Don't Squeeze My Charmin," based on the TV ads for the popular household product.

In the seventies, Walker recorded sporadically for RCA, Capitol, and SHELBY SINGLETON's revived Plantation label, with little success. He became a popular performer in Las Vegas and made an attempted (unsuccessful) comeback in 1986 with a new album for MCA.

◄ WALKER, CINDY

(born c. 1925, Mexia, TX)

Cindy Walker was one of country music's leading songwriters, writing over five hundred songs, many of which became hits for artists from ROY ORBISON to GENE AUTRY and BOB WILLS. She also had a brief recording and performing career in the forties and early fifties.

Walker was supported in her love of music by her piano-playing mother, Oree, who wrote all of her daughter's music down and accompanied her in many of her performances. The pair came to Hollywood in the late thirties, and Walker was an immediate hit when paired with Gene Autry in the C-grade cowflick *Ride Tenderfoot Ride*. She started making musicals in the early forties and so impressed Bing Crosby that he recorded her "Lone Star Trail" and arranged for her to audition for Decca Records. In 1944 she had a hit with her own "When My Blue Moon Turns to Gold Again," which has since become a BLUEGRASS standard.

After the war, Cindy hooked up with legendary WESTERN SWING bandleader Bob Wills, staying with him until the early fifties. She provided Wills with many of his better postwar hits, including "Bubbles in My Beer," "Miss Molly," "Cherokee Maiden," and "You're from Texas." In 1954 mother and daughter returned to their hometown of Mexia, Texas, where Cindy continued to write hits. Other notable Walker numbers include "Dream Baby," a big hit for Roy Orbison, "I Don't Care," originally cut by WEBB PIERCE and recently revived by RICKY SKAGGS, "Blue Canadian Rockies," cut by Gene Autry and covered by GRAM PARSONS when he was a member of the BYRDS, HANK SNOW's "The Gold Rush Is Over," and JIM REEVES's "Distant Drums."

◀ WALKER, FRANK

(born c. 1890, Fly Summit, NY; died 1965)

Frank Walker was one of the pioneering country record producers who signed such legendary acts from the SKILLET LICKERS to HANK WILLIAMS.

A World War I veteran, Walker was originally a banker who switched to booking concerts. He was hired by the Columbia Phonograph Company, as it was then known, in 1921. In 1923, he signed blues great Bessie Smith to the label, his first major contracting coup. He was put in charge of the company's country-music catalog in 1925, and traveled many times through the South arranging recording sessions, working primarily in Atlanta and Dallas. After recording the duo of Gid Tanner and Riley Puckett in New York in 1924, he put together the Skillet Lickers band featuring the two musicians. He also scripted and supervised their famous series of musical-comedy sketches, including the twelve-part "Corn Licker Still in Georgia," which were tremendously successful. He arranged for the recordings of the Skillet Lickers's main rival, CHARLIE POOLE and the North Carolina Ramblers, along with more citified country singers like VERNON DALHART. His recordings of CAJUN accordionist Louis Falcon in 1928 are said to be the first commercial recordings of this style of music.

Walker left Columbia to work in a similar capacity for RCA from 1938 to 1945 and then finished his musical career with a bang at MGM, signing a then-unknown country crooner named Hank Williams.

◀ WALKER, JERRY JEFF

(born 1942, Catskill Mountains, NY)

Jerry Jeff Walker is a one-hit songwriter who was associated with the mid-seventies OUTLAW scene in Texas and has had sporadic success as a performer.

Coming from a musical family, Walker's grandparents played in an upstate New York square-dance band and his mother and aunt performed in a local tight-harmony trio reminiscent of the Andrews Sisters. He spent most of his high-school years playing basketball, although he quit school when he was sixteen to wander around the country, eventually ending up as a streetsinger in New Orleans. He returned home to finish his schooling, and became interested in the FOLK REVIVAL music of PETE SEEGER and WOODY GUTHRIE, as well as the reissued recordings of JIMMIE RODGERS.

Walker performed on the folk coffeehouse circuit in the East and Midwest through the mid-sixties, until he met SINGER/SONGWRITER Bob Bruno who introduced him to the nascent Austin, Texas folk scene. The two joined forces in a shortlived folk-rock outfit, Circus Maximus, which recorded one album for Vanguard Records and performed sporadically.

In the late sixties, Walker's big break came in the form of a radio appearance on alternative New York radio station WBAI. Accompanied by DAVID BROMBERG, he performed his self-penned ballad, "Mr. Bojangles," inspired by a cellmate he met one night in Texas while sleeping off a drinking spree. The song was popularized over the station, and in 1971 was a big hit for the NITTY GRITTY DIRT BAND. It also earned Walker his first recording contract with Atlantic.

His first recordings were far from successful, and by the mid-seventies Walker was back in Austin. His homemade recordings were issued in 1973 by MCA Records, introducing a brief period of chart success. His second album from this period featured a cover of GUY CLARK's "LA Freeway," which was a minor hit for him.

Walker continued to record and perform through the seventies, gaining a reputation for high living and erratic performances. His voice grew huskier, probably due at least partially to his increased alcohol intake, although Walker today claims that his boozin' and partyin' image was somewhat exaggerated to fit his outlaw persona.

Walker's career in the eighties and early nineties has mostly been limited to club dates around Austin and occasional tours. He still is living off his one hit song and his image as an outlaw. His performances, however, continue to be unpredictable, ranging from god awful to listenable.

Select Discography
Driftin' Way of Life, Vanguard 73124. Reissue of 1969 album featuring Nashville session men Charlie McCoy and "Pig" Robbins.
Great Gonzos, MCA 10381. Selected cuts from MCA albums from the mid-seventies.
Live at Gruene Hall, Rykodisc 10123. 1989 live recording.

◀ WARD, WADE

(born Benjamin Wade Ward, 1892, Saddle Creek, VA; died 1971)
One of the great old-time BANJO players, Ward was part of a historic Virginia family who were active in making music for generations.

Born near Independence, Virginia in the Southwest corner of the state, Ward came from a Scotch-Irish family who had settled in the area at least as early as 1840. Wade's family moved when he was ten to a farm known as Peach Bottom Creek which was Ward's home for the remaining sixty-nine years of his life. His father, Enoch, was a fiddle player, but he had already stopped playing when his youngest son was born, and his mother knew many of the traditional mountain ballads and songs; however, it was Wade's elder brother, David Crockett Ward (known as Crockett), twenty years his senior, who was the key musical influence on his life. Crockett was a fine fiddle player and began teaching his younger brother the rudiments of banjo and fiddle playing when he was an early teen.

Although professionally a farmer all of his life, Ward began performing as a part-time musician from an early age. First, he worked with his elder brother playing for dances, festivals, and other special occasions. When he was in his twenties, Ward began a life-long association with a local auction house; his job was to attract customers with his music. He formed his first band to play at local land auctions with the team of fiddler Van Edwards and his GUITAR picking son, Earl. The guitar was a relatively new instrument in the region, and it changed the style of music playing from the old-time modal dance music to one more suited to modern chord harmonies. Ward also changed, switching from the older style clawhammer banjo style he had learned from his brother to a three-finger picked style most closely associated with popular recording artist CHARLIE POOLE.

In the early twenties, Ward's elder brother Crockett left the family farm to work in nearby Galax as a carpenter. By the early thirties, Crockett's son Fields Ward was an accomplished guitarist and vocalist, and, along with Wade, they began playing as a trio. Local fiddler "Uncle" Eck Dunford hooked up with the group to form what would be known as the Bog Trotters Band; the fifth member, Doc Davis on autoharp, was a friend of Dunford's who joined the group in the mid-thirties. The group was "discovered" by noted folklorist JOHN LOMAX and his son Alan, and recorded for the Library of Congress in 1937; for the next few years, they were prominent not only in their home region but also in the budding FOLK REVIVAL, because Alan featured them on his radio broadcasts promoting traditional folk music.

The band continued to play informally through the early fifties, when Fields left the region for a job in Maryland. At the same time, Crockett suffered from a stroke and did not play the fiddle again. In the mid-fifties, folklorists interested in the Bogtrotters band came into the region, including MIKE SEEGER and the team of Jane Rigg, Eric Davidson, and Paul Newman. The latter group was most instrumental in recording Ward through the mid-sixties; he was now primarily working with local fiddler Glen Smith. Ward's distinctive, yet simple, banjo style made him an instant celebrity in the folk revival days, and his style was widely emulated. His good humor and deep repertoire of traditional music also made him a popular performer, and he continued to record, perform, and appear at festivals until his death in 1971. Fields Ward has recorded as a singer/guitarist sporadically during the seventies for various folk labels.

Select Discography

Uncle Wade, Folkways 2380. Tribute album featuring fine playing from the sixties.

◀ WARINER, STEVE

(born 1954, Indianapolis, IN)

Originally a COUNTRYPOLITAN artist, Wariner's career has blossomed in the new country era of the late eighties, with his tough, rockin' original compositions complemented by his fine GUITAR work.

Raised in Indiana, Wariner was inspired to play guitar by his father who had his own amateur country band. The younger Wariner began performing while still in high school; after finishing his schooling, he worked as a bass player for DOTTIE WEST for three years, followed by two-and-a-half years with BOB LUMAN before signing as a solo artist to RCA in 1977. His first release, the self-composed "I'm Already Taken," was a minor hit for him, and later was covered by CONWAY TWITTY.

In the late seventies and early eighties, Wariner was produced to sound like a GLEN CAMPBELL clone. He did not perform much of his own material, and his releases were bathed in a pop-country backup that really wasn't suited to him. However, he did manage to break through in 1982 with the number-one hit, "All Roads Lead to You," while still recording in this style.

It was in the mid-eighties, when he changed to more progressive producers, that he finally hit his stride, beginning with a remake of Bob Luman's "Lonely Women Make Good Lovers" in 1984, and his first number one since 1982, "Some Fools Never Learn" from a year later. Wariner cowrote his next hit with John Hall (lead vocalist for the pop group Orleans), "You Can Dream of Me," from 1986, which had a pop/contemporary sound thanks to the presence of Orleans as backup vocalists, and the glitzy production of Tony Brown. Wariner's success led to an invitation to write a new theme song for TV's *Who's the Boss?*!

Wariner continued to move in a pop-rock direction from 1987's "Small Town Girl," cowritten by session pianist John Jarvis who had cut his musical teeth as a sideman for Rod Stewart (although his country credentials were strong too; he tickled the ivories on GEORGE STRAIT's novelty hit "All My Exes Live in Texas" from the same year).

After a couple of more pop-ish hits under the hands of Brown, Wariner switched to producer Jimmy Bowen and scored a hit in 1989 with the countrified "Where Did I Go Wrong," his second self-written number-one song. This was followed by his jazzy "I Got Dreams," cowritten with Bill LaBounty, which featured Wariner's scat singing (a novelty for a country recording).

In the early nineties, Wariner moved to Arista and further hits, including 1992's number-one song "The Tips of My Fingers" and "Like a River to the Sea" from a year later.

Select Discography
Life's Highway, MCA 31002. 1986 album.
Greatest Hits, Vols. 1 and 2, MCA 42032/10357. The first collection draws on his recordings from 1985 to 1987, the second takes him up to 1991.
I Am Ready, Arista 18691. 1991 album.

◀ WATSON, DOC

(born Arthel Watson, 1923, Deep Gap, NC)

Watson is a mellow-voiced singer/guitarist who is one of the most talented flatpickers, influencing an entire generation of players, including TONY RICE and countless others.

Coming from a musical family and blind from birth, Doc early on showed capabilities on a number of instruments. Inspired by his idol MERLE TRAVIS, he began playing fiddle tunes and elaborate melody fills on the GUITAR. By the late fifties, he was working in a local band playing electric lead guitar on ROCKABILLY, country, and pop songs.

Folklorist Ralph Rinzler discovered Watson while recording old-time BANJO player CLARENCE "TOM" ASHLEY. Watson was brought North and soon began performing and recording with his son, Merle (born 1949; died 1985), on second guitar. He became a major star on the FOLK-REVIVAL circuit, recording with JEAN

RITCHIE and also as a duet with BLUEGRASS mandolinist BILL MONROE, although these recordings were never legally released until 1993.

Watson's big break came when he was included on the sessions for *Will the Circle Be Unbroken*, the NITTY GRITTY DIRT BAND's homage to country music legends. Watson's vocals were prominently featured, as well as his legendary flatpicking. He was immediately signed to the Poppy label, where he recorded two Grammy-winning LPs that suffered from far more cluttered productions than his earlier work for folk-label Vanguard Records.

Watson's repertoire was always a mix of traditional country songs, tin-pan alley novelties, country songs from recordings made from the twenties through the fifties, and favorite songs from the repertoires of other performers like JIMMIE RODGERS and even bluesman Mississippi John Hurt who Watson came to admire while both men were performing at folk festivals in the sixties. Son Merle added a strong blues influence when, influenced by Southern rockers the Allman Brothers, he took up slide guitar. Doc's relaxed vocal style, typical of the Kentucky/North Carolina region where he was born, and warm stage presence made him immediately accessible to urban audiences in ways many traditional artists are not.

Although he remains active as a performer, the death of his son Merle from a farm accident in the mid-eighties devastated him and he went into semiretirement.

Select Discography

Doc Watson Family, Smithsonian/Folkways 40012. Reissue of fine early-sixties album featuring Doc with his relatives.

The Essential, Vanguard 45/46. Various cuts from Vanguard albums and live cuts from the Newport Folk Festival.

Pickin' the Blues, Flying Fish 70352. 1983 album featuring Merle playing lots of slide guitar.

My Dear Old Southern Home, Sugar Hill 3795. 1992 album featuring backup by the Nashville Bluegrass Band.

◀ WATSON, GENE

(born 1943, Palestine, TX)

Watson is another difficult-to-characterize SINGER/SONGWRITER from the wilds of Texas who has had only minor success on the country charts while developing a cult following.

Born in Palestine, he was raised in Paris, Texas. At sixteen, he made his first recordings for Uni Records in a teen-pop style. Four years later, he moved to Houston in search of a musical career, singing at night at The Dynasty Club while working as an auto-body repairman by day. After a regional hit with 1975's "Love in the Afternoon," he was picked up by Capitol Records.

He continued to record in a solid HONKY-TONK mold for several labels, scoring hits with 1979's "Farewell Party" (his backup band was renamed the Farewell Party Band in honor of this number three country hit), the honky-tonk anthem "Should I Go Home (Or Should I Go Crazy)" from a year later, and particularly 1981's "Fourteen Carat Mind," his sole number-one country hit. He has continued to record through the eighties and early nineties with moderate success, but his un-willingness to change his style to bow to contemporary tastes has made him mostly a cult figure on the edges of mainstream country.

Select Discography

Greatest Hits, Curb 77393. His first hits drawn from Capitol recordings made in the mid-seventies.

Greatest Hits, MCA 31128. Hits from the late seventies and early eighties.

Back in the Fire, Warner Bros. 23832. 1989 comeback album.

◀ WEAVER BROTHERS AND ELVIRY, THE

(Leon "Abner" Weaver [mandolin, guitar, fiddle, saw]; Frank "Cicero" Weaver [banjo, saw]; Elviry [born June Petrie, 1891; died 1977; piano, mandolin, ukulele])

The Weaver Brothers and Elviry were a country-novelty trio who performed in tent and traveling shows, vaudeville, and eventually films.

The two brothers portrayed country rubes, with Leon beginning the act around 1902, bringing his brother in soon after, and enlisting June Petrie some eleven years later. Leon is thought to have been the first performer to play the musical saw on the vaudeville stage. While the brothers clowned around, Elviry acted the part of the put-upon wife, with her deadpan, exasperated facial expressions the perfect foil to the brother's broad humor. Around 1927, Elviry formed The Home Folks, a country harmony group that toured with the trio made up of various members of their extended families. Initially married to Leon, Petrie then married Frank, without apparently disrupting the teamwork.

The group became a model for country comedy acts and, through their exten-sive touring, were quite influential on establishing the image of "hayseed" char-acters. They also performed a wide variety of material, from comic instrumentals and songs to traditional heart songs; Elviry was particularly well-known for her rendition of "Just Tell Them That You Saw Me," the tearjerking story of a good woman gone wrong.

◀ WEEPER

A weeper is a song dripping with heavy sentiments, often dealing with romantic loss, death, or betrayal.

Overly sentimental songs have long been favorites in country circles, although it's sometimes difficult for the outsider to determine just how seriously these songs are meant to be taken. Songs of orphaned children, lost mothers, betrayed lovers, train wrecks, coal-mining disasters, flood, fire, and famine seem to win the hearts and ears of country audiences, no matter what the decade. Perhaps because life in the rural South was so difficult—with deep poverty, disease, and little oppor-tunity for improvement daily facts of life—the country audience gravitated towards music that had a strong "blue" or sad component. The very first country hit—

VERNON DALHART's recording of "The Wreck of the Old 97"—falls squarely in this category; despite an upbeat tune, the song tells of an unmitigated disaster, a train wreck that took the lives of the devoted engineer and his colleagues. Other classic weepers of the early country era include many of the BLUE SKY BOYS' hit recordings ("The Sweetest Gift, A Mother's Smile" tells of how a prisoner waits anxiously for his mother's visit, not to gain "parole or pardon, no sacks of silver, or any gold, you see," but rather the gift of her smile) as well as many classics by the CARTER FAMILY ("Bury Me Beneath the Willow" tells of an unrequited lover's request to be buried "under the weeping willow tree" so that "maybe then she'll [his beloved will] think of me.")

In the period after World War II, when honky-tonks became centers of hard drinkin' and hell raisin', a new crop of weepers arose. HANK WILLIAMS's "Your Cheatin' Heart" is a typical song in the new style; it's weepy content is matched by the "crying" sound of the steel guitar and Williams's very emotional delivery (he sounds as if he's about to break down in tears). Often, the songs tell of a young man who is lured to his doom by a "HONKY-TONK angel," a loose woman who hangs out at a bar hoping to ensnare and lead astray the dedicated, hard-working country boy (needless to say, this scenario stretched the truth, since many young country boys were looking for trouble in the bars). One of the many classics in this genre is "She's More to Be Pitied Than Scolded," which muses philosophically on the plight of the barroom beauty (with the immortal chorus "She's more to be pitied than scolded/She needs to be loved, not despised/Too much beer and wine, too many good times/The lure of the honky-tonk wrecked her young life"). HANK THOMPSON's "Wild Side of Life" is a classic of this genre, and it inspired the first great weeper sung by a female, KITTY WELLS's answer song, "It Wasn't God Who Made Honky Tonk Angels," which finally presented the woman's point of view.

The sixties saw the weeper formula become an almost exclusively female domain. Stronger female vocalists, like TAMMY WYNETTE, had hits with big-lunged ballads like "Stand By Your Man," but songs like Wynette's "D-I-V-O-R-C-E," telling of the painful breakdown of a marriage which a mother tries to hide from the prying ears of her children, are more typical of the women's repertoire of the period.

Although no-holds-barred weepers are not as often heard today, the tradition lives on in various guises, ranging from the more upbeat ("Forever and Ever Men" by RANDY TRAVIS, with its vow of eternal love, verges on the bathetic) to songs mixed with a mid-seventies SINGER/SONGWRITER sensibility ("The River" by GARTH BROOKS), to pop-rock weepers (K. D. LANG's duet with ROY ORBISON on his classic "Crying," a teen-pop hit of the early sixties in the weeper tradition), to big-throated pop ballads like "Something in Red" by LORRIE MORGAN. Still, some artists continue to cut out-and-out weepers, like SHELBY LYNNE's early hits "The Hurtin' Side" and "I Love You So Much It Hurts," and even ROSANNE CASH's more cerebral numbers like "The Wheel" hint at weeper conventions of the past.

Following some other critics, I sometimes refer to "two-" or "three-hanky" weepers; these weepers are so sentimental that the listener would need the stated number of hankies to make it through the song!

◀ WELLS, KITTY

(born Muriel Deason, 1919, Nashville, TN)

One of the pioneering female country vocalists, Wells's fifties tear-drenched ballads put women on the country music map. Previously, solo female vocalists were few and far between; most Nashville executives felt the recording-buying public for country music was too conservative to accept a woman singing about lovin', cheatin', and losin'. The popularity of Wells's recordings changed this attitude, and paved the way for PATSY CLINE's great success at the decade's end.

Deason began performing on local radio with her sisters and a cousin as The Deason Sisters in 1936. A year later, she wed Johnny Wright, a talented musician. Soon after, she began performing with Johnny along with her sister-in-law, Louise Wright, as Johnny Wright and The Harmony Girls. In 1939, Johnny added Jack Anglin (who had married Louise) to the band to form the Tennessee Hillbillies (later the Tennessee Mountain Boys). In 1942, Jack was drafted, so Johnny began performing with his wife as a duo; at this time, he christened her "Kitty Wells," taking her stage name from the folk ballad "Sweet Kitty Wells." After the war, Jack reunited with Johnny to form the popular country duo, JOHNNY AND JACK. In 1947 they joined the *Louisiana Hayride* radio program, which made their reputation, winning them a contract with RCA in Nashville.

In 1949 Kitty began recording gospel numbers backed by Johnny and Jack's band, with little success. Meanwhile, the duo's recordings sold well. Semiretired as a housewife, she was lured back into the studio for one more try at recording in 1952. Paul Cohen, a Decca label executive, wanted her to record a woman's answer song to the immensely popular HANK THOMPSON song "Wild Side of Life." "It Wasn't God Who Made Honky Tonk Angels" rightfully asserted that men had to share the blame for the "fallen women" who frequented the rough-and-tumble backwoods bars. The song shot up the country charts, making Wells's reputation.

Through the fifties and sixties, Wells proved she was no one-hit wonder. On solo recordings ("I Can't Stop Loving You," "Mommy for a Day," "Heartbreak U.S.A."), and duets with RED FOLEY ("One by One," "As Long As I Live") she honed her image as the gutsy good girl (sometimes gone wrong). Her vocal style and personality were far more laidback than traditional country female performers, like COUSIN EMMY or MARTHA CARSON, who tended to whoop it up on stage and recordings. Instead, she sang in a style that was closer to fifties mainstream pop, although her voice embodied a heart-tugging regret that was pure country.

Although Wells continued to record from the mid-sixties through the seventies, her major hit-making years were over. She continued to tour and perform for her loyal fans with her longtime husband, appearing occasionally on the Opry, and the duo operate their own museum in their suburban Nashville home.

Select Discography

The Queen of Country, Bear Family 15638. Four CDs featuring all of Wells's RCA and Decca recordings from 1949 to 1958, with an illustrated booklet by Charles Wolfe.

Country Music Hall of Fame, MCA 10081. Reissues Decca recordings cut between 1952 and 1965, including all of her hits in the heartache genre.

◀ WEST, DOTTIE

(born Dorothy Marie Marsh, 1932, near McMinnville, TN; died 1991)

West was one of the popular exponents of the NASHVILLE SOUND during the sixties and seventies.

Raised in a tiny farm community, West was inspired to become a musician by her fiddling father. She made her debut on local radio when she was twelve, although she had not yet decided to make music a career. She enrolled at Tennessee Technical College where she began performing with guitarist Bill West on radio and at dances; the couple were married in 1953 and relocated to the Cleveland, Ohio, area. Dottie appeared on Ohio's *Landmark Jamboree*, a Western-style TV show, during the fifties, as well as performing with singer Kathy Dearth, aka Kathy Dee, as The Kay-Dots, a vocal duo who blended country-styled harmonies with pop material.

In 1958 Dottie began traveling to Nashville on weekends, securing a recording contract with the BLUEGRASS-oriented Starday label a year later, and then with the jazz label Atlantic. She moved permanently to Nashville in 1961, and had her first big break in 1963 when JIM REEVES had a hit with her song "Is This Me?" She was signed to RCA and producer CHET ATKINS, and the duo produced her first hit, the self-written "Here Comes My Baby," a year later, leading to membership in the GRAND OLE OPRY. This was followed by other hits in the typical Nashville Sound style of the day, replete with oohing choruses, including 1966's "Would You Hold It Against Me?" and "Paper Mansions" from a year later.

Always a plaintive vocalist, West began turning out a slew of hanky-wringing hits. She even recorded a theme album in 1966 called *Suffer Time*, chronicling, in the words of the liner notes, the story of "an eternal loser"! West produced some classic Kleenex soakers, including 1968's "If You Go Away," two original songs, the maudlin 1969 hit, "Clinging to My Baby's Hand" and 1970's "The Cold Hand of Fate," and 1971's "Once You Were Mine" and "Six Weeks Every Summer," telling of the "heart-wrenching" guilt of a single parent.

West's popularity as a singer and songwriter reached its height in 1973 when she was invited by Coca-Cola to write a series of jingles for the popular brew; one of them, "Country Sunshine," became a big hit in that year. Her solo hits came more sporadically after the mid-seventies, although she still managed a couple of number ones, including "A Lesson in Leavin' " from 1980 and "Are You Happy Baby" and "What Are We Doin' in Love" from a year later, the later an uncredited duet with KENNY ROGERS.

At the same time, West became a popular duet partner, first singing with Justin Tubb, and then DON GIBSON, before forming a very successful partnership with Kenny Rogers, recording several racy titles between 1978 and 1981. However, West's career slowed in the eighties, culminating in the foreclosure of her Nashville mansion in 1990, and a couple of failed marriages (she had divorced original husband Bill West in 1972 to marry several younger musicians and associates in succession); a bankruptcy filing and public auction followed in 1991. Just as she was about to make a comeback, West was killed in an automobile accident on her way to the *Grand Ole Opry*. Daughter SHELLY WEST was also a popular country singer.

Select Discography
Greatest Hits, Curb 77555.

◀ WEST, SHELLEY

(born 1958, Cleveland, OH)

Daughter of popular chanteuse DOTTIE WEST, Shelley had some hits in a similar COUNTRYPOLITAN style to her mother before fading from the scene.

Shelley got her start as a backup singer in her mother's road show, beginning when she was sixteen years old. She married Allen Frizzell, who worked in her mother's band, in 1978. Frizzell came from another country dynasty, with brother LEFTY FRIZZELL a noted country crooner and brother DAVID FRIZZELL an up-and-coming star. In fact, David and Shelley teamed up as a duo by 1979, and began touring on the West Coast.

In 1980, the duo hit it big with "You're the Reason God Made Oklahoma," featured in Clint Eastwood's film *Any Which Way You Can*. Follow-up hits included "A Texas State of Mind," "Another Honky-Tonk Night on Broadway," and "I Just Came Here to Dance," all in the country-pop style that was then prevalent. Shelley went solo in 1983, having another number-one hit with her version of "José Cuervo," a song that supposedly boosted sales of the popular tequila by twenty-seven percent! In the same year, she divorced Frizzell. In 1985, she remarried and abandoned her musical career.

◀ WEST, SPEEDY

(born Wesley Webb West, 1924, Springfield, MO)

West was a pioneering recording artist on the PEDAL STEEL GUITAR, whose duets with Jimmy Bryant recorded in the fifties remain some of the finest country instrumentals of all time.

Born in Missouri, West took up the steel guitar when he was thirteen years old. After serving in World War II, he settled in Southern California, where he found work with SPADE COOLEY's and HANK PENNY's bands. In 1948 West is said to have been the first steel player to switch to the newly introduced pedal steel guitar. In the early fifties, he became a regular on CLIFFIE STONE's *Hometown Jamboree* TV and radio shows, as well as beginning a long association as a studio musician and solo artist with Capitol Records. Hooking up with Jimmy Bryant—the two became known as the "Flaming Guitars"—they produced some wonderful instrumentals. It is said that neither heard the other's work before they entered the studio, and the spontaneous, good-natured fun of classics like 1953's "Speedin' West" and "Stainless Steel" from a year later remain classics of their kind.

Through the fifties, Speedy was much in demand in sessions for both pop and country acts, and as a performing artist. Rather than sitting passively at the pedal steel guitar, he developed an energetic stage act, making him one of the more glitzy of steel players. In 1960 he helped a young artist name LORETTA LYNN get her start by producing her first record, "I'm a Honky Tonk Girl," for the tiny Zero label. Later in the sixties, he relocated to Tulsa, Oklahoma, where he worked as a consultant to Fender Guitars while running a recreational vehicle business and playing on the side. In 1981 a debilitating stroke ended his performing career, although he continued to be a presence at steel-guitar conventions.

◀ WESTERN SWING

Western swing is a unique combination of stringband music with jazz styles. It was born in the Texas/Oklahoma region in the late twenties. There, musicians were influenced by blues and jazz recordings, as well as early pop crooners, to form an amalgam of traditional country sounds with a swinging accompaniment.

The band credited with creating this sound was the LIGHT CRUST DOUGHBOYS in 1931 and 1932, featuring fiddler BOB WILLS and vocalist MILTON BROWN. Soon, Wills and Brown formed their own bands. Although Brown's band was in many ways hotter than Wills, it was short-lived (Brown died in the mid-thirties following an automobile accident); meanwhile, Wills's band mushroomed into a full jazz ensemble, with a large horn section and the crooning vocals of Tommy Duncan. The band's instrumentation also included smooth steel guitar, ragtime-influenced piano, and often twin harmony fiddling (Wills's fiddling was fairly primitive and he usually took a backseat to the more modern stringmen he employed). Wills's repertoire was made up of popular songs, blues, traditional fiddle tunes (often jazzed up), and big-band standards.

A second wave of Western swing came in the late forties in Southern California, where many Western musicians had settled after the war to appear in the countless B, C, D, and F grade cowpoke films that the lesser Hollywood studios (particularly Republic) were busily churning out. Wills's postwar band returned to the stripped-down sound of his original unit, now featuring electric guitar, steel guitar, and even electric MANDOLIN (played by Tiny Moore), with various vocalists (Wills had fired Duncan in 1948 in a fit of anger). Another popular California-based band was led by SPADE COOLEY.

The fifties and sixties were lean times for the music. But then, in the early seventies, new, young bands began playing the music, like ASLEEP AT THE WHEEL, introducing a new generation to the Western swing sound. Meanwhile, country superstar MERLE HAGGARD recorded an entire album in homage to Wills's music, and then brought the star out of retirement for his famous last session in 1973. A slew of reissues of early recordings in the seventies, eighties, and nineties have made even the lesser-known bands famous once again.

◖ WHITE, LARI

(born 1966, Dunedin, FL)

A perky NEW-COUNTRY songstress, White comes from a country-gospel background. Her career has been championed by RODNEY CROWELL, who employed her as a backup singer and produced her first successful album.

White has been singing and performing since age four, when she performed with her parents as a gospel trio (her grandfather was a primitive Baptist minister). With the arrival on the scene of a younger brother, the group became known as the White Family Singers, performing primarily gospel material for church and community groups. Secular music crept into the act when the two children began performing a medley of ELVIS PRESLEY tunes, and found that the audience enjoyed seeing them ape the master's moves.

Lari performed in her teen years with a local rock band, also performing Broadway tunes at talent shows, and earning a scholarship at the University of Miami in music engineering and voice. She began writing her own material, while working in local clubs and recording background vocals and advertising jingles. She checked out the music scenes in Los Angeles, Chicago, and New York, finally arriving in Nashville in 1988. She appeared on TNN's *You Can Be a Star*, a televised amateur talent contest, winning first prize. Soon after, she signed with Capitol and released a single, "Flying Above the Rain," that had some local popularity; she also signed as a songwriter with RONNIE MILSAP's publishing group and began studying acting.

White spent the late eighties appearing in Nashville dinner theaters while waiting for her big break. An ASCAP showcase created interest in her songwriting, and then in 1991 she was invited by country-rocker Rodney Crowell to sing backup on his summer tour. She signed with RCA in 1992, and Crowell agreed to produce her debut album.

The good-natured White still brings a wholesome religiosity to her music, even though she might be belting out a HONKY-TONK lament. Her big hit so far is 1993's "What a Woman Wants," not exactly a liberation anthem, although not as regressive as some country songs.

Select Discography
Lead Me Not, RCA 66117. Her debut LP.

◖ WHITES, THE

(Buck [mandolin, guitar, piano, vocals]; Sharon [guitar, vocals]; Cheryl [bass, vocals])

The Whites are a family band who have gone through many permutations in their nearly thirty-year existence, from BLUEGRASS group to mainstream country to gospel.

Father Buck was Oklahoma-born and Texas-raised, playing both HONKY-TONK styled piano and bluegrass/WESTERN SWING on MANDOLIN, becoming something of a legend in the area; his claim to fame as a recording artist in the fifties was that he was the pianist on the session that produced Slim Willet's "Don't Let the Stars Get in Your Eyes" in 1952. He retired to take a job as a pipefitter in Arkansas, but took up music again when his two daughters, Sharon and Cheryl, began playing guitars and singing as preteens. Along with wife Pat Goza White, they formed The Whites as a bluegrass group in 1966. Five years later, Buck retired from his day job, and the family relocated to Nashville in search of success.

They made their first recording in 1972 for the bluegrass/country label County Records as Buck White and the Down Home Folks, a fairly straightforward recording in the progressive bluegrass style that was popular at the time. Buck also made some recordings on his own as a mandolinist in the mid-seventies, thanks to a renewal of interest in the instrument created by the jazz-tinged recordings of DAVID GRISSMAN. The trio moved into a solid country direction with their 1978 album, *Poor Folks Pleasures*, issued by the more pop-oriented division of County, Sugar Hill. They toured with EMMYLOU HARRIS a year later, where Sharon met her future husband, RICKY SKAGGS, who was then serving as Harris's musical director.

The Whites had their greatest chart success in the early through mid-eighties, beginning with 1981's rerecording of "Give Me the Pillow You Dream On." Most of their hits were remakes of fifties WEEPERS, prominently featuring Sharon's lead vocals with Buck and Cheryl limited pretty much to harmonizing. In 1984 the group joined the GRAND OLE OPRY, and four years later switched directions slightly by cutting an all-gospel album (both Skaggs and Sharon White have become fundamentalist Christians).

All in all, the Whites are a sweet-tempered harmony group who, while not enjoying chart-busting success, have brought an element of traditional family harmonizing back to country music.

◀ WHITLEY, KEITH

(born 1954, Sandy Hook, KY; died 1989)
One of the finer new country performers, Whitley's career was sadly cut short when he died of alcohol poisoning at age thirty-four.

Whitley began performing from a young age, working on local radio by the time he was nine. Along with high-school buddy RICKY SKAGGS, he developed a love of the traditional music of the STANLEY BROTHERS; the two formed a duo that so impressed Ralph Stanley that he asked them to join his band in 1971. Whitley remained with Stanley for six years as lead vocalist, and then performed with J. D. CROWE in his PROGRESSIVE BLUEGRASS band, The New South, from 1977 to 1982. A year later, he moved to Nashville, and was signed to RCA, one of the first new traditionalists to record.

Unlike Skaggs, who kept one foot in traditional country, Whitley embraced whole-heartedly more mainstream Nashville sounds. He wed LORRIE MORGAN, daughter of well-known country singer GEORGE MORGAN; she would achieve her greatest success as a performer after Whitley's death. His first hit came in 1986 with "Miami, My Amy," which reached number fourteen on the country charts, followed two years later by his first number one, "Don't Close Your Eyes," from

Whitley's third album, the first that he coproduced and the first that he felt really reflected his sound. The same album produced two other hits, "When You Say Nothing At All," written by the popular Paul Overstreet-Don Schlitz songwriting team, as well as "I'm No Stranger to the Rain" which wasn't released until early 1989. Already suffering from alcoholism, Whitley was found dead at home in May of 1989. His death made him something of a country-music martyr, like many other artists who die young, helping propel his posthumous hits "I Wonder Do You Think of Me," shortly after his death, and "I'm Over You," a year later, to the top of the charts. A 1994 memorial album featuring many NEW-COUNTRY stars attests to Whitley's continued stature, at least among his fellow musicians.

Select Discography

I Wonder Do You Think of Me, RCA 9809. His last album, completed just before his death due to alcoholism, with fine steel guitar by Paul Franklin and a whole slew of beer-soaked laments.

◀ WHITLEY, RAY

(born 1901, Atlanta, GA; died 1979)

A popular singing cowboy and songwriter, Whitley provided GENE AUTRY with many of his biggest hits, including "Back in the Saddle Again."

After serving in the navy, Whitley settled in the New York area, where he worked as an electrician and steelworker while playing music on the side. He successfully auditioned for the New York–based WHN *Barn Dance* in the early thirties, and became cohost of the show with TEX RITTER by the middle of the decade. He began recording for the budget ARC label as well as bigger Decca Records, producing hits with his version of JIMMIE RODGER's "Blue Yodel Blues" and the topical "Last Flight of Wiley Post." He was among the first cowboy performers to use the newly introduced "jumbo"-size Gibson SJ-200, which became the standard instrument for cowpokes everywhere.

Whitley was one of the first of the singing cowboys to head West, settling in Hollywood in 1936. Between 1938 and 1942, he made a series of shorts for RKO as well as appearing as the musical sidekick to cowboy star Tim Holt. His last film appearance was as the ranch manager in James Dean's swansong, *Giant*.

Meanwhile, Whitley hooked up with noted producer FRED ROSE, and the duo cowrote a number of horsey classics for singer Gene Autry, including "Back in the Saddle Again," "Lonely River," "I Hang My Head and Cry," and "Ages and Ages Ago." In the fifties, Whitley gave up performing to become a manager, working for a later incarnation of the SONS OF THE PIONEERS and popular cowpoke JIMMY WAKELY. His later years were spent appearing at cowboy film festivals; he died in 1979.

◀ WHITMAN, SLIM

(born Otis Dewey Whitman, Jr., 1924, Tampa, FL)

Anyone who suffered from insomnia in the late seventies and early eighties is surely familiar with the late-late-night TV ads for Slim Whitman, the artist whose records have "outsold Elvis." His wooden demeanor, heavily greased-back hair, and mechanical GUITAR strumming gave miles of smiles to everyone addicted to country kitsch. Despite the lowball charm of his commercials, Whitman was laughing all the way to the bank, with his direct-mail sales generating enough income to keep him supplied with Brylcream for many years to come.

Beginning as a professional baseball player, Whitman began singing in local bars in the late forties to augment his income. This led to a contract with RCA in 1949, where he scored moderate success with Western-flavored numbers like "Casting My Lasso in the Sky." In 1952 he joined Imperial, where he immediately scored with "Indian Love Call," the hoary old chestnut that had previously been a hit for Jeanette MacDonald and Nelson Eddy. Whitman's high tenor voice, augmented by frequent yodeling on this record, was a novelty on country and pop charts. He continued to record pop songs with a Western theme through the mid-fifties.

Although Whitman's U.S. popularity dried up, he remained tremendously successful in England and Europe, where his lonesome vocals and heavy use of crying steel guitar seemed just the thing for wannabe Western wranglers. His latter day fame in the U.S. came with the successful television marketing campaign of the early eighties.

Select Discography

The Best of Slim Whitman, 1952–1972, Rhino 70976. All the Slim you need in one handy package.

◀ WHITTIER, HENRY

(born William Henry Whittier, 1892, near Fries, VA; died 1941)

Whittier was one of the first to record traditional mountain songs, most closely associated with "The Wreck of the Old 97," which was covered by citified country singer VERNON DALHART to become country music's first million seller.

A mill worker, Whittier was also a multi-instrumentalist who was most skilled as a harmonica player, but also played fiddle, organ, piano, and GUITAR. Not a particularly talented singer, he made some test recordings for the General Phonograph Corporation in 1923 (who owned the OKeh label) which were considered to be so bad that they were thought to be unreleasable. However, when FIDDLIN' JOHN CARSON scored a hit with "Little Old Log Cabin in the Lane," also released by OKeh, the company reconsidered and issued Whittier's recordings, including "The Wreck of the Old 97," in 1924.

Whittier's best recordings were made as one half of the team of Grayson and Whittier. George Bannon Grayson was a blind fiddler/vocalist, and the duo made some fine recordings between 1927 and 1929, including several songs that have entered the BLUEGRASS repertoire, most notably the instrumental "Lee Highway

Blues." The Depression ended their recording career, although the duo continued to work together until Grayson was killed in an automobile accident in the mid-thirties. Whittier also recorded as an accompanist to the female fiddle player ROBA STANLEY, and led band recordings under the name of the Virginia Breakdowners.

Although only a passable guitarist and not the greatest singer, the success of Whittier's recordings showed the skeptical New York recording executives that there was a market for country music, and along with pioneers like John Carson, he paved the way for the next generation of performers.

◀ WILBURN BROTHERS

(Doyle born 1930, Thayer, MO; died 1982; Teddy born 1931)

A kind of watered-down LOUVIN BROTHERS, the Wilburn Brothers had considerable success in the fifties and sixties releasing a series of pleasant if somewhat predictable recordings. They are best remembered for helping launch the career of LORETTA LYNN by featuring her on their mid-sixties syndicated country music show.

Originally part of a musical family act featuring their parents, brothers, and older sister, the group began performing locally, eventually gaining enough fame to be invited to perform on the GRAND OLE OPRY in 1941. Soon after, the group moved to the *Louisiana Hayride* radio show, remaining there until 1951 when the brothers were drafted into the army. On their return from service in 1953, they struck out as a duo, linking up with WEBB PIERCE and FARON YOUNG for package tours. They signed with Decca, releasing a series of antiseptic hits, from 1956's "Go Away With Me" through the early sixties discs "Trouble's Back in Town," "Tell Her No," "It's Another World," and "Hurt Her Once for Me." They also recorded covers of country and pop-ish items, even cutting a cover of Nat King Cole's cover of "Answer Me My Love." Many of their later recordings were marred by the inclusion of choruses and tinklin' keyboards that make mid-sixties Nashville records such a chore to listen to today.

In the early sixties, they founded their own talent agency with Smiley Wilson, the Wil-Helm Agency, complementing their Sure-Fire Music publishing operation. These two businesses made them powerful brokers on the Nashville scene, along with their regular TV appearances on their own variety program. They published many of Loretta Lynn's early classics, until business disagreements led to a nasty separation in the early seventies. The duo continued to perform on the Opry until brother Doyle died after battling cancer in 1982, when Teddy left performing to focus on the family business.

Select Discography

Retrospective, MCA 25990. Their best-known hits.

◀ WILD ROSE

(c. 1988–ongoing: Wanda Vick [vocals, many instruments]; Pam Gadd [banjo, vocals]; Pam Perry [guitar, vocals]; Kathy Mac [bass]; Nancy Given [drums])

Wild Rose is a NEW-COUNTRY quintet who emphasize their perky good looks and up-tempo harmonies.

The group has a fine pedigree, with each member an accomplished instrumentalist, despite the still-prevalent stereotype that women are not capable string-benders. Both Gadd and Perry come out of the New Coon Creek Girls (named in honor of the original thirties-era band led by LILY MAE LEDFORD), with Vick and Given alumni of PORTER WAGONER's Right Combination, an all-girl combo featured on his Opry performances, and Mac coming from a Nashville-based female night-club outfit known as Tina Carroll and The Nashville Satins. Although they have somewhat of a more traditional flavor than other Nashville-based outfits, they carry forward in their music a strong tradition of Nashville-pop styles.

Although made up of women, the group is not particularly feminist in their choice of material (like, for example, CATHY FINK's Blue Rose band), nor in their dress, which is typical glitzy Nashville stage garb. With their well-puffed hair and cheerful stage manner, they appeal strongly to the traditional values of their audience (i.e., although they are performing women, they don't threaten their audience by questioning a woman's role as basically being limited to home and hearth). Still, the fact that they all play their own instruments and emphasize their talents as performers has been inspirational to other female performers working their way up the ranks. The band first broke through with "Breakin' New Ground" in 1989, followed by "Going Down Swinging."

Select Discography

Breaking New Ground, Liberty 93885. Their debut album.

◀ WILKIN, MARIJOHN

(born Marijohn Melson, 1918, Sanger, TX)

Wilkin is a well-known country songwriter, famous for "Long Black Veil" and countless other classics of the late fifties and sixties.

Born in Texas, Wilkin came to Nashville when she was already forty years old, taking a job playing piano in a local bar while signing up as a house songwriter for one of Nashville's many music factories. Her big breaks came a year later, when LEFTY FRIZZELL had a major hit with her "Long Black Veil" and STONEWALL JACKSON was equally lucky with "Waterloo." She wrote "P.T. 109," a 1962 hit for future sausage-monger JIMMY DEAN, a patriotic, story song relating President Kennedy's achievements in World War II; the profits enabled her to open her own music publishing house, Buckwood, the first Nashville music publisher owned by a woman.

Although Wilkin lapsed into a period of heavy drinking, Buckwood became a center for young singer/songwriters who were not acceptable to the Nashville establishment, such as KRIS KRISTOFFERSON. Kristofferson helped Wilkin out of her slump by cowriting with her 1974's "One Day at a Time," which was eventually recorded by over two hundred artists. Wilkin took this as a sign that the Lord had bigger plans for her, and since the mid-seventies has been exclusively writing and performing gospel music.

◀ WILLIAMS, DON

(born 1939, Floydada, TX)

Williams is nicknamed "The Gentle Giant" for his relaxed, crooning vocal style; he was most popular during the COUNTRYPOLITAN craze of the seventies, when pop-style balladry was big business in Nashville.

The son of an automobile mechanic, Williams was taught guitar by his mother, and began playing as a teenager in the rocking country styles that were popular at the time. After finishing high school and serving in the army, Williams began performing as a duo at nights with a friend named Lofton Kline; they hooked up with another local performer, Susan Taylor, to form the Pozo Seco Singers in 1964. A year later, they broke through on the pop charts with "Time." The group remained together until 1971, with a few more minor pop hits.

Williams followed Taylor to Nashville to work as a songwriter in support of her nascent solo career in the early seventies. There he hooked up with producer Allen Reynolds who worked for noted recording engineer/performer JACK CLEMENT. Clements had just formed his own JMI label, and quickly signed Williams. Williams had minor hits with his first two releases, but then hit it big with 1974's "We Should Be Together," leading to a contract with ABC/Dot, and his first number one, "I Wouldn't Want to Live If You Didn't Love Me."

The hitmaking continued through the seventies, all characterized by simple productions emphasizing Don's laid-back vocalizing. His resonant baritone voice led him to be compared with JIM REEVES, and like another country hit maker of the era, KENNY ROGERS, he managed somehow to combine pop schmoozing with enough country sentiments to appeal to a fairly broad audience. Other typical Williams hits include the bathetically romantic "Til the Rivers All Run Dry," co-written with Wayland Holyfield, from 1976; 1977's "I'm Just a Country Boy," written by Marshall Baker and Fred Hellerman (who was one of the founders of the first great FOLK-REVIVAL group, the Weavers), which became a signature tune for the singer; 1979's upbeat good-ol'-boy anthem "Tulsa Time" (which was covered by Eric Clapton a year later for the pop charts!); and his biggest seller, 1980's "I Believe in You."

The eighties saw a slowing of Williams career, although he continued to turn out records in his patented style. After a successful duet with EMMYLOU HARRIS on "If I Needed You" in 1981, he released the Bible-belt thumper "Lord, I Hope This Day Is Good," a 1982 number-one country record. This was followed by 1983's "If Hollywood Don't Need You," given a boost by its references to celebrities like Burt Reynolds with whom Williams had worked in the films *W. W. and the Dixie Dancekings* and *Smokey and the Bandit II*. His sound changed slightly in 1984 with

"That's the Thing About Love" which featured light sax playing by Nashville sessionman Jim Horn.

Williams retired for a while in the mid-eighties due to continuing back trouble, but returned to recording again for new label Capitol in 1986. His last number one came that same year with "Heartbeat in the Darkness," cowritten by AMAZING RHYTHM ACES vocalist Russell Smith. It was an unusual song for Williams, with its slight R&B flavor, but he managed to mold it into his distinctive laidback schmoozy style. Williams switched to RCA in 1989, and had a number-two hit a year later with "Back in My Younger Days." Dedicated to life on his farm near Nashville, Williams continues to perform and record, although his hitmaking days are more or less over.

Select Discography

Greatest Hits, Vol. 1–4, MCA 31249/31172/31247/31248.

◀ WILLIAMS, HANK

(born Hiram Williams, 1923, Georgiana, AL; died 1953)

Williams was America's greatest HONKY-TONK performer, whose unaffected singing style and bluesy songs that were tinged with a rough sense of humor revolutionized country music after World War II. His early death insured him a permanent place in country music's pantheon of stars, just as all martyred heroes are given posthumous fame.

Born in rural Alabama, Williams and his family were poor dirt farmers who relocated to metropolitan Greenville. Here, Williams first heard the blues performed by streetsinger Rufe Payne; like many other white country artists, Williams's life was changed by this exposure to black traditional music. Around 1937, the family relocated to Montgomery where Williams made his first public appearance, leading to a regular spot on local radio. He formed his first band, the Drifting Cowboys, a name that he would use for his backup band throughout his career. He also composed "Six More Miles (to the Graveyard)," a blues that for the first time showed his unique sense of gallows humor.

The war years were spent in Mobile, Alabama, shipyards, with a return to music with a new band, featuring a young female singer, Audrey Sheppard Guy, who was to become his first wife (and mother of HANK WILLIAMS, JR.). In 1946, Williams signed with Nashville power-broker FRED ROSE, who became the mastermind behind his successful career. He signed with MGM in 1947, charting with his first release, the bluesy and ballsy "Move It On Over," and his first honky-tonk anthem, "Honky Tonkin'." Williams could even transform religious material into his own unique style, making a hit out of the fundamentalist hymn "I Saw the Light."

In August 1948, Williams was invited to join the prestigious *Louisiana Hayride* radio program, second only to the GRAND OLE OPRY in popularity among rural listeners. This spread his sound throughout the Southwest, and helped propel his cover of the twenties novelty number "Lovesick Blues" into a number-one country hit in 1949. An invitation to join the *Grand Ole Opry* followed, elevating Williams to the heights of country stardom.

Despite his increasing dependence on alcohol and painkillers (he suffered from spina bifida and was in almost constant pain), Williams continued to churn out the hits through the remaining three years of his life. The savvy Rose also peddled Williams's songs to more mainstream performers, so that his "Cold, Cold Heart" was a hit for Tony Bennett (!), "Hey Good Lookin' " scored for Frankie Laine, and Jo Stafford made a hit out of the CAJUN novelty number "Jambalaya."

By mid-1952, hard drinking and drug use caught up with the star. He was expelled from the Opry and his marriage ended in divorce. He quickly remarried in a lavish ceremony, but his life was soon over. He died in the back of a car on the way to a performance on New Year's Day 1953. As often happens, his death propelled his final recordings, "Your Cheatin' Heart" and the novelty "Kaw-Liga," to the top of the country charts.

Like many other performers who die young, Williams's death cast a long shadow. His recordings have been in print continuously since his death, and remain staples on jukeboxes across the country. His first wife Audrey tried to mold his son into his image, so that Hank Williams, Jr., spent his early performing years aping his father's manner and performing his songs. Meanwhile, legends about the life and times of Williams continue to circulate, occasionally even making headlines in the tabloids.

Select Discography

40 Greatest Hits, Polydor 233. Good overall introduction to his MGM/Sterling label recordings.

The Original Singles Collection . . . Plus, Polydor 194. Most of the hits on three-CD package with superior sound. All of Hank Williams's Sterling/MGM recordings have been reissued on an eight-volume set from Polydor, catalogued 548/551/554/557/633/634/749/752.

Health and Happiness Shows, Polydor 862. Radio shows prepared for broadcast in the early fifties; some repetition of material across the eight shows, but an interesting document nonetheless. Nicely packaged.

Rare Demos, Country Music Foundation 067. Reissues Hank performing just with his own guitar accompaniment, with great notes by Bob Pinson; originally on two LPs, CMF 006 and 007.

◀ WILLIAMS, HANK, JR.

(born Randall Hank Williams, 1949, Shreveport, LA)

Son of the legendary country musician, Williams has toiled in the shadow of his famous father for many years, often suffering in more ways than one from the comparison. Following a brush with death in the mid-seventies after an accident while mountain climbing, Williams was reborn as a hell-raising, country OUTLAW, an image that by the early nineties was also proving to be somewhat confining for the singer.

Williams's career was shaped by his manipulative mother, Audrey, who hoped to make him truly a junior version of his famous father. Even though she had separated from Hank senior before his death (and he had remarried), Audrey tended the flame for the elder songster, using his fame to further her own rather weak singing career. Hank junior was featured in her road shows, always performing his daddy's material. Hank's old record label, MGM, participated in this ghoulish scam by having the younger Williams record near letter-perfect renditions of his father's songs.

By the late sixties, Williams was bridling at his mother's management of his career and the limitations of being a Hank senior clone. He had a number of hits in which he commented on his strange situation, including 1966's "Standing In the Shadows (of a Very Famous Man)." He also began to write songs in a plain-spoken, straightforward style, and befriended the Nashville outlaws, including WILLIE NELSON and WAYLON JENNINGS, who were seeking to return country music to its purer roots. In 1974 Williams left Nashville to live in Alabama, recording his breakthrough album, *Hank Williams Jr. and Friends*, featuring country-rockers like CHARLIE DANIELS and Chuck Leavell. The album shocked his record label while it announced his new freedom from the slick Nashville sound. In 1977 Williams transformation was completed when he switched from his father's label to Warner Brothers, who marketed him as a hell-raisin' country-rocker.

Williams had a slew of hits for the Warners label, particularly in the late seventies and early eighties, starting with 1978's "I Fought the Law" capped by his "All My Rowdy Friends" single and video in 1981, which featured Hank joined by country, rock, and blues musicians. Hank cultivated a born-to-boogie image, which led to albums that seemed to be recorded in hyperdrive. By the late eighties, the unstoppable party sound was beginning to wear thin, and Williams seemed to be searching for a new direction. One of the strangest career moves was the 1992 "duet" with his dead daddy in the video/single "There's a Tear in My Beer," in which, through the "miracle" of overdubbing and computer editing, Williams, Jr., was able to sing and perform along with his long-gone dad. This was followed by the alcohol-drenched "Hotel Whiskey," a duet with NEW-COUNTRY star CLINT BLACK that takes the rowdy imagery of country honky-tonking to new, scary depths. Where the young Williams's rowdy image used to seem to be partially a put-on, it seems as if the star himself has been absorbed by it and can't shake it off, even though its usefulness and timeliness has ended. The younger Williams is in danger of becoming a country anachronism or, worse, a country embarrassment, which would be a sad ending to what has proved to be a distinguished career against some mighty difficult odds.

Select Discography

Living Proof, Mercury 320. Traces his MGM recording career from 1964 to 1975, when finally he began to emerge from out of the shadow of his father and take on his own personality as a redneck rocker.

Bocephus Box, Curb/Carbicorn 45104. His post-MGM career as a rowdy redneck.

◀ WILLIAMS, LEONA

(born Leona Helton, 1943, Vienna, MO)

Leona Williams is a country SINGER/SONGWRITER who was married to MERLE HAG-
GARD in the late seventies and early eighties, performing as his duet partner through
that period.

Williams came from a musical family and performed with her four brothers,
seven sisters, and parents as the Helton Family from an early age. At age fifteen,
she got her own radio show called *Leona Sings* that was broadcast out of Jefferson
City, Missouri, and soon after wed drummer Ron Williams. They were hired by
LORETTA LYNN to work in her road band, with Leona playing bass and singing and
her husband playing drums.

As a country vocalist, Williams was signed to Hickory in 1968, scoring minor
hits in 1969 with "Once More" and the novelty "Country Girl with Hot Pants On"
in 1971. In 1975 she joined Haggard's road show, replacing his estranged wife
BONNIE OWENS as his duet partner; the pair were married in 1978. They recorded a
duet album together in 1983, the same year their divorce came through, ironically
called *Heart to Heart*.

Although Williams went on to record for a number of labels as a solo artist
through the eighties, her music did not chart and she is not active today.

◀ WILLIAMS, LUCINDA

(born 1953, Lake Charles, LA)

New country SINGER/SONGWRITER Williams is best known for her song "Passionate
Kisses," a 1992 hit for MARY CHAPIN CARPENTER.

The daughter of a college professor/poet, Williams was raised in a number of
Southern university towns. She began as a blues and country singer, covering songs
by traditional country artists like her namesake, HANK WILLIAMS. She recorded two
albums for Folkways Records in the late seventies, the first all traditional material,
the second all her own songs, which gained some attention. She began focusing
on her own brand of semi-confessional singer/songwriter material, relocating to
Los Angeles by the mid-eighties where she recorded her first pop-styled album for
the punk-rock label Rough Trade in 1989. She switched to Chameleon/Elektra in
the early nineties, which rereleased her Rough Trade album as well as a new
recording, *Sweet Old World*, in 1992.

As of yet, Williams has won her audience mainly on the fringes of country. With
a raspy voice and a confessional style reminiscent of mid-seventies Joni Mitchell,
she appeals to an upscale, yuppified audience rather than down-and-dirty
rednecks.

Select Discography

Ramblin'/Happy Woman Blues, Smithsonian Folkways 40042/40003. Reissues her
two Folkways albums.

Lucinda Williams, Chameleon 61387. Reissue of her first Rough Trade album from 1988.

Sweet Old World, Chameleon 61351. 1992 release.

◀ WILLIAMS, TEX

(born Sol Williams, 1917, Ramsey, IL; died 1986)

Tex Williams was a talking-blues singer most famous for his 1947 recording of "Smoke, Smoke, Smoke that Cigarette," which he cowrote with guitarist MERLE TRAVIS.

Williams was born in rural Illinois and by the age of thirteen was performing locally as a one-man band on radio and at local venues. He spent most of the thirties in a variety of country and cowboy outfits touring the Western states. By late in the decade, he had settled in Hollywood, where he found employment in the movies as a singing cowboy. He joined up with SPADE COOLEY in the early forties, playing bass and singing lead on Cooley's biggest hit, "Shame, Shame On You." In 1946 the entire band defected with Williams as their leader, signing with the young Capitol label; a year later, they provided Capitol with its first million-seller in "Smoke, Smoke, Smoke That Cigarette." The band produced some exciting sides for Capitol through their last classic hit, 1949's "Bluebird on Your Windowsill."

Although Williams's band was hot and stayed together, with various personnel, through the mid-sixties, he was unable to equal his first hits in subsequent recordings. He opened his own club, the Tex Williams Village, in Newhall, California, while the band toured extensively, backing Tex as well as more pop-flavored vocalists. Many of Williams's later fifties and early sixties recordings featured truly dreadful, Hollywood orchestra accompaniments, and his singing was reduced to a barely recognizable croak. After closing his club in 1965, Williams went solo, recording sporadically for a number of labels, having his last (minor) hit in 1972 with "The Night Miss Nancy Ann's Hotel for Single Girls Burned Down."

◀ WILLIG, FOY

(born Foy Willingham, 1915, Bosque County, TX; died 1978)

Willig was an early cowboy star who led the often underrated Western band the Riders of the Purple Sage.

Willig began his career while in high school, performing on local radio as a pop crooner and in a gospel quartet. He worked his way to New York by the early thirties, where he had his own radio program sponsored by Crazy Water Crystals from 1933 to 1935. He then returned to Texas, working for a while as a radio announcer, before heading West to the allure of the burgeoning Los Angeles–based music scene.

In 1943 the first Riders of the Purple Sage was formed, and the group grew by the late forties into a large congregation, featuring two accordions, fiddle, clarinet, and some swinging steel guitar. They first recorded for the small Majestic label, having hits with the now classic "Cool Water" and "No One to Cry To," and then moved to Capitol where they recorded the classic "Ghost Riders in the Sky." Besides appearing in a zillion C-grade Western films, they also performed live with ROY ROGERS and the pop trio the Andrews Sisters.

Willig disbanded the group in 1952 and more or less retired from performing, although they did make some "reunion" recordings in the late fifties. By the seventies, Willig had come out of retirement to cash in on performances at Western film conventions, where he continued to work until his death in 1978.

◀ WILLIS, KELLY

(born c. 1959, Austin, TX)

Quavering-voiced ROCKABILLY revivalist Willis gained much media attention outside of country circles but has failed so far to make much of an impression on either the country or pop charts.

Discovered by earnest SINGER/SONGWRITER NANCI GRIFFITH, fellow Texan Willis has a much perkier style, reviving a rockabilly sound and repertoire (one of her first covers was of JANIS MARTIN's fifties hit "Bang Bang"). There are many who admire her blues-tinged delivery, although I find her studied country hiccuping and quivering voice a bit grating. She has also covered the songs of many of her fellow Texan singer/songwriters, including STEVE EARLE and JOE ELY. Her best recording so far is a cover of MARSHALL CRENSHAW's breezy rocker, "Whichever Way the Wind Blows."

Willis is sort of a female DWIGHT YOAKAM; she tries hard to recreate a traditional sound but doesn't yet have the depth to do it justice.

Select Discography
Bang Bang, MCA 10141. 1991, second album.
Kelly Willis, MCA 10789. Her third album, from 1993.

◀ WILLIS BROTHERS, THE

(Guy [guitar, vocals] born Alex Willis, 1915, Arkansas; died 1981; Skeeter [fiddle] born 1917, Coalton, OK; died 1976; Vic [accordion, piano] born 1922, Schulter, OK; died 1995)

The Willis Brothers were a pleasant country trio who scored a few mid-sixties hits, particularly 1964's truckers' anthem "Give Me Forty Acres."

The group began its life performing under the name of the Oklahoma Wranglers, originally on radio out of Shawnee, Oklahoma, and then, in 1940, moving to Kansas City, Missouri. With a break for service in World War II, their fame grew steadily, and they performed on the GRAND OLE OPRY in the postwar years until 1949, when they left to tour with EDDY ARNOLD's road shows. In 1946 they backed a young unknown singer in his first sessions for tiny Sterling records; he was HANK WILLIAMS, and he went on to bigger and better things soon after.

Somewhat unusually for a country trio, the group prominently featured Vic's pleasant pop-flavored accordion, and their stage show played off the personalities of serious Guy, the frontman, versus Skeeter, known as the "smilin' fiddler." Like many other outfits of the day, their harmonies and musical orientation drew as much inspiration from mainstream pop as they did from any tenuous connection with country traditions.

In the mid-sixties, the group signed with Starday Records, a small BLUEGRASS-specialty label out of Nashville that was cashing in big on the craze for TRUCK-DRIVING SONGS. The Willises provided hits with a few numbers in this vein, along with humorous country songs like 1967's "Somebody Loves My Dog."

In 1976, Skeeter died of cancer and Guy retired, leaving Vic to lead a more pop-influenced trio, noted for his burbling accordion and the group's close harmonies.

Select Discography
24 Great Truck Drivin' Songs, Deluxe 7809. Cassette-only release of mid-sixties material.

◀ WILLS, BOB

(born 1905, Limestone County, TX; died 1975)
Wills was the father of modern WESTERN SWING, a hybrid music that combined old-time country fiddling and songs with jazz, blues, boogie-woogie, and even Mexican-American sounds into a musical dialect that is still strongly identifiable today. Although only a moderately talented musician himself, Wills singlehandedly shaped the most important band in this style, the Texas Playboys, and his characteristic "Ah-ha" interjections and introduction of the various instrumentalists made their recordings immediately recognizable and vastly successful.

Wills was the son of an old-time fiddler/cotton farmer, who introduced his son to the traditional fiddle tunes of the Southwest. At the same time, Wills can remember hearing black field workers singing alongside him in the cotton fields, and so his youth was equally influenced by the traditional hollers and blues that they performed, as well as the jazz sounds newly introduced on records and radios. By 1932, Wills, a passable old-time fiddler himself, was a member of the LIGHT CRUST DOUGHBOYS, based in Fort Worth, a band sponsored by Burrus Mills, makers of Light Crust Dough, with MILTON BROWN, the other seminal name in Western swing, as vocalist. By 1933, he had his own band, the Texas Playboys, based in Tulsa; two years later they were signed by Vocalion.

Wills's new band was defined by two distinctive elements: the newly introduced electric "steel" guitar and the smooth vocalizing of singer TOMMY DUNCAN. Steel guitarist Leon McAuliffe (born 1917; died 1988) was responsible for the group's big hit, "Steel Guitar Rag"; his burbling solos were a trademark of the early Wills recordings, and he was often introduced by Wills's high falsetto shout of "Take it away, Leon." Duncan blended a mainstream sensibility with an affinity for the blues of JIMMIE RODGERS. The band also featured the fine boogie-influenced piano playing of Al Stricklin, and a loping bass-and-drum rhythm section that predicted the shuffle beat of later country boogie outfits. By the end of the thirties, the group had grown to include a large brass section, rivaling the popular big bands of the day in size and sound.

World War II spelled the end of the big bands of the thirties, and Wills turned to working with a smaller outfit out of his new home, Southern California, where he moved to appear in a number of forgettable D-grade Hollywood Westerns. Singer Tommy Duncan was expelled from the ranks in 1948 and was replaced by a series of lead vocalists, male and female, who were similarly modern in their approach. The new Wills band featured the swing-influenced fiddles of Johnny Gimble, Louis Tierney, and Joe Holley, steel-guitarists Herb Remington and Noel Boggs, electric guitarist Eldon Shamblin, and electric mandolinist "Tiny" Moore. The pared-down Wills's band made an excellent series of recordings for MGM in the late forties and early fifties, which in many ways were more exciting than his big-band sides of the late thirties.

Wills continued to work and record sporadically through the fifties and sixties, most notably recording two reunion LPs with singer Tommy Duncan in 1961 and 1962. Championed by country performer MERLE HAGGARD, who made a tribute LP to Wills in 1970, he came out of semiretirement to supervise one last session, just before his stroke in 1973 and his death two years later.

Different Texas Playboys have continued to perform in the seventies and eighties, one band led by Leon McAuliffe and another led by Wills's brother, Johnnie Lee (born 1912; died 1984), who recorded the original version of "Rag Mop" in 1948 (later a hit for the Mills Brothers). Another brother, Billy Jack (born 1926), worked as a drummer, bassist, and vocalist for Bob's band before forming his own group in 1949 along with mandolinist Tiny Moore, known as Billy Jack Wills and the Western Swing Band. They had the most progressive sound of any of the Western bands, with a jazz and R&B bent that was rarely heard in Western Swing; the group folded in 1954 when its members rejoined Bob Wills's ensemble.

Wills was also a talented songwriter, whose most notable composition was "San Antonio Rose," although he also transformed several traditional fiddle tunes ("Liza Jane," "Ida Red," and others) into swinging, pop confections.

Select Discography

Anthology: 1935–1973, Rhino 70744. Two-CD set spanning Wills's entire recording career.

The Essential, Columbia/Legacy 48958. Prewar recordings by Wills and his biggest bands.

Tiffany Transcriptions, Vols. 1–9, Kaleidoscope 16/19/20/21/25/27/29/32/35. Wonderful 1946 to 1947 recordings made for radio, with a tight combo featuring Herb Remington on steel guitar and vocalist Tommy Duncan. Start with volume 2, *The Best of . . .* Avoid like the plague Kaleidoscope 6002, *Tiffany Transcriptions with The McKinney Sisters*, where Wills and company back these saccharine popsters.

The Longhorn Recordings, Bear Family 15689. Twenty-three recordings cut by Wills in 1964, including twelve wonderful solo old-time fiddle tunes played by Wills himself.

◖ WISEMAN, MAC

(born Malcolm B. Wiseman, 1925, near Waynesboro, VA)

Unique among country artists, Wiseman has managed to straddle the division between BLUEGRASS and commercial country throughout his career, maintaining a traditional sound in his arrangements and choice of material. His fuzzy-voiced tenor is immediately recognizable in whatever genre of music he records.

Wiseman was born in rural Virginia in the Shenandoah Valley, where he was surrounded by old-time country music. He studied classical music at the Shenandoah Conservatory in Dayton, and then worked as an announcer at a small radio station out of Harrisburg, Pennsylvania. His first break as a singer came performing with MOLLY O'DAY after World War II. In the late forties, he hooked up briefly with Lester Flatt and Earl Scruggs, who had just left BILL MONROE's band. In 1950 Wiseman joined Monroe as lead vocalist, working for him for about a year.

A year later, Wiseman was signed as a solo act to Dot Records; six years later, he was hired as a house producer for the company, running their country-music division through the early sixties. Wiseman's first hit recordings were of the sentimental "Tis Sweet to Be Remembered" and "Shackles and Chains," both accompanied by a hybrid country/bluegrass band, featuring two fiddlers playing in harmony (something Wiseman borrowed from the popular WESTERN SWING style). In 1959 he had his biggest hit with the WEEPER "Jimmy Brown the Newsboy."

In the sixties, Wiseman continued to record in a traditional country vein, even though the NASHVILLE SOUND was beginning to encroach on his (and most other) recordings. He left Dot for Capitol in the early sixties, followed by a stint with MGM and then RCA. When Lester Flatt split from Earl Scruggs (because Scruggs wanted to record more popular music) in 1969, Wiseman teamed up with his old friend, recording a number of traditional bluegrass albums, first for RCA and then CMH. This return to bluegrass won him new friends on the traditional music circuit.

After Flatt died, Wiseman remained a popular touring attraction, returning to performing straight country, although he recorded only rarely. In 1986, when MCA revived the Dot label, he returned for an album in the style of his late-fifties recordings.

Select Discography

Early Dot Recordings, County 113. Bluegrass-flavored sessions from the fifties.
Teenage Hangout, Bear Family 15694. Dot label recordings from the fifties when the label encouraged him to record in the teen-pop mode; somehow, Wiseman makes these songs sound like traditional bluegrass numbers!
Grassroots to Bluegrass, CMH 9041. 1990 recordings.

◖ WOOD, DEL

(born Polly Adelaide Hendricks, 1920, near Nashville, TN; died 1990)

Wood was one of the few female instrumentalists to become a major GRAND OLE OPRY star, whose 1951 million-selling recording of "Down Yonder" made this ragtime piano piece a country standard.

Born on a farm just north of Nashville, Wood was raised in a working class neighborhood of the city. Already a talented pianist by high school age, she worked as a song plugger in local music shops during the forties, as well as taking a job in state government. In 1951 her recording of "Down Yonder," originally a ragtime composition of the twenties that was also turned into a jazzy fiddle tune by Gid Tanner and the SKILLET LICKERS, was a major hit both on the pop and country charts. This led to an invitation to perform on the *Grand Ole Opry* in 1953, where she remained until her death. Her jazzy piano stylings were influential on another young ivory pounder, JERRY LEE LEWIS. She recorded many albums, often with typical Nashville pop backings but was most popular thanks to her Opry appearances.

◀ WOOLEY, SHEB

(born 1921, Erick, OK)

Country comedian who often recorded under the alter-ego of Ben Colder, Wooley is best known to fans of fifties Westerns as Pete Nolan from TV's *Rawhide* and the hard-drinking villain, Ben Miller, from *High Noon*.

Wooley was born and raised on an Oklahoma farm, and came by his horsemanship skills honestly. After World War II, he worked for a short time in Nashville before landing his own radio show out of Fort Worth, Texas. This led, two years later, to an MGM contract and his first recordings, many made with excellent West Coast sidemen in a WESTERN SWING/country-boogie style. Wooley spent much of the fifties in Hollywood, appearing in over thirty films and 105 episodes of *Rawhide*. His first major hit was the novelty country-pop crossover, "Purple People Eater" of 1958, followed by "That's My Pa." Capitalizing on his success as a comedian, he began recording as Ben Colder in the early sixties, having hits with such schlock comedy classics as 1962's "Don't Go Near the Eskimos," "Harper Valley P.T.A (Later That Same Day)"—a 1968 answer song to Jeannie C. Riley's hit, "Harper Valley P.T.A.", and 1971's "Fifteen Beers Ago." He largely disappeared from the recording scene in the seventies.

Select Discography

The Best of Comedy, Richmond 2126. Cassette-only reissue of "Ben Colder's" big country comedy discs.

◀ WORK, JIMMY

(born 1924, Ohio)

A fine HONKY-TONK recording artist and songwriter, Work never achieved the success he deserved, although several of his songs have become country classics.

Born in Ohio but raised on a farm on the Kentucky/Tennessee border, Work left home to seek employment in Detroit, where he made his fist recordings in the early fifties. One of his first and best-known songs was "Tennessee Border," which was covered by HANK WILLIAMS, leading to a contract with Decca for Work. Followed by a couple of years of unsuccessful recording for a variety of labels, Work signed with Dot in 1954, scoring with his own "Making Believe" a year later, which was also a major hit in a cover version by KITTY WELLS. He also recorded fine up-tempo material including "Tom Cattin' Around," the ever-popular folk classic "Rock Island Line," and his ultimate honky-tonk WEEPER "That's What the Jukebox Plays." Work remained with Dot through 1956 and then retired from music making, returning to the life of a farmer on the Tennessee border.

Select Discography
Making Believe, Bear Family 15651. All of Work's recordings cut between 1945 and 1959.

◀ WRIGHT, MICHELLE

(born 1961, Toronto, Canada)

Wright is a chesty, big-throated singer who hit it big with the pop-glitz ballad "Take It Like a Man" in 1992.

Like her countrymate SHANIA TWAIN, Wright was trained as an all-around enter-tainer; her mother was a Toronto-based lounge singer and raised her daughter to be a performer. From her teen years, Wright toured Canada with various pop and country bands, honing her performance skills while also developing a bad habit of heavy drinking. Also like Twain, she recognized that country music was a growth business for good-looking singers who could blend girl-next-store wholesomeness with just a tinge of playful bad girl sass. Wright overcame her drinking problem and in the early nineties relocated to Nashville, where she was immediately signed to a recording contract. Her first single, "Take It Like a Man," was just sultry enough to be a major hit; the video for the song promoted Wright as a bombshell, with lots of cleavage and pouty lips. Not surprisingly for the ex-showgirl, Wright's road show emphasizes costumes and glitter over song and substance.

Select Discography
Michelle Wright, Arista 8627. 1990 debut album.

◀ WYNETTE, TAMMY

(born Virginia Wynette Pugh, 1942, near Tupelo, MS)

The ultimate sixties country crooner, Wynette will always be best known for her hit "Stand By Your Man," which set the course of women's liberation back by several hundred years but (nonetheless) remains a classic country WEEPER.

Raised by her grandparents in rural Mississippi, Wynette showed early musical talents, learning to play several instruments as well as singing. She joined her mother in Birmingham, Alabama, during her teen years, and was married for the first time at age seventeen; the marriage ended by the time she was twenty. Wy-nette worked as a beautician during the day, and club singer at nights, to support her three children. Local success led to a regular featured slot on the *Country Boy Eddy Show*, and then on PORTER WAGONER's popular syndicated country program.

Wynette came to Nashville in the mid-sixties in search of a career, auditioning for several labels while working as a singer and song plugger. Ace producer BILLY SHERRILL recognized her potential and signed her to Epic, where she had an immediate hit with 1966's "Apartment Number 9," followed by the racy (for the time) "Your Good Girl's Gonna Go Bad." Wynette's good-girl-on-the-edge-of-going-bad image was underscored in a series of hits, including "I Don't Wanna Play House" from 1967 (about a woman reluctant to participate in an affair with a married man) and "D-I-V-O-R-C-E" from 1968 (where a battling husband and wife try to hide "the facts" about their deteriorating marriage from the kids who apparently were not too swift as spellers). Oddly enough, the same year brought "Stand By Your Man," the ultimate beat-me-whip-me-but-I'll-still-be-true-to-you saga, with Wynette's powerful delivery subtly changing the song's message (it's hard to believe that the big-lunged Wynette would stay home and bake cookies while her husband slept around!). 1969 brought more hits with "Singing My Song" and "The Ways to Love a Man."

In 1968 Wynette began a seven-year stormy relationship with hard-drinkin' country star GEORGE JONES, making for excellent tabloid headlines. The duo often recorded together, including an album of duets from 1972 (with a hit in 1973 with "We're Gonna Hold On") and again in 1976, hitting it big with "Golden Ring" and "Near You" (even though they divorced in 1975); they reteamed in 1980, scoring a hit with "Two-Story House." Meanwhile, Tammy continued to record through the seventies, scoring major hits through the middle of the decade, including 1972's "Bedtime Story" (which sounded like a combination of the instrumental part of "Stand By Your Man" and the children's theme of "I Don't Wanna Play House") and "My Man (Understands)" (which clones the sentiments of "Stand By Your Man"), 1973's "Kids Say the Darndest Things" (perhaps the only country song to take its title from Art Linkletter!), 1974's "Another Lonely Song" (which brought Wynette to tears because of the line "I shouldn't give a damn," which she felt was sinful), and her last solo number-one country hit, "You and Me" from 1976. Many of these songs were cowritten by producer Sherrill and were carefully crafted to fit Wynette's image.

By the early to mid-eighties, Wynette's career was in the doldrums. The increasingly pop orientation of Sherrill's production was ill-suited to her basically HONKY-TONK style, and she was reduced to singing warmed over pop songs like "Sometimes When We Touch" (a duet with Mark Grey). An attempt to remake her for the NEW-COUNTRY generation in 1987 on her album *Higher Ground*, produced by Steve Buckingham and featuring a duet with RICKY SKAGGS, was a critical, if not financial, success. Wynette even dipped to self-parody, recording with the English-based technorock group KLF, scoring a British hit in 1992 with "Justified and Ancient."

At the end of 1993, Wynette was hospitalized suffering from a serious infection; she has been battling stomach problems for many years, and this ailment appeared to be related to these problems. However, she was soon back on the road performing again.

Select Discography

Tears of Fire: 25th Anniversary Collection, Epic 52741. Supplants earlier Greatest Hits collections; a complete overview of her career from a 1964 demo of "You Can Steal Me" through her early-nineties comeback with technorockers KLF.
Higher Ground, Epic 40832. 1987 album featuring new country stars Ricky Skaggs, Vern Gosdin, and VINCE GILL in the backup band.

Y.

◀ **YEARWOOD, TRISHA**

(born 1964, Georgia)

Yearwood is a talented NEW-COUNTRY singer whose career so far shows the perils of being overhyped. A big hit single came right out of the gate, but Yearwood has had difficulty following it up, while her handlers seem intent on molding her into a more mainstream pop chanteuse.

The daughter of a small-town banker father and schoolteacher mother, Trisha had an ordinary, "white-bread" childhood. She came to Nashville in 1984 after two years of junior college to pursue a music-business degree at Belmont College. She interned at the publicity department at MTM Records, and began doing demo and studio work, where she met another young unknown, GARTH BROOKS. Brooks invited her to back him up on his first albums, as well as to tour as his opening act. She was signed to a solo deal in 1991, producing the megahit "She's in Love with the Boy," an up-tempo ballad that Yearwood literally belted out. This was followed by the sultry "Wrong Side of Memphis," along with a duet with Garth on the suggestive "Like We Never Had a Broken Heart."

Mega-agent Ken "We Are the World" Kragen took Yearwood under his professional wing in 1992. He had helped shape KENNY ROGERS's career from pure country into pop superstardom, complete with movie deals, lucrative gigs in Vegas, and chart-topping pop records. Kragen urged Yearwood to lose some weight, signed her up to a high-visibility contract with Revlon to promote her own perfume, and oversaw the making of her second album. Surprisingly, although the album was well received critically, Yearwood did not achieve the same chart success she had originally and is in danger of becoming a one-hit wonder. It may be that her fans felt she was turning away from pure country too quickly in search of greener fields.

Still, Yearwood is an excellent singer whose instincts are to pursue more traditional material. With the right producers and handlers, there's no reason why she can't return to her former glory as a new-country queen.

Select Discography

Trisha Yearwood, MCA 10297. 1991 debut that was the most important new-artist release since RANDY TRAVIS's first way back in 1986.

Hearts in Armour, MCA 10641. Trisha goes a bit more mainstream, including a duet with Don Henley on "Walkaway Joe."

◀ YOAKAM, DWIGHT

(born 1956, Pikeville, KY)

Yoakam is a Southern California–based country singer who was one of the first NEW-COUNTRY stars. Yoakam uses traditional country symbols—his oversized cowboy hat, boots, and jeans, and songs about Cadillacs, women, whiskey, and hard livin'—to offer a nostalgic, slightly bemused spin to his material. His band is a typical pseudo-ROCKABILLY outfit, with a heavy GUITAR-bass-drum sound augmented by country fiddling, based on the country HONKY-TONK sound created by BUCK OWENS and MERLE HAGGARD in the Bakersfield, California, region in the fifties. Yoakam's biggest hits have been "Guitars, Cadillacs, and Hillbilly Music" and his cover of ELVIS PRESLEY's "Suspicious Minds," part of the soundtrack for the 1992 film *Honeymoon in Vegas.*

Yoakam does have real country roots; born in Kentucky, where his father was serving in the military, the family relocated to Cincinnati when Dwight was two, where many other Appalachian families came in the fifties in search of a better life. The family continued to visit relatives in Kentucky throughout Dwight's childhood, traveling down Route 23, the link between Cincinnati and the upper South immortalized in Yoakam's song "Readin', Rightin', Rt. 23." After completing high school and spending a couple of years as a philosophy major at Ohio State, Yoakam moved to Los Angeles. There, he became a fixture in the local punk-rock scene; his retro looks and sound seemed to fit in better with a punk sensibility than it did in the day's middle-of-the-road country.

Yoakam's late-seventies and early-eighties hits won him a cult following in rock, pop, and country circles. Although he has continued to produce minor hits on the country charts, Yoakam stands apart from other new-country acts in his slightly ironic take on the country image. His image is both an homage to the urban cowboy and a satire of it, and his music has a disturbing underside that seems to question the country ethos.

By the way, *Rolling Stone* magazine revealed in 1993 that, under the oversized hats, Yoakam is almost completely bald!

Select Discography

Guitars, Cadillacs, etc., Reprise 25372. His major-label debut LP, which first introduced his sound to a wide audience.
This Time, Reprise 45241. His 1993 album.

◀ YODELING

Yodeling, or a sudden change from a chest voice to a falsetto head voice, originated centuries ago in the Swiss mountains and probably entered the repertory of Southern country musicians through traveling tent shows of the nineteenth century.

Country music scholars commonly believe the first singer to make a record featuring yodeling was RILEY PUCKETT, the popular Georgia country artist, but it is JIMMIE RODGERS who popularized the yodeling style in his famous recordings of the late twenties and early thirties. Scores of yodeling cowboys came along in the wake of Rodgers's popularity, spearheaded by such famous horsy film stars as GENE AUTRY and ROY ROGERS. BOB WILLS in his WESTERN SWING bands used a kind of modified yodel, an expressive "Ah-ha," to express his pleasure at the band's performance, and BILL MONROE introduced the falsetto break into BLUEGRASS music. The "yee-hah" often shouted out by semi-inebriated fans at bluegrass or country concerts is a kind of mock yodel. Popular R&B vocalist Aaron Neville says he was influenced to create his semiyodeling vocal technique by listening to Gene Autry when he was a youngster. And GEORGE JONES created a kind of reverse yodel, where he suddenly drops into the low bass from his normal vocal range as a means of adding emphasis to a song, a trick picked up by RANDY TRAVIS and GARTH BROOKS among countless others. In a recent twist, Wylie and the Wild West have had a minor hit with "Yodelin' Fool," featuring traditional yodeling set to a ROCKABILLY beat.

Actually, traditional Southern mountain singing styles have long featured sudden shifts from normal to falsetto voice. For example, North Carolina ballad singer Dillard Chandler often broke into a short falsetto yelp at the end of a stanza, a kind of vocal hiccup that resembles a mini-yodel. Just as yodeling developed as a means of communication in the Alps, "hollerin' " was used among Southern mountaineers to communicate across vast distances or to call in the animals. The annual hollerin' contests still held in Spivey Corners, North Carolina, feature much vocalizing that could be called "yodeling."

While the Swiss usually yodel for joy, Jimmie Rodgers introduced the yodel as a lonesome or "blue" expression, coming as it did at the end of a verse in songs like "T.B. Blues." Southern musicians have transformed the yodel into one of the most expressive of all musical techniques.

◀ YOUNG, FARON

(born 1932, Shreveport, LA)

Young was a fifties-era honky-tonker who became a sixties-era country music mainstay and industrywide mover and shaker.

Born in Shreveport, Young was raised on a small farm outside of town. He began playing GUITAR from an early age and was already a competent country performer when he entered high school. After a brief stab at college in the early fifties, Young's musical career interrupted his education. He was signed to the popular *Louisiana Hayride* radio program, where he met another future crooner, WEBB PIERCE, and the duo were soon touring Southern honky-tonks and clubs.

In 1951 Young was signed to Capitol, having hits with the barroom tearjerkers "Tattle Tale Tears" and "Have I Waited Too Long." Young spent two years in the army from 1952 to 1954, but in the middle of his army service (primarily as an entertainer for the troops) he was invited to join the GRAND OLE OPRY. After his service, he scored his biggest hits, including 1955's country anthem, "Live Fast, Love Hard and Die Young." More HONKY-TONK standards followed, including 1956's "I've Got Five Dollars and It's Saturday Night," 1958's "That's the Way I Feel," and

1959's "Country Girl." In 1958, Young made his big-screen debut with FERLIN HUSKY and Zsa Zsa Gabor in *Country Music Holiday*, and appeared in the biopic, *Daniel Boone*.

In the sixties, Young entered the mainstream Nashville music-business world with a vengeance. While his recordings continued, they tended to be conventional middle-of-the-road country crooning (1967's "I Guess I Had Too Much to Dream Last Night" is an example of his excesses in this period). Meanwhile, he founded the influential trade-music paper, *Music City News*, opened his own music publishing company, *and* his own Nashville-based racetrack.

The seventies saw Young performing less as his importance as a businessperson grew. While he still had hits in the first half of the decade, his music making later dropped off. By the eighties, he was recording only rarely, but still maintained a regular presence on the Opry, starred on country-music TV specials, and continued to make personal appearances.

Select Discography

The Capitol Years, Bear Family 15493. Five CDs featuring 157 songs, with notes by Colin Escott. All the hits and everything else he waxed for this label.
Live in Branson, MO, USA, LAserLight 137. Young c. 1993 performing his old tunes for his old fans.

◀ YOUNG, NEIL

(born 1945, Toronto, Ontario, Canada)

Neil Young is another pop/rock star who, like BOB DYLAN and GRAM PARSONS, has dipped into country music from time to time during a long and often mercurial career. Beginning as a folk revivalist in his native Canada, Young's first break came as a member of the influential folk-rock band Buffalo Springfield from 1966 to 1968. He began a solo career in 1969, while also performing with the influential vocal group Crosby, Stills, Nash, and Young during 1970 and 1971 and sporadically over the next few decades, as well as leading the grunge-rock group Crazy Horse.

Young's first solo efforts showed strong country influences, particularly 1970's *After the Gold Rush*, with its mournful cover of DON GIBSON's "Oh Lonesome Me" and Young's own country classic, "Only Love Can Break Your Heart." His followup LP, *Harvest*, provided Young's biggest commercial success, featuring the top-forty hit "Heart of Gold." Most of the rest of Young's work in the seventies was more rock-oriented, although he returned to acoustic folk/rock on 1978's *Comes a Time*.

In the early eighties, a series of mercurial career swings saw Young take on synth-pop, blues-rock, and even ROCKABILLY; a reunion with Crazy Horse followed and a return to heavy-duty rock and roll with a political edge. Then, in another about-face, Young returned to country on 1992's *Harvest Moon*, with its minor nostalgic title hit.

Young's reedy tenor vocals, politically edged material, and his career-long refusal to fit into a single mold have all been influential on country performers who are also looking for ways to break the often stifling mold of industry expectations.

He has also been a prime mover behind Farm Aid, the series of concerts master-minded by WILLIE NELSON to aid Middle America's smaller farmers. Still, he has hardly won an appreciable country audience, appealing instead to a core group of aging hippies and yuppies who are attracted to country's primal and highly personal sound.

Select Discography

After the Gold Rush, Reprise 2283.

Harvest, Reprise 2277.

Harvest Moon, Reprise 45057. 1992 release that earned Neil a Grammy nomination.

◀ YOUNG, STEVE

(born 1942, Alabama)

OUTLAW SINGER/SONGWRITER Young has had a spotty recording career; beloved by WAYLON JENNINGS and his fiercely devoted fans, he has yet to break through to recognized success.

Born in Alabama, Young began performing in a folk singer/songwriter style, recording for A&M, Rounder, and Mountain Railroad records through the mid-seventies. His A&M album featured contributions from California folk-rockers like ex-Byrdsmen GENE CLARK and CHRIS HILLMAN along with legendary country-rocker GRAM PARSONS. His "big break" came in 1976 when he was signed to RCA, thanks to the support of Waylon Jennings for whom he had provided the 1973 hit "Lonesome, On'ry, and Mean." His best-known song, "Seven Bridges Road," was a minor, mid-seventies hit for the EAGLES. However, RCA didn't know what to do with him, and he languished at the label. Since then, Young has bounced around somewhat, appearing occasionally on smaller labels, still maintaining a cult following.

Select Discography

Solo/Live, Watermelon 1004. Nice acoustic show from 1991 on which he performs most of his best-known material.

BIBLIOGRAPHY

Abrahams, Roger, and George Foss. *Anglo-American Folksong Style.* Englewood Cliffs, NJ: Prentice-Hall, 1968.

Ahrens, Pat. *Union Grove: The First Fifty Years.* Union Grove, NC: Union Grove Old Time Fiddle Convention, 1975.

Albert, George, and Frank Hoffman. *The Cash Box Country Singles Chart, 1958–1982.* Metuchen, NJ: Scarecrow Press, 1984.

Anderson, Bill. *Whisperin' Bill.* Nashville, TN: Longstree Press, 1990.

Artis, Bob. *Bluegrass.* New York: Hawthorn Books, 1975.

Atkins, Chet, with Bill Neeley. *Country Gentleman.* Washington, D.C.: Regnery, 1974.

Biracree, Tom. *The Country Music Almanac.* New York: Prentice-Hall, 1993.

Bufwack, Mary A., and Robert K. Oermann. *Finding Her Voice: Women in Country Music.* New York: Crown, 1993.

Burton, Thomas, ed. *Tennessee Traditional Singers.* Knoxville: University of Tennessee Press, 1981.

Cantwell, Robert. *Bluegrass Breakdown: The Making of the Old Southern Sound.* Urbana: University of Illinois Press, 1984.

Carawan, Guy and Candie. *Voices from the Mountains.* New York: Alfred A. Knopf, 1975.

Clarke, Donald. *The Penguin Encyclopedia of Popular Music.* New York: Penguin Books, 1990.

Cohen, John, Mike Seeger, and Hally Wood. *Old-time String Band Songbook.* New York: Oak Publications, 1976.

Cohen, Norman. *Long Steel Rail: The Railroad in American Folksong.* Urbana: University of Illinois Press, 1981.

Country Music Foundation Staff. *Country: The Music and the Musicians.* New York: Abbeville Press, 1988.

———. *Country Music Hall of Fame and Museum Book.* Rev. ed. Nashville, TN: Country Music Foundation, 1987.

———. *Encyclopedia of Country Music.* New York: Schirmer Books, forthcoming.

Cusic, Don. *Randy Travis.* New York: St. Martins Press, 1990.

———. *Reba: Country Music's Queen.* New York: St. Martins Press, 1991.

Dellar, Fred, and Alan Cackett. *The Harmony Illustrated Encyclopedia of Country Music.* Rev. ed. New York: Harmony Books, 1986.

Delmore, Alton. *Truth Is Stranger Than Publicity.* Nashville, TN: Country Music Foundation, 1987.

Denisoff, R. Serge. *Waylon: A Biography*. New York: St. Martins Press, 1984.

Eichenlaub, Frank and Patricia. *The All American Guide to Country Music*. Castine, ME: Country Roads, 1992.

Escott, Colin, and Martin Hawkins. *Good Rockin' Tonight: The Sun Records Story*. New York: St. Martins Press, 1989.

Escott, Colin, with George Merritt and William MacEwen. *Hank Williams: The Biography*. Boston: Little, Brown, 1994.

Fong-Torres, Ben. *Hickory Wind: The Life of Gram Parsons*. New York: Pocket Books, 1991.

Fowler, Gene, and Bill Crawford. *Border Radio*. New York: Limelight Editions, 1990.

Gentry, Linnell. *A History and Encyclopedia of Country Western and Gospel Music*. New York: Scholarly Reprints, 1972 (reprint of 1961 edition).

Ginnel, Cary. *The Decca Hillbilly Discography*. Westport, CT: Greenwood Press, 1989.

———. *Milton Brown and the Founding of Western Swing*. Urbana: University of Illinois Press, 1994.

Greene, Archie. *Only a Miner*. Urbana: University of Illinois Press, 1972.

Gregory, Hugh. *Who's Who in Country Music*. London: Weidenfeld and Nicolson, 1993.

Gruhn, George, and Walter Carter. *Acoustic Guitars and Other Fretted Instruments: A Photographic History*. San Francisco: GPI Books/Miller Freeman, 1993.

Guralnick, Peter. *Last Train to Memphis: The Rise of Elvis Presley*. Boston: Little, Brown, 1994.

———. *Lost Highway: Journeys and Arrivals of American Musicians*. Boston: David R. Godine, 1979.

Hagan, Chet. *Country Music Legends in the Hall of Fame*. Nashville, TN: Country Music Foundation, 1982.

———. *The Grand Ole Opry*. New York: Henry Holt, 1989.

Haggard, Merle, and Peggy Russell. *Sing Me Back Home*. New York: Timescape Books, 1981.

Hardy, Phil, and Dave Laing. *The Faber Companion to 20th-Century Popular Music*. London: Faber and Faber, 1990.

Hemphill, Paul. *The Nashville Sound: Bright Lights and Country Music*. New York: Simon and Schuster, 1970.

Hoffman, Frank and George Albert, eds. *The Cash Box Country Album Charts, 1964–1988*. Metuchen, NJ: Scarecrow Press, 1989.

Hood, Phil, ed. *Artists of American Folk Music*. New York: Morrow, 1986.

Hume, Margaret. *You're So Cold I'm Turning Blue: Guide to the Greatest in Country Music*. New York: Penguin, 1982.

Jones, Loyal. *Minstrel of the Appalachians: The Story of Bascom Lamar Lunsford*. Berea, KY: Appalachian Consortium Press, 1982.

———. *Radio's Kentucky Mountain Boy: Bradley Kincaid*. Berea, KY: Applachian Center, Berea College, 1988.

Jones, Louis M. ("Grandpa"), with Charles K. Wolfe. *Everybody's Grandpa: Fifty Years Behind the Mike*. Knoxville: University of Tennessee Press, 1984.

Jones, Margaret. *Patsy: The Life and Times of Patsy Cline*. New York: HarperCollins, 1994.

Kingsbury, Paul, ed. *Country on Compact Disc: The Essential Guide to the Music*. New York: Grove Press, 1993.

Klein, Joe. *Woody Guthrie: A Life*. New York: Knopf, 1980.

Kochman, Marilyn, ed. *The Big Book of Bluegrass*. New York: Quill, 1985.

Lornell, Kip. *Virginia's Blues, Gospel and Country Records, 1902–1943*. Lexington: University Press of Kentucky, 1989.

Lomax, John. *Adventures of a Ballad Hunter*. New York: Macmillan, 1947.

Lynn, Loretta, and George Vesey. *Coal Miner's Daughter*. Chicago: Contemporary Books, 1985.

Malone, Bill C. *Country Music USA*. Rev. ed. Austin: University of Texas Press, 1985.

———. *Singing Cowboys and Musical Mountaineers*. Athens: University of Georgia Press, 1993.

Malone, Bill C., and Judith McCulloh, eds. *Stars of Country Music: Uncle Dave Macon to Johnny Rodriguez*. Urbana: University of Illinois Press, 1975.

Mandrell, Barbara, and George Vesey. *Get to the Heart: My Story*. New York: Bantam, 1990.

Marshall, Rick. *Encyclopedia of Country & Western Music*. New York: Simon and Schuster, 1988.

Mason, Michael, ed. *The Country Music Book*. New York: Scribner, 1985.

McCall, Michael. *Garth Brooks*. New York: Bantam, 1991.

Milsap, Ronnie, and Tom Carter. *Almost Like a Song*. New York: McGraw-Hill, 1990.

Morton, David C., and Charles K. Wolfe. *Deford Bailey: A Black Star in Early Country Music*. Knoxville: University of Tennessee Press, 1990.

Nash, Alanna. *Behind Closed Doors: Talking with the Legends of Country Music*. New York: Knopf, 1988.

Nelson, Willie. *Willie: An Autobiography*. New York: Pocket Books, 1989.

Paris, Mike, and Chris Comber. *Jimmie the Kid: The Life of Jimmie Rodgers*. New York: Da Capo, 1977.

Parton, Dolly. *My Story*. NY: HarperCollins, 1994.

Porterfield, Nolan. *Jimmie Rodgers: The Life & Times of America's Blue Yodeler*. Urbana: University of Illinois Press, 1979.

Price, Steven D. *Old as the Hills: The Story of Bluegrass Music*. New York: Viking, 1975.

———. *Take Me Home*. New York: Praeger, 1974.

Pruett, Barbara. *Marty Robbins: Fast Cars and Country Music*. Metuchen, NJ: Scarecrow Press, 1990.

Quain, Kevin, ed. *The Elvis Reader: Texts and Sources on the King of Rock 'n' Roll*. New York: St. Martins Press, 1992.

Riddle, Almeda. *A Singer and Her Songs*, ed. Roger Abrahams. Baton Rouge: Louisiana State University Press, 1970.

Riese, Randall, and Neal Hitchens. *Nashville Babylon: The Uncensored Truth and Private Lives of Country Music's Greatest Stars*. New York: Congdon and Weed, 1988.

Rinzler, Ralph, and Norman Cohen. *Uncle Dave Macon: A Bio-Discography*. Los Angeles: John Edwards Memorial Foundation, 1970.

Rodgers, Carrie. *My Husband, Jimmie Rodgers*. Nashville, TN: Country Music Foundation, 1975.

Rogers, Jimmie N. *The Country Music Message: All About Lovin' and Leavin'*. Englewood Cliffs, NJ: Prentice-Hall, 1983.

Rooney, Jim. *Bossmen: Bill Monroe and Muddy Waters*. New York: Da Capo, 1989.

Rorrer, Clifford. *Charlie Poole and the North Carolina Ramblers*. 2nd ed. North Carolina: Self-published, 1992.

Rosenbaum, Art. *Folk Visions and Voices: Traditional Music and Song in North Georgia*. Athens: University of Georgia Press, 1983.

Rosenberg, Neil V. *Bluegrass: A History*. Urbana: University of Illinois Press, 1985.

————. *Bill Monroe and His Blue Grass Boys*. Nashville, TN: Country Music Foundation, 1974.

Russell, Tony. *The Carter Family*. London: Old Time Music, 1973.

Sandberg, Larry and Dick Weissman. *The Folk Music Sourcebook*. Rev. ed. New York: Da Capo, 1989.

Savoy, Ann. *Cajun Music: Reflection of a People*. Lafayette, LA: Self-published, 1989.

Scott, Frank, and Al Ennis. *The Roots and Rhythm Guide to Rock*. Pennington, NJ: A Cappella Books, 1993.

Seeger, Mike, with Ruth Pershing. *Talking Feet*. Berkeley, CA: North Atlantic Books, 1992.

Shelton, Robert. *No Direction Home: The Life and Music of Bob Dylan*. New York: Morrow, 1986.

Shelton, Robert, and Burt Goldblatt. *The Country Music Story*. New York: Castle Books, 1971.

Snow, Hank. *The Hank Snow Story*. Urbana: University of Illinois Press, 1994.

Stambler, Irwin, and Grelun Landon. *The Encyclopedia of Folk, Country, and Western Music*. 2nd ed. New York: St. Martins Press, 1984.

Tasson, Myron, et. al. *Fifty Years at the Grand Ole Opry*. New York: Pelican, 1975.

Tichi, Cecelia. *High Lonesome: The American Culture of Country Music*. Chapel Hill: University of North Carolina Press, 1994.

Townsend, Charles S. *San Antonio Rose: The Life and Music of Bob Wills*. Urbana: University of Illinois Press, 1976.

Tribe, Ivan M. *Mountain Jamboree: Country Music in West Virginia*. Lexington: University of Kentucky, 1984.

————. *The Stonemans*. Urbana: University of Illinois Press, 1993.

Vaughan, Andrew. *Who's Who in the New Country Music*. New York: St. Martins Press, 1990.

Webb, Robert Lloyd. *Ring the Banjer! The Banjo in America; From Folklore to Factory*. Boston: MIT Museum, 1981.

Whitburn, Joel. *Joel Whitburn's Top Country Singles 1944–1988*. Menomenee Falls, WI: Record Research, 1989.

Wiggins, Eugene. *Fiddlin' Georgia Crazy: Fiddlin' John Carson, His Real World and His World of Songs*. Urbana: University of Illinois Press, 1987.

Williams, Jett, and Pamela Thomas. *Ain't Nothing Sweet as My Baby: The Story of Hank Williams's Lost Daughter*. New York: Harcourt Brace Jovanovich, 1990.

Wolfe, Charles K. *Tennessee Strings: The Story of Country Music in Tennessee*. Knoxville: University of Tennessee Press, 1977.

————. *The Grand Ole Opry: The Early Years*. London: Old Time Music, 1978.

————. *Kentucky Country Folk and Country Music*. Lexington: University of Kentucky Press, 1982.

Wright, John. *Travellin' the Highway Home: Ralph Stanley and the World of Traditional Bluegrass Music*. Urbana: University of Illinois Press, 1993.

INDEX

Page numbers that appear in **bold** type refer to main entries.